Italy
day BY day

1st Edition

by Sylvie Hogg & Stephen Brewer

WILEY

Wiley Publishing, Inc.

> Gladiatorial battles, like the one depicted in this mosaic, thrilled audiences throughout the Roman Empire.

Contents

PAGE 100

PAGE 153

PAGE 171

PAGE 240

PAGE 288

PAGE 326

PAGE 365

PAGE 398

PAGE 430

PAGE 488

PAGE 621

PAGE 12

PAGE 588

PAGE 615

PAGE 677

PUBLISHED BY

Wiley Publishing, Inc.

111 River St., Hoboken, NJ 07030-5774

ISBN 978-0-470-43210-5

Frommer's®

Editorial by Frommer's

EDITOR
Naomi P. Kraus

PHOTO EDITOR
Cherie Cincilla

CARTOGRAPHERS
Guy Ruggiero & Roberta Stockwell

CAPTIONS
Donald Strachan

COVER PHOTO RESEARCH
Richard Fox

COVER DESIGN
Paul Dinovo

Produced by Sideshow Media

PUBLISHER
Dan Tucker

MANAGING EDITOR
Megan McFarland

PROJECT EDITOR
Amy K. Hughes

PHOTO RESEARCHERS
John Martin, Paula Trotto

DESIGN
Kevin Smith, And Smith LLC

SPOTLIGHT FEATURE DESIGN
Em Dash Design LLC

For information on our other products and services or to obtain technical support, please contact our Customer Care Department within the U.S. at 800/762-2974, outside the U.S. at 317/572-3993 or fax 317/572-4002.

Wiley also publishes its books in a variety of electronic formats. Some content that appears in print may not be available in electronic formats.

MANUFACTURED IN CHINA

5   4   3   2

How to Use This Guide

The Day by Day guides present a series of itineraries that take you from place to place. The itineraries are organized by time (The Best of Tuscany & Umbria in 1 Week), by region (The Portofino Peninsula), by town (Taormina), and by special interest (Ancient Rome). You can follow these itineraries to the letter, or customize your own based on the information we provide. Within the tours, we suggest cafes, bars, or restaurants where you can take a break. Each of these stops is marked with a coffee-cup icon ☕. In each chapter, we provide detailed hotel and restaurant reviews so you can select the places that are right for you.

The hotels, restaurants, and attractions listed in this guide have been ranked for quality, value, service, amenities, and special features using a **star-rating system.** Hotels, restaurants, attractions, shopping, and nightlife are rated on a scale of zero stars (recommended) to three stars (exceptional). In addition to the star-rating system, we also use a kids icon to point out the best bets for families.

The following **abbreviations** are used for credit cards:

AE American Express   **DISC** Discover
V Visa   **DC** Diners Club
MC MasterCard

A Note on Prices

Frommer's lists exact prices in local currency. Currency conversions fluctuate, so before departing consult a currency exchange website such as **www.oanda.com/convert/classic** to check up-to-the-minute conversion rates.

In the "Take a Break" and "Best Bets" sections of this book, we have used a system of dollar signs to show a range of costs for 1 night in a hotel (the price of a double-occupancy room) or the cost of an entree at a restaurant. Use the following table to decipher the dollar signs:

COST	HOTELS	RESTAURANTS
$	under $150	under $15
$$	$150–$250	$15–$25
$$$	$250–$350	$25–$40
$$$$	$350–$450	$40–$50
$$$$$	over $450	over $50

How to Contact Us

In researching this book, we discovered many wonderful places—hotels, restaurants, shops, and more. We're sure you'll find others. Please tell us about them, so we can share the information with your fellow travelers in upcoming editions. If you were disappointed with a recommendation, we'd love to know that, too. Please email us at frommersfeedback@wiley.com or write to:

Frommer's Italy Day by Day, 1st Edition
Wiley Publishing, Inc.
111 River Street
Hoboken, NJ 07030-5774

Travel Resources at Frommers.com

Frommer's travel resources don't end with this guide. **Frommers.com** has travel information on more than 4,000 destinations. We update features regularly, giving you access to the most current trip-planning information and the best airfare, lodging, and car-rental bargains. You can also listen to podcasts, connect with other Frommers.com members through our active reader forums, share your travel photos, read blogs from guidebook editors and fellow travelers, and much more.

An Additional Note

Please be advised that travel information is subject to change at any time—and this is especially true of prices. We suggest that you write or call ahead for confirmation when making your travel plans. The authors, editors, and publisher cannot be held responsible for the experiences of readers while traveling. Your safety is important to us, so we encourage you to stay alert and be aware of your surroundings.

About the Authors

Sylvie Hogg (chapters 1, 4, 5, 6, 12, and 13) has been dutifully traipsing the *bel paese*, in the name of research for American and British travel guides, for the past decade. The Eternal City and all things ancient Roman are her first love, though she also confesses a serious weakness for the natural splendor of the Bay of Naples and the wine of southern Tuscany. She lives in Kansas City, Missouri, with her husband, Tim. They had their first child, a *bambino*, in July 2009.

Stephen Brewer (chapters 1, 2, 3, 7, 8, 9, 10, 11, 14, 15, and 16) is an editor and writer who has worked in magazines, books, radio, and corporate communications for almost three decades. He had his first sip of a real cappuccino in Rome in the early 1970s and has been savoring the pleasures of Italy ever since.

Acknowledgments

Sylvie: I would like to thank my husband Timmy, for taking on such odious chores as accompanying me to Capri as we researched this book, and Quint, who was conceived during the writing of this book and provided invaluable editorial perspective from inside the womb.

Stephen: I offer special thanks to Stefano, Elena, Marilena, and Victoria for adding so much to this book with their hospitality and advice. I'm also grateful to Amy Hughes for her many contributions and deep knowledge of Italian culture. Naomi Kraus, my editor, was wonderfully supportive and skillfully shaped the book from its conception, and I thank her for choosing me as one of the writers on such a plum assignment. With fondest memories, I also acknowledge my hosts and traveling companions for many years, Jim and Louise Tansey, who created a beautiful home on a Tuscan hillside, and Mary Beth Brewer, for whom Italy was a passion, a profession, and an endless source of pleasure. The three of you accompany me in spirit every step of the way.

About the Photographers

Vanessa Berberian discovered her passion for travel photography while studying classical archaeology in Italy; she currently works as a commercial photographer in London. **Raffaele Capasso** studied at the European Institute of Design and Visual Arts in Rome and currently lives in Naples. Roman native **Riccardo De Luca** has been covering Italy since 1997; his photos have appeared in *The Herald Tribune, Le Monde,* and other international publications. Sicilian native **Sandro Di Fatta**'s work has spanned the globe and been exhibited in several galleries. **Cristina Fumi** won a camera at age 8 and then turned her shutterbug hobby into a second career after 15 years as a tour leader. The work of **Giuseppe Piazza** has appeared in publications all over the United States and Europe, including *Time, Stern,* and *Le Monde.*

1

The Best of Italy

The Best of Northern Italy

0 _____ 50 mi

0 _____ 50 km

Favorite Italy Moments
Ravenna mosaics **22**
Accademia (Venice) **17**
Grand Canal (Venice) **17**
Lago di Garda **14**
The Cinque Terre **23**

SWITZERLAND

St. Moritz

Glurns

A2

Locarno

Sondrio

ALPS

Matterhorn

Monte Bianco

A40

Courmayeur

1

VALLE D'AOSTA

Aosta

A5

2 *Gran Paradiso*

Parco Nazionale del Gran Paradiso

Biella

Lugano

Lago Maggiore

10

Stresa

Varenna

11

Bellagio

Lecco

Lago di Como

Lago d'Iseo

Lago di Garda

Como

A2

12 Bergamo

Sirmione

14

Brescia

A4

Desenzano

LOMBARDY

9 **Milan**

A8

Lodi

A7

A1

Cremona

Vercelli

Po

A32

Avigliana

3

7

Turin

A21

6

Asti

PIEDMONT

Pinerolo

A6

Barolo

5

Cuneo

Pavia

8

Voghera

Tortona

A26

A7

Piacenza

Po

EMILIA-ROMAGNA

Parma

19

Reggio Emilia

LIGURIA

Genoa

Portofino

A15

A12

Savona

Gulf of Genoa

Finale

Vernazza

23

Portovenere

La Spezia

Carrara

Massa

Viareggio

Lucca

A11

FRANCE

A10

Ventimiglia

4

San Remo

MONACO

A8

Ligurian Sea

Pisa

Livorno

Piombino

Elba

Favorite Small Cities & Towns
Ferrara **21**
Mantua **18**
Bellagio **11**

Best Scenic Drives & Rides
Strada delle Dolomiti (Bolzano) **13**

Most Scenic Places
Parco Nazionale del Gran Paradiso **2**
The Cinque Terre **23**

Best Markets
Piazza delle Erbe & Piazza
della Frutta (Padua) **16**
Rialto (Venice) **17**
Piazza Campo del Palio (Asti) **6**

Festivals & Events
Biennale d'Arte Contemporanea
e Architettura (Venice) **17**
Carnevale (Venice) **17**

Best Museums
Gallerie dell'Accademia (Venice) 17
Pinacoteca di Brera (Milan) 9
Accademia Carrara (Bergamo) 12
Museo Egizio (Turin) 7

Best Ancient Ruins
Arena (Verona) 15

Best Churches & Cathedrals
Battistero & Duomo (Parma) 19
Basilica di San Marco (Venice) 17
Santa Maria dei Miracoli (Venice) 17
Duomo (Milan) 9

Best Architecture
Certosa di Pavia (Pavia) 8
Galleria Vittorio Emanuele II (Milan) 9
Palazzo Borromeo (Lago Maggiore) 10
Palazzo del Tè (Mantua) 18
Stupinigi (Turin) 7

Favorite Works of Art
Mosaics (Ravenna) 22
Camera degli Sposi (Mantua) 18
The Last Supper (Milan) 9

Favorite Small Inns
B & B Locanda Borgonuovo (Ferrara) 21
Ca' della Corte (Venice) 17
Oltre il Giardino (Venice) 17

Best Luxury Hotels
Grand Hotel et de Milan (Milan) 9
Gritti Palace (Venice) 17
Royal Hotel (San Remo) 4

Top Food & Wine Experiences
Venice 17
The Langhe Wine Route 5

Best Castles & Monasteries
Castello Sforzesco (Milan) 9
Castello di Fenis (Aosta) 1
Sacra di San Michele (Avigliana) 3

Best Piazzas
Campo Santi Giovanni e Paolo (Venice) 17
Piazza delle Erbe & Piazza
   dei Signori (Verona) 15
Piazza San Carlo (Turin) 7
Piazza San Marco (Venice) 17

Memorable Dining Experiences
Fini (Modena) 20
Antiche Carampane (Venice) 17
Bea Vita (Venice) 17
Le Bistrot de Venise (Venice) 17
Aquila Nigra (Mantua) 18

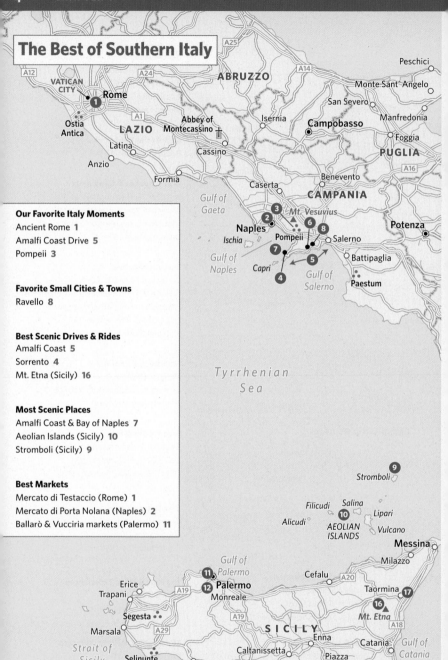

The Best of Southern Italy

0 50 mi
0 50 km

*Adriatic
Sea*

Vieste

*Gulf of
Manfredonia*

A14

Bari

PUGLIA

Alberobello

Brindisi

Matera

Taranto

Lecce

Metaponto

BASILICATA

*Gulf of
Taranto*

CALABRIA

Paola

Cosenza

Crotone

Catanzaro

*Ionian
Sea*

A3

Villa San Giovanni

**Reggio di
Calabria**

*Strait of
Messina*

Best Castles & Monasteries
Castel Sant'Angelo (Rome) **1**
Castel Nuovo (Naples) **2**

Best Piazzas
Piazza del Duomo (Siracusa) **15**

Best Museums
Capitoline Museums (Rome) **1**
Galleria Borghese (Rome) **1**
Vatican Museums (Rome) **1**
Museo Archeologico Nazionale
(Naples) **2**

Best Ancient Ruins
Colosseum (Rome) **1**
Hadrian's Villa (Rome) **1**
Ostia Antica (Rome) **1**
Palatine Hill (Rome) **1**
Pompeii **3**
Parco Archeologico della Neapolis
(Siracusa) **15**
Valley of the Temples
(Agrigento) **13**

Best Churches & Cathedrals
St. Peter's Basilica (Rome) **1**
Cathedral (Monreale) **12**

Best Architecture
Pantheon (Rome) **1**
Villa d'Este (Rome) **1**

Favorite Works of Art
Apollo and Daphne (Rome) **1**
Mosaics, Villa Romana del Casale
(Piazza Armerina) **14**

Favorite Small Inns
Villa Laetitia (Rome) **1**
Costantinopoli 104 (Naples) **2**
Villa Ducale (Taormina) **17**

Best Luxury Hotels
Palazzo Sasso (Ravello) **8**
Santa Caterina (Amalfi) **6**

Top Food & Wine Experiences
Rome **1**
Naples **2**

Memorable Dining Experiences
Perilli (Rome) **1**

Festivals & Events
Christmas & Easter (Rome) **1**

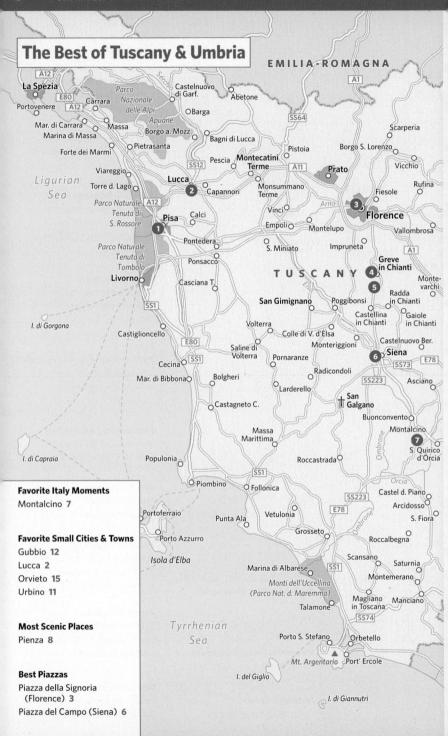

The Best of Tuscany & Umbria

EMILIA-ROMAGNA

A12

La Spezia
Portovenere
E80
A12
Carrara
Mar. di Carrara
Marina di Massa
Massa
Forte dei Marmi
Pietrasanta
Viareggio
Torre d. Lago
Lucca ②
Pisa ①
Livorno

Ligurian Sea

Parco Nazionale delle Alpi
Apuane

Sérchio
Castelnuovo di Garf.
Barga
Borgo a. Mozz.
Bagni di Lucca
Abetone

SS64

A1

Pistoia
Pescia
Montecatini Terme
SS12
Capannori
Monsummano Terme
Vinci
Calci
Empoli
Pontedera
Ponsacco
Montelupo
S. Miniato

Parco Naturale Tenuta di S. Rossore
A12

Parco Naturale Tenuta di Tombolo

Casciana T.

A11
Prato
Scarperia
Borgo S. Lorenzo
Vicchio
Fiesole
Rufina
Florence ③
Vallombrosa
Impruneta
Greve in Chianti ④
⑤
Montevarchi
A1

Arno

TUSCANY

I. di Gorgona

Castiglioncello
E80
SS51
Cecina
Mar. di Bibbona
Volterra
Saline di Volterra
Colle di V. d'Elsa
Monteriggioni
Pornaranze
Radicondoli
Bolgheri
Larderello
Castagneto C.
San Galgano
Massa Marittima

San Gimignano
Poggibonsi
Castellina in Chianti
Gaiole in Chianti
Radda in Chianti
Castelnuovo Ber.
Siena ⑥
E78
SS73
SS223
Asciano
Buonconvento
Montalcino ⑦
S. Quirico d'Orcia

I. di Capraia

Roccastrada

Ombrone

Populonia
SS1
Piombino
Follonica
Portoferraio
Porto Azzurro
Punta Ala
Vetulonia
Grosseto
Orcia
Castel d. Piano
Arcidosso
S. Fiora
Roccalbegna

Isola d'Elba

SS223
E78

SS1
Marina di Albarese
Monti dell'Uccellina (Parco Nat. d. Maremma)
Scansano
Montemerano
Magliano in Toscana
Talamone
Saturnia
Manciano
SS74

Tyrrhenian Sea

Porto S. Stefano
Orbetello
Mt. Argentario
Port' Ercole
I. del Giglio
I. di Giannutri

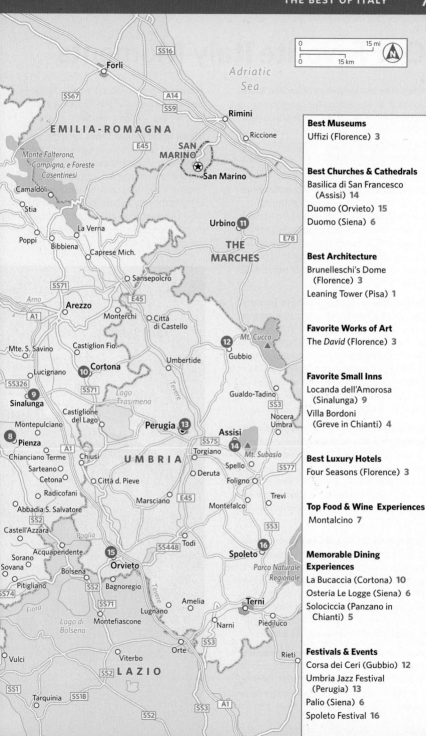

Best Museums
Uffizi (Florence) **3**

Best Churches & Cathedrals
Basilica di San Francesco
  (Assisi) **14**
Duomo (Orvieto) **15**
Duomo (Siena) **6**

Best Architecture
Brunelleschi's Dome
  (Florence) **3**
Leaning Tower (Pisa) **1**

Favorite Works of Art
The *David* (Florence) **3**

Favorite Small Inns
Locanda dell'Amorosa
  (Sinalunga) **9**
Villa Bordoni
  (Greve in Chianti) **4**

Best Luxury Hotels
Four Seasons (Florence) **3**

Top Food & Wine Experiences
Montalcino **7**

**Memorable Dining
Experiences**
La Bucaccia (Cortona) **10**
Osteria Le Logge (Siena) **6**
Solociccia (Panzano in
  Chianti) **5**

Festivals & Events
Corsa dei Ceri (Gubbio) **12**
Umbria Jazz Festival
  (Perugia) **13**
Palio (Siena) **6**
Spoleto Festival **16**

Our Favorite Italy Moments

Absorbing the splendors of ancient Rome.
Spend a full day among the magnificent ruins
of the ancient city, from the heights of the
Palatine to the valley of the Colosseum, and
let nostalgia for the glorious and heady days
of imperial Rome overcome you. See map p 4,
①; p 78.

Being dazzled by the mosaics in Ravenna.
The brilliance of the mosaics glittering
within Byzantine churches and monuments
is especially touching because the heavenly
and earthly scenes are so painstakingly and
sincerely rendered—a last hurrah before Europe
slipped into the Dark Ages. See map p 2, ㉒;
p 336.

Taking time for food and wine in Tuscany. Give
the sightseeing a break and concentrate on
gluttony in all its forms when visiting this most
picturesque and bountiful of Italian regions.
Build lazy lunches into your itinerary, stop in
at every deli that looks appealing, and sample
all the wines, cured meats, and cheeses you
possibly can. Our favorite of many options?
Montalcino. See map p 6, ⑦; p 234.

**Standing in front of your favorite painting or
sculpture in any museum.** Here in the world's
richest repository of Western art, you can take
your pick from hundreds of masterpieces. One
of our favorites is Carpaccio's *Story of St. Ursula,*
a color-saturated, action-packed medieval
travelogue in Venice's Accademia. See map
p 2, ⑰; p 371, ⑨.

Cruising on the Grand Canal. Even Venetians
take their noses out of their newspapers for
the trip, and it doesn't matter how many times
we've done it, either—we can't take our eyes
off the *palazzi* lining the banks or keep from
musing on the fact that Marco Polo, Casanova,
and Byron once slipped down the storied
waterway, too. See map p 2, ⑰; p 362.

**A trip on a steamer up the western shore of
Lago di Garda.** The boat passes villas and gardens
and pulls into one pretty town after another.
Medieval Gargnano is especially picturesque, and
around Limone sul Garda the shores are planted

with lemon groves. Most dramatically, the Alps
form a solid curtain at the northern end of the
lake. See map p 2, ⑭; p 441, ④.

Hiking in the Cinque Terre. Sure, the paths can
be packed, and American-accented English
too often disturbs the getaway experience, but
scene after scene of the azure sea, vineyards
clinging to hillsides, and mirage-like villages
hugging the rocky coast are just stunning. A big
plus: You can hike until your body screams "No
more!" then make the return trip by train. See
map p 2, ㉓; p 540.

The heart-stopping and jaw-dropping Amalfi Coast drive. Even the rapturous view from the sea of this spectacular coastline doesn't prepare you for the unbeatable rush of riding a bus along the death-defying curves of the Via Amalfitana. With rugged mountains on one side and sheer drop-offs to the water on the other, it's a thrill ride that goes on for 30km (18 miles). See map p 4, **5**; p 568, **1**.

Going back in time in Pompeii. No other archaeological site is so thoroughly transporting: Frozen in time by the eruption of Mt. Vesuvius in A.D. 79, ancient Pompeii is astonishingly intact, evoking an uncanny sense of familiarity in many who wander the sophisticated ruins of the buried city. See map p 4, **3**; p 588.

> PAGE 1 *Piazza San Marco at night, Venice.*
  THIS PAGE *The Colosseum's dramatic exterior features Doric, Ionic, and Corinthian columns.*

Our Favorite Small Cities & Towns

> *Bellagio, from the Latin for "between lakes," has a spectacular promontory location on Lake Como.*

Gubbio. This beautifully preserved, compact agglomeration of pastel, crenellated buildings set against a steep green hill looks like it was plucked out of a 15th-century painting. See map p 6, ⑫; p 264, ⑩.

Lucca. Justly famous for its pristine circuit of town walls, Lucca is much more than a medieval time capsule: The town perpetuates the elegance of the late 19th and early 20th centuries, with stately shopfronts and the spirit of a gentler bygone era. See map p 6, ②; p 274.

Orvieto. A warren of medieval streets and a spectacular Duomo, all improbably perched on a porous stone bluff, it never fails to impress, nor does a glass of the town's famous Orvieto Classico. See map p 6, ⑮; p 258, ❶.

Urbino. The ideal Renaissance city straddles a pair of ridges in the foothills of the Apennines, a harmonious apparition of towers, walls, and domes amid the rolling hills of the Marches. Duke Federico da Montefeltro and his son, Guidobaldo, oversaw one of Italy's most enlightened courts from their elegant palace,

now filled with the collections of the Galleria Nazionale delle Marche. See map p 6, ⑪; p 310, ❸.

Ferrara. The centerpiece of this Renaissance city of rose-colored brick is the imposing castle of the Este family, who endowed Ferrara with palaces, gardens, and intrigues, including those of their most famous duchess, Lucrezia Borgia. See map p 2, ㉑; p 332.

Mantua. Surrounded by the sweeping, lake-like curve of the River Mincio and built around three beautiful piazzas, Mantua is remote and rather dreamy, locked in a Renaissance world of its own. See map p 2, ⑱; p 472.

Bellagio. This medieval town of stepped streets on a promontory in Lago di Como is surrounded by gardens and lakeside villas, and backed by the Alps plunging into the deep waters. See map p 2, ⑪; p 432, ❸.

Ravello. Just when you thought the Amalfi Coast couldn't possibly get any more stunning, along comes Ravello, with views that trump all and sultry gardens, too. See map p 4, ❽; p 622.

The Best Scenic Drives & Rides

Strada delle Dolomiti. One of Europe's most scenic drives rises and falls through the mountains for 110km (66 miles) between Bolzano and Cortina. Along the route are many vistas that take in dozens of spindly, snow-capped peaks, 18 of them rising more than 3,000m (10,000 ft.). See map p 2, ⑬; p 436, ③.

Amalfi Coast Drive. The two-lane road that clings to the hillside—forested mountains to one side, plunging cliffs and the azure Mediterranean to the other, and sublime views in every direction—is the most exciting attraction on the Amalfi Coast. Public transportation (the blue SITA bus) is the classic way to experience the drive. See map p 4, ⑤; p 568, ①.

Campania by water. The most fun way to jaunt around Campania—and the only way to reach Capri, apart from a helicopter—is by ferry (*traghetto, nave*) or hydrofoil (*aliscafo*). Naples and Sorrento are the main ports, with dozens of departures daily in high season. See map p 4, ④; p 631.

Mt. Etna, Sicily. Europe's largest active volcano isn't beautiful, per se, but a trip to the top of this awesome peak—made via a thrilling cableway ride and all-terrain vehicle—is the experience of a lifetime. See map p 4, ⑯; p 645, ⑤.

> The winding stretch of coastal road between Sorrento and Amalfi is one of Europe's classic drives.

The Most Scenic Places

> *From its scenic seaside perch, Positano is a great jumping-off point for Amalfi Coast adventures.*

Southern Tuscany. Olive groves, vineyards, cypresses, wine towns, and wheat fields studded with farmhouses capture the beauty and essence of Tuscany. Pienza is an especially good place to hit. See map p 6, **8**; p 252.

Parco Nazionale del Gran Paradiso. The 703 sq. km (173,000 acres) of valleys, plateaus, and peaks rise and fall across the former hunting grounds of King Vittorio Emanuele. Crystal-clear lake waters reflect the Gran Paradiso peaks, and some 4,000 ibex, along with chamois, badgers, and other mountain-dwelling creatures, roam the park. See map p 2, **2**; p 500, **4**.

The Cinque Terre. Steep seaside cliffs have defied road builders, and a trail follows the unspoiled coastline through stunning panoramas, fragrant pine groves, and hillsides terraced with vineyards to connect the region's five villages. See map p 2, **23**; p 540.

Amalfi Coast & Bay of Naples. Rugged coastlines of staggering dimension, vertiginous views more breathtaking than any photo can convey, and the imposing cone of Mt. Vesuvius make the Amalfi Coast and the Bay of Naples, including the island of Capri, the most magnificent landscape in Italy. See map p 4, **7**; p 568.

Aeolian Islands, Sicily. The shores tend to be pebbly inlets or vertical rock faces, but they are riddled with beautiful swimming coves that are best reached by renting your own motorboat. See map p 4, **10**; p 664.

Stromboli, off Sicily. An active but sluggish volcano emits puffs of smoke and lava all the time, and a nighttime trek to the summit provides views of fiery red lava flowing toward the sea. See map p 4, **9**; p 666, **7**.

The Best Markets

> *The atmospheric alleys of Palermo host two of Italy's most colorful, and chaotic, street markets.*

Mercato di Testaccio, Rome. The good-natured haggling, the emphatic gesturing, and the banter between customers and vendors of fresh produce and more is a priceless snapshot of daily Roman life. See map p 4, **1**; p 76, **4**.

Piazza delle Erbe & Piazza della Frutta, Padua. These two adjoining squares in the city center house one of Italy's largest and liveliest markets; produce is on offer in Piazza delle Erbe, and clothing and housewares in Piazza della Frutta. See map p 2, **16**; p 414, **4**.

Rialto, Venice. The commercial heart of Venice for more than 1,000 years is a sea of stalls piled high with fruit, vegetables, fish, and souvenirs; the bustle of the place brings to mind old Shylock's oft-quoted question in *The Merchant of Venice:* "What news on the Rialto?" See map p 2, **17**; p 360, **5**.

Piazza Campo del Palio, Asti. A market that takes over this large square on Wednesday and Saturday mornings provides an excellent introduction to the food and wine for which

Asti and the surrounding region is famous— bags of Arborio rice, piles of hazelnuts and apples, *toma* and *Castelmagno* cheeses, truffles, and, of course, bottles of Asti Spumante, Moscato, and Barbera. See map p 2, **6**; p 518, **7**.

Mercato di Porta Nolana, Naples. The prime spot to witness Naples's ancient (and theatrical) tradition of buying and selling is this seafood market, where open-air stands glisten with such silvery *pesce azzurro* as anchovies and tuna, wriggly octopus and squid glare at you from ice-packed trays, and fresh clams and mussels huddle together in great watery vats. See map p 4, **2**; p 604, **7**.

Ballarò & Vucciria markets, Palermo. Nowhere is Palermo's multicultural pedigree more evident than at its boisterous street markets that go on for blocks and blocks, hawking everything from spices to seafood to sides of beef to toilet paper to handicrafts to electronics. See map p 4, **11**; p 670, **3**.

The Best Castles & Monasteries

Castel Sant'Angelo, Rome. Hadrian's mausoleum from the 2nd century A.D. has been a fortress for popes and a prison—the very one where Puccini's Tosca was incarcerated, and the view from the terrace high above the Tiber is as dramatic as the opera's finale. See map p 4, ❶; p 98, ❶.

Castello Sforzesco, Milan. Milan's medieval bastion of power became a center of Renaissance culture and now houses museums filled with works by Leonardo da Vinci and Michelangelo and other treasures. See map p 2, ❾; p 461, ❻.

Castello di Fenis, near Aosta. The largest and best preserved of the many castles that once guarded trade routes along the Valle d'Aosta is surrounded by tall double walls and many round and square towers; an inner courtyard is decorated with frescoes depicting St. George slaying the dragon and other scenes from legend. See map p 2, ❶; p 499, ❷.

Sacra di San Michele, near Avigliana. This monastery dedicated to the archangel is precariously perched atop Mt. Pirchiriano, piercing the clouds at 960m (3,150 ft.), and riddled with a labyrinth of view-affording terraces, steep staircases, and narrow lanes. See map p 2, ❸; p 490, ❷.

Castel Nuovo, Naples. Visitors who arrive in Naples by boat are greeted by the turrets, crenellated parapets, deep moat, and overall storybook appearance of this massive 13th-century fortress overlooking the bay. See map p 4, ❷; p 609, ⓴.

> The mountain now crowned by the Sacra di San Michele has been inhabited since the Stone Age.

The Best Piazzas

> *Siracusa, an important Greek city 2,500 years ago, was the home of the mathematician Archimedes.*

Piazza della Signoria, Florence. The monumental heart of Florence is dominated by the imposing gray bulk of Palazzo Vecchio, one of the most formidable medieval monuments in all of Italy, and graced with a copy of Michelangelo's *David* as well as other ancient and Renaissance statuary. See map p 6, ❸; p 182, ❷.

Piazza del Campo, Siena. The most beautiful piazza in Italy is dramatically shaped like a sloping scallop shell or fan, divided into nine sections in honor of the Council of Nine, who ruled Siena during its golden age, and graced with a copy of the original Fonte Gaia (Fountain of Joy), created by the city's own Jacopo della Quercia. See map p 6, ❻; p 290, ❶.

Campo Santi Giovanni e Paolo, Venice. Bartolomeo Colleoni, a 15th-century mercenary, rides across one of Venice's most beautiful squares astride an equestrian monument by Verrocchio, and the Church of Santi Giovanni e Paolo is the final resting place of 25 doges, entombed in marble splendor. See map p 2, ❶⑦; p 376, ❺.

Piazza San Marco, Venice. Napoleon called this civilized square the "drawing room" of Europe, and the Piazza, as it's simply known, is where Venetians and their visitors converge to sip a cappuccino or cocktail on the outdoor terraces of some of Europe's grandest cafes. See map p 2, ❶⑦; p 350, ❺.

Piazza delle Erbe & Piazza dei Signori, Verona. The site of the Roman forum is now Verona's central square, the venue for a daily market; the adjoining Piazza dei Signori was once the scene of assemblies of the medieval citizens' council. Walking between these two beautiful squares involves a risk—a whalebone suspended in the Arco della Costa (Arch of the Rib) will fall on anyone who has never told a lie. See map p 2, ❶⑤; p 418, ❺.

Piazza San Carlo, Turin. Elegant arcades are lined with fine shops, chocolatiers, and cafes whose terraces provide an outdoor living room for the Torinese. See map p 2, ❼; p 484.

Piazza del Duomo, Siracusa. Sicily's most beautiful piazza is baroque, operatic, and surrounded by lovely churches and palaces. See map p 4, ❶⑤; p 676, ❶.

The Best Museums

> *Raphael's* Marriage of the Virgin, *on display in Milan's Pinacoteca di Brera.*

Capitoline Museums, Rome. Michelangelo-designed buildings house some of the most important Roman sculptures in the world, as well as fine works by Caravaggio, Titian, Tintoretto, and Guido Reni. See map p 4, **①**; p 89, **⑧**.

Galleria Borghese, Rome. The collections at this 17th-century garden estate are modestly sized but come close to perfection, with astonishing marble sculptures by Bernini and Canova and paintings by Caravaggio, Titian, and Raphael. See map p 4, **①**; p 84, **②**.

Vatican Museums, Rome. The richest museum of ancient and Renaissance art in the world is enthralling in its quantity and quality. Standouts are the *Laocoön* and other ancient sculptures, the Raphael Rooms (Stanze di Raffaello) and Michelangelo's frescoes in the Sistine Chapel, and the rest of the collections range from mummies to moon rocks. See map p 4, **①**; p 88, **③**.

Uffizi, Florence. One of the world's greatest museums shows off countless iconic works of Renaissance art—including Leonardo da Vinci's *Annunciation* (with an angel that could be the Mona Lisa's brother), Michelangelo's *Holy Family,* Sandro Botticelli's *Birth of Venus,* and Peter Paul Rubens's voluptuous nudes. See map p 6, **③**; p 174.

Gallerie dell'Accademia, Venice. Three former religious buildings house a vast repository of Venetian art from the Byzantine to the rococo. Veronese's *Feast in the House of Levi,* Carpaccio's *St. Ursula,* and Gentile Bellini's *Procession in St. Mark's Square* are just a few of the many treasures. See map p 2, **⑰**; p 370, **⑨**.

Pinacoteca di Brera, Milan. Renaissance works from northern and central Italy—the Montefeltro Altarpiece, painted by Piero della Francesca for the duke of Urbino; Andrea Mantegna's *Dead Christ;* Raphael's *Marriage of the Virgin;* and *Finding the Body of St. Mark* by Tintoretto—are among the masterpieces that hang in Milan's finest art gallery. See map p 2, **⑨**; p 461, **⑤**.

Accademia Carrara, Bergamo. A walk through the galleries is a survey of the great Italian masterpieces. Many are from the 15th century, the golden age of the Early Renaissance, and Botticellis, Bellinis, Mantegnas, Titians, and Tiepolos appear one after another. See map p 2, **⑫**; p 477, **④**.

Museo Egizio, Turin. Turin's Egyptian collection is second only to the one in Cairo, with such prizes as the tomb of the royal architect Ka and his bride, a black basalt statue of Rameses II, and legions of mummies. See map p 2, **⑦**; p 510, **⑧**.

Museo Archeologico Nazionale, Naples. The echoey halls of this enormous Renaissance palazzo house artifacts from Pompeii and other sites buried by the eruption of Mt. Vesuvius, from baking equipment and surgical instruments to eye-popping erotic frescoes. The museum's other star attraction is the renowned Farnese collection of ancient sculpture. See map p 4, **②**; p 605, **⑩**.

The Best Ancient Ruins

Colosseum, Rome. With its elegant, enduring bulk and former function as a theater for gory contests between men and animals, the Flavian amphitheater (A.D. 72–80) never fails to impress. See map p 4, **1**; p 80, **8**.

Hadrian's Villa, outside Rome. The emperor's summer retreat was an architectural fantasy of pools, an aquarium, and walls of water. See map p 4, **1**; p 142, **2**.

Ostia Antica, outside Rome. At the extensive ruins of the port of ancient Rome, baths, a theater, apartments, and even a public latrine richly evoke life in the ancient city. See map p 4, **1**; p 146.

Palatine Hill, Rome. Nothing recalls the glory of ancient Rome like these massive brick ruins, studded by umbrella pines. This is where Rome began—where Romulus killed Remus in 753 B.C.—and where emperors and other wealthy Romans built their palaces and private entertainment facilities. See map p 4, **1**; p 80, **6**.

Arena, Verona. When the best-preserved Roman arena in the world was built in the 1st century A.D., the entire population of Verona could squeeze in for gladiator shows and mock naval battles. The amphitheater is still filled to its 20,000-person capacity when operas are performed on evenings in July and August. See map p 2, **15**; p 416, **1**.

Pompeii. The most famous ancient Roman city besides the capital itself was buried by the eruption of Mt. Vesuvius and, frozen in time, preserves a fascinating look at life as it was in A.D. 79. See map p 4, **3**; p 588.

Parco Archeologico della Neapolis, Siracusa. Spread across the vast ruins of ancient Siracusa are the gigantic Teatro Greco (Greek Theater); the Orecchio di Dionisio ("Ear of Dionysius," a tall and vaguely ear-shaped cave where the Greek tyrant Dionysius supposedly kept and eavesdropped on prisoners); the Anfiteatro Romano (Roman Amphitheater); and an artifact-filled museum. See map p 4, **15**; p 677, **5**.

Valley of the Temples, Agrigento. Sicily's most celebrated archaeological site preserves a proud group of temples from the 5th century B.C., as well as houses, streets, and tombs—all set on a ridge amid olive and almond trees and overlooking the sea. See map p 4, **13**; p 650, **7**.

> *Agrigento's Greek Temple of Concord has been standing since the 5th century B.C.*

The Best Churches & Cathedrals

> Churches harbor some of Italy's most intriguing architecture and revolutionary art. St. Peter's Basilica, Vatican City, is pictured.

St. Peter's Basilica, Rome. The incomprehensibly voluminous basilica of the Vatican is packed with incalculable riches, from the marble and gold that cover its every surface to such masterpieces as Michelangelo's *Pietà* and Bernini's Baldacchino. See map p 4, ❶; p 66, ❽.

Basilica di San Francesco, Assisi. From a commanding position at the end of Umbria's most pious hill town, this proud 13th-century church honors the monk who preached and led a life of poverty and whose life is depicted in Giotto's magnificent fresco cycle. See map p 6, ⓮; p 268, ❶.

Duomo, Orvieto. The facade of what may be the most beautiful Gothic church in Italy is a confection of polychrome marble, all pointed arches and spiky spires, and the interior contains fine frescoes by Luca Signorelli. See map p 6, ⓯; p 258, ❶.

Duomo, Siena. The architectural gem of Siena's golden age is the work of many architects and artists, who created a facade of colored bands of marble, an elaborately designed floor, and rich carvings and frescoes throughout. See map p 6, ❻; p 292, ❺.

Battistero & Duomo, Parma. The octagonal baptistery clad in pink marble and rising in five graceful tiers from an airy piazza is the greatest Italian Romanesque work, the creation of Benedetto Antelami. Correggio painted one of his great masterpieces in the cupola of the adjacent Duomo, where the Virgin and her entourage seem to float right through the top of the church into an Easter-egg-blue Heaven. See map p 2, ⓳; pp 326–327, ❶–❷.

Basilica di San Marco, Venice. Venice's Byzantine extravaganza is a shrine to the city's patron saint, and the multidomed, mosaic-paved Basilica begun in the 11th century still evokes the might of the Venetian republic. Beyond the glittering facade, more than 3.8 sq. km (1½ sq. miles) of colorful glass-tile mosaics sparkle and bedazzle with rich renditions of the religious rank and file, and the treasures include gilded bronze horses and other plunder from the Crusades. See map p 2, ⓱; p 368, ❸.

Santa Maria dei Miracoli, Venice. A top contender for the most beautiful church in Venice is sheathed in gleaming white marble; the effect is especially stunning when the exterior is lit at night. See map p 2, ⓱; p 374, ❹.

Duomo, Milan. A great accomplishment of the early Renaissance and one of the largest churches in Christendom was a work in progress for 6 centuries. The facade, with its 140 pinnacles and many tiers of statuary, was not completed until the 19th century, under the orders of Napoleon when he marched into town in 1805 and had himself crowned king of Italy on the high altar. See map p 2, ❾; p 456, ❶.

Cattedrale, Monreale. The Arab-Norman cathedral is best known for its dazzling 12th-century mosaics—perhaps the greatest artistic treasure in all of Sicily—and the cloister surrounded by 228 columns. See map p 4, ⓬; p 646, ❶.

The Best Architecture

Pantheon, Rome. The best-preserved and most elegant ancient building in Rome—if not the world—was built and possibly designed by Hadrian from A.D. 118 to 125 and is crowned with a 44m-wide (143-ft.) dome, poured in concrete almost 2,000 years ago and never structurally modified. See map p 4, **1**; p 102, **11**.

Villa d'Este, Rome. Whimsical grottoes, rushing flumes, and reflecting pools lace the gardens of the pleasure palace of Renaissance noble and cardinal Ippolito d'Este. See map p 4, **1**; p 142, **1**.

Brunelleschi's Dome, Florence. Filippo Brunelleschi's iconic dome (1420–36) is one of the world's most magnificent examples of Renaissance architecture, and on a climb to the top you'll experience the inventive double-shell design firsthand as you squeeze between the interior and outer domes. See map p 6, **3**; p 179, **2**.

Leaning Tower, Pisa. The very word "Pisa" conjures images of a jauntily askance, ornate white marble cylinder, framed by sunny blue skies and as iconic of Italy as pizza and tomato sauce. A view and a photo session do not suffice: Climbing the tower is one of Italy's most exhilarating experiences. See map p 6, **1**; p 220, **1**.

Certosa di Pavia, Pavia. This city south of Milan was a court for the ruling Visconti and Sforza families, and at the Certosa they are entombed behind a facade of richly colored marble, amid frescoes, paintings, and elaborate statuary. Cistercian monks reside at the Certosa in two-story cottages—each with its own garden plot—that surround the enormous cloister. See map p 2, **8**; p 448, **7**.

Galleria Vittorio Emanuele II, Milan. The glass-covered shopping arcade at the center of Milan, tucked between the Duomo and La Scala and inaugurated in 1867, is the prototype for shopping malls around the world. Milanese are proud to refer to their landmark as the *"Salotto di Milano"* (Living Room of Milan). See map p 2, **9**; p 457, **2**.

Palazzo Borromeo, Lago Maggiore. The gardens and palace built for a distinguished line of Milanese cardinals and counts on a rocky outcropping in Lago Maggiore are insanely excessive but a marvel to behold. See map p 2, **10**; p 440, **2**.

Palazzo del Tè, Mantua. On the monumental archway at the entrance to the pleasure palace of Federico II Gonzaga, the keystone appears to be falling out of place—a foreshadowing of the whimsy that lies in the salons beyond, where every surface is covered with frescoes and stuccos. See map p 2, **18**; p 474, **3**.

Stupinigi, Turin. Filippo Juvarra had more than a simple lodge in mind when in 1729 he created this retreat amid the Savoy hunting grounds: 137 rooms and 17 galleries are strung out along four angled wings off an oval-shaped main hall topped by a bronze stag. See map p 2, **7**; p 503, **2**.

> *Pisa's* torre pendente, *or Leaning Tower, has lurched almost since its first stones were laid in 1173.*

Our Favorite Works of Art

> *Bernini's* Apollo and Daphne *freezes the moment when the smitten god catches up with the object of his love—and she begins transforming into a tree.*

Apollo and Daphne, **Rome.** The emotionally charged work—capturing the moment in the myth of Apollo and Daphne when the nymph turns into a laurel tree to escape the amorous pursuit of the young god—is the most arresting example of Gian Lorenzo Bernini's sculptural virtuosity, which seems to defy the physical limitations of marble. See map p 4, ❶; p 84, ❷.

The *David,* Florence. The sculpture that Michelangelo considered to be his masterpiece captures the biblical hero with an expression of self-possession and tension, menace and vulnerability, that seems to change before your eyes. See map p 6, ❸; p 159, ❽.

Mosaics, Ravenna. From 550 to 750, Ravenna flourished as the western seat of the Byzantine Empire, and the most striking evidence of the city's former power can be found in the brilliant mosaics that shine within its churches and other landmarks. See map p 2, ㉒; p 336.

Camera degli Sposi, Mantua. One of the greatest fresco cycles of the Renaissance is an almost photographic record of life at a Renaissance court and one of the few such works that Andrea Mantegna painted to come through the ages intact. See map p 2, ⓲; p 472, ❶.

***The Last Supper,* Milan.** For his fresco on the refectory wall of the church of Santa Maria delle Grazie, Leonardo da Vinci used perspective to create the illusion that the room extends right into the painting and depicted the apostles and Christ with dramatic intensity—creating one of the world's most memorable images. See map p 2, ❾; p 462, ❼; p 22.

Mosaics, Villa Romana del Casale, Piazza Armerina. The most amazing and extensive mosaic cycle from the Roman world—many of wild beasts—pave the floors of the ruins of the country estate of a 4th-century-A.D. nobleman in Sicily. See map p 4, ⓮; p 642, ❷.

Our Favorite Small Inns

> *The Villa Ducale has one of the best perches in Sicily.*

Villa Laetitia, Rome. Suites set in the lush garden of a 100-year-old villa are decorated with 19th- and 20th-century antiques and offer such amenities as kitchens and, in most, outdoor space. See map p 4, **①**; p 135.

Locanda dell'Amorosa, near Sinalunga. An enchanting world unto itself, surrounded by vineyards, lawns, and ancient cypresses, offers country comfort in a 14th-century manor. See map p 6, **⑨**; p 231.

Villa Bordoni, near Greve. An incredibly stylish place in the Chianti countryside also has a wonderful on-site restaurant. See map p 6, **④**; p 225.

B&B Locanda Borgonuovo, Ferrara. A stylish apartment in an old building around the corner from Castello Estense provides Ferrara's most charming accommodations, stylishly furnished with Art Deco pieces. See map p 2, **㉑**; p 335.

Ca' della Corte, Venice. Behind a welcoming entrance court is one of Venice's most charming small inns, with extremely comfortable, character-filled rooms, a roof terrace, and a garden. See map p 2, **⑰**; p 402.

Oltre il Giardino, Venice. The former home of Gustav Mahler's widow, Alma, is tucked into a luxuriant garden next to a canal, and the beautifully refurbished guest rooms are an idyllic and intimate retreat. See map p 2, **⑰**; p 407.

Costantinopoli 104, Naples. A stay in this Art Nouveau palazzo at the back of a private courtyard is guaranteed to make you fall in love with Naples. See map p 4, **②**; p 610.

Villa Ducale, Taormina. A sunny inn perched high above town offers well-appointed rooms, many with terraces, and jaw-dropping views of Mt. Etna. See map p 4, **⑰**; p 683.

LEONARDO'S *LAST SUPPER*

Anatomy of a Masterpiece

BY STEPHEN BREWER

LEONARDO DA VINCI painted *The Last Supper* on the back wall of the refectory of the church of Santa Maria delle Grazie in Milan between 1495 and 1498, capturing the moment when Christ says to his 12 apostles, "One of you which eateth with me shall betray me" (Mark 14:18). Many other painters have executed the same scene, but none has managed to evoke the psychological depth, emotional drama, and touching humanity that Leonardo achieved. The painting has deteriorated severely over the years, was used for target practice by Napoleon's troops, and was rattled by World War II bombs. It's now preserved in a climate-controlled environment. See p 462, **❼**.

THE APOSTLES are arranged in groups of three, a sign of the Holy Trinity. There are three windows at the back of the painting, and the shape of Christ suggests a triangle.

THE ARCH above the window behind Christ is placed so that it forms a halo above his head.

Fragile Beauty

A wall painting such as *The Last Supper* would normally have been done as a fresco, in which paint is applied to wet plaster so the two dry together to create a permanent bond. Leonardo invented a new technique, applying tempera (egg yolk and vinegar) and oil paint to dry plaster. The experiment was unsuccessful, and the painting has been deteriorating since it was finished. A restoration completed in 1999 preserved what was left of Leonardo's original, but few of the master's true colors remain, and many of the shapes and lines have been altered over the centuries. It is a testimony to the genius of Leonardo that the work continues to evoke the raw power of this important moment for the Christian faith.

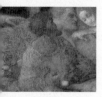

JUDAS clutches a purse, presumably filled with silver he was awarded for betraying Christ. He is part of the group, but cast in shadows, and he leans away from Christ.

CHRIST All elements in the composition direct the eye to Christ's head. Christ is perfectly calm, while the apostles react with varying aspects of anger and shock.

THE DOOR In 1662 a door was cut into the wall, and the section of the painting showing Christ's feet, which Leonardo had positioned to symbolize the crucifixion, was removed.

JOHN, to the left of Christ, looks effeminate. It has been suggested that the figure is Mary Magdalene, who some scholars believe was Christ's wife. It may simply be that young John was still beardless and soft-skinned.

The Best Luxury Hotels

> *The frescoed Presidential Suite at the Four Seasons in Florence.*

Four Seasons, Florence. One of Florence's newest hotels (opened in 2008) is also the most luxurious, with a 4.5-hectare (11-acre) private garden with outdoor pool, the frescoed surroundings of the beautifully restored Palazzo della Gherardesca, and the best staff in town. See map p 6, ❸; p 205.

Gritti Palace, Venice. Doge Andrea Gritti built this palazzo on the Grand Canal in 1525, and the sheen of luxury hasn't faded since. See map p 2, ⓱; p 405.

Grand Hotel et de Milan, Milan. This bastion of luxury lives up to its name thanks to its refined atmosphere, a very discreet staff, and a perfect location near La Scala. See map 2, ❾; p 468.

Royal Hotel, San Remo. A grand hotel set amid palm-shaded lawns and lovely gardens above the sea pampers guests in style and recalls the town's end-of-the-19th-century heyday. See map p 2, ❹; p 559.

Palazzo Sasso, Ravello. A Moorish peach palazzo is supremely comfortable and well appointed, yet refreshingly down to earth and surrounded by terraced gardens overflowing with bougainvillea. See map p 4, ❽; p 623.

Santa Caterina, near Amalfi. A stunning natural setting, informal atmosphere, and sea-facing terraces are complemented by a swimming deck and the best breakfast spread in the region. See map p 4, ❻; p 630.

The Top Food & Wine Experiences

> *Cold cuts like* coppa, prosciutto crudo, *and* pancetta *are just three of the many ways Italians like to cure a pig.*

Cheap eats in Rome. Instead of a sit-down lunch, grab a savory pizza *farcita* (pizza bread sandwich stuffed with your choice of veggies, cheeses, or meats) or *pizza al taglio* (pizza by the slice). Come sundown, it's *aperitivo* time (happy hour) at most Roman bars and lounges—that means a free buffet of tasty Italian specialties for anyone who buys a drink. See map p 4, ❶; p 127.

Montalcino. The hill town, surrounded by wineries that make Brunello di Montalcino, is filled with bars serving the mighty red alongside Tuscan delicacies. Montalcino's 14th-century fortress houses the excellent Enoteca La Fortezza. See map p 6, ❼; p 278.

Spritzing in Venice. Find a square, pull up a chair at a cafe table, and enjoy a spritz—a splash of Aperol in Prosecco—accompanied by *cicchetti,* little portions of cheese, fried calamari, olives, and other appetizers. See map p 2, ⓱; p 395.

The Langhe Wine Route. The hills of the Langhe that roll away to the south of Alba are carpeted with vineyards that produce some of Italy's finest wines and are topped with castles and villages, most with an *enoteca* (wine bar) or two. See map p 2, ❺; p 521, ❻.

Pizza in Naples. Pizza was invented in Naples, and the particular style of dough, tomato sauce, and mozzarella used in the city isn't replicated anywhere else in the world. The two best places to try the local specialty are Da Michele and Gino Sorbillo. See map p 4, ❷; p 605.

The Most Memorable Dining Experiences

> Osteria Le Logge, a pharmacy in the 19th century, one of Italy's finest eateries in the 21st.

Perilli, Rome. Step back in time and enjoy the old-school atmosphere at this beloved institution of Roman *ristorazione*. See map p 4, ①; p 128.

La Bucaccia, Cortona. Rustic tradition meets elegant flourish at this cavelike temple of Cortonese cuisine, run by the passionate Magi family. Ingredients are rigorously local, and the flavors are swoon-inducing. See map p 6, ⑩; p 273.

Osteria Le Logge, Siena. The best veal steaks in town and memorable pastas are served in refined, old-fashioned environs. See map p 6, ⑥; p 295.

Solociccia, Panzano in Chianti. Carnivores will want to craft their travel plans around the 4 days each week that this Tuscan temple of meat is open; the generous prix fixe meal consists of six courses of lovingly prepared, succulent meats infused with local herbs. See map p 6, ⑤; p 238.

Fini, Modena. One of Italy's most noted restaurants produces its own salamis, hams, and other ingredients that show up in the house specialties, accompanied by wine from Fini's own vineyards. See map p 2, ⑳; p 317.

Antiche Carampane, Venice. It's almost impossible to find, but excellent and exotic seafood pastas and sophisticated fish preparations make the effort worthwhile. See map p 2, ⑰; p 398.

Bea Vita, Venice. A canalside meal in a quiet backwater includes homemade pastas and fresh fish and meat in innovative preparations. See map p 2, ⑰; p 398.

Le Bistrot de Venise, Venice. Ages-old Venetian recipes and rare, special-production wines are paired for a memorable dining experience in sophisticated surroundings. See map p 2, ⑰; p 399.

Aquila Nigra, Mantua. A Renaissance feast of such local specialties as eel and pike from the Mincio is served in a fresco-bedecked convent. See map p 2, ⑱; p 475.

Can't Miss Festivals & Events

> *Carnevale, originally Venice's last meat feast before Lent, has grown into Italy's most recognizable festival.*

Christmas & Easter, Rome. The Church is at its most ceremonious, with liturgical productions from the Vatican to the Colosseum that put Hollywood to shame. See map p 4, ❶; p 719; p 721.

Corsa dei Ceri (Race of the Candles), Gubbio. In one of Italy's greatest medieval traditions, the town's patron, St. Ubaldo, is honored each May 15 with an uphill race to his sanctuary—at breakneck speed, and with a twist: Runners carry huge wooden candles . . . and St. Ubaldo's always wins. See map p 6, ⓬; p 264, ❿.

Umbria Jazz Festival, Perugia. Every July, the Umbria Jazz Festival brings world-class musicians to stages all over town. See map p 6, ⓭; p 720.

Palio, Siena. Two times a year, on July 2 and August 16, jockeys fly around Siena's dirt-filled *campo* three times with the goal of winning Europe's most daring horse race. See map p 6, ❻; p 293.

Spoleto Festival (Festival dei Due Mondi), Spoleto. The beautiful Umbrian town hosts music, dance, and theater events every June and July, showcasing the world's top performers. See map p 6, ⓰; p 719.

Biennale d'Arte Contemporanea e Architettura, Venice. One of the world's most prestigious exhibits of contemporary art takes over pavilions in the Giardini Pubblici in odd years, architecture in even years. See map p 2, ⓱; p 719.

Carnevale, Venice. Masked revelers roam the streets and waterways for 10 days before Ash Wednesday, making this the best or worst time to come to Venice, depending on your view of crowds and bacchanals. See map p 2, ⓱; p 718.

2
Strategies for Seeing Italy

Strategies for Seeing Italy

No matter how many days or weeks you allot to your Italian travels, you will inevitably end up lamenting, "So much to see and do, so little time." With a little strategizing, however, you can make the most of your time. The overriding rule, however, is this: Relax and be prepared to let the many-faceted wonders of Italy and Italian life sweep you away.

> PREVIOUS PAGE Spectacular gardens front the villas overlooking scenic Lake Como. THIS PAGE Lingering over your caffè—here in Florence's Piazza della Signoria—is an essential part of the experience in Italy.

Tip #1: Leave the driving to someone else
The Italian love affair with the car is legendary, but as it is with any difficult companion, you'll probably find life easier without one. Renting a car is expensive, and gasoline is pricey (it costs more than twice what it does in the United States). Many city centers are closed to private cars, and parking is almost impossible in Rome and Florence, as well as in such smaller cities as Siena and Bologna. On the plus side, it's easy to get around most regions by train—all major cities, as well as such places as the resorts of Liguria, are well connected by train service, while buses pick up the slack to serve many small towns, and ferries and hydrofoils ply the lakes and seacoasts. You might want a car to tour such places as the remote corners of the

Tuscan countryside or inland Sicily, but in those cases you can probably get by with renting one for a day or two.

Tip #2: Stay put Packing and unpacking and checking into and out of hotels can be time-consuming and a hassle. So, settle into one place for a spell. Many cities and towns are surprisingly close to one another and well connected by train, so it's often easy to use one city as a base and travel out from there. From Venice, for instance, it's easy to make day trips as far afield as Verona, Ferrara, Ravenna, and Bologna, all of which are well under 2 hours away. From Rome it's easy to visit Assisi, Orvieto, and other towns in Umbria. A rail pass (p 725) can make it especially easy and economical to hop on and off trains to explore

> *Enjoy the local specialities—here, Parma's hams and cheeses.*

a region. Plus, many hotels provide discounts for longer stays, and long-term guests are often treated to a delight that money can't buy—a generous dose of hospitality.

Tip #3: Travel light Just ask anyone who's dragged a suitcase over the countless bridges of Venice—lugging your baggage around, up, and down station steps and along city streets, is inconvenient, to say the least, if not painful, just as using taxis and paying porters gets to be an annoying expense. Bring only what you can comfortably carry, and you'll be amazed at how much easier your travels through Italy are. If you forget something, all the better—that's a good excuse to shop for one of those enticing items that fill shop windows throughout the country.

Tip #4: Eat well for less You don't need to spend a fortune to eat well in Italy, where good food is in abundance and even the most humble fare is often prepared with pride. Lunch won't cost more than 3€ if you grab a square of pizza or a simple panino. You'll soon learn that each town has its own delicious fast-food fare, such as Genoa's *farinata,* chickpea flour that's brushed with olive oil, sprinkled with sea salt, baked, cut into circles, and filled with spinach, ricotta, and other stuffings. Come sundown, *aperitivi* are often accompanied by a free buffet of tasty Italian specialties. In Venice, a spritz is served with your choice of tapas-like *cicchetti,* olives, little morsels of salami and cheese, fried calamari, and other tidbits that cost about 2€ a plate.

Tip #5: Take advantage of special events Wherever you go in Italy, you can usually find some good entertainment—concerts, festivals, walking tours, food fairs, wine tastings, outdoor movies, processions . . . something always seems to be happening in Italian towns and cities. The tourist information office in any town is usually a good source for information on local events, and your hotel will probably also be in the know. Italy famously hosts some of the world's most noted festivals and other events, from the Spoleto Festival of Two Worlds to the Venice Biennale to Rome's summer opera season in the Baths of Caracalla and Verona's summertime operas in the Roman arena. You may want to plan your trip around one of these big blowouts, in which case you should reserve hotel rooms and purchase tickets well in advance.

Tip #6: Go online Most Italian hotels, museums, and other tourist-oriented operations now have websites, often with English versions. You can book anything from a hotel room to an opera ticket for La Scala (www.teatroallascala.org) online, making your Italian travels much easier than they were in the days when we were dependent on the whims of errant letters of inquiry and erratically operating ticket offices. Hotel websites treat you to views of the rooms—never trust one that doesn't show guest room shots. One especially useful Web resource is http://trenitalia.com, where you can find times and prices for trains operating throughout Italy.

You can stay connected even if you don't want to lug a laptop around and if your Blackberry doesn't function in Italy. Many Italian hotels have computers for public use, and Internet cafes are fairly easy to come by in most towns and cities; remember that in Italy you must present a passport or another form of identification in order to use a public computer.

Tip #7: Be a culture vulture You don't have to be an art historian to appreciate Italy's vast repository of art. Simply open yourself to the experience of seeing some of the greatest artworks and architectural landmarks of the Western world. You may well join the legions of tourists who have been transported by the power of the *David* or *The Last Supper.* Many museums offer free gallery tours, often in English, that will enhance the experience, or at least provide English-language brochures and in-gallery cards highlighting their collections.

Tip #8: Don't overbook your days You'll get a lot more out of your experiences if you see two museums a day instead of four, allow three days in a city instead of rushing through on a whirlwind tour in a single afternoon. Keep in mind, too, that summertime heat in Italy, especially in the south, can be enervating, so slacken your place to accommodate.

Tip #9: Expect the unexpected Allow time to let things happen in Italy. You may well find that you want to spend a few extra moments in front of a museum masterpiece, strolling through a public garden, or just sitting on the rim of a fountain in a piazza. Leave time for the unexpected. A walk through a market checking out cheeses you've never tasted before can take up the entire morning; an unknown street can lead you to a church you've never visited or a part of town you've never explored.

Tip #10: Remember, "When in Rome . . ." One of the great pleasures of being in Italy is to fall in with the rhythm of the Italian way of life. Linger at a cafe over a cappuccino; allow 2 hours for lunch, even longer for dinner; or join the Italians on an evening *passeggiata,* when the point is simply to stroll without a destination in mind. Who knows? These simple concessions to a different schedule may well be the highlight of your trip, and you'll soon notice that art and architecture aren't the only visual treats in Italy. Sitting in a piazza watching Italian drama swirling around you, in all its Technicolor clichés—kids playing, lovers holding hands, women hanging out of windows—is one of the great pleasures of being in this country where life tends to be much more public than it does in the United States and the United Kingdom.

> *Rome's Baths of Caracalla make a dramatic backdrop for summer orchestral concerts and grand operas like* Aïda.

3
The Best
All-Italy
Itineraries

The Best of Italy in 1 Week

Italy in a week? You will whet your appetite, and have a head-spinning experience doing so. A full 7 days allows just enough time to see some of the greatest art and architecture of the Western world, explore some evocative historical sites, and get a taste for *la dolce vita*. There's no need to rent a car because you'll be traveling from city to city by train (don't bother with a rail pass—buying individual tickets is cheaper), but do bring a pair of sturdy walking shoes.

START Fly into Rome's Fiumicino or Ciampino airport.

1 Rome. Start your first day in this ancient city on the **Capitoline Hill** (p 62, **1**), where Michelangelo designed the star-patterned **Campidoglio** square and surrounding buildings of the **Capitoline Museums** (p 89, **8**), and the south-facing terraces provide a majestic view over the **Roman Forum** (p 82). From here the route leads down into this center of Western civilization for almost a thousand years, and then up the **Palatine Hill** (p 80, **6**), where Rome began and where the wealthiest citizens once lived. Then it's on to the massive, remarkably well-preserved theater of slaughter that is the **Colosseum** (p 80, **8**). Your final stop in ancient Rome treats you to the elegance that this ancient civilization achieved—the **Pantheon** (p 102, **11**), perhaps the best-

> PREVIOUS PAGE *Torre del Mangia, overlooking Siena's Piazza del Campo.* THIS PAGE *Neptune is the central figure in Rome's Trevi Fountain, the construction of which took 30 years.*

0   100 mi
0   100 km

Turin Vercelli Bergamo **Trento** Belluno
PIEDMONT   **FRIULI-**
         Alessandria **Milan** Brescia **VENETO** **VENEZIA**
Cuneo   LOMBARDY Verona Vicenza Treviso **GIULIA** SLOVENIA
         Pavia Cremona Padua
FRANCE   Piacenza Mantua **Venice** ❸ **Trieste**
         Savona   Gulf of
LIGURIA **Genoa** Reggio Modena Ferrara Venice
Imperia   EMILIA-ROMAGNA
         La Spezia **Bologna** Ravenna CROATIA
Ligurian Lucca Prato ❷ Forlì
  Sea   Pisa   Rimini BOSNIA AND
         Livorno Arno **Florence** SAN   HERZE-
                        TUSCANY MARINO Pesaro GOVINA
                        Siena Arezzo Ancona Adriatic
         Corsica   **Perugia** THE   Sea
         (FRANCE) Grosseto MARCHES
                        UMBRIA ❶ Rome
                        Viterbo Terni ❷ Florence
                        LAZIO Rieti **L'Aquila** ❸ Venice
                        VATICAN Pescara
Tyrrhenian Sea CITY **Rome** ❶ ABRUZZO

Train Tip

Though advance train reservations (a must on most high-speed trains) before you leave for Italy can be more expensive than those made in Italy, your time is at a premium on this tour and you don't want to be left without a seat, so if you're going to Italy during the busy summer season or around the holidays, make train reservations before you leave home. See p 723 for more on train travel in Italy.

preserved structure to come from the ancient world and graced with a magnificent dome of poured concrete. A few afternoon hours in the **Vatican Museums** (p 88, ❸) allow you time to see some of the world's best ancient sculpture, including the *Laocoön* and *Apollo Belvedere* as well as two of Italy's greatest Renaissance accomplishments, the **Raphael Rooms** (Stanze di Raffaello) and Michelangelo's frescoes in the **Sistine Chapel.** You'll have time and energy for a brief look inside **St. Peter's Basilica** (p 66, ❽) and a look at **Castel Sant'Angelo** (p 98, ❶) before freshening up before dinner—

> *The ancient construction secrets behind the dome of the Pantheon have intrigued visitors for millennia.*

always a delight in Rome, especially when it's followed up by a stroll through the **Piazza Navona** (p 100, ⑥) and past the floodlit **Trevi Fountain** (p 67, ⑬).

On your second day, spend the morning wandering the picturesque squares and alleys of **Trastevere** (p 110) and **Campo de' Fiori** (p 104, ①), Rome's oldest and most authentic quarters. Have lunch, then cross town to feast your eyes on the masterpieces of baroque sculpture and painting in the **Galleria Borghese** (p 84, ②). Go for a stroll through the **Villa Borghese** (p 72, ⑧), making your way to the Pincio terraces and their enchanting view over the city and the Vatican. Finish the day in the Tridente district below the **Spanish Steps** (p 73, ⑭), where shopping, sipping wine, and dining are the main pursuits. ⊙ **2 days.**

From Rome's Stazione Termini, take a late-morning train on Day 3 to Florence's Stazione Santa Maria Novella. Trains run twice an hour—make sure you reserve a seat in advance—and the trip takes about 95 minutes.

② **Florence.** After you've checked into your hotel, hit the ground running, because an introduction to the city's remarkable art and architecture will pack an afternoon with visits to the **Uffizi** (p 174), the **Accademia** (p 159, ⑧) to see Michelangelo's *David,* and finally, **Brunelleschi's Dome,** the **Battistero,** and **Campanile di Giotto** at the Piazza del Duomo (p 178). As the day begins to wane, make your way across the **Ponte Vecchio** (p 182, ①) to the panoramic **Piazzale Michelangelo** (p 159, ⑩) to watch the sun set over the city's domes and red-tile rooftops. Top it all off with dinner in an authentic Tuscan *buca* (cellar).

Spend the next morning wandering through **Oltrarno** (p 186), the district on the left bank of the Arno, to the **Palazzo Pitti** (p 168, ①), where galleries are filled with Renaissance works and painting and sculpture by later European masters. Spend the rest of your afternoon strolling through the **Giardino di Boboli** (p 187, ⑮).

On your last morning in Florence visit the **Medici Chapels** (p 173, ⑪), where Michelangelo's grand sculptures honor the

> *The marble stripes and lozenges of Florence's Duomo predate the Renaissance.*

> *Where most towns have a Main Street, Venice has the Grand Canal.*

powerful Florentine clan, and the **Basilica di San Lorenzo** (p 172, ⑩), the great work of Filippo Brunelleschi. ⏱ 2½ days.

Board a Eurostar Italia train (reservations a must!) bound for Venice's Stazione Santa Lucia so that you'll arrive there by midafternoon. Trip time is approximately 3 hours.

❸ **Venice.** A perfect introduction to this water-dependent city is a trip up the **Grand Canal** (p 362), the S-shaped, 3.2km-long (2-mile) stretch of busy waterway, lined with palazzi, that has been the city's main street for more than a thousand years. Then step into the **Basilica di San Marco** (p 368, ❸), glittering with Byzantine mosaics, before joining Venetians for a cocktail in one of the legendary cafes of **Piazza San Marco** (p 350, ❺), the civilized square that Napoleon called the "drawing room" of Europe. After dinner stroll over to the **Ponte di Rialto** (p 358, ❸) to watch the gondolas slip beneath your feet and fall under the spell of the shimmering reflections of the palazzi on the waters of the Grand Canal.

Begin Day 6 amid the bustle of the Rialto markets, then set off on a tour of some of the city's greatest repositories of art. **Santa Maria Gloriosa dei Frari** (p 372, ⑬) is one of the largest churches in Venice and one of the city's great treasure troves, with masterworks by Titian and Giovanni Bellini. The nearby **Scuola Grande di San Rocco** (p 372, ⑫) is lavishly decorated by Tintoretto, and the **Scuola Grande dei Carmini** (p 370, ⑪) is a masterpiece designed by architect Baldassare Longhena. Come lunchtime,

restore yourself in **Campo Santa Margherita** (p 356, ❾), a welcoming square filled with cafes and market stalls, then spend the afternoon exploring the masterpieces in the **Accademia** (p 370, ❾), the **Peggy Guggenheim Collection** (p 354, ❸), and the new **Centro d'Arte Contemporanea de Punta della Dogana** (p 354, ❷). Take a look inside the massive church of **Santa Maria della Salute** (p 354, ❶) before enjoying the sweeping views of the lagoon, the Grand Canal, and the Giudecca Canal from the Dogana, then join Venetians in a sunset *passeggiata* along the Zattere.

Your final day in Venice might begin with a visit to the **Palazzo Ducale** (p 369, ❷), the palace where the doges lived and ruled, then off into the backwaters of the city to amble at leisure, perhaps setting a rambling course to see the jewel-like little **Church of Santa Maria dei Miracoli** (p 374, ❹), tucked away on a small canal and sheathed in white marble, and **Campo Santi Giovanni e Paolo** (p 358, ❶), a sunny square graced with an equestrian monument by Verrocchio. In the afternoon, take to the waters of the lagoon and visit one or two of the nearby islands: **Murano** (p 382, ❷), for glass; **Burano** (p 384, ❸), for lace; or **Torcello** (p 384, ❹), the most peaceful, a deserted little island where past residents left behind the glorious, mosaic-paved **Basilica di Santa Maria Assunta** (p 372, ⑮). ⏱ 2½ days.

Fly home out of Venice's Aeroporto Marco Polo.

The Best of Italy in 2 Weeks

Two weeks allow a little more time to see Italy at your leisure, and a bit more of it, too. Even so, you will probably find that you could spend much more time in any of the places you visit on this itinerary. On the plus side, this entire itinerary can be done via rail and public transportation (a rail pass is recommended, p 724).

> The gardens of Ravello's Villa Cimbrone were laid out in 1905 by Lord Grimthorpe, designer of London's Big Ben.

START Fly into Rome's Fiumicino or Ciampino airport.

1 Rome. For your first 2 days in Rome, see my suggestions on p 36, **1**. On your third day, leave the city center for a visit to the **Catacombe di San Callisto** (p 74, **1**) and a walk along the history-saturated **Via Appia Antica** (p 113, **7**). Then, spend some time exploring some of the city's less-trafficked neighborhoods, such as the **Aventine** (p 77, **7**), the **Jewish Ghetto** (p 77, **8**; p 107, **12**–**16**), or **Monti** (p 77, **10**). ☉ 3 days.

On the morning of Day 4, take a Eurostar Italia (reserve in advance) train from Stazione Termini to Naples's Stazione Centrale (trip time: 1 hr. 21 min.). Change there to the Circumvesuviana train to Sorrento (trip time: 1 hr).

2 Sorrento. We recommend you use this lively resort town and transportation hub as a base for exploring the Amalfi Coast. You'll arrive here in time for a late afternoon swim at one of its beaches and a walk through town. At night, grab a bite and a drink on **Piazza Tasso** (p 624, **1**) and watch the world go by. ☉ 1 day, including travel time.

On the morning of Day 5, head to the Circumvesuviana train station and catch an Amalfi-bound SITA bus. At the Amalfi terminus, switch to the bus to Ravello (try to get a seat on the right side of the bus for the best views). Travel time is 1½ hours, including waiting time in Amalfi.

3 Ravello. The journey to Ravello, on local bus service, is part of the fun. You ride on a two-lane

1 Rome
2 Sorrento
3 Ravello
4 Amalfi
5 Positano
6 Capri
7 Pompeii
8 Naples
9 Florence
10 Siena
11 Bologna
12 Venice
13 Verona

road that clings to the vertiginous hillside, with nothing but a skilled driver and a guardrail standing between you and a 150m (500 ft.) drop to the sea. The views of verdant hillsides and the azure sea help dispel vertigo and raw fear. Ravello's main attraction is **Villa Cimbrone** (p 622, 3), where sumptuous gardens provide panoramic views up and down the coast. ⏱ 2 hr.

Hop back aboard the SITA bus and return to Amalfi.

4 **Amalfi.** This once maritime power is now a bustling little place that offers more of a realistic view of life on the coast than some of its more picturesque neighbors. Do stop in at its 13th-century **Duomo** (p 628, 1), whose ornate Moorish-influenced facade hides an elaborate baroque interior. ⏱ 2 hr.

> *Capri's Blue Grotto is accessible only by boat.*

Take a SITA bus to Positano (trip time: 30 min.).

⑤ **Positano.** Positano is one of the most undeniably romantic spots on earth, where colorful houses cling to a hillside above a beach and harbor. A visit here is less about seeing the sights and more about soaking up the local atmosphere. Follow the labyrinth of narrow lanes downhill to the harbor, where you can board a boat back to Sorrento. ⏲ At least 1 hr. See p 618.

On Day 6, from Sorrento's Marina Piccola, board a hydrofoil or ferry to Capri. Allow 30 minutes to 1 hour for the crossing.

⑥ **Capri.** A full day on this fabled island will let you fully explore its natural wonders. Hike to the **Arco Naturale** or along **Via Pizzolungo** (p 614, ⑦) if you're physically up to it—you'll be afforded remarkable views of the sea and outcroppings. If you prefer to avoid the hike, head to the town of Anacapri and take a chairlift up to the top of the island's highest point, **Monte Solaro** (p 615, ⑩). For more gorgeous views, walk down Via Tragara to see the famed **Faraglioni** (p 612, ③), and then shop your way through the **boutiques of Capri town** (p 612, ②). And no trip to Capri is complete without a touristy but memorable trip by sea into the **Blue Grotto** (p 614, ⑧). ⏲ 1 day.

Early in the morning of Day 7, check out of your hotel in Sorrento and board the Circumvesuviana train to Pompeii/Scavi. The train station has luggage storage facilities.

⑦ **Pompeii.** Spend most of the day witnessing the fascinating vestiges of life in A.D. 79, when Mt. Vesuvius erupted and buried this city in ash, preserving it for the ages. Pompeii's must-see **Villa of the Mysteries** (p 593, ⑲) is justifiably famous for its magnificent frescoes. ⏲ 5 hr., including travel time.

From Pompeii, take the Circumvesuviana train to Naples (trip time: 45 min.).

⑧ **Naples.** Arrive in Naples in time for a late afternoon visit to the **Museo Archeologico Nazionale** (p 605, ⑩), filled with artifacts and mosaics recovered from Pompeii and Herculaneum, and also explore the harbor and *centro storico*. End the day enjoying one of Naples's great culinary contributions, pizza, at either **Da Michele** or **Gino Sorbillo** (p 605). ⏲ 2 hr.

On Day 8, take an early morning train out of Naples to Florence's Stazione Santa Maria Novella (trip time: 3 hr. 15 min.). You'll spend the next 3 nights in Florence.

> *Lush bougainvillea and impossible terraces make romantic Positano more than just a sleepy fishing village.*

⑨ Florence. ⏲ 2½ days. See p 38, ②.

On the afternoon of Day 10, take a train to Siena (trip time: 1 hr. 22 min.) for a quick excursion.

⑩ Siena. Start your afternoon off in the **Piazza del Campo** (p 290, ①), the monumental square at the center of the city. A climb to the top of the **Torre del Mangia** (p 291, ②) for the views across the city to the rolling Chianti countryside is a must. Next, take a quick look at the collections of the **Palazzo Pubblico & Museo Civico** (p 291, ③), especially its frescoed Sala della Pace. Top off your visit with a stop at the dramatic **Duomo** (p 292, ⑤), perhaps the most beautiful of all of Italy's Gothic cathedrals. ⏲ 4 hr.

On Day 11, take an early morning train out of Florence to Bologna (trip time: 1 hr.). Store your luggage in the train station.

⑪ Bologna. It's not on the well-worn tourist track, but Bologna is one of Italy's best-preserved medieval cities and the seat of the oldest university in Europe. A short walking tour, much of it under the arcades that cover the city's sidewalks, shows off Piazza Maggiore, surrounded by sturdy brick palaces and the **Basilica di San Petronio** (p 318, ①); the **Church of San Giacomo Maggiore** (p 320, ⑤), where the chapel of the Bentivoglio family is decorated with frescoes by Lorenzo Costa that vividly depict a day in the life of a Renaissance court; the **Pinacoteca Nazionale** (p 321, ⑥), a vast repository of works by Bolognese artists and other masters; and the **Basilica di San Domenico** (p 322, ⑧), where the tomb of Bologna's own St. Dominic was crafted by Michelangelo and other artists over several centuries. ⏲ 4 hr.

From Bologna, board an afternoon train to Venice's Stazione di Santa Lucia (trip time: 1 hr. 40 min.). You'll spend your remaining time in Italy based in Venice.

⑫ Venice. ⏲ 2½ days. See p 39, ③.

On the afternoon of Day 14, take a train excursion (trip time: 1 hr. 30 min.) to Verona.

⑬ Verona. It's famous for its star-crossed lovers Romeo and Juliet, but Verona is an alluring place even without these romantic

> *Verona's largely intact arena hosted real gladiators in the days of the Roman Empire.*

associations, laying claim to the best-preserved Roman **arena** (p 416, ①) in the world; the **Teatro Romano** (p 419, ⑧), a beautiful Roman theater offering stunning views; the 12th-century **San Zeno Maggiore** (p 418, ③), with a triptych by Andrea Mantegna; and, of course, the **Casa di Giulietta** (p 419, ⑦)—the house where Shakespeare's heroine is said to have lived and hailed her lover from the balcony. ⏲ 3 hr.

Fly home out of Venice's Aeroporto Marco Polo.

THE GREAT
CHURCHES

Italy's Seven-Century Building Spree

BY STEPHEN BREWER

BETWEEN THE 11th and 17th centuries Italy saw a great building spree, as massive churches rose in the middle of most cities of any size and wealth. The designs were based on basilicas, or halls that the ancient Romans used as public meeting places; indeed, many of Italy's grandest churches, including St. Peter's in Rome, are known as basilicas, while the term *cathedral* refers to a church that is the seat of a bishop. Whatever the churches are called, most are laid out on an east–west axis, with the entrance on the west end so the congregation faces east, the direction of the rising sun, from which Christ is predicted to return to Earth. The main body of a church is the nave, Latin for ship, as the cathedral is seen as a ship carrying the populace through the stormy seas of life on Earth. No matter what they look like, all cathedrals are intended to awe believers with the majesty of God, and they continue to inspire awe as treasure troves of some of Italy's greatest art and architecture.

Outside Palermo
CATTEDRALE DI MONREALE
One of the finest examples of Arab-Norman architecture in the world was completed in 1182 by French crusaders who occupied Sicily. Pointed exterior arches are inlaid with marble, richly colored glass mosaics carpet nearly every inch of the interior, and the cloisters are surrounded by 216 white marble columns. See p 646, **①**.

Venice
BASILICA DI SAN MARCO
The most famous Byzantine church in the world, completed in 1093, is modeled after the Hagia Sophia in Istanbul and other Eastern Orthodox churches. Built in the shape of a Greek cross and crowned with ornate domes and towers, San Marco is awash inside and out with glittering mosaics. See p 368, **③**.

Parma
DUOMO DI PARMA
In the 12th century, church builders were still borrowing techniques from the Romans. The high walls, small windows, and columns with decorated capitals in the cathedral in Parma are typical of the Romanesque; Parma's cathedral is also graced with a stunning baptistery (pictured). See p 327, **②**.

Siena
CATTEDRALE DI SANTA MARIA DELL'ASSUNTA
With its high arches, large windows, and tall campanile, Siena's massive Duomo, completed in 1263, is a fine example of the Italian Gothic. The facade is largely the work of Giovanni Pisano, master architect of the age, and the carved pulpit in the black-and-white striped interior is by his father, sculptor Nicola Pisano. See p 292, **⑤**.

Rome
ST. PETER'S BASILICA
The most important church in Christendom is the greatest architectural achievement of the Renaissance. Michelangelo was the master architect, building upon the work of such notables as Donato Bramante and Raphael. The dome is the tallest in the world but slightly smaller than Brunelleschi's dome in Florence. See p 66, **⑧**.

Bible Lessons

Whatever the style, most Italian cathedrals serve as a Poor Man's Bible, in which the illiterate could learn the Scriptures through biblical stories portrayed in carvings, frescoes, and even stained glass. A fearsome scene of the Last Judgment, a warning to sinners to repent before it is too late,

nearly always also makes an appearance.

The South in 12 Days

In many ways, the south is especially evocative of Italy and Italian life—stunning seacoasts, azure seas, palm trees, clamorous cities, ancient ruins, seafood, and pizza. If these are the sights and sensations you associate with Italy you won't be disappointed, because you'll encounter all of the above in Rome and the lands to the south. This 12-day tour begins in Rome, includes a stop to enjoy Naples and the Amalfi Coast, and ends in Sicily.

START Fly into Rome's Fiumicino or Ciampino airport.

1 **Rome.** For your first 2 days in Rome, see my suggestions on p 36, **1**. On your third day, leave the city center for a visit to the **Catacombe di San Callisto** (p 74, **1**) and a walk along the history-saturated **Via Appia Antica** (p 113, **7**). Then, spend the afternoon in the quieter corners of the *centro storico*, wandering the **Jewish Ghetto** (p 77, **8**; p 107, **12**–**16**), **Isola Tiberina** (p 108, **18**), or **Monti** (p 77, **10**). ⏱ 3 days.

On the morning of Day 4, take a Eurostar Italia (reserve in advance) train from Stazione Termini to Naples Stazione Centrale (trip time: 1 hr. 21 min.).

2 **Naples.** Walk through the city's fascinating seafood market, the **Mercato di Porta Nolana** (p 604, **7**), where the denizens of the deep are as much a part of the show as the wheeling and dealing that is an honored tradition in this old mercantile city. Then move off to explore the pedestrian-friendly and very lively **Spaccanapoli** (p 602, **1**) section of town. Once you're done above-ground, take a tour of **Napoli Sotterranea** (p 605, **8**), the Neapolitan "underworld," where a fascinating 90-minute itinerary takes you through ancient quarries, a Greco-Roman theater, cisterns and aqueducts, and caves that were used as air-raid shelters in World War II. In the afternoon, visit the **Museo Archeologico Nazionale** (p 605, **10**), where

> *The pace of life is a little slower in Italy's deep south; here, the coast near Taormina, Sicily.*

1 Rome
2 Naples
3 Amalfi Coast
4 Pompeii
5 Capri
6 Palermo
7 Siracusa
8 Taormina

Turin
Vercelli
PIEDMONT
Alessandria
Cuneo
Savona
LIGURIA
Imperia
Genoa
Bergamo
Milan
LOMBARDY
Brescia
Pavia
Piacenza
Cremona
Mantua
Reggio
Modena
Ferrara
EMILIA-ROMAGNA
Bologna
La Spezia
Lucca
Prato
Forlì
Ravenna
Pisa
Livorno
Arno
Florence
TUSCANY
Siena
Arezzo
Grosseto
Viterbo
UMBRIA
Perugia
Tiber
Terni
Rieti
LAZIO
VATICAN
CITY
Rome
Trento
TRENTINO-
ALTO ADIGE
Belluno
Verona
Vicenza
VENETO
Treviso
Padua
Venice
Gulf of
Venice
FRIULI-
VENEZIA
GIULIA
Trieste
Ligurian
Sea
Corsica
SAN
MARINO
Pesaro
Ancona
THE
MARCHES
Adriatic
Sea
L'Aquila
Pescara
ABRUZZO
MOLISE
Campobasso
CAMPANIA
Ischia
Naples
Salerno
Potenza
BASILICATA
Bari
APULIA
Taranto
Brindisi
Lecce
Area of
inset
Tyrrhenian Sea
Gulf of
Taranto
AEOLIAN
ISLANDS
Palermo
CALABRIA
Catanzaro
Messina
Reggio di
Calabria
Mt. Etna
Taormina
SICILY
Ionian Sea
Syracuse
(Siracusa)
Rimini

Naples
Ottaviano
A30
A3
Mt. Vesuvius
VESUVIUS
NATIONAL PARK
Herculaneum
E45
Pompeii
Pompei
A3
E45
Gulf of
Naples
Monti Lattari
Ravello
Sorrento
Positano
Amalfi
THE AMALFI COAST
Anacapri
Capri
Capri

0   10 mi
0   10 km

0   100 mi
0   100 km

> *Norman, Arabic, and baroque influences combined to create the unique architectural mix that is Palermo.*

the many ancient artifacts, from household implements to jewelry, and mosaics on display are good preparation for the remarkable ruins you'll see at Pompeii. Finish your day off with some first-rate pizza at either **Da Michele** or **Gino Sorbillo** (p 605).

On your second morning, start your day with a Neapolitan breakfast at **Caffè Gambrinus** (p 609, ⑲). Then head off to the Vomero neighborhood (take one of the city's famous funiculars) and the **Certosa di San Martino** (p 606, ⑫), which combines phenomenal views of the bay with fabulous baroque art. If you have time, squeeze in a tour of the **Museo di Capodimonte** (p 606, ⑪ and its famous Galleria Farnese—loaded with world-class art. ⏱ 1½ days.

On the afternoon of Day 5 board the Circumvesuviana train to Sorrento, where you'll spend the next 3 nights.

❸ **Amalfi Coast.** ⏱ 1½ days, including travel time. See pp 40–42, ❷–❺.

You can sleep in a little on Day 7, then take the Circumvesuviana train to Pompeii/Scavi.

❹ **Pompeii.** ⏱ 1 day. See p 42, ❼.

On Day 8, from Sorrento's Marina Piccola, board a hydrofoil or ferry to Capri. Allow 30 minutes to 1 hour for the crossing.

❺ **Capri.** ⏱ 1 day. See p 42, ❻.

Rise early on Day 9 and take the Circumvesuviana train from Sorrento to Naples (trip time: 1 hr.) and transfer at Stazione Centrale to a bus to Capodichino airport, from which you'll catch a flight to Palermo (trip time for a direct flight: 1 hr.).

❻ **Palermo.** On your first day in this colorful city, start with a visit to the souklike **Vucciria** (p 670, ❸) market, where Palermo's rich history as a cultural crossroads is gloriously apparent, then spend the afternoon walking around the **Kalsa** (p 671, ❻) district, the oldest and most fascinating part of the city. The churches of **San Cataldo & La Martorana** (p 671, ❺) show off Arab-Norman architecture, and in **Santa Maria dello Spasimo,** trees have grown out of the floor through the church's open brick vaults. Duck into the **Oratorio di San Lorenzo** (p 673) for an eyeful of fabulous baroque stuccoes, then end the day with a nightcap at the bar of the **Grand Hotel et des Palmes** (p 674), a relic of decadent old Palermo.

In the morning, take in the 12th-century Byzantine mosaics at the **Cappella Palatina** (part of the **Palazzo dei Normanni**—see p 668, ❶), and then make the trip out by bus to **Monreale** (p 646, ❶) to compare them with the dazzling 12th-century mosaics in this hill town's Arab-Norman **Cattedrale;** the vast scale of Monreale's mosaics creates the more astonishing impression. ⏱ 1½ days.

On the afternoon of Day 10, rent a car in Palermo. Siracusa is 258km (161 miles) from Palermo and trip time is a little over 3 hours. From Palermo, take the E90 east to the A19 toward Catania. Merge onto the E45, then head south along the SS114 to Siracusa and follow the signs into the city.

> *Iridescent Byzantine mosaics were added to Palermo's Cappella Palatina in the 1100s.*

7 Siracusa. Arrive in Siracusa in time to explore the city's *centro storico* on Ortigia Island, stopping at **Piazza del Duomo** (p 676, **1**) and the **Fonte Aretusa** (p 676, **2**).

Spend the morning of Day 11 exploring Siracusa's fantastic **Parco Archeologico della Neapolis** (p 677, **5**), whose lush grounds include the **Teatro Greco** and **Anfiteatro Romano,** as well as ancient caves and quarries. If you have time for a museum visit, the artifacts at the **Museo Archeologico Regionale Paolo Orsi** (p 678, **6**) are a natural complement to the ruins in the archaeological park. In the afternoon, make the trip down to the small hill town of **Noto** (p 650, **6**), Sicily's crown jewel of baroque delights. A rebuilding in the early 18th century enlivened Noto with a fanciful *barocco* style, complete with curving staircases and ornate balconies. ⏱ 1½ days.

Depart Siracusa on Day 11 so you'll arrive in Taormina before darkness sets in. Head 119km (74 miles) north on the A18, then follow signs to Taormina, where you'll spend your last evening in Italy. Trip time is 1½ hours.

8 Taormina. Your final day in Sicily comes with a chance to relax: You'll want to visit the **Teatro Greco-Romano** (p 680, **2**), one of the most spectacular ancient theaters in the world, but other than that the pastimes are soaking

> *Corso Umberto is the setting for Taormina's nightly* passeggiata.

up the sun on the beach at **Mazzarò** (p 682), reveling in the glorious views up and down the coast, and joining the festive *passeggiata* on **Corso Umberto** (p 680, **1**). ⏱ 1 day.

From Catania airport (45 min. south of Taormina on A18), you can connect via air to many European hub cities.

Great Cities & Towns of the North

Florence is just the tip of the iceberg on this 2-week jaunt—after a stop in the center of the Renaissance, you'll embark on a trip through many of Italy's other treasure-filled cities. And it's not just art you'll enjoy. You'll also experience the vibrant pulse of Italian urban life, dine well on the cuisine of Emilia-Romagna and Lombardy, and discover just how varied and richly textured Italy can be. This trip is geared to train travel—the difficulty of driving and parking in these pedestrian-oriented cities makes a car a hindrance. A rail pass is recommended (p 724).

START Fly into Florence's Peretola airport.

① **Florence.** ⏱ 2½ days. See p 38, **②**.

On the afternoon of Day 3, store your luggage at Stazione Santa Maria Novella, then take a train to Pisa. Trip time is 1 hour.

② **Pisa.** Pay your respects to the **Leaning Tower** (p 220, **①**), one of Italy's most famous and beloved landmarks. ⏱ 3 hr.

Return to Stazione Santa Maria Novella in time to collect your luggage and take a Eurostar Italia train (reservation required) to Bologna. Total trip time is about 2 hours.

③ **Bologna.** One of Italy's best-preserved medieval cities is filled with art and monuments, and, thanks to the oldest university in Europe, it's a lively and energetic city with plenty of informal restaurants in which to enjoy its legendary cuisine. Much of your touring will be along the city's 34km (21 miles) of arcades, built in the Middle Ages to encourage leisurely discourse. ⏱ 1 day. See p 43, **⑪**.

On the morning of Day 5, take a train from Bologna to Parma (trip time: 55 min.).

④ **Parma.** An excursion to Parma is a foodie's paradise; don't leave without sampling some of the city's namesake ham and cheese. But there's more to the city than just food. Its remarkable pink octagonal **Battistero** (baptistery, p 326, **①**), by Benedetto Antelami, is unquestionably the greatest Italian Romanesque work.

> Piazza Maggiore, the heart of medieval Bologna, is a popular meeting spot for students at Europe's oldest university.

Florence
Pisa
Bologna
Parma
Modena
Ravenna
Ferrara
Venice
Verona
Mantua
Milan

And the **Duomo** (p 327, ❷) is graced by a three-dimensional fresco by Correggio, whose grasp of perspective was way ahead of his time. Another Correggio masterpiece that's a must-see is the dining room of the **Camera di San Paolo** (p 328, ❹), where the intimate surroundings offer up a close view of the artist's wit and skill. ⏱ **5 hr.**

From Parma, take an afternoon local train (trip time: 30 min.) to Modena.

❺ **Modena.** Another opportunity to sample the local cuisine—perhaps a wedge of Parmigiano topped with the local specialty, *aceto balsamico*? Do stop in at Modena's 12th-

> *The hams of Parma are key to the cuisine of Emilia-Romagna.*

century **Duomo** and its bell tower (p 314, ❷), both of them masterpieces of the European Romanesque. ⏱ 2 hr.

Return to Bologna for the evening. On the morning of Day 6, take a regional train (trip time 1 hr. 20 min.) to Ravenna.

❻ **Ravenna.** Step back to the Byzantine era in this city, whose churches and landmarks dazzle visitors with their famous mosaics. Many of these—including the **Basilica di San Vitale** (p 336, ❶), the **Mausoleo di Galla Placidia** (p 338, ❷), and the **Basilica di Sant'Apollinare Nuovo** (p 338, ❸)—are easily accessed off the Piazza del Popolo. Some of Ravenna's most impressive yet charming mosaics adorn the otherwise austere **Chiesa di Sant'Apollinare in Classe** (p 340, ❼), in a landlocked suburb that was once the city's busy port and easily reached by bus. You can also take a plunge in the sea from a string of beaches just to the east of town, and the city center, closed to traffic, comes alive with strollers in the early evening. ⏱ 6 hr.

Return to Bologna for the evening. On the morning of Day 7 check out of your hotel and head via local train (trip time: about 30 min.) to Ferrara. Store your luggage at the station.

❼ **Ferrara.** A Renaissance city of rose-colored brick, Ferrara is one of the most beautiful in all of Italy. The preferred mode of transport along the old streets and around the park that tops the town walls is by bicycle, so rent one and pedal around for a bit to get a feel for the city. Among the impressive residences left behind by the Este family that ruled here from the 13th to the 17th centuries are the massive **Castello Estense** (p 332, ❶), with a decidedly bloody reputation; and the **Palazzo Schifanoia** (p 334, ❸), a retreat that's home to an especially noteworthy cycle of Renaissance frescoes. ⏱ 5 hr.

From Ferrara, take either an evening regional or Eurostar Italia (reservations necessary) train to Venice's Stazione Santa Lucia (trip time: 1½ hr.).

❽ **Venice.** ⏱ 3 days. See p 39, ❸.

On the morning of Day 11, take a regional train to Verona (trip time: 1 hr. 10 min.). Store your baggage at the station.

❾ **Verona.** ⏱ 4 hr. See p 43, ⓭.

Take a regional train to Mantua (trip time: 1 hr.), where you'll spend the afternoon and Day 12.

❿ **Mantua.** Set into a wide curve of the River Mincio, which often shrouds the city in mists, Mantua is a Renaissance time warp, built around three stage-set-like squares and dominated by the formidable castle of the ruling Gonzaga family. They filled their **Palazzo Ducale** (p 472, ❶) with works by Mantegna

> *Parma's Duomo, opposite the octagonal baptistery, is embellished with frescoes by local painter Antonio da Correggio.*

> *The Galleria Vittorio Emanuele II is home to the most stylish shopping in über-fashionable Milan.*

and other great artists, and built a remarkable pleasure palace, the **Palazzo del Tè** (p 474, ③), at the edge of town. ⊕ 1 day.

On the afternoon of Day 12, board a regional train for Milano Centrale (trip time: 2 hr.).

⑪ **Milan.** It's a sprawling metropolis that's got a rep for business and wouldn't win a beauty contest when compared with other cities in Italy. But Milan has an energy level that few other Italian cities can match, and it's not without its charms. It's a pilgrimage site for opera buffs, art lovers, and serious fashionistas. As an added bonus, many of its sights are concentrated in a relatively small area, making a visit here a reasonably carefree experience.

Pay your respects first at the ornate **Duomo** (p 456, ①), the third-largest church in Christendom. Other must-sees in the city include **Santa Maria delle Grazie** (p 462, ⑦), where Leonardo da Vinci's *The Last Supper* graces the refectory (procure tickets before you leave home); the **Pinacoteca di Brera** (p 461, ⑤), the city's finest art gallery; the **Castello Sforzesco** (p 461, ⑥), the ducal palace of Milan's Renaissance rulers that now houses a remarkable assemblage of seven museums; **La Scala** (p 460, ③), the world's most famous opera house; and the **Galleria Vittorio Emanuele II** (p 457, ②), the glass-enclosed shopping arcade that practically set the standard for the modern shopping mall.

With your time remaining in Milan, you might want to take in the **Museo Poldi Pezzoli** (p 460, ④), where works by Botticelli and Bellini hang in a 19th-century palazzo, and the **Pinacoteca Ambrosiana** (p 463, ⑫), an enticing collection of Caravaggios, Brueghels, and other Renaissance works. Step into **Santa Maria presso San Satiro** (p 465, ⑬), where Donato Bramante's *trompe l'oeil* creates an illusion of columns and arches. Two churches west of the Duomo evoke the 4th century, when Milan was a capital of the Western Empire: the **Basilica di Sant'Ambrogio** (p 462, ⑨) and **San Lorenzo Maggiore** (p 463, ⑪), the oldest church in Milan. You can't properly do Milan without exploring its high-fashion side, and the epicenter of world fashion is the **Quadrilatero della Moda** (Fashion Rectangle, p 466), the boutique-filled blocks between Via della Spiga, Via Montenapoleone, Via Manzoni, and Via Sant'Andrea. A walk past the flagship shops of Italian and other European designers offers a peek at what styles will soon be in vogue and explains why Italians—the Milanese especially—are so well dressed. ⊕ 2 days.

Fly home from Milan's Malpensa airport.

The Scenic North in 1 Week

Scenery, and much of it, is the highlight of this itinerary, which begins in the Dolomites and ends on the shores of the Mediterranean in one of Italy's most beautiful regions, the Cinque Terre. The route also takes in a lake that has been inspiring royalty, composers, poets, and the rest of us for centuries. A car is a must for the start of this itinerary; rent one in either Milan or Venice (whichever gateway is more convenient for you) and head up to Cortina.

START Fly into Venice or Milan, then rent a car and drive to Cortina d'Ampezzo.

❶ Cortina. Italy's most famous ski resort is surrounded by the stunning Dolomite peaks, which you can ascend on a series of thrilling funicular trips that depart right from town. ⏲ 1 day. See p 436, **❹**.

From Cortina, head west on the Strada delle Dolomiti (p 436, **❸**) to Bolzano. Distance: 110km (66 miles).

❷ Bolzano. Half the fun of visiting Bolzano is getting there by way of one of Europe's most scenic drives through the mountains between Cortina and Bolzano. The town itself, however, is full of alpine charm, as well as medieval churches and castles. The town's most famous resident these days is **Ötzi the Iceman** (p 435), who wandered the mountains 5,300 years ago and was discovered in an ice field north of Bolzano in 1991.

A second day in Bolzano allows time to make the ascent by funicular to Altopiano del Renon, a mountain plateau with dizzying views of the surrounding countryside. ⏲ 2 days. See p 434, **❶**.

From Bolzano, on Day 4 head south on the A22/E45, then on the SS450; head west on the A4 (to Milan) and then north on the SR11 to Sirmione. Distance: 156km (98 miles).

❸ Lago di Garda. Drop down to the plains again, to the shores of Lago di Garda. Using either of the two prettiest towns on the lake as your base, Gargnano or Sirmione, set out by boat to enjoy such sights as the **Giardino Botanico Hruska** in Gardone (p 442); **Il Vittoriale degli Italiani,** the lakeside estate of Gabriele d'Annunzio near Salò; and the **Grotte di Catullo,** the extensive ruins of a villa complex on the lakeshore at Sirmione. ⏲ 1 day. See p 441, **❹**; p 444, **❹**; p 445, **❻**.

> Portofino's upscale harbor may be the prettiest spot on the Ligurian riviera.

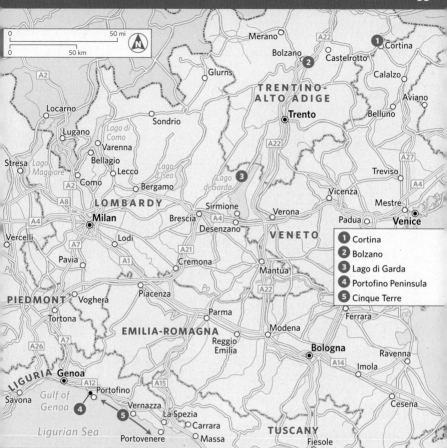

From Sirmione, on Day 5 head west on the A4 (to Milan), then southwest on the A21 to the A7 to Genoa. Distance: 267km (167 miles). Drop off your car in Genoa (it's now a liability) and take a local train to Rapallo (trip time: 30 min.).

④ **Portofino Peninsula.** This scenic stretch of seaside boasts three appealing towns: **Rapallo, Santa Margherita,** and the smallest and prettiest, **Portofino.** The shores and trails of this stunning region cross pine and olive-tree studded landscapes to seaside abbeys and remote coves. Upon arriving, spend the afternoon in Rapallo, then explore the others on the morning of Day 6. All the towns are easily connected by train, so getting from one to the other is a breeze. ⏱ 1½ days. See p 560.

On the afternoon of Day 6, take a regional train from Rapallo to Monterosso (trip time:

about 45 min.). Travel within the Cinque Terre is strictly by foot, local train, or boat.

⑤ **Cinque Terre.** There are few places in Italy more scenic than the isolated and rugged coast of the "Five Lands." Spend the rest of your time in Italy taking in the beauty of **Monterosso al Mare, Vernazza, Corniglia, Manarola,** and **Riomaggiore.** Hiking, swimming, and contemplating the region's magnificent landscapes are the major activities. The best way to appreciate the scenery is to hike the **Sentiero Azzurro** (Blue Trail), which follows one of Europe's most beautiful and unspoiled coastlines. ⏱ 1½ days. See p 540.

Both Milan and Florence are about 3 hours by train from Monterosso; you can fly out of either gateway.

4

Rome

RIPPA·L·F·COS·TERTIVM·FECIT

13 Favorite Moments

When it comes to experiencing the best of Rome, sun-drenched days at the Colosseum are only the beginning—the Eternal City virtually bombards you with ways to enjoy yourself, from the visual to the gastronomical. Get off the tourist track, and accept the fact that there's traffic and pollution. With its unrivalled concentration of art and history, romantic scenery, and vibrant people, Rome embraces all with a monumental, irresistible charm. Here are the most sublime moments in our ongoing love affair.

> PREVIOUS PAGE Rome is warm enough to allow alfresco dining for much of the year—here with a view of the Pantheon. THIS PAGE Michelangelo's soaring dome for St. Peter's Basilica is the tallest in the world.

① Gazing over the ruins of the Roman Forum and Palatine from the Capitoline Hill terraces in the evening and, from there, strolling down Via dei Fori Imperiali, where strategically placed floodlights cast dramatic glows over solitary columns and the arches of the Colosseum. The ruins of Rome at night are disarmingly spectacular. See p 82.

② Taking your lover to the Pincio Terraces, whose theatrical ivy-covered stone balustrades and views are virtually unchanged since the Renaissance, when maidens, courtiers, and the occasional knave no doubt met here for trysts and double-crossings. See p 73, ⑩.

③ After a long day of sightseeing, joining the rest of Rome for an *aperitivo* at one of the outdoor bars on Campo de' Fiori. Have a seat, praise Bacchus for having created inexpensive, drinkable wine, and watch the world go by. See p 104, ①.

④ Treading the ancient paving stones along the leafy Via Appia Antica, and leaving the hustle and bustle of the city's *centro* far behind. Umbrella pines and farmland that seem to be steeped in antiquity perfume the air, transporting you back to the time when this was Rome's Regina Viarum (Queen of Roads). See p 112.

⑤ Riding a scooter, half-fearing for your life, on a sunny day, over the broad cobblestone avenues of Rome's archaeological areas, past twisted pines and 2,000-year-old ruins. A thrill ride and history lesson all in one.

⑥ Loading up on gourmet goodies at Volpetti At this shrine to Italian meats and cheeses, you can put together a picnic for yourself or pick up souvenirs such as specialty oils and pâtés for your foodie friends back home. See p 76, ⑥.

> Rent a scooter and zip your way around the city to see Rome as the Romans do.

7 **Standing along the high, western rim of the Circus Maximus** and absorbing the view from the pine trees across to the ruins of the Palatine Hill. As you do, imagine being one of 300,000 fans cheering on the raucous ancient Roman chariot races. See p 81, **10**.

8 **Mastering the art of taking a caffè at a real Roman bar.** Walk in to the bar, greeting all with a smile and "*Buon giorno.*" Pay for your drink at the *cassa,* and take your receipt to the bar counter. Slip a .10€ or .20€ tip on top of the receipt, and place your order with the *barista.* Drink your coffee as the Romans do—standing up at the bar.

9 **Going to the Capitoline Museums' Palazzo Nuovo** in late afternoon on a crisp winter day, when no one else is there. Your only companions are half-drunk, smirking fauns and busts of Hadrian and Homer. See p 89, **8**.

10 **Taking your first step over the threshold of St. Peter's Basilica.** When the ethereal light of the low afternoon sun is broken into celestial beams by the basilica's well-placed windows, Bernini's stained-glass dove of the Holy Spirit against the church's terminal apse flickers with searing tones of amber. See p 66, **8**.

11 **Mixing with locals at the lively Mercato di Testaccio.** No other market in the city has such a strong sense of community: Yuppies and jovial retirees shuffle from stall

> Try (everything) before you buy at the corner of gastronomic heaven known as Volpetti.

to stall, passionately debating the latest political scandal—or soccer (football) league standings—while they expertly pick out the freshest culinary delights. See p 76, **4**.

12 **Encountering Bernini's sculptures at Galleria Borghese.** Grimace in determination as the *David* does against daunting adversary Goliath, or gape at the amazing detail of *Apollo and Daphne.* The paintings and ceiling frescoes throughout the gallery make for colorful counterpoints. See p 84, **2**.

13 **Hydrating with free, ice-cold spring water from a *nasone* fountain.** All around town, these cast-iron hydrants provide a continuous flow of fresh and clean drinking water from the same sources that fed the ancient Roman aqueducts. In the heat of summer, there's no better way to cool down. See p 101.

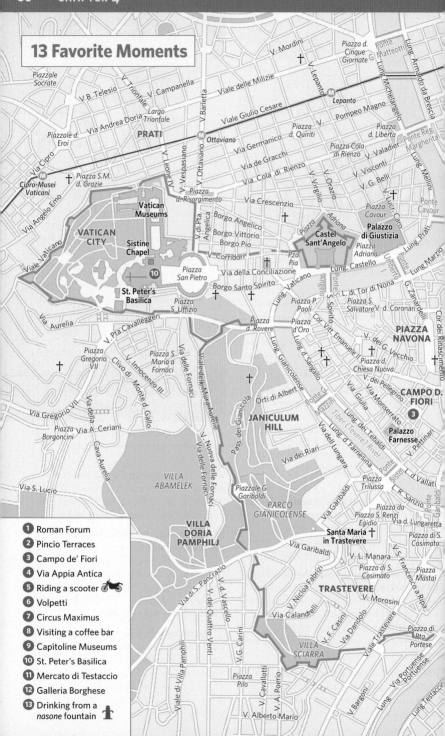

13 Favorite Moments

The Best of Rome in 1 Day

Seeing the top sights of Rome in 1 day requires an early start and late bedtime, discipline, and a bit of stamina, but it's actually quite doable. This "greatest hits" itinerary begins with an overview of the highlights of ancient Rome; after lunch, head across town and spend a few hours at the Vatican. Conclude your day with a leisurely evening walking tour of the gorgeously floodlit fountains and piazzas of the *centro storico* (historic center).

> *Rome's Pantheon, dating from the 2nd century A.D., is the final resting place of Renaissance artist Raphael.*

START Take bus 30, 40, 62, 64, 70, 87, 95, 170, 492, or 571 to Piazza dell'Aracoeli and climb the stairs to Piazza del Campidoglio.

❶ ★★★ **Capitoline Hill.** The most sacred of Rome's hills was given its present look in the 1500s, when Michelangelo designed the star-patterned **Campidoglio** square and surrounding buildings of the **Capitoline Museums** (p 89, ❽). The western slopes of the hill, with their steep red tufa walls and tangled vegetation, still look much the same as they would have in the

primordial days before the rise of Rome. Don't miss the majestic view of the Roman Forum from the south-facing terraces on either side of the bell-towered Palazzo Senatorio (city hall). ⏱ 15–30 min. Bus: 30, 40, 62, 64, 70, 87, 170, 492, or 571.

❷ ★★★ **Roman Forum (Foro Romano).** While the Forum is not one of the better-preserved archaeological sites of ancient Rome, it is the most historically significant. The Forum was the nerve center of the most powerful Western

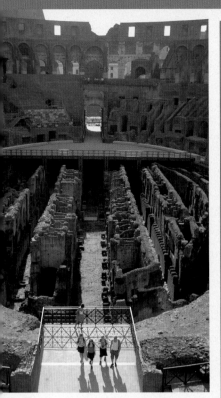

> *Wild animals were caged below floor level prior to their entry into the Colosseum's bloody arena.*

civilization in history for the better part of a thousand years, where political decisions were made, public speeches were heard, and market activities took place. The remains here—of 2,000-year-old temples, law courts, and victory monuments—are impressive but skeletal. ⏲ 1 hr. See p 82.

❸ ★★★ 🄺 **Palatine Hill.** Nothing recalls the glory of ancient Rome like the massive brick ruins, studded by umbrella pines, of the Palatine Hill. This is where Rome began—where Romulus killed Remus in 753 B.C.—and where the wealthiest Romans lived throughout the Republic. During the age of the Roman Empire, the Palatine was the exclusive residence of the imperial family. What remains here are the phenomenally extensive brick skeletons of the 1st-century-A.D. Domus Flavia, an architectural marvel that had extravagant gardens, fountains, secret passageways, racetracks, and grandiose audience halls. ⏲ 1 hr. See p 80, ❻.

❹ ★★★ 🄺 **Colosseum.** The Flavian amphitheater (A.D. 72–80) never fails to impress—for its elegant, enduring bulk, and its disturbing former function as a theater of slaughter. In the empire's heyday, games were held almost every other day; in times of special celebration, games could last for weeks or months on end. Free *tesserae* (tickets) were distributed to about 65,000 Romans, who could be seated in the arena in a matter of minutes, thanks to an efficient system of 80 numbered *vomitoria* (entrance/exit passageways). Against slashing swords and gnashing lions' teeth, gladiators and *bestiarii* (animal fighters) fought to the death, hoping to someday win their freedom. A visit inside the massive structure is certainly rewarding, but

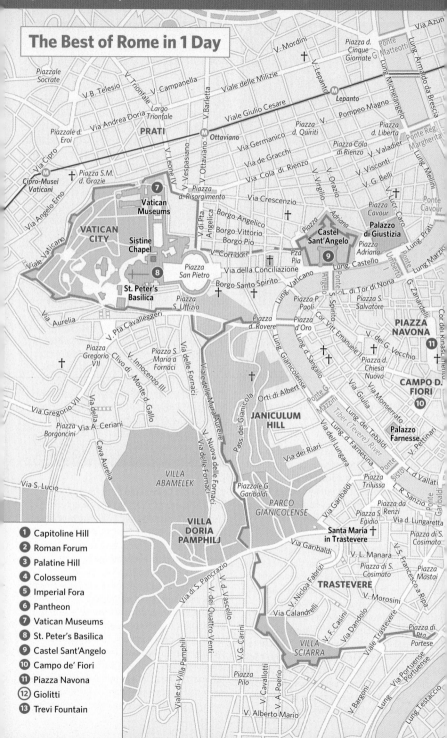

The Best of Rome in 1 Day

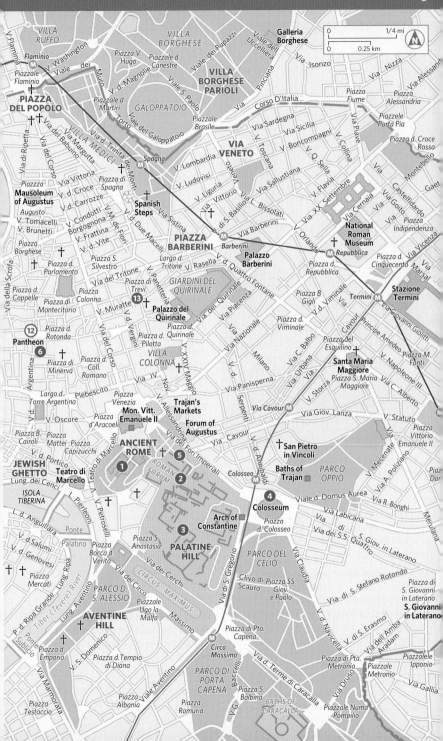

> *The Belvedere Torso is just one of the artistic highlights of the Vatican Museums.*

the spread of the Roman Empire, which ultimately reached as far east as Iran (Parthia). ⏱ 30 min. Admission free. Via dei Fori Imperiali.

6 ★★★ **Pantheon.** As the best-preserved and most elegant ancient building in the city—if not the world—the Pantheon (Temple to All Gods) merits multiple visits. It was built and possibly designed by Hadrian in A.D. 118–125 in a form governed by circles and squares—shapes that, as Vitruvius wrote (and Leonardo immortalized in his drawing *Vitruvian Man*), the human body most naturally occupies. The Pantheon's perfectly hemispherical poured concrete dome is 43m (141 ft.) tall and wide, 1m (3 ft.) wider than the dome of St. Peter's. Raphael is buried here. ⏱ 15–30 min. See p 102, **11**.

Take a taxi from the Pantheon to the Vatican Museums.

7 ★★★ **Vatican Museums.** After lunch, the crowds leave the Vatican, making it much more pleasant to explore. Make sure you see the starring ancient sculptures—the gut-wrenching emotion and dynamism of *Laocoön,* the transcendent composure of *Apollo Belvedere*—in the Pio-Clementine section of the museums, and then hightail it for the Vatican's biggest guns, the Stanze di Raffaello (Raphael Rooms) and Michelangelo's frescoes in the Sistine Chapel. The art here, by two of the greatest painters in history, is a triumph of Renaissance achievement: bold in color, lofty in concept, and monumental in scale. ⏱ 1½ hr. See p 88, **3**.

8 ★★★ **St. Peter's Basilica.** The incomprehensibly voluminous Vatican basilica is packed with incalculable riches, from the marble and gold that cover its every surface to masterpieces like Michelangelo's *Pietà* and Bernini's Baldacchino. ⏱ 45 min. Piazza San Pietro. ☎ 06-69881662. Free admission to church; dome 6€. Church: daily 7am–7pm (can vary with papal appearances or religious holidays); dome: daily 8am–6pm.

9 ★★ kids **Castel Sant'Angelo.** The view at dusk of this mausoleum-turned-fortress, from Ponte Sant'Angelo—where angels by Bernini wince and moan—is not to be missed. ⏱ 15 min. See p 98, **1**.

By now, it's at least 5pm—a good time to rest up at your hotel before heading back out for

if you're pressed for time, a walk around the exterior is fine. If there's a long queue, buy your tickets at the Palatine (p 80, **6**) and then go straight to the Colosseum turnstiles. ⏱ 30–45 min. See p 80, **8**.

5 ★★ **Imperial Fora.** Mussolini blazed the broad thoroughfare of Via dell'Impero—now Via dei Fori Imperiali—to trumpet the glories of his ancient forebears and propagate his own ambitions of empire. Along the east side of the boulevard, the ruins of the forums built by emperors Nerva, Augustus, and Trajan can be seen protruding from the ancient street level, 7.6m (25 ft.) below. On the west side, near the Colosseum, don't miss the fascinating marble maps (also from the Fascist period) charting

> *A nighttime view of the imposing Castel Sant'Angelo, once the mausoleum of the emperor Hadrian.*

dinner and the evening portion of the tour. If it's after 6, and you're feeling energetic, skip the hotel break and proceed directly to ⑩.

⑩ ★★★ **Campo de' Fiori.** By early evening (6–6:30pm), this square in the very heart of the *centro storico* is abuzz with all kinds of people taking an *aperitivo* at the many outdoor bars. (I recommend **Vineria Reggio,** p 140, and **Taverna del Campo,** p 129.) Later in the evening, it's a younger scene. Campo de' Fiori and nearby Piazza Navona are also prime zones for dinner. ⏱ 1 hr. See p 104. Bus: 30, 40, 62, 64, 70, 87, 116, or 492.

⑪ ★★ **Piazza Navona.** The most famous baroque square in Rome, built on the site of the ancient Stadium of Domitian athletic arena, boasts Bernini's fantastic Fountain of the Four Rivers and Borromini's Church of Sant'Agnese in Agone, as well as the smaller Fountain of the Moor and Fountain of Neptune. The cafes here are unabashedly touristy, but the setting sure is pretty. ⏱ 20–30 min. See p 92, ❶, and p 100, ❻. Bus: 30, 40, 62, 64, 70, 87, 116, or 492.

⑫ 🍴 ★★ **Giolitti.** At the city's best-loved gelato shop, the setting is elegant and the ritual is fun. Pay the cashier up front, then negotiate your way through the crowds in back, where servers scoop up enormous helpings of almost 100 flavors. Via degli Uffici del Vicario 40. ☎ 06-6991243. $.

⑬ ★★★ kids **Trevi Fountain.** Rome's most celebrated fountain, designed by Nicola Salvi and built from 1732 to 1762, is impressive enough during the day, but at night, the floodlights make it look so gorgeous that you won't even mind the crowds. ⏱ 20 min. Piazza di Trevi. Bus: 62, 85, 95, 175, or 492.

MICHELANGELO'S
PIETÀ
Anatomy of a Masterpiece

BY SYLVIE HOGG

MICHELANGELO'S first large-scale sculptural work (executed in 1498 and 1499, when the artist was 24) was, along with his *David*, his finest achievement in marble. Meaning "piety," *Pietà* was a common subject in Italian Renaissance art and represents the Virgin Mary holding her crucified son, Jesus Christ. Michelangelo's take on the theme was all about grace, not grief, while still conveying the spiritual pathos of the moment. Michelangelo carved the *Pietà* from a single piece of Carrara marble and signed it—the only work he ever left his name on—in Latin on the sash across Mary's chest. Five hundred years later, it's still widely regarded as the greatest work of Christian art ever created.

The *Pietà* is displayed, as it has been for five centuries, in St. Peter's Basilica in the Vatican (p 66, **8**), Rome.

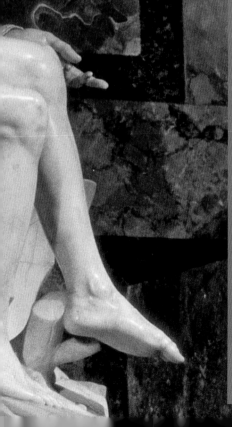

COMPOSURE
There is no overwhelming grief in Mary's face, only gentle sorrow, as she looks down at her son's lifeless body. Emotional restraint was a hallmark of High Renaissance classicism.

IDEAL BEAUTY
Mary would have been nearly 50 when Jesus was crucified, but Michelangelo gave her the face of a young woman. This may be the artist's idea of a pure soul untainted by sin; or it may be a portrait of Michelangelo's own mother, who died when he was a young boy.

BALANCE
A strong pyramidal shape gives balance to a composition that would otherwise be top-heavy. Mary's disproportionately large lower half is cleverly hidden beneath heavy draping.

MASTERY OF THE MEDIUM
The draping of Mary's marble garments is expertly sculpted, yet not exaggerated to the point of simply showing off the artist's virtuosity.

DIGNITY
Michelangelo gave Christ dignity in death: The wounds in his chest, hands, and feet are minimized, and his body is not the grotesquely emaciated figure typical of similar art of this era.

The Best of Rome in 2 Days

On your second day, spend the morning wandering the picturesque squares and alleys of Trastevere and Campo de' Fiori, Rome's oldest and most authentic quarters. In the afternoon, feast your eyes on the baroque masterpieces in the Galleria Borghese, then stroll through the Villa Borghese, making your way to the Pincio terraces and their enchanting views. Finish your tour in the elegant Tridente district below, where such *dolce vita* activities as shopping, drinking, and eating abound.

> Santa Maria in Trastevere was built on the site where a spring is said to have come to life on Christ's birth.

START Take bus 23, 271, or 280 to Lungotevere degli Anguillara, and walk to Piazza di Santa Cecilia; or take bus H, 780, or tram 8 to Piazza G. G. Belli, and walk.

① ★ Santa Cecilia. This peaceful basilica—an 18th-century reworking of a medieval church—is dedicated to the patron saint of music, who was martyred here in the 3rd century A.D. (According to tradition, her executors tried to chop off her head three times—the maximum number of attempts allowed—but she survived for several more days, singing softly the praises of God all the while.) Inside, altar mosaics dazzle, and fragments of Pietro Cavallini's wonderful 13th-century fresco of *The Last Judgment* can be seen at limited times. Cecilia was exhumed from her tomb in the crypt here in 1599, long enough for Stefano Maderno to sculpt the lovely (but disturbing—her throat is slashed) statue of the saint's still-uncorrupted body below the altar. ⊙ 20 min. Piazza di Santa Cecilia. ☎ 06-5899289. Admission free. Daily 9:30am-12:30pm and 4-6:30pm. Cavallini frescoes: Tues, Thurs 10am-noon; Sun 11:30am-12:30pm. Bus: 23, 271, 280, 780, or H. Tram: 8.

② ★★ Piazza & Basilica di Santa Maria in Trastevere. The first church in Rome dedicated to the Virgin Mary is spectacular inside and out, with a landmark Romanesque brick bell tower, colorful frescoes, mosaics, and loads of recycled ancient marbles. The eponymous square in front of the church acts as a kind of common living room for the neighborhood. ⊙ 20 min. See p 93, **⑦**, and p 110, **⑤**. Piazza di

1 Santa Cecilia
2 Piazza & Basilica di Santa Maria in Trastevere
3 Ombre Rosse
4 Via Giulia
5 Piazza Farnese
6 Campo de' Fiori
7 Galleria Borghese
8 Villa Borghese
9 Caffè delle Arti
10 Pincio Terraces
11 Cafe at Casina Valadier
12 Piazza del Popolo
13 Enoteca Antica di Via della Croce
14 Spanish Steps

> *They're mobbed at almost any hour, but the Spanish Steps are still a must for visitors.*

Santa Maria in Trastevere. ☎ 06-5814802. Free admission. Daily 7:30am–9pm. Bus: 23, 271, 280, or H. Tram: 8.

③ 🍽 ★ **Ombre Rosse.** This cafe with a porchlike view over a charming piazza is more stylish than the average neighborhood bar, but still frequented by born-and-bred, local *trasteverini.* Piazza Sant'Egidio 12. ☎ 06-5884155. $.

④ ★★ **Via Giulia.** Bearing straight toward the Vatican from Ponte Sisto, this former pilgrim route is home to many art galleries and high-end, original boutiques. Via Giulia's most fetching feature is an arch—with overgrown ivy draped luxuriously toward the cobblestones—that spans the road behind Palazzo Farnese. ⏱ 15 min. Bus: 23, 271, or 280.

⑤ ★★ **Piazza Farnese.** Sophisticated Piazza Farnese is where locals come to read the newspaper or push a stroller in peace, against the stately, yellow-brick backdrop of 16th-century Palazzo Farnese. ⏱ 15 min. See also p 93, ⑨, and p 106, ❸. Bus: 23, 30, 40, 62, 64, 70, 87, 116, 271, 492, or 571. Tram: 8.

⑥ ★★★ **Campo de' Fiori.** Rome's market square par excellence, the *campo* is the perfect embodiment of the myth of Italy. Every morning from Monday to Saturday, the square hosts a lively fruit, vegetable, and trinket bazaar. By early evening, in the same place where grocery shoppers eyed *pachino* tomatoes a few hours before, Rome's bright young things are scoping out each other over sparkling wine and effervescent conversation. ⏱ 20–30 min. See also p 93, ❿, and p 104, ❶. Bus: 23, 30, 40, 62, 64, 70, 87, 116, or 492. Tram: 8.

⑦ ★★★ **Galleria Borghese.** Reel in amazement at sculptures by Bernini (and other masterpieces) at one of the world's most outstanding small museums. Visits must be booked at least 1 day in advance; opt for the 1 or 3pm time slots. ⏱ 1 hr. See also p 84, ❷. Piazzale Scipione Borghese. ☎ 06-32810. www.galleriaborghese.it. Reservations required. Admission 8.50€ plus 2€ booking fee. Tues–Sun 9am–7pm (last visit 5pm). Bus: 116 or 910.

⑧ ★★ kids **Villa Borghese.** Go for a relaxing stroll among the refreshing greenery of Rome's most central public park. Boats can be rented at the picturesque *laghetto.* It's also a popular spot for jogging and cycling; bikes can be rented at several kiosks throughout the park for about 5€ per hour. ⏱ 1 hr. Daily 6am–sunset. Metro: Spagna. Bus: 52, 53, 63, 116, or 910. Tram: 3 or 19.

⑨ 🍵 **Caffè delle Arti** is much nicer than your average museum cafeteria. An open-air terrace, it's a secluded and relaxing spot for midafternoon refreshments or an early evening *aperitivo*. A rich buffet brunch is available on Sundays. At the Galleria Nazionale d'Arte Moderna. Via Gramsci 73. ☎ 06-32651236. $$.

⑩ ★★ **Pincio Terraces.** The utterly tryst-worthy Pincio gardens have secluded corners, umbrella pine bowers, and spectacular stone balustrades overlooking the rooftops of the *centro* and across to St. Peter's. ⏱ 30 min. Metro: Flaminio.

⑪ ★★ **Cafe at Casina Valadier.** In good weather, settle into a canvas divan at this panoramic alfresco cafe for a glass of Prosecco. The garden setting, surrounded by the trees of the Villa Borghese, is sublime. ⏱ 30 min. Piazza Bucarest. ☎ 06-69922090. www.casinavaladier.it. Drinks from 7€. Daily 10am–10pm.

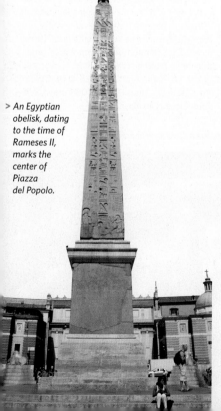

> *An Egyptian obelisk, dating to the time of Rameses II, marks the center of Piazza del Popolo.*

> *Romans do their morning shopping at Campo de' Fiori, the "field of flowers," and other outdoor markets.*

⑫ ★★ **Piazza del Popolo.** Romans and tourists alike bask in the late afternoon sun that floods this vast, traffic-free oval space just below the Pincio. Graced in the center by a massive, hieroglyphed pink granite obelisk, the "square of the people" is perfect for idling and gelato-licking, and a fitting introduction to the good-life Tridente district that spreads out pronglike to the south. ⏱ 15 min. See also p 92, ③. Metro: Flaminio.

⑬ 🍷 ★★ **Enoteca Antica di Via della Croce.** Grab a bar stool or sidewalk seat and enjoy some wine and tantalizing plates of meats, cheeses, and olives at this friendly wine bar. A favorite of expats living in Rome. Via della Croce 76B. ☎ 06-6790896. $$.

⑭ ★★★ **Spanish Steps.** De rigueur on any visitor's itinerary, but prepare to contend with mobs of gelato-wielding tourists and Casanovas trawling the square for naïve foreign females. Luckily, neither taints the overall beauty of the glamorously upsweeping Spanish Steps (which were actually designed and funded by the French). At the base of the 18th-century stairs, the sunken Barcaccia ("bad boat") fountain is by Pietro Bernini (Gian Lorenzo's father). The climb to the high terrace covers 12 curving flights of steps of varying width—you'll trip if you don't watch where your feet are—but the view from the top is exhilarating. Come between 2am and 6am (or just during off season), and you'll enjoy that rarest of Roman treats—having the fabulous stage of the Spanish Steps to yourself. ⏱ 30 min. Metro: Spagna.

The Best of Rome in 3 Days

One of the best and most surprising things about Rome is how quickly you can escape the urban chaos and enjoy the rustic tranquillity of the city's greener areas, just a few miles away from the tourist hordes. On Day 3, you'll visit catacombs, walk along the history-saturated Via Appia Antica, and head up to the leafy Aventine for peace, quiet, and gorgeous city views. Back in the *centro storico*, take a walk through the Jewish Ghetto and Isola Tiberina, before wrapping up the day in medieval Monti, one of the liveliest and most authentic neighborhoods in the *centro storico*.

START Take bus 118 or a taxi to the Catacombe di San Callisto on the Via Appia Antica (the entrance is 3.2km/2 miles south of Porta San Sebastiano gate). You'll need bus 118 or a taxi to get from the Via Appia to Testaccio. Everything else is walkable, but as always in Rome, comfortable shoes are key.

1 ★★★ kids **Catacombe di San Callisto.** Nineteen kilometers (12 miles) and four levels of hand-dug tunnels make up the underground network of Rome's largest catacombs, home to the tombs of half a million Christians, buried here from the 1st to the 4th centuries A.D. Near the start of the tour, you'll visit the Crypt of the Popes, where nine fathers of the early church are buried, as well as the cenotaph of St. Cecilia. In grand Roman fashion, the tour concludes with a walk through a labyrinth of 20m-high (65-ft.) tunnels, whose walls are perforated up to the ceiling with *loculi* (tomb niches). It's phenomenally impressive (and uncannily reminiscent of college library stacks). ⏱ 1 hr. Via Appia Antica 110–126. ☎ 06-5130151. Admission 6€. Thurs–Tues 8:30am–noon, 2:30–5pm. Closed Feb. Bus: 118.

> *Isola Tiberina is joined to the Jewish Ghetto and Trastevere by two ancient bridges.*

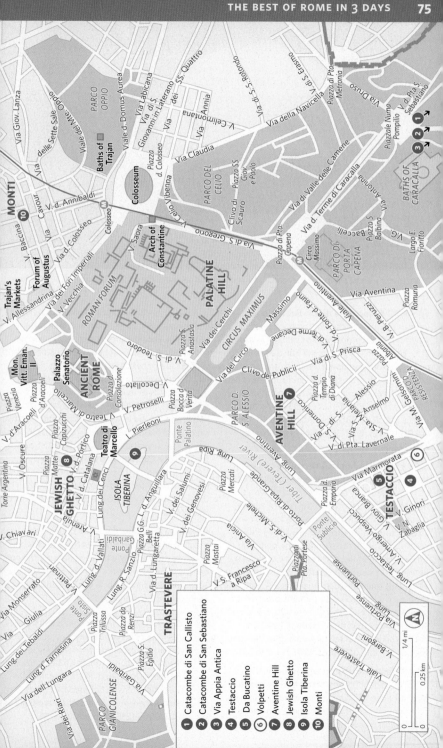

MONTI

Baths of Trajan

PARCO OPPIO

Trajan's Markets

Forum of Augustus

V. dei Fori Imperiali

Colosseum

Arch of Constantine

ROMAN FORUM

PALATINE HILL

Mon. Vitt. Eman. II

Palazzo Senatorio

ANCIENT ROME

CIRCUS MAXIMUS

PARCO DEL CELIO

PARCO DI PORTA CAPENA

BATHS OF CARACALLA

AVENTINE HILL

Teatro di Marcello

JEWISH GHETTO

ISOLA TIBERINA

TRASTEVERE

TESTACCIO

Tiber (Tevere) River

1. Catacombe di San Callisto
2. Catacombe di San Sebastiano
3. Via Appia Antica
4. Testaccio
5. Da Bucatino
6. Volpetti
7. Aventine Hill
8. Jewish Ghetto
9. Isola Tiberina
10. Monti

N

1/4 mi
0   0.25 km

> *Rome's early Christians buried their dead in the underground tunnels of the catacombs, south of the city center.*

2 ★★ kids **Catacombe di San Sebastiano.** If your third day in Rome falls on a Wednesday, when the Catacombe di San Callisto (above) are closed, the Catacombe di San Sebastiano, just a few minutes down the road, are a good plan B. There's a cluster of beautifully stuccoed and painted pagan tombs here in addition to the typical catacomb niches. ⏱ 1 hr. Via Appia Antica 136. ☎ 06-7850350. Admission 6€. Mon–Sat 9am–noon, 2:30–5pm. Closed mid-Nov to mid-Dec. Bus: 118.

3 ★★★ kids **Via Appia Antica.** Few places in Rome transport you to ancient times as well as the old Appian Way, whose black basalt flagstones still bear the wheel ruts of ancient cart traffic. The best atmosphere is along the stretch south of the tomb of Cecilia Metella, where a rustic, agrarian landscape opens up on either side of the 4th-century-B.C. highway. Between residential properties whose street addresses enviably read "Via Appia Antica" the scenery is scattered with remains of ancient tombs and villas, and shepherds drive flocks of sheep right across the "Queen of Roads." It's hard to believe you're still well within the confines of the city of Rome. ⏱ 1 hr. See also p 112.

4 ★★ **Testaccio.** Anchored by an artificial hill made of ancient pottery castoffs and populated by salt-of-the-earth *romani de Roma*, the authentic neighborhood of Testaccio oozes character. You'll want to be here by noon so that you can

visit the covered **Mercato di Testaccio,** in Piazza Testaccio, where locals shop for produce and more—the good-natured haggling, the emphatic gesturing, and the banter between customers and vendors is a priceless snapshot of daily Roman life. The market is open Monday through Saturday from 8am to 1pm. Before or after lunch (see **5** and **6**), go for a walk past the old slaughterhouse and around Monte Testaccio (you can still see the potsherds that make up the hill at the corner of Via Galvani and Via Zabaglia). Also here is the peaceful **Cimitero Acattolico,** or Protestant Cemetery (Via Caio Cestio 6; ☎ 06-5741900; donation expected; Tues–Sun 9am–4:30pm). ⏱ 1½ hr. Metro: Piramide. Bus: 30, 60, 75, 95, 118, or 170. Tram: 3.

5 ★★ **Da Bucatino.** For a classic Testaccio meal, it's hard to beat the hearty pastas at this down-home and lively trattoria, around the corner from the busy market. ⏱ 1 hr. See p 124. Via Luca della Robbia 84–86. ☎ 06-5746886. Entrees 7€–15€. Lunch & dinner Tues–Sun.

6 🍴 ★★ **Volpetti.** If you prefer a quick bite to a full lunch, Rome's best deli will make you simple panini stuffed with their divine cheeses and cured meats. Or head around the corner to Volpetti Più, their cafeteria-style offshoot with hot prepared foods and tables where you can eat. Via Marmorata 47. ☎ 06-5742352. Closed Sun. $–$$.

> *Produce is piled high at the Mercato di Testaccio.*

7 ★★ **Aventine Hill.** Oblivious to the noise of the city all around it, the Aventine Hill is mostly residential and home to several churches with dignified and simple red-brick exteriors and grassy grounds—a welcome contrast to the fussy baroque style and cramped quarters of so many Roman churches. The 5th-century-A.D. church of Santa Sabina is cavernous and calming—a sublime example of the basilican form. Visit the Parco Savello for splendid views over Trastevere and St. Peter's. ⏱ 1 hr. Metro: Circo Massimo. Bus: 30, 60, 75, 81, 95, 118, 175, or 628. Tram: 3.

8 ★★ **Jewish Ghetto.** This medieval quarter along the Tiber (Tevere) is where Roman Jews were confined from the 16th to the 19th centuries. Many tourists miss the Ghetto, but from towering ancient ruins such as the Teatro di Marcello, to such sculptural gems as the **Fountain of the Tortoises** in Piazza Mattei, to the triumphant Synagogue, this small area has a lot to see. ⏱ 45 min. See also p 107, **12**–**16**. Bus: 30, 40, 62, 64, 70, 81, 87, 170, 271, 492, or 628. Tram: 8.

9 ★★ **Isola Tiberina (Tiber Island).** This boat-shaped protuberance in the middle of the river between the Ghetto and Trastevere is an oasis of calm; ever since the Greek god of medicine, Aesculapius, washed up here disguised as a snake, the island has been the city's sanctuary

> *A charming architectural detail from the Fountain of the Tortoises, at the heart of Rome's Jewish Ghetto.*

of medicine. Check out the lower promenade (water level permitting), with its great views of the ancient bridges nearby. ⏱ 30 min. Bus: 23, 30, 40, 62, 64, 70, 81, 87, 170, 271, 280, 492, or 628. Tram: 8.

10 ★★ **Monti.** Even though it's mere blocks from the Roman Forum and the Colosseum, most tourists skip right over this area because it doesn't contain many actual "sights." All the better for you: Its charming streets and piazzas are filled with fun, casual places to eat and drink—whether you're in the mood for a pizza or a serious bottle of wine—where you can mix with real Romans. Pedestrian-only Piazza Madonna dei Monti is the hub of the community, and La Bottega del Caffè (p 126) its best alfresco cafe. ⏱ 2-3 hr. Bus: 75, 85, 87, 175, 571. Metro: Cavour.

Ancient Rome

In towering brick or crumbling marble, the awe-inspiring ruins of ancient Rome are concentrated in the archaeological park south of the *centro storico*. Here, in an undulating topography drenched in history and dotted with umbrella pines, are such famed sights as the Forum and the Colosseum, as well as the most sacred hills of Rome: the Capitoline and the Palatine. Bring a bottle of water and a picnic, and wear comfortable shoes for this half- or full-day tour. In summer, avoid these sites during the intense heat of midday. For the best collections of art recovered from these ruins, see p 84.

START Take bus 30, 95, 170, or 628 to Via del Teatro di Marcello, or take bus 40, 62, 64, 70, 87, or 492 to Via dell'Aracoeli or Piazza Venezia, and walk.

1 ★ **Teatro di Marcello.** The familiar arches of this 1st-century-B.C. theater, used for plays and concerts, inspired the design of the Colosseum, built 100 years later. ☉ 10 min. Via del Teatro di Marcello.

2 ★★ **Capitoline Hill.** Analogous to the Acropolis in Athens, this was the citadel and religious nerve center of ancient Rome. Atop this spur of red tufa, augurs monitored the flight of birds for omens, and traitors were hurled from the infamous Tarpeian Rock. The temple of Jupiter here, now lost, dominated the Roman skyline for centuries. In 390 B.C., the Gauls attempted to storm the capitol under cover of darkness and the dense vegetation here, but the sacred geese of Rome, kept in a pen nearby, detected their movement and sounded the alarm, thwarting the raiders. (The Capitoline guard dogs, who slept through it, were later crucified.) ☉ 45 min. See p 89, **8**, for the Capitoline Museums.

3 ★★ **Trajan's Forum.** Majestic and overtly phallic, the 40m-high (130-ft.) marble **Trajan's Column** was dedicated in A.D. 113 to commemorate the Romans' victory over Dacia (modern Romania). The spiral band of reliefs depicts all stages of the military campaign, down to the finest detail. The most dominant feature in Trajan's Forum is the massive, concave-fronted, brick structure known as **Trajan's Markets.** Built on three levels, the markets

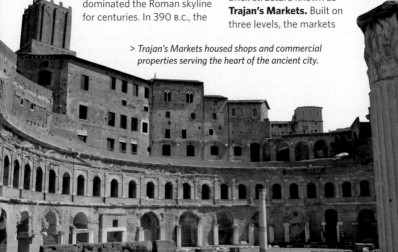

> *Trajan's Markets housed shops and commercial properties serving the heart of the ancient city.*

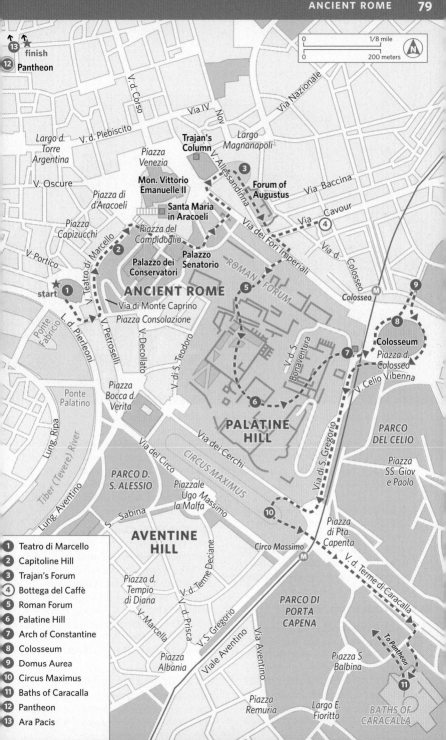

1 Teatro di Marcello
2 Capitoline Hill
3 Trajan's Forum
4 Bottega del Caffè
5 Roman Forum
6 Palatine Hill
7 Arch of Constantine
8 Colosseum
9 Domus Aurea
10 Circus Maximus
11 Baths of Caracalla
12 Pantheon
13 Ara Pacis

> *The Colosseum stands as a monument to the grandeur and savagery of ancient Rome.*

housed 150 shops and commercial offices.
🕐 45 min. Via IV Novembre 94. ☎ 06-6790048.
Admission 6.50€. Daily 9am–6pm. Bus: 30, 40,
62, 64, 70, 85, 87, 95, 170, 175, or 492.

④ 🍴 **Bottega del Caffè,** a busy alfresco
cafe just up the hill from the Forum (and
a world away from the predatory tourist
snack carts down there), is a good spot
to grab a bite and people-watch. **Piazza
Madonna dei Monti 5 (at Via dei Serpenti).**
☎ 393-9311013. $–$$.

❺ ★★★ **Roman Forum.** See p 82.

❻ ★★★ kids **Palatine Hill.** It was here that the
she-wolf nursed Romulus and Remus, and
where, in 753 B.C., Romulus killed Remus to
found Roma. Later, emperors and other ancient bigwigs built their palaces and private
entertainment facilities here. Nowadays, it's a
sprawling, crowd-free archaeological garden,
with enormous, honeycomb-like brick ruins

in every direction and views over the Circus
Maximus. 🕐 45 min. Entrances near Arch of Titus
and at Via di San Gregorio 30. ☎ 06-6990110.
11€ (includes Roman Forum & Colosseum). Daily
9am–1 hr. before sunset. Metro: Colosseo. Bus: 60,
75, 85, 87, 95, or 175. Tram: 3.

❼ ★ **Arch of Constantine.** Decorated largely
with sculpture looted from earlier emperors'
monuments, this arch was dedicated in A.D.
315 to commemorate the Battle of the Milvian
Bridge (A.D. 312), in which Constantine
defeated his co-emperor, Maxentius, after
having a vision of the Christian cross. The
superstitious Constantine legalized Christianity
in A.D. 313 with the Edict of Milan, ending
centuries of persecution. 🕐 15 min.

❽ ★★★ kids **Colosseum.** Occupying the
masses' free time with escapist, high-
testosterone spectacles, the games at the
Flavian amphitheater were the most extreme
sport of antiquity. Inaugurated in A.D. 80

> *An ultramodern museum inaugurated in 2006 houses the Ara Pacis, which dates from 9 B.C.*

over the site of Nero's lake, the Colosseum hosted 65,000 fans every other day with its gory contests between men and animals. The enormous amphitheater was supported entirely on radial and lateral arches. Below, an ingenious system of 32 elevator shafts and trapdoors kept the action constant. In A.D. 523, well after the rise of Christianity, the fights ended for good. The pockmarks that riddle the travertine walls indicate where metal-hungry Lombards gouged into the stone in the 9th century to extract the lead fasteners between the blocks. ⏱ 45 min.; crowded until late afternoon—buy tickets at the Roman Forum or Palatine Hill to skip the queue. Piazza del Colosseo. ☎ 06-7005469. 11€ (includes Roman Forum & Palatine). Daily 9am–1 hr. before sunset. Metro: Colosseo. Bus: 60, 75, 85, 87, 95, or 175. Tram: 3.

⑨ ★★ Domus Aurea. The maniacal emperor Nero snatched up most of the city land that burned in the catastrophic fire of A.D. 64 and built himself a palace that extended from the Palatine to the Oppian Hill, where the underground ruins of the "Golden House" can now be visited. See p 96, ②.

⑩ ★ kids Circus Maximus (Circo Massimo). Before there was Russell Crowe in *Gladiator,* there was Charlton Heston in *Ben-Hur.* In the world of ancient Roman sports, it was the chariot races at the Circus Maximus that held fans—300,000 of them—most in thrall. ⏱ 15 min. Metro: Circo Massimo. Bus: 30, 60, 75, or 95. Tram: 3.

⑪ ★★ Baths of Caracalla. Luxurious bathing complexes, like those built by Caracalla in A.D. 212 below the Aventine Hill, were as integral to the Romans' daily life as shuffling through the Forum on business or watching gladiators slug it out in the Colosseum. The shady ruins here are an ideal place to relax. ⏱ 45 min. Viale delle Terme di Caracalla 52. ☎ 06-39967700. 6€. Tues–Sun 9am–1 hr. before sunset, Mon 9am–2pm. Metro: Circo Massimo. Bus:118. Tram: 3.

⑫ ★★★ Pantheon. Still almost wholly intact, this 2nd-century-A.D. temple to all the gods with a hemispherical concrete dome and 16 monolithic granite columns is the best example of Roman architecture that history has handed down. ⏱ 15 min. See p 102, ⑪.

⑬ ★★ Ara Pacis. Housed in a strikingly modern, Richard Meier–designed pavilion along the riverbank, this 9 B.C. "Altar of Peace" is one of the most important works of Roman relief sculpture in the world. It was commissioned when the emperor Augustus returned triumphant from his military endeavors in Gaul and Spain. The museum structure, opened in 2006, is the first work of new architecture in the *centro storico* since the Fascist period. ⏱ 30 min. Lungotevere in Augusta. ☎ 06-0608. Admission 6.50€. Tues–Sun 9am–7pm.

The Roman Forum

The Forum Romanum was the beating heart of republican and imperial Rome and the most important civic space in the Western world for much of antiquity. Roman people carried out their daily religious, political, and commercial activities in its temples, basilicas, and markets. From the late Middle Ages, dirt, debris, and cow manure accumulated in the Forum, reaching a height of 9m (30 ft.) by the 1890s, when systematic excavations began.

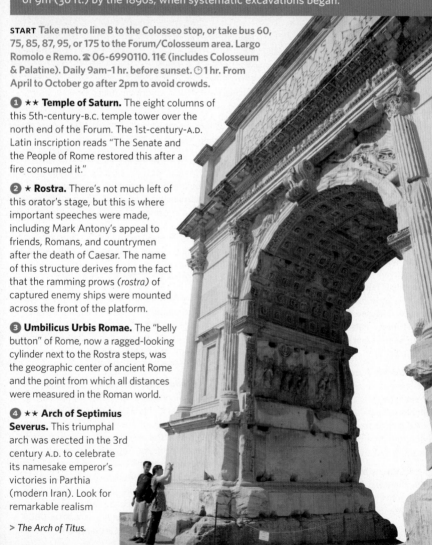

START Take metro line B to the Colosseo stop, or take bus 60, 75, 85, 87, 95, or 175 to the Forum/Colosseum area. Largo Romolo e Remo. ☎ 06-6990110. 11€ (includes Colosseum & Palatine). Daily 9am–1 hr. before sunset. ☉ 1 hr. From April to October go after 2pm to avoid crowds.

1 ★★ **Temple of Saturn.** The eight columns of this 5th-century-B.C. temple tower over the north end of the Forum. The 1st-century-A.D. Latin inscription reads "The Senate and the People of Rome restored this after a fire consumed it."

2 ★ **Rostra.** There's not much left of this orator's stage, but this is where important speeches were made, including Mark Antony's appeal to friends, Romans, and countrymen after the death of Caesar. The name of this structure derives from the fact that the ramming prows (*rostra*) of captured enemy ships were mounted across the front of the platform.

3 **Umbilicus Urbis Romae.** The "belly button" of Rome, now a ragged-looking cylinder next to the Rostra steps, was the geographic center of ancient Rome and the point from which all distances were measured in the Roman world.

4 ★★ **Arch of Septimius Severus.** This triumphal arch was erected in the 3rd century A.D. to celebrate its namesake emperor's victories in Parthia (modern Iran). Look for remarkable realism

> *The Arch of Titus.*

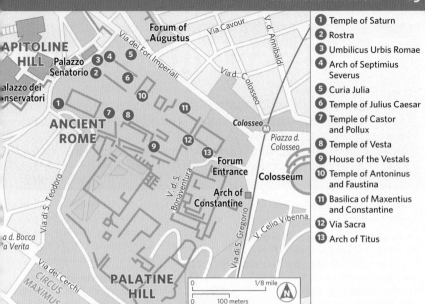

1. Temple of Saturn
2. Rostra
3. Umbilicus Urbis Romae
4. Arch of Septimius Severus
5. Curia Julia
6. Temple of Julius Caesar
7. Temple of Castor and Pollux
8. Temple of Vesta
9. House of the Vestals
10. Temple of Antoninus and Faustina
11. Basilica of Maxentius and Constantine
12. Via Sacra
13. Arch of Titus

the reliefs of Roman soldiers leading away
anacled Parthians.

★★ Curia Julia. The tall brick hall is where the
oman senate met, and was preserved through
e ages thanks to its conversion to a Christian
urch in the 6th century. (The Curia was built in
9 B.C., so this isn't the same senate house where
lius Caesar was stabbed in 44 B.C.).

★ Temple of Julius Caesar. It once had a six-
olumned front, but all that's left of this temple to
e most famous Roman in history is its podium.
nder its green metal roof is the rocky mound
here Caesar's funeral pyre burned for 7 days
44 B.C., culminating in the appearance of a
met. The Romans interpreted the streaking
lestial body as the soul of Caesar flying on the
ck of an eagle, after which he was apotheo-
zed and venerated here.

★ Temple of Castor and Pollux. The pic-
resque *tria columna* of this temple to the twin
orsemen, or Dioscuri, have helped centuries of
ets imagine the splendor of Rome in its heyday.

★ Temple of Vesta. A curved grouping of
naller columns in this area are the ruins of the
cred enclosure where the six Vestal Virgins
nded the eternal flame of Rome.

★ House of the Vestals. The only people

who lived in the Forum were the Vestal Virgins.
Their refectory-type residence now consists
of a rectangular courtyard with a shallow pool,
surrounded by brick ruins of living quarters.

10 ★★ Temple of Antoninus and Faustina.
Six columns in striking *cipollino* ("little onion")
marble mark the entrance to this 2nd-century-
A.D. temple dedicated to an emperor and his
wife. The structure survives because it was
reconsecrated as a church in the medieval
period. The bat-wing frontispiece is baroque.

**11 ★★★ Basilica of Maxentius and
Constantine.** The three soaring vaults of this
spectacular 4th-century-A.D. basilica represent
only one-third of the law court's original size.
Much of it crumbled in the earthquake of
1349. This is also where the colossal statue of
Constantine (p 89, 8) used to stand.

12 ★★ Via Sacra. The sacred way, still paved
with many of its original basalt flagstones, is the
route all official processions took into the Forum.
Along the way, there are bowers of laurel (bay)
where you can smell the very leaves from which
Roman victory crowns were made.

13 ★★ Arch of Titus. Sculptural reliefs on the
inside of this triumphal arch (A.D. 81), which
marks the southern entrance to the Forum,
glorify the sack of Jerusalem.

The Best Museums

As if all the open-air attractions weren't enough to keep you busy, Rome also bombards you with museums of every kind at every turn. Out of the more than 100 museums in the city, those listed here are my favorites for all-around interest, from rich troves of ancient sculpture (removed from the archaeological sites) to intimate family collections of Renaissance and baroque art to Fascist-era didactic museums.

START Take tram 2, 3, or 9 to Villa Giulia and walk to the museum.

1 ★★ **Etruscan Museum at Villa Giulia.** Pope Julius III's gorgeous Mannerist villa houses priceless artifacts from the civilization that ruled Italy before the Romans. A charming his-and-hers tomb, the Marriage Sarcophagus, may be the single star piece here, but take time to peruse all of this quiet museum to appreciate the real sophistication of the Etruscans. My favorite displays are the gold jewelry pieces,

which feature intricate designs of animals and floral motifs made of impossibly tiny granules of gold. ⏱ 45 min. Piazza Villa Giulia (at Viale delle Belle Arti). ☎ 06-3226571. Admission 4€. Tues–Sun 9am–7pm. Tram: 2, 3, or 19.

2 ★★★ **Galleria Borghese.** Immensely entertaining and mercifully manageable size, the collection at this 17th-century garden estate is museum perfection. Ancient Roman mosaics in the entrance salon depict gory scenes between gladiators and wild animals. In Room 1, Canova's portrait of Napoleon's sister, *Pauline Bonaparte* (1805–08), lies topless on a marble divan. (Notice how realistic the depressions in the mattress are.)

> *The harrowing fate of a Trojan priest is immortalized in marble in the Vatican's* Laocoön.

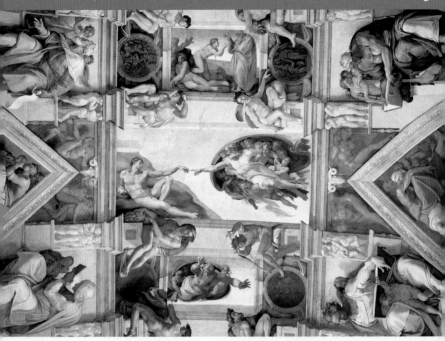

> *Michelangelo's iconic frescoed ceiling of the Sistine Chapel was completed in 1512.*

Bernini's staggeringly skillful sculptures in Rooms 2 to 4 are so realistically rendered that their subjects seem to be breathing. His *David* (1623–24, Room 2) is a dynamic portrait of the biblical hero, totally baroque in contrast to Michelangelo's more famous *David* in Florence. *Apollo and Daphne* (1622–25, Room 3) is Bernini's most outstanding work, depicting the myth when the fleeing maiden turns into a laurel tree to escape the amorous pursuit of Apollo. The emotion and miniscule details in the work are marvelous. Finally, Bernini's *Rape of Persephone* (1621–22, Room 4) is celebrated for the realism of Hades' fingers pressing into Persephone's thighs. Her squirming feet convincingly convey struggle.

The paintings by Caravaggio in Room 8 range in tone from luscious (*Boy with a Basket of Fruit*, 1594) to strident and grisly (*David and Goliath*, 1610). Renaissance masterpieces such as Raphael's *Deposition* (1507) and Titian's *Sacred and Profane Love* (1514) hang casually upstairs in the *pinacoteca*, along with Correggio's erotic *Danäe* (1531). ⏲ 1 hr. See p 72, ❼.

> *Bad boy of the baroque, Caravaggio painted his vision of* The Sick Bacchus *in 1591 (now at Galleria Borghese).*

The Best Museums

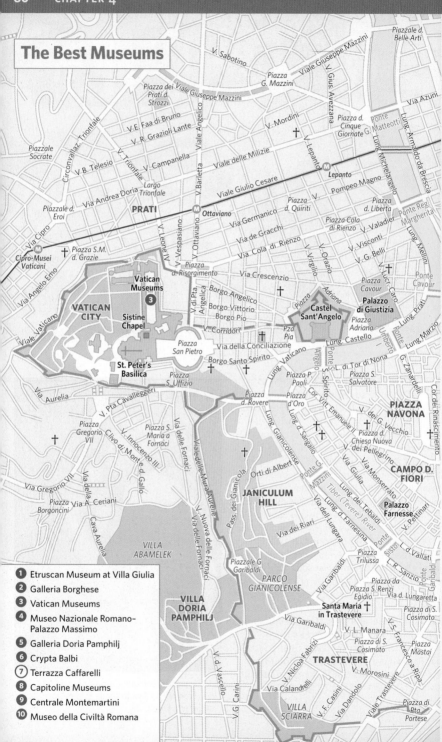

1. Etruscan Museum at Villa Giulia
2. Galleria Borghese
3. Vatican Museums
4. Museo Nazionale Romano–Palazzo Massimo
5. Galleria Doria Pamphilj
6. Crypta Balbi
7. Terrazza Caffarelli
8. Capitoline Museums
9. Centrale Montemartini
10. Museo della Civiltà Romana

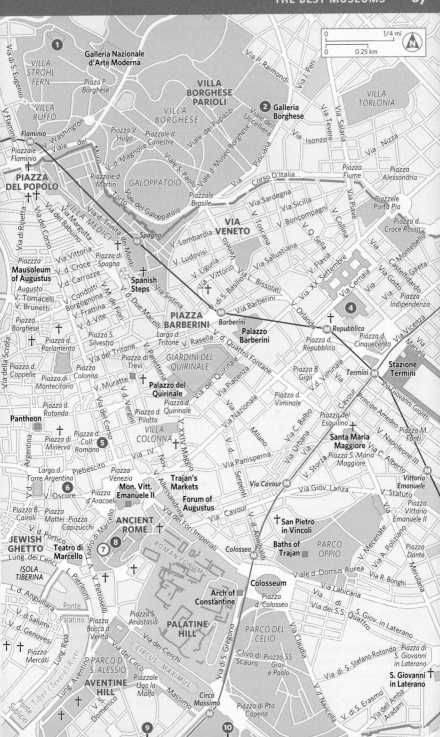

> *The Vatican Museums' Gallery of the Maps was the cutting edge of cartography in the 16th century.*

SITE GUIDE
PAGE 91

③ ★★★ Vatican Museums (Musei Vaticani). The richest museum of ancient and Renaissance art in the world is enthralling in its quantity and quality, and aggravating in its utter lack of explanatory signage. As a rule, the important stuff is where the crowds are, but try to resist the riptide of tour groups that washes headlong toward the Sistine Chapel, skipping a ton of fabulous art along the way. The museum guidebook—or, better yet, the CD-ROM audio guide—can make your meander through these masterpiece-packed halls vastly more meaningful. (The museums' website, **http://mv.vatican.va**, is also an excellent source of background information.)

④ ★★ Museo Nazionale Romano–Palazzo Massimo. An embarrassment of ancient riches—paintings, mosaics, statues, and inscriptions—are displayed in this bright and airy palazzo near the train station. Frescoes teeming with delightful animal and vegetable motifs, rescued from the bedrooms and dining rooms of Roman villas, are the highlight here, and totally unique among Rome's museums. ⏱ 1 hr. Largo di Villa Peretti 1 (at Via Giolitti). ☎ 06-48903501. Admission 6.50€. Tues–Sun 9am–7pm. Metro: Termini. Bus: 40, 64, 70, 170, 175, or 492.

⑤ ★★ Galleria Doria Pamphilj. The patinated halls of this noble palace still smell like the 17th century. Masterpieces collected by the Doria Pamphilj family—one of the most influential in Roman history—include works by Caravaggio, Guercino, Raphael, and Titian, and Velázquez's famous portrait of Pope Innocent X Pamphilj (1650). In the last, the intense, ruthless eyes of the pope are startling, but Innocent X was apparently quite pleased with his depiction. Admission includes a highly entertaining audio tour, narrated by the living princes themselves, who frankly dish on what paintings they like and which they can't stand. ⏱ 1 hr. Via del Corso 305. ☎ 06-6797323. Admission 8€. Fri–Wed 10am–5pm. Bus: 30, 40, 62, 64, 70, 85, 87, 95, 170, or 492.

★★ Crypta Balbi. A largely unsung period [in] Rome's history—the Middle Ages—is the [o]bject of most of the finds at this intimate [m]useum, opened in 2000 on the site of a 13th [c]. theater that was continuously used for [v]arious functions throughout the centuries. [●] 45 min. Via delle Botteghe Oscure 31. ☎ 06-[6]9967700. Admission 6.50€. Tues–Sun 9am–[7:]45pm. Bus: 30, 40, 62, 64, 70, 87, 170, 492, or 571.

☕ ★ **Terrazza Caffarelli,** the Capitoline Museums' cafe, has fresh sandwiches and drinks—and a commanding view of the *centro storico*. Non-museum-goers can access the cafe from the northern wall of Palazzo dei Conservatori. Piazza del Campidoglio. $–$$.

★★★ Capitoline Museums (Musei Capito-[li]ni). In the Michelangelo-designed buildings [o]f Piazza del Campidoglio are some of the [m]ost important Roman sculptures in the world. [T]he Palazzo dei Conservatori houses the 5th-[c]entury-B.C. bronze *Capitoline She-wolf*, mascot [o]f Rome, in Room 4, and in the courtyard, the [p]hotogenic fragments of the colossal statue of [C]onstantine (which used to stand in the Ba[s]ilica of Maxentius and Constantine; p 83, ⑪). [T]he *pinacoteca* has a number of fine works by [C]aravaggio, Titian, Tintoretto, and Guido Reni.

Across the square in the Palazzo Nuovo [a]re the majestic 2nd-century-A.D. bronze of [M]arcus Aurelius on horseback (the statue in [t]he square out front is a copy of this amazingly [p]reserved original), haunting busts of emperors [a]nd philosophers in Rooms 4 to 5, and myriad [m]arble fauns and satyrs throughout. In winter, [w]hen the museum is practically empty, you [a]lmost feel as if these ancient creatures' eyes [a]re following you. Not to be missed, the pon-[d]erous tufa blocks of the *tabularium* (Roman [a]rchive hall, 78 B.C.) connect the two wings of [t]he museums and offer dramatic views over the [F]orum. ◷ 1½ hr. Best in late afternoon. Piazza del [C]ampidoglio. ☎ 06-67102071. Admission 6.50€. Tues–Sun 9am–8pm. Bus: 30, 40, 62, 64, 70, 87, [9]5, 170, or 492.

★★ Centrale Montemartini. Works from [t]he Capitoline Museums' collection of ancient [s]culpture that were too big or numerous to [i]nsert in those halls have been installed in a [d]ecommissioned electric plant south of the

> Michelangelo designed the Capitoline Museums to glorify the sculpture of ancient Rome.

centro. The "Venus in the Boiler Room" effect here, of luminous marble against dark metal machinery, is aesthetic genius. ◷ 30 min. Via Ostiense 106. ☎ 06-5748030. Admission 4.50€. Tues–Fri 9:30am–7pm. Bus: 23, 271.

⑩ ★★★ kids **Museo della Civiltà Romana.** It's worth the subway ride to Mussolini's fantasy urban development project, EUR (Esposizione Universale Roma), to see the enormous, 1:250 scale **model of ancient Rome** at this field-trip favorite. The rest of the museum is filled with smaller-scale reproductions of ancient structures and fascinating engineering feats, like the aqueducts and construction of the Colosseum. There are also full-size replicas of the reliefs of Trajan's Column, all at eye level. ◷ 1½ hr, including transportation to and from. Piazza Agnelli 10. ☎ 06-5926135. Admission 6.50€. Tues–Fri 9am–2pm; Sat–Sun 9am–7pm. Metro: EUR-Fermi.

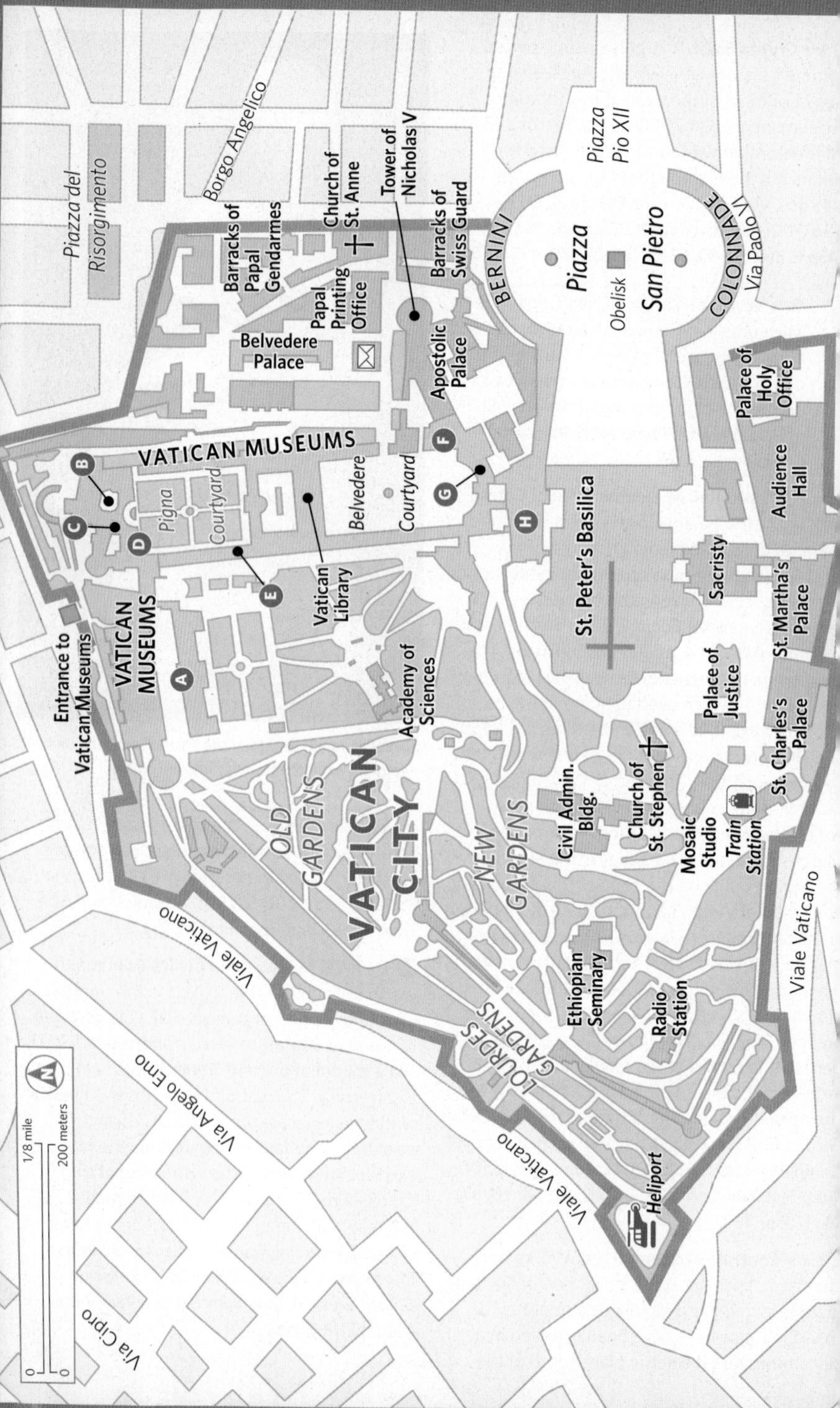

Piazza del Risorgimento

Borgo Angelico

Barracks of Papal Gendarmes

Church of St. Anne

Tower of Nicholas V

Barracks of Swiss Guard

Belvedere Palace

Papal Printing Office

Apostolic Palace

VATICAN MUSEUMS

Pigna Courtyard

Belvedere Courtyard

BERNINI

Piazza Pio XII

COLONNADE

Via Paolo V

Piazza

Obelisk

San Pietro

Palace of Holy Office

Audience Hall

Entrance to Vatican Museums

VATICAN MUSEUMS

Vatican Library

Academy of Sciences

St. Peter's Basilica

Sacristy

St. Martha's Palace

OLD GARDENS

VATICAN CITY

NEW GARDENS

Civil Admin. Bldg.

Church of St. Stephen

Mosaic Studio

Palace of Justice

St. Charles's Palace

Train Station

Viale Vaticano

Viale Vaticano

LOURDES GARDENS

Ethiopian Seminary

Radio Station

Viale Vaticano

Heliport

Via Angelo Emo

Via Cipro

1/8 mile

200 meters

SITE GUIDE

③ Vatican Museums

Start your tour in the Ⓐ ★★ **Pinacoteca** (picture gallery), home to Raphael's *Transfiguration* (1520; his last painting), in Room 8; Leonardo's enigmatic *St. Jerome* (1482), in Room 9; and Caravaggio's eerie, green-fleshed *Deposition* (1604), in Room 12. In the Pio-Clementino museum of classical statuary, the open-air Ⓑ ★★★ **Octagonal Courtyard** houses the exquisite marble ★★ *Apollo Belvedere,* a paragon of classical composure (this work is a 2nd-c.-A.D. copy of a 5th-c.-B.C. original). In radical stylistic contrast, the stunning 1st-century-A.D. ★★★ *Laocoön* (Lay-*ah*-koh-on) captures the very height of human vulnerability. The sculpture depicts the fate of a Trojan priest who was suspicious of the Trojan horse and asked his people to "beware of Greeks bearing gifts." The Greek-favoring gods, angered, sentenced him to death by sea serpents. Moving back inside the museum halls, you'll come upon the Ⓒ ★ *Belvedere Torso.* This single marble torso inspired Michelangelo's rendering of Christ in *The Last Judgment,* in the Sistine Chapel. The Ⓓ ★ **Museo Etrusco** upstairs has knockout gold breastplates from the 2,500-year-old Regolini-Galassi tomb. The vivid blue and green frescoes in the Ⓔ ★★ **Gallery of the Maps** are a wonderfully detailed cartographical record of 16th-century Italy. Pink-tinged frescoes (1522–25) by Giulio Romano in the Ⓕ ★ **Sala di Costantino** are a tribute to Christianity toppling paganism—quite literally in the ceiling panel, where a marble statue of a pagan god falls and

shatters before a gilded cross. The frescoes in the Ⓖ ★★★ **Stanze di Raffaello** (Raphael Rooms, 1506–17) are second only to the Sistine Chapel in terms of importance. Exquisite scenes such as *The School of Athens* and *The Liberation of St. Peter* display the harmony of color and balance of composition that were the hallmark of High Renaissance classicism and Raphael's mastery. After the Raphael Rooms, a wrong turn and confusing signs can take you downstairs to the Vatican's dreadful modern art collection; stay to the left for the direct route to the Ⓗ ★★★ **Sistine Chapel** (Cappella Sistina), where Michelangelo's spectacular frescoes very much live up to the hype. After a restoration in the 1980s and '90s, they're more eye-popping than ever. On the ceiling (1508–12), the stories of creation, Adam and Eve, and Noah are told in nine frames, surrounded by faux architectural elements and medallions. On the altar wall, the swirling *Last Judgment* (1535–41) is much more fire-and-brimstone, reflecting the anger and disappointment of Michelangelo's later years. Exit the museums via the right rear door of the Sistine Chapel to go straight to St. Peter's. Exit via the left door to return any rented audio guides. ⊙ 2 hr. Go after 12:30pm in high season. Viale Vaticano. ☎ 06-69883333. http://mv.vatican. va. Admission 14€ adults, 8€ students. Audio guide 6€. Mon–Sat 8:30am–4pm (exit 6pm). Last Sun of month open 8:30am–12:30pm (exit by 2pm). Closed Catholic holidays—check website for most up-to-date schedule.

The Best Piazzas

Giving every city neighborhood its own alfresco salon, with newsstands, cafes, and room to breathe, the piazza is one of the great Italian urban inventions. In Rome, some are grandiose gifts to the city from politically minded popes; others are the result of streets meeting at odd angles; but the best piazzas are those where Romans act out their daily pageants, fully aware of their dramatic backdrops. Plan on spending an entire day wandering these gathering spots.

START Take bus 30, 40, 62, 64, 70, 87, 116, or 492 to Corso Vittorio Emanuele II or Corso Rinascimento.

① ★★ **Piazza Navona.** This theatrical baroque platter retains the shape of the ancient stadium over which it was built (p 97, ⑧). Vying for your attention at the center of the oval are Bernini's dynamic Fountain of the Four Rivers and Borromini's haughty Church of Sant'Agnese in Agone. Cafes and restaurants abound on the square, but you'll never find locals dining here. Piazza Navona is at its best

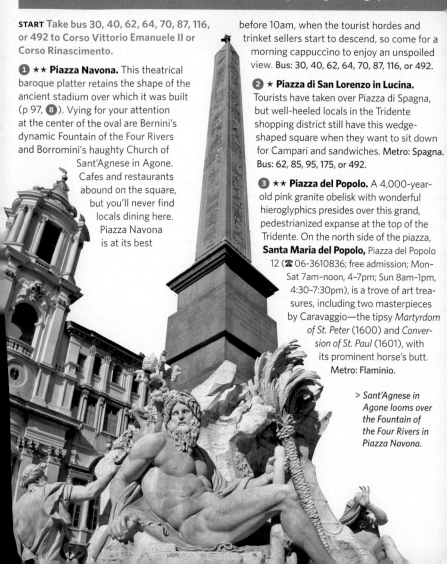

before 10am, when the tourist hordes and trinket sellers start to descend, so come for a morning cappuccino to enjoy an unspoiled view. Bus: 30, 40, 62, 64, 70, 87, 116, or 492.

② ★ **Piazza di San Lorenzo in Lucina.** Tourists have taken over Piazza di Spagna, but well-heeled locals in the Tridente shopping district still have this wedge-shaped square when they want to sit down for Campari and sandwiches. **Metro: Spagna.** Bus: 62, 85, 95, 175, or 492.

③ ★★ **Piazza del Popolo.** A 4,000-year-old pink granite obelisk with wonderful hieroglyphics presides over this grand, pedestrianized expanse at the top of the Tridente. On the north side of the piazza, **Santa Maria del Popolo,** Piazza del Popolo 12 (☎ 06-3610836; free admission; Mon-Sat 7am-noon, 4-7pm; Sun 8am-1pm, 4:30-7:30pm), is a trove of art treasures, including two masterpieces by Caravaggio—the tipsy *Martyrdom of St. Peter* (1600) and *Conversion of St. Paul* (1601), with its prominent horse's butt. **Metro: Flaminio.**

> *Sant'Agnese in Agone looms over the Fountain of the Four Rivers in Piazza Navona.*

Both baroque artist Caravaggio and Florentine goldsmith Cellini supposedly committed murder in Piazza Campo de' Fiori.

D'Angelo, an old-fashioned coffee bar and pastry and light snack shop, has an elegant feel and parlor-style seating (which will cost a bit more than counter service). **Via della Croce 30.** ☎ 06-6782556. $–$$.

★★ **Piazza di Spagna.** Sure, it's a zoo, but the thousands of tourists and flashy locals who flood this gorgeous square—framed by the Spanish steps, palm trees, brightly colored palazzi, and designer shops galore—must be on to something, right? The fountain at the base of the steps is called La Barcaccia ("bad boat"). **Metro: Spagna.**

★ **Piazza Mattei.** A scrappy little square in the old Jewish Ghetto charms all with its endearing 16th-century Fontana delle Tartarughe (Fountain of the Tortoises), begun in 1588 by Giacomo della Porta and Taddeo Landini and given its namesake reptiles by Bernini in 1638. The shabby-chic *boîte* here, Bartaruga (p 137), is a fun place to stop in for a cocktail. **Bus:** 23, 30, 40, 62, 63, 64, 70, 87, 170, 280, or 492.

★★ **Piazza di Santa Maria in Trastevere.** The crossroads of daily life in village-y Trastevere meets all criteria: a sprinkling of cafes and restaurants, children with *nonna* in tow, a graceful fountain, and a big church. **Bus:** H, 23, 280, or 780. **Tram: 8.**

⑧ ★ **Bar Marzio,** a typical Roman coffee bar, has outdoor tables offering a prime view across the square to the splendid facade of Santa Maria in Trastevere. **Piazza di Santa Maria in Trastevere 15.** ☎ 06-5816095. $.

⑨ ★★ **Piazza Farnese.** Just steps away from the buzz of the Campo de' Fiori, Piazza Farnese is elegant, sedate, and open, graced on its west side by the stately Palazzo Farnese, designed in part by Michelangelo and now the French embassy. The fountains here are granite bathtubs filched from the Baths of Caracalla (p 81, ⑪) in the 1500s and topped by the Farnese family emblem, the iris. **Bus:** 23, 30, 40, 62, 64, 70, 87, 116, 280, or 492. **Tram: 8.**

⑩ ★★★ **Campo de' Fiori.** With a produce market in the morning and a booming social scene at its many bars in the evening, this former "field of flowers" is the liveliest square in the *centro storico*. **Bus:** 30, 40, 62, 64, 70, 87, 116, or 492. **Tram: 8.**

⑪ ★★★ **Piazza della Rotonda.** Despite a 9m (30-ft.) rise from the surrounding ground level, the 2nd-century-A.D. Pantheon still stands, awesomely imposing, at the southern end of this square. Stop by in the late evening for a drink, when the atmosphere is more intimate and tourist-free. **Bus:** 30, 40, 62, 64, 70, 85, 87, 95, 116, or 175. **Tram: 8.**

The Best Piazzas

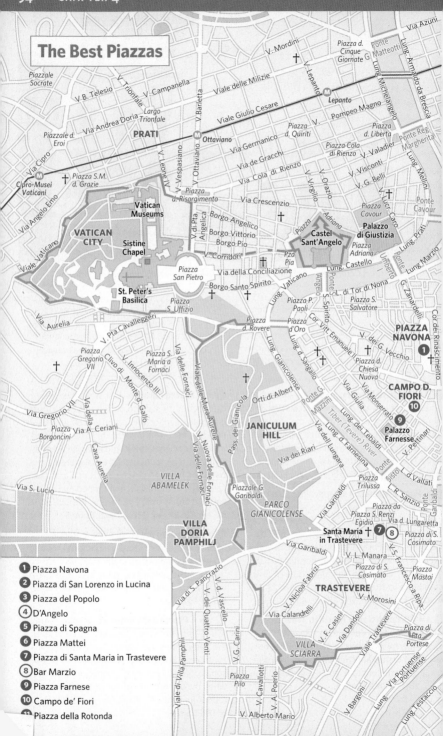

Underground Rome

In a city whose street level has risen about 9m (30 ft.) since the days of the Caesars, it's only natural that a whole other Rome should exist hidden away beneath the modern buildings. The catacombs are well known, but there are many other subterranean sites that offer a fascinating descent into the bowels of history.

> The macabre Crypt of the Capuchin Monks is decorated with the remains of 4,000 of the order's brethren.

START Take bus 118 or a taxi to the Catacombs of San Callisto on the Via Appia Antica.

1 ★★ kids **Catacombs of San Callisto.** Of Rome's 65 known catacombs—networks of hand-dug tunnels that became massive "dormitories" for the dead—only a handful are open to the public. The catacombs of San Callisto are the largest, with 500,000 burial niches (loculi). See p 74, **1**; and p 697.

Take a taxi to the Domus Aurea.

2 ★★ **Domus Aurea.** The cavernous halls of Nero's former pad, the "Golden House," feature grottoes with fake stalactites, frescoed rooms, and the famed octagonal dining room. ⏲ 45 min. Via della Domus Aurea. ☎ 06-39967700. Reservations required. Admission 6.50€. Wed–Mon 9am–7:45pm. Metro: Colosseo. Bus: 60, 75, 85, 87, 95, or 175. Tram: 3.

3 ★★ kids **Excavations of San Clemente.** This lasagna-like layering of churches is the best place in Rome to understand the city's archaeological evolution. Descend 18m (60 ft.) through medieval and paleo-Christian layers to the lowest level, where adherents of the ancient cult of Mithras met and performed grisly rituals. ⏲ 30 min. Via di San Giovanni in Laterano. ☎ 06-70451018. Admission 5€. Mon–Sat 9am–12:30pm, 3–6pm; Sun 10am–12:30pm, 3–6pm. Metro: Colosseo. Bus: 60, 75, 85, 87, 95, or 175. Tram: 3.

4 🍴 ★ **Amarcord** is a casual spot to pick up a custom-made piadina (flatbread sandwich), a specialty of Fellini's native Rimini. Via di San Giovanni in Laterano 164. ☎ 347-7679342 Closed Sun. $.

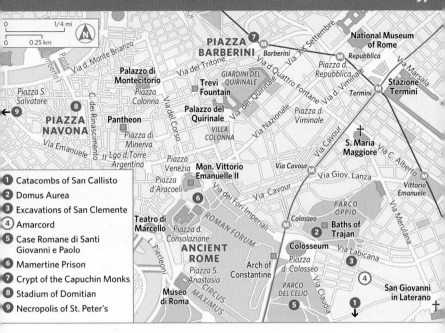

1. Catacombs of San Callisto
2. Domus Aurea
3. Excavations of San Clemente
4. Amarcord
5. Case Romane di Santi Giovanni e Paolo
6. Mamertine Prison
7. Crypt of the Capuchin Monks
8. Stadium of Domitian
9. Necropolis of St. Peter's

5 ★★ Case Romane di Santi Giovanni e Paolo.
Recent excavations beneath this Romanesque church on the Caelian Hill revealed extensive 1st-century-A.D. Roman houses with splendid wall frescoes as well as ancient city streets.
⏱ 45 min. Piazza Santi Giovanni e Paolo 13. ☎ 06-70454544. www.caseromane.it. Admission 6€. Thurs–Mon 10am–1pm, 3–6pm. Metro: Colosseo. Bus: 60, 75, 85, 87, 95, or 175. Tram: 3.

6 ★ Mamertine Prison (Carcere Mamertino).
Under the church of San Giuseppe dei Falegnami, just outside the Roman Forum, these dank rock chambers are where the most formidable enemies of Rome, such as the Gallic chieftain Vercingetorix, were imprisoned—and later strangled after being paraded before the public during the Romans' triumphal celebrations.
⏱ 15 min. Clivo Argentario 1. ☎ 06-6792902. Donation expected. Daily 9am–noon, 2:30–5pm. Bus: 60, 85, 87, 95, or 175.

7 ★★★ Crypt of the Capuchin Monks. This macabre, but oddly pleasing church crypt is decorated with thousands of artfully arranged monks' bones. Each chapel (of the Pelvises, the Skulls, the Femurs and Tibias), is a bizarre diorama where propped-up monks, still in their desiccated skin and cassocks, strike cautionary poses. In the last chapel, a chilling *memento mori* reads: "What you are now, we used to be. What we are now, you will be." ⏱ 20 min. Via Veneto 27. ☎ 06-4871185. Donation expected. Daily 9am–noon, 3–6pm. Metro: Barberini. Bus: 62, 95, 116, 175, or 492.

8 ★★ Stadium of Domitian. At the northern end of Piazza Navona, explore the fascinating remains of the 1st-century-A.D. athletic venue that gave the square its oblong shape. ⏱ 45 min. Piazza di Tor Sanguigna 16. ☎ 06-67103819. Admission 6€. Sat–Sun 10am–1pm or by appointment. Bus: 70, 87, 116, or 492.

9 ★★★ Necropolis of St. Peter's. Hushed-voiced priests lead you into the ancient level—15m (50 ft.) below the immense Vatican basilica—where bones believed to be St. Peter's were found in the 1940s. Book this unforgettable descent into early Christian history far in advance. ⏱ 45 min. Ufficio Scavi. ☎ 06-69885318. Fax 06-69885518. uffscavi@ fabricsp.va. Admission 10€. Tours Mon–Sat 9am–5pm. Under-12s not admitted. Book at least 1 month in advance.

Piazza Navona & the Pantheon

On this walking tour, prepare to switch sightseeing gears quickly in the most central part of the old city—quiet, labyrinthine alleys abruptly give way to imposing monuments and knockout postcard panoramas, and a slew of nonchalant-looking churches stash away some of the city's most celebrated works of art. The masters of the Roman baroque—architect Francesco Borromini, architect/sculptor Gian Lorenzo Bernini, and painter Caravaggio—were all very active in this area in the 17th century.

START Take bus 40, 62, or 74 to Castel Sant'Angelo/Piazza Pia.

1 ★★★ kids **Castel Sant'Angelo.** Rome's hamburger of history started out as Hadrian's mausoleum in the 2nd century A.D. and was converted in the Middle Ages into a fortress for the popes, who then gave themselves apartments here in the Renaissance. Its final incarnation, as a prison, lasted through the end of the 19th century, long enough to inspire Puccini's *Tosca*. Be sure to climb all the way up to the highest terrace—looking straight down over the Tiber is as soaring and dramatic as an operatic finale. ⏱ 1 hr. Lungotevere Castello 50. ☎ 06-6819111. Admission 7€. Tues–Sun 9am–7pm.

2 ★★ **Ponte Sant'Angelo.** The angels studding this bridge to Castel Sant'Angelo are copies of original sculptures by Bernini. Each figure holds an instrument of the passion of Christ; their masterfully rendered emotions run the gamut from introverted sorrow to wrenching pain to that Bernini warhorse, the parted-lips swoon. Best at night. Between Castel Sant'Angelo and Lungotevere Sant'Angelo.

3 ★ **Via dei Coronari.** This charming little street was formerly part of a pilgrim route to the Vatican; today, it's lined with antiquarians' shops and intersected by dozens of quaint alleys, with hidden trattorias and artists' studios.

> *Cafes and restaurants ring Piazza Navona and its fantastical fountains.*

> *Fashionable locals crowd the sidewalk cafes of Via della Pace.*

4 ★ **Via della Pace area.** Via della Pace bisects the web of streets, known as the "triangle of fun," between Via dei Coronari and Via del Governo Vecchio. By day, motorcycle mechanics rub shoulders with Roman nobility; by night, Roman hipsters flock to the area's countless eateries and *boîtes*.

5 🍽 ★ **Bar della Pace.** The chic and the restless flutter in and out of this eternally fashionable cafe from morning to night, but I recommend you stay a while—it's a prime spot for reading, postcard-writing, and ogling the lovely Santa Maria della Pace, just down the street. Via della Pace 3-7. ☎ 06-6861216. $-$$.

6 ★★★ **Piazza Navona.** Rome's grandest baroque square is the stage for an architectural smack-down between Borromini and Bernini. Weighing in on the western side of the oblong piazza is Borromini's **Sant'Agnese in Agone** (1653-57, see **7** below), a small church whose proud bearing is enhanced by its telescoping bell towers, oversized dome, and concave facade—a popular baroque feature, designed to draw in passersby. A bare basin for centuries, the **Fountain of Neptune** (Fontana di Nettuno) was only given its namesake figure and fanciful decoration in the 1800s. In the center, Neptune engages an octopus in fierce battle as unfazed duos of seahorses, nymphs, and aquatic cherubs cavort around the fountain's edge. In the center of the square, Bernini's action-packed, obelisk-crowned **Fountain of the Four Rivers** (Fontana dei Quattro Fiumi, 1651) is a feisty competitor, with four reclining figures representing the Danube, Plate, Ganges, and Nile. The fountain's base is a mass of travertine, hewn in the pre-weathered, organic style so favored in the 17th and 18th centuries. And any baroque sculptor worth his salt would sooner be caught dead than design a fountain that didn't include cavorting animals—today, overheated tourists and mentally unstable locals splash (illegally) alongside Bernini's "hippopotamus" (which is just a horse, wading) and river serpents. Between Borromini and Bernini, who wins? After 350 years, the jury is

The Eternal Drinking Water City

There's no excuse for being dehydrated in Rome. At the height of the Roman Empire, 11 aqueducts brought the city 25 million gallons of water a day for its baths, ornamental fountains, and basic utilities. That tradition of hydro-abundance continues in modern Rome: There are monumental fountains everywhere you look, and one of the city's most generous gifts to tourists and citizens alike is its free, perfectly drinkable spring water, in the form of *nasoni*.

In almost every piazza in town, on countless side streets, and in archaeological sites, you'll see these cast-iron hydrants marked SPQR, whose curved pipes emit a continuous stream of water into a drain below. These hydrants are properly called *fontanelle* ("little fountains") but in Roman slang, they're *nasoni* ("big noses"), for the shape of the spigots.

Naturally, many newcomers' first question is: Is it really safe to drink this water? The answer is an emphatic yes. Fontanelle draw on spring water in the hills outside the city—the same sources the ancients tapped for their aqueducts, minus the lead pipes—that tastes better and is cleaner than Rome's tap water, which is also potable. (Only a handful of fountains around town, mostly in the parks, are not potable, in which case they're clearly marked *acqua non potabile.*) What's more, the water issuing from the fontanelle is always ice-cold, even in the height of summer.

Once you have a plastic water bottle, you can just keep refilling it at nasoni all over town—for free. If you don't have a bottle handy, here's how the pros do it: Simply block up the bottom of the spigot with your finger, and the stream of water will come out a small hole in the top of the curved pipe, like a drinking fountain. Be careful with this method, though, as some nasoni are quite powerful and will shoot water all over you if you completely block up the bottom of the pipe. Of course, in July or August, this might feel very refreshing.

When you master drinking from a nasone, it's time to move onto the big, ornamental fountains of Rome. No, we're not recommending you drink from their dirty basins, but from the side jets of water that feed fountains such as the Trevi and the Barcaccia at Piazza di Spagna. These jets are the same as nasone water, fresh and clean. Tradition even holds that the water supply for the Barcaccia guarantees eternal youth for all who drink it.

> *The corridors of the Galleria Doria Pamphilj are exquisitely decorated and furnished.*

⑦ ★ Sant'Agnese in Agone. Borromini's broad, flamboyant facade belies this church's rather small interior. Through a door marked SACRA TESTA to the left of the altar, there's a reliquary holding the chimpanzee-sized skull of St. Agnes, martyred here in the 4th century A.D. ⏱ 15 min. Piazza Navona. No phone. Free admission. Tues–Sun 9am–noon, 4–7pm.

⑧ ★ Sant'Agostino. On the left wall, Caravaggio's *Madonna dei Pellegrini* (1604) shocked contemporaries with its frank depiction of dirty-footed pilgrims. On a pillar nearby, Raphael's meaty *Isaiah* (1512) recalls the frescoes of the Sistine Chapel. ⏱ 20 min. Piazza Sant'Agostino. ☎ 06-68801962. Free admission. Daily 8am–noon, 4–7:30pm.

⑨ ★★ San Luigi dei Francesi. Revolutionary for their high-keyed emotions and contrived play of light, Caravaggio's three *Life of St. Matthew* altarpieces (1603), displayed here, are some of his greatest masterpieces. ⏱ 20 min. Piazza San Luigi dei Francesi. ☎ 06-688271. Free admission. Daily 8:30am–12:30pm; Mon–Wed, Fri–Sun 3:30–7pm.

⑩ ★ Sant'Ivo alla Sapienza. Borromini always created drama in his architecture by employing elements of curvaceous tension; here, an upside-down marble tornado of a dome crowns a dizzying, star-shaped church. ⏱ 15 min. Corso Rinascimento 40. Free admission. Interior open only Sun 9am–noon.

⑪ ★★★ Pantheon. Hands down the most masterful architectural feat of ancient Rome, the Pantheon is almost perfectly preserved. The porch consists of 16 monolithic Egyptian granite columns, weighing 82 tons each. Inside, the 44m-wide (143-ft.) dome—poured in concrete in the 120s A.D. and never structurally modified—is pierced by a 9m-wide (30-ft.) oculus, open to the sky. While most ancient buildings lost their marbles to the popes, the Pantheon's floor and brick walls retain their rich revetment of yellow marble and purple porphyry. The tombs of Raphael and the Savoia monarchs are also here. ⏱ 30 min. Best in early morning or late afternoon, and in the rain. Piazza della Rotonda. ☎ 06-68300230. Free admission. Daily 9am–6pm, until 7:30pm in summer.

still out—but if you look up at the left bell tower of the Church of Sant'Agnese in Agone, a devastatingly superb statue of St. Agnes, placed there after the fountain's completion, seems to have the last laugh. Nine meters (30 ft.) below the baroque fountains and churches located here is the site where the ancient *agones* (athletic competitions) were held in the Stadium of Domitian (p 97, ⑧). In the medieval period, the Romans called this space *platea in agona* ("place of competition"), which later evolved into the modern appellation, Piazza Navona.

12 ★★ **Piazza della Minerva.** In front of the Gothic church Santa Maria Sopra Minerva, an Egyptian obelisk—one of 13 in Rome—is supported on the back of a plucky elephant, sculpted by Bernini. Also in this neighborhood, Via dei Cestari and Via Santa Chiara are home to most of Rome's religious outfitters, with their fabulous window displays of gem-encrusted chalices and the latest in liturgical couture.

13 ★ **Sant'Ignazio.** The focal point of this tight and tidy baroque square is the Jesuit church of St. Ignatius, famous for its illusionistic "dome," frescoed on the church's flat roof by Andrea Pozzo in 1626. ⏱ 15 min. Piazza di Sant'Ignazio. ☎ 06-6794406. Free admission. Daily 7:30am–12:15pm, 4–7pm.

14 ★★ **Piazza di Pietra.** The impressive row of columns here were the north wall of the 2nd-century-A.D. Temple of Hadrian, a plastic model of which can be seen in a showcase window across the square.

15 🍽 ★ **Gran Caffè La Caffettiera,** an elegant coffee and snack bar (and Internet hot spot), is especially cozy in winter. Piazza di Pietra 65. ☎ 06-6798147. $.

16 ★ **Piazza di Montecitorio.** On this sloping square in front of the Bernini-designed lower house of Parliament, dapper *carabinieri* (army police) survey the scene for terrorists—and eligible foreign women. The 2,600-year-old obelisk, moved here in 1751, was the shadow-casting *gnomon* of Augustus's sundial (9 B.C.), an approximation of which is inlaid in bronze over the square.

17 ★ **Column of Marcus Aurelius.** Dismissed by some art historians as a cheap imitation of Trajan's Column (p 78, **3**), this 30m-high (100-ft.) marble shaft (A.D. 180–193) depicts Marcus Aurelius's military exploits in Germany. Piazza Colonna.

18 ★★ **Galleria Doria Pamphilj.** This collection, whose audio guide is read (in English) by a living Pamphilj prince, has an enviable array of 16th- and 17th-century canvases, as well as Velázquez's famously soul-exposing portrait of Pope Innocent X Pamphilj. ⏱ 1 hr. Piazza del Collegio Romano 2. ☎ 06-6797323. www.doria pamphilj.it. Admission 8€. Fri–Wed 10am–5pm.

> *TOP* Bernini's elephant supports an Egyptian obelisk at the center of Piazza della Minerva. *BOTTOM* One of the Four Rivers, part of the sculptor's grandiose 1651 fountain in Piazza Navona.

Campo de' Fiori & the Jewish Ghetto

Unpretentious, workaday, and totally picturesque, the area around Campo de' Fiori is the best place in the *centro storico* (historic center) to see Roman daily life at its most authentic. Locals far outnumber tourists, and you can't walk a few steps without coming across a coffee bar, wine shop, or neighborhood trattoria. The Jewish Ghetto has left its dark days behind and become a vibrant, rewarding place to explore, with remnants of every era of Roman history. The Isola Tiberina and the riverbank here offer rustic charm and some of the city's most interesting, unsung sights.

START Take bus 30, 40, 62, 64, 70, 87, 116, 492, 571, or 628 to Corso Vittorio Emanuele II, or tram 8 to Largo Argentina.

1 ★★★ **Campo de' Fiori.** Bustling with energy night and day, and welcoming all, Campo de' Fiori is the beating heart of the *centro storico.* In the morning, the stalls of the city's most famous fruit and vegetable market sell produce to top chefs and local housewives. At night, all and sundry descend on the piazza's cafes and wine bars for the evening *aperitivo.*

2 ★★ **Craftsmen's Streets.** Many of the streets in the *centro storico* are named for the crafts practiced by artisans there throughout the ages; the best examples of these lie north of the *campo.* On Via dei Cappellari, medieval hatmakers have been replaced by furniture workshops, where old men (and some young) make table legs on lathes powered by foot pedals. Off Via del Pellegrino, tiny Arco degli Acetari (Vinegar-Makers' Arch) is the ramshackle, ocher-walled corner featured on so many Roman postcards.

> *Via del Portico d'Ottavia once marked the boundary of Rome's Ghetto, and still sports shop signs in Hebrew.*

1. Campo de' Fiori
2. Craftsmen's Streets
3. Piazza Farnese
4. Via Giulia
5. Galleria Spada
6. Via dei Giubbonari
7. Roscioli
8. Sant'Andrea della Valle
9. Area Sacra di Largo Argentina
10. Piazza Mattei
11. Piazza Margana
12. Via del Portico d'Ottavia
13. Forno del Ghetto
14. Synagogue
15. Portico d'Ottavia
16. Largo 16 Ottobre
17. Teatro di Marcello
18. Isola Tiberina
19. Ponte Rotto
20. Cloaca Maxima
21. Temples of Hercules and Portunus
22. Bocca della Verità

> *The persecution of Rome's Jews, which began in the 16th century, is remembered in a museum inside the Synagogue.*

③ ★★ Piazza Farnese. Serene Piazza Farnese enjoys the same Renaissance harmony as its namesake architectural feature, the dignified and imposing 16th-century Palazzo Farnese. The square and its immediate vicinity have recently become some of the most sought-after real estate in the city, with fabulous flats that accommodate visiting film stars on location in Rome.

④ ★★ Via Giulia. The dead-straight path of Via Giulia—for many, the most beautiful street in Rome—was cleared by Pope Julius II in the 1500s to give pilgrims a fail-safe passage to the Vatican. The picturesque ivy-covered arch that spans the street was to be part of a private bridge—never completed—for the Farnese family, connecting Palazzo Farnese with the Villa Farnesina, across the river in Trastevere.

⑤ ★ Galleria Spada. Private galleries with works by Titian and other Renaissance masters are almost a dime a dozen in Rome; what makes the Spada especially worth a visit is the uncannily deceptive Galleria del Borromini, a corridor only 9m (30 ft.) long that appears to be three times that length. ⏱ 30 min. Piazza Capo di Ferro 3. ☎ 06-6874896. Admission 5€. Tues–Sun 9am–7pm. Bus: 23, 30, 40, 62, 64, 70, 87, 116, 280, or 492. Tram: 8.

⑥ ★ Via dei Giubbonari. Shopaholics rejoice—this narrow, cobblestone thoroughfare is bursting with up-and-coming fashion boutiques, gourmet food stores, and street vendors.

⑦ 🍴 ★★ Roscioli. Stop into this beloved bakery for a square of *pizza bianca,* or choose from a vast assortment of freshly made savory and sweet pastries. Via dei Chiavari 34. ☎ 06-6864045. $.

⑧ ★ Sant'Andrea della Valle. The second highest dome in Rome—after St. Peter's—rests atop this excellent 16th-century basilica, where Puccini set the first act of *Tosca.* ⏱ 15 min. Corso Vittorio Emanuele II 6. ☎ 06-6861339. Free admission. Daily 8am–noon, 4:30–7:30pm.

⑨ ★ Area Sacra di Largo Argentina. During the excavation fever of the 1930s, Mussolini evicted hundreds of Romans who were living here and ordered archaeologists to dig. What you see here today, 9m (30 ft.) below street level, are four republican-era temple foundations and a much-hyped though visually underwhelming fragment of the senate house (Curia Pompei) where Julius Caesar was stabbed on the ides of March, 44 B.C. Ruins open by appointment only. ☎ 06-67103819. Fax 06-6790795. Admission 2.10€.

⑩ ★★ Piazza Mattei. One of Rome's most prized possessions, the 17th-century Fontana delle Tartarughe (Fountain of the Tortoises) lies tucked away in this little quadrangle, where you'll often find film crews shooting and art students sketching its picturesquely patinated centerpiece. On the south side of the square, the funky **Bartaruga** (p 137) is a cool spot for a cold drink.

⑪ ★ Piazza Margana. This textbook example of a charming Italian square comes complete with geraniums spilling out of window boxes, pretty alfresco cafe/restaurant—and, if you look carefully down tiny Via di Tor Margana, a gun-barrel view of Trajan's Column, 500m (½ mile) away.

② ★ **Via del Portico d'Ottavia.** Formerly the eastern boundary of the Jewish Ghetto, this bumpy, busy street is now the principal thoroughfare of the modern neighborhood, with shop signs in Hebrew alluding to the community's heritage.

③ ★ **Forno del Ghetto.** It's hard to resist the sweet smells of almonds, cinnamon, and ricotta emanating from this tiny Jewish bakery, run by three gruff matrons. Cookies and candied cakes are sold by the kilo and are best eaten fresh out of the oven. **Via del Portico d'Ottavia 1.** ☎ 06-6878637. Items from 1€. Sun–Thurs 9am–7:30pm. Fri 9am–sundown.

④ ★★ **Synagogue.** Rome's gorgeous, palm-treed *sinagoga* is a particularly triumphant edifice in this part of town. It was built in the 1890s over land that was once the most squalid part of the Ghetto, shortly after the decree that ended Jewish segregation. Inside the temple is the Museo d'Arte Ebraica, with vivid exhibits documenting the persecution of Jews in Rome from 1555—when the papal bull, *Cum nimis absurdum,* established the Ghetto laws—through the Nazi occupation of the 1940s. ⏱ 30 min. Lungotevere Cenci 15. ☎ 06-68400661. Admission 6€. Sun–Thurs 9am–4:30pm (until 7pm May–Aug), Fri 9am–1:30pm.

⑤ ★ **Portico d'Ottavia.** Poking up from the ancient level at the end of Via del Portico d'Ottavia are the impressive remains of a *propylaeum* (gate to a temple precinct) built by Augustus, and named for his sister, in 23 B.C. Today, the portico is the monumental entry to the modest medieval Church of Sant'Angelo in Pescheria, where Jews were forced to attend Catholic Mass during the Ghetto period. The pavement outside was the site of Rome's *pescheria* (fish market) for centuries, hence the name of the church. On the left side of the portico there's a marble plaque left over from the *pescheria* days: The inscription states that for any fish measuring longer than the plaque, the excess length (from the head down) must be tithed to the church. ⏱ 15 min. Free admission. Excavations daily 9am–5pm.

> *The vibe is artsy but unpretentious at Bartaruga in Piazza Mattei.*

⑯ ★ **Largo 16 Ottobre.** In front of the Portico d'Ottavia ruins, a plaque on the wall commemorates the place where, on the night of October 16, 1943, Roman Jews were rounded up by Nazi troops and deported to the concentration camps of Auschwitz and Birkenau. Of the 3,091 men, women, and children deported, only 15 survived.

⑰ ★★ **Teatro di Marcello.** With a 15,000-spectator capacity, this 13 B.C. theater was the main ancient Roman venue for plays,

> *The Fiat 500 and the Vespa have kept Rome moving for decades.*

concerts, and the occasional public execution. In the 1300s, the Savelli family built a fortress on top of the ponderous ruins, which they then converted into a palace during the Renaissance. Above the ancient travertine arches, the apartments are still inhabited by modern princes and *contessas.* Many newcomers to Rome mistake this building for the Colosseum; although the theater is much smaller than the Colosseum, its familiar-looking design of superimposed travertine arches inspired the look of the Colosseum, built 100 years later. ⏱ 15 min. Free admission. Excavations daily 9am–5pm.

🔞 ★★ **Isola Tiberina.** In 391 B.C., a snake slithered onto the shores of Tiber Island; at the same time, a decade-long plague in Rome ended. Ever since, the river island has been a sanctuary of medicine, with the Fatebenefratelli hospital today occupying the majority of the real estate here. The ancient Romans, in a moment of fancy, sculpted the island to look like a ship; part of the "hull" (a fragment of carved travertine) can still be seen on the lower esplanade, a favorite sunning spot of Romans on their lunch breaks. Stairs to the lower esplanade are located west of the main entrance to the hospital. In summer, outdoor movies are shown and snack bars set up down here during the Isola del Cinema film festival (www.isoladelcinema.com). ⏱ 30 min.

🔞 ★ **Ponte Rotto.** Stranded in the middle of the river below Isola Tiberina is the single arch of the 142 B.C. Ponte Rotto, or "broken bridge," which fell and was rebuilt so many times that the city finally abandoned it when it collapsed in 1598. From the neighboring modern bridge, Ponte Palatino, wheel ruts can still be seen on the Ponte Rotto's roadway. **No access.**

🔟 **Cloaca Maxima.** A gaping arch in the riverbank walls under the eastern end of the Ponte Palatino is the mouth of the 6th-century-B.C. "great sewer," constructed to drain the moisture from the swampy valley of the Roman Forum. According to some archaeologists, the underground waterway is still navigable, with secret access hatches in unlikely parts of the city. **Interior open by appointment only.** ☎ 06-67103819. Admission 2.10€.

🔢 ★ **Temples of Hercules and Portunus.** In a beautiful setting, among oleanders and fountains on a grassy rise near the riverbank, these two republican-era temples survive

Converting from pagan to Christian use saved the Temples of Hercules and Portunus.

because of their reconsecration as churches. For centuries, the round temple (of Hercules) was known as the Temple of Vesta because the only other known round temple was that of Vesta in the Roman Forum. The rectangular temple was dedicated to Portunus, god of port activity; in antiquity, the most important cargo coming to Rome, such as columns for the Forum, or lions for the Colosseum, was unloaded from river barges here. **No access.**

2 ★ kids **Bocca della Verità (Mouth of Truth).** Propped up at the end of the portico of the Church of Santa Maria in Cosmedin (which has a fantastic Romanesque bell tower and unusual Greek Orthodox interior) is an ancient sewer cover known as the Mouth of Truth that is supposed to bite off the hands of liars. In the spirit of Gregory Peck and Audrey Hepburn in *Roman Holiday,* tourists line up all day to take pictures of themselves with their hands in the mouth slot—cheesy, but a Roman rite of passage. ⏱ **15 min. Queue shortest before 1pm. Piazza della Bocca della Verità. ☎ 06-6781419. Free admission. Daily 9am–5pm.**

> *According to legend, Santa Maria in Cosmedin's Mouth of Truth will close on the hand of a liar.*

Trastevere

Separated from the rest of the old city by the river, picturesque Trastevere has strived to maintain its own identity since ancient times, when it was dubbed Trans Tiberim (Across the Tiber). Although expatriates have relocated here in droves, the district still has its insular character and village-y appeal.

> The soaring, mosaic-replete interior of the Romanesque Santa Maria in Trastevere.

START Take bus 23, 271, 280, 780, H, or tram 8 to Piazza G. G. Belli (Lungotevere degli Anguillara/Viale Trastevere).

1 ★ **Vicolo dell'Atleta.** The "alley of the athlete"—as tiny as streets get in Rome—has a facade of a 13th-century synagogue, now the restaurant Spirito di Vino (p 128).

2 ★★ **Santa Cecilia.** See p 70, **1**.

3 ★ **San Francesco a Ripa.** Home to Bernini's overtly sexual *Beata Ludovica Albertoni* (1674). ⏱ 15 min. Piazza San Francesco d'Assisi 88.

☎ 06-5819020. Free admission. Daily 7:30am–noon, 4–7pm.

4 **Via dei Fienaroli.** Dense ivy blankets the walls of this pretty street, hiding numerous interesting bookshops and cafes.

5 ★★ **Piazza & Basilica di Santa Maria in Trastevere.** The hub of daily life in Trastevere is graced by the magnificent church of Santa Maria in Trastevere, with 22 recycled Roman columns lining the nave and sparkling mosaics adorning the apse. Legend has it the church was built over the spot where a fountain of oil miraculously

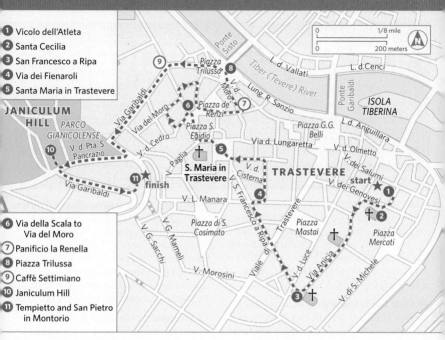

1 Vicolo dell'Atleta
2 Santa Cecilia
3 San Francesco a Ripa
4 Via dei Fienaroli
5 Santa Maria in Trastevere

6 Via della Scala to
  Via del Moro
7 Panificio la Renella
8 Piazza Trilussa
9 Caffè Settimiano
10 Janiculum Hill
11 Tempietto and San Pietro
  in Montorio

bubbled up in 38 B.C., apparently heralding the coming of Christ. The piazza's handsome fountain, by Carlo Fontana, is somewhat blighted by vagrancy. See p 70, 2, and p 93, 7.

6 ★ **Via della Scala to Via del Moro.** This warren of gnarled streets (Vicolo del Cedro, Vicolo del Bologna, Piazza de' Renzi) is the most charming part of old Trastevere, where clotheslines are strung over narrow alleys, parking jobs reach new heights of ingenuity, and neighbors chat animatedly.

7 ★★ **Panificio la Renella,** purveyor of *pane* to all restaurants and households in the vicinity, is a bread bakery that also has excellent pizza by the slice, bar stools to sit on, and a community message board. Via del Moro 15–16. ☎ 06-5817265. $.

8 **Piazza Trilussa.** This is the point of egress for all the tiny streets in the area, and where pedestrian Ponte Sisto leads across the Tiber toward Campo de' Fiori. Several cafes and bars, such as Freni e Frizioni (p 137), in this vicinity draw huge crowds of young people most evenings.

9 ★ **Caffè Settimiano,** in the shadow of the old Porta Settimiana (a gate in the 3rd-c.-A.D. Aurelian Walls), is a wonderful place to rest your feet, read the paper, and watch *trasteverini* go by. Via di Porta Settimiana. ☎ 06-5810468. $.

10 ★★★ **Janiculum Hill.** The hike to the top of the Gianicolo—the highest point in central Rome—is steep, but well worth the spectacular views, tree-lined promenades, and clear air. Don't miss the fabulously inviting 17th-century Fontanone dell'Acqua Paola. Take Via Garibaldi to Via di Porta San Pancrazio and climb the steps to the Passeggiata del Gianicolo.

11 ★ **Tempietto and San Pietro in Montorio.** In the courtyard of this church is Donato Bramante's round Tempietto (1508), one of Rome's greatest, and least visited, architectural treasures. Built to honor the martyrdom of St. Peter (which took place down the hill at the Vatican, not up here), the beautifully proportioned Tempietto is a masterpiece of High Renaissance classicism. ⏲ 15 min. Piazza San Pietro in Montorio 2. ☎ 06-5813940. Free admission. Tempietto daily 10am–noon, 2–4pm.

Via Appia Antica

The most important of Rome's famous ancient roads, the rustic Via Appia Antica (Appian Way) is home to most of the city's catacombs and is a world away from the bustle of the *centro*. Visit the catacombs where Roman Christians were buried, then continue south, where a landscape steeped in antiquity should leave you spellbound. Walking and biking on the Via Appia is best on Sundays, when the ancient road is closed to vehicle traffic.

START Take bus 118 (from Metro Circo Massimo or Piramide) to the Porta San Sebastiano stop. (Or, if you start at the catacombs, take 118 to the Catacombe di San Callisto or Basilica San Sebastiano stops.) Or take a taxi (10–15 min. from the city center, 15€–20€). Allow 3–4 hours for the trip.

1 Porta San Sebastiano. This massive brick gateway is left over from Rome's 3rd-century-A.D. fortification. It marks the start of Via Appia Antica's southbound route. Inside, the **Museo delle Mura** has exhibits on Roman defense systems. ⏱ 30 min. Via di Porta di San Sebastiano 18. ☎ 06-70475284. Museum admission 2.60€. Tues–Sun 9am–7pm (until 5pm Nov–Mar).

The next mile of the Via Appia is visually underwhelming and plagued with traffic; take bus 118 five stops (about 1.6km/1 mile) south to the catacombs, where the landscape is greener and quieter.

2 kids Catacombs of San Callisto. The most impressive and extensive of Rome's catacombs. ⏱ 1 hr. See p 74, **1**.

3 kids Catacombs of San Sebastiano. More intimate than San Callisto, with an interesting cluster of pagan tombs. ⏱ 1 hr. See p 76, **2**.

4 Villa and Circus of Maxentius. A 5-minute walk south of San Sebastiano, the ruins of a 4th-century imperial country estate and circus (chariot racetrack, which held 10,000 spectators) offer awe-inspiring views of Cecilia Metella (**5**) among the umbrella pines. ⏱ 30 min. Via Appia Antica 153. Admission 2.60€. Tues-Fri, Sun 9am–1:30pm; Sat 9am–1 hr. before sunset.

5 Mausoleum of Cecilia Metella. The best view of this cylindrical tomb of a 1st-century-B.C. socialite is from the middle of the Circus of Maxentius (**4**) or the road. The Via Appia was the Rodeo Drive of tombs in antiquity, and Cecilia Metella's was only one of hundreds of marble-clad sepulchers that used to crowd the roadside. The other tombs, dismantled in the Middle Ages for their materials, are now little more than brick stumps. ⏱ 15 min. Via Appia Antica 161. Admission 6€. Tues–Sun 9am–1 hr. before sunset.

> OPPOSITE PAGE *The Porta San Sebastiano marks the start of the Via Appia Antica.* THIS PAGE *Motor-powered traffic is banned from the flagstones of the ancient road on Sundays.*

Tour Tip

Enjoy Rome offers a 3-hour bus and walking tour of the Via Appia, including the stupendous aqueduct park off Via Appia Nuova, otherwise hard to reach. Call for tour times. ☎ 06-4451843.

⑥ Bar Caffè dell'Appia Antica & Bike Rentals.
A bike ride can be a very pleasant way to see the Appia Antica, provided you start here and ride south, where vehicle traffic is light to nonexistent. This informal coffee bar rents bikes by the hour. The Via Appia is bumpy, but you can travel as far as 3km (2 miles) on the ancient road, viewing ruins and rural life, and not worry about getting lost—the Appia's path is due south and dead straight. Via Appia Antica 175. ☎ 338-3465440. Bikes 3€ per hour. Tues–Sun 8:30am–7pm.

⑦ Via Appia Antica. The leafy, 3km (2-mile) segment beginning at Cecilia Metella is the Appia at its most evocative. Private villas on either side of the road eventually give way to ruins-strewn fields and the occasional flock of sheep. You'll need to walk for at least 500m (⅓ mile) to appreciate the change of scenery; beyond that, it's somewhat repetitive—umbrella pines, tomb stumps—but still wonderfully soaked in history. ⏱ At least 1 hr.

Public transportation is spotty at the southern end of the road; return by foot or bike to ⑥. From there, catch bus no. 660 to Metro San Giovanni, or call a taxi (☎ 06-3570) from the bar.

① Porta San Sebastiano
② Catacombs of San Callisto
③ Catacombs of San Sebastiano
④ Villa and Circus of Maxentius
⑤ Mausoleum of Cecilia Metella
⑥ Bar Caffè dell'Appia Antica & Bike Rentals
⑦ Via Appia Antica

Rome Shopping Best Bets

Best Multilabel Boutique
Gente, Via del Babuino 81 (p 115)

Best Stylish & Affordable Shoes
Martina Novelli, Piazza Risorgimento 38 (p 119)
Posto Italiano, Via Giubbonari 37A (p 119)

Best Street for Contemporary Fashion
Via dei Giubbonari, off Campo de' Fiori (p 106)

Best Accessories at Good Prices
COIN, Via Cola di Rienzo 173 (p 118)

Best Museum Store
Capitoline Museums, Piazza del Campidoglio
(p 119)

Best Teen Threads
Brandy Melville, Via Cola di Rienzo 136 (p 115)

Best Kitchen Gadgets
c.u.c.i.n.a., Via Mario de' Fiori 65 (p 118)

Best Toys and Children's Books
Città del Sole, Via della Scrofa 65 (p 119)

Best Gourmet Foods
Franchi, Via Cola di Rienzo 204 (p 119)
Volpetti, Via Marmorata 47 (p 119)

Best Local Market
Mercato di Testaccio, Piazza Testaccio (p 119)

Best Gifts
Modigliani, Via Condotti 24 (p 118)

Best Bookstore
Anglo American Book Co., Via della Vite 102
(p 115)

**Best Street for High-Fashion
Window-Shopping**
Via Condotti (p 118)

> Volpetti is the top spot in town for gourmet picnic fare.

Rome Shopping A to Z

Apparel & Accessories

Brandy Melville VATICAN

Sort of like Abercrombie meets Juicy Couture, this Italian label with a cultlike following is where Rome's privileged teens go for striped T-shirts, tanks, leggings, and underwear. **Via Cola di Rienzo** 36 (at Via Orazio). ☎ 06-3211622. AE, MC, V. Metro: Ottaviano. Bus: 70, 81. Map p 116.

Ethic PANTHEON

A favorite of 20- and 30-something Roman women, with reasonably priced boho-chic pieces in saturated colors and adherent cuts. Via del Pantheon 46–47 (at Piazza della Maddalena). ☎ 06-68803167. (Branch at Piazza Cairoli 7–12, at Via Giubbonari. ☎ 06-68301063.) AE, MC, V. Bus: 30, 40, 62, 64, 70, 85, 87, 95, 116, 175, or 492. Map p 116.

★ **Gente** SPANISH STEPS

A microcosm of the Via Condotti boutiques, with more affordable denim and accessories.

Modigliani ships handcrafted gifts all over the world.

Via del Babuino 81 (at Piazza di Spagna). ☎ 06-3207671. AE, MC, V. Metro: Spagna. (Branch at Via Cola di Rienzo 277, Vatican area.) Map p 116.

★ **Murphy & Nye** PIAZZA DEL POPOLO

Roman men love to dress as if they're on a back-up crew for a major regatta. Join 'em with threads from this trendy, nautical-inspired sportswear boutique. **Via del Corso 26–27** (near Piazza del Popolo). ☎ 06-36004461. AE, MC, V. Metro: Flaminio. Map p 116.

Books & Music

★★ **Anglo American Book Co.** SPANISH STEPS

English-language titles of all kinds are sold here, but the selection is particularly strong on art and architecture. Via della Vite 102 (at Via Mario de' Fiori). ☎ 06-6795222. AE, MC, V. Metro: Spagna. Map p 116.

★ **Feltrinelli Libri e Musica** PANTHEON

This national chain has bar-code-scanning CD-listening stations and a great travel section. Largo di Torre Argentina 5A–6 (at Corso Vittorio

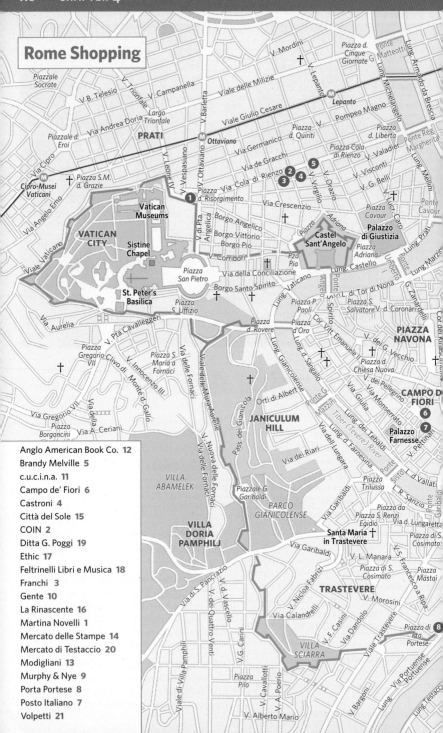

Rome Shopping

> *Stove-top coffeemakers are among the kitchen gadgets on sale at c.u.c.i.n.a.*

Emanuele II). ☎ 06-68803248. AE, MC, V. Bus: 30, 40, 62, 64, 70, 87, or 492. Map p 116.

Department Stores

★ COIN VATICAN

It's underwhelming if you're used to the U.S. or U.K. department store standard, but COIN does have some great finds in its accessories and housewares sections. Via Cola di Rienzo 173 (at Via Paolo Emilio). ☎ 06-700020. AE, MC, V. Metro: Ottaviano. Map p 116.

★ La Rinascente SPANISH STEPS

Similar to COIN but larger and more central, Rinascente is a good bet when you need to buy a last-minute leather wallet or silk scarf for someone back home. Largo Chigi 20 (at Via del Corso). ☎ 06-6797691. AE, MC, V. Bus: 62, 63, 85, 95, 175, or 492. Map p 116.

High Fashion Boutiques

All roads lead to Rome; the roads around the Spanish Steps lead to credit card debt. Every big-name designer has a presence here: The main drag is **Via Condotti,** but **Piazza di Spagna, Via del Babuino,** and **Via Borgognona** are also chockablock with luxury labels.

Design & Home Furnishings

★★ c.u.c.i.n.a. SPANISH STEPS

At this shrine to stainless-steel cookware and kitchen gadgets, you can pick up authentic Bialetti stove-top coffeemakers, mini parmigiano graters, and all gauges of ravioli cutters. Via Mario de' Fiori 65 (at Via delle Carrozze). ☎ 06-6791275. www.cucinastore.com. AE, MC, V. Metro: Spagna. Map p 116.

★★★ Modigliani SPANISH STEPS

From Murano wineglasses to hand-painted Tuscan platters, the fine merchandise at this four-story tabletop-goods store makes great gifts that can be shipped anywhere in the world. Via Condotti 24 (at Via Bocca di Leone). ☎ 06-6785653. www.modigliani.it. AE, MC, V. Metro: Spagna. Map p 116.

Food & Wine

★★ Castroni VATICAN

This coffee bar extraordinaire has bulk candy, caviar, fine wines, and all manner of oils and vinegars. A godsend for many expats, Castroni also stocks hard-to-get foreign foodstuffs such as Bisquick and Vegemite. Via Cola di Rienzo 196–198 (at Via Terenzio). ☎ 06-6874383. AE, MC, V. Metro: Ottaviano. Map p 116.

★★ Franchi VATICAN

One of the top two gourmet delis in town (Volpetti is the other), Franchi has every cheese and cured meat under the sun. At lunch, hot prepared food (including heavenly *supplì*—balls of rice, tomato sauce, and mozzarella, breaded and fried) is available to go. Via Cola di Rienzo 204 (at Via Terenzio). ☎ 06-6874651. AE, MC, V. Metro: Ottaviano. Map p 116.

★★ Volpetti TESTACCIO

Foodies, prepare to swoon—the aromas of cheese and cured meat here beckon like at no other deli in Rome. The enthusiastic staff will let you taste everything. There's an amazing selection of honeys, vinegars, Italian spirits, pâté, preserves, infused oils, and truffled items galore. Via Marmorata 47 (at Via Alessandro Volta). ☎ 06-5742352. AE, MC, V. Metro: Piramide. Bus: 23, 30, 75, 95, 271, or 280. Tram: 3. Map p 116.

Markets

★★ Campo de' Fiori

This historic produce market is still a Roman institution and well worth a visit, though kitschy souvenirs have begun to take over what used to be the city's most authentic fruit-and-veggie bazaar. Mon–Sat 7am–2pm. No credit cards. Bus: 30, 40, 62, 64, 70, 87, or 492. Map p 116.

★★ Mercato delle Stampe SPANISH STEPS

Here you'll find wonderfully worn antique books, old engravings, vintage magazines, and their loving dealers. Largo della Fontanella Borghese. No credit cards. Metro: Spagna. Bus: 81. Map p 116.

★★ Mercato di Testaccio See p 76, .

★ Porta Portese TRASTEVERE

Unless you're in the market for a Turkish casino ashtray or a dot-matrix printer, you'll find Rome's biggest flea market more spectacle than working shopping experience. Via Portuense from Piazza Porta Portese to Via Ettore Rolli. Sun only, 7am–2pm. No credit cards. Bus: 23, 271, or 280. Tram: 3 or 8. Map p 116.

Shoes

★★ Martina Novelli VATICAN

Delightfully opinionated shopgirls will help women choose the right pair at this hip, mostly affordable shoe store near the Vatican. Piazza Risorgimento 38 (at Via Ottaviano). ☎ 06-39737247. AE, MC, V. Bus: 23, 81, 271, or 492. Tram: 19. Map p 116.

★★ Posto Italiano CAMPO DE' FIORI

This friendly "Italian place" stocks well-priced and current shoes and boots for men and women. Via Giubbonari 37A (off Campo de' Fiori). ☎ 06-6869373. (Branch: Viale Trastevere 111. ☎ 06-58334820). AE, MC, V. Bus: 30, 40, 62, 64, 70, 87, or 492. Map p 116.

Stationers

★★ Ditta G. Poggi PANTHEON

Amid tubes of oil paint and stencils at this 180-year-old art supplies store, you might stumble across charming 1950s composition books (at 1950s prices) and the odd Italian BEWARE OF DOG sign. Via del Gesù 74–75 (at Via Piè di Marmo). ☎ 06-6793674. www.poggi1825.it. AE, MC, V. Bus: 30, 40, 62, 64, 70, 87, or 492. Map p 116.

Toys

★★ Città del Sole PANTHEON

Italy's excellent educational toy and children's books chain invites even adults to spend hours browsing its wonderful merchandise. Teach junior some *italiano* with translated versions of Dr. Seuss and *Where the Wild Things Are.* Via della Scrofa 65. ☎ 06-68803805. AE, MC, V. Bus: 30, 70, 87, 492, or 628. Map p 116.

Rome Restaurant Best Bets

Best All-Around *Cucina Romana* Experience
Perilli $$ Via Marmorata 39 (p 128)

Best Understatedly Cool, Insider Spots
Maccheroni $$ Via delle Coppelle 44 (p 127)
Fiaschetteria Beltramme $$ Via della Croce 39 (p 126)

Best Bare-Bones *Hostaria*
Da Bucatino $$ Via Luca della Robbia 84–86 (p 124)

Best Boisterous Lunch
Enoteca Corsi $ Via del Gesù 87 (p 125)

Best Outdoor Tables
Antica Pesa $$$ Via Garibaldi 18 (p 121)
La Veranda $$$ Borgo Santo Spirito 73 (p 127)

Best For Serious Oenophiles & Food Snobs
Casa Bleve $$ Via del Teatro Valle 48–49 (p 121)
Enoteca Cavour 313 $$ Via Cavour 313 (p 125)

Best Paparazzi Haunt
Due Ladroni $$$ Piazza Nicosia 24 (p 124)

Best Quick Lunch Near the Ruins
La Bottega del Caffè $ Piazza Madonna dei Monti 5 (p 126)

Best For Romance
Il Bacaro $$$ Via degli Spagnoli 27 (p 126)

Best Coffee
Bar Sant'Eustachio $ Piazza di Sant'Eustachio 82 (p 121)

Best Seafood, But It'll Cost Ya
Quinzi e Gabrieli $$$$ Via delle Coppelle 5 (p 128)

Best Modern Roman Dining
'Gusto $$–$$$ Piazza Augusto Imperatore 7, 9, 28 (p 126)

> *Casa Bleve specializes in exquisite plates of delicacies to accompany its fine wines.*

Rome Restaurants A to Z

★★ **Al Girarrosto Toscano** VATICAN *GRILL*
Carnivores go wild for the succulent perfection of this restaurant's Tuscan-style grilled meats. Via Germanico 58–60 (at Via Vespasiano). ☎ 06-39723373. Entrees 10€–20€. AE, MC, V. Lunch & dinner Tues–Sun. Metro: Ottaviano. Bus: 23 or 492. Tram: 19. Map p 122.

★★ **Antica Pesa** TRASTEVERE *ROMAN*
Refined *signori e signore* trek halfway up the Janiculum Hill to this charmer with a reliable traditional menu and a lovely interior garden, a converted bocce court. Via Garibaldi 18 (at Via del Mattonato). ☎ 06-5809236. Entrees 12€–20€. AE, MC, V. Dinner Mon–Sat. Bus: 23, 271, or 280. Map p 122.

★★★ **Bar Sant'Eustachio** PANTHEON *COFFEE*
Its blue-script neon sign is a beacon for coffee snobs in search of the richest, creamiest brew in the city. The *gran caffè* is the specialty. Piazza di Sant'Eustachio 82 (south side of square). ☎ 06-

6561309. Coffee 1.50€–4€. No credit cards. Daily 8:30am–1am. Bus: 30, 40, 62, 64, 70, 87, 116, or 492. Map p 122.

★★ **Casa Bleve** PANTHEON *WINE BAR*
Lavish spreads of cheeses, meats, olives, and other delicacies at this ambitious *enoteca*-and-more resemble a Renaissance feast—with a vaulted and columned room to match. Via del Teatro Valle 48–49 (off Corso Vittorio Emanuele II). ☎ 06-6865970. www.casableve.it. Entrees 8€–18€. AE, MC, V. Lunch & dinner Tues–Sat. Bus: 30, 40, 62, 64, 70, 87, 116, or 492. Tram: 8. Map p 122.

★★★ **Checchino dal 1887** TESTACCIO *ROMAN*
Often mischaracterized as an offal-only joint, this establishment, opened in 1887, is a special-night-out type of place, serving wonderful *bucatini all'amatriciana* and veal saltimbocca—as well as hearty plates of, *er,* heart and other slaughterhouse castoffs. Via di Monte Testaccio 30 (at Via Galvani). ☎ 06-5746318.

> *Lunch is a boisterous affair at Enoteca Corsi.*

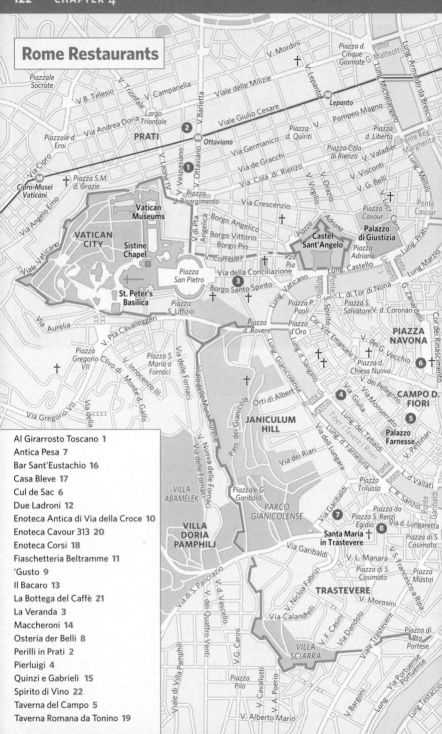

Rome Restaurants

Al Girarrosto Toscano **1**
Antica Pesa **7**
Bar Sant'Eustachio **16**
Casa Bleve **17**
Cul de Sac **6**
Due Ladroni **12**
Enoteca Antica di Via della Croce **10**
Enoteca Cavour 313 **20**
Enoteca Corsi **18**
Fiaschetteria Beltramme **11**
'Gusto **9**
Il Bacaro **13**
La Bottega del Caffè **21**
La Veranda **3**
Maccheroni **14**
Osteria der Belli **8**
Perilli in Prati **2**
Pierluigi **4**
Quinzi e Gabrieli **15**
Spirito di Vino **22**
Taverna del Campo **5**
Taverna Romana da Tonino **19**

> *A pizza bread sandwich from Aristocampo makes a cheap and tasty picnic lunch.*

www.checchino-dal-1887.com. Entrees 16€–30€. AE, MC, V. Dinner Tues–Sat. Metro: Piramide. Bus: 23, 95, 170, or 280. Tram: 3. Map p 125.

★ **Cul de Sac** PIAZZA NAVONA *WINE BAR*
Cozy and lively, this popular *enoteca* has a mind-boggling selection of cheeses and cold cuts, savory Mediterranean salads and hors d'oeuvres, and wines by the glass or bottle. Piazza Pasquino 73 (at Via del Governo Vecchio). ☎ 06- 68801094. Entrees 8€–13€. MC, V. Lunch Tues–Sun, dinner daily. Bus: 40, 62, 64, 70, 87, or 492. Map p 122.

★★ kids **Da Bucatino** TESTACCIO *ROMAN*
The best place in Testaccio for a casual Roman meal. In this authentic *hostaria,* you'll be treated like family, and you'll get to watch the antics of the many local families who eat here regularly. Via Luca della Robbia 84–86 (at Via Bodoni). ☎ 06-5746886. Entrees 7€–15€. AE, MC, V. Lunch & dinner Tues–Sun. Bus: 23, 75, 271, or 280. Tram 3. Map p 125.

★★ **Due Ladroni** SPANISH STEPS *ITALIAN*
Italian gossip mags always feature a few grainy photos of celebs dining at this classy but unpretentious restaurant, where the standard pastas and meat dishes are solid, and the waiters have the tip-enhancing quality of treating you as if you might be famous. Piazza Nicosia 24 (off Via di Ripetta). ☎ 06-6896299. Entrees 14€–24€. AE, MC, V. Lunch & dinner Mon–Sat. Bus: 87, 280, 492, or 628. Map p 122.

Dining Tips

You might think that finding good food in Rome, the capital of Italy, is a given, right? Not so fast. While there are many wonderful places to eat in this city, some restaurants whose lifeblood is a revolving population of tourists slack off in their preparations and don't always use top-quality ingredients. We'd hate for you to waste your time, money, or calories on mediocre food, so in this chapter, we've given you our top recommendations for different cuisine types, price ranges, and levels of formality. However, should you strike out on your own, keep these guidelines in mind:

1. Don't eat at any restaurant where the menu is translated into five languages (or, worse yet, where the menu is simply photographs of spaghetti drowning in red sauce).

2. Avoid restaurants where waitstaff is overly solicitous of passersby. If their restaurant is so great, why do they need to hustle you in off the street?

3. Most restaurants located right on the main piazzas are big-time tourist traps. Stick to the smaller squares and side streets.

4. Do as the Romans do. If you follow the locals (they're the ones who go out after 8pm), you'll be in good shape.

5. Never order priced-by-weight seafood without first confirming what it will actually cost you. That baked turbot might come back to haunt you once you see the insane 100€ charge for it on your bill.

6. Keep your budget on track by having only one restaurant meal per day. (See "Snacking as the Romans Do," p 127.)

7. Double-check your bill: I hate to admit it, but there are just enough unscrupulous waiters out there to make this un-vacation-like step worth the effort. Even locals sometimes get charged for items they never ordered, or for dishes they ordered but that were never brought out.

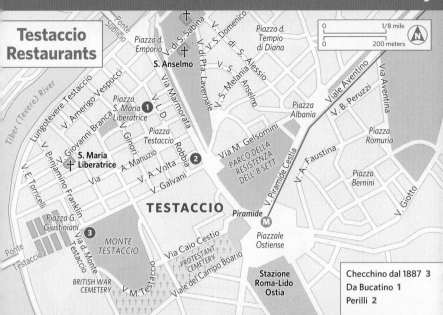

Testaccio Restaurants

Checchino dal 1887 **3**
Da Bucatino **1**
Perilli **2**

★ **Enoteca Antica di Via della Croce** SPANISH STEPS *WINE BAR* A prime spot to rest your feet after shopping around the Spanish Steps. There's a long bar, table service in back and outside, great antipasti, and dozens of wines by the glass. Via della Croce 76b (at Via Bocca di Leone). ☎ 06-6790896. Entrees 10€–16€. AE, MC, V. Lunch & dinner daily. Metro: Spagna. Map p 122.

★★ **Enoteca Cavour 313** MONTI *WINE BAR* Serious foodies can stop into this handsome gem near the Forum for plates of the highest quality prosciutto, carpaccio, cheese, vegetable dishes, and, of course, wine. Via Cavour 313 (at Via dell'Agnello). ☎ 06-6785496. Entrees 10€–18€. AE, MC, V. Lunch & dinner daily. Closed Sun Jun–Aug. Metro: Cavour or Colosseo. Bus: 75, 85, 87, 175, 571. Map p 122.

★★ **Enoteca Corsi** PANTHEON *ROMAN* At this terrific remnant of early-20th-century Rome, government office workers settle into cramped tables to eat hearty, messy dishes sloshing dangerously close to their Zegna ties and Armani shirts. The loud and lively scene—and the prices—are a time warp back to more carefree days. Via del Gesù 87 (near Via del Plebiscito). ☎ 06-6790821. Entrees 7€–12€. MC, V. Lunch Mon–Sat. Bus: 30, 40, 62, 64, 87, 492, 571. Map p 122.

> *Antipasti, pizzas, and creative cuisine are available all day at 'Gusto.*

> *La Bottega del Caffè is the perfect choice for a light lunch in Monti.*

★★ **Fiaschetteria Beltramme** SPANISH STEPS *ROMAN* Chic locals, expats, and visitors in the know brave the no-phone, no-reservations policy at this homey spot, run by cool women, for one of the most satisfying casual dining experiences in the *centro*. The menu offers a nice mix of cold, lighter plates and traditional Roman dishes—the *carbonara* is outstanding. A few communal tables nicely accommodate solo diners. Via della Croce 39 (at Via Belsiana). No phone. Entrees 10€–18€. No credit cards. Lunch & dinner Mon–Sat. Metro: Spagna. Map p 122.

★ kids **'Gusto** SPANISH STEPS *CREATIVE ITALIAN/PIZZA* This conglomerate of hip modern restaurants has several locations on a Fascist-era piazza. The pizzeria (at no. 9) is buzzy and kid-friendly; the new "fish and vegetables" restaurant (no. 28) is fresh and airy, with two whitewashed dining levels and fantastic, unique pastas. It's one of few places in Rome where you can have a sit-down meal any time of day. Piazza Augusto Imperatore 7, 9, and 28, Via della Frezza 16. ☎ 06-3226273. www.gusto.it. Entrees 8€–22€. AE, MC, V. Open daily; exact hours vary by location. Metro: Flaminio or Spagna. Bus: 913. Map p 122.

★★ **Il Bacaro** PANTHEON *ITALIAN* When you want to escape the chaos of central Rome, this romantic and low-key spot on a hidden back street offers respite from the traffic and tourist crush. Insanely delicious *primi* and *secondi* (such as *tortelli* with Taleggio and pumpkin) are a welcome departure from strictly traditional Roman fare. Via degli Spagnoli 27 (off Via della Scrofa). ☎ 06- 6872554. www.ilbacaro.com. Entrees 12€–21€. AE, MC, V. Lunch & dinner Mon–Sat. Bus: 30, 62, 70, 81, 87, 116, or 492. Map p 122.

★ **La Bottega del Caffè** MONTI *LIGHT FARE/PIZZA* The social epicenter of newly hip Monti has tons of outdoor tables and a laid-back vibe—no one cares whether you order a full meal or just a cappuccino. Perfect for lunch between touring ruins, or for a late-night bite after hitting the bars in the area. Piazza Madonna dei Monti 5 (at Via dei Serpenti). ☎ 393-9311013. Entrees 7€–14€. AE, MC, V. Lunch

Snacking as the Romans Do (and Saving Money)

Romans don't eat restaurant meals at both lunch and dinner (a surefire way to blow your budget), so why should you? With these alternate methods for satisfying hunger, you'll save a bunch of euros and get to sample the many facets of Roman food culture.

PANINI & PIZZA INSTEAD OF LUNCH

Any time of day, grab a savory *pizza farcita* (pizza bread sandwich stuffed with your choice of veggies, cheeses, or meats) from **Aristocampo** (Campo de' Fiori 30, open late), **Frontoni** (Viale Trastevere 52, closed Sun), or **Burro e Alici** (Via della Mercede 34, near the Spanish Steps), or squares of pizza at any *pizza al taglio* joint that smells good (I like **Panificio Renella**, at Via del Moro 15–16 in Trastevere, but there are fine spots all over town). Most of these places have some sort of seating—when in Rome, resting your feet is essential! For a more bare-bones experience, any *alimentari* (grocer's) will make you a simple panino (with meat and or cheese only; Romans don't do condiments) for around 2.50€. Take it to Villa Borghese, or to a grassy site such as the Palatine or Baths of Caracalla, for a picnic later in the day.

APERITIVO INSTEAD OF DINNER

Come sundown, it's *aperitivo* time (happy hour) at most Roman bars and lounges—that means a free buffet of tasty Italian specialties for anyone who buys a drink. In other words, an 8€ Prosecco entitles you to a whole dinner's worth of food—and no one frowns upon going back for seconds and thirds.

THE LEAST EXPENSIVE SIT-DOWN MEAL

Of course, the reality is that after long days of Roman sightseeing, even budget-minded travelers just want to be served something and linger at a table. In which case, simply head to the nearest pizzeria—they are everywhere in Rome. A basic *margherita* (mozzarella, basil, and tomato sauce) pizza will cost you about 5€ and a liter of house wine is 8€. Note that Roman pizzas are traditionally thin-crusted, unlike Naples-style pizza, which has a more pillowy dough. Many pizzerias are open only for dinner.

> *Thin-crusted Roman pizzas differ slightly from the Neapolitan version, but you'll always find a classic* margherita.

& dinner daily. Metro: Cavour. Bus: 60, 75, 85, 87, or 175. Map p 122.

★★ **La Veranda** VATICAN *CREATIVE ITALIAN*
A gorgeous frescoed hall gives way to leafy terraces at this wonderfully patinated place, a favorite of the Vatican press corps and visiting cardinals. On the menu, look for inventive dishes such as *tonnarelli* with ricotta and cinnamon. Borgo Santo Spirito 73 (at the Hotel Columbus). ☎ 06-6872973. Entrees 13€–28€. AE, MC, V. Lunch & dinner daily. Bus: 23, 40, 62, 64, or 271. Map p 122.

★★ **Maccheroni** PANTHEON *ITALIAN*
Popular with Roman scenesters, this trendy spot is also one of the best dining values in Rome, offering simple but perfectly executed dishes (such as pasta *all'amatriciana* and chicken *alla cacciatora*) at humane prices. Via delle Coppelle 44 (at Via degli Spagnoli).

> *Due Ladroni is popular with Rome's celebs.*

☎ 06-68307895. www.ristorantemaccheroni.com. Entrees 10€–16€. AE, MC, V. Lunch & dinner daily. Bus: 30, 62, 70, 81, 87, 116, or 492. Map p 122.

★ 🄺🄸🄳🅂 **Osteria der Belli** TRASTEVERE SARDINIAN/SEAFOOD Proprietor Leo keeps locals and visitors alike happy with a knockout sauté of clams and mussels, spaghetti *alla pescatora,* and grilled swordfish. The energetic indoor-outdoor spot gets especially lively on Friday nights, when boozy old-timers settle in for their fish fix. Piazza Sant'Apollonia 9–11 (at Via della Lungaretta). ☎ 06-5803782. Entrees 9€–15€. AE, MC, V. Lunch & dinner Tues–Sun. Bus: 23, 271, 280, 780, or H. Tram: 8. Map p 122.

★★ **Perilli** TESTACCIO ROMAN
Step back in time and enjoy the old-school atmosphere at this beloved institution of Roman *ristorazione.* Zero pretense, just formally attired waitstaff who treat you with the right amount of informality, and serve you un-fooled-around-with renditions of Roman classics. Going to Perilli is an event, like a play with many acts, so you really *should* get the *antipasto, primo, secondo,* and *dolce,* or you'll be missing out on the full experience. Via Marmorata 39 (at Via Galvani). ☎ 06-5742415. Entrees 9€–16€. AE, MC, V. Lunch & dinner Thurs–Tues. Reservations recommended. Bus: 23, 75, 95, 170, or 280. Tram: 3. Map p 125.

★ **Perilli in Prati** VATICAN ROMAN
An excellent alternative to the tourist-trap eateries that plague the Vatican area, this family-run trat (it's the younger, quieter relative of Perilli in Testaccio) offers spot-on renditions of Roman classics such as *gricia* pasta (with pig cheek, sheep's-milk cheese, and pepper) and warm service. Via Otranto 9–11 (at Viale Giulio Cesare). ☎ 06-3700156. www.perilliinprati.it. Entrees 9€–16€. AE, MC, V. Lunch & dinner Mon–Fri; dinner Sat. Metro: Ottaviano. Bus: 23. Tram: 19. Map p 122.

★ **Pierluigi** CAMPO DE' FIORI ITALIAN
Popular with older, well-heeled locals and tourists, this trusty indoor-outdoor trat does a mean octopus *soppressata* and *tagliata di manzo* (tender beef strips on a bed of arugula). Piazza de' Ricci 144 (at Via Monserrato). ☎ 06-6861302. Entrees 10€–20€. AE, MC, V. Lunch & dinner Tues–Sun. Bus: 23, 40, 64, 116, 271, 280, or 571. Map p 122.

★★★ **Quinzi e Gabrieli** PANTHEON SEAFOOD
Local VIPs and visiting movie stars come here for the absolute best (and most expensive) seafood pastas and entrees in town. Lunch tasting menus are a bit easier on the wallet. Via delle Coppelle 5 (at Via degli Spagnoli). ☎ 06-6879389. www.quinziegabrieli.it. Entrees 20€–35€. AE, MC, V. Lunch & dinner Mon–Sat. Bus: 30, 70, 87, 116, or 492. Map p 122.

★★ **Spirito di Vino** TRASTEVERE ROMAN
In a former medieval synagogue atop a 2nd-century street, the Catalani family does exceptional modern and ancient Roman cuisine (such as *maiale alla Mazio,* a favorite pork dish of Julius Caesar's) and other plates as warm and comforting as the ambience. Via

> Da Bucatino, in Testaccio, is a favorite with locals seeking an informal meal.

dei Genovesi 31 (at Vicolo dell'Atleta). ☎ 06-5896689. Entrees 15€–24€. AE, MC, V. Dinner Mon–Sat. Bus: 23, 271, 280, 780, or H. Tram: 8. Map p 122.

★ **Taverna del Campo** CAMPO DE' FIORI CAFE/WINE BAR This trendy lunch and *aperitivo* spot on Campo de' Fiori has terrific, garlicky sandwiches, cheap cocktails and *vino* by the glass, and free peanuts. Snag a front-row table, don your fashionista sunglasses, and watch the pageant go by. Campo de' Fiori 16 (at Via dei Baullari). ☎ 06-6874402. Sandwiches 4.50€–6€. No credit cards. Tues–Sun 8am–1am. Bus: 30, 40, 62, 64, 70, 87, 492, or 571. Map p 122.

★ **Taverna Romana da Tonino** ANCIENT ROME ROMAN Sink your teeth into succulent roast lamb and other hearty *secondi* at this inexpensive, homey trat near the Forum. Come early or be prepared to wait. Via Madonna dei Monti 79 (at Via dell'Agnello). ☎ 06-4745325. Entrees 8€–14€. No credit cards. Lunch & dinner Mon–Sat. Metro: Cavour. Bus: 60, 75, 85, 87, or 175. Map p 122.

> Romans appreciate the simple alfresco dining at Maccheroni.

Rome Hotel Best Bets

Best "Only in Rome" Hideaway
Inn at the Roman Forum $$$$ Via degli Ibernesi 30 (p 134)

Best Stylish Retreat
Villa Laetitia $$$ Lungotevere delle Armi 22–23 (p 135)

Best Cheap & Centrally Located
Sole al Biscione $ Via del Biscione 76 (p 135)
Ivanhoe $ Via dei Ciancaleoni 50 (p 134)

Best for Hobnobbing with Hotshots
Hotel de Russie $$$$ Via del Babuino 9 ·(p 134)
Portrait Suites $$$$ Via Bocca di Leone 23 (p 135)

Best Vacation Rental Agency
Roman Reference $–$$$ (p 134)

Best for Families
Aldrovandi Palace $$$ Via Ulisse Aldrovandi 15 (p 131)
Lancelot $$ Via Capo d'Africa 47 (p 134)

Best Gem in an Overpriced Area
Modigliani $$–$$$ Via della Purificazione 42 (p 134)

Best in an Authentic Roman Neighborhood
Santa Maria $$ Vicolo del Piede 2 (p 135)

Best Escape from Vespa Drone
Aventino Hotels Group $$–$$$ Via S. Melania 19 (p 131)

> *The candle-lit roof terrace at the Portrait Suites has a view of the Spanish Steps.*

Rome Hotels A to Z

★ Adriatic VATICAN
The simple but spacious rooms here are perfect for budget- conscious travelers who want a convenient location but not a lot of amenities. Via Vitelleschi 25. ☎ 06-68808080. www. adriatichotel.com. 42 units. Doubles 90€–130€. AE, MC, V. Bus: 23, 40, 271, or 280. Map p 132.

★ kids Aldrovandi Palace VILLA BORGHESE
Occupying some seriously prized (and gorgeous) real estate, this classy hotel boasts a swimming pool and all modern amenities. Via Ulisse Aldrovandi 15. ☎ 06-3223993. www. aldrovandi.com. 135 units. Doubles 250€–500€. AE, MC, V. Bus: 52 or 53. Tram: 3 or 19. Map p 132.

★★ Aventino Hotels Group AVENTINE
Of these three converted villas on the prestigious Aventine Hill, the San Anselmo is the chicest and most luxurious, the Aventino has cheerful 1930s appeal, and the Villa San Pio is like visiting your long-lost, old money Roman relatives. Via S. Melania 19. ☎ 06-5745231. www.aventinohotels.com. 100 units (in the Aventino Hotels Group). Doubles 230€–400€. AE, MC, V. Metro: Circo Massimo. Bus: 95 or 175. Tram: 3. Map p 132.

★★ Caesar House ANCIENT ROME
Done up in a Roman palette of crimsons and golds, this family-run guesthouse has luxurious, homey rooms, some with picture-window views over ruins and rooftops. Warm hospitality makes this a personal, intimate place that's hard to leave. Via Cavour 310. ☎ 06-6792674. www. caesarhouse.com. 7 units. Doubles 170€–270€. AE, MC, V. Bus: 75, 85, 87, 175, 571. Map p 132.

★ Forte SPANISH STEPS
The location, on one of Rome's loveliest streets, can't be beat. The smallish rooms are comfortable and (mostly) contemporary, and the prices are certainly low for this part of town. Via Margutta 61. ☎ 06-3207625. www. hotelforte.com. 21 units. Doubles 156€–256€. AE, MC, V. Metro: Spagna. Map p 132.

> *Simplicity reigns at Trastevere's top lodging, Santa Maria.*

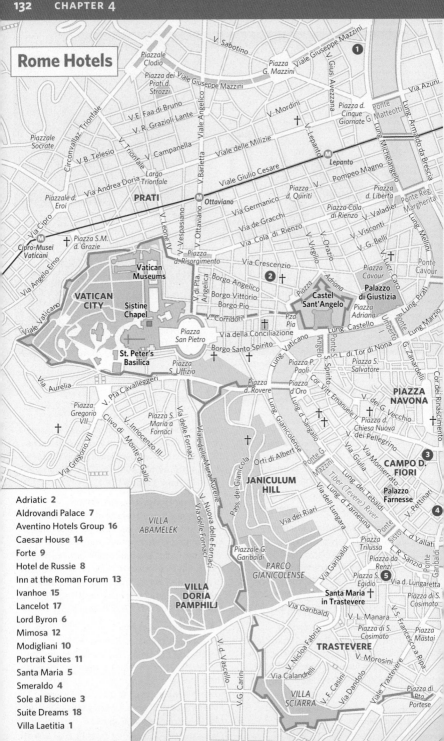

Rome Hotels

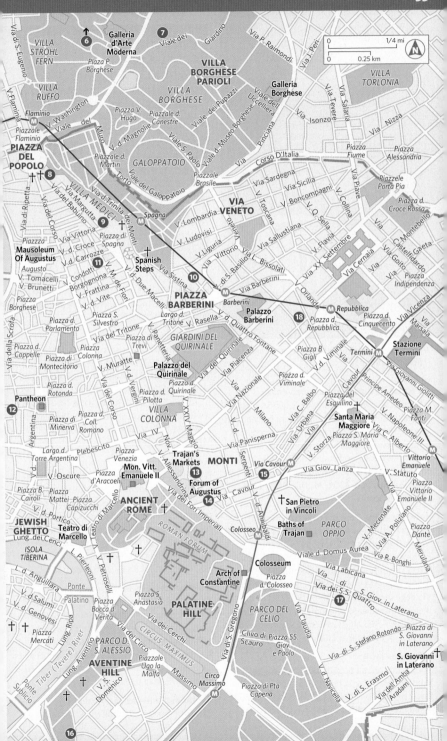

> *A nighttime view from the terrace of the Inn at the Roman Forum.*

★★ Hotel de Russie PIAZZA DEL POPOLO
It has the best location of Rome's five-star hotels, a clean neoclassical look, and tons of high-profile guests. The hotel's U-shape encloses a fabulous terraced garden, with bars, restaurants, and grottos sweeping up toward the Pincio. Via del Babuino 9. ☎ 06-328881. www.hotelderussie.it. 125 units. Doubles from 450€. AE, DC, MC, V. Metro: Flaminio. Map p 132.

★★★ Inn at the Roman Forum ANCIENT ROME
At this boutique inn on a silent side street, rooms are tastefully luxurious, with spacious bathrooms. The Master Garden Rooms (from 450€) have private patios, and the hotel's roof lounge has views of the Campidoglio. Via degli Ibernesi 30. ☎ 06-69190970. www.theinnattheromanforum.com. 15 units. Doubles 210€–600€. AE, MC, V. Metro: Cavour. Bus: 75, 85, 87, 175, 571. Map p 132.

★ Ivanhoe MONTI
The rooms are all private, but there's a hostel-like feel to this basic but friendly inn in the heart of the hip Monti neighborhood. Those willing to rough it a bit can save by booking

rooms without private bath. Via dei Ciancaleoni 50. ☎ 06-486813. www.hotelivanhoe.it. 20 units. Doubles 80€–140€. AE, MC, V. Metro: Cavour. Bus: 75, 85, 87, 175, 571. Map p 132.

★ kids Lancelot COLOSSEUM
This friendly hotel with surprisingly large and bright doubles (and free Wi-Fi) attracts a veritable United Nations of return guests. Full- and half-board options are great for families on a budget. Via Capo d'Africa 47. ☎ 06-70450615. www.lancelothotel.com. 60 units. Doubles 150€–254€. AE, MC, V. Metro: Colosseo. Bus: 60, 75, 87, 175, or 571. Map p 132.

★★ Lord Byron VILLA BORGHESE
Bordering Villa Borghese, in Rome's most prestigious residential area, this elegant palazzo oozes Art Deco style. Guest rooms are romantic, sleek, and chic; book a renovated room, as some floors have yet to be updated. Via Giuseppe de Notaris 5. ☎ 06-3220404. www.lordbyronhotel.com. 34 units. Doubles 330€–500€. AE, MC, V. Tram: 3, 19. Map p 132.

kids Mimosa PANTHEON
This budget stalwart in the heart of the *centro storico* enjoys great word of mouth, so book early. There are larger units suitable for families with small children. Via di Santa Chiara 61. ☎ 06-68801753. www.hotelmimosa.net. 11 units. Doubles 77€–118€. MC, V. Bus: 40, 62, 64, 70, 87, 492, or 571. Map p 132.

★★ Modigliani PIAZZA BARBERINI
Cheerful Roman hospitality and fantastic

> *Ultra-stylish Villa Laetitia.*

value near the top of the Spanish Steps. Accommodations are clean and classic; west-facing rooms on the 5th and 6th floors have heart-stopping views. Owners Marco and Giulia are a delight. Via della Purificazione 42. ☎ 06-42815226. www.hotelmodigliani.com. 23 units. Doubles 155€–197€. AE, MC, V. Metro: Barberini. Bus: 62, 95, 175, 492. Map p 132.

★★★ **Portrait Suites** SPANISH STEPS

Fashionistas with money to spare, look no further than this swanky boutique guesthouse. The candle-lit roof terrace is the epitome of modern Roman fabulousness. Superb staff. Via Bocca di Leone 23. ☎ 06-69380742. www.lungarnohotels.com. 15 units. Suites from 700€. AE, MC, V. Metro: Spagna. Map p 132.

★★ **Santa Maria** TRASTEVERE

An amazing find in hotel-deprived Trastevere, the Santa Maria feels like a 16th-century motel, with simple chalet-style rooms and a pretty courtyard with orange trees. Vicolo del Piede 2. ☎ 06-5894626. www.htlsantamaria.com. 19 units. Doubles 175€–260€. AE, MC, V. Bus: 23, 271, or 280. Tram: 8. Map p 132.

★ **Smeraldo** CAMPO DE' FIORI

Well-priced but cramped, this *centro storico* "emerald" has a few shining facets, including Internet access and air-conditioning in rooms (a rarity in this price range), and a pretty roof garden. Vicolo dei Chiodaroli 9. ☎ 06-6875929.

www.smeraldoroma.com. 50 units. Doubles 100€–160€. AE, MC, V. Bus: 40, 62, 64, 70, 87, 492, or 571. Map p 132.

★ **Sole al Biscione** CAMPO DE' FIORI

Rooms are basic (and can be loud when school groups lodge here), but the multilevel courtyard garden, open to all guests, overflows with Roman charm. Via del Biscione 76. ☎ 06-68806873. www.solealbiscione.it. 60 units. Doubles 100€–160€. No credit cards. Bus: 40, 62, 64, 70, 87, 492, or 571. Map p 132.

★★ **Suite Dreams** REPUBBLICA

This boutique inn just west of Termini station offers modern design and warm service. Large and bright rooms (and gorgeous bathrooms) have a sleek and clean look that's a haven from the city chaos outside. 15 units. Via Modena 5. ☎ 06-48913907. Doubles 130€–180€. AE, DC, MC, V. Map p 132.

★★★ **Villa Laetitia** PRATI

Set in the lush and tranquil back garden of a 100-year-old villa, each suite at Anna Fendi's first Roman lodging venture is decorated with 19th- and 20th-century antiques and original pieces by the likes of Picasso and Lagerfeld. All have kitchens, and all but one unit has outdoor living space. Lungotevere delle Armi 22–23. ☎ 06-3226776. www.villalaetitia.com. 15 units. Doubles 150€–350€. AE, MC, V. Tram: 19. Map p 132.

Rome Nightlife & Entertainment Best Bets

Best Bar for Getting Wasted on 3€ Glasses of Wine
Vineria Reggio, Campo de' Fiori 15 (p 140)

Best Pub
Cork's Inn, Via delle Tre Cannelle 8 (p 141)

Best Aperitivo Hour
Société Lutèce, Piazza Montevecchio 17 (p 137)
Freni e Frizioni, Via del Politeama 4-6 (p 137)

Best Intimate Alfresco Spot
Le Coppelle 52, Piazza delle Coppelle 52 (p 137)

Best Club-Hopping Zone
Monte Testaccio (p 141)

Best Live Music
Big Mama, Vicolo di San Francesco a Ripa 18 (p 140)

Best Gay Disco
Alibi, Via di Monte Testaccio 40-47 (p 140)

Best Entertainment, Period
Soccer games at Stadio Olimpico, Viale dello Stadio Olimpico (p 141)

Best Performing Arts Center
Auditorium–Parco della Musica, Viale Pietro di Coubertin (p 140)

Best Summer Festival
Villa Celimontana Festival Jazz, Piazza della Navicella (p 141)

Best Meet Market
Campo de' Fiori (p 104)

Best Wine & Cheese Bar
Al Vino Al Vino, Via dei Serpenti 19 (p 137)

Best for Living La Dolce Vita
Baths of Caracalla, Viale delle Terme di Caracalla (p 141)

Best Excuse to Get Dressed Up
Teatro dell'Opera, Via Firenze 72 (p 140)

> *The busy bar at Al Vino Al Vino.*

Rome Nightlife & Entertainment A to Z

Bars & Lounges

★★ Al Vino Al Vino MONTI
Cozy and convivial, this excellent wine bar feels like the neighborhood's living room. Great selection of antipasti, meats, and cheeses, too. Via dei Serpenti 19 (near Via Panisperna). ☎ 06-485803. Metro: Cavour. Bus: 75. Map p 138.

★★ Bartaruga JEWISH GHETTO
A dark room with sagging armchairs and bright frescoes, sassy bar staff, and stiff drinks. The scene is artsy and intellectual but unpretentious. Piazza Mattei 9. ☎ 06-6892299. Bus: 23, 271, or 280. Tram: 8. Map p 138.

★★ Freni e Frizioni TRASTEVERE
"Brakes and Clutches" is a former mechanic's garage turned nighttime hot spot, with an ethnic-inflected *aperitivo* spread (think curried risotto). Via del Politeama 4–6 (near Piazza Trilussa). ☎ 06-58334210. Bus: 23, 271, or 280. Map p 138.

> *The modern Auditorium–Parco della Musica is known for refined acoustics.*

★ Le Coppelle 52 PANTHEON
This lounge catches all the evening traffic coming or going to the hip restaurants in the vicinity. On balmy nights, the outdoor tables on the intimate square are prized real estate. Piazza delle Coppelle 52 (off Via delle Coppelle). ☎ 06-6832410. Bus: 30, 40, 62, 64, 70, 87, 492, or 571. Map p 138.

★★ Société Lutèce PIAZZA NAVONA
One of the first bars to introduce the northern Italian *aperitivo* phenomenon to Rome, this stylish, laid-back spot is great for drinking and snacking before, or instead of, dinner. Piazza Montevecchio 17 (off Via dei Coronari). ☎ 06-68301472. Bus: 30, 70, 87, 492, 628. Map p 138.

★★ Taverna del Campo CAMPO DE' FIORI
Roman hipsters ebb and flow through its outdoor tables from the *aperitivo* hour (6–7pm) till closing (2am), leaving peanut shells in their wake. Campo de' Fiori 16 (at Via Baullari). ☎ 06-6874402. Bus: 30, 40, 62, 64, 70, 87, 116, or 492. Tram: 8. Map p 138.

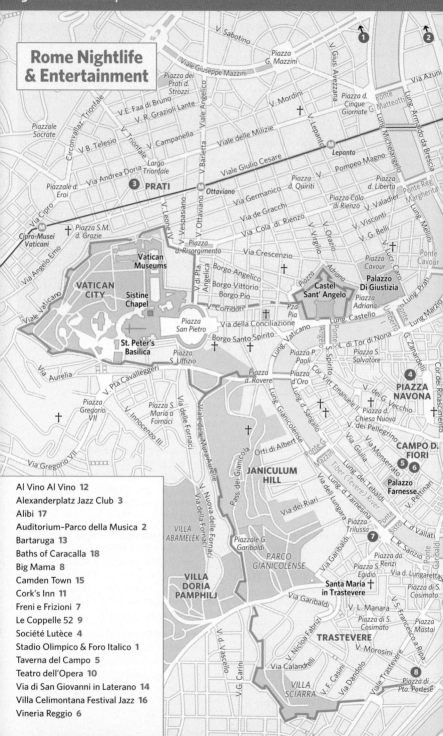

Rome Nightlife & Entertainment

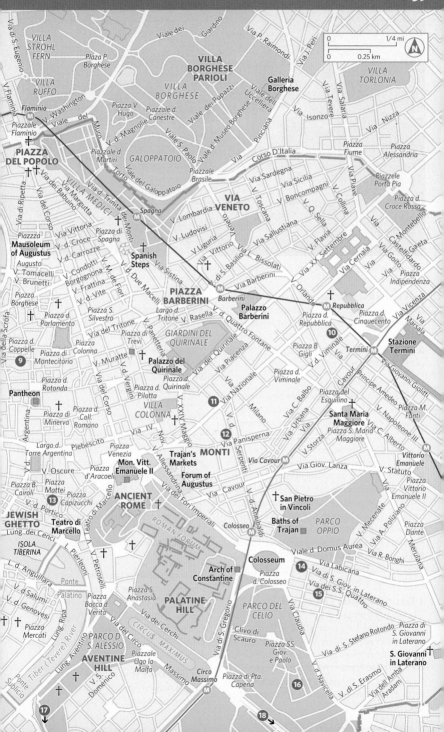

> *The Lazio soccer team and their bitter local rivals Roma both play at the Stadio Olimpico.*

★★ **Vineria Reggio** CAMPO DE' FIORI
Night after night, this super-cheap, social Campo de' Fiori drinking spot perpetuates *la dolce vita*. **Campo de' Fiori 15 (at Via Baullari).** ☎ 06-68803268. Bus: 30, 40, 62, 64, 70, 87, 116, or 492. Tram: 8. Map p 138.

Classical Music

★★ **Auditorium–Parco della Musica** NORTH-ERN SUBURBS This exciting new multipurpose center for the arts, designed by world-renowned architect Renzo Piano, brings a refreshing breath of modernity to Rome. Some say the three lead-roofed concert halls look like giant beetles, but the architecture is undeniably dramatic and the acoustics outstanding. The schedule features lots of folk singer-songwriter acts along with the traditional Accademia di Santa Cecilia symphony performances. Great cafes on site, too. **Viale Pietro di Coubertin (Corso Francia/Viale Tiziano).** ☎ 199-109-783 (in Italy) or 06-3700106 (outside Italy). www.auditorium.com. Tickets from 15€. Bus: M, 53, 217, or 910. Tram: 2. Map p 138.

★ **Teatro dell'Opera** REPUBBLICA
The theater's ornate 19th-century interior is a perfect setting for a sophisticated Roman night out. Recent productions have included *Carmen, La Fanciulla del West,* and such ballets as *Il Lago dei Cigni (Swan Lake)* and *Lo Schiaccianoci (The Nutcracker)*. **Via Firenze 72 (at Via del Viminale).** ☎ 06-481601. www.operaroma.it. Tickets 15€–115€. Map p 138.

Gay & Lesbian

★★ **Alibi** TESTACCIO
Consistently good gay disco with an infamously heavy pickup scene; music is a happy mix of house and techno. In summer, the dancing spills out to the club's fabulous rooftop. **Via di Monte Testaccio 40–47 (at Via Galvani).** ☎ 06-5743448. www.alibionline.it. Metro: Piramide. Bus: 23, 30, 75, 95, 170, or 280. 12€–15€ cover (Fri–Sat only). Map p 138.

★★ **Via di San Giovanni in Laterano** COLOSSEUM
In the past few years, this side street just up from the Colosseum (and across from the old gladiators' barracks) has emerged as *the* bar strip for gays and lesbians, with several casual outdoor cafes where same-sex couples are the norm. There's even a petition in city hall to rename the road "Gay Street." **Between Piazza del Colosseo and Via Celimontana.** Map p 138.

Live Music

★ **Alexanderplatz Jazz Club** PRATI
Smooth and classy, this low-ceilinged jazz joint is one of the best in Italy. In summer, the club sponsors the super-fab jazz festival at Villa Celimontana. **Via Ostia 9 (at Via Leone IV).** ☎ 06-39742171. 8€ cover. Metro: Ottaviano. Map p 138.

★★ **Big Mama** TRASTEVERE
With a reassuring reek of beer, this subterranean blues club is the closest thing in

me to a honky-tonk. Top-notch blues, rock,
d soul acts guarantee a good time, so the
all, sticky wooden tables go fast. Vicolo di
ancesco a Ripa 18 (at Via San Francesco a Ripa).
06-5812551. 8€–12€ cover. Bus: 23, 271, 280,
0, or H. Tram: 3 or 8. Map p 138.

bs

Camden Town COLOSSEUM

wners Alberto and Carlo welcome a loyal
ung crowd nightly for pints and sporting
ents. Friendly, English-speaking staff, and a
ely scene at the bar and tables. Via Ostilia
A (at Via Capo d'Africa). ☎ 06-7096322.
etro: Colosseo. Bus: 75, 81, 175. Tram: 3. Map
138.

★ Cork's Inn PIAZZA VENEZIA/MONTI

is secluded indoor-outdoor joint counts lots
Roman and expat regulars. All major sports
e shown, but it's first and foremost a rugby
r. A great place to while away a mild evening,
earing jeans and flip-flops. Via delle Tre
annelle 8 (off Via Nazionale). ☎ 06-6990986.
s: 40, 64, 70. Map p 138.

mmer Venues

★★ Baths of Caracalla SOUTH OF COLOSSEUM

ttend a production of *Aïda* here, amid
e towering ruins of the 3rd-century-A.D.
ldarium, and you'll know the meaning of *la
olce vita*. Viale delle Terme di Caracalla. July–
ug only. www.operaroma.it. Ticket prices vary.
etro: Circo Massimo. Bus: 30, 118, or 628. Map
138.

★ Villa Celimontana Festival Jazz SOUTH

F COLOSSEUM In this gorgeous 16th-century
ark, a summer-long festival offers nightly
zz, blues, and rock acts, as well as temporary,
iniature versions of some of Rome's top
staurants. Piazza della Navicella (at Via
audia). ☎ 06-5897807. For table bookings,
6-77073799. www.villacelimontanajazz.com.
ckets around 20€. Metro: Colosseo. Bus: 60, 75,
, 87, 175, or 271. Tram: 3. Map p 138.

ports

Stadio Olimpico & Foro Italico NORTHERN

BURBS There is no better place to soak
modern Roman culture than at the
occer stadium. The Olimpico, Rome's
,000-capacity venue, is where the AS Roma
nd SS Lazio *Serie A* (premier league) teams
ay at least once a week from September to

Clubs of Monte Testaccio

Want to sample Rome's club scene but
not sure where to start? **Monte Testaccio,**
ancient Rome's pottery dump, is ringed
with discos and lounges for all tastes,
ages, and noise levels. Simply head for the
three streets (Via Galvani, Via di Monte
Testaccio, and Via Zabaglia) skirting the
artificial mountain, and see what looks
good to you. A few of my favorite standbys
are **Metaverso** (Via di Monte Testaccio
38A, ☎ 06-5744712), **Joia** (Via Galvani
20, ☎ 06-5740802), and **Caffè Latino** (Via
di Monte Testaccio 96, ☎ 06-57288556).
Check the weekly listings mag *Roma C'è*
to see what's on where. For all Testaccio
clubs, take the metro to Piramide, or bus
23, 30, 75, 95, 170, or 280, or tram 3. After
midnight, take bus N10.

June. The rest of the athletics complex here, the
Foro Italico, is dotted with umbrella pines and
Fascist-era mosaics and statues. The Italian
Open is played here, as well as other sporting
events and big-name concerts. Foro Italico/
Viale dello Stadio Olimpico. ☎ 06-3237333 (box
office). Tickets 20€–120€. Bus: 32, 271, or 280.
Tram: 225. Map p 138.

Tivoli

The most classic Roman day trip, Tivoli lies about 32km (20 miles) west of the city and is home to the fountain-filled 16th-century Villa d'Este and the fantastically unique ancient ruins of Hadrian's Villa—not bad for a hill town in the *provincia*. Both sites are under the UNESCO World Heritage protectorate.

> *Ippolito d'Este, of Ferrara's noble family, commissioned the fountains of the Villa d'Este in 1550.*

START Take metro line B to Ponte Mammolo, then a Cotral bus to Tivoli (Villa d'Este). Transportation to Tivoli can be slow; allow a full day.

① ★★★ **Villa d'Este.** It's all about the fountains, fountains, and more fountains at this pleasure palace, commissioned in 1550 by Renaissance noble and cardinal Ippolito d'Este. Throughout the lush gardens, whose steep slopes offer breathtaking views back toward Rome, there are whimsical grottoes, rushing flumes, and reflecting pools everywhere you turn. Subtler and more bizarre gurgling "trees" also delight. Gian Lorenzo Bernini's musical fountain, Fontana dell'Organo, "performs" a baroque interlude several times throughout the day. ⏱ 45 min. Piazza Trento 1. ☎ 0774-312070 or 199-766166 (toll-free from Italy). Admission 6.50€. Tues–Sun 9am–6:15pm May–Sept; 8:30am–4pm Oct–Apr. From Rome: Cotral bus from Metro Ponte Mammolo, about 45 min. From Villa Adriana, regional bus to Tivoli, about 15 min.

② ★★★ **Hadrian's Villa (Villa Adriana).** Hadrian's sprawling estate (A.D. 118–34) was as much a summer retreat from the stifling air in Rome as it was a place where the emperor could fulfill all his fantasies in architecture, having been inspired by things he had seen in Greece and Egypt.

Near the entrance, the ★ **Stoa Poikile** pool was once surrounded by a shady colonnade where Hadrian and his friends would walk around after meals to stimulate digestion. The delightfully inventive ★★★ **Teatro Marittimo** was where the emperor meditated on a private

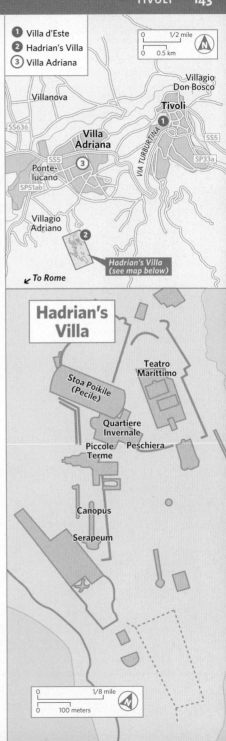

Hadrian kept himself fit by swimming laps in the Greek-inspired moat at his villa.

island" and swam laps in the moat, which owed with aqueduct water to create resistance. he ★ **Peschiera** was a giant aquarium, handy or seafood dinners this far inland. The attached **Quartiere Invernale** (Winter Palace) has ome of its heating system intact, as well as reat views toward Rome. At the ★ **Piccole erme** (Small Baths), look for marvelous tuccoes on the ceiling vaults. At the far end of he site, the exquisite ★★★ **Canopus,** a long pool vith broken Assyrian arcades and statuary of Nile creatures, terminates in the ★★ **Serapeum,** dining room whose front "wall" was a thin heet of water, fed by an aqueduct above, that ooled the air. ⏱ 1½ hr. Villa Adriana (Tivoli). ☎ 0774-382733. 6.50€. Daily 9am–6:30pm Apr–ept; 9am–5pm Oct–Mar. From Rome: Cotral bus to Villa Adriana from metro station Ponte Mammolo, bout 45 min. From Villa d'Este (Tivoli town), egional bus to Villa Adriana, about 15 min.

③ 🍽 **Villa Adriana,** an elegant country dining room, is perfect for lunch before or after touring Hadrian's Villa, and much better than most of the tourist-clogged places you'll find up in Tivoli town proper. Reservations are recommended. **Via di Villa Adriana 222.** ☎ **0774-535028. $$-$$$.**

Nero
Reign
A.D. 54–68

> Had his step-brother killed.

> Had his mother killed.

> Had his first wife killed; also kicked his second wife in the stomach while she was pregnant, causing her death. Motive: The unborn child was a potential threat to Nero's power.

> Blamed Christians for the Great Fire of A.D. 64 that destroyed two-thirds of the city of Rome (depicted on this page). Then, seeing a real estate opportunity, built his "Golden House" over half of the newly available, charred lands.

> Considered himself an uncommonly gifted poet and musician; competed in arts competitions that he invariably won (by bribing or threatening the judges).

> Killed himself in A.D. 68, uttering "What an artist dies in me" as his last words.

ROMAN EMPERORS' HALL OF INFAMY

A Who's Who of Dubious Achievements

BY SYLVIE HOGG

From the inbred Julio-Claudian dynasty that ruled during Rome's Golden Age to the tyrants and lame ducks of the "troubled" 3rd century A.D., this rap sheet goes to show that even the most scandal-embroiled politicians of today have nothing on the depraved, megalomaniacal, and downright bizarre policies and R-rated personal habits of some of the more prominent fathers of Western Civilization.

MOST UNDIGNIFIED DEATH
Caracalla
Reign A.D. 211–217

> Upon the death of his father, emperor Septimius Severus, Caracalla and his younger brother Geta inherited the throne. Within a year, Caracalla had Geta killed and issued the Damnatio Memoriae, ordering Geta's name and likeness to be erased anywhere they appeared.
> Eventually assassinated by a bodyguard while urinating on the side of a road in Asia Minor.
> Historian Edward Gibbon called him "the common enemy of all mankind."

MOST DEBAUCHED
Tiberius
Reign A.D. 14–37

> Never wanted to be emperor; he only came to power after the first two heirs of Augustus died and the Julio-Claudian family had no other choice.
> Preferred island life to the city grind and built 12 imperial palaces on Capri, including the cliff-side Villa Jovis (p 582). Visitors who angered him were hurled from a precipice to the sea 330m (1,000 ft.) below.
> Known for debauchery, he filled his bathtubs with minnows so that they would nibble on his naked parts while he soaked.

MOST INCESTUOUS
Caligula
Reign A.D. 37–41

> Nearly emptied the imperial coffers to build a 3km-long (2-mile) temporary floating wooden bridge—all to spite a soothsayer.
> Insisted on being referred to as a god (none other than Jupiter) in public proceedings.
> Slept with each of his three sisters and prostituted them out to other men.
> Named his beloved horse a senator.
> Assassinated by a (human) senator in cahoots with the Praetorian Guard.

MOST BELLIGERENT
Commodus
Reign A.D. 180–192

> Immortalized by Joaquin Phoenix in *Gladiator*. The depiction of Commodus's character is probably accurate.
> Commodus preferred the sporting life to statecraft and spent most of his time sparring with gladiators and animals in the arena.
> Claimed, on an enormous bronze statue of himself dressed as Hercules, that he had defeated 1,000 men.
> Strangled to death in his bathtub by a wrestler named Narcissus when a plot to poison him failed.

WORST DEATH
Maximinus "Max" Thrax
Reign A.D. 235–238

> Killed by his troops, who preferred to be ruled by Max's next in line, a 13-year-old boy who became Emperor Gordian III.
> His head was severed and carried into Rome as a trophy, while Max's underfed troops ate the rest of his body.

Ostia Antica

The port of ancient Rome lay where the Tiber flowed into the Mediterranean (*ostia* is "mouth" in Latin). The seacoast receded, and the river course changed, leaving Ostia Antica landlocked and obsolete. Surrounded by trees and rarely crowded, the ruins are varied, extensive, and fun to explore, even better than Pompeii for understanding how the ancients used to live. The visit can easily be done in half a day, or combined with a trip to the beach at Ostia Lido for a full day's excursion. Bring a picnic, or eat at the site's pleasant cafe.

> Now landlocked, the "port" of Ostia Antica was once Rome's gateway to the seas.

START Take the Ostia-Lido train from Porta San Paolo (Piramide station of metro line B). Allow 5 hours for round-trip transportation and a leisurely tour of the site.

1 Tombs. The road leading into the ancient town proper is lined with tombs; as was the custom throughout Rome, burials had to be outside the city walls.

2 ★ Theater. The first large structure you'll encounter is this (heavily restored) ancient theater, where Greek and Roman plays are still performed during summer festivals.

3 ★★★ Forum of the Corporations. Behind the theater, don't miss this wonderful former square where the shops of various importers have mosaics that indicate their cargo, from oil to elephants. A fascinating window onto the sophisticated commercial trade of Ostia.

4 ★★ The Mill. Here, heavy basalt grinding stones (that were turned by blindfolded donkeys) and bread ovens are still in place.

5 ★★ Thermopolium. These hard-to-find ruins once served as a stylish snack bar, serving hot and cold food and drinks—a bit like an ancient version of Starbucks.

6 ★ Forum Baths. Notice especially the pipes that heated the marble-clad walls of these baths, where the ancient residents of Ostia came to wash up, work out, and gossip about each other.

7 ★★ Forica. This tour-group magnet was the public latrine, with neat rows of toilets still open to the sewer below (now neutral smelling).

8 ★ Apartments. All over the site, modest-to-extravagant apartment clusters are open for wandering—be sure to visit the posh ★ **Garden**

> Ostia *is Latin for "mouth," and marked the point where the Tiber met the Mediterranean.*

Apartments, the ★ **Insula of the Charioteers,** and the ★ **House of the Dioscuri.**

9 ★★ **Mithraeum.** This creepy chamber is found under the Baths of Mithras and was where 2nd-century-A.D. initiates of the god of Mithras performed rituals.

10 ★★ **Baths of Porta Marina.** Check out the hilarious ancient mosaics of bodybuilders here—the campy vanity is priceless. Like the Forum Baths, these *terme* were an important place for hygiene, exercise, and socializing.

11 **Ostia Lido.** Just a few stops on the train from Ostia Antica is Rome's closest seashore. (Get off at Cristoforo Colombo or Stella Polare.) The water here is far from sparkling, but it's lively, with plenty of beach clubs (and dark sand that Romans say accelerates tanning). Dozens of *stabilimenti* (beach clubs with restaurants) line the shore here; daily fees are about 15€ and include use of a beach chair, umbrella, showers, and changing rooms. At the ★★ *spiaggia libera,* or "free beach" (take bus no. 7 from Cristoforo Colombo train station), you'll find rugged dunes and wider stretches of sand, which make for a much more attractive setting, but there are few facilities.

Practical Information

The Ostia Antica site (☎ 06-56358099) is at Viale dei Romagnoli 117. Admission costs 6.50€. It's open April to October Tuesday to Sunday from 9am to 6pm and November to March from 8:30am to 4pm.

1 Tombs
2 Theater
3 Forum of the Corporations
4 The Mill
5 Thermopolium
6 Forum Baths
7 Forica
8 Apartments
9 Mithraeum
10 Baths of Porta Marina
11 Ostia Lido

Rome Fast Facts

Accommodations Booking Services

Italian hotel reservations website **Venere** (http://en.venere.com/hotels_rome) works with a wide range of properties and often has great last-minute bargains that can save you up to 75% off rack rates. There are **Hotel Reservation** service desks at Fiumicino and Ciampino airports and at Termini station (for all, ☎ 06- 6991000; www.hotelreservation.it; daily 7am–10pm) that can help you out in a pinch.

For short-term vacation rentals in Rome—a fantastic and money-saving way to experience the city—check out **Roman Reference** (☎ 06-48903612; www.romanreference.com). **Bed & Breakfast Italia**, Corso Vittorio Emanuele II 284 (☎ 06-6878618; www.bbitalia.it), has a dizzying array of accommodations, ranging from private apartments in historic palazzi to more spartan sleeps with shared bathrooms.

American Express

The Rome office of AmEx, offering foreign exchange and travel services, is at Piazza di Spagna 38 (☎ 06-67641). It's open Monday to Friday 9am to 5:30pm, and Saturday 9am to 12:30pm.

ATMs

Banks with cash machines (*bancomat*) can be found on every major square and along main streets in rentral Rome. Italy generally uses 4-digit PINs; if you have a 6-digit number, check with your bank before you leave.

Dentists & Doctors

Most hotels or your consulate can provide a list of English-speaking doctors and dentists. For emergencies or medical attention outside office hours, go to the nearest hospital's *pronto soccorso* (emergency room); they'll treat your immediate problem for free and give you a short course of prescription drugs if needed. Hospitals abound in Rome. **Ospedale Fatebenefratelli,** Piazza Fatebenefratelli 2, Isola Tiberina (☎ 06-68371), is one of the best. For dental emergencies, head to **Ospedale Dentistico George Eastman**, Policlinico medical complex, Viale Regina Elena 287B (☎ 06-844831). **Ospedale Bambino Gesù,** Piazza Sant'Onofrio 4 (☎ 06-68591), on the Janiculum Hill, is central Italy's premier pediatric hospital.

Emergencies

For general emergencies, call ☎ **112** for the Carabinieri or ☎ **113** for the Polizia. Call ☎ **114** for an ambulance and ☎ **115** for the fire department

Getting There

By air, most people arrive at Rome's **Fiumicino airport** (Leonardo da Vinci), which is served by many international carriers as well as European airlines. Some charter or low-cost airlines fly into Rome's smaller airport, **Ciampino.** There is a direct train from Fiumicino to Roma-Termini station (11€); a taxi is 40€. From Ciampino, there is a coach bus to Roma-Termini (8€); a taxi is 30€. Rome is also easy to reach by train from elsewhere in Italy or Europe: All high-speed, Eurostar, InterCity, and most regional trains stop at Roma-Termini. If you're coming by car, Rome lies off the A1 autostrada; whether you're coming from north or south, simply follow the exits marked "Roma Centro." Driving in Rome is not recommended, as nonresident traffic can't enter the *centro storico,* and parking is either very difficult to find or expensive.

Getting Around

While Rome isn't exactly small, there's so much to see along the way that walking is the *best* way to soak it all up. To cover longer distances, or when your feet get sore, Rome's **ATAC** (☎ 800-431784; www.atac.roma.it) system of public buses, metro lines, and trams offers comprehensive coverage of the city. You can buy tickets (*biglietti*) at tobacco stores (*tabacchi*), in metro stations, and at some newsstands. Single tickets are 1€ and good for 75 minutes. Daily tickets cost 4€, 3-day tickets are 11€, and weekly tickets are 16€. All tickets must be validated in the time-stamping machines when you board. See "Taxis," below, for information on getting around by cab.

Internet Access

Almost all hotels now have a public Internet terminal; many nicer hotels also have Wi-Fi, which often works only in certain guest rooms or just the lobby. Some hotels offer these services for free, while others carry a daily or hourly charge (as much as 10€ per hour in some fancier hotels), so it's a good idea to clarify the fee before you navigate away.

Rome also has plenty of Internet points where you can log on for about 5€ to 6€ an hour. **Internet Train** (www.internettrain.it) is a chain with several convenient locations: Via dei Pastini 21 (near the Pantheon; ☎ 06-97606735); Piazza Sant'Andrea della Valle 3 (near Largo Argentina; no phone). All branches are open Monday to Friday 10am to 11pm and Saturday to Sunday from 10am to 8pm.

Pharmacies

Italian *farmacie* will fill foreign prescriptions with little or no hassle. They're also where you buy over-the-counter medicines like ibuprofen or cough syrup, feminine hygiene products, and even sunblock. *Farmacie* are recognizable by a neon green or red cross and are usually open 8am to 1:30pm and 3:30 to 8pm. A few pharmacies, like those at Piazza Cinquecento 49–53 and at Via Nazionale 228, are open late. There's a 24-hour pharmacy at Via Barberini 49 (off Piazza Barberini).

For optical care (glasses repair, contact lens solution), go to an *ottica,* which can be found on nearly every block in Rome.

Police

To report a lost or stolen article, such as a wallet or passport, visit the local police *questura* or Carabinieri *caserma* in your location. Rome's Termini train station has Polizia and Carabinieri offices where you can file a report. More centrally located, there's also a Carabinieri station at Piazza Venezia. See also "Emergencies," p 148.

Post Office

Stamps (*francobolli*) can be purchased at most tobacco stores (*tabacchi*), and postcards and letters can be mailed from either your hotel or the red letterboxes mounted on walls around town. Do note that mail service in Rome is notoriously slow.

Safety

Rome is a generally safe city, especially in the touristed *centro,* but there are plenty of vagrants around the train station, especially on Sundays. Be very vigilant for gypsies and pickpockets in and around the train station, on any crowded bus (especially the 64) or metro train (especially line A), and in dense tourist areas.

Taxis

Taxis are required by law to pick up fares only at taxi stands, which are located in major squares and at main tourist sites. Be sure your cab has the red SPQR insignia on the driver's door, and always insist on the metered fare (except for the airport; see below). Taxis can also be requested by phone (☎ 06-3570, 06-6645, 06-4994). Fares within the city typically range from 6€ to 20€. The fare to or from the airport costs 40€ (flat rate to and from Fiumicino) or 30€ (flat rate to and from Ciampino). These flat airport-to-city-center rates are only valid when going to or leaving from within the old Aurelian Walls; otherwise, the metered fare applies. Add the tip by rounding up to the next whole euro—if the fare is 7.40€, leave the driver 8€.

Telephones

Italy phased out its coin phones long ago. Phone booths (*cabine*) take the *scheda telefonica* (plastic phone card) only, sold in denominations of 2.50€, 5€, and 7.75€ at *tabacchi*. Break off the perforated corner, and insert the card to get a dial tone. (Even if you have a prepaid long-distance calling card, you must insert a *scheda telefonica* to open the line.) Local calls (beginning with 06) usually cost .10€ to .20€; calls to Italian cell phones (beginning with 328, 338, 339, 340, 347, 348, and so forth) are wildly expensive—more than 1€ per minute.

Toilets

City-maintained public toilets are rare; those that do exist are often far from sanitary. Cafes, bars, and restaurants are required by law to let even noncustomers use their restrooms, so don't be shy; just ask politely for the *bagno*.

Tours

Enjoy Rome, Via Marghera 8A (☎ 06-4451843; www.enjoyrome.com), offers a wide range of educational and entertaining group and private walking tours. For a more in-depth, academic experience, the specialized, small-group tours organized by **Context Rome** (☎ 888/467-1986 toll-free from the U.S., ☎ 06-4820911 in Italy, www.contextrome.com) are outstanding.

Visitor Information

The city of Rome tourist bureau, Via Parigi 5 (☎ 06-36004399; www.romaturismo.com), provides free maps (the excellent *Charta Roma*), events info, pamphlets, and tips on public transportation, although they don't sell bus tickets. You'll also find green tourist board kiosks, providing the same services, around town.

5
Florence

13 Favorite Moments

The consummate open-air museum that is Florence presents visitors with myriad opportunities to revel in the glories of the city's rich heritage. The very stones that Michelangelo and the Medici tread are still underfoot, and centuries of artistic patronage are in plain view on every street corner. While you're here, however, don't forget to break away from the tourist pack and discover the simpler pleasures that make bella Firenze such a civilized, elegant place all these hundreds of years later.

> PREVIOUS PAGE The tower of the Palazzo Vecchio rises above Florence's busiest square, the Piazza della Signoria. THIS PAGE Detail from Birth of Venus, by Florentine Renaissance painter Sandro Botticelli, now at the Uffizi.

① **Climbing Giotto's campanile.** The climb to the top of the Duomo's dome gets a lot more traffic, but for even more excellent views, head next door to the cathedral's 14th-century bell tower. The 414-step ascent is airier and more congenial, and set to the unforgettable sound of those enormous bronze bells ringing every 15 minutes. See p 180, **③**.

② **Having cocktails at the rooftop of the Continentale hotel.** Whether you start an evening or end it there, the intimate and trendy SkyBar, just above the Ponte Vecchio, has drop-dead dramatic views of Florence's Renaissance domes and medieval crenellations. See p 211.

③ **"Studying" Renaissance art history in the Uffizi.** Gaze in awe as masterpiece after iconic masterpiece appears before your eyes at the life-size encyclopedia of painting that is Florence's most celebrated art gallery. See p 174.

④ **Enjoying the shade and greenery of the Giardino di Boboli.** Florence's gorgeous "green lung" makes for a beautiful counterpoint to all the culture-vulturing you'll be doing in this city. Wander down the manicured avenues and listen to the gurgling fountains, then climb up to the Fortezza di Belvedere for awesome panoramas. See p 187, **⑤**.

⑤ **Wandering around Oltrarno.** Just off the main thoroughfare that connects Ponte Vecchio to Palazzo Pitti and the Giardino di Boboli, step into a quieter, funkier, and more authentic Florence in the back streets of the city's "left bank." Grab a snack at Piazza Santo Spirito. See p 186.

⑥ **Laying your eyes on the David.** The ubiquitous postcards and marble copies of the world's most famous sculpture are no substitute for the real thing: Michelangelo's colossal rendering of the biblical hero must be seen in person. See p 159, **⑧**, and p 171.

⑦ **Taking in the splendor of Piazza della Signoria.** Whether you splurge on a

> *Brunelleschi's dome (105m/351 ft. tall) and Giotto's bell tower (81m/269 ft.) punctuate the Florentine skyline.*

cappuccino at Café Rivoire or find a free place to sit down, Florence's most magnificent square is a masterpiece of theatrical proportions, with the imposing Palazzo Vecchio dominating one end and a show-stopping lineup of sculpture in the Loggia dei Lanzi. See p 169, **3**.

8 Escaping the crowds in Fiesole. Florence's classic day trip destination isn't exactly undiscovered, but the fresh air and Roman sights in this hill town make for a wonderful break from duking it out with tourist hordes in the city below. See p 214.

9 Surveying the city from Piazzale Michelangelo at twilight. From this balustraded terrace high above central Florence, you'll get those million-dollar views of twinkling lights and silhouetted Renaissance landmarks pictured on so many postcards and tourism posters. See p 159, **10**.

10 Indulging your inner carnivore. As Italian cities go, Florence is the best for meat-lovers. Throw cardiac caution to the wind and devour a *bistecca alla fiorentina*—the dinosaur-sized

Florentine T-bone steak—at a traditional *ristorante* like Buca Mario. See p 200.

11 Discovering the Basilica di San Lorenzo complex. The unfinished facade belies the wonders inside the city's most diverse religious building. In the main church, admire Bronzino's action-packed *Martyrdom of St. Lawrence,* then go around back to see the Medici Chapels and Michelangelo's Laurentian Library. See p 172, **10**.

12 Getting a sandwich. It may be a simple pleasure, but Florence is a truly great panino town, which can save you a lot of money. Try the famed *bagnato* (boiled beef dip) at Nerbone or one of the many meat-and-cheese offerings at student favorite Antico Noe. See p 203.

13 Department store shopping at COIN or La Rinascente. Florence has plenty of unapproachably priced designer goods, but everyone can snag something uniquely Italian in these midrange department stores, whether it's a new belt or a kitchen gadget. See pp 191, 194.

13 Favorite Moments

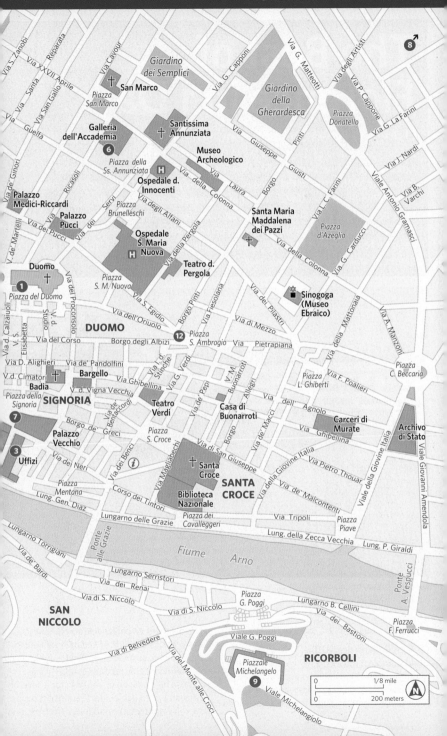

Via S. Zanobi
Via XXVII Aprile
Reparata
Via Cavour
Giardino dei Semplici
Via G. Matteotti
Via degli Artisti
Via P. Capone
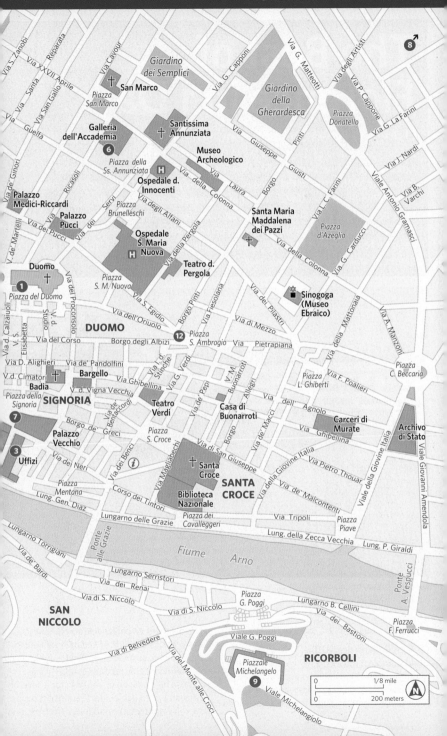
San Marco
Piazza San Marco
Via Santa
Via San Gallo
Giardino della Gherardesca
Piazza Donatello
Via G. La Farini
Via J. Nardi
Galleria dell'Accademia
Santissima Annunziata
Via Giuseppe
Via B. Varchi
Piazza della Ss. Annunziata
Museo Archeologico
Giusti
Viale Antonio Gramsci
Via de' Ginori
Palazzo Medici-Riccardi
Ricasoli
Ospedale d. Innocenti
Via della Colonna
Via L. C. Farini
Piazza d'Azeglio
Palazzo Pucci
Via dei Servi
Piazza Brunelleschi
Borgo
Santa Maria Maddalena dei Pazzi
Via G. Carducci
Via de' Pucci
Via dei
Via degli Alfani
Via della Pergola
Via della Colonna
Ospedale S. Maria Nuova
Duomo
Via dei Proconsolo
Teatro d. Pergola
Piazza S. M. Nuova
Via S. Egidio
Via del Pilastri
Via A. Manzoni
Piazza del Duomo
Via dell'Oriuolo
Sinagoga (Museo Ebraico)
Via della Mattonaia
Via d. Calzaiuoli
Studio
DUOMO
Borgo Pinti
Via Fiesolana
Via di Mezzo
Via
Via del Corso
Borgo degli Albizi
Piazza S. Ambrogio
Pietrapiana
V. d. Cimatori
Via D. Alighieri
Via de' Pandolfini
Via d. Stinche
Via G. Verdi
Via M. Buonarroti
Piazza L. Ghiberti
Via F. Poalieri
Piazza C. Beccaria
Badia
Bargello
Via Ghibellina
Via de' Pepi
V. M. Allegri
del'
Agnolo
SIGNORIA
Piazza della Signoria
V. d. Vigna Vecchia
Teatro Verdi
Casa di Buonarroti
Via de' Macci
Borgo
Carceri di Murate
Archivo di Stato
Palazzo Vecchio
Via de' Bentaccordi
Piazza S. Croce
Via di San Giuseppe
Via Ghibellina
Uffizi
Borgo de' Greci
Via dei Neri
Via de' Benci
Santa Croce
Viale della Giovine Italia
Via Pietro Thouar
Viale Giovanni Amendola
Piazza Mentana
Via Maglabechi
Biblioteca Nazionale
SANTA CROCE
Via della Giovine Italia
Via de' Malcontenti
Lung. Gen. Diaz
Corso dei Tintori
Piazza dei Cavalleggeri
Via Tripoli
Piazza Piave
Lungarno Torrigiani
Lungarno delle Grazie
Lung. della Zecca Vecchia
Lung. P. Giraldi
Ponte alle Grazie
Fiume Arno
Ponte A. Vespucci
Via de' Bardi
Lungarno Serristori
Via dei Renai
Piazza G. Poggi
Lungarno B. Cellini
Piazza F. Ferrucci
SAN NICCOLO
Via di S. Niccolo
Via di S. Niccolo
Via dei Bastioni
Via di Belvedere
Viale G. Poggi
RICORBOLI
Via del Monte alle Croci
Piazzale Michelangelo
Viale Michelangiolo

0   1/8 mile
0   200 meters

The Best of Florence in 1 Day

Using every waking hour and steely discipline, you can actually see many of the highlights of Florence in one jam-packed day. This "greatest hits" tour begins with a one-two punch of Florence's can't-miss museums, with visits to the masterpiece-packed Uffizi and then the Accademia to see Michelangelo's *David*. After lunch on medieval Piazza della Signoria, you'll take in the city's majestic ecclesiastical complex: the Duomo, the baptistery, and Giotto's bell tower. Do some shopping on your way to the Ponte Vecchio, then head up to panoramic Piazzale Michelangelo in time for sunset. Top it all off with dinner at an authentic Tuscan *buca* (cellar).

> *The Ponte Vecchio was the only one of Florence's medieval bridges left standing by the retreating German army in 1944.*

START Take bus A, B, 14, or 23 to the Uffizi.

1 ★★★ **Galleria degli Uffizi.** This is one of the world's greatest museums, where room after room, you'll confront countless iconic works of Renaissance art—including Leonardo da Vinci's *Annunciation* (with an angel that could be Mona Lisa's brother), Michelangelo's *Holy Family*, Sandro Botticelli's *Birth of Venus*, Peter Paul Rubens's voluptuous nudes, and more. Prebooking your ticket is highly recommended—it's essential in high season or you're in for a several-hour wait just to get inside. (Serious art devotees will want to make multiple visits here, but

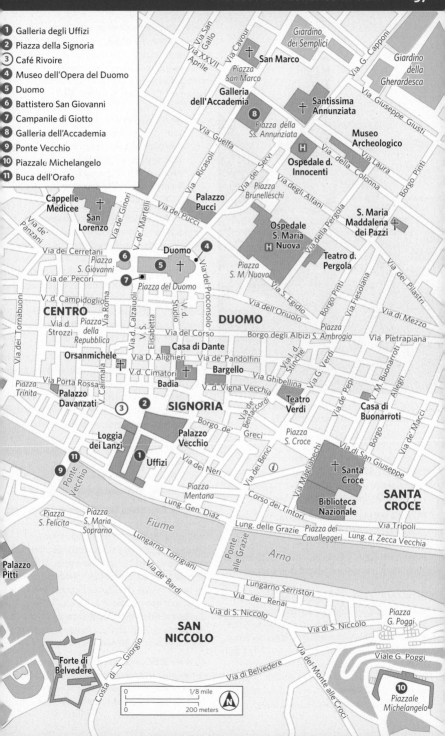

1 Galleria degli Uffizi
2 Piazza della Signoria
3 Café Rivoire
4 Museo dell'Opera del Duomo
5 Duomo
6 Battistero San Giovanni
7 Campanile di Giotto
8 Galleria dell'Accademia
9 Ponte Vecchio
10 Piazzale Michelangelo
11 Buca dell'Orafo

> *Café Rivoire, opposite the Palazzo Vecchio, has one of the best-located terraces in the city.*

Nearby, the twisted composition of Giambologna's *Rape of the Sabines,* is one of the great Mannerist sculptures. Many of these works are rewarding to view from multiple angles, so take advantage of the fact that the Loggia is not roped off. 🕐 30 min. See p 169, ❸.

❸ 🍽 ★ **Café Rivoire.** This alfresco cafe is touristy and overpriced, but the prime views are worth the price. Perfect for light fare, a *spremuta* (fresh-squeezed orange juice), or a pick-me-up *caffè*. Piazza della Signoria 4R (at Via Vaccherecchia). ☎ 055-212412. $–$$$.

❹ ★★ **Museo dell'Opera del Duomo.** For connoisseurs of Renaissance sculpture, this museum across from the Duomo is a shrine, hosting everything from an unfinished, heart-wrenching *Pietà* by Michelangelo to its premier attraction—the restored panels of Lorenzo Ghiberti's original *Gates of Paradise* from the baptistery (❻). Upstairs, don't miss the delightful marble reliefs from the *cantoria* by Luca della Robbia. 🕐 1 hr. See p 181, ❺.

❺ ★★ kids **Duomo.** Consecrated in 1436, one of Europe's most majestic cathedrals rests under Filippo Brunelleschi's revolutionary dome, a triumph of engineering over gravity. The symbol of Florence itself, it's a tourist stamping ground of horrendous proportion—but justifiably so. It's part church, part candy cane, part zebra—in stripes of marble-white, bottle-green, and pink. The interior, by contrast, is spartan, but with one of Europe's most classic views from the top of the cupola. 🕐 45 min. See p 178, ❶.

❻ ★★★ **Battistero San Giovanni.** The exterior of the baptistery gets the most attention—masterful replicas of the original bronze doors hang on three sides. The most famous pair, widely credited with having launched Renaissance art, are Ghiberti's *Gates of Paradise* on the east side (facing the Duomo, and where most tour groups swarm). It's also well worth ducking inside the building for a quick look at the stunning 13th-century mosaics covering the domed ceiling. 🕐 30 min. See p 181, ❹.

❼ ★★★ kids **Campanile di Giotto.** An ideal companion to Brunelleschi's dome, this Gothic bell tower was completed at the end of the 14th century long after Giotto, its creator, had

if art appreciation isn't your top priority while in town, you can skip the Uffizi on a 1-day tour of Florence and use these hours for shopping and wine-sipping instead.) 🕐 2½ hr. See p 174.

❷ ★★★ kids **Piazza della Signoria.** The monumental heart of Florence is dominated by the imposing bulk of Palazzo Vecchio, one of the most formidable medieval monuments in all of Italy. Its thin tower looms tall over the city like a merciless sentry. Piazza della Signoria is also an open-air museum of sculpture, where a copy of Michelangelo's *David* stands (the original used to stand here before being moved to the Accademia, ❽). The 14th-century Loggia dei Lanzi, along the south side of the square, is filled with ancient and Renaissance statues (the most sublime is Benvenuto Cellini's *Perseus* holding aloft the severed head of Medusa, his foot firmly planted on her decapitated body).

died (in 1337). Walk 414 steps to the top of the campanile for a panoramic view of the Duomo and Florence and the surrounding hills. It's actually a better vista than that from the top of the Duomo, since the top of the campanile affords a dramatic close-up view of the dome of the cathedral itself. ⏱ 30 min. See p 180, ③.

⑧ ★★ **Galleria dell'Accademia.** After seeing the famous paintings in the Uffizi in the morning, it's time to lay your eyes on the most famous sculpture in the world—the utterly mesmerizing *David* by Michelangelo (p 171). You've seen pictures and kitschy replicas of the 9m-tall (17-ft.) nude all over the world, but nothing compares to beholding David "in the flesh." This monumental icon of youthful male beauty is a stellar example of Michelangelo's humanism and completely deserving of all the hype. As with the Uffizi, it's smart to reserve your ticket in advance to avoid the often lengthy (and shadeless) queue. ⏱ 15 min., without a wait. Via Ricasoli 60. ☎ 050-2388609. Admission 8€. Tues–Sun 8:15am–7pm. Bus: B, D, or 12.

⑨ ★ **Ponte Vecchio.** The Ponte Vecchio, as its name suggests, is the city's oldest bridge; its latest incarnation dates to 1345, but the shops along it have been taking advantage of all the foot traffic since at least the 12th century. Originally occupied by blacksmiths, butchers, and tanners, the shops that flank the bridge have mostly sold gold and silver since the reign of the Medici. Sunset is the ideal time to cross. ⏱ 30 min. See p 182, ①.

⑩ ★★ **Piazzale Michelangelo.** For a final *arrivederci* to Florence, take a taxi to its most panoramic piazza, laid out in 1885. From this balustraded terrace, the city of the Renaissance unfurls before you. View it at twilight as the lights of the city twinkle on. In the center of the square is a monument to Michelangelo; the charming church nearby is San Miniato al Monte. ⏱ 30 min.

⑪ ★ **Buca dell'Orafo.** For your final meal in Florence, head to this famous cellar restaurant, set in the former workshop of a Renaissance goldsmith. It's on an arched alleyway near the Ponte Vecchio. The Tuscan cuisine is served at communal tables, and if you want to dine with locals, book a late table. ⏱ 2 hr. See p 200 for full restaurant details.

> *TOP* Raphael's *Madonna del Cardellino, in the Uffizi's collection, is named for the goldfinch held by the infant Christ and John the Baptist.*
> *BOTTOM* *San Miniato al Monte, one of the city's truly ancient places, is part of the scenery at Piazzale Michelangelo.*

The Best of Florence in 2 Days

On your second day in Florence, spend the morning wandering Oltrarno, the district on the left bank of the Arno. The great attraction here is the Palazzo Pitti and the adjacent Giardino di Boboli. Even if you take all morning, you will see only a part of the Palazzo Pitti's great collection of art, which encompasses works by Renaissance and later European masters. Stroll through the Boboli gardens before a typical Oltrarno trattoria lunch, and then head back to the "right bank" for a grand array of treasures. The latter includes the Medici Chapels (with Michelangelo's grand sculptures), Filippo Brunelleschi's Basilica di San Lorenzo, and the art-filled town hall, Palazzo Vecchio.

> *The lavish rooms of the Palazzo Pitti's Galleria Palatina were decorated with rich Medici tastes in mind.*

START Take bus D, 11, 36, 37, or 68 to the Palazzo Pitti.

① ★★ **Palazzo Pitti.** This 15th-century Medici palace on the south side of the Arno is second only to the Uffizi in its wealth of artwork. The Galleria Palatina on the second floor, with its marvelous collection of paintings, is reason enough to go to Florence; I'd visit for the Raphaels alone. And the Palatina just primes you for what's to come: the city's most extensive coterie of museums—including exhibitions of costume, modern art, and even the Medici's private digs. ⊙ 2 hr. See p 168, **①**.

② ★ ᴋɪᴅѕ **Giardino di Boboli.** Laid out between 1549 and 1656, this is Europe's grandest Renaissance garden. After a stroll through the garden, make the short climb to the star-shaped bastions of the Fortezza di Belvedere

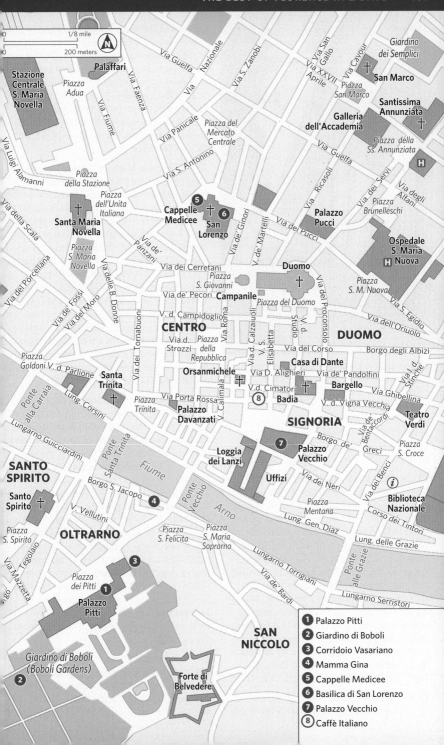

1 Palazzo Pitti
2 Giardino di Boboli
3 Corridoio Vasariano
4 Mamma Gina
5 Cappelle Medicee
6 Basilica di San Lorenzo
7 Palazzo Vecchio
8 Caffè Italiano

> *The arcades of the Vasari Corridor track the riverbank before crossing the Arno above the Ponte Vecchio.*

for a panoramic view of the city and its Renaissance spires. Before departing, stroll down the stunning Viottolone, an avenue of pines and cypresses. ⏱ 1 hr. See p 187, ⑤.

❸ Corridoio Vasariano (Vasari Corridor).

After Cosimo I de' Medici (1519–1574) moved to the Palazzo Pitti, he commissioned Giorgio Vasari to build a private aboveground tunnel to the Uffizi. The corridor, built in 1565, runs along the Arno from the Palazzo Pitti to the Ponte Vecchio, crosses the river above the bridge shops, then continues on to the museum that once served as the Medici offices. The walkway, sometimes called the Medici Skywalk, is lined with paintings and windows offering unique vistas. ⏱ 1 hr. ☎ 055-2654321 for information; ☎ 055-294883 for reservations. Admission 8.50€. Reservations required for admission (by guided tour only). Tues–Sun 8:15am–7pm. Tours Tues, Wed, Fri–Sun. Bus: A, B, 23, or 71.

❹ ★★ Mamma Gina. This is the most famous—and one of the best—trattorias on the

left bank of the Arno, ideal for a luncheon stopover after the Pitti and the Boboli garden. One of the succulent pasta dishes along with a garden salad makes for an ideal repast before you venture into the sun again. After lunch, you can head across the Ponte Santa Trinità bridge back to the *centro storico* (historic center) of Florence. Borgo San Jacopo 37R. ☎ 055-2396009. www.mammagina.it. Entrees 13€–20€. AE, DC, MC, V. Closed Sun.

❺ ★★ Cappelle Medicee (Medici Chapels).

The big deals here are the celebrated Medici tombs by Michelangelo. Regrettably, those creations honored unworthy members of the Medici clan, Giuliano and Lorenzo II. Nevertheless, the great artist portrayed them as model princes of the Renaissance: Michelangelo's idealized rendering of Giuliano de' Medici (1453–1478) gives no indication that this was a deranged young man who died an early death. Giuliano's tomb also features Michelangelo's *Night* and *Day,* two allegorical figures that are some of the most monumental pieces of sculpture in the world (though *Night* shows the artist's absurd disregard for realistic female anatomy—its widely spaced "breasts" make Pamela Anderson look like an all-natural gal). ⏱ 15 min. See p 173, ⑪.

❻ ★★★ Basilica di San Lorenzo. Although the

facade was never finished, some of the greatest artists and architects, including Brunelleschi, worked to create this splendid church between the 15th and 17th centuries. Walk up the nave to explore the **Vecchia Sacrestia** (Old Sacristy), Brunelleschi's grand creation and one of the first and finest works of the early Renaissance—made all the more enthralling by the 1460 pulpits of Donatello. On the left side of the church, Agnolo Bronzino's 1569 ***Martyrdom of St. Lawrence*** is a rather ridiculously, but highly entertaining (it's filled with nudes flexing their muscles pointlessly), depiction of the patron saint of grilled meats (no kidding) getting barbecued. As if this weren't bait enough, the **Biblioteca Medicea Laurenziana** (Laurentian Library) was designed for the Medici by Michelangelo himself. ⏱ 1 hr. See p 172, ⑩.

❼ ★★ Palazzo Vecchio. Having 2 days in

Florence gives you time to actually go inside the dominant building on Piazza della Signoria, Palazzo Vecchio. This massive 13th-century palace has been the town hall for 700 years, putting

The Medici Clan

You can't walk far in Florence without overhearing a tour guide spouting the name of the city's most influential family—the Medici (pronounced "*Meh*-dee-chee"). Beginning in the 14th century with Averardo (Bicci) de' Medici, the clan rose to power with the fortune they made in the banking business. Considering that, for a time, the Medici were the wealthiest family in all of Europe, their influence in their hometown of Florence was all-consuming.

Lorenzo "the Magnificent" de' Medici (1449–92; pictured above, center) is perhaps the most well known member of the family. His tenure as a civic leader endowed Florence with countless works of art and architecture, and he was the chief patron of Leonardo da Vinci and Michelangelo when they were in Florence. The Uffizi Gallery was started by the Medici (it was originally where they had their offices, or *uffizi*), and they were also the moneybags behind the Giardino di Boboli. The Medici also produced three popes, Leo X and Clement VII, who ruled both Rome and Florence for nearly two decades in the 16th century, as well as Leo XI.

If, while you're walking around Florence (or Tuscany, or Rome), you see a coat of arms with balls (anywhere from 5 to 8 of them) on it, that's the Medici insignia; wherever it appears, that work of art or architecture was financed by Florence's most illustrious family. What the balls represent is an ongoing matter of debate: They may be coins or even pills, as *Medici* means "doctors" and the earliest ancestors were in the medical profession.

> *The Laurentian Library, next to San Lorenzo, is famed for Michelangelo's Renaissance staircase.*

to shame other city halls around the world. A highlight is the **Salone dei Cinquecento** (Hall of the 500), where the great council met. It's filled with Vasari frescoes. The star attraction is **Michelangelo's *Victory*,** originally intended for the tomb of Pope Julius. 🕐 1 hr. See p 170, ❹.

⑧　🍸 **Caffè Italiano.** Ease into the Florentine night by heading north of Piazza della Signoria to this secret hideaway in the historic core. If you're rushed, stay downstairs and drink at the stand-up bar. Head upstairs for a more leisurely evening spent at dark wooden tables. Service is a disaster, but when your order comes, expect some of the best coffee and desserts in town. My favorite? *Caffè-choc*—that's espresso laced with pure bitter chocolate powder. **Via della Condotta 56R.** ☎ 055-291082. $$.

The Best of Florence in 3 Days

A third day in Florence gives you a glimpse of even more of the city's treasures, from the world's greatest repository of Renaissance sculpture in the Museo Nazionale del Bargello to the scientific wonders at the Museo di Storia della Scienza. Few dare to sneak out of Florence without paying a visit to the Basilica di Santa Maria Novella and the Basilica di Santa Croce, two of Europe's grandest churches. To escape tourists for a spell, head for the hills, for a romantic dinner in the hill town of Fiesole.

> Michelangelo's Bacchus, *hewn from marble in the 1490s, is a treasure of the Bargello.*

START **Take bus A, 14, or 23 to the Bargello.**

① ★★ **Museo Nazionale del Bargello.** This is a vast repository of some of the most famous Renaissance sculpture ever created, including Donatello's *John the Baptist* and his own bronze *David.* The Bargello also contains, along with countless other works, Michelangelo's *Bacchus*—a masterful rendering of the Roman god of wine in an inebriated state (note his tipsy pose). ⏲ 1 hr. See p 170, **⑤**.

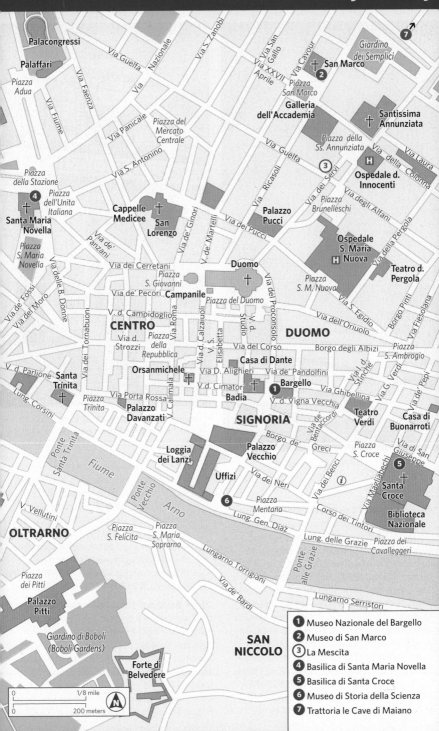

1 Museo Nazionale del Bargello
2 Museo di San Marco
3 La Mescita
4 Basilica di Santa Maria Novella
5 Basilica di Santa Croce
6 Museo di Storia della Scienza
7 Trattoria le Cave di Maiano

> *The cloisters at the Franciscan Basilica di Santa Croce.*

> *The recently restored facade of Santa Maria Novella is typical of the Tuscan Romanesque style.*

2 ★★ **Museo di San Marco.** This convent and cloisters are a museum honoring Fra Angelico (1395–1455). Cosimo il Vecchio de' Medici chose Angelico to build and decorate this new convent, where he also lived, and where Girolamo Savonarola—the monk famed for his "bonfire of the vanities"—later resided as well. The Cloister of St. Anthony was designed by Michelozzo di Bartolomeo. Angelico's famous *Last Judgment* and his sober masterpiece, *Annunciation,* are filled with a pacifying power, as are the walls of the monks' cells, which are decorated with scenes that foster meditation. ⏲ 45 min. Piazza San Marco 1. ☎ 055-294883. Admission 4€. Tues–Fri 8:30am–1:50pm; Sat 8:15am–6:50pm. Bus: 1, 6, 7, 10, 11, 17, or 20.

3 🍷 ★ **La Mescita.** Florentines call La Mescita a *fiaschetteria* (a cheap joint for wine and food), while Americans might call it a "dive." By any name, it makes the best sandwiches in this part of town. It's worth fighting for a table at this crowded, bustling joint, where you'll eat alongside Florentines and risk getting booted if you occupy a table for too long. Via degli Alfani 70R (at Via dei Servi). ☎ 055-7591604. $. Bus: 31 or 32.

4 ★★ **Basilica di Santa Maria Novella.** Built by the Dominicans (construction began in 1246), this church is filled with some of Tuscany's grandest frescoes, notably the late-14th-century paintings by Andrea di Bonaiuto in the Cappellone degli Spagnoli (Chapel of the Spanish; it was used by the court of Eleonora of Toledo). Other treasures include the famous *Crucifix* by Filippo Brunelleschi. ⏲ 30 min. See p 173, **12**.

> *The interior of Santa Croce is decorated with frescoes by Giotto, Taddeo Gaddi, and others.*

5 ★★ **Basilica di Santa Croce.** Locals call it "the Westminster Abbey of Tuscany," because this 14th-century church contains the tombs of the Renaissance's brightest lights—most notably Michelangelo and Galileo. Author John Ruskin made a classic comment about Santa Croce: "Wait then for an entirely light morning: rise with the sun and go to Santa Croce, with a good opera glass in your pocket." The vast, barnlike church is surprisingly (and naturally) well lit. ⏱ 1 hr. See p 183, **4**.

6 ★ **Museo di Storia della Scienza.** This science museum houses such treasures as the lens Galileo used to discover four moons of Jupiter; an alchemist's laboratory; Galileo's right hand and middle finger, stolen when he was being buried at Santa Croce; and amazingly realistic anatomical wax models. The 18th-century

surgical implements will make you cringe. ⏱ 1 hr. Piazza dei Giudici. ☎ 055-2653130. Admission 4€. June–Sept Mon, Wed–Fri 9:30am–5pm; Tues and Sat 9:30am–1pm. Off season Mon, Wed–Sat 9:30am–5pm; Tues 9:30am–1pm. Bus: 13, 23, 62.

7 ★ **Trattoria le Cave di Maiano.** For your final good-bye to Florence, take a 15-minute ride to this converted farmhouse, where Florentines escape the city heat on summer nights. The hearty regional cuisine—such as chicken roasted under a brick with peppers, and succulent pastas—is the finest in the area. Many adventurous diners walk the entire 8km (5 miles) back to Florence, with the city lights, twinkling in the distance, to lead the way. *Note:* You can stop at any point along the way and board bus 7 back to town. ⏱ 4 hr., including dinner and the walk. For full details on the restaurant, see p 203.

The Best Art & Architecture

It's a hackneyed but apt description: Florence is one of the greatest open-air museums in the world. Within the compact core of the old city, there are literally hundreds of churches, historic palaces, museums, and galleries that are architectural landmarks in their own right and stash away some of the most groundbreaking and influential works of Western painting and sculpture. From the thronged halls of the Uffizi to the intimate rooms of the Museo dell'Opera del Duomo to such open-air troves as Piazza della Signoria, this Renaissance-focused tour will keep art lovers busy for several days.

> In the Loggia dei Lanzi, Cellini's bronze Perseus holds aloft the head of Medusa.

START **Take bus D, 11, 36, 37, or 68 across the Arno to Piazza dei Pitti.**

❶ ★★ **Palazzo Pitti.** Luca Pitti, a rich importer of French fabrics, wanted a palace to outclass the Medici's—and in that he got his wish. Niccolò Macchiavelli hailed this palace as "grander than any other erected in Florence by a private citizen." When the Pittis went broke, the Medici moved in, making it the most splendid palace in Europe until Louis XIV built Versailles. In the 19th century, the Palazzo Pitti sheltered the Italian royal family, when Florence was the capital. Victor Emmanuel III gave it to the state, which turned it into a series of world-class museums.

Climb 140 steps and enter the ★★★ **Galleria Palatina.** Head here if you have to skip everything else. It's filled with masterpieces from the High Renaissance and later eras, collected by the Medici. The most famous painting is Raphael's *Madonna of the Chair,* one of the six most renowned paintings in Europe. Baroque sumptuousness defines the ★ **Appartamenti Reali,** homes to the kings of Savoy. Note Michelangelo da Caravaggio's *Portrait of a Knight of Malta.* In the shadow of the Renaissance rooms, the ★ **Galleria d'Arte Moderna** showcases the Macchiaioli, the 19th-century school of Impressionist painters in revolt against academicism. The **Galleria del Costume** is filled with 18th- to 20th-century clothing, including historic wardrobes such as Eleonora of Toledo's burial dress. On the ground floor, **Museo degli Argenti** is a camp glorification of the Medici

1 Palazzo Pitti
2 Uffizi
3 Piazza della Signoria
4 Palazzo Vecchio
5 Museo Nazionale del Bargello
6 Cantinetta dei Verrazzano
7 Piazza del Duomo
8 Galleria dell'Accademia
9 Museo Archeologico
10 Basilica di San Lorenzo
11 Cappelle Medicee
12 Basilica di Santa Maria Novella

household wares, with treasures in ivory and silver, among other metals. It's ostentatious but fun. ⏱ 2 hr. Piazza dei Pitti (across the Arno off Via Guicciardini). ☎ 055-2388611. www.firenzemusei.it. Galleria Palatina 6.50€ adults, 3.25€ children. Other museums 5€ adults, 2.50€ children. Tues–Sun 8:15am–6:45pm. Bus: D, 11, 36, 37, or 68.

2 ★★★ **Uffizi** ⏱ 3 hr. See p 174.

3 ★★ kids **Piazza della Signoria.** The center of civic life in Florence for centuries, this landmark square appropriately stands in the historic core dominated by the Palazzo Vecchio (4), the town hall. Michelangelo's *David* in front of the palace is a copy, but the late-14th-century **Loggia dei Lanzi** is an open-air museum that boasts plenty of original master works,

> Raphael's Madonna of the Chair *is in the Palazzo Pitti's collection.*

> *Giorgio Vasari's frescoes embellish the Salone dei Cinquecento in the Palazzo Vecchio.*

including Benvenuto Cellini's *Perseus* holding the severed head of Medusa. Ammannato's controversial fountain of Neptune inspired this chant in the 16th century: *Ammannato, Ammannato, che bel marmo hai rovinato!* (What beautiful marble you've ruined!) ☺ 1 hr. Open 24 hr. Bus: A, B, 23, or 71.

④ ★★★ Palazzo Vecchio. This "Old Palace" became home to Cosimo I and the Medici in 1540, but it dates to the 13th century, when it was built by Gothic master builder Arnolfo di Cambio. (Di Cambio's 92m/308-ft. landmark tower, which still graces the Florentine skyline, was an engineering feat in its day.) The highlight of the interior is the **Salone dei Cinquecento** (Hall of the 500), frescoed by Giorgio Vasari and his assistants in the 16th century. (Alas, wax-pigment frescoes by Leonardo melted when braziers were brought in to speed up the drying process.) Michelangelo's sculpture *Victory* survives, thankfully, along with Donatello's famous bronze group, *Judith Slaying Holofernes,* created in 1455. You can also visit the private apartments of Eleonora of Toledo, the Spanish wife of Cosimo I, and

the chamber where religious zealot Girolamo Savonarola endured a dozen torture sessions, including "twists" on the rack. ☺ 1 hr. Piazza della Signoria (at Via Vacchereccia). ☎ 055-2768465. Admission 6€. Mon–Wed and Fri–Sun 9am–7pm; Thurs 9am–2pm. Ticket office closes 1 hr. before palace. Bus: A, B, 23, or 71.

⑤ ★★ Museo Nazionale del Bargello. This grim fortress—once a place for public hangings—centers around a courtyard with a loggia and portico. The second-floor sculpture collection is the Renaissance's finest, including Donatello's *David* (the first freestanding nude since the Roman era), two Donatello versions of *John the Baptist,* and a less famous *David* by Michelangelo. Also here is Michelangelo's delightfully tipsy *Bacchus.* Cup in hand, about to reel over backwards, he looks like he's trying, and comically failing, to pass a field sobriety test. ☺ 1½ hr. Via del Proconsolo 4 (at Via Ghibellina). ☎ 055-294883. www.sbas.firenze.it. Admission 5€. Daily 8:30am–1:50pm. Closed 2nd and 4th Mon and 1st, 3rd, and 5th Sun of each month. Bus: A, 14, or 23.

The World's Most Famous Sculpture

If Michelangelo (1475–1564) were alive today and giving advice on what to see in Italy, he'd tell you to skip his famous frescoes at the Sistine Chapel (p 88, **3**) but urge you to queue up at the Accademia in Florence for the ★★★ *David.* Why? Michelangelo hated painting—a two-dimensional medium that, while requiring a certain amount of skill, was nonetheless an "additive" art. The "subtractive" art of sculpture, on the other hand, as Michelangelo saw it, was a divine enterprise, in that it involved seeking out and bringing form to a spirit that lived in the marble. And because Michelangelo famously preferred the male anatomy to the female form (in art, anyway; whether that extended to his personal life is a matter of debate) he may well have considered *David* his most triumphant masterpiece in his long and prolific career.

Michelangelo began the 5m-tall (17-ft.) David in 1501 and completed it in 1504. What set Michelangelo's apart from other Davids was that the slain Goliath wasn't in the picture. Michelangelo chose to capture an ambiguous moment (is it before he fought Goliath, or just after he killed him?), but it's this combination of self-possession and tension on his face that makes the David so striking in person. The face looks a little bit different from each angle—here menacing, there vulnerable—and in this way, almost seems to be running through a subtle range of emotions before your eyes. From the neck down, David is relaxed yet powerful, in the idealized style favored during the High Renaissance. His stance is called *contrapposto* ("counterpoised"), an elegant position that goes back to ancient Greek sculpture, where one leg supports the body and the other bent leg is engaged only as a gentle buttress. *Contrapposto* also means that one hip is higher and one shoulder is lower, creating a slight S-curve on David's right side. (Try it at home in the mirror.) Of course, many eyes in the Accademia inevitably fall to David's private parts—*il pisello*, as Italians euphemistically and diminutively call it. Why David wasn't better endowed by Michelangelo is yet another matter of scholarly debate. (Why David, a Jew, isn't circumcised is because that was the custom in Italian Renaissance art.) The only real criticism one can make is about the exaggerated size of David's head and right hand, but that's because the work was originally intended to go along the roof of the Duomo, where it would have looked more proportional to viewers below. That Duomo plan was scrapped, and David was placed in Piazza della Signoria as a symbol of the grit of the Florentine Republic. He stood for 369 years in front of Palazzo Vecchio (where the copy stands now) before being moved inside the Accademia (p 159, **8**) in 1873.

> *Donatello's bronze David, in the Bargello, was the first freestanding male nude sculpted since ancient Rome.*

⑥ 🍷 ★ **Cantinetta dei Verrazzano.** Stop in for a glass of Chianti and a focaccia at this local outpost of the Chianti winery (p 236), which serves savory snacks and cold platters along with their fine wines (2€–8€ by the glass). Via dei Tavolini 18–20R (at Via dei Calzaiuoli). ☎ 055-268590. $$. Bus: A.

⑦ ★★ kids **Piazza del Duomo.** At the most colorful architectural complex in the city, the dome, the bell tower, the baptistery, and the church itself all merit visiting. Check out the Museo dell'Opera del Duomo (p 181, ⑤) to see Ghiberti's baptistery doors as well as all the works of art that used to decorate the cathedral. See p 178 for details.

⑧ ★★ **Galleria dell'Accademia.** Sure, there are other important works of art here, including some unfinished *Slaves* by Michelangelo, but the real reason you brave the line to get in here is to see the ★★★ *David.* See p 159, ⑧, and "The World's Most Famous Sculpture," p 171.

⑨ ★★ **Museo Archeologico.** A marvelous palazzo is home to one of the world's greatest collections of Egyptian and Etruscan artifacts, much of it collected by the Medici. "The great looter," Tuscan grand duke Leopold II, added to this treasure trove in the 1830s. The astonishingly well-preserved *Arezzo Chimera* (a lion with a goat protruding from its back) is a 5th-century masterpiece. Room XIII contains the celebrated *Idolino,* a nude bronze lad (perhaps a Roman statue created during the time of Christ). 🕐 1 hr., 15 min. Via della Colonna (off Piazza della Santissima Annunziata). ☎ 055-23575. Admission 4.15€. Nov–Aug Mon 2–7pm; Tues, Thurs 8:30am–7pm; Wed, Fri–Sun 8:30am–2pm. Sept as above and also Sat 9pm–midnight. Oct as above except for Sun (9am–8pm). Bus: 6, 31, or 32.

⑩ ★★ **Basilica di San Lorenzo.** The overall effect of this basilica, which houses the tombs of many a Medici (see also Cappelle Medicee, ⑪), is almost Byzantine; one Bulgarian critic called it "a Florentine Hagia Sophia looming over a souk" (a reference to the nearby Mercato di San Lorenzo; p 185, ⑩). The Medici shelled out big bags of gold for it, however, even though the facade was never finished. Brunelleschi designed the Old Sacristy, where Donatello created two pulpits with dramatic bronze panels in the nave. Also here is Agnolo Bronzino's fabulously camp fresco of the ★★ *Martyrdom of St. Lawrence,* with the saint languishing rather Zen-like on the gridiron as the flames rage below him, and barely clad figures around him strike exaggerated poses that serve only to flaunt their ridiculous muscles. ⊙ 1 hr. Piazza San Lorenzo (at Via del Canto dei Nelli). ☎ 055-216634. Free admission. Daily 10am–5pm. Bus: 1, 6, 7, 11, 17, 33, 67, or 68.

⑪ ★★ Cappelle Medicee (Medici Chapels). Make a fast trek to the Sagrestia Nuova, Michelangelo's first realized architectural work—begun in 1520, but left unfinished until 1534. On the left, the tomb of Lorenzo, Duke of Urbino, bears the artist's reclining figures representing *Dawn* and *Dusk*. On the right, the tomb of Giuliano, Duke of Nemours (and youngest son of Lorenzo the Magnificent), features Michelangelo's allegorical figures of *Day* and *Night*. Michelangelo's New Sacristy was intended as an addition to Brunelleschi's Old Sacristy in San Lorenzo proper (⑩). Michelangelo never completed the other two tombs commissioned to him, but in 1521 he did finish the deeply moving *Madonna and Child,* for the tomb of Lorenzo "the Magnificent" de' Medici. ⊙ 15 min. Piazza Madonna degli Aldobrandini 6 (behind San Lorenzo where Via del Gigli and Via Faenza converge). ☎ 055-2388602. Admission 6€. Daily 8:15am–4:30pm. Closed 2nd and 4th Sun and 1st, 3rd, and 5th Mon of each month. Bus: 1, 6, 7, 11, 17, 33, 67, or 68.

⑫ ★★ Basilica di Santa Maria Novella. The green and white marble facade was created in the 15th century. The interior dates to the 13th century. By the 1800s, this Romanesque and Gothic structure in the city of the Renaissance had become "the church for foreigners," attracting expatriate literati, including Percy Bysshe Shelley, Henry James, Ralph Waldo Emerson, even Henry Wadsworth Longfellow. Giovanni Boccaccio used the church for scenes in his *Decameron.* Of the many frescoes adorning the church, Domenico Ghirlandaio's are the finest. Ostensibly, they depict scenes in the lives of the Virgin Mary and St. John the Baptist, but they're also a dazzling portrait of everyday life in Renaissance Florence. If time remains, visit the cloisters and the splendid Spanish Chapel, frescoed by Andrea di Bonaiuto in the 14th century. ⊙ 45 min. Piazza Santa Maria Novella (at Via della Scala). ☎ 055-215918. Free admission to church, 2.70€ to cloisters and Spanish Chapel. Church Mon–Thurs 9:30am–5pm; Fri 1–5pm; Sat 9:30am–5pm; Sun 1–5pm. Cloisters and Spanish Chapel Sat and Mon–Thurs 9am–5pm; Sun 9am–2pm. Bus: A, 6, 9, 11, 36, 37, or 68.

> *Masaccio, Ghirlandaio, Filippino Lippi, and other masters contributed to the decoration of Santa Maria Novella's Gothic interior.*

> *The Arezzo Chimera, now in the Museo Archeologico, is one of the best-preserved bronzes left by the Etruscans.*

The Uffizi

Once the Medici business offices, the Galleria degli Uffizi is one of the world's greatest art museums. No place has a more extensive collection of Renaissance masterpieces—including Michelangelo's *Holy Family,* Leonardo da Vinci's *Annunciation,* and Sandro Botticelli's *Birth of Venus.* Most of the year, advance booking is essential to avoid the long queue; see "Museum Info," below. Oh, and you'll impress the locals if you get the pronunciation right: It's "Oo-*feed*-see," not "You-*feetsy.*"

> *Ambrogio Lorenzetti's* Presentation at the Temple *was painted six years before the artist perished from the plague.*

Museum Info

The Uffizi is at Piazzale degli Uffizi 6, at Via Lambertesca (☎ 055-23885; www. polomuseale.firenze.it/English/Uffizi). It's open Tuesday to Sunday from 8:15am to 6:50pm. Admission is 6.50€. Reservations are strongly recommended; contact Firenze Musei (☎ 055-294883; www.firenzemusei.it).

START Take the A, B, 23, or 71 bus to Piazzale degli Uffizi 6 (at Via Lambertesca).

1 Room 2: This salon showcases the works of Giovanni Cimabue (1240–1302), often called the father of modern painting, and his pupil, Giotto (1276–1337)—both rebels from Byzantium. Still linked to Byzantine art, Cimabue's *Santa Trinità Maestà* (1280) approaches realistic painting. Three decades later, Giotto painted the greatest *maestà* of them all, the *Ognissanti Madonna.*

2 Room 3: This is a showcase of 14th-century Sienese master paintings—none finer than Simone Martini's *Annunciation* (1313), showing a horrified Mary learning of her imminent immaculate conception. The Lorenzetti brothers, Pietro and Ambrogio, also created masterpieces displayed in this room, before the Black Death of 1348 claimed their lives; the chief work is Ambrogio's *Presentation at the Temple* (1342).

3 Room 7: Renaissance innovations in painting were possible in part because of Masaccio (1401–28) and Paolo Uccello (1397–1475) and their revolutionary use of perspective. Look at Uccello's *Battle of San Romano* (1456), depicting a Florentine victory over the Sienese army. A rare piece by Masaccio (he was dead at 27) is *Madonna and Child with St. Anne* (1424).

4 Room 8: Numerous paintings by Fra Filippo Lippi (1406–1469) are showcased here. One of our favorites is *Madonna and Child with Angels*—a portrait of the randy monk's mistress.

5 Rooms 10–14: These rooms feature the most famous paintings in Florence, Sandro Botticelli's *Birth of Venus* and *Primavera (Allegory of Spring).*

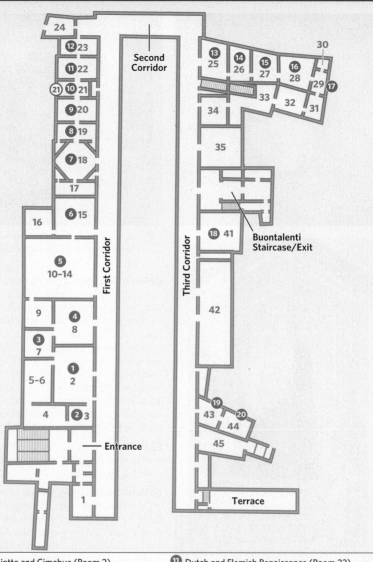

1 Giotto and Cimabue (Room 2)

2 14th-century Sienese paintings (Room 3)

3 Masaccio and Uccello (Room 7)

4 Fra Filippo Lippi (Room 8)

5 Botticelli (Rooms 10-14)

6 Da Vinci and Verrocchio (Room 15)

7 La Tribuna (Room 18)

8 Perugino and Signorelli (Room 19)

9 Dürer (Room 20)

10 Venetian Masters (Room 21)

11 Dutch and Flemish Renaissance (Room 22)

12 Mantegna and Correggio (Room 23)

13 Michelangelo and Florentine artists (Room 25)

14 Raphael and del Sarto (Room 26)

15 Fiorentino and Pontormo (Room 27)

16 Titian (Room 28)

17 Il Parmigianino (Room 29)

18 Rubens (Room 41)

19 Caravaggio (Room 43)

20 Rembrandt (Room 44)

21 Uffizi Café

> *Michelangelo's* Holy Family *is one of very few panel paintings made by the Florentine genius.*

7 **Room 18:** Called *La Tribuna*, this octagonal room is the most lavish salon, made of lapis lazuli for air, red walls for fire, green *pietre dure* for earth, and mother-of-pearl for water. Its showcase is the *Medici Venus*, a copy of a Greek original. The baroque artist Agnolo Bronzino painted the celebrated portrait of Eleonora of Toledo, wife of Cosimo I. When the Medici tombs were opened in 1857, her body was discovered buried in the same satin dress she wore in the painting. You can also view Raphael's *St. John the Baptist in the Desert* (1518).

8 **Room 19:** Perugino's (1446–1523) *Madonna* and his stern *Portrait of Francesco delle Opere* shine brightest here.

9 **Room 20:** This gallery exhibits paintings of Germans who worked in Florence. Albrecht Dürer (1471–1528) was the master of the German Renaissance. Contrast his *Adam and Eve* with the one by Lucas Cranach (1472–1553). Dürer's work is a study of the body; Cranach's shows a more erotic bent. Dürer's *Adoration of the Magi* is not to be missed. Hans Bruegel (1568–1625) is represented by his *Il Grande Calvario*, a Calvary scene.

> *TOP Caravaggio's* Medusa *is a typically dark self-portrait.* BOTTOM *Giotto's 14th-century* Ognissanti Madonna.

6 **Room 15:** Art lovers flock here to see the stunningly beautiful *Annunciation* by Leonardo da Vinci (1452–1519) and his master Andrea del Verrocchio (1435–88). Leonardo is believed to have painted the angel on the far left and the landscape, from 1472 to 1475. The *Baptism of Christ* is by Verrocchio.

10 **Room 21:** Venetian masters of the 15th century shine in this *sala*—especially Giovanni Bellini

11 **Room 22:** Dutch and Flemish paintings of the Renaissance, including more German works, grace this gallery. Our favorite is *Portrait of Sir Richard Southwell* by Hans Holbein the Younger (1497–1543).

> *View Leonardo's* Annunciation *from the lower right to appreciate the artist's mastery of perspective.*

12 Room 23: This gallery is a showcase for Andrea Mantegna's triptych of the *Adoration of the Magi, Circumcision,* and *Ascension* painted from 1463 to 1470. There are also three noted works by Antonio da Correggio (1489–1534).

13 Room 25: This gallery houses Michelangelo's only painting in Florence—a *tondo* (round painting) of the Holy Family, often called the *Doni Tondo* (1506–08). The muscular forms show Michelangelo's preference for sculpture. He even designed the elaborate frame.

14 Room 26: This salon of High Renaissance painting is dominated by the serene *Madonna del Cardellino* by Raphael (1483–1520), one of the world's most celebrated works. Another remarkable version of the Virgin is *Madonna of Harpies* by Andrea del Sarto (1486–1530), one of the first Mannerists.

15 Room 27: Early Florentine Mannerism reaches a fever pitch in this room dedicated to Rosso Fiorentino (1485–1541), del Sarto's star pupil. Fiorentino is best appreciated in his *Moses Defends the Daughters of Jethro* (1523), which owes a heavy debt to Michelangelo. Del Sarto's other Mannerist pupil, Jacopo Pontormo (1494–1557), is represented by his *Supper at Emmaus.*

16 Room 28: This *sala* is dedicated to Titian Vercellio (1488–1566). Of all the postcards sold at the Uffizi, none—not even Botticelli's *Primavera*—tops the sale of Titian's *Venus of Urbino,* lounging nude on her bed.

> *Fra Filippo Lippi's* Madonna and Child with Angels *was painted around 1455.*

17 Room 29: The late Mannerist master Il Parmigianino (1505–40) dominates this gallery. His *Madonna and Child* (nicknamed "Madonna of the Long Neck," for obvious reasons) is one of the most celebrated paintings in the Uffizi.

18 Room 41: This room is dedicated to Peter Paul Rubens (1577–1640) and his voluptuous nudes. You can also see his fat *Baccanale.*

19 Room 43: Michelangelo da Caravaggio is the star painter here, especially his marvelous *Medusa,* painted with oil on cloth.

20 Room 44: Compare the two self-portraits by Rembrandt—one in his youth, the other as a senior citizen.

㉑ Uffizi Café. This bar atop the loggia serves cold drinks and espresso. $.

Piazza del Duomo

There are five major elements to the Opera di Santa Maria del Fiore (or "OPA," as it's abbreviated everywhere), each with a separate entrance but all worth your time, money, and physical effort. Given the number of sightseeing components here, it's a good idea to break up your Duomo doings over the course of a few days. If you're like most visitors, you'll find your way back here over and over without even trying: That giant russet dome and those amazing candy stripes of green and pink marble are like homing signals for aimlessly wandering tourists.

> You can spy Brunelleschi's giant dome from just about anywhere in the city.

START Take bus 1, 6, 14, 17, 22, 23, 36, 37, or 71 to Piazza del Duomo.

1 ★★ kids **Il Duomo (Cattedrale di Santa Maria del Fiore).** The world's largest cathedral in its day, Florence's Duomo is still the second longest church in Italy (behind St Peter's Basilica in the Vatican). From 1294 to 1436, builders labored and taxpayers paid for the work, but the flamboyant neo-Gothic structure wasn't complete until the 19th century. The facade is a confection of marble stripes—green, white, and pink—that's either garish or gorgeous, depending on your opinion. In more subdued patterns, the candy-stripe effect of the colored marble continues along the sides and back of the church. But it's the dome (**2**) that Brunelleschi imposed over the church that is the Duomo's singular masterpiece. Walking inside the cathedral, you may be struck by how barren it looks. The only major works of art in here are the grand-scale but otherwise unremarkable frescoes in the dome by Giorgio

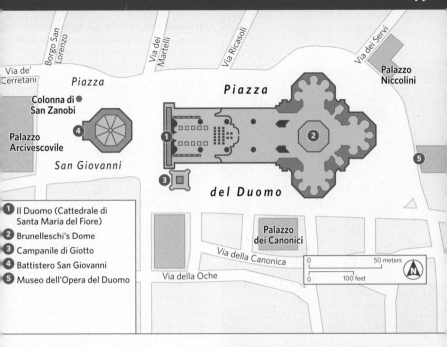

1 Il Duomo (Cattedrale di Santa Maria del Fiore)
2 Brunelleschi's Dome
3 Campanile di Giotto
4 Battistero San Giovanni
5 Museo dell'Opera del Duomo

Vasari and Federico Zuccari. ⏱ 20 min. ☎ 055-2302885. Free admission. Mon–Wed, Fri 10am–5pm; Thurs 10am–3:30pm; Sat 10am–4:45pm; Sun 1:30–4:30pm.

2 ★★★ kids **Brunelleschi's Dome.** At 105m (351 ft.), Filippo Brunelleschi's iconic dome (1420–36) is one of the most magnificent examples in the world of Renaissance architecture, and climbing it is one of the great joys of visiting Florence. Entrance is along the north outside wall of the Duomo (to the left and back, if you're looking at the facade). There are 463 steps in all—most of which are spiraling, or slanted, or steep, and without handrails—and the passageways are narrow, especially near the top, where traffic going up and down must pass each other in a single, tight corridor. At the halfway point, you emerge into a bird's-eye view (through a high Plexiglas barrier) over the unfinished interior of the church. The rest of the way up, you'll experience Brunelleschi's inventive double-shell design firsthand, as you actually climb between the two shells, with the convex wall of the interior "dome" on your right and the concave wall of the outer dome on your left. (There's no clear right of way in the dome section of the ascent and descent, and

> When Michelangelo first saw Ghiberti's bronze baptistery door panels he supposedly exclaimed, "Oh, door worthy of heaven!"

> *Vertigo-sufferers may not appreciate the view to Giotto's campanile from the dome.*

del Duomo (Porta della Mandorla, north side of the church). www.operaduomo.firenze.it. Admission 6€. Sun–Fri 8:30am–7pm; Sat 8:30am–5:40pm; entrance allowed until 40 min. before closing.

③ ★★★ kids **Campanile di Giotto.** On designs by early Renaissance master Giotto, the first stone of this bell tower was laid in 1334. Giotto died in 1337, and construction labored on for another 20 years (halting in 1348 during the devastating Black Death) under architects Andrea Pisano and Francesco Talenti, who completed the tower in 1359 with only one departure from Giotto's original design: They left off his spire, which would have made the tower's total height 122m (400 ft.)—taller, even, than the yet-to-be-dreamed-up dome of Brunelleschi. I recommend climbing both the dome of the Duomo and the bell tower, but if you only have time for one, do the bell tower. For one, it's less crowded and less claustrophobic than the dome ascent, with more open areas where you can rest (or, ahem, appreciate the views from various heights while you also catch your breath). The bell tower is also a slightly easier climb, with 414 steps to the dome's 463, and a height of 81m (269 ft.) to the dome's 105m (351 ft.). But what makes the campanile so thrilling is the dazzling perspective on Brunelleschi's dome. Even the glimpes of the dome that you catch through the campanile's quadrifoliate windows as you trudge up the stairs are postcard-worthy. If you're here when the tower's five bells chime—their Italian names translate to Big, Tipsy, Finished, Priestling, and Shrieker—it's even more gleeful. Throughout the day, the chimes go off every 15 minutes, starting on the hour. On Fridays and Saturdays from June to October, you can even go up at night and see the tops of Florence's most formidable monuments dramatically floodlit. ⏱ 30 min. Piazza del

you can get stuck in a hunched over position for several minutes waiting for the path to clear: Of course, that's part of the adventure, but serious claustrophobes be warned.) For your exertion, you're rewarded with a sublime open-air view at the top. The panorama takes in not only every major monument of Florence but also the gently rolling hills that ring the city, each with its own fairy-tale skyline bathed in that strangely solid Tuscan light. The only thing that's missing from this view is the dome itself: looking down on it from this perch is not nearly as dramatic as looking across at the dome from a similar height, but for that, there's the campanile (**③**). On your way back down through the dome, there's a room that displays some of the original tools that were used for lifting materials up to this construction site in the sky. Note that there can be a wait of up to an hour to get into the dome in high season; come early in the morning or an hour before closing (when the light is the best anyway) to avoid the worst crowds. ⏱ 30 min., without a wait. Piazza

Rest Break

The Opera del Duomo opened the **Centro Arte e Cultura,** Piazza San Giovanni 7 (☎ 055-282226), in 2008. It caters mostly to groups, but individuals can also book guided tours to the Duomo and related monuments here. Of particular interest to the visitor, however, are the state-of-the-art restrooms: Pay an .80€ fee and you've got a guaranteed immaculate toilet—not always easy to find in Italy.

> The cavernous interior of the Duomo includes side-by-side equestrian frescoes by Paolo Uccello and Andrea del Castagno.

Duomo (at the northern end of Via dei Calzaiuoli). ☎ 055-2302885. Admission 6€. Summer nighttime visits are 7€ and include admission to the baptistery. Daily 8:30am–7:30pm; June–Oct Fri and Sat 7pm–11pm. Last admission 40 min. before closing.

④ ★★★ Battistero San Giovanni. This 11th- and 12th-century octagonal baptistery, named after St. John the Baptist, is visited mainly for its gilded bronze doors. The doors here are copies; the originals are in the Duomo museum (**⑤**). The most magnificent are Lorenzo Ghiberti's 1425 east doors, illustrating scenes from the Old Testament. The typically critical Michelangelo hailed these doors as "The Gates of Paradise." It's a wonder more visitors don't go inside the baptistery, as the monumental 13th-century mosaics covering the dome are well worth the small entrance fee. ⏱ 15 min. Piazza San Giovanni (off Piazza del Duomo). ☎ 055-2302885. Admission 3€. Mon–Sat noon–7pm; Sun 8:30am–2pm. Last admission 30 min. before closing.

⑤ ★★ Museo dell'Opera del Duomo. The "loot" ripped from the Duomo, the baptistery, and Giotto's campanile ended up at this intimate museum behind the cathedral. Ghiberti's *Gates of Paradise* from the baptistery are on display in the courtyard. Upstairs, don't miss the delightful marble

reliefs from the *cantoria* by Luca della Robbia: Cherubs clash cymbals with joyful abandon and belt ecclesiastical music karaoke-style. An unfinished *Pietà* by Michelangelo, originally intended for the artist's tomb, is on the mezzanine. Throughout the museum are interesting models and illustrations of the cathedral's long and complex evolution. ⏱ 1 hr. Piazza del Duomo 9 (at the eastern end of the cathedral). ☎ 055-2302885. Admission 6€. Mon–Sat 9am–7:30pm; Sun 9am–1:30pm. Last admission 40 min. before closing.

A Good Read

The story of how Brunelleschi, a 15th-century clockmaker, won the commission to design the dome and how he went about engineering the unprecedented feat is one of the great tales of Renaissance ingenuity. Pick up a copy of Ross King's *Brunelleschi's Dome* (Penguin, 2001) before you visit; it's a riveting and short read that explains all the ingenious methods and custom-made machinery that went into erecting the dome (as well as the juicy politics behind it) and describes, in wonderful detail, daily life in Renaissance Florence.

The Centro Storico

In Florence's historic core—a flat, compact area known as the *centro storico*—you can wander stone streets that remain essentially the same as they were when Michelangelo, Leonardo da Vinci, and Galileo trod these paths. Mornings are the best, most authentic time to stroll the *centro storico*, especially in summer (when it can get very crowded and uncomfortable later in the day). To fully visit all the attractions below would take 2 days—even 3 if you tend to linger over great art.

> The facade of Santa Croce was a 19th-century addition to the Franciscans' Florence headquarters.

START Take bus B to Ponte Vecchio.

1 ★★ **Ponte Vecchio.** Built in 1354, the Ponte Vecchio's medieval character endures, despite the modern commerce of astronomically priced jewelry it supports. Italy's greatest goldsmith, Benvenuto Cellini (1500–1571) is memorialized in a statue at the midpoint of the bridge—he was one of many jewelers who replaced the medieval butchers and tanners who originally traded here. Ponte Vecchio means "old bridge," and in fact, it is the only truly old bridge left in Florence. Notice, as you look up and down the Arno from here, that all the other bridges spanning the river are much

more modern: During World War II, every Florentine bridge except the Ponte Vecchio was bombed and destroyed by the Germans during their retreat from the city in 1944. But because of the beauty and history of Ponte Vecchio, the German forces spared it, supposedly on express orders from Hitler himself. ⏱ 15 min. Open 24 hr.

2 ★★ kids **Piazza della Signoria.** Pedestrians can't help but be drawn into this L-shaped square, dominated by the towered and crenellated Palazzo Vecchio (p 170, **4**). The Loggia dei Lanzi showcases much of Florence's best open-air sculpture, including Benvenuto

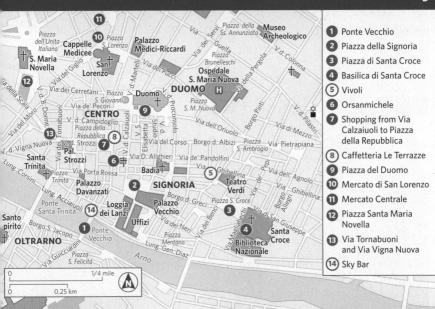

Cellini's masterful *Perseus,* and a copy of Michelangelo's *David.* Although it's certainly a prime tourist destination, Piazza della Signoria remains a place where real Florentines also enjoy spending free time. You'll see them having coffee at Café Rivoire (p 158, ③) on Sundays, or on weekday mornings, sitting and reading the newspaper under a statue on the loggia, or just taking their dogs for "art-historical" walks across the grand expanse of flagstones.

③ ★★ **Piazza di Santa Croce.** This square is the heart of one of the most happening parts of the *centro storico.* The Santa Croce quarter has the city's highest concentration of stylish, high-quality, and (usually) reasonably priced restaurants, many with international flavor (an influence of the large foreign student population in this zone).

④ ★ **Basilica di Santa Croce.** Behind a faux-Gothic facade lies a soaring church interior that became the pantheon of Florence when the tombs of Galileo, Michelangelo, and Machiavelli, among other Renaissance luminaries, were placed here along the nave. Santa Croce also contains a galaxy of great Renaissance sculpture, such as Donatello's famous *Crucifixion.* Check out Filippo

> *Away from the piazzas, you can still discover quiet corners of the* centro storico.

> *Parma ham, dried porcini, and fresh produce—you'll find them all at the Mercato Centrale.*

Brunelleschi's Cappella dei Pazzi, a masterpiece of Renaissance design, and take in Giotto's masterful 1320 frescoes depicting the life of St. Francis. The "tomb" of Dante here is actually a cenotaph; he's buried in Ravenna. ⏱ 30 min. Piazza Santa Croce (entrance along north side of church). Admission 4€. Church Mon–Sat 9:30am–5pm; Sun 1–5:30pm. Museum and cloisters Mon–Sat 9:30am–5:30pm; Sun 1–5:30pm.

⑤ 🍴 ★★★ **Vivoli.** This *gelateria*, a block west of Piazza Santa Croce, serves what many call the world's best ice cream. Choose from fruity flavors like fig and melon, or richer ones like chocolate or zabaglione, which tastes like eggnog. Via Isole delle Stinche 7R (at Via della Vigna Vecchia). ☎ 055-292334. Closed Jan and 3 weeks in Aug. $.

⑥ ★★ **Orsanmichele.** A Gothic grain warehouse turned church turned museum (upstairs), the landmark building contains fine frescoes by Sandro Botticelli as well as a bronze copy of Donatello's marble of *St. George*, the first relief carving to create the illusion of per-spective. In the nearby Church of Orsanmichele you can feast your eyes on such works as Lorenzo Ghiberti's bronze of *St. John the Baptist* (1413–16), the first life-size bronze of the Renaissance, and Donatello's remarkable *St. Mark* in marble (1411–13). ⏱ 45 min. Via Arte della Lana 1 (at Via dei Calzaiuoli). ☎ 055-284944. Free admission. Church hours erratic; call for information. Museum daily 9–11:45am; Sat–Sun 1–1:45pm (but don't count on these hours).

⑦ ★★ **Shopping from Via dei Calzaiuoli to Piazza della Repubblica.** Make no mistake: A huge part of Florence's appeal is its tantalizing boutiques. These pedestrianized streets just south of the Duomo are my favorite place to shop—where you'll find midrange (that is, affordable) Italian chains selling everything from trendy hosiery to fashion knitwear to men's clothing basics. In this vicinity, there are also two department stores (COIN and La Rinascente, p 191) with fun home accessories departments. If you're looking for high-end designer shops, you'll find a few in this area, although most of those big-name boutiques are on Via Tornabuoni and Via Vigna Nuova (⑬).⏱ 1 hr.

⑧ ☕ **Caffetteria Le Terrazze.** Take the elevator to the 5th floor in the La Rinascente department store for coffee and wonderful views of the Florentine skyline. Piazza della Repubblica 1. ☎ 055-219113. $$.

⑨ ★★ **Piazza del Duomo.** Florence's monumental, tourist-mobbed cathedral square is a hub through which all foot and motor traffic passes at least once daily. ⊙ 30 min. See p 178.

⑩ ★ **Mercato di San Lorenzo.** No first trip to Florence is complete without buying something at this open-air market, where vendors hawk colorful leather goods, flashy fashion accessories, and Florentine stationery. There are some good buys here if you weed out the poorly crafted leather items, but be sure to haggle—it's expected! ⊙ 45 min. Piazza San Lorenzo to Via dell'Ariento. Tues–Sat 8am–8pm.

⑪ ★ **Mercato Centrale.** This grand cast-iron and glass structure—built in the late 19th century and inspired by Paris's Les Halles—houses two lofty floors of market stalls, where many Florentines and restaurateurs do their daily grocery shopping. Butchers, fishmongers, deli counters, and bakeries are on the ground floor; the fruit and vegetable stalls are upstairs. For a simple, classic Florentine lunch, have a *bagnato* (like a French dip beef sandwich) at Nerbone, at stand #292. ⊙ 30 min. Entrances at Via dell'Ariento and Piazza del Mercato Centrale. No phone. Free admission. Mon–Fri 7am–2pm.

⑫ ★ **Piazza Santa Maria Novella.** As this guide was being researched, exciting work was well underway to requalify and pedestrianize this lively square behind the church of the same name. The grassy center here was originally laid out in the 16th century to resemble a Roman circus—an annual chariot race, the *Palio dei Cocchi,* took place here until the late 19th century, with the two obelisks marking the turning points of the track. In recent years, Piazza Santa Maria Novella had become a snarl of traffic and haunt of vagrants, but the new project to clean up and pedestrianize the square augurs well for the open space, surrounded by some of the city's finest hotels. ⊙ 15 min. See p 173, ⑫, for details on the church.

⑬ ★ **Via Tornabuoni and Via Vigna Nuova.** If only to gape in awe at the merchandise (and prices!) in the windows, it's worth a stroll down

> *Shopping is a pleasure in fashionable Florence.*

the toniest shopping streets in Tuscany, where every Italian and international designer worth his or her salt has a boutique. Toward the river, where Via Tornabuoni opens up to a wedge-shaped widening, you can't miss the imposing facade of the palazzo that is the world flagship of Salvatore Ferragamo, the famed luxury-goods maker that is headquartered in Florence. In the basement of the 13th-century palace, shoe-lovers should seek out the ★★ **Museo Salvatore Ferragamo,** Palazzo Feroni-Spini, Via Tornabuoni 2 (☎ 055-3360456; free admission; Mon–Fri 9am–1pm, 2–6pm). ⊙ 1 hr.

⑭ ☕ ★★ **SkyBar.** Cap off all your *centro storico* traipsing with a glass of something festive at the rooftop SkyBar. The canopied terrace offers views in every direction from its sleek canvas divans. In the Continentale hotel, Vicolo dell'Oro 6a. ☎ 055-27262. $$.

Oltrarno

Away from the beaten path between Ponte Vecchio and Palazzo Pitti, the "left bank" of Florence casually hides away quiet neighborhood piazzas, stylish restaurants, and, this being Florence, churches with magnificent Renaissance art and architecture. In addition to the sights we mention below, take time to follow your curiosity down side streets—you might just discover a new favorite boutique or wine bar.

> Oltrarno, Florence's "other side of the Arno," is a choice neighborhood for an aperitivo or dinner.

START Take bus D, 11, 36, 37, or 68 across the Arno to Piazza dei Pitti. Walk a few blocks northwest to Piazza Santo Spirito.

1 ★ **Piazza Santo Spirito.** A refuge for foot traffic in Oltrarno, this wide-open square is lined with restaurants, coffee bars, and newsstands. The eponymous **church** here is notable for its glorious Renaissance interior by Brunelleschi (his trademark mathematical proportions and use of gray *pietra serena* abound) as well as its blank facade.

Unfortunately, the center of this piazza has become slightly unsavory at night, so stick to daytime, or the always-busy (and safe) perimeter cafes. ⏱ 20 min. Piazza Santo Spirito. ☎ 055-210030. Free admission to church for 5 min., then donation requested. Daily 8am–noon; Thurs–Tues 4–6pm Bus: D, 11, 36, 37, or 68.

2 ★ **Santa Maria del Carmine.** The main draw at this church, which was rebuilt in a high baroque style after a fire in 1771, is the ★★ **Cappella dei Brancacci,** with its wonderful

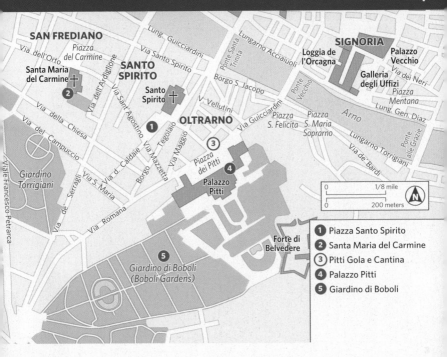

1 Piazza Santo Spirito
2 Santa Maria del Carmine
3 Pitti Gola e Cantina
4 Palazzo Pitti
5 Giardino di Boboli

cycle of early-15th-century frescoes by Masolino and Masaccio (some were finished by Filippino Lippi) depicting events from the life of St. Peter. Look for the groundbreaking realism of certain scenes, such as the cripple in *St. Peter Healing the Sick with His Shadow* (on the left side of the center wall), or the high-keyed shame—and nudity—of Adam and Eve in the *Expulsion from the Garden of Eden* (on the left edge of the chapel's left wall). ⏱ 30 min. Piazza del Carmine. ☎ 055-2768224. Free admission to church; 6€ to view Brancacci chapel. Mon–Sat 10am–5pm; Sun 1–5pm. Bus: D, 11, 36, 37, or 68.

3 🍷 **Pitti Gola e Cantina.** Coping with the masses at Palazzo Pitti is a lot less stressful if you stop at this cozy wine bar first for a light snack and a glass of Chianti. Piazza dei Pitti 16. ☎ 055-212704. $$.

4 ★★ **Palazzo Pitti.** You need only wander around Oltrarno for a few minutes before you're bound to catch sight of the long, imposing facade (in faux "unfinished" brown masonry) of this former residence of the Medici. Nowadays, the enormous building houses several

museums, the most important of which is the Galleria Palatina with its masterpieces from the Renaissance and beyond. ⏱ 1½ hr. See p 168, 1.

5 ★ kids **Giardino di Boboli.** The great landscape artist Tribolo laid out these Renaissance gardens, through which the Medici romped, in the 16th century. Since opening to the public in 1776, Boboli has become the most famous and dazzling garden of Tuscany, filled with splashing fountains and elegant statuary. A fountain depicting an obese Bacchus astride a turtle is a copy of a statue depicting Pietro Barbino, Cosimo I's court jester. Lucky for them, modern Florentines (with ID that proves their residency) enjoy free admission to the gardens and their relaxing tree-lined lanes year-round. ⏱ 1 hr. Piazza dei Pitti (at Via Romana). ☎ 055-2651838. Admission 6€, including entrance to Museo degli Argenti (p 168, 1). June–Aug daily 8:30am–7:45pm; Apr–May and Sept–Oct daily 8:30am–6:30pm; Nov–Feb daily 8:15am–4:45pm; Mar daily 8:15am–5:30pm. Closed the 1st and last Mon of each month. Ticket office closes 1 hr. before gardens. Bus: D, 11, 36, 37, or 68.

CRAZY FOR *CALCIO*

Soccer Is Italy's Ruling Sport BY SYLVIE HOGG

ON A SCALE of things integral to an Italian's life, *calcio* (soccer) falls somewhere between mamma and pasta. The amount of press and media coverage dedicated to pre- and post-game commentary and analysis is mind-boggling. Often before they can walk or talk, Italians already have a squadra del cuore (favorite team) that will bring them ecstasy or, more often, a profound sense of betrayal for a lifetime. To understand modern Italy, forget monuments and museums: You've got to go to the stadium.

Italian Soccer Leagues

The "big league" of Italian soccer is Serie A, in which 20 teams compete (the lineup changes yearly; the 4 lowest ranked teams are downgraded to the mortifying Serie B, whereas the 4 best performing teams in Serie B get moved up into the A ranks). The season of 38 games (each team plays another twice: once at home, once away) runs from September to May. Teams get 3 points for a win, 1 for a tie, and whoever has the most points by the end of the season wins the league title (*scudetto*).

Every other summer, the Italian national team competes in either the World Cup or the European Cup, and the summers when no soccer is on are a time of national unease. Certainly, Italians were thrilled when team Italia brought home the World Cup trophy in 2006, but it was nothing compared to the soul-lifting sense of triumph that comes from your own club, such as A.S. Roma or A.C. Milan, winning the *scudetto*.

Calcio Lingo for Beginners

PALLA, PALLONE ball
ATTACCANTE striker/forward
CENTROCAMPISTA midfielder
DIFENSORE defender/fullback
PORTIERE goalkeeper (literally, doorman)
ARBITRO referee, though *imbecille* and other derogatory

terms are also commonly used
FALLO foul
PARTITA game/match
TIFOSO fan
GOOOOOOOOOOO-OOOOOOOOOL the happiest or saddest word in the Italian language, depending on who scored.

Star Players

ROBERTO BAGGIO One of the top Italian players of the century, the popular Il Divin Codino (the divine ponytail) played for the national team and for clubs all over Italy.

PAOLO MALDINI The legendary defender played his entire career for A.C. Milan (1984–2009) and was part of the national team from 1988 to 2002.

FRANCESCO TOTTI The captain of A.S. Roma since 1997 and a national Italian team member since 1998. He is the top scorer in Roma club history.

DIEGO MARADONA The scrappy Argentine forward played for Napoli (and led them to two league championships). A phenom on the field, he is adored by all Italian soccer fans.

GABRIEL BATISTUTA The dashing Argentine striker scored 200 goals in 12 years of Italian league play (1991–2003), mostly for Fiorentina.

Where to Catch a Game

AT THE STADIUM Buy tickets at the stadium (major cities usually have at least one team) a few hours before game time or ask at your hotel. Pick one team to root for and get your colors right. Have a nearby fan teach you some chants. Seating is a free-for-all—the spot printed on your ticket is probably already taken, so just find a seat nearby. The clock doesn't stop, and there are no Jumbotron replays: Plan on staying put in your seat, eyes glued to the field, except at halftime.

AT A BAR Your best bet for watching a match on TV is at the local bar. Arrive early if you want a seat.

Florence Shopping Best Bets

Best Apothecary-Style Perfumery
Antica Farmacia Santa Maria Novella, Via della Scala 16N (p 191)

Best Art Books
Franco Maria Ricci, Via delle Belle Donne 41R (p 191)

Best Modern Art Gallery
Galleria Masini, Piazza Goldoni 6R (p 191)

Best Aspirational Lifestyle Store
Lungarno Details, Vicolo dell'Oro/Lungarno Acciaiuoli (p 195)

Best Clothing for Men
Giorgio Armani, Via Tornabuoni 48 (p 194)

Best Department Store
La Rinascente, Piazza della Repubblica 1 (p 194)

Best Florentine Paper Goods
Pineider, Piazza della Signoria (p 196)

Best Food Store
Pegna, Via dello Studio 8 (p 195)

Best Home Accessories
Bartolini, Via dei Servi 30R (p 195)

Best Local Market
Mercato di San Lorenzo, Piazza San Lorenzo (p 196)

Best Shoes for Men and Women
Bologna, Piazza San Giovanni 13-15 (p 196)

Best Shopping Street for a Weak Economy
Via dei Calzaiuoli (p 195)

Best Unmistakably Florentine Designer
Emilio Pucci, Via Tornabuoni 20R (p 194)

> *The shop Bologna is the best place in Florence to buy leather shoes.*

Florence Shopping A to Z

Art

★★★ **Galleria Masini** SANTA TRINITÀ
Florence's oldest gallery is the best, representing more than 500 of the country's most avant-garde painters. **Piazza Goldoni 6R.**
☎ 055-294000. www.masiniart.com. AE, DC, MC, V. Bus: A, B, 14, or 23.

Beauty Products

★ **Antica Farmacia del Cinghiale** SIGNORIA
For 3 centuries, this apothecary has been dispensing herbal teas, fragrances, and potpourris. Its skin care products were used by the mistresses of the Medici. **Piazza del Mercato Nuovo 4–5R.** ☎ 055-282128. AE, MC, V. Bus: A, B, 23, or 71.

★★ **Antica Farmacia Santa Maria Novella**
SANTA MARIA NOVELLA   Herbal secrets known to the Medici are still sold here in a wonderfully antique atmosphere—potpourris, perfumes, scented soaps, and more. **Via della Scala 16N.** www.smnovella.it . AE, MC, V. Bus: A, 6, 9, 36, 37, or 68.

> *Handmade stationery makes a great Florentine gift.*

Books

★ **Franco Maria Ricci** SANTA MARIA NOVELLA
Florence's best art bookshop also sells homemade stationery and arts and crafts. **Via delle Belle Donne 41R.** ☎ 055-283312. AE, DC, MC, V. Bus: A, 6, 9, 11, 36, 37, or 68.

★ **Paperback Exchange** DUOMO
New and used titles, all in English. **Via dell'Oche 4R.** ☎ 055-293460. www.papex.it. AE, DC, MC, V. Bus: A or C.

Ceramics & Pottery

★★ **Richard Ginori** SESTO FIORENTINO
Exquisite porcelain and refined bone china are sold in a western suburb. Good buys in Murano glass. **Via Giulio Cesare 21, Sesto Fiorentino.**
☎ 055-420491. www.richardginori1735.com. AE, DC, MC, V.

Department Stores

★ **COIN** SIGNORIA
This department store in a 16th-century palazzo sells everything from affordable clothing for men and women, to Italian-designed kitchenware, to MAC cosmetics. **Via dei Calzaiuoli 56A.** ☎ 055-280531. www.coin.it. AE, MC, V. Bus: A, B, 23, or 71.

Florence Shopping

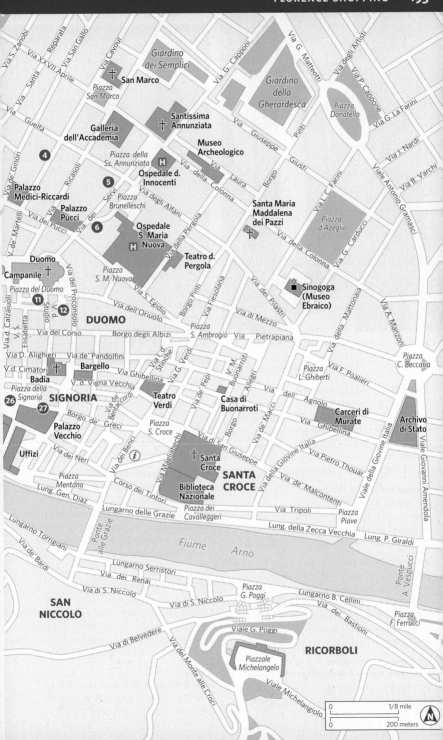

> Be sure to haggle for your leather goods at the Mercato di San Lorenzo.

VAT Refund

Visitors from non-European Union countries who spend 155€ or more at any one shop are entitled to a value-added tax (VAT) refund that can save them 11% to 13%. To get a refund, pick up a tax-free form from the retailer. There's a Forex office on Piazza San Giovanni where you can get most of your refund immediately (you'll need your passport and the tax-free form). Otherwise, present your unused purchases for inspection at the airport Customs office (*dogana*) or your point of departure. The inspector will stamp your form, enabling you to pick up a cash refund (minus a commission) there. There's often a long line for the cash refund, however, which can be a problem if you're on your way to a flight. To avoid this, you can also drop the postage-paid, preaddressed envelope and **customs-stamped** form in the mail and you'll receive the VAT refund by bank check or credit/debit card refund, though it may take several months.

★★ La Rinascente REPUBBLICA
This six-story emporium sells top Italian designers at affordable prices. The home section on the top floor is small but packed with Italian bed and bath linens, kitchenware, and picture frames. Piazza della Repubblica 1. ☎ 055-219113. AE, DC, MC, V. Bus: 22, 36, or 37.

Fashion for Men & Women

★★ Aspesi SANTA TRINITÀ
Understated, wearable clothing for the chic women of Florence. Via Porta Rossa 81–83R. ☎ 055-287987. AE, DC, MC, V. Bus: 22, 36, or 37.

★★ Emilio Pucci SANTA TRINITÀ
Even Marilyn Monroe left a request to be buried in her favorite Pucci dress. Today the bright, busy patterns of this local fashion house are in vogue again. Via Tornabuoni 20R. ☎ 055-2658082. www.pucci.com. AE, DC, MC, V. Bus: B, 6, 11, or 36.

★★★ Giorgio Armani SANTA TRINITÀ
Expensive, tailored men's wear and accessories that are always in fashion. Via Tornabuoni 48. ☎ 055-2658121. www.giorgioarmani.com. AE, DC, MC, V. Bus: B, 6, 11, or 36.

★★ Gucci SANTA TRINITÀ
The legendary designer label began in Florence in 1904 and is still turning out highly coveted handbags, shoes, and ready-to-wear for men and women. Via Tornabuoni 73R. ☎ 055-264011. www.gucci.com. AE, DC, MC, V. Bus: B, 6, 11, or 36.

★ Italian Appeal OLTRARNO
Look for the Helvetica lettering that looks uncannily similar to that of American Apparel: This is a great place for fashion-forward women to find inexpensive and trendy knitwear, skirts, trousers, and accessories. Via Guicciardini. No phone. AE, MC, DC, V. Bus: D, 11, 36, or 37.

Gourmet Food

★ I Sapori del Chianti DUOMO
If you're not visiting the Chianti region on this trip (or you were there and didn't get a chance to stock up on its savory treats), this shop has local oils, wines, salami, and condiments of all kinds. Via dei Servi 10. ☎ 055-2382071. AE, MC, DC, V. Bus: 1, 7, 25, or 33.

★ La Bottega dell'Olio PONTE VECCHIO
The finest olive oils from all of Italy, plus balsamic vinegars, oil-cured vegetables

> *Honey flavored with chestnuts is a Tuscan delicacy.*

and pâtés. Olive oil–based soaps, olive oil dispensers and cruets, and olive-wood kitchen items round out the *oliva-mania*. Piazza del Limbo 2R. ☎ 055-27268000. AE, DC, MC, V. Bus: D, 11, 36, 37, or 68.

★★ Pegna DUOMO
No cutesy gourmet shop trappings here—it's more like an upscale convenience store, the best one-stop shop in the *centro* for gourmet pâtés, jams, olive oil, wine, and charcuterie. Via dello Studio 8. ☎ 055-282701. www.pegna.it. AE, DC, MC, V. Bus: 1, 7, 25, or 33.

Housewares
★★ Bartolini DUOMO
This delightful maze of a place sells classic and modern china, stemware, cutlery, and kitchen gadgets for amateurs and professionals alike. An institution for Florentine wedding registries. Via dei Servi 30R. ☎ 055-211895. AE, DC, MC, V. Bus: 1, 7, 25, or 33.

★ Lungarno Details PONTE VECCHIO
Chic bath emulsions and other stylish interior accents found in the Lungarno Hotels group guest rooms are sold in this bright showroom. Vicolo dell'Oro/Lungarno Acciaiuoli. ☎ 055-27268000. AE, DC, MC, V. Bus: D, 11, 36, 37, or 68.

Leather
★ Beltrami SANTA TRINITÀ
This world-famous, Florence-based leather-maker offers polished and timeless footwear, handbags, belts, briefcases, and luggage. Via della Vigna Nuova 70R. ☎ 055-2877779. AE, DC, MC, V. Bus: A.

> *Florence's flagship department stores, COIN and La Rinascente, are great places to shop for housewares and linens.*

★★ Bojola REPUBBLICA/SAN LORENZO
A leading retailer of Florentine leather goods. The store pioneered the '60s trend of combining leather and cotton fabric. Via dei Rondinelli 25R. ☎ 055-211155. www.bojola.it. AE, DC, MC, V. Bus: A, 6, 11, 12, 36, 37, or 68.

Shopping Tip

Florence is known for its showrooms of famous designers and also for its artisan workshops, turning out jewelry and leather merchandise of the highest quality. The most fashionable shops—and the most expensive—are clustered along **Via Tornabuoni** in the center of town. **Via della Vigna Nuova** is the other fashionable shopping street. For the rest of us, **Via dei Calzaiuoli** and its side streets are even more fun, with outlets of all the Italian fashion boutiques that carry more affordable, everyday buys.

> *Shoes and bags are the stars at Salvatore Ferragamo's flagship store on Via Tornabuoni.*

★ Il Bisonte SANTA TRINITÀ

Soft leather goods in the most supple and luxurious of textures. Slouchy totes and duffles look safari-ready. **Via del Parione 31R.** ☎ 055-215722. AE, DC, MC, V. Bus: A.

Markets

★ Mercato Centrale SAN LORENZO

Florence's grand covered food market is the place to stock up on groceries if you've rented an apartment, or if you just want to pick up picnic fixings and people-watch. **Piazza del Mercato Centrale. Bus: 1, 6, 7, 11, 33, 67, or 68.**

★★ Mercato di San Lorenzo SAN LORENZO

At the most bustling market in Tuscany, vendors hawk quality leather goods, stationery, even gourmet food items. Haggling is the norm, and lots of fun. **Piazza San Lorenzo. Bus: 1, 6, 7, 11, 33, 67, or 68.**

Paper & Stationery

★★ Il Papiro DUOMO

Exquisite paper products, photo frames, and more. **Via Cavour 55R.** ☎ 055-6499151. www.ilpapirofirenze.it. AE, DC, MC, V. Bus: 1, 7, 25, or 33.

★★★ Pineider SIGNORIA

Since 1774, customers from Napoléon to Elizabeth Taylor have ordered personal stationery, greeting cards, and handcrafted diaries here. **Piazza della Signoria.** ☎ 055-284655. www.marcus.com. AE, DC, MC, V. Bus: B or D.

Prints & Engravings

★ Giovanni Baccani SANTA TRINITÀ

Collectors have been flocking to "The Blue Shop" since 1903 for exquisite prints, engravings of old Florentine scenes, triptychs, and handmade frames and boxes. **Via della Vigna Nuova 75F.** ☎ 055-214467. AE, DC, MC, V. Bus: A.

Shoes

★★ Bologna DUOMO

The window displays at this well-known shop are tough to resist, with of-the-moment boots, sneakers, and everything in between, for trendy men and women. **Piazza San Giovanni 13–15.** ☎ 055-290545. www.calzoleriabologna.com. AE, DC, MC, V. Bus: 22, 36, or 37.

★★ Calvani REPUBBLICA

The hottest contemporary Italian and European designers are represented here, though you could cut the snobbery of the sales staff with a knife. **Via degli Speziali 7R.** ☎ 055-2654043. AE, DC, MC, V. Bus: 22, 36, or 37.

★★ Salvatore Ferragamo SANTA TRINITÀ

Shoes are the big thing at this Florence-based maison, with some world-class apparel and accessories for men and women. **Via Tornabuoni 14R.** ☎ 055-292123. www.salvatoreferragamo.it. AE, DC, MC, V. Bus: B, 6, 11, 32, or 36.

Florence Restaurant Best Bets

Best Wine Bar
Fuori Porta $$ Via del Monte alle Croci 10R
(p 201)

Most Quintessential Florentine Trattoria
Sabatini $$ Via de' Panzani 9A (p 203)

Best Family Favorite
Sostanza $ Via del Porcellana 25R (p 203)

Most Stylish Newcomer
Sant'Agostino 23 $$ Via Sant'Agostino 23R
(p 203)

Best Panini
Antico Noe $ Volta di San Piero 6R (p 203)

Best Casual Pasta & Pizza
Borgo Antico $$ Piazza Santo Spirito 6R (p 200)

Best Pasta-Sampling Menu
Acqua al Due $$ Via della Vigna Vecchia 40R
(p 200)

Best Roast Meats
Il Latini $$ Via dei Palchetti 6R (p 201)

Best High-Concept *Cucina Fiorentina*
Cibrèo $$$$ Via Verrocchio 8R (p 200)

Best Countryside Dining
Da Delfina $$ Via della Chiesa, Artimino
(p 201)

Best Farmhouse Dining
Trattoria le Cave di Maiano $$ Via della Cave
16, Fiesole (p 203)

Most Authentic Florentine Cuisine
Ganino $ Piazza dei Cimatori 4R (p 201)

Best Antipasti
Il Pennello $ Via Dante Alighieri 4R (p 201)

Best Ice Cream
Vivoli $ Via Isole delle Stinche 7R (p 203)

> Stop at the wine bar Fuori Porta during an evening visit to Piazzale Michelangelo.

Florence Restaurants

Piazzalle di
Porta at Prato

**SAN
JACOPINO**

Via Montebello

Via Soferino

Via della Scala

Via B. Rucellai

Il Prato

Via d. Orti

Via Jacopo
da Diacceto

Via Luigi Alamanni

**Teatro
Comunale**

Via Palestro

Via Curtatone

Palacongressi

Via Guelfa

Palaffari

**Stazione
Centrale
S. Maria
Novella**

Piazza
Adua

Via Faenza

Via Fiume

Via Panicale

Via Nazionale

Via

Piazza
della Stazione

Piazza
dell'Unità
Italiana

Via S. Antonino

**Cappelle
Medicee**

Piazza del
Mercato
Centrale

Piazza S.
Lorenzo

**San
Lorenzo**

(i)
**S. Maria
Novella** ✝

Via della Scala

Via Palazzuolo

Piazza
S. Maria
Novella

Via de Panzani

Via del Giglio

Via dei Cerretani

Piazza

S. Giovanni

Ognissanti ✝

Via delle B. Donne

Via de' Pecori

CENTRO

V. d. Campidoglio

Piazza

Via Roma

Lung. Santa Rosa

Ponte A. Vespucci

Lungarno Amerigo Vespucci

Piazza
d'Ognissanti

Borgo Ognissanti

Piazza

Via de' Fossi

Via del Moro

Via del Tornabuoni

Via d. Strozzi

Piazza
della
Repubblica

**Palazzo
Strozzi**

**Orsan-
michele** ✝

Porta
S. Frediano

Fiume

Lungarno

Piazza
di Cestello

Soderini

Ponte alla Carraia

Via della Vigna Nuova

V. d. Parione

Goldoni

**Palazzo
Corsini**

**Santa
Trinita** ✝

Lung. Corsini

Piazza
Trinita

Via Porta Rossa

Borgo Ss. Apostoli

**Palazzo
Davanzati**

V. Calimala

**Loggia
dei Lanzi**

Arno

SAN FREDIANO

Piazza
del Carmine

Lungarno Guicciardini

Via Santo Spirito

Via dei Serragli

Via dell'Ardiglione

**SANTO
SPIRITO**

**Santa Maria
del Carmine** ✝

Via Sant'Agostino

**Santo
Spirito** ✝

Piazza
S. Spirito

Via Mazzetta

Borgo Tegolaio

Lung. Acciaiuoli

Ponte S. Trinita

Borgo S. Jacopo

Ponte Vecchio

V. Vellutini

OLTRARNO

Via Guicciardini

Piazza
S. Felicita

Piazza
S. Maria
Soprarno

Via della Chiesa

Via del Campuccio

Via Romana

Borgo

Via Maggio

⑩ Piazza
dei Pitti

**Palazzo
Pitti**

**Forte di
Belvedere**

Giardino di Boboli
(Boboli Garden)

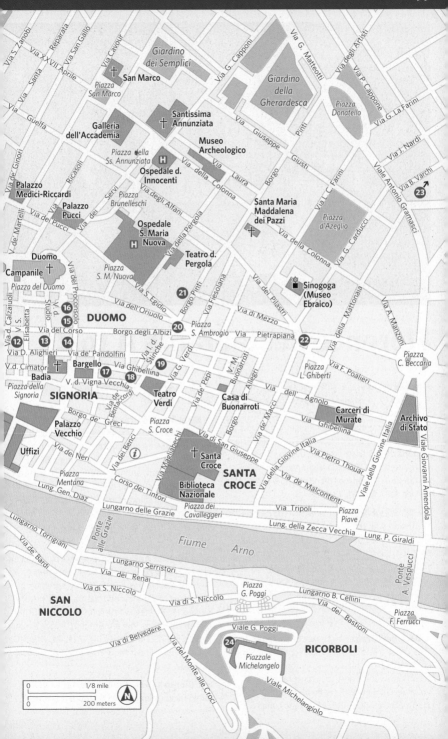

Florence Restaurants A to Z

★ **Acqua al Due** SIGNORIA *TUSCAN*
Assaggini (2–4 small tastings) within each menu category are the big deal here, and despite all the hype this place gets, the food's still quite good and prices fair. Don't miss the signature pasta sampler, but also try the steak with blueberry. **Via della Vigna Vecchia 40R.** ☎ 055-284170. Entrees 8€–20€. AE, DC, MC, V. Dinner daily. Bus: 14, 23, or 71.

★★ kids **Borgo Antico** OLTRARNO *TUSCAN/PIZZA*
With sidewalk tables on a pedestrianized square, this local favorite is a hip and casual spot for reliable Tuscan standards, monster salads (the *insalatone* of shrimp, avocado, and mozzarella is the best), and especially scrumptious pizzas. **Piazza Santo Spirito 6R.** ☎ 055-210437. Entrees 8.50€–18€. AE, DC, MC, V. Lunch and dinner Mon–Sat. Bus: D, 6, 11, 36, 37, or 68.

★ **Buca dell'Orafo** PONTE VECCHIO *FLORENTINE*
This cellar trattoria once housed a Renaissance goldsmith. Now, locals and visitors here share communal tables and Tuscan peasant food. **Volta dei Girolami 28R (at Ponte Vecchio).** ☎ 055-213619. Entrees 10€–18€. AE, MC, V. Lunch &

dinner Tues–Sat. Closed Aug and 2 weeks in Dec. Bus: 23 or 71.

★ **Buca Mario** SANTA MARIA NOVELLA *FLORENTINE/TUSCAN* It may be filled with more tourists than locals, but this ristorante has wonderful old-school appeal. Bring a big appetite for meat, and the white-shirted veteran waiters will bring you one of the best *bistecche alla fiorentina* (Florentine T-bone steak) in the city. **Piazza Ottaviani 16R.** ☎ 055-214179. Entrees 10€–18€; 28€ for steak. Dinner daily; lunch Sat–Sun. AE, MC, V. Bus: 6, 11, 36, 37, or 68.

★ **Cantinetta Antinori** SANTA MARIA NOVELLA *FLORENTINE/TUSCAN* For 600 years, the Antinori family has dazzled with ingredients and wines from their own farms and vineyards, served in the elegant surroundings of a 15th-century palazzo. **Palazzo Antinori, Piazza Antinori 3.** ☎ 055-292234. Entrees 14€–22€. AE, DC, MC, V. Lunch and dinner Mon–Fri. Closed Aug. Bus: 6, 11, 36, 37, or 68.

★★ **Cibrèo** SANTA CROCE *MEDITERRANEAN*
Fabio Picchi's innovative restaurant is one of Florence's finest, but be warned: There's no

> ### Dining Tip
> Reservations are recommended at all Florence restaurants except the most casual sandwich or pizza places.

pasta here. Simple soups share the menu with such ventures as fricasseed cockscombs and innards in an egg. Nearby Cibreino is less costly, but the "intellectual" clientele factor is just as high. Via Verrocchio 8R. ☎ 055-2341100. Entrees 20€–36€. AE, DC, MC, V. Lunch and dinner Tues–Sat. Closed late July to early Sept. Bus: B or 14.

★★ **Da Delfina** ARTIMINO *TUSCAN*
In a medieval walled village 15 minutes (9km/5½ miles) from Florence, Da Delfina draws city folk to feast on dishes made with produce from nearby fields. Via della Chiesa, Artimino (near Carmignano). ☎ 055-8718119. Entrees 13€–16€. No credit cards. Lunch Tues–Sun; dinner Tues–Sat. From Santa Maria Novella, take the Signa train, then a cab for 5 min.

★★ **Fuori Porta** RECORBOLI *TUSCAN*
Near the outskirts of the center on the south side of the Arno, one of the city's best *enoteche* (wine taverns) offers 650 labels. Some 50 are sold by the glass, with a limited food menu. Via del Monte alle Croci 10R. ☎ 055-2342483. Small plates 6.50€–10€. AE, MC, V. Lunch and dinner daily. Closed Aug 10–20. Bus: 13.

★ **Ganino** DUOMO *FLORENTINE*
Savvy foodies patronize this intimate tavern halfway between the Duomo and the American Express office. The chefs deliver reliably praise-worthy victuals, from succulent pastas to Tuscan white beans and juicy T-bones. Piazza dei Cimatori 4R. ☎ 055-214125. Entrees 8€–20€. AE, DC. Lunch and dinner Mon–Sat. Bus: 14, 23, or 71.

★★ kids **Il Latini** SANTA TRINITÀ *FLORENTINE* At this local dive festooned with prosciutto thighs, diners feast at communal tables on dishes such as *arrosto misto*—slabs of assorted meats fresh off the grill. It's touristy, but lots of fun nevertheless. Via dei Palchetti 6R. ☎ 055-210916. Fixed price 35€. AE, DC, MC, V. Lunch and dinner Tues–Sun. Closed 2 weeks in Aug. Bus: C, 6, 11, 36, 37, or 68.

★ **Il Pennello** DUOMO *FLORENTINE/ITALIAN*
Florence's oldest trattoria is still going strong,

> *OPPOSITE PAGE Intimate dining at La Giostra. THIS PAGE, TOP TO BOTTOM Gelato at Vivoli; Acqua al Due; the kitchen at Il Latini.*

> The well-stocked bar at Cibrèo.

with hot young Tuscan chefs and a vast antipasti table. Via Dante Alighieri 4R. ☎ 055-294848. Entrees 8.50€–16€. AE, DC, MC, V. Lunch and dinner Tues–Sat. Closed 3 weeks in Aug. Bus: 14, 22, or 23.

★ **La Giostra** DUOMO/SANTA CROCE *TUSCAN* A Hapsburg prince with Medici blood welcomes guests to this adventurous restaurant, with a number of dishes based on Hapsburg family recipes—some more successful than others. Borgo Pinti 12R. ☎ 055-241341. Entrees 12€–24€. AE, DC, MC, V. Lunch and dinner daily. Bus: A, B, C, 14, 23, 71 or 80.

★ **Le Mossacce** DUOMO *TUSCAN/FLORENTINE* Midway between the Duomo and the Bargello, this classic *osteria* from 1942 hires trustworthy waiters eager to recommend Florence's best cannelloni or chestnut flour cake. Via del Proconsolo 55R. ☎ 055-294361. Main courses 5€–10€. AE, DC, MC, V. Lunch and dinner Mon–Fri. Closed Aug. Bus: 14.

★ **Nerbone** SAN LORENZO *PANINI/TUSCAN* This 1872 five-table dive has the best *bagnato* (boiled beef sandwich dipped in meat juices) in town. Mercato Centrale (Via dell'Ariento entrance, stand #292). ☎ 055-219949. Entrees 4€–8€. No credit cards. Lunch Mon–Sat. Closed 2 weeks in Aug. Bus: 12, 25, 31, or 32.

★ **Osteria del Caffè Italiano** SANTA CROCE *WINE BAR/TUSCAN* Umberto Montano's wine bar, in a 13th-century palazzo, has the city's best Tuscan *salumi* (cured meats) and fine wines by the glass. Via Isole delle Stinche 11–13R. ☎ 055-289368. Entrees 11€–25€. MC, V. Lunch and dinner Tues–Sun. Bus: A or 14.

★ **Paoli** DUOMO *TUSCAN/ITALIAN* Between the Duomo and Piazza della Signoria, this 1824 restaurant in 13th-century digs is touristy, but the Italian cuisine is superb. Via dei Tavolini 12R. ☎ 055-216215. Entrees 11€–19€. AE, DC, MC, V. Lunch and dinner Wed–Mon. Closed 3 weeks in Aug. Bus: A.

★★ **Pitti Gola e Cantina** OLTRARNO *WINE BAR/ TUSCAN* The perfect spot to rest your feet and refuel after a visit to the Palazzo Pitti, this friendly place with library-like shelves of interesting wines has cheese plates, tasty pastas, and prized Tuscan meats. Piazza dei Pitti 16. ☎ 055-212704. Entrees 8.50€–18€. AE, DC, MC, V. Breakfast, lunch and dinner Tues–Sun. Bus: D.

★ **Sabatini** SANTA MARIA NOVELLA
FLORENTINE/INTERNATIONAL Tripe and
beefsteak fans flock to this quintessential
Florentine trattoria. Via de' Panzani 9A. ☎ 055-
211559. Entrees 12€–30€. AE, DC, MC, V. Lunch
and dinner Tues–Sun. Bus: 1, 6, 14, 17, or 22.

★★ **Sant'Agostino 23** OLTRARNO *TUSCAN/
CREATIVE* A dark, brasserie-style dining room
sets the stylish mood for this hot spot (there
are a few outside tables, too). The Parisian
influence extends to the menu design, meaning
you can nosh on salads, or hearty meat dishes,
or antipasti, without feeling the linear rigor of
a typical Italian menu. Via Sant'Agostino 23R.
☎ 055-210208. Entrees 8€–18€. AE, DC, MC, V.
Lunch and dinner daily. Bus: D.

★ **Sostanza** SANTA MARIA NOVELLA
FLORENTINE Known as *il troia* (the trough), this
trattoria serves huge portions of peasant food
at crowded communal tables. Via del Porcellana
25R. ☎ 055-212691. Entrees 8€–18€. No credit
cards. Lunch and dinner Mon–Fri. Closed Aug and
2 weeks at Christmas. Bus: 12.

★ **Trattoria le Cave di Maiano** FIESOLE *TUSCAN*
This former farmhouse is known for its herb-
flavored roast lamb and homemade ice cream
with raspberries. Via delle Cave 16 (between
Florence and Fiesole). ☎ 055-591133. Entrees
9€–20€. Fixed-price lunch 30€–65€. AE, DC, MC,
V. Lunch and dinner daily. Closed 1 week in Feb.
Bus: 7.

★★★ kids **Vivoli** SANTA CROCE *GELATO*
Aficionados would argue that gelato is in fact
a food group, and whether you want to make a
meal, afternoon pick-me-up, or dessert of the
frozen stuff, Vivoli is the best place in town—some
say the world. Via Isole delle Stinche 7R. ☎ 055-
239334. From 3€. Tues–Sun 9am–1am. Closed
Aug. No credit cards. Bus: A, B, C, 14, 23, 71, or 80.

★ kids **Yellow** DUOMO *PIZZA/ITALIAN*
The buzzy and warm, warehouse-sized dining
room is full of booths, perfect for families or
groups. The pizzeria fare is filling (though
pastas and sides are actually better than the
pizzas), and kids love that there are fries on the
menu. Service is quick and friendly, and tabs
are mercifully low. Via del Proconsolo 39. ☎ 055-
211766. Entrees 5€–12€. AE, DC, MC, V. Lunch and
dinner daily. Bus: A.

> *Steak—bistecca—is a Florentine specialty.*

Panini and Picnic Fixings

If you're not in the mood for a full meal, or
just prefer an impromptu outdoor lunch,
there are some excellent places where you
can stop for a budget-friendly sandwich or
great picnic fixings.

★★ **Antico Noe,** Volta di San Piero 6R
(☎ 055-2340838; bus A, B, C, 14, 23, 71, or
80), is a student-favorite stand-up joint (on
an arched alley off Piazza San Pier Maggiore
in Santa Croce). Choose from a menu of
over 20 savory sandwiches with generous
helpings of meat, cheese, vegetables,
and unique condiments. There are a few
tables outside where you can eat (if you
can brave the questionable types hanging
about) or just take away. It's open for lunch
(and occasionally dinner) Monday through
Saturday.

The aisles of gourmet grocery ★★ **Pegna**
(p 195) are packed with picnic-worthy
items, from pâtés to fresh country bread,
and the deli counter will slice up specialty
cheese and meats to order. Bottles of wine
and cold beverages are also available.

Florence Hotel Best Bets

Best Boutique Hotel
Continentale $$$$ Vicolo dell'Oro 6A (p 205)

Best Luxury Hotel
Four Seasons $$$$ Borgo Pinti 99 (p 205)

Best for the Budget
Pensione Maria Luisa de' Medici $ Via del Corso 1 (p 209)

Best for Art Lovers
Relais Uffizi $$ Chiasso del Buco 16 (p 209)

Best Hospitality & Value
Davanzati Hotel $$ Via Porta Rossa 5 (p 205)

Poshest Location
Helvetia & Bristol $$$$ Via dei Pescioni 2 (p 208)

Best for Return Visitors Who Want to Feel Like Locals
Loggiato dei Serviti $$ Piazza Santissima Annunziata 3 (p 208)

Best Tower
Torre Guelfa $$ Borgo Santi Apostoli 8 (p 209)

Best Vintage Charm for Penny-Pinchers
La Scaletta $ Via Guicciardini 13 (p 208)

Best Near the Ponte Vecchio
Berchielli $$$ Lungarno Acciaiuoli 14 (p 205)
Hermitage Hotel $$ Vicolo Marzio 1 (p 208)

Best for Aesthetes
J. K. Place $$$ Piazza Santa Maria Novella 7 (p 208)

Most Welcoming
Mario's $ Via Faenza 89 (p 208)

Best Palazzo Living
Monna Lisa $$ Borgo Pinti 27 (p 208)

Largest Rooms
J and J $$$ Via di Mezzo 20 (p 208)

> *Guest bedroom at the upscale Helvetia & Bristol.*

Florence Hotels A to Z

★★ **Berchielli** PONTE VECCHIO
Even the standard doubles are big and bright at this traditional hotel, and the deluxe units have views of the Arno and Ponte Vecchio. Welcoming staff and a comfy lounge make it a haven after a busy day of sightseeing. Lungarno Acciaiuoli 14. ☎ 055-264061. www.berchielli.it. 76 units. Doubles 305€–380€. AE, DC, MC, V. Bus: 6 or 17.

★★ **Continentale** PONTE VECCHIO
Of the four Ferragamo-owned Lungarno Hotels in town, this is the most contemporary in style. Clean lines and white linens make the small rooms seem larger than they are, and there are scores of luxurious amenities. Some rooms have incredible views over the top of the Ponte Vecchio. Vicolo dell'Oro 6A. ☎ 055-27262. www. lungarnohotels.com. 48 units. Doubles 340€–470€. AE, DC, MC, V. Bus: B.

★★ **Davanzati Hotel** SIGNORIA
The father and son who run this boutique inn are always on hand with great tips for enjoying Florence. Unwind and mix with other guests

during the complimentary happy hour. Rooms are cozy and immaculate, though bathrooms are nothing special, and all come equipped with a laptop with free Wi-Fi. Room 100 is a contemporary loft-style unit perfect for families. Via Porta Rossa 5. ☎ 055-286666. www. hoteldavanzati.it. 21 units. Doubles 120€–312€ w/ breakfast. AE, DC, MC, V. Bus: A.

★★★ **Four Seasons** NORTHEAST OF CENTER
The top luxury property in Florence, thanks to three major assets: its own 4.5-hectare (11-acre) private garden with outdoor pool; its location inside a painstakingly restored historic Renaissance palace with gorgeous common areas and graceful guest rooms; and the best staff in town. Borgo Pinti 99. ☎ 055-26261. www. fourseasons.com. 117 units. Doubles 500€–800€. AE, DC, MC, V. Bus: A, 6, 31, or 32.

★★ **Grand Hotel** SANTA MARIA NOVELLA/ SANTA TRINITÀ The Grand is truly sumptuous—with large bathrooms and Renaissance or Empire bedrooms done in vibrant silks, brocades, frescoes, and antiques.

> *The lounge at J. K. Place.*

Florence Hotels, Nightlife & Entertainment

Piazzale di Porta at Prato

SAN JACOPINO

Via della Scala

Via Jacopo da Diacceto

Via Luigi Alamanni

Via B. Rucellai

Via Palestro

Via Soferino

Via Montebello

Il Prato

Via d. Orti

Via Curtatone

Via della Scala

Via Palazzuolo

Teatro Comunale

Stazione Centrale S. Maria Novella

Piazza Adua

Palaffari

Palacongressi

Via Guelfa

Via Faenza

Via Nazionale

Via Panicale

Piazza del Mercato Centrale

Piazza della Stazione

Piazza dell'Unità Italiana

S. Maria Novella

Piazza S. Maria Novella

Via S. Antonino

Via de' Panzani

Via del Giglio

Cappelle Medicee

Piazza S. Lorenzo

San Lorenzo

Via dei Cerretani

Piazza S. Giovanni

Via de' Pecori

CENTRO

V. d. Campidoglio

Via de' Tornabuoni

Via d. Strozzi

Piazza della Repubblica

Via Roma

Via Calzaiuoli

Orsanmichele

Ognissanti

Piazza d'Ognissanti

Lungarno Amerigo Vespucci

Borgo Ognissanti

Via di Fossi

Via del Moro

Via delle B. Donne

Via della Vigna Nuova

V. d. Parione

Palazzo Strozzi

Piazza Trinita

Via Porta Rossa

Palazzo Davanzati

Borgo SS. Apostoli

Lung. Santa Rosa

Ponte A. Vespucci

Lungarno

Fiume

Porta S. Frediano

Piazza di Cestello

Borgo San Frediano

Via dell'Orto

SAN FREDIANO

Ponte alla Carraia

Palazzo Corsini

Santa Trinita

Lung. Corsini

Arno

Lungarno Guicciardini

Lungarno Soderini

Piazza del Carmine

Santa Maria del Carmine

Via dell'Ardiglione

Via del' Serragli

Via Sant'Agostino

Via della Chiesa

Via del Campuccio

Via de' Leoni

SANTO SPIRITO

Piazza S. Spirito

Santo Spirito

V. Vellutini

Borgo Tegolaio

Via Mazzetta

Via Maggio

Via Romana

Piazza dei Pitti

Palazzo Pitti

Borgo S. Jacopo

OLTRARNO

Via Guicciardini

Piazza S. Felicita

Piazza S. Maria Soprarno

Ponte Vecchio

Loggia dei Lanzi

Lung. Acciaiuoli

Ponte S. Trinita

Ponte Vecchio

Giardino di Boboli (Boboli Garden)

Forte di Belvedere

Costa di S. Giorgio

0   1/8 mile
0   200 meters

N

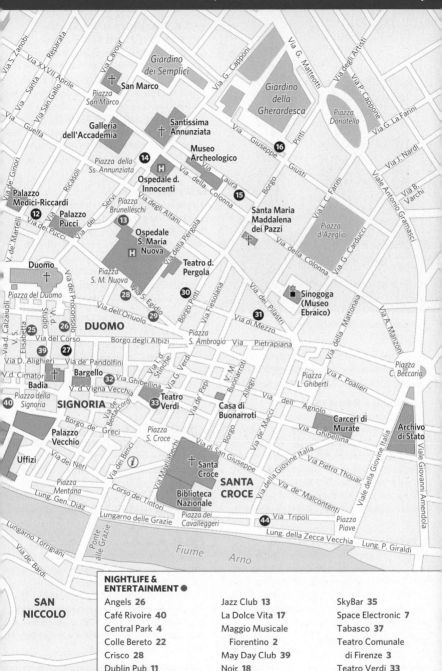

NIGHTLIFE & ENTERTAINMENT ●

Angels **26**
Café Rivoire **40**
Central Park **4**
Colle Bereto **22**
Crisco **28**
Dublin Pub **11**
Fiddler's Elbow **9**
Full-Up **32**
Gilli's **24**

Jazz Club **13**
La Dolce Vita **17**
Maggio Musicale
  Fiorentino **2**
May Day Club **39**
Noir **18**
Procacci **20**
Rio Grande **1**
Santa Maria
  de' Ricci **25**

SkyBar **35**
Space Electronic **7**
Tabasco **37**
Teatro Comunale
  di Firenze **3**
Teatro Verdi **33**
Tenax **5**
Tin Box Club **29**
Yab **23**

> *Simple decor in the always-friendly Davanzati Hotel.*

Piazza Ognissanti 1. ☎ 800-3253589 or 055-288781. www.starwoodhotels.com. 107 units. Doubles 330€–430€. AE, DC, MC, V. Bus: 6 or 17.

★★ Helvetia & Bristol REPUBBLICA

This restored Belle Epoque palazzo has lavish bedrooms with period furniture and elegant bathrooms with acres of Carrara marble. The location opposite the imposing medieval Palazzo Strozzi is one of the fanciest in town. Via dei Pescioni 2. ☎ 888-7700447 or 055-211686. www.royaldemeure.com. 67 units. Doubles 288€–400€. AE, DC, MC, V. Bus: 6, 11, 22, 36, or 37.

★ Hermitage Hotel PONTE VECCHIO

The Hermitage has a terrace over the Arno and small to midsize rooms with 17th- to 19th-century antiques; some bathrooms have Jacuzzis. Vicolo Marzio 1. ☎ 055-287216. www.hermitagehotel.com. 28 units. Doubles 120€–245€ w/breakfast. MC, V. Bus: B.

★★ J and J SANTA CROCE

This 16th-century former monastery, with vaulted ceilings and frescoes, has some of the city's largest rooms. Via di Mezzo 20. ☎ 055-26312. www.jandjhotel.com. 20 units. Doubles 283€–315€ w/breakfast. AE, DC, MC, V. Bus: A.

★★ J. K. Place SANTA MARIA NOVELLA

This refined hotel is set up like a private townhouse, with a ground floor that's a maze of luxurious common areas. Bedrooms are less sumptuous (the "Classic" doubles are quite small) but handsome and well designed. Simple touches such as free juice in the lounge all day and free hotel-wide Wi-Fi add to the relaxed hospitality. Piazza Santa Maria Novella 7. ☎ 055-2645181. www.jkplace.com. 20 units. Doubles 350€–500€ w/breakfast. AE, DC, MC, V. Bus: 14 or 23.

La Scaletta OLTRARNO

If you like vintage charm, check into this aging palazzo across the Arno and hang out on its flower-bedecked terrace, with a 360-degree view of the city. Guest rooms are rather dark but spacious enough, with European-basic bathrooms. Via Guicciardini 13. ☎ 055-283028. www.hotellascaletta.it. 13 units. Doubles 75€–150€ w/breakfast. MC, V. Bus: D, 11, 36, or 37.

★ Loggiato dei Serviti ACCADEMIA

A monastery in 1527, this comfortably elegant hotel has evocative beamed or vaulted ceilings and terra-cotta floors on one of the city's most beautiful squares. Piazza Santissima Annunziata 3. ☎ 055-289592. www.loggiatodeiservitihotel.it. 29 units. Doubles 150€–205€ w/breakfast. AE, DC, MC, V. Bus: 1, 7, or 17.

★ Mario's SANTA MARIA NOVELLA

This little, spotless, home-style city inn has small to midsize bedrooms stylishly decorated and furnished for your comfort; some have small private gardens. Via Faenza 89. ☎ 055-216801. www.hotelmarios.com. 16 units. Doubles 82€–170€ w/breakfast. AE, DC, MC, V. Bus: 10, 13, or 17.

★ kids Monna Lisa DUOMO/SANTA CROCE

Behind a severe facade, this art-laden 14th-century palazzo with a large back garden takes top prize for old-world elegance. One might half expect da Vinci to drop in for a stay. The new Limonaia wing is more modern and airy. Borgo Pinti 27. ☎ 055-2479755. www.monnalisa.it. 45 units. Doubles 199€–390€ w/breakfast. AE, DC, MC, V. Bus: A, 6, 31, or 32.

★ Morandi alla Crocetta NORTHEAST OF CENTER

In a 16th-century convent, this *pensione* evokes the era when British travelers sought private home–like lodgings with family heirlooms.

The Noble Suite at the Four Seasons.

Exposed brick archways in the walls of some rooms create a cozy, nostalgic feel. Via Laura 50. ☎ 055-2344747. www.hotelmorandi.it. 10 units. Doubles 177€–220€. AE, DC, MC, V. Bus: 6, 7, 10, 17, 31, or 32.

★ **Pensione Maria Luisa de' Medici** DUOMO
This B&B in a 1645 palazzo is one of the city's most desirable, with baroque art that contrasts strikingly with the modernist furniture. The bedrooms are large and the hospitality is memorable, but all but two rooms have shared bathrooms, and it's a three-story climb (there's no lift) to reach the pensione. Via del Corso 1. ☎ 055-280048. 9 units. Doubles 80€–95€ w/ breakfast. No credit cards. Bus: A, 14, or 23.

★ **Relais Uffizi** PONTE VECCHIO/SIGNORIA
Right next to the Uffizi, this hotel is a great value, in a 15th-century building with homey, midsize to large rooms and marble baths. Chiasso del Buco 16. ☎ 055-2676239. www. relaisuffizi.it. 10 units. Doubles 140€–250€ w/ breakfast. AE, DC, MC, V. Bus: A, B, 23, or 71.

★ **Residenza dei Pucci** DUOMO
This restored 19th-century town house has ample rooms with high ceilings, French tapestries, four-poster beds, and marble baths. Via dei Pucci 9. ☎ 055-281886. www. residenzadeipucci.com. 12 units. Doubles 80€–170€. AE, MC, V. Bus: 1, 6, 14, or 17.

★ **Ritz** SANTA CROCE
This family-run budget hotel near the Uffizi has snug, comfy rooms overlooking the Arno and a view of Fiesole from the roof terrace. Lungarno della Zecca Vecchia 24. ☎ 055-2340650. www. hotelritz.net. 32 units. Doubles 100€–200€ w/ breakfast. AE, DC, MC, V. Bus: 23.

★ **Tornabuoni Beacci** SANTA TRINITÀ
In a 16th-century palace, this timeworn favorite faces another century with genteel grace. The roof terrace bursts with flowers and panoramas. Via Tornabuoni 3. ☎ 055-212645. www.hoteltornabuonibeacci.com. 28 units. Doubles 150€–280€ w/breakfast. AE, DC, MC, V. Bus: B, 6, 11, or 36.

★★ **Torre Guelfa** PONTE VECCHIO
Florence's tallest privately owned tower graces this 14th-century palazzo near the Ponte Vecchio. Rooms have canopied iron beds. Borgo Santi Apostoli 8. ☎ 055-2396338. www.hoteltorreguelfa.com. 21 units. Doubles 150€–210€ w/breakfast. AE, MC, V. Bus: D, 11, 36, 37, or 68.

Florence Nightlife & Entertainment Best Bets

Best Cocktails at Sunset
SkyBar, Continentale hotel, Vicolo dell'Oro 6A (p 211)

Best Aperitivo
Colle Bereto, Piazza Strozzi 5R (p 211)

Best Cafe
Gilli's, Piazza della Repubblica 39R (p 212)

Best Chic People-Watching
Noir, Lungarno Corsini 12–14R (p 211)

Best Club
Rio Grande, Viale degli Olmi 1 (p 212)

Best Gay Bar
Tabasco, Piazza Santa Cecilia 3 (p 213)

Best Irish Pub
Dublin Pub, Via Faenza 27R (p 213)

Best Jazz
Jazz Club, Via Nuova de' Caccini 3 (p 213)

Best Live Music
Tenax, Via Pratese 46A (p 213)

Best Opera & Ballet
Teatro Comunale di Firenze, Corso Italia 16 (p 213)

Best Summer Festival
Maggio Musicale Fiorentino, Corso Italia 16 (p 213)

Best Dance Party for Foreign Students
Space Electronic, Via Palazzuolo 37 (p 212)

Best for Staring at Gorgeous Art & Architecture
Café Rivoire, Piazza della Signoria 4R (p 212)

Best Intimate Church Concerts
Santa Maria de' Ricci, Via del Corso at Via Sant'Elisabetta (p 213)

> *Cocktails at Colle Bereto.*

Florence Nightlife & Entertainment A to Z

Bars & Lounges

★ Angels DUOMO

A good bet when you just want a drink in a sleek setting and not the whole "scene" of a Florentine night out, this bar/restaurant different rooms to suit your mood, cocktails and wines by the glass or bottle, and late-night snacks. Via del Proconsolo 29-31 ☎ 055-2398762. Bus: 14, 23, or 71.

★★ Colle Bereto REPUBBLICA

A big, enclosed sidewalk veranda at this lounge bar attracts a hip crowd, especially for its 7pm to 9pm *aperitivo* (happy hour). The small, indoor area upstairs is table-service only, with a small area for dancing to DJ-spun tunes. Piazza Strozzi 5R. ☎ 055-283156. Bus: A or 22.

★ La Dolce Vita OLTRARNO

The owners covered the walls in mirrors so that beautiful people can dazzle themselves. Piazza del Carmine. ☎ 055-284595. Bus: D.

> *The discothèque Central Park is a summer favorite with Florentine clubbers.*

★ May Day Club DUOMO

The recorded music is cutting edge. Antique radios provide the decor for a young crowd. Occasional Japanese porn night with kinky-shaped sushi. Via Dante Alighieri 16R. ☎ 055-2381290. www.maydayclub.it. No cover. Bus: A.

★★ Noir SANTA TRINITÀ

This riverside bar may not exactly overlook the Arno, but that doesn't keep the chic masses from flooding the eternally popular disco-lounge every night of the week. Lungarno Corsini 12-14R ☎ 055-210752. Bus: B.

★★ SkyBar PONTE VECCHIO

The best view in the city—a 360-degree panorama that takes in dramatic perspectives on the city's best medieval and Renaissance architec-

Map Note

For a map denoting the locations of all listings in this section, see p 207.

> *Café Rivoire sits on the prime real estate of Piazza della Signoria.*

ture—is from this rooftop bar at the Continentale hotel (p 205). Watching the sunset from here is epic. Its tentlike covering and comfy sofas make it perfect in all seasons. **In the Continentale hotel, Vicolo dell'Oro 6A. ☎ 055-27262. Bus: B.**

Cafes

★ Café Rivoire SIGNORIA

The tables of this classy cafe open onto one of the world's most beautiful squares. Stick to the light snacks and drinks and ignore the main dishes. **Piazza della Signoria 4R. ☎ 055-214412. Bus: A, B, 23, or 71.**

★★ Gilli's REPUBBLICA

Dating from 1789, this is the oldest, most beautiful cafe in Florence. *Risorgimento* leaders convened here in the 1850s to plot the unification of Italy. **Piazza della Repubblica 39R. ☎ 055-213896. Bus: A or 22.**

★★ Procacci SANTA TRINITÀ

This darling cafe/bar is beloved by fashionistas. Its specialty is a *panino tartufato,* an egg-shaped roll filled with white truffle paste. **Via Tornabuoni 64R. ☎ 055-211656. Bus: A or 22.**

Discos & Clubs

★ Central Park WEST OF CENTER

Florence's best summer disco, with fabulous outdoor dance floors among its gardens. Expect to pay 15€ in cab fare to get home. **Via Fosso Macinante. ☎ 055-353505. No cover. Bus: 1, 9, 26.**

Full-Up SIGNORIA

Sugar daddies meet hot models in this old cellar with a small dance floor blasting recorded music. It's a favorite expat dance club and piano bar. **Via della Vigna Vecchia 23-25R. ☎ 055-293006. 5€–20€ cover. Bus: A, 14, or 23.**

★★ Rio Grande WEST OF CENTER

The most popular dance club with an older crowd. Music is mostly Latino. **Viale degli Olmi 1. ☎ 055-331371. www.rio-grande.it. 16€ cover, including first drink. Bus: P.**

Club, Cafe & Concert Tips

Italian clubs are cliquey—people usually go in groups to hang out and dance exclusively with one another. Plenty of flesh is on display, but single travelers hoping to find random dance partners may often be disappointed.

Florence no longer has a glitterati or intellectuals' cafe scene. But if you want designer pastries and cappuccino served to you while you people-watch on a piazza, its high-toned cafes will do.

Florence is wanting for the musical cachet or grand opera houses of Milan, Venice, or Rome, but the city has two symphony orchestras and a fine music school in Fiesole. Florence's public theaters are respectable, and most major touring companies stop in town on their way through Italy. Tickets for all cultural and music events are available through **Box Office,** Via Alamanni 39 (☎ 055-210804; www.boxol.it).

Space Electronic SANTA MARIA NOVELLA
Karaoke bar, pub, American-style bar, dance floor? One thing's sure: The second floor is definitely a disco with a space capsule hovering overhead. A rite of passage for foreign study participants and those wishing to recapture those bygone days. Via Palazzuolo 37. ☎ 055-293082. 15€ cover, including first drink. Bus: 26, 7, or 35.

Yab REPUBBLICA
This 1980s-style disco with surly bouncers and a velvet rope is popular with 20-somethings. Monday nights draw an older crowd. Via Sassetti 5R. ☎ 055-215160. 20€ cover, including first drink. Bus: A or 22.

Gay Clubs

Crisco DUOMO
The most famous cruising skin bar in Tuscany. Mr. Right is waiting. Via Sant'Egidio 43R. ☎ 055-480580. 9€–15€ cover. Bus: 1 or 3.

Tabasco SIGNORIA
The oldest gay dance club in Italy lives up to its very name, with smoke machines, strobe lights, and Tuscan studs. Piazza Santa Cecilia 3. ☎ 055-213000. www.tabascogay.it. 10€–13€ cover. Bus: A, B, 23, or 71.

Tin Box Club DUOMO
The hottest dark room in Tuscany—for *young* gay men only. Via dell'Oriuolo 19-21R. ☎ 055-466387. 10€ cover. Bus: 1 or 3.

Irish Pubs

Dublin Pub SANTA MARIA NOVELLA Now that the Irish pub rage has calmed down somewhat in Florence, this remains one of the best of the lot. Via Faenza 27R. ☎ 055-293049. Bus: A, 1, 11, 12, 36, 37, or 68.

Fiddler's Elbow SANTA MARIA NOVELLA
With tables set in a dark paneled room and outside on the square, this old favorite showcases live Celtic music on many nights, an open mic night on Thursdays, and broadcasts all major sporting events. Piazza Santa Maria Novella 7R. ☎ 055-215056. Bus: 14 or 23.

Jazz

Jazz Club DUOMO
The best live jazz in town (concerts Tues–Sat only), in a basement with rickety tables and a fun-loving clientele. In summer the action moves to Parco di Villa Fabbricotti. Via

> *Outdoor summer music events are a staple of the Tuscan festival calendar.*

Nuova de' Caccini 3. ☎ 055-2479700. www.jazzclubfirenze.com. Membership 5€. Bus: A.

Live Music

★★ Tenax PERETOLA
Tuscany's premier venue for rock and grunge bands. Via Pratese 46A. ☎ 055-308160. www.tenax.org. 20€–25€ cover. Closed mid-May to Sept. Bus: 29 or 30.

Opera & Ballet

★★★ Teatro Comunale di Firenze WEST OF CENTER Florence's main cultural venue for opera, ballet, and classical concerts. It's also the home of the Maggio Musicale Fiorentino (see below). Corso Italia 16. ☎ 055-2779350. Tickets 15€–150€. Bus: B.

★★ Teatro Verdi SANTA CROCE
This is Tuscany's major hall for dance, classical music, opera, and ballet, often with star performers. Via Ghibellina 99. ☎ 055-2396242. Tickets 18€–90€. Bus: A.

Summer Festivals

★★★ Maggio Musicale Fiorentino WEST OF CENTER This festival of opera, dance, and classical music is Italy's biggest and best. Teatro Comunale di Firenze, Corso Italia 16. ☎ 055-2779350. www.maggiofiorentino.com. Apr–July. Tickets 15€–150€. Bus: B.

Free Organ Concerts

Every night, in the church of **Santa Maria de' Ricci**, Via del Corso at Via Sant'Elisabetta (☎ 055-215044), there's a free organ concert at 9:15pm. The music consists of mostly classical and liturgical standards, with a few selections per night accompanied by opera soloists.

Fiesole

Fresh air and a gentler atmosphere await in this romantic hill town just northeast of central Florence. Fiesole (pronounced "fee-*eh*-zo-lay") also offers a chance to explore fascinating Roman ruins and take a meal at one of the area's best country dining rooms. Good news for the time-strapped: This most classic of Florentine "day" trips can be done in 4 hours. Piazza Mino, at the center of this small town, is where you'll find most of Fiesole's cafes and restaurants.

> *Fiesole's Villa le Balze was donated by John D. Rockefeller's granddaughter to Georgetown University.*

START **Take bus 7 from Stazione Santa Maria Novella or Via de' Cerretani in Florence.**

1 ★ **Cattedrale.** The most prominent feature on the Fiesolano skyline is the crenellated clock and bell tower of its main church; the interior of the cathedral is cool and understated, with black and white bands of stone and refreshingly few ornate details. ⊕ 15 min. Piazza Mino. No phone. Free admission. Daily 9am–noon, 3–6pm.

2 ★★ **Teatro Romano (Roman Theater and Archaeological Museum).** Fiesole's roots are even more ancient than Florence's, and at this romantically overgrown archaeological site, you can romp over not only Roman ruins but some remains of Etruscan Faesulae, too. The 1st-century-B.C. **Roman Theater** is the chief attraction here (and where many open-air concerts are held during the Estate Fiesolana; see box). The theater seats 3,000 today, as it

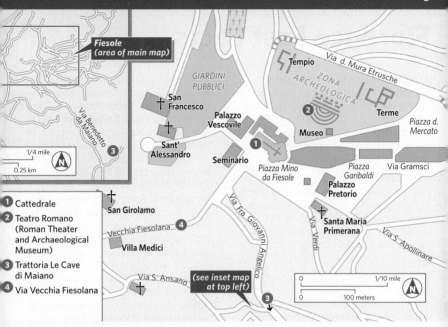

Festival Tip

If you're in town between late June and August, try to catch an event during the **Estate Fiesolana.** Much of this summer festival takes place in the gorgeous setting of the Roman Theater and features classical and other music concerts, ballet and theater performances—even film screenings. For information, visit the tourist office at Piazza Mino 36–37 (☎ 055-598720), or check the festival's website at www.estatefiesolana.it. Most tickets cost around 15€.

Map Legend

1. Cattedrale
2. Teatro Romano (Roman Theater and Archaeological Museum)
3. Trattoria Le Cave di Maiano
4. Via Vecchia Fiesolana

probably did in antiquity. Also in the area are three rebuilt arches of Fiesole's Roman baths, as well as a stretch of the 4th-century-B.C. Etruscan walls. The archaeological museum here includes lots of Etruscan funerary urns and Roman architectural fragments, as well as an important collection of Greek vases from the 8th to the 4th centuries B.C., from Puglia. ⏱ 1 hr. Via Portigiani 1. ☎ 055-59118. Admission 6.50€. Easter–Oct daily 9:30am–7pm; winter Wed–Mon 9:30am–5pm.

3 ★ **Trattoria le Cave di Maiano.** If you're up for a hearty sit-down lunch or dinner, this is the best kitchen in town. See p 203.

4 ★★★ **Via Vecchia Fiesolana.** The hilly areas around Fiesole offer lovely country strolls, perfect for working off a meal or earning your next gelato break. The best is the twisty, downhill walk along Via Vecchia Fiesolana, where you'll have marvelous vistas of the Florentine skyline all to yourself between patinated stone walls and cypress groves. Along the way, you'll pass the panoramic gardens of **Villa Medici,** Via Mantellini (☎ 055-59164), built in the 15th century for Cosimo il Vecchio. Under the humanistic patronage of Lorenzo the Magnificent, this secluded estate became a beehive for 16th-century intellectuals. Farther along, and now owned by Georgetown University, is **Villa Le Balze,** Via Vecchia Fiesolana 26 (☎ 055-59208). Admission to both villas is free; and both are nominally open Monday to Friday, though hours are erratic; call ahead, or just stop by and try your luck. At the bottom of Via Vecchia Fiesolana lies the hamlet of San Domenico, most notable for the 15th-century church where Fra Angelico was a monk and left several paintings and frescoes. From here, Via di San Domenico continues all the way back to Florence. Complete the journey on foot, or hop on bus 7 back to the city center. ⏱ 2–3 hr. Via Vecchia Fiesolana to Via San Domenico.

Florence Fast Facts

Accommodations Booking Services
FlorenceBy (no phone; www.florenceby.com) offers a wide range of options, from budget hotels in the *centro* to luxury farmhouses in the suburbs. For carefully selected apartments in great locations, try **Italianize Me** (☎ 055-7879162; www.italianizeme.com).

American Express
Florence's AmEx office is a few blocks north of Piazza della Signoria at Piazza Cimatori/Via Dante Alighieri 22R (☎ 055-50981). It's open Monday to Friday 9am to 5:30pm, and Saturday 9am to 12:30pm.

ATMs
Central Florence has banks with ATMs (*bancomat*) in every square and every few blocks on major streets. Italy generally uses 4-digit PINs; if you have a 6-digit number, check with your bank before you leave.

Dentists & Doctors
For general medical care, Dr. Stephen Kerr keeps an office at Piazza di Mercato Nuovo 1 (☎ 335-836-1682 cell or 055-288-055 office), with office hours Monday to Friday from 3 to 5pm without an appointment. Your consulate can also provide a list of English-speaking doctors and dentists. For emergencies, or if you need medical attention outside of doctors' office hours, go to the *pronto soccorso* (emergency room) at the nearest hospital, where they'll treat your immediate problem for free and give you a short course of prescription drugs if necessary.

Emergencies
For general emergencies, call ☎ **112** for the Carabinieri or ☎ **113** for the Polizia. Call ☎ **114** for an ambulance and ☎ **115** for the fire department. For a medical emergency that doesn't require an ambulance, see "Dentists & Doctors," above. To report lost or stolen items, see "Police," p 217.

Getting There
BY PLANE Visitors flying to Florence will either arrive at Florence's **Peretola** (it's officially named Amerigo Vespucci airport, though locals never call it that; ☎ 055-3061300; www.aeroporto.firenze.it), 5km (8 miles) northwest of the city center, which is served by European carriers, or at **Pisa's Galileo airport** (☎ 050-849300; www.pisa-airport.it), which is served by some long-haul flights (such as Delta's nonstop from New York–JFK). From Peretola, there's a direct bus (4.50€; 20 min.) to central Florence (Santa Maria Novella station). From Pisa airport to Santa Maria Novella, there's a direct train (5.60€; 1 hr). **BY TRAIN** By train, Florence is easy to reach from anywhere in Italy and from several European cities: All high-speed, Eurostar, Inter-City, and most regional Tuscan trains stop at the Santa Maria Novella station (☎ 055-2352595; www.grandistazioni.it). **BY CAR** Florence lies just west of the **A1** (Italy's main north-south autostrada or superhighway). Once in Florence, a car is a liability and parking impossible, so plan to park it on the outskirts of town, or better yet, return it to the rental agency as soon as you arrive in the city.

Getting Around
Central Florence is compact, flat, and best explored on foot. For example, the walk between Palazzo Pitti in Oltrarno and the Duomo (one of the longer distances you're likely to cover in one stretch) only takes about 20 minutes. **ATAF** (☎ 055-5650222; www.ataf.net) is Florence's public transportation authority, and city buses are reliable and clean. Tickets are 1€ and good for 1 hour; purchase them at a *tabacchi* (tobacco store) or a newsstand. In most cases, however, you won't need to take any buses unless you're going up to Piazzale Michelangelo (bus 12 or 13) or to the hill town of Fiesole (bus 7).

Internet Access
Almost all hotels now have a public Internet terminal where guests can sign on; many nicer hotels also have Wi-Fi, which often only works in certain guest rooms or just the lobby. Some hotels offer these services for free, while others carry a daily or hourly charge that can be quite high (as much as 10€ per hour in some fancier

hotels), so it's a good idea to clarify the fee before you navigate away. Being a university town, central Florence also has plenty of Internet points where you can log on for about 5€ to 6€ per hour. **Internet Train** (www.internettrain.it) is one such chain with several convenient locations: Via de' Benci 36R (near Santa Croce); Via Porta Rossa 38R (near Piazza della Repubblica); Via Guelfa 54/56 (near San Lorenzo); and Borgo San Jacopo 30R (in Oltrarno), all open until 11pm or midnight.

Pharmacies

Italian *farmacie* will fill foreign prescriptions with little or no hassle. They're also where you buy over-the-counter medicines such as ibuprofen or cough syrup, feminine hygiene products, and even sunblock. *Farmacie* are recognizable by a neon green or red cross and are usually open 8am to 1:30pm and 3:30 to 8pm. There's a 24-hour pharmacy inside Santa Maria Novella train station.

For optical care (glasses repair, contact lens solution), go to an *ottica* (optical shop), which can be found on nearly every block in Florence.

Police

To report a lost or stolen article, such as a wallet or passport, visit the local police *questura* or Carabinieri *caserma* in your location. Florence's Santa Maria Novella train station has Polizia and Carabinieri offices where you can file a report. See also "Emergencies," p 216.

Post Office

The central post office is at Via Pellecceria 3 (☎ 055-2736481). Stamps (*francobolli*) can be purchased at most *tabacchi* (tobacco stores), and postcards and letters can be mailed from your hotel or the red letterboxes mounted on walls around town.

Safety

Florence is a generally safe city, especially in the tourist-heavy *centro*. Women walking alone, even at night, will rarely feel threatened, though it's a good idea to stick to well-lit streets and piazzas where other pedestrians are present. Be vigilant for pickpockets in and around the train station and in crowded tourist areas such as Piazza del Duomo or in the line for the Uffizi.

Taxis

Florence is so small and walkable that you'll usually only need a taxi for hauling luggage to and from the airport or train station. Expect to pay about 10€ between the train station and city-center hotels, and around 25€ for airport trips. Hotels and most restaurants will call a cab for you, and there are clearly marked taxi ranks outside the airport and train station. If you need to call one yourself, the biggest taxi dispatcher in town is **Radio Taxi** (☎ 055-4242). If they're busy, try ☎ 055-4798, 055-4390, or 055-4499.

Telephones

Italian phone booths (*cabine*) take the *scheda telefonica* (plastic phone card) only, sold in denominations of 2.50€, 5€, and 10€ at *tabacchi*. Break off the perforated corner, and insert the card to get a dial tone. (Even if you have a prepaid long-distance calling card, you must insert a *scheda telefonica* to open the line.) Local calls (beginning with 055) usually cost .10€ to .20€; calls to Italian cell phones (beginning with 328, 338, 339, 340, 347, 348, and so forth) are wildly expensive—more than 1€ per minute.

Toilets

The new Duomo visitor center in Piazza San Giovanni 7 has the only decent public toilets (the fee is .80€) in central Florence; avoid the ones at the train station at all costs. Otherwise, just stop in at the nearest bar/cafe and ask politely to use the *bagno*. You don't need to be a paying customer for this privilege in Italy.

Visitor Information

The official website of the Florence Tourist Board is www.firenzeturismo.it. The board also has walk-in offices at the train station (☎ 055-212245; Mon–Sat 8:30am-7pm, Sun 8:30am-2pm), at Via Cavour 1R (☎ 055-290832; Mon–Sat 8:30am-6:30pm), and at Peretola airport (☎ 055-315874; daily 8:30am-8:30pm).

6
Tuscany
& Umbria

The Best of Tuscany & Umbria in 3 Days

If you only have 3 days to explore the area, stick to Tuscany.
A survey tour of four of the region's most iconic destinations is quite satisfying,
though you'll be changing hotels every day. Using Lucca as a base for your
first day, start with a morning excursion to Pisa—the Leaning Tower is a thrill
in person—then spend the afternoon taking in Lucca's elegant *fin de siècle*
atmosphere. The next morning, make your way to Chianti Country, where you'll
find country roads, castles, and wine-tasting opportunities galore. On your third
day, explore Italy's greatest medieval masterpiece—the city of Siena.

> PREVIOUS PAGE *Poppies and cypress trees, San Quirico, Tuscany.* THIS PAGE *The towering moments of Siena, including the Torre del Mangia, left, and the Duomo, right, are visible from the surrounding hills.*

START Pisa (25km/16 miles south of Lucca;
100km/62 miles west of Florence). Trip
length: 3 days.

❶ **Pisa.** It's a rite of passage for all who set
foot in Tuscany: Though admittedly a tourist
trap, the ★★★ **Leaning Tower** is a must-do.
Since you'll have only the morning in Pisa, however, it's absolutely essential that you prebook

your tower tickets (see "The Nuts & Bolts of
Climbing," p 222, for detailed information).
Follow our Pisa recommendations in "The Best
of Tuscany & Umbria in 1 Week" (p 228, ❷)
for climbing the Leaning Tower and visiting the
Battistero (baptistery) and Duomo. You'll need
to allow 4 to 5 hours total for seeing the sights
of Pisa and round-trip travel from Lucca, so it's
a good idea to get an early start.

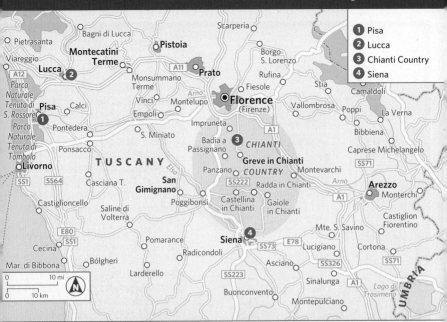

1 Pisa
2 Lucca
3 Chianti Country
4 Siena

Travel Tip

For detailed information on sights and recommended hotels and restaurants, see Lucca (p 274), Siena (p 290), and "Where to Stay & Dine in Chianti Country" (p 225).

After you've summited the tower and seen the other superb ecclesiastical monuments here, head up to Lucca, where you'll spend the afternoon and evening of Day 1.

Lucca is 25km (16 miles) northeast of Pisa. By car, take the SS12.

2 **Lucca.** Once you return from Pisa, there's no time to waste. You'll only have an afternoon and evening in elegant Lucca, but with a little discipline, you'll be able to cover a lot of ground and see, taste, and hear the best of what this truly unique Tuscan city has to offer.

Start by renting a bicycle from ★ **Antonio Poli,** Piazza Santa Maria 42 (☎ 0583-493787; daily 8:30am–8pm), and go for a ride atop Lucca's panoramic ★★ **Passeggiata delle Mura**—a wide paved path that goes all the way around the city on Lucca's medieval fortification walls. The ride takes less than an hour. After that, grab a midafternoon snack to tide you over until dinner.

> San Michele in Foro, in the Piazza San Michele, was built on the site of Lucca's Roman-era forum.

The Nuts & Bolts of Climbing

Climbing the Leaning Tower of Pisa shouldn't be missed by anyone able-bodied enough to ascend its 300 spiraling steps. But to ensure a smooth Pisa experience and keep to your schedule, book your tower visit ahead of time. Otherwise, you could be in for several hours' wait or even find that all the tickets are sold out for that day, especially in summer.

Advance (prepaid) tickets must be booked at least 16 days but no more than 45 days ahead of your visit. This service is only available online at www.opapisa.it or in person at the box offices on Piazza dei Miracoli. Tickets cost 17€ in advance (guaranteeing you a set entrance time) or 15€ at the box office (but with no guarantee that you'll be able to climb the tower that day). Entrance times are every half-hour, and you must arrive punctually or risk being turned away. As a rule, plan to be at Piazza dei Miracoli at least 30 minutes before your appointed entrance time.

When you book online, you'll be sent a voucher that you need to print out and bring with you to either of the box offices *(biglietterie)* on the edges of Piazza dei Miracoli. If you have a prepaid voucher, you can go directly to the front of the line and pick up your entrance ticket—be prepared to show some form of photo identification.

You'll have to deposit any handbags, backpacks, umbrellas, etc., in the bag drop area along the north side of Piazza dei Miracoli. Even the smallest purses must be checked, though you can bring a camera with you. The bag drop service is free of charge and monitored by security personnel.

Now, you just have to wait for the clock to strike your appointed entrance hour. Pisa's tower isn't the tallest in Italy, but it does require considerable physical effort. For many, the sense of imbalance that comes from climbing the spiral stairs of a seriously tilting edifice is the most challenging part. The ascent takes about 10 minutes, but it takes another 5 minutes or so to recover from the dizziness. At the uppermost terrace, serious vertigo-sufferers will want to keep away from the low edge, which cantilevers thrillingly over the grassy piazza.

The tower is open "all day" every day, but the hours change a bit throughout the year (10am–5pm Nov–Feb, except between Dec 25 and Jan 7, when it's open from 9am–6pm; 9am–6pm Mar 1–Mar 13; 9am–7pm Mar 13–Mar 21 and all of Oct; 8:30am–8:30pm Mar 21–Jun 15 and all of Sept; and 8:30am–11pm Jun 16–Aug 31).

> *Sangiovese is the staple grape of Tuscany's great reds, Chianti and Brunello.*

> *Lucca's Via Fillungo is where* lucchesi *come to shop or take an evening passeggiata.*

For this, Lucca presents a number of tasty options, but I recommend getting a couple slices of freshly baked focaccia at ★★ **Amedeo Giusti** (p 276, ❾) or, if the market is open in Piazza San Michele, a *frate lucchese* (lemon-flavored doughnut, dipped in sugar and optional Nutella) or two at the **Nelli** kiosk.

Once you've been fortified by one of these local specialties, climb the ★★ **Torre Guinigi** (p 276, ❽) for spectacular views of Lucca's layout

and the surrounding countryside. One of the most prominent features of the Lucchese skyline, this 44m (144 ft) brick tower has a little grove of ilex trees growing on top of it. Spend what's left of the afternoon or early evening walking around the *centro storico.* Join the shopping parade on and around **Via Fillungo,** with its fabulous Art Nouveau shopfronts. If possible, attend a **Puccini concert** in the church of San Giovanni. In the morning, say goodbye to Lucca with a cappuccino on ★ **Piazza dell'Anfiteatro.**

From Lucca, drive east on the A11 autostrada toward Florence (Firenze). Outside Florence, take the A1 south to the Raccordo FI-SI, following signs to Siena. Exit at Tavarnelle, following signs east to Greve in Chianti (99km/62 miles total).

❸ **Chianti Country.** On the morning of Day 2, drive east to the Chianti, the roughly diamond-shaped territory between Florence and Siena where Italy's most popular red wine, Chianti, is made. The hilly, forested region doesn't have a lot of "sights"—it's more about driving around, touring wineries, and eating and drinking well. Using the driving directions from Lucca above, you'll enter the Chianti from its western edge and drive east (past the unsightly industrial town of Sambuca) along a winding country road, following signs for Greve. After about 5km (3 miles) on that road, you'll arrive at the 11th-century ★ **Badia a Passignano** (see p 235, ❷, for tastings at this Antinori estate).

> The shell-shaped Piazza del Campo has been the vibrant center of Sienese life since the middle ages.

> Offerings at the shop of Dario Cecchini, "The Butcher of Tuscany," who also runs three restaurants for meat lovers.

After Badia a Passignano, continue east toward Greve (another 8km/5 miles) through a gorgeous landscape of dense woods and sunny vineyards. ★ **Greve in Chianti** (often referred to as just "Greve") is the largest town and unofficial capital of the Chianti. It's worth a quick stop here to walk around the arcaded main square, Piazza Matteotti, and pick up some regional meats and cheeses at the famous deli ★★ **Macelleria Falorni,** Piazza Matteotti 66–71 (☎ 055-854363; Mon–Sat 8am–1pm, 3:30–6:30pm; Sun 10am–1pm; 3–7pm), or taste some local vintages at their high-tech wine bar ★ **Le Cantine di Greve,** Galleria delle Cantine 2 (☎ 055-8546404).

As you move on, bear in mind that the main road that bisects Greve is the SS222, or "Chiantigiana" highway, which runs north-south through Chianti and is the fastest, best-paved route in the region. As a rule, it takes about 90 minutes to travel way up or down the Chiantigiana, though this can double in summer thanks to traffic. Other Chianti roads are twisty and often unpaved, so distances that look relatively short on the map actually take quite a while to cover.

In **Panzano,** 5km (3 miles) south of Greve on the SS222, meat lovers should—no, *must*—pay a visit to legendary butcher Dario Cecchini's shop, ★★★ **Antica Macelleria Cecchini,** Via XX Luglio 11 (☎ 055-852020; Sun–Tues, Thurs 9am–2pm; Fri–Sat 9am–6pm). Even if it's before noon, Dario and his staff will ply you with complimentary country red wine and divine crostini. See "The Butcher of Tuscany," p 238, for more information and for details about his three restaurants in Panzano.

For lunch, head south on the SS222, then take the turnoff to the left (about 1.5km/1 mile beyond Greve), following signs to Lamole. This road will take you up, up, and up, past the Vignamaggio estate, where Kenneth Branagh's *Much Ado About Nothing* was filmed. After about 8km (5 miles), you'll reach the tiny village of Lamole, which is perched like an eagle's nest over central Chianti, with breathtaking views over the green valley you just climbed. Settle in for a relaxing meal at the ★★ **Ristoro di Lamole,** Via di Lamole 6 (☎ 055-8547050; entrees 10€–18€; daily for lunch & dinner Mar–Dec; closed Jan–Feb), whose shaded, panoramic terrace is a blissful place to try fresh local pastas and meat dishes.

After lunch, visit a winery (see p 236 for recommendations).

As for evening activities, don't plan on sleeping too far from where you'll eat. Driving long distances on narrow, unlit Chianti roads after a big dinner is stressful—especially with the very real possibility of encountering a wild boar.

From Greve, take the SS222 south to Siena (42km/26 miles).

④ **Siena.** Italy's most magnificent medieval city is compact enough that you can do the highlights in one full, but not frantic, day. As you start to walk around Siena, you'll quickly realize that all roads lead to ★★★ **Piazza del Campo,** the shell-shaped piazza where the Palio (p 293) takes place each summer, and where the ★★ **Palazzo Pubblico** and ★★ **Torre del Mangia** strike formidable figures in the Tuscan sky.

In Palazzo Pubblico, the ★★★ **Museo Civico** (p 291, ③) has the city's most spectacular frescoes. Next, head for the ★★★ **Duomo** (p 292, ⑤), with its dazzling Gothic facade of multi-colored marble, and climb to the top of the ★★ **Museo dell'Opera Metropolitana** (p 292, ⑥) for vertiginous views.

Spend the rest of the afternoon wandering the streets and ancient *contrade* (mascotted

Where to Stay & Dine in Chianti Country

Conveniently located near Greve (3km/2 miles up a dirt road), the ★★★ **Villa Bordoni** (pictured), Via San Cresci, Loc. Mezzuola (☎ **055-8547453;** www.villabordoni.com; doubles 170€–295€), is a very stylish place with beautiful, rustic grounds and a friendly atmosphere. The wonderful on-site restaurant—the owners of the hotel are a Scottish couple who are chefs first and foremost— eliminates the problem of having to drive anywhere for dinner. Between Panzano and Radda, ★★ **Villa Rosa di Boscorotondo,** Via San Leolino (☎ **055-852577;** www. resortvillarosa.it; doubles 80€–140€), is a 19th-century inn with great country character and fantastic value.

★★ **La Cantinetta di Rignana,** Loc. Rignana (☎ **055-852601;** Wed–Mon for lunch & dinner; entrees 8€–15€), is a classic country tavern with a folksy dining room and a glassed-in terrace with views of the surrounding vineyards. Handmade egg pastas with rich sauces, wonderful grilled meats, and outstanding desserts will have you rolling out the door. ★★★ **Solociccia** is a carnivore's dream, but it's open only 3 nights a week. See "The Butcher of Tuscany" on p 238 for more information.

neighborhoods that compete in the Palio) of the Y-shaped city, ducking into churches like ★ **San Domenico** (p 293, ⑦) and **San Francesco** (p 293, ⑧). Toast your 3 days in Tuscany at the **Enoteca Italiana** (Fortezza Medicea, Via Camollia 72; ☎ 0577-236012; wines by the glass from 3€; cold dishes from 7.50€; Mon noon–8pm, Tues–Sat noon–1am).

The Best of Tuscany & Umbria in 1 Week

Having a full week to spend in Tuscany and Umbria is much better than 3 days, but it's a Pandora's box of options—so many hill towns, so much countryside, so much to eat and drink, and still, such (relatively) little time. Follow our itinerary below, from Lucca to Perugia, for the best cross section of what these two neighboring regions have to offer, from sightseeing and country driving to wine tasting and gastronomic indulgences. Fortunately, the distances between each stop aren't great, meaning you can divide your time between two to three hotels over the course of your trip.

> The hills of southern Tuscany are an essential part of any 1-week itinerary in the region.

Travel Tip

For detailed information on sights and recommended hotels and restaurants, see individual town listings later in this chapter.

START Lucca (77km/48 miles west of Florence on the A11). Trip length: 7 days.

1 Lucca. Lucca is justly famous for its pristine circuit of town walls, but there are other walled towns in Italy. What ultimately strikes you as you explore this most sophisticated small city in Tuscany is that Lucca is truly a breed apart.

First of all, in a region where hill towns are the norm, Lucca is flat. You won't find any 45-degree-angle streets, which makes Lucca a delight to walk, though bicycles are the favorite mode of transportation. A bike ride along the walls (p 274, **1**) is *the* must-do on a trip Lucca.

Second, while most Tuscan towns tend to have a similarly medieval look, Lucca is a time capsule of a different kind. Instead of transporting you back 800 years to an era of jousting and plagues, Lucca perpetuates the elegance of the late 19th and early 20th centuries, with immaculate shopfronts still bearing original Art Nouveau signs in etched and gilded glass. Even the Lucchese themselves seem imbued with the spirit of a gentler, bygone era. And when you see the dense green hills that surround Lucca, it's clear you're not in sun-kissed, "postcard" Tuscany. Lucca is closer to the Cinque

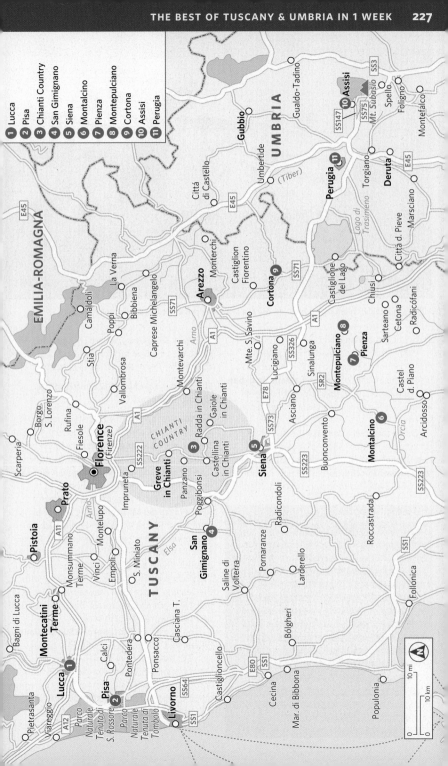

> *Pisa's Piazza del Duomo (or Campo dei Miracoli) was laid out in the city's 12th-century heyday.*

Terre of Liguria than it is to Siena.

With a full day to spend in Lucca, follow our recommendations on p 221, **2**, but add a visit to the interior of the ★★ **Cattedrale di San Martino** (p 275, **5**), take a longer bike ride around town, and enjoy a leisurely lunch somewhere.

Opera fans can also make the 30-minute drive to the western shore of melancholy Lake Massaciuccoli to see the very interesting **Villa Museo Puccini,** Torre del Lago Puccini (☎ 0584-341445; admission 7€; daily 10am–12:30pm, 3–5:30pm), where Lucca native Giacomo Puccini lived for 30 years and composed *La Bohème, Tosca,* and *Madama Butterfly.*

From Lucca, take the SS12 south to Pisa (25km/16 miles).

2 Pisa. No matter how touristy it seems, you just can't come all the way to Tuscany and not see the ★★★ **Leaning Tower.** Like an evening gondola ride in Venice or the Blue Grotto in Capri, it's an indelible, albeit expensive, travel experience you'll be glad you had.

Upon arrival in Pisa, make a beeline for ★★★ **Piazza dei Miracoli** (aka Campo dei Miracoli or Piazza del Duomo), and pick up your prebooked tickets for the Leaning Tower (see "The Nuts & Bolts of Climbing," p 222, for details). There are separate entrance fees for the Duomo and Battistero, which along with the Leaning Tower itself make for a rather expensive morning (24€ total). But if your budget permits, they're all worth seeing.

The Gothic ★★ **Battistero di San Giovanni,** Piazza del Duomo (☎ 050-560547; admission 5€; Nov–Feb daily 9am–4:20pm; Mar & Oct daily 9am–5:30pm; Apr–Sept daily 8am–7:30pm), merits a visit both for its 13th-century pulpit by Nicola Pisano, and for its renowned acoustics (see "Good Vibrations," left). It's also Italy's largest baptistery at 34m (112 ft.)

Good Vibrations

Don't leave Pisa without experiencing the amazing acoustics of the Battistero. Thanks to the particular curvature of the Gothic dome, sounds can be sustained in here for an exceptionally long time. Every half-hour, a baptistery attendant ducks under the ropes in the center of the baptistery to demonstrate these acoustics: he or she first sings a loud, clear note and lets it echo around the building and fade. Then, the attendant sings a string of several notes a half-octave apart. Those notes resonate and linger long after they're sung, "playing" simultaneously and making it sound as if the singer is in harmony with himself.

in diameter, and if you count the bronze statue of St. John atop the dome, it's only 1m (3 ft.) shorter than the Leaning Tower—56m (184 ft.) vs. the tower's height of 57m (187 ft.) on the high side.

Pisa's ★★ **Duomo** or **Cattedrale,** Piazza dei Miracoli (☎ 050-560547; admission 2€; Apr–Sept daily 10am–7:30pm, Sun opens at 1pm; Mar & Oct Mon–Sat 10am–5:30pm, Sun 1–5:30pm; Nov–Feb Mon–Sat 10am–12:45pm and daily 3–4:30pm), is one of the finest Romanesque cathedrals in Tuscany. The interior is as impressive as the exterior: the banded light-and-dark stone masonry has been left exposed for the most part, save for a few frescoes and Cimabue's monumental 1302 mosaic of *Christ Pantokrator* in the apse.

There's another, even more fanciful Pisano **pulpit** here (by Giovanni this time, who finished it in 1311), with wonderful sculptural details and marble-lion column bases.

Perhaps the most eye-catching feature of the church interior, however, is the enormous **bronze chandelier** hanging near the altar. On a drafty Sunday in 1581, so the legend goes, a 17-year-old Galileo was bored during Mass and, instead of paying attention to the liturgy, began watching the lamp swinging in the breeze. Observing that the lamp always took the same amount of time to complete one swing no matter how far it swung from side to side, Galileo came up with his pendulum theory.

The rest of Pisa is not particularly attractive or interesting, so don't feel guilty about moving on once you've seen the sights of Piazza dei Miracoli. Plan to be on the road toward Chianti Country by early afternoon.

From Pisa, head north on the SS1/Via Aurelia, then east on the A11 autostrada toward Florence. Outside Florence, take the A1 south to the Raccordo FI-SI, following signs to Siena. Exit at Tavarnelle, following signs east to Greve in Chianti (125km/78 miles total).

❸ **Chianti Country.** With any luck, your 90-minute drive from Pisa has been uneventful, and you'll arrive at your Chianti hotel, where you'll be spending the next 2 nights, by midafternoon. Time permitting, stop at ★ **Badia a Passignano** (p 235, ❷) on your way into the heart of the Chianti. If you're staying in the countryside, take a walk down a gravel road to

> *Gregorian chant is a daily ritual for the Augustinian monks of the Sant'Antimo abbey, near Montalcino.*

stretch those Leaning Tower–stiffened legs. Or do your strolling in "downtown" ★ **Greve**—a lap or two of the town's main square, Piazza Matteotti, is de rigueur—and stop in at ★ **Le Cantine di Greve** (p 224) for some Chianti

Vernaccia di San Gimignano

With all the ruby-colored Chianti, Brunello, and Vino Nobile flowing around Tuscany, it's easy to forget that there is a venerable white wine produced in the region, too. San Gimignano's golden-hued Vernaccia has been made for more than a millennium—some say the grapevines even date back to Etruscan times—and was the favorite drink of such Renaissance artists as Michelangelo. Sample the crisp and complex wine in San Gimignano at the lively **Da Gustavo,** Via San Matteo 29 (☎ 0577-940057; daily 8am–8pm; closed Nov and Feb).

> *Giant oak barrels help mature the wine at Chianti's Castello Verrazzano.*

the day, you'll have a more enjoyable experience. San Gimignano's major attractions only take a few hours. Visit the **Collegiata** (p 288, ❷), the most important church in town, and climb the **Torre Grossa** (p 288, ❸)—at 54m (175 ft.), it's a bit less taxing than the Leaning Tower of Pisa—for sweeping panoramas of the countryside and a fun bird's-eye view of San Gimignano itself. If you have enough time and morbid curiosity, the **Museo della Tortura** (p 288, ❹) is another worthwhile spot that kids tend to find interesting. Close off your visit with an *aperitivo* at popular bar **Da Gustavo** (see "Vernaccia di San Gimignano," p 229). If you opt to have dinner here, it makes sense to stay in San Gimignano overnight, as opposed to returning to a Chianti hotel—an hour's drive away—for a second night.

From San Gimignano, head east on the SP1, past Poggibonsi, then head southeast on the SR2/SR68 onto the Firenze-Siena Superstrada and follow signs for Siena (42km/26 miles).

❺ **Siena.** On Day 4, follow the same itinerary for seeing the highlights of Siena as on p 225, ❹. After indulging in a wonderful dinner (try ★★★ **Osteria Le Logge**, p 295, for a truly special night out), spend the night here—in town, we love Palazzo Ravizza (p 294).

From Siena, take the SR2/Via Cassia south to Montalcino (44km/25 miles).

❻ **Montalcino.** On the morning of Day 5, plan to visit a Brunello winery (recommendations on p 240, but we're partial to the charming family at ★★★ **Poggio Antico**), but make sure you finish your tour by 12:15pm, which gives you plenty of time to drive to, and park at, the ★★★ **Abbazia di Sant'Antimo** (p 278, ❷) and attend the Gregorian chant service at 12:45pm. After Sant'Antimo, have lunch in Montalcino (we especially recommend ★★ **Taverna del Grappolo Blu**, p 279) and visit the fortress and its *enoteca,* where you can sample glasses or buy bottles from all producers in the Brunello consortium.

From Montalcino, take the SR2 toward San Quirico d'Orcia, then the SP146 east to Pienza (24km/15 miles total).

❼ **Pienza.** The Renaissance stage set of pocket-size Pienza takes less than an hour to see (parking and walking to the *centro* included).

tasting. For dinner, try one of the places listed in "Where to Stay & Dine in Chianti Country" (p 225). If the idea of an all-meat extravaganza excites you, don't miss a chance to dine at one of Dario Cecchini's restaurants in nearby **Panzano** (see "The Butcher of Tuscany," p 238).

On Day 3, visit a winery in the morning (recommendations on p 236) and have lunch at ★★ **Ristoro di Lamole** (p 225). After lunch, drive to San Gimignano for a few hours' tour of Tuscany's "medieval Manhattan."

From Greve in Chianti, take the SS222 south to Castellina in Chianti, then head due west on SR429, go around Poggibonsi, then head west on the SP1 and follow signs to San Gimignano (approx. 45km/28 miles total).

❹ **San Gimignano.** San Gimignano's betowered *centro storico* (of the original 70 towers, only 13 remain) is swarmed by day-trippers from morning to midafternoon, so if you arrive later in

> *The Sangiovese grape is known as "Brunello" in the wine hills around Montalcino.*

While there, buy some local *pecorino di Pienza* sheep's-milk cheese.

Spend the nights of Days 5 and 6 in the same spot. Both Montepulciano (p 280) and Pienza (p 286) are good bases, but the best property in the area, where you'll be based for 2 nights, is ★★★ **Locanda dell'Amorosa,** near Sinalunga (see box, right).

From Pienza, continue east on the SP146 to Montepulciano (14km/9 miles).

⑧ **Montepulciano.** The morning of Day 6, visit a Vino Nobile winery, like ★★★ **Cantine Dei** or ★★★ **Avignonesi** (p 255), and then have lunch at ★★ **La Grotta** in Montepulciano (p 281) or Cortona (273). They're not related, but both towns have recommended restaurants with an identical name—which means "The Cave."

From Montepulciano, take the SP326/SP32 to Cortona (33km/21 miles).

⑨ **Cortona.** Spend the afternoon of Day 6 in the steepest town in Tuscany and site of Frances Mayes's *Under the Tuscan Sun.* Cortona is a delight to explore, though it's essential to wear good walking shoes and to understand that

"steep" means *steep!* The town's unique pottery makes for good shopping opportunities.

From Cortona, take the SS71 south and then the Raccordo Autostradale Bettolle-Perugia toward Perugia (across the northern shore of Lago di Trasimeno), then the SS147 from Perugia to Assisi (69km/43 miles total).

Spending the Night near Pienza

Romantico doesn't even begin to describe the storybook ★★★ **Locanda dell'Amorosa**—an enchanting world unto itself, surrounded by vineyards, lawns, and ancient cypresses. Most guest rooms at this 14th-century manor are located in a brick courtyard where wisteria spills from the second-story arcade. The old stable is the hotel's restaurant, and the old cellars are the well-used *osteria* (wine bar). Country comfort, not limitless luxury, is the idea here, and you'll never want to leave it. Località l'Amorosa (10km/6 miles south of Sinalunga). ☎ 0577-677211. www.amorosa.it. 25 units. Doubles from 248€. AE, DC, MC, V.

10 **Assisi.** On the morning of your seventh and final day in the region, pay a visit to Umbria's number-one attraction—the birthplace of St. Francis and home of the stunning, eponymous ★★★ **Basilica di San Francesco** (p 268, **1**). A few hours are sufficient to marvel at the frescoes by Giotto and Cimabue in the upper church and to have lunch at the inimitable ★★★ **La Stalla** (p 271), a converted barn just outside the walls of Assisi that excels in roasted meats and other succulent home-style cooking.

From Assisi, take the SS147 to Perugia (24km/15 miles).

11 **Perugia.** Wind up your weeklong tour in Umbria's most happening city. Visit the impressive collections at the ★★★ **Galleria Nazionale** (p 283, **3**) and do some archaeological spelunking in the medieval ghost town beneath ★★★ **La Rocca Paolina** (p 284, **5**), then join the masses on **Corso Vannucci**—the communal promenade where Italy's most entrenched *passeggiata* ritual takes place nightly.

> TOP The Rocca Maggiore citadel affords a view over Assisi, including the campanile of San Francesco (left). BOTTOM Eerie medieval streets below what's left of Perugia's Rocca Paolina.

Renting a Villa

Villas are an increasingly popular way to stay in Tuscany and Umbria, and for good reason. In contrast to hotels, a vacation rental gives you room to spread out, the freedom to do your own thing, and the fun of living temporarily *all'italiana*. A rental car is essential for all but a handful of villas.

Villas can also save you money. You'll end up spending less on meals out, since you'll have a kitchen and dining area where you can cook feasts with local gourmet goodies. And if you're in a group, you'll save even more as you defray the rental fees over a larger number of people. The majority of villas have swimming pools, washing machines, DVD players, and satellite TV; units with reliable Internet connections are rare. Of course, villas don't come with concierges, continental breakfasts, or daily maid service. But at a minimum, all villas come with emergency contact information and local resources if any issues should arise.

As with any real estate, location is key. Find out the following before booking:

- Is it close to a main road? Country roads are fun but slow—for relaxed day trips around the region, it pays to have easy access to the thoroughfares that serve greater Tuscany and Umbria. On the flip side, steer clear of anything too close to the autostrada.

- Are there a food market, pharmacy, coffee bar, and gas station within a 5- to 10-minute drive? A bit of seclusion is great; too much is a hassle.

- What's the topography like? You're more likely to get that gorgeous cliché of sun-drenched fields and cypress-lined lanes near Montalcino and Montepulciano, while in Chianti Country and the Lucca area you'll find more mountainous, forested terrain. The Valdichiana, near Cortona, is flatter farmland and is more industrialized in parts.

Keep in mind that the noble-sounding names—*Tenuta* this, or *Poggio* that—of some listings may suggest something loftier than the reality. Sure, plenty of properties are truly estatelike, but others are blandly modern. When you do arrive at even the most idyllic properties, don't expect fairy-tale surroundings in every direction: There are bound to be modern intrusions, like the monstrous new hospital that blights the view to the south. Anticipate them, and they won't ruin your vacation.

Some agencies we like: U.K.-based **Tuscany Now** (☎ 020-7684-8884; www.tuscanynow. com), which charges from 1,600€ per week for a four-person villa. **In Tuscany** (☎ 0577-630257; www.intuscany.net) asks from 1,000€ per week for a four-person villa. **Your Tuscany** (☎ 06-68809301; www.yourtuscany. com) has high-end villas from 2,600€ per week for a property that sleeps six.

Tuscany & Umbria for Food & Wine Lovers

Gastronomes celebrate the fertile, sun-baked countryside of Tuscany for its olive groves; for its Chianina cattle, acclaimed for producing the most succulent beefsteaks in Europe; and for its grapes, which give forth world-famous wines like Chianti and Brunello. With such a bounty of fresh, locally available ingredients, Tuscany is a region of simply prepared, rural cuisine—known as *cucina povera*. Umbria, to the east, shares that tradition, with truffles and porcini adding their distinctive earthy flavors. This movable feast was designed to help you experience these regions at their most delicious.

START Lucca (77km/48 miles west of Florence on the A11). Trip length: 7 or more days.

1 Lucca. The most enjoyable eating in Lucca is the snacking you do as you walk around. The focaccias at bakery ★★ **Amedeo Giusti** (p 276, **9**) are legendary and come in all flavors. Line up at the street-facing window to place your order. The pastries at **Pasticceria Taddeucci** (p 276, **7**) are so beautifully presented that it almost seems a crime to eat them. **Antico Caffè di Simo** (p 275, **4**) is one of the most elegant coffee bars in all of Tuscany—all dark wood and antique glass and mirrors, it's a 19th-century relic that once served the great Giacomo Puccini his morning cappuccino. If the open-air market on Piazza San Michele

Travel Tip

For detailed information on sights and recommended hotels and restaurants, see the individual town listings later in this chapter.

is up and running when you're in Lucca, head for the **Nelli** cart (p 276, **6**) and try the *frate lucchese* (an unforgettable, lemony doughnut).

From Lucca, drive east on the A11 autostrada toward Florence. Outside Florence, take the A1 south to the Raccordo FI-SI, following signs to Siena. Exit at Tavarnelle, following signs east to Greve in Chianti (99km/62 miles total).

> Though codified only in 1716, Chianti has been produced in the same hills since at least the 7th century.

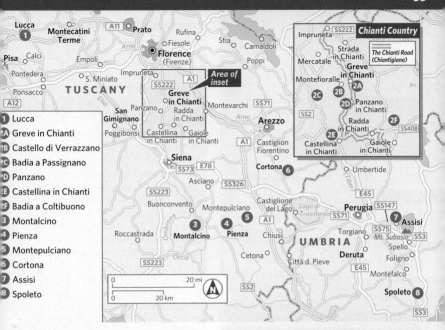

2 Chianti Country. Against a quintessential Tuscan landscape—with medieval wine castles and fields of gray-green olive groves—the Chianti Country south of Florence is home to some of Italy's best wineries and finest food producers, restaurants, and markets. You'll want to spend at least 2 days here. A good center for touring the area is its unofficial capital, **A ★ Greve in Chianti.** The Greve tourist information center is at Viale Giovanni da Verrazzano 33 (☎ 055-8546287).

Just north of Greve on the SS222, follow the signs to **B ★★★ Castello di Verrazzano** (p 236), a Chianti producer that offers a wonderful lunch feast at communal tables.

Head back to Greve, then follow signposts out of town .6km (1 mile) west toward Montefioralle. A signposted, potholed road beyond Montefioralle continues for about 30 minutes to **C ★ Badia a Passignano,** a 212-hectare (530-acre) property amid some of the best vineyards for producing Chianti. The estate belonged to Vallombrosan monks for centuries but was purchased by the Antinori family in 1987. You can visit the *bottega* (small store) on the grounds, purchase wines, and tour the historic cellars. Tastings are offered daily from 10:30am to noon and from 4:30 to 5pm (☎ 055-8071278).

Enjoying the Grape

Visiting wineries will be one of the highlights of your trip to this region, so it's important that you plan ahead. Reserve your visits well in advance, as many wineries offer only one tour per day, and only on weekdays. Visits are easily booked via the wineries' websites—the wineries we recommend are listed in boxes later in this chapter, after each of Tuscany's three winemaking regions: Chianti, Montalcino, and Montepulciano.

Due to the nature of Tuscan roads (always allow 30 min. more than you think you need!), the length of tours (they're never rushed), and the limited opening hours of most estates, you can realistically visit only one or two wineries a day. But every town has a well-stocked *enoteca* (wine bar and shop) where you can sample glasses (or buy bottles) of all the regional vintages.

From Montefioralle, follow the signposts south along a secondary road into **D Panzano,** a distance of 8.2km (5 miles). At the epicenter of Chianti Country, it's hailed as a *paese dei golosi* (village of gourmands). Foodies flock to the best butcher of Tuscany, **★★★ Antica**

> *THIS PAGE Some Tuscan reds can age well for decades. OPPOSITE PAGE Chianti's robust bouquet is a perfect complement to the region's hearty cooking.*

Macelleria Cecchini (see "The Butcher of Tuscany," p 238)—the de facto community center, where news is dispensed about whatever food events are happening.

From Panzano, follow the signs 13km (8 miles) to ⓔ **Castellina in Chianti,** home to the region's finest wine restaurant: ★★★ **L'Albergaccio,** Via Fiorentina (☎ 0577-741042; entrees 14€–25€; Fri–Tues lunch & dinner). At this restored stone barn, with a summer garden terrace, the wine list is unrivaled in Tuscany. Antipasti are prepared according to the season. Treats unique to the place include ravioli stuffed with salt cod and aromatic wood pigeon simmered in Chianti.

For our final stopover, follow the signs east to Radda in Chianti. Continue east a distance of 21km (13 miles) to ⓕ ★★★ **Badia a Coltibuono** (☎ 0577-749031; lunch & dinner daily, closed Jan 8–Mar 4). This is one of the great Chianti estates, made famous by its owner, Lorenza de' Medici (the maven of Italian cuisine). It is cel-

Chianti's Best Winery Tours & Tastings

Chianti is famous for—what else?—its Chianti red wines. To really experience the best of this varietal, we suggest stopping in at the following wineries.

Castello di Verrazzano NEAR GREVE
There's a convivial atmosphere at this lofty estate—the birthplace of explorer Giovanni da Verrazzano. The classic tour (18€) through the panoramic gardens and cellars takes 90 minutes and includes tastings of several wines, olive oil, and balsamic vinegar, even a souvenir glass. The "Wine & Food Experience" (48€) lasts 3½ hours and concludes with an excellent Tuscan home-style lunch served at communal tables. Via San Martino in Valle 12, Greti, 5km (3 miles) north of Greve. ☎ 055-854243. www.verrazzano.com. Classic wine tour Mon–Fri 10am. Tour & lunch Mon–Sat 11am. AE, DC, MC, V. Reservations required.

Fonterutoli NEAR CASTELLINA IN CHIANTI
This estate has its own medieval *borgo* (village), and the *enoteca* welcomes drop-in visitors all day for its inexpensive tastings (5€ for four wines; 6€ for six wines). Guided winery tours, which last 90 minutes and must be booked in advance, are offered weekdays at 10am and 3pm from April to October, and 11am and 3pm November to March. The cost is 14€ with a tasting of three wines, or 16€ with tasting of five wines. Borgo di Fonterutoli, 5km (3 miles) south of Castellina on SR222. ☎ 0577-741385. www.fonterutoli.it. Enoteca hours: Apr–Oct Mon–Wed, Sat 9am–7pm, Thurs, Fri 9am–8pm, Sun 10am–1pm, 2–7pm; Nov–Mar Mon, Sat 9:30am–12:30pm, 1:30–6:30pm, Tues–Fri 9:30am–6:30pm, closed Sun. AE, DC, MC, V.

ebrated for its Chiantis, virgin olive oils, and its cooking school. Fresh herbs and seasonal produce dominate the menu in the restaurant, the best place in Tuscany to order Chianina beef.

From Greve in Chianti, continue south on the SS222 toward Siena, then follow signs for the SR2 toward Rome and Montalcino (84km/55 miles total).

The Butcher of Tuscany

Foodies of the carnivorous persuasion, take heed: Your mother ship is in the heart of the Chianti region. In the one-stoplight town of Panzano, south of Greve, the butcher shop ★★★ **Antica Macelleria Cecchini,** Via XX Luglio 11 (☎ 055-852020; Sun–Tues, Thurs 9am–2pm; Fri–Sat 9am–6pm), is fondly known as the "Uffizi of Meat." Hands-on proprietor Dario Cecchini has been profiled in books and magazines and become something of a local celebrity, but the reality is that Dario is a hardworking artisan who is at his tiny shop every day it's open, often blaring classical music as he lovingly threads rosemary sprigs through balls of freshly ground beef. The place, where visitors are plied with free wine and *crostini,* is often packed. Still, despite the carnival atmosphere surrounding his Panzano storefront, his meats are serious business, sourced by top gourmet restaurants from Florence to Siena.

Of course, not everyone who visits Panzano has a kitchen where they can cook up Dario's meat preparations: That's where Dario's restaurants come in.

It started with ★★★ **Solociccia,** Dario's celebratory "only meat" place across from the butcher shop. Patrons sit at communal tables and are treated to six meat courses, which may include Cecchini's signature *tonno del Chianti* (Chianti "tuna"—which is actually delicate pork) or "sushi" (steak tartare), plus generous side dishes of Tuscan fare, country wine, and military-grade after-dinner liqueurs. For lovers of meat and convivial dining, there is no more memorable restaurant in Tuscany. Via XX Luglio/Via Chiantigiana 5. Prix fixe 30€. AE, MC, V. Dinner Thurs–Sat at 7pm and 9pm; lunch Sun at 1pm.

Steak isn't served at Solociccia, but it's the main event at ★★ **L'Officina della Bistecca** (The Steak Shop). Bring an empty stomach, as these expertly executed slabs of beef are positively dinosaur-sized. Via XX Luglio 11. Prix fixe 50€. AE, MC, V. Dinner Fri and Sat at 8pm; lunch Sun at 1pm (other times by reservation only).

If you're only in Panzano for a midday detour, there's ★★ **MacDario,** Cecchini's take on "fast food" Tuscan-style. Here, huge and juicy burgers are served with thick-cut, garlic-and-sage Tuscan "fries." Via XX Luglio 5. Meals start at 10€. AE, MC, V. Lunch Mon–Tues and Thurs–Sat.

---

❸ **Montalcino.** This medieval hill town yields Brunello di Montalcino, one of the greatest wines in the world. Many wineries welcome visitors, and the town is filled with wine shops and *enoteche* (wine cellars).

To sample the town's foodstuffs, including its gourmet honey and its pecorino cheese, go to ★★ **Enoteca La Fortezza** (p 278, ❶). While in Montalcino, be sure to try Brunello's "younger brother," Rosso di Montalcino, made of the same grapes as its more famous counterpart.

Taking far less time to age, this is a fruity red with Brunello's flavor and a much lower price tag.

For recommendations on visiting Brunello wineries, see p 240 or check with the wine consortium at the center of town, inside the **Palazzo Comunale,** Costa del Municipio 1 (☎ 0577-848246; Tues–Sat 10am–7pm; Sun noon–6pm).

From Montalcino, take the SR2 toward San Quirico d'Orcia, then the SP146 east to Pienza (24km/15 miles total).

> *Pecorino di Pienza, made from ewe's milk, is aged or flavored in a variety of ways.*

4 Pienza. The gastronomic claim to fame of this tiny 15th-century village, the "ideal Renaissance city," is its cheese—pecorino di Pienza—made from the milk of local ewes. The official store of the only licensed producer of this cheese, **Caseificio Pienza SOLP,** is in the *centro storico* at Via Dogali 6 (☎ 0578-748695). Depending on which variety you choose (fresh, semi-aged, and mature) and what flavor (herbed, truffled, and so on), the store staff can make suggestions about what to pair the pecorino with, whether cured meats or honey.

From Pienza, drive east to Montepulciano, following SS146 (14km/9 miles).

5 Montepulciano. This ancient town of Etruscan origin, dominating the hills of the Valdichiana, is celebrated for its violet-scented, orange-speckled ruby wine, Vino Nobile di Montepulciano, in production since the 8th century. Although Brunello from nearby Montalcino (see above) is beefier and considered number one by most connoisseurs, the eminently drinkable Vino Nobile is a better companion to a wider range of foods.

As is the case with the Montalcino wine, a younger and less expensive Rosso di Montepulciano exists. It is aged for a shorter period and sold sooner.

A visit to the intimate ★★★ **Cantine Dei** winery (see "Montepulciano's Best Winery Tours & Tastings," p 255) is a wonderful way to get acquainted with Montepulciano's wine tradition and winemakers' relationship with the land.

From Montepulciano, take the SP326/SP32 to Cortona (33km/21 miles).

6 Cortona. Just blocks from Cortona's main square, ★★★ **La Bucaccia** (p 273) is one of my favorite places to eat in Tuscany. You can't help but fall in love with the Magi family, who owns and operates the cavelike restaurant: Their enthusiasm and passion for Cortonese cooking are infectious. Romano handles the dining room, while Agostina heads up the kitchen, making absolutely everything from scratch. Even their young daughter Francesca lends a hand (though not too late on school nights), serving customers like a seasoned pro. While

Montalcino's Best Winery Tours & Tastings

Montalcino is home of the exalted Brunello and more humble Rosso di Montalcino. We suggest stopping in at the following wineries.

Altesino NORTH OF MONTALCINO
Altesino offers tours and tastings (of a Brunello, a Rosso di Montalcino, and a Super-Tuscan) for 10€. Upon reservation, you can also have a light lunch. Località Altesino 54 (12km/7K miles north of Montalcino). ☎ 0577-806208. www.altesino.it. Daily 10am–6pm; advance booking recommended. AE, DC, MC, V.

Castello Banfi SOUTH OF MONTALCINO
If the tasting-room setup here—with elegant accessories for sale along with wines, oils, and vinegars—reminds you of the big California wineries, it's because Banfi is American-owned. Tours (from 10€ with tasting) take you through the state-of-the-art cellars (a 5-min. drive from the castle). Castello di Poggio alle Mura. Sant'Angelo Scalo (20km/12 miles south of Montalcino). ☎ 0577-840111. www.castellobanfi.com. AE, DC, MC, V.

Poggio Antico SOUTH OF MONTALCINO
Our favorite Brunello winery is this award-winning estate run by the charming Gloder-Montefiori family. The attached **Ristorante di Poggio Antico** is a destination in its own right, turning out top-notch "revisited" Tuscan cuisine. Località I Poggi (3km/2 miles south of Montalcino). ☎ 0577-848044. www.poggio antico.com. Tours and tastings from 10€ (reservations requested): Mon–Fri 9am–1pm, 2:30–6pm; Sat–Sun by appointment. AE, DC, MC, V.

> *Much of Tuscany's famed produce is cultivated in the fertile provinces of the southwest.*

the clientele tends to be mostly travelers, the atmosphere is warm and authentic. From *antipasto* to *dolce,* this is one dining experience you'll remember for a very long time.

From Cortona, take the SS71 south and then the Raccordo Autostradale Bettolle-Perugia toward Perugia (across the northern shore of Lago di Trasimeno), then the SS147 from Perugia to Assisi (69km/43 miles total).

7 Assisi. You might not think of Assisi as a culinary destination—it's a religious and artistic destination first and foremost, with the Basilica of St. Francis drawing millions of visitors each year. But just outside the old city gates is an Umbrian barbecue joint of sorts, ★★★ **La Stalla** (p 271). This rough-and-tumble spot ranks right up there with the great culinary experiences in Italy. Fashioned out of old livestock stalls, it's a meat-lover's place, so vegetarians and cholesterol-watchers should skip straight to **8**.

From Assisi, take the SS147, SS75, and SS3 south to Spoleto (46km/29 miles).

> Crostini con trito di coniglio, *or toasted bread with minced rabbit.*

8 **Spoleto** The unofficial headquarters of the Umbrian black truffle (*tartufo nero*) has a number of great places to sample the coveted tubers in pastas or shaved over grilled meats. **Via Arco di Druso,** in the heart of old Spoleto, also has some great delis where you can pick up picnic supplies of local meats and cheeses. The best dining in town is the aptly named ★★★ **Il Tartufo,** Piazza Garibaldi 24 (☎ 0743-40236; entrees 10€–26€; set menus without wine 30€–35€; AE, DC, MC, V; lunch & dinner Tues–Sat; Sun lunch; closed last 2 weeks in July; reservations required). It's a modern and airy place where the menu is a happy minefield of truffles and porcini mushrooms, which lend their inimitable earthy flavors to polentas and meat dishes.

> *Wine buffs will find a well-stocked* enoteca *in most Tuscan towns.*

A GRAPE GUIDE

Italy's Wine-Making Regions

BY STEPHEN BREWER

GRAPEVINES GROW all over Italy, and an estimated one million vineyards carpet the landscape. The most widely recognized wines, and many connoisseurs say the best, are the legendary Italian reds—Barolo and Barbaresco from Piedmont, and Chianti and Brunello di Montalcino from Tuscany. That, of course, doesn't mean that Italy doesn't also produce many superb whites, or that excellent wines don't show up just about everywhere you go in this country. Here's a brief guide to the grapes that flourish in the different regions and the wines they yield.

Key Grape-Growing Regions

① PIEDMONT
The Nebbiolo grape shows up in Barolo, the full-bodied king of Italian reds, and the lighter Barbaresco. Moscato grapes yield sparkling Asti Spumante and the lesser-known but delicious Moscato d'Asti, a dessert wine.

② ABRUZZO
The Trebbiano grape produces the crisp, gentle white Trebbiano d'Abruzzo, and from the Montepulciano d'Abruzzo grape comes the dry red wine of the same name.

③ VENETO
The white Prosecco grape yields the light sparkling wine of the same name. Valpolicellas are smooth reds made primarily from the Corvina grape.

④ EMILIA-ROMAGNA
Lambrusco grapes yield the region's famous red of the same name—a little fizzy, a little sweet, and tastier than might be expected.

⑤ TUSCANY
Tuscany's much-loved red wines are almost entirely based on the Sangiovese grape, with Chianti Classico, Brunello di Montalcino, Rosso di Montalcino, and Vino Nobile wines from the town of Montepulciano leading the pack. Vernaccia from San Gimignano, made from the Vernaccia grape, is one of the region's most notable whites.

⑥ LAZIO
Sparkling white Frascati, produced in the town of the same name in the hills above Rome, is made from a blend of Trebbiano and Malvasia grapes.

⑦ SICILY
Full-bodied Nero d'Avola is made from the grape of the same name. Sicilian whites made from the Catarratto grape are reliably crisp and good.

Be Label-Conscious

Always look for "DOC" and "DOCG" designations on wine labels. The first, Denominazione di Origine Controllata, means the wine is produced in a specific growing area and adheres to certain standards. The second designation adds the words "e Garantita," and imposes a more rigorous standard. Italy has some 260 DOC designations and 36 DOCG designations—most of the DOCGs are in Piedmont and Tuscany. "IGT," Indicazione Geografica Tipica, is a designation for wines that are not subject to DOC and DOCG standards but are nonetheless recognized for high quality; among these are the finely crafted and delicious Super Tuscans.

Sip from the Source

The website of the Movimento Turismo del Vino (www.movimentoturismovino.it) lists major Italian growing regions and suggests itineraries in each for visits to wineries that welcome visitors. It also sponsors Cantine Aperte, one day a year (May 31) when some 800 wineries around the country are open to the public, with tours and tastings.

The Best Art & Architecture in Tuscany & Umbria

While most of Tuscany's individual masterpieces of art are in museums and churches in Florence and Siena, where the works were commissioned and created, you'll still find plenty of dazzling buildings and magnificent frescoes in the towns and countryside of Tuscany and Umbria. Arezzo has a first-rate repository of work by Piero della Francesca. Giotto's St. Francis frescoes in Assisi are among the most important in the history of art. Architectural interest in these regions comes in well-preserved medieval towns, isolated abbeys, and in the unique design of pint-size cities like Lucignano and Pienza.

START Lucca is 77km (48 miles) west of Florence on the A11. Trip length: 7 days.

1 Lucca. Inside its thick swath of Renaissance walls, bordered by gardens, Lucca still thrives within its medieval street plan. For architecture buffs, it's one of the most richly rewarding cities of Tuscany. Its Romanesque churches, best appreciated for their facades, exemplify the Pisan-Romanesque style, richly embroidered with polychrome marble insets and relief carvings by visiting Lombardian and Pisan sculptors. The main attractions include the ★★ **Duomo,** or **Cattedrale di San Martino** (p 275, **5**), with its green and white marble facade designed by Guidetto da Como; and the exceptionally tall **San Michele in Foro**—another stellar example of Luccan influence on the Pisan-Romanesque style and one of region's most beautiful church exteriors, with its delicately twisted columns and arcades.

Before the Pisan style of architecture swept through town here, the Luccan-Romanesque style prevailed. The church of **San Frediano** is a prime example, graced with white marble from the ancient Roman amphitheater.

Travel Tip

For detailed information on sights and recommended hotels and restaurants, see the individual town listings later in this chapter.

> *San Gimignano once had 70 towers, but only one, the Torre Grossa, can be scaled today.*

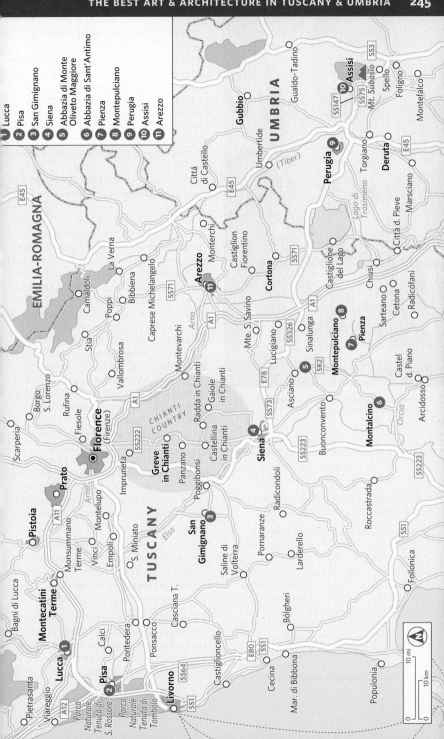

> *Among the treasures inside Pisa's Duomo is Giovanni Pisano's 1311 pulpit.*

In general, the streets of the old town, **Città Vecchia**, are full of Gothic and Renaissance palazzi and other delights. The town is well worth an entire day of your trip.

From Lucca, take the A11 west to the SS1 and follow signs to Pisa (25km/16 miles).

2 Pisa. With its Leaning Tower, Pisa introduced the world to the Pisan-Romanesque style of architecture and sculpture—which flourished from the 11th to the 13th centuries, when the Pisan Republic was a powerful maritime city-state. Gothic sculpture flourished here as well, at the hands of sculptor Nicola Pisano (1220–80) and his son, Giovanni Pisano (1250–1315).

Touring Pisa is easy; its foremost monuments center around the ★★★ **Piazza del Duomo**, the city's historic core (also known as the Campo or Piazza dei Miracoli, or Field of Miracles). There's not a lot more to the town after you've spent a few hours taking in the sites on the main square.

The heavy, white marble ★★★ **Leaning Tower** (see "The Nuts & Bolts of Climbing," p 222), of course, is the most compelling structure, with its six floors of circular galleries. It's famous for its tilt and its beauty, but also for the experiments Galileo conducted there (he dropped his mismatched balls from the top of the leaning side). Construction began in 1173 in the pure Romanesque style, and continued until 1350. Stainless steel cables keep the tower from toppling.

The prototype for the Pisan-Romanesque style, the ★★ **Duomo**, Piazza del Duomo 17 (☎ 050-560547; admission 2€; Nov–Feb Mon–Sat 10am–12:45pm, 3–4:30pm, Sun 3–6:30pm; Oct, Mar Mon–Sat 10am–5:30pm, Sun 1–5:30pm; Apr–Sept Mon–Sat 10am–7:30pm), is an even greater treasure, particularly its west front with its four tiers of graceful marble columns. The fine Romanesque bronze panels on the south transept door date to the 12th century. The interior is also an impressive achievement and there is a stunning pulpit, carved by Giovanni Pisano from 1302 to 1311.

The nearby ★★ **Battistero**, Piazza del Duomo (☎ 050-560547; admission 5€; Nov–Feb daily 9am–4:20pm; Mar and Oct daily 9am–5:30pm; Apr–Sept daily 8am–7:30pm), is another stellar example of the Pisan-Romanesque style. The roof is crowned by an unusual Gothic dome with four doorways, each decorated with fine carving. Papa Pisano carved the impressive pulpit.

If time remains, check out the **Museo dell'Opera del Duomo,** now the home of sculptures that were removed from the Piazza del Duomo for safekeeping. Some from the Romanesque period are masterpieces by unknown artists.

From Pisa, head east along the Strada Grande Comunicazione Firenze-Pisa-Livorno, then go south on the SR429. Near the town of Certaldo, cut southwest, following signs for San Gimignano (86km/54 miles total).

3 San Gimignano. Visitors can journey back to the Middle Ages in San Gimignano, Italy's best-preserved medieval town. Although San Gimignano is unique in appearance today, towns throughout central Italy looked much like it during the Middle Ages.

Thirteen of 70 original towers are still standing since the town's heyday, from the 11th to

The World's Tipsiest Tower

When Guglielmo and Bonanno Pisano laid the foundations of their city's bell tower in 1173, little did they know that centuries after their lifetime, the very word "Pisa" would conjure images in the minds of people worldwide of a jauntily askance, ornate white marble cylinder. When the Leaning Tower was finally completed in 1390, its architects had unknowingly created an indelible Italian icon—one that rakes in over 10,000€ in entrance fees every day.

Thanks to a particularly bad patch of shifting Pisan subsoil (which is watery from the Arno and sandy all over town), the tower was already leaning when builders reached the third level, in 1185. Work on the tower ground to a halt. After a century of hemming and hawing and engineers' head-scratching, Giovanni di Simone took the reins on the project in 1275 and resumed construction. To correct the lean, his solution was to build a banana-like curve into the cylindrical structure that would help it reach a more vertical profile. That curve worked to some extent and is still visible today; problem was, the foundation kept sinking, and the tower kept tipping.

By 1990, the tower's lean was about 4.6m (15 ft.) off the vertical, and the mayor of Pisa ordered the tower closed to visitors indefinitely. Since then, a series of delicate endeavors to shore up the tower's foundations have succeeded in righting the tower a mere .6m (2 ft.) closer to vertical. Still plenty off-kilter to attract the tourist masses, but not so precarious as to come crashing down over Piazza dei Miracoli, the tower reopened to the public in 2001. Though its prominent lean looks disconcerting to prospective climbers (or to anyone standing to its southwest), the tower is now stable—like a pole that's been hit by a car, it would probably suffer catastrophically if anyone tried to jiggle it back into place.

For the best "Look, I'm holding up the Leaning Tower!" photo op, head to the southern flank of the cathedral. Walk over to the northeastern part of the square for the infinitely more amusing "Look, I'm body-slamming the Leaning Tower!" shot.

And for the record, most locals just call it the *torre di Pisa* ("tower of Pisa"). Perhaps because calling it the *torre pendente* ("leaning tower") would be acknowledging the obvious truth, that the town's biggest attraction is, well, defective.

> *Siena's Duomo is striking, from its Romanesque-Gothic facade to its marble-striped, exuberantly decorated interior.*

> *A detail from Lorenzo Lotto's 1527 Nativity, part of the collection in Siena's Pinacoteca Nazionale.*

the 13th centuries. More than defensive strongholds, the towers stood as symbols of a family's prestige and worth; the taller the tower, the more powerful the ruling dynasty.

From San Gimignano, go east on the S324 to Poggibonsi and take the Raccordo FI-SI south to the signposted exits for Siena (40km/24 miles total).

❹ **Siena.** After Florence, Siena holds more pleasures for art and architecture lovers than any other Tuscan town. Our hurried tour calls for only 1 day here, but at least 2 days are preferable.

In the Middle Ages, Siena rivaled Florence as an art center until the Renaissance, when Sienese artists clung to Greek and Byzantine formulas and fell behind the times. Duccio di Buoninsegna and Simone Martini were pioneers in bringing greater realism to the more static Byzantine style with the flowing lines and expressive human features in their work. But the Black Death of 1348 also dealt a crippling blow to artistic aspirations in Siena.

Nicola and Giovanni Pisano, who both worked on the ★★★ **Duomo** (p 292, ❺), were the first proponents of Gothic architecture in town. The Duomo is also a treasure trove of

> *"Benedict Leaves His Parents,"* a panel from the Life of St. Benedict *fresco cycle at Monte Oliveto Maggiore.*

Tuscan and Sienese art with Nicola Pisano's 13th-century pulpit an undisputed masterpiece.

The ★ **Pinacoteca Nazionale** (p 293, ❾) is the greatest repository of Sienese art. It's not the Uffizi, but it houses an extensive collection of masterpieces created between the 13th and 16th centuries. Here you'll see works by all Siena's most famous artists, including Duccio and the great Simone Martini, the Lorenzetti brothers, Domenico Beccafumi, and Il Sodoma.

The ★★ **Palazzo Pubblico** houses the Sala della Pace (p 291, ❸) with Ambrogio Lorenzetti's fresco masterpieces *The Effects of Good and Bad Government.*

Some of the city's greatest art is on display at the ★★ **Museo dell'Opera Metropolitana** (p 292, ❻), which is especially strong on works by Duccio and Jacopo della Quercia, a towering figure in Gothic art.

From Siena, take the SP438 toward Asciano, then follow the SP451 to Monte Oliveto Maggiore (37km/23 miles total).

❺ ★★ **Abbazia di Monte Oliveto Maggiore.** The ★★★ **panoramic drive** from Siena to this 14th-century Benedictine abbey is among the most beautiful in Tuscany, taking in the dramatic clay hills of the Crete Senesi. Upon arrival at the splendidly secluded monastery complex (you'll enter on foot via drawbridge), a steep wooded path takes you down past the old fishpond to the abbey itself. The *chiostro grande*

(central cloister) is the main art-historical attraction here, with its fantastic **Life of St. Benedict fresco cycle** by Luca Signorelli and Il Sodoma. The 36 compelling scenes, begun in 1497, were finished in 1508. While at the abbey, have a look at the refectory, where you can see tables set—with bottled water and condiments—for the monks' communal meals. If you're here in late afternoon, consider staying for Vespers (Mon–Sat 6:15pm; Sun 6:30pm), which is recited in Gregorian chant. You can buy and taste Monte Oliveto wine in the abbey's cellar. Monte Oliveto Maggiore, Chiusura. ☎ 0577-718567. Daily 9:15am–noon, 3:15pm–5pm (until 6pm May–Oct). Free admission.

From the Abbazia di Monte Oliveto Maggiore, take the SS451 toward Buonconvento, then SR2 south to Montalcino (25km/16 miles total). The Abbazia di Sant'Antimo is just south of Montalcino.

❻ ★★★ **Abbazia di Sant'Antimo.** If you ignore the classically Tuscan patchwork valley of cypress groves and wheat fields that surround it, this 12th-century abbey looks like it could be in France. Its simple Gothic bones and unfussy travertine construction are a marvelous example of Romanesque restraint. Filtered sunlight gives the dusky stone interior of Sant'Antimo a magical quality, and a real quietness that's hard to find in Italian churches. It's not completely devoid of embellishment, however: The

> *The Basilica di San Francesco complex in Assisi is composed of a Gothic upper church counterpoised by an intimate Romanesque lower church below it.*

column capitals and bases have reliefs carved in luminous alabaster. Artistic accolades aside, the main reason many people visit the abbey is to hear Gregorian chant—Sant'Antimo is an active monastery and one of few in Italy where the friars still recite the liturgy in this ancient style. There are at least three Gregorian chant services at Sant'Antimo daily; see p 278, **❷**, for the schedule and complete information about visiting the abbey.

From the Abbazia di Sant'Antimo, head back past Montalcino and take the SP14/SP146 east to Pienza (15km/9 miles).

❼ Pienza. This honey-colored village owes its overall look to Pope Pius II, who was born here in 1405. He set out to transform Pienza into a model Renaissance mini-city and succeeded admirably. Bernardo Rossellino, a protégé of the great Renaissance theorist Leon Battista Alberti, carried out the pope's mandate, creating a light-filled ★★ **Duomo** (p 286, **❷**) with a Renaissance facade, the ★ **Palazzo Piccolomini** (Rossellino's masterpiece), and a main square that remains a Renaissance jewel.

Critics of the Vatican denounced all the money spent and called Pienza "the pope's folly." Pius died before the work was complete,

but his achievement endures, helping to lure fans of great architecture to Tuscany.

From Pienza, drive east to Montepulciano, following SS146 (14km/9 miles).

❽ Montepulciano. One of the region's highest hill towns, its architecturally harmonious medieval streets open onto panoramic views of the countryside. Spend a day wandering and discovering its treasures, beginning with the parade of Renaissance palazzi flanking its main street, the "Corso."

The chief attractions are the ★★ **Duomo,** ★★ **Palazzo Neri-Orselli,** ★★ **Palazzo Nobili-Tarugi,** and ★★ **Tempio di San Biagio** (a masterpiece of High Renaissance architecture); everything centers around the monumental ★ **Piazza Grande.** See p 280 for more details.

Montepulciano makes the best place in the area to stay for the night (see p 281 for our suggestions).

From Montepulciano, cut east on the SP10 and SP32 to the Raccordo Autostradale Perugia-A1, following signs to Perugia (67km/42 miles).

❾ Perugia. The 30 rooms of the impressive ★★★ **Galleria Nazionale** (p 283, **❸**) comprise Umbria's finest repository of paintings, including

> St. Francis Renounces Worldly Goods, *one of Giotto's frescoes in Assisi's upper church.*

works by hometown artists Perugino and Pinturicchio. Perugia's other great site of architectural (and archaeological) interest is ★ **La Rocca Paolina** (p 284, ⑤), the underground cavity beneath Piazza Italia, where an entire swath of the medieval city was covered in the 16th century to make way for a papal fortress. It's now a freely accessible public exhibition space that, together with the paintings hanging in the Galleria Nazionale, sheds light on what life must have been like in Perugia 700 years ago.

From Perugia, take the SS147 to Assisi (24km/15 miles).

⑩ **Assisi.** Religious pilgrims and lovers of art flock to Assisi for one reason: to go to the ★★★ **Basilica di San Francesco** (p 268, ①). No matter your faith or background in art history, one look at Giotto's delightful ★★★ **Life of St. Francis frescoes** (1295–1300) in the upper church, and you'll be a convert. After the devastating 1997 earthquake, the frescoes were cleaned up and restored to remarkable brilliance, and each scene—*Expulsion of the Demons from Arezzo,* or *St. Francis Preaching to*

the Birds—absorbs you with its loving detail and lively use of color.

From Assisi, follow signs back to Perugia, then take the Raccordo Autostradale Perugia-A1 to the west, and then the A1 north toward Florence (115km/72 miles). Take the Arezzo exit and follow signs into the city, another 9km (5½ miles) after exiting the autostrada.

⑪ **Arezzo.** Arezzo marks the start of the **Piero della Francesca trail.** Della Francesca was a visionary early Renaissance master artist who created a dramatic style and explored the geometry of perspective. Born in the early 15th century, he spent his life painting and writing books on geometry and perspective until he went blind at the age of 60.

In the morning in Arezzo, you can visit his fresco masterpiece, the *Legend of the Holy Cross* (1452–66) on the walls of the apse at the ★★★ **Basilica di San Francesco** (p 266, ①). Treated with great realism, these frescoes evoke the Renaissance ideal of serenity and, in their subtle lighting techniques, a sense of timelessness.

The Best of Southern Tuscany

Siena and the sweep of countryside to the southeast, from Montalcino to Cortona, are the stuff of Tuscan coffee-table books and best-selling memoirs. Whether you're looking for olive groves, vineyards, cypresses, or wheat fields studded with farmhouses, all the Tuscan stereotypes are perpetuated here. Southern Tuscany is also one of the most activity-filled parts of the region, with options ranging from wine touring in Montalcino and Montepulciano to taking the thermal waters in Bagno Vignoni.

START Siena is 75km (47 miles) south of Florence on the Raccordo Firenze-Siena. Trip length: 5 days.

1 Siena. In stark contrast to Florence, where the rush of modern life and mass tourism has somewhat blighted the city's Renaissance splendor, Siena has preserved its time-capsule atmosphere despite an annual onslaught of visitors. Ever since the 14th century, when the Black Death wiped out most of the population and rendered Siena a minor player on the political map, the city has jealously guarded its traditions—like its 17 ancient *contrade* (neighborhoods) that proudly bear names like

Travel Tip

For detailed information on sights and recommended hotels and restaurants, see the individual town listings later in this chapter.

"Caterpillar" and "Porcupine" and compete against each other in the two Palio horse races each summer—and remained Italy's most showstopping medieval city. It's home to the most dramatic square in the country, ★★★ **Piazza del Campo,** and its ★★★ **Duomo** (p 292, **5**) is one of the most splendid cathedrals anywhere. Spend a day traipsing

> The extraordinary landscape of southern Tuscany is defined by two valleys, the Val d'Orcia and Valdichiana.

1. Siena
2. Abbazia di Monte Oliveto Maggiore
3. Montalcino
4. San Quirico d'Orcia
5. Bagno Vignoni
6. Pienza
7. Montepulciano
8. Cortona

between the *terzi* ("thirds") of Siena, which are splayed out like the letter Y on three ridges that converge at Il Campo. Peer into the doorways of *contrada* headquarters for a taste of the medieval rituals that still live on here.

Siena is also the gateway to what many consider the visual definition of Tuscany—the southern part of it. The town's proximity to everything on this tour (except for Cortona, which is 73km/45 miles away) makes it a good base for exploring southern Tuscany, though Montepulciano and Pienza are just as convenient and offer more of a country feel.

From Siena, drive southeast along SP438 toward Asciano, then follow signs to Monte Oliveto Maggiore (37km/23 miles total).

2 ★★ Abbazia di Monte Oliveto Maggiore.
It's amazing how quickly the scenery changes once you head southeast out of Siena along the SP438. Here, in the famous Crete Senesi, a carpet of greenish-gray clay soil covers the gently rolling hills, imparting a different, otherworldly color to the landscape depending on how the light catches it. After Asciano, the ridge-hugging drive to the abbey gets even more thrilling—just beyond the shoulders of the road, escarpments of clay plunge precariously down to the valley below.

Spending the Night near Montalcino

The most luxurious lodging in the region is at ★★★ **Castello Banfi–Il Borgo,** below the castle at the Banfi winery. In the recently restored buildings of this medieval village *(borgo),* supremely comfortable guest rooms feature country-chic furniture and linens, and in the enormous bathrooms, you'll find soaps and lotions made from Banfi grapes. Il Borgo's isolation, however, 20km (12 miles) from Montalcino, means you may end up eating many meals at Banfi's own, rather formal restaurants. Poggio alle Mura, Sant'Angelo Scalo (take SP14 toward S. Angelo Scalo, then follow signs for Castello Banfi). ☎ 0577-877700. www.castellobanfiilborgo.com. 14 units. Doubles 320€–580€; suites from 580€ w/buffet breakfast. AE, DC, MC, V.

> *Lush, rolling contours and cypress-studded ridges are typical of the Val d'Orcia.*

The monks who chose the site for the 14th-century Abbazia di Monte Oliveto Maggiore were certainly good judges of real estate. The brick complex occupies the end of a heavily wooded ridge, with valley views for 270 degrees. The principal attraction at the abbey is the *Life of St. Benedict* **cycle of frescoes** by Luca Signorelli and Il Sodoma in the central cloister, but it's just as rewarding to walk around the serene grounds, which remain refreshingly cool and shady even in the height of summer. Free tastings of wine—made by the Benedictine brothers here—are offered in the abbey's cellar. See p 249, ⑤, for visitor information.

From Monte Oliveto Maggiore, take the SS451 toward Buonconvento, then SR2 south to Montalcino (25km/16 miles total).

③ **Montalcino.** The medieval hill town from which slopes of Brunello vineyards radiate is one of the most happening, yet still authentic, small cities in Tuscany, with lively restaurants and cafes, and opportunities galore to sample the king of Tuscan wine, Brunello di Montalcino. Climb

Spending the Night in Bagno Vignoni

If you find the waters so relaxing that you want to spend the night in Bagno Vignoni, try the old-world ★ **Hotel Posta Marcucci,** a family-run place where a night's stay includes use of the hotel's own thermal pool, Piscina Val di Sole. Loc. Ara Urcea 43. ☎ 0577-887112. www.hotelpostamarcucci.it. 36 units. Doubles start at 164€. AE, MC, V.

> *San Quirico was once an important stop on the pilgrim route linking Canterbury (in England) with Rome.*

the ramparts of the old fortress for stunning Val d'Orcia views, then taste some local vintages at ★★ **Enoteca La Fortezza** (p 278, ❶), set in a corner of the fortress walls. The town also makes a fine base for exploring Montepulciano and Pienza.

From Montalcino, take the SR2 east to San Quirico d'Orcia (15km/9 miles).

❹ **San Quirico d'Orcia.** It's overlooked by most on the Montalcino-Pienza-Montepulciano circuit, but San Quirico d'Orcia is nevertheless one of the Val d'Orcia's most beautiful towns and worth passing through on your way out of Montalcino. As you wander around, don't miss the ★★ **Horti Leonini,** Piazza della Libertà (☎ 0577-897506). These 16th-century gardens, laid out as a resting place for pilgrims on their way to Rome, have perfect geometric patterns of box hedges—it's a surprisingly sophisticated spot to come across in such a sleepy town.

From San Quirico d'Orcia, continue south on the SR2 to Bagno Vignoni (5km/3 miles).

❺ **Bagno Vignoni.** Instead of a piazza at the center of this hamlet, there's an ancient pool of steaming mineral water. The town's history as a

Montepulciano's Best Winery Tours & Tastings

Visitors flock to vineyards around Montepulciano to try the locally produced Vino Nobile. Our favorites are listed below.

Avignonesi VALIANO
The best-known Vino Nobile di Montepulciano is made here. The tours, led by highly informative guides, take you through Avignonesi's 19th-century cellars and wind up with a leisurely seated tasting. Fattoria Capezzine, Valiano (15km/9 miles east of Montepulciano, or 8km/5 miles south of Cortona). ☎ 0578-724304. www.avignonesi.it. Tour & tasting free of charge (reservations required): Mon–Fri 10:30am, noon, and 3pm. AE, DC, MC, V.

Cantine Dei EAST OF MONTEPULCIANO
With her rock 'n' roll spirit, proprietress Caterina has an enthusiasm about her wines that is contagious. The tasting (10€) includes the estate's own extra-virgin olive oil, the best and least acidic in Tuscany. Villa Martiena, 3km (2 miles) east of Montepulciano. ☎ 0578-716878. www.cantinedei.com. Tour & tasting 10€ (reservations required): Mon–Fri 9:30am–12:30pm, 2:30–5:30pm. AE, DC, MC, V.

> *The Valdichiana is the home of Chianina cattle, the only beef permitted in authentic* bistecca alla fiorentina.

spa destination goes back to the Roman period, when the hot springs here were recognized for their therapeutic properties. Bagno Vignoni's thermal waters are rich in bicarbonate, sulfate, alkaline-earth elements, iron, and zinc, and soaking in them is reputedly beneficial for joint and respiratory problems. The medieval setting in the idyllic Val d'Orcia is certainly an antidote to stress, in any case, and the old-fashioned health-institution feel of some of the buildings is a fun throwback.

Visitors wishing to partake of the spa experience can go to the **Antiche Terme di Bagno Vignoni,** Piazza del Moretto 12 (☎ 0577-887635; www.termebagnovignoni.it; June–Oct 8am–1pm), or the **Piscina Val di Sole** at the Hotel Posta Marcucci (☎ 0577-887112; www.piscinavaldisole.it;

Oct–Mar 10am–5pm, Apr–Sept 9:30am–1pm, 2–6pm; closed Thurs), where day-use of the pools and a locker costs about 15€. Massages, mud wraps, and other treatments are available, too.

From Bagno Vignoni, head back north on the SR2, then take the SS146 to Pienza (15km/9 miles total).

⑥ Pienza. Park your car on the outskirts of this tiny village and walk into what looks like a stage set for a Renaissance play—the tawny beige streets seem too perfect and picturesque to be real. Pienza was given its ideal-city layout and perfectly proportioned buildings under the humanist Pope Pius II, who was born here in 1405. Stroll down **Via dell'Amore,** and take in

Spending the Night near Cortona

Among the best country inns in the valley below Cortona is ★★ **Villa Baldelli.** The furnishings make you feel like a noble at this welcoming and warm country house with wonderful old stone floors and high, beamed ceilings. The extensive grounds include a pool and a 3-hole practice green. San Pietro a Cegliolo 420 (5km/3 miles north of Cortona). ☎ 0575-612406. www.relaisvillabaldelli. com. 15 units. Doubles 199€–250€ w/buffet breakfast. AE, DC, MC, V.

> There's hardly a flat street in Montepulciano.

the romantic panorama over golden rolling hills studded with cypresses to the south: it was here that much of *The English Patient* was filmed.

Peek your head in the ★★ **Duomo** (p 286, ❷), whose spire and nave have a Germanic feel. (Pius spent many years in Germany and praised how light-filled the churches there were.) Trattoria ★ **Latte di Luna,** Via San Carlo 2–4 (☎ 0578-748606), at the eastern end of Corso Rossellino, is a great spot for lunch or dinner, but even if you don't have time for a full meal, there are dozens of shops in town that sell the local sheep's milk cheese, pecorino di Pienza, in its many flavored varieties.

From Pienza, take SS146 east to Montepulciano (14km/9 miles).

❼ **Montepulciano.** The narrow main street snakes its way to the top of this hill town, where the high ★ **Piazza Grande** is studded with Renaissance and medieval monuments (though the best single monument here is actually just outside the walls, the ★★ **Tempio di San Biagio**). The views from the walls are epic, and nearby, there are several wineries where you can learn about the production of, and taste, the local specialty, Vino Nobile di Montepulciano (see "Montepulciano's Best Winery Tours & Tastings," p 255, for recommendations). Montepulciano is also conveniently located near the A1 autostrada, making it a popular base or detour when traveling in Tuscany or Umbria, but don't expect much nightlife beyond a few older tourists and locals out for a leisurely evening stroll.

From Montepulciano, take the SP16/SP326/ SP32 to Cortona (33km/21 miles).

❽ **Cortona.** Writer Frances Mayes put Cortona on tourists' radar when her memoir about buying and fixing up Villa Bramasole, on the outskirts of town, became an international bestseller. And except for a stifling spell between June and July, we're pleased to report that the "Tuscan Sun" effect has not ruined Cortona. Its streets and piazzas are pristine and unspoiled, and in the town's steep (and I do mean steep) upper reaches, there are still local families that raise livestock in pens adjacent to their medieval houses. Cortona has some wonderful places to eat—★★★ **La Bucaccia** (p 273) is the best—and in the valley below the town, there are several comfortable country inns that make good bases for exploring the area.

The Best of Umbria

Like so much of central Italy, Umbria has an undulating topography that's studded with hill towns, but its generous supply of cultural, natural, and gastronomic delights is just far enough off the beaten path to feel more authentic. Umbria is often compared with Tuscany—and there are enough similarities to have earned it the overused "the new Tuscany" moniker—but on the whole, it's a greener and more rustic region that's far less inundated by tourists.

START Orvieto is 165km (103 miles) south of Florence and 120km (75 miles) north of Rome on the A1. Trip length: 4–5 days.

1 Orvieto. A steep plug of red tufa (volcanic rock) rises out of the plains of southern Umbria. Atop it, the city of Orvieto—its warren of medieval streets and spectacular Duomo improbably perched on the bluff—never fails to impress. Many first-time visitors to Italy have already had some introduction to the place—in the form of its dry white wine, Orvieto Classico.

A bright red funicular railway connects the bus and train station and parking lots of Orvieto Scalo with Orvieto proper. Once you've reached the "summit," the streets have a coziness and gentility that serve as an appropriate introduction to the feel of so many Umbrian towns. Shoppers will find beautiful ceramics

Travel Tip

For detailed information on sights and recommended hotels and restaurants, see the individual town listings later in this chapter.

and fashion in the boutiques of Via Garibaldi and Corso Cavour.

Chief among Orvieto's cultural attractions is its 14th-century ★★★ **Duomo,** Piazza del Duomo (☎ 0763-341167; free admission to church, 3€ for Chapel of San Brizio; daily 7:30am–12:45pm, 2:30–7:15pm)—perhaps the most beautiful Gothic church in Italy. Its facade is a confection of polychrome marble, all pointed arches and spiky spires, while the sides and rear of the church (which seems about ready to plunge off the cliff behind it) feature horizontal

> The plug of tufa rock supporting Orvieto has served as wine cellar, pigeon coop, and World War II bomb shelter.

1 Orvieto
2 Todi
3 Cascata Le Marmore
4 Spoleto
5 Fonti del Clitunno
6 Norcia
7 Montefalco
8 Spello
9 Assisi
10 Gubbio
11 Perugia
12 Lago di Trasimeno

bands of black and white stone. The gorgeous interior of the cathedral contains frescoes by Luca Signorelli, in the Chapel of San Brizio, and an important Catholic relic—an altar cloth stained supposedly with the blood of Christ, from the miraculous 1263 Mass at Bolsena—in the Chapel of the Corporal.

Orvieto is also a town with deep Etruscan roots. The Etruscans carved a remarkable series of tunnels, cellars, wells, and secret passageways into the tufaceous foundation of their city. ★★ **Orvieto Underground,** in the tourist office at Piazza Duomo 24 (☎ 0763-344891), runs tours of these tunnels that are not only fascinating but a great way to escape summer heat. Tours depart daily at 11am, 12:15, 4, and 5:15pm and cost 5€.

Last but not least, climb the ★ **Torre del Moro** (Via Duomo/Corso Cavour; ☎ 0763-344567; 2.60€; Nov–Feb daily 10:30am–1pm, 2:30–5pm; Mar–Apr and Sept–Oct daily 10am–7pm; May–Aug 10am–8pm) for commanding views of the surrounding plains and the labyrinthine layout of Orvieto itself.

From Orvieto, go south on the SS205, then follow the SS448 to Todi (39km/24 miles total).

> The facade of Orvieto's Duomo, the "Golden Lily of Cathedrals," includes four carved reliefs by Lorenzo Maitani.

> *Todi's Santa Maria della Consolazione is laid out on a Greek cross plan.*

❷ **Todi.** While there is no shortage of contenders for the title of "Quaintest Town in Italy" in Tuscany and Umbria, Todi just might take the prize. Not only that, the Italian press has declared their Umbrian jewel the "most livable city in the world." This town takes less than half a day to explore, though you might want to stay around for a meal at ★★ **Ristorante Umbria,** Via S. Bonaventura 13 (☎ 075-8942737; entrees 6€–14€; lunch & dinner Wed–Mon; reservations recommended).

All the sights of Todi are clustered around the sloping and impossibly picturesque ★ **Piazza del Popolo** (often used as a movie set in the role of "cloyingly perfect Italian square"). The light-pink Gothic **Duomo** (☎ 075-8943041; free admission; daily 8:30am–12:30pm, 2:30–6:30pm) sits atop a flight of stairs at the northern end of the square. Palazzo del Popolo houses the city's **Museo e Pinacoteca** (☎ 075-8956216; admission 3.10€; Tues–Sun 10:30am–1pm, 3–5pm), which contains a saddle that belonged to tough-as-nails Anita Garibaldi, on the southeast side of the square.

Next, head to Todi's most celebrated church, ★★★ **Santa Maria della Consolazione,** Via della Consolazione at Via della Circonvallazione, just west of the city walls (no phone; free

admission; Wed–Mon 9:30am–12:30pm, 2:30–5pm), a domed Renaissance work, possibly by Bramante, with a Greek cross plan and polygonal apses on each side that create impressive vaulted effects on the stuccoed interior.

From Todi, go south on the SS3 to Terni, then follow signs to Cascata Le Marmore (51km/32 miles total).

❸ ★★ **Cascata Le Marmore.** Among its many natural attractions, Umbria has the highest waterfall (165m/541 ft.) in Europe. Granted, the three-tiered falls were carved in part by the ancient Romans, and today they're controlled by the hydroelectric power company, but they're nevertheless magnificent. Unless you are here at the right time, you'll be disappointed, as the falls are "turned off" most of the day, reduced to a weak, creeklike flow. But at certain scheduled times per day (go to www.marmorefalls.it for details), an alarm heralds imminent deluge, the gates are opened upstream, and the falls come alive spectacularly for an hour or more.

Plan to arrive at least 30 minutes early to be in position for the full show, and count on heavy traffic on the surrounding roads when the falls are switched on, especially on weekends in summer. At the top of the falls, there's an observatory with powerful views over the falls. You can also follow paths up and along the sides of the falls where, in parts, you'll get soaked when the falls are in full swing. Do not leave children unattended here.

Adventure seekers can also raft in the area—contact **Rafting Le Marmore** (☎ 330-753420; www.raftingmarmore.com) for more information on available excursions.

From Cascata Le Marmore, head back toward Terni, then take the SS3 north to Spoleto (37km/23 miles total).

4 Spoleto. Sedate Spoleto has a number of interesting architectural and culinary attractions that make it well worth a few hours' detour.

On the outskirts of town, admire the magnificent ★ **Ponte delle Torri,** which consists of 10 towers resting in a perfectly V-shaped, verdant canyon of ilex trees. The bridge may have been built in the 13th century, to carry water to upper Spoleto, over a preexisting Roman aqueduct. In his *Italian Journey,* Goethe waxed rhapsodic about the bridge—apparently he thought the whole thing was Roman—and his praise-filled words are preserved in a bronze plaque along the western end of the bridge. From the belvedere there, in the morning, you can witness the otherworldly sight of the Ponte delle Torri slicing the sunlight.

Inside the city walls, skip the lower town, but do take time to visit the upper town, which, after a series of handsome ascending streets, culminates in Piazza del Duomo. There, the 12th-century cathedral of ★ **Santa Maria Assunta** (☎ 0743-44307; free admission; 8am–1pm, 3–5:30pm) has frescoes by Fra Filippo Lippi. Behind it to the east is the well-preserved **Rocca Albornoziana fortress.**

Spoleto really comes to life during the **Festival dei Due Mondi,** or Two Worlds Festival (www.

> TOP *Spoleto's Ponte delle Torri rises above the Tessino River, which has been spanned since Roman times.* BOTTOM *An Orvieto "Classico" is made with grapes from the original, and best, growing zone.*

Spending the Night in Norcia

If you get carried away indulging in Norcia's culinary delights, consider staying overnight at **Palazzo Seneca,** a handsome new guesthouse done up in a modern style reminiscent of the W chain. Via Cesare Battisti 12. ☎ 0743-817434. www.palazzoseneca.com. 24 units. Doubles from 160€. AE, DC, MC, V.

> *THIS PAGE The quaint streets of Todi are at Umbria's geographical center.* OPPOSITE PAGE *A team hoists its "candle" in Gubbio's Corsa dei Ceri, an annual local festival since the 12th century.*

festivaldispoleto.it), which brings big international names in music, dance, theater, and cinema to the Umbrian hill town from mid-June to mid-July.

Truffle lovers should make a point to have lunch or dinner at **Il Tartufo** (p 241, ❽), Spoleto's unofficial temple of the prized tuber, serving up dishes that make generous use of its black and white varieties year-round.

From Spoleto, take the SS3 north and follow signs to Campello sul Clitunno or Fonti del Clitunno (5km/3 miles).

❺ **Fonti del Clitunno.** Postcards and tourism brochure photographs of this natural spring surrounded by lush gardens prepare you for something a bit more paradisical than the reality, but this is still a valid stop on your way around central Umbria. The park is great for stretching car-stiffened legs, and the lake in the middle—it's the crystal-clear source of the Clitunno River—is quite pretty. In the dead of winter, when the trees are barren, it's missable. Loc. Pissignano. ☎ 0743-275085. Admission 2€. Daily 10am-12:30pm, 2:30–5:30pm, 9am–8pm in summer.

From Fonti del Clitunno, follow the SS3 south to the SS685, then pick up the SS209 (marked as SR320 in places) to Serravalle, then take the SS209, then SS396 into Norcia (47km/29miles total).

❻ **Norcia.** One caveat about driving 45 minutes east to this town: It's the Italian capital of pork butchery (a *norcineria,* anywhere in Italy, is a butcher who specializes in pig and boar meat), and that particular claim to fame remains the biggest draw for outsiders. If you're not into *salame,* prosciutto, and the like, you might not enjoy this stop as much, though Norcia is also known for its nonmeat delicacies like lentils, chocolate, and truffles.

Norcia was the hometown of St. Benedict (and his less celebrated twin sister, St.

Scholastica), and his church, the 13th-century **San Benedetto** (no phone; free admission; daily 8am–noon, 3–6pm), was built over the site where they were born in 480.

Although Norcia is nearly surrounded by the imposing Monti Sibillini, the town itself is flat. All the better, I say, for going from meat shop to meat shop and stocking up on picnic supplies.

Norcia has been a pioneer in the butchery arts since the 13th century—and according to a grisly, perhaps apocryphal chapter of its history, medieval stage parents would bring their aspiring-singer sons to Norcia to become castrati under the same knives that quartered pig flesh for human consumption.

From Norcia, follow the exact directions from Fonti del Clitunno to Norcia (above) in reverse then head north on the SS3, following signs west to Montefalco (60km/38 miles total).

❼ **Montefalco.** Thanks to its enviable position high in the central part of the region, Montefalco has earned the nickname Ringhiera dell'Umbria, or "Balcony of Umbria." It's worth a drive up

Spending the Night in Montefalco

A favorite hotel here is ★★★ **Villa Zuccari,** a 16th-century villa with a breezy, retro resort feel; huge grounds; and a swimming pool. Loc. San Luca. ☎ 0742-399402. www.villazuccari.com. 39 units. Doubles 110€–190€. AE, DC, MC, V.

here just to check out the breathtaking views, but Montefalco is also an oenological destination of some note. The local red, Sagrantino di Montefalco, is a DOCG appellation (reserved for only the most important regional wines like Brunello and Barolo). One of the most acclaimed producers of it is ★ **Rocca di Fabbri,** Loc. Torre di Montefalco (☎ 0742-378802), where you can tour the winery and taste Sagrantino by appointment.

From Montefalco, head north toward Bevagna, then bear right on SR316, following signs for Spello (20km/13 miles).

⑧ **Spello.** The most remarkable feature of this medieval hill town is its imposing circuit of ★★ **fortification walls,** in which several sets of Roman gates date back over 1,600 years. Spello also loves its flowers—which manifests itself in a preponderance of window boxes spilling forth with geraniums and wisteria.

But Spello's real demonstration of its floral prowess is in the yearly festival **Le Infiorate di Spello.** The *infiorata* tradition is one repeated in many towns around Italy, in which tons upon tons of flower petals, in every color imaginable, are arranged over the city streets and squares in fragrant tapestries and reproductions of famous works of art. Spello's *infiorata* takes place the week after Corpus Christi. For more information, see www.infioratespello.it.

From Spello, take SS75 north to SS147 into Assisi.

⑨ **Assisi.** See p 268 for details on visiting Assisi.

From Assisi, head west on the SS75, then north on the SP147/SP175/SS298 to Gubbio (48km/30miles).

⑩ **Gubbio.** Gubbio is the most visually impressive city in Umbria. More than any other well-preserved medieval town nearby, Gubbio truly looks like it was plucked out of a 15th-century

> *You'll see flowers growing all over Spello in the weeks running up to the Infiorate festival.*

painting. Something about its compact agglomeration of pastel, crenellated buildings, set against a steep green hill, produces this rather unreal, Christmas-card effect.

The slender, towered ★★ **Palazzo dei Consoli** is the dominant feature of the skyline. It rests on an arched foundation and houses city hall as well as the ★ **Museo Civico,** Piazza Grande (☎ 075-9274298; admission 3€; daily 10am–1:30pm, 2–5pm), which houses the prized Eugubine Tablets, bronze inscriptions in an ancient Umbrian language that attest to the very ancient roots of Gubbio.

Like many an Umbrian city, Gubbio produced a saint. St. Ubaldo is revered at the eponymous church on the high hill, Monte Ingino, behind Gubbio, and one of Italy's greatest medieval traditions is the annual ★★ **Corsa dei Ceri** (Race of the Candles), held each May 15 in honor of Ubaldo. Standard-bearers for each of Gubbio's three parishes race up the hill on foot, carrying huge wooden "candles," to the sanctuary of St. Ubaldo.

Spending the Night in Gubbio

If you wish to overnight in Gubbio, your best bet is the classic ★★ **Bosone Palace,** which has character-filled rooms in an historic palace at reasonable prices. Via XX Settembre 22. ☎ 075-9220688. www.mencarelligroup. com. 30 units. Doubles from 110€. Suites 150€–190€. AE, DC, MC, V.

Astonishingly, the racers cover the 4km/2½-mile distance in less than 10 minutes while shouldering their sacred cargo. It's a day of great feasting and merriment that should not be missed if you're in Umbria around this time. Even if you can't make it to Gubbio in mid-May, visitors can reach St. Ubaldo's church via the **Funivia** (☎ 075-9273881; admission 5€; call for hours), a chairlift of sorts where you don't actually sit down but stand in birdcage-like baskets.

From Gubbio (42km/26 miles), go south on the SS298 to Perugia.

Perugia. See p 282 for details on visiting Perugia.

From Perugia, head west on the Raccordo Autostradale Perugia-A1, then head south on the SS71 to Castiglione del Lago (47km/29 miles).

Lago di Trasimeno. The summer playground of Umbria draws many European holidaymakers to its shores from June to August, but even out of season, the 128 sq. km (80 sq. mile) lake is worth a quick look. Its historical claim to fame is as the site where, in 217 B.C., Hannibal and the Carthaginian army routed the Romans in the Second Punic War.

The lake's main resort town, ★ **Castiglione del Lago,** isn't all that big, but it does have lakefront dining and cafes that make for a

> Gubbio's medieval character has been well preserved.

> The shallow, calm expanses of Lago di Trasimeno abound in fishing and boating opportunities.

good stopover. In summer, you can go for a dip at its beaches—the best are just south of Castiglione—but to really experience the lake as locals do, go for a fishing charter and see if you can reel in some eel or trout. Contact the **Alba Trasimeno** fishing cooperative at ☎ 075-8476005; from 55€ per person. You can also take a ferry to ★ **Isola Maggiore,** in the center of the lake, where life rewinds at least 50 years.

Spending the Night in Lago di Trasimeno

Lake Trasimeno boasts one of Umbria's most stylish villa-hotels, ★★★ **I Capricci di Merion,** located in the very same territory north of the lake where Hannibal trounced the Roman army. Via Pozzo 21. Tuoro sul Trasimeno. ☎ 075-825002. www.capriccidimerion. com. 9 units. Doubles 130€–160€. AE, MC, V.

Arezzo

Famous native sons of this historic, bustling, and prosperous town include the poet Petrarch (1304-74); architect and author Giorgio Vasari (1512-74); and Roberto Benigni, who brought Arezzo to a world audience as director and star of *Life Is Beautiful*. Time here is best spent strolling the medieval core and Piazza Grande, but don't miss the frescoes of Piero della Francesca in Basilica di San Francesco.

> *Detail from Piero della Francesca's* Legend of the True Cross *cycle in the Basilica di San Francesco.*

START Arezzo is southeast of Florence on the A1. Just follow the directional signs to the city. Trip length: 81km (50 miles).

① ★★★ **Basilica di San Francesco.** Between 1452 and 1466, Piero della Francesca painted *The Legend of the True Cross*—a series of frescoes that proved to be an art-history milestone. Each is remarkable for its grace, ascetic severity, brilliant colors, and dramatic light effects—"the most perfect morning light in all Renaissance painting," said Sir Kenneth Clark. ⏱ 30 min. Piazza San Francesco. ☎ 0575-20630 or 0575-900404 for reservations (25 people admitted every 30 min). Admission 6€. Daily 8:30am-noon and 2-6pm.

② **Casa di Vasari.** The first art historian—who chronicled the lives of Michelangelo, da Vinci, and others—Vasari bought this house in 1540. The charming frescoes are his own. ⏱ 30 min. Via XX Settembre 55. ☎ 0575-40901. 2€ adults, 1€ ages 17 and under. Wed-Mon 9am-7pm; Sun 9am-1pm.

③ ★ **Museo Statale d'Arte Medievale e Moderna.** Our favorite works are Vasari's *Esther's Wedding Banquet* and the frescoes by Spinello Aretino, but the 13th- to 18th-century majolica somehow overshadow the art. ⏱ 45 min. Via San Lorentino 8. ☎ 0575-409050. Admission 4.90€ adults, 2.90€ ages 18-25; free 17 and under. Tues-Sun 9am-6pm.

④ ★ **Santa Maria della Pieve.** This 12th-century church near **Piazza Grande** is a stellar example of the Pisan-Romanesque style. Its chief treasure is Pietro Lorenzetti's polyptych *Madonna and Child with Saints*. ⏱ 30 min. Corso Italia 7. ☎ 0575-377678. Free. Daily 8am-7pm May-Sept; 8am-noon and 3-6pm Oct-Apr.

⑤ ★★★ **Busatti.** Founded in 1842, this is a mecca for exquisite textiles and handmade fabrics. ⏱ 15 min. or more. Corso Italia 48. ☎ 0575-355295. www.busatti.com. AE, DC, MC, V.

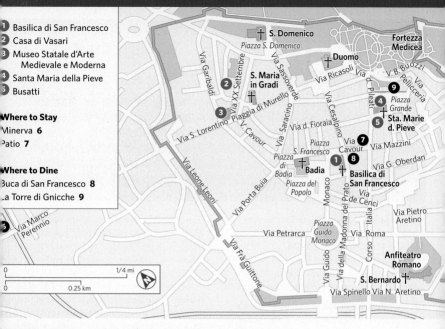

1. Basilica di San Francesco
2. Casa di Vasari
3. Museo Statale d'Arte Medievale e Moderna
4. Santa Maria della Pieve
5. Busatti

Where to Stay
Minerva **6**
Patio **7**

Where to Dine
Buca di San Francesco **8**
La Torre di Gnicche **9**

Where to Stay & Dine

Buca di San Francesco CENTRO STORICO *TUSCAN/ARETINE* Arezzo's finest restaurant is in the frescoed cellar of a palazzo from the 1300s. In its 7th decade, it's still keeping alive "the memory of the old Tuscan flavors." Via Francesco 1. ☎ 0575-23271. Entrees 8€–15€. AE, DC, MC, V. Lunch & dinner Wed–Mon. Closed 2 weeks in Aug.

La Torre di Gnicche CENTRO STORICO *TUSCAN* This overly decorated little dive is a Tuscan tavern with a vengeance—the kind from the 1950s, when the region was being discovered by the postwar generation. The cookery is fresh but unrefined. Try the local cheese and cold cuts, onion soup, or tripe. Piagga San Martino 8. ☎ 0575-352035. Entrees 6€–12€. AE, DC, MC, V. Lunch & dinner Thurs–Tues.

Minerva CENTRO STORICO This postwar structure is a bastion of modern comfort, with a touch of Italian style and elegance. Midsize rooms are soundproof, with large windows. Via Fiorentina 4. ☎ 0575-370390. www.hotel-minerva.it. 130 units. Doubles 93€–150€ w/breakfast. AE, DC, MC, V.

> *Giorgio Vasari designed the loggia on Piazza Grande under which atmospheric cafes now shelter.*

★★ Patio CENTRO STORICO
It has an odd name, but for atmosphere, this ambitious hotel in the 18th-century Palazzo de' Giudici is our local favorite. Each of the large units is dedicated to one of Bruce Chatwin's travel books, with furniture from the country it represents— say, Emperor Wu-Ti-style from China. Via Cavour 23. ☎ 0575-401962. www.hotelpatio.it. 7 units. Doubles 145€–180€ w/breakfast. AE, DC, MC, V.

Assisi

As the birthplace of Italy's patron saint, St. Francis, this Umbrian hill town draws plenty of Catholic pilgrims. Art lovers flock here for the spectacular frescoes by Giotto in the Basilica di San Francesco. The atmosphere in the pink-gray stone streets of Assisi is pious and quiet, making this a fine overnight choice for tranquillity-seekers; otherwise, you can see Assisi in half a day. If you're planning to stay, book well in advance, especially between Easter and October.

START Assisi is 128km (80 miles) east of Siena on the Raccordo Autostradale Siena-Bettolle-Perugia and the SP247. It's 171km (106 miles) southeast of Florence on the A1, Raccordo A1-Perugia, and SP247. Assisi is 24km (15 miles) east of Perugia on the SS75.

① ★★★ **Basilica di San Francesco.** The majestic church on the lower rim of Assisi, overlooking the valley beyond, is an awe-inspiring sight inside and out, but St. Francis—the monk who preached and led a life of poverty—would probably be dismayed to have such a grandiose church built to honor him. Much of the basilica which was begun in 1228, only 2 years after Francis's death (and before he was officially canonized), was damaged in the earthquake of 1997, but it was speedily restored.

Giotto's fresco cycle of the ★★★ *Life of St. Francis,* in the upper church, is absolutely wonderful, with touching and intimate scenes that are a priceless window onto the life and teachings of the love-all-and-live-without-wealth friar. The cryptlike lower church, where the tomb of St. Francis is located, has low vaulted ceilings and less celebrated frescoes by Sienese painters

> *The paved approach to Assisi's basilica is named after the church's probable architect, Brother Elias.*

Map Labels

- San Francesco
- Piazza Sup. di San Francesco
- Piazza Inf. di San Francesco
- Via Frate Elia
- Porta S. Francesco
- Via Metastasio
- Via San Francesco
- Via Fontebella
- Piazza Unità d'Italia
- Via G. P. Nicolini
- Porta S. Pietro
- Via Borgo San Pietro
- San Pietro
- Via Ancaiani
- Via Vittorio Emanuele II
- Viale Marconi
- Porta S. Giacomo
- Rocca Maggiore
- V. Seminario Fortini
- Via S. Paolo
- S. Maria Minerva
- Piazza del Comune
- V. Brizi
- Ch. Nuova
- Via A. Cristofani
- Via Apollinare
- Porta del Sementone
- Porta Moiano
- Via Vittorio Emanuele II
- Porta Perlici
- P. Perlici
- V. Villamena
- Rocca Minore
- Anfiteatro Romano
- Piazza S. Rufino
- Duomo
- Piazza Matteotti
- Via S. Gabriele dell'Addolorata
- Via del Corso Mazzini
- V. Sant'Agnese
- Piazza S. Chiara
- Santa Chiara
- Via Borgo Aretino
- Via Carceri
- Porta Cappuccini
- Viale Umbertto
- Porta Nuova
- V. d. Fortezza
- Vicolo D. Castello
- Via di...
- SS147
- 1/10 mile
- 100 meters

1. Basilica di San Francesco
2. Tempio di Minerva
3. Rocca Maggiore
4. Eremo delle Carceri & Monte Subasio

Where to Stay

Hotel La Rocca **5**
Residenza d'Epoca San Crispino **6**
Umbra **7**

Where to Dine

La Fortezza **8**
La Stalla **9**
Osteria Piazzetta delle Erbe **10**

Assisi remains an important place of pilgrimage for the devout as well as for admirers of the philosophy of St. Francis and the artworks of Giotto.

> St. Francis Chases the Demons from Arezzo, *one of Giotto's panels from the Gothic upper church.*

Through the lower church, you can also enter a chapel (hours vary) containing dozens of Francis's personal effects. ⏱ 45 min. Piazza Superiore di San Francesco/Piazza Inferiore di San Francesco. ☎ 075-819001. Free admission. Lower Church: Daily 6am–7pm. Upper Church: Daily 8:30am–6pm.

② ★ **Tempio di Minerva.** In the square that overlies Assisi's ancient Roman forum, six columns from a 2,000-year-old temple to Minerva (now the church of Santa Maria Sopra Minerva) sit cheek by jowl with the town's medieval Torre Civica (Civic Tower). ⏱ 5 min.

③ ★★ **kids Rocca Maggiore.** The citadel dominates the skyline of Assisi. Climb up here for the best views of the valley and commanding views of the Basilica di San Francesco. ⏱ 1 hr. Via della Rocca. ☎ 075-815292. Admission 3€. Daily 7am–sunset.

④ ★★ **Eremo delle Carceri & Monte Subasio.** St. Francis fans shouldn't miss this hermitage

The Story of St. Francis

In terms of holiness and reverence among Catholic Italians today, St. Francis ranks right up there with Mary and Jesus. Born Giovanni Francesco di Bernardone in 1181, St. Francis was the son of a wealthy local merchant and like the stereotypical spoiled rich kid, spent much of his youth drinking and gambling and wearing fancy clothing. By his mid-20s, however, Francis had tired of the carousing lifestyle. He found religion and began preaching the virtues of the simple life without material wealth. He founded the Friars Minor (the Franciscan order), who lived in the wilderness near Assisi and greeted those they met—whether human, animal, or plant—with uplifting songs.

Even for non-Catholics, Francis's values are hard not to like. Among his teachings was the notion that everything from the animals to the trees to the smallest bird is worthy of love and respect. This flower-child attitude shows through a beautifully simple poem and prayer to the elements Francis wrote, called "Canticle of the Creatures," or "Brother Sun, Sister Moon," which you'll see copies of everywhere around town. Giotto's *Preaching to the Birds* fresco in the upper church of the Basilica di San Francesco touches on this theme.

Although later saints were also blessed with the stigmata, Francis was the first to receive the "gift," in 1224, and the miracle pretty much cinched his sainthood. After a life spent traveling as far as Spain, Morocco, Egypt, and Palestine to preach simplicity and a return to kindliness, Francis died near his hometown in 1226. Within 2 years he was made a saint, and in 1939 he was proclaimed the official patron saint of Italy. He's also the patron saint of animals (which are honored on his feast day, Oct 4) and the environment.

4km (2½ miles) east of Assisi's walls, where Francis came to live when he had his religious awakening. The caves, or cells (*carceri*), here are where he and his followers lived. This is also a great jumping-off point for nature lovers, as the hiking paths of Monte Subasio are accessible here, too. ⏱ 1 hr. Via delle Carceri. ☎ 075-812301. Free admission. Daily 6:30am–7pm.

Where to Stay & Dine

★ **Hotel La Rocca** CENTRO STORICO
On a cozy side street at the east end of town, this is a well-run budget hotel with simple, spacious rooms. A basic on-site restaurant offers half- or full-board options. Via Porta Perlici 27. ☎ 075-812284. www.hotelarocca.it. 27 units. Doubles from 52€. AE, DC, MC, V.

★★ **La Fortezza** CENTRO STORICO *CREATIVE UMBRIAN* Scrumptious, soul-warming dishes like *cannelloni all'assisiana* (with veal *ragù* and parmigiano) and *coniglio in salsa di mele* (rabbit in a currylike sauce of white wine, saffron, and apples) make this one of the best choices on a chilly day. Vicolo della Fortezza/Piazza del Comune. ☎ 075-812418. Entrees 6€–12€. AE, DC, MC, V. Lunch & dinner Fri–Wed.

★★★ **La Stalla** EASTERN OUTSKIRTS *UMBRIAN/ BARBECUE* It's worth coming to Assisi if only for a meal at this raucous and rustic barn, one of my all-time-favorite places to eat in Italy. After an invigorating 15-minute walk along a country road to reach the place, you'll settle into rickety communal tables in former livestock stalls, where the scents of grilled meat and wood smoke hang heavy in the air. With prices as low as these, order with abandon. They'll bring you plenty of the house *vino rosso* to wash it all down. Via Santuario delle Carceri 24. ☎ 075-812317. Entrees 4€–7€. No credit cards. Lunch & dinner Tues–Sun. Reservations recommended.

★★ **Osteria Piazzetta delle Erbe** CENTRO STORICO *UMBRIAN* One of the most consistently delicious restaurants within Assisi proper serves lighter, creative takes on traditional Umbrian fare, such as pasta dumplings with pear and pecorino. The atmosphere is warm and friendly. Via San Gabriele dell'Addolorata 15b. ☎ 075-815352. Entrees 8€–14€. AE, DC, MC, V. Lunch & dinner Tues–Sun.

★★★ **Residenza d'Epoca San Crispino** CENTRO STORICO Five-star rooms don't exist in this ascetic town, but the boutique-style accommodations here offer something approaching luxury. Most units have vaulted ceilings that incorporate the original brickwork of the palazzo

> *Tuscany is known for simple, country fare that complements the local wine.*

and panoramic views over the countryside. Spa treatments are available at its sister property, Resort & Spa San Crispino. Via Sant'Agnese 11. ☎ 075-8155124. www.assisiwellness.com. 7 units. Double-occupancy suites 160€–220€, prices lower for longer stays. AE, DC, MC, V.

★★ **Umbra** CENTRO STORICO
This comfy, old-style hotel has a great garden out back and a good on-site restaurant. Via degli Archi 6. ☎ 075-812240. www.hotelumbra.it. 25 units. Doubles from 100€. AE, DC, MC, V.

Cortona

Medieval Cortona is one of Tuscany's steepest hill towns, clinging to the slopes of a hill planted with olive groves, opening onto views of Lake Trasimeno. Frances Mayes's *Under the Tuscan Sun,* which takes place in Cortona, has brought many more visitors here, but the town remains quiet and romantic. The main pleasure here is wandering up narrow streets to discover hidden gardens and churches.

> *The 13th-century Palazzo Comunale provides the architectural backdrop to Cortona's bustling downtown.*

START Cortona is southeast of Florence on the SS69 to the SS71. From Arezzo, take the SS71 and turn off for Cortona at Camucia and follow the signs. By train, get off at Camucia or Terontola. Trip length: from Florence 105km (63 miles); from Arezzo 34km (22 miles).

1 ★ Museo dell'Accademia Etrusca. Cortona's Etruscan collection, housed in a 13th-century mansion, includes an oil lamp chandelier from the late 4th century B.C. ⏲ 40 min. Piazza Signorelli 9. ☎ 0575-637235. www. accademia-etrusca.org/museo. Admission 4.20€ adults, 2.50€ ages 17 and under. Apr–Sept daily 10am–7pm; Oct–Mar Tues–Sun 10am–5pm.

2 ★★ Museo Diocesano. This museum is Cortona's chief attraction, with a splendid array of paintings from the Florentine and Sienese schools, including pieces by Luca Signorelli and Fra Angelico. ⏲ 1 hr. Piazza del Duomo 1. ☎ 0575-62830. Admission 5€, 3€ ages 14 and under. Daily 9:30am–1pm and 3:30–7pm (closes at 5pm in winter).

3 ★ Via Jannelli. Jutting wooden beams support the second and third floors on this picture-perfect alley just inside the Etruscan walls. ⏲ 5 min.

4 ★ Piazza Pescaia. This wooded triangle is the heart of residential Cortona. In the tiny streets

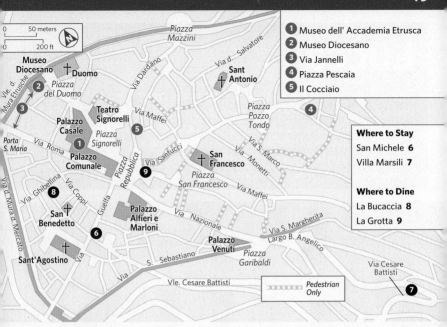

1 Museo dell' Accademia Etrusca
2 Museo Diocesano
3 Via Jannelli
4 Piazza Pescaia
5 Il Cocciaio

Where to Stay
San Michele 6
Villa Marsili 7

Where to Dine
La Bucaccia 8
La Grotta 9

that radiate from the garden square, you'll find such diminutive gems as the churches of ★ **San Niccolò** and **San Cristoforo,** and the ★ **convent of Santa Chiara.** Listen for the clucking of hens—some *cortonesi* still raise their own chickens right inside the city walls. ⏲ 30 min.

5 ★ **Il Cocciaio.** The best shop in town for Cortona's famous ceramic patterns of green, cream, and dark yellow. ⏲ 15 min. or more. Via Benedetti 24. ☎ 0575-605294. AE, DC, MC, V.

Where to Stay & Dine

★★★ **La Bucaccia** CENTRO STORICO *TUSCAN*
Rustic tradition meets elegant flourish at this convivial and cavelike temple of rigorously local Cortonese cuisine run by the passionate Magi family. Via Ghibellina 17. ☎ 0575-606039. Entrees 7€–16€. AE, DC, MC, V. May–Oct dinner daily; Nov–Apr dinner Tues–Sun. Lunch Sat–Sun year-round. Reservations highly recommended.

★ **La Grotta** CENTRO STORICO *TUSCAN*
Come for a wide menu of tasty *casalinga* (home-cooking) in cozy chambers lined with stone and brick. The tender, flavorful Florentine steaks are the most affordable in town. Piazza Baldelli 3. ☎ 0575-630271. Entrees 5.50€–8€. AE, DC, MC, V. Lunch & dinner Wed–Mon.

★★ **San Michele** CENTRO STORICO
This government-rated, 4-star hotel in an 11th-century palace has vaulted ceilings with *pietra serena* arches, small to midsize rooms under wood-beamed ceilings, and antique furnishings. The tower rooms are ideal for lovers. Via Guelfa 15. ☎ 0575-604348. www.hotelsanmichele.net. 50 units. Doubles from 150€ w/breakfast. AE, DC, MC, V.

★★ **Villa Marsili** OUTSKIRTS
With dignified lounges and finely furnished, frescoed bedrooms, this former gentleman's residence from 1786 is the coziest nest in town, with outdoor gardens. Via Cesare Battisti 13. ☎ 0575-605252. www.villamarsili.net. 27 units. Doubles 160€–230€ w/buffet breakfast. AE, DC, MC.

Lucca

Set within massive walls, Lucca is its own elegant world where time has stood still—not in the typically Tuscan Middle Ages, but in the stylish early 1900s. Lucca also has splendid medieval and Renaissance architecture, as well as one very beloved native son in composer Giacomo Puccini. The town makes a good base for exploring northern Tuscany as well as the Cinque Terre, only an hour away. Spend at least 2 nights here.

> *The curve of Piazza dell'Anfiteatro traces the outline of Lucca's ancient Roman amphitheater.*

START Lucca is west of Florence on the A11, past Prato, Pistoia, and Montecatini. It's northeast of Pisa on the SS12. There are frequent direct trains to Lucca from both Florence and Pisa. Trip length: from Florence 77km (48 miles); from Pisa 25km (16 miles).

1 ★★ kids **Ancient Walls.** Planted with plane, chestnut, and ilex trees, Lucca's medieval fortifications make for one of Tuscany's great city walks. The wide path on top is a city park, the ★★ **Passeggiata delle Mura,** stretching for 4.9km (2⅔ miles). You can also explore the ramparts by bike (see below). ⏱ **90 min. on foot 30 min. by bike.**

2 ★ **Antonio Poli.** Hit the Passeggiata delle Mura (see above, **1**) in style, on a neon green

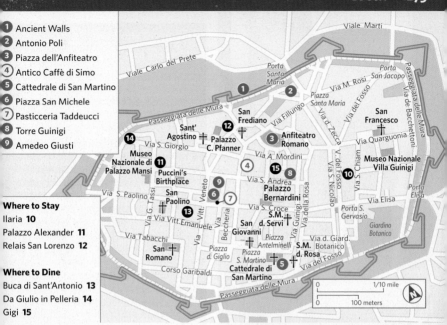

1. Ancient Walls
2. Antonio Poli
3. Piazza dell'Anfiteatro
4. Antico Caffè di Simo
5. Cattedrale di San Martino
6. Piazza San Michele
7. Pasticceria Taddeucci
8. Torre Guinigi
9. Amedeo Giusti

Where to Stay
Ilaria **10**
Palazzo Alexander **11**
Relais San Lorenzo **12**

Where to Dine
Buca di Sant'Antonio **13**
Da Giulio in Pelleria **14**
Gigi **15**

or Barbie-pink bike from this laid-back rental shop near the tourist office. The basic cost is 2.50€ per hour. Piazza Santa Maria 42. ☎ 0583-493787. Daily 8:30am–8pm.

3 ★ Piazza dell'Anfiteatro. The foundations of what were the grandstands of a Roman amphitheater today support an ellipse of attractive medieval houses and cafes. ⏲ 15 min.

4 🍷 Antico Caffè di Simo. This is the most famous cafe in town. Even Puccini came here for a drink, perhaps contemplating his next opera, against the same, now-antique backdrop of faded mirrors, brass, and marble. Via Fillungo 58. ☎ 0583-496234. $.

5 ★★ Cattedrale di San Martino. The ornate, asymmetrical Duomo was consecrated in 1070 but took centuries to finish. The interior was given a Gothic dress in the 14th to 15th centuries. In the left transept is Jacopo della Quercia's ★★ **Tomb of Ilaria del Carretto** (ca. 1406), his earliest surviving masterpiece and the first sculptural creation of the Renaissance to use Roman decorative motifs. The Duomo is also filled with great art by Italian masters including a *Last Supper* by Tintoretto (third altar on the right). ⏲ 40 min. Piazza San Martino.

> The unfinished facade of the Cattedrale di San Martino is rich in Gothic stonework.

> *The summit of Torre Guinigi affords a panorama over the city and the Apennine range beyond.*

☎ 0583-957068. Cathedral, free admission; 3.50€ to sacristy, inner sanctum, and Duomo museum. Apr–Oct daily 10am–6pm; Nov–Mar Mon–Fri 10am–2pm, Sat–Sun 10am–5pm.

6 ★ **Piazza San Michele.** What was once ancient Lucca's Roman forum is now its most happening square, with market stalls selling fashion and food items many days. On those market days, make a beeline to the **Nelli** cart, famous for its *frate lucchese* (a lemon-hinted doughnut dipped in sugar and optional Nutella, 1€ each). The 12th-century church here, **San Michele in Foro,** has an eye-popping facade. ⏱ 30 min. Piazza San Michele (off Via Caldera). ☎ 0583-48459. Free admission. Daily 9am–noon and 3–5:30pm.

7 🍴 **Pasticceria Taddeucci.** This 19th-century pastry shop is most famous for its *Buccellato.* The ring-shaped hard cake with

Giacomo Who?

Lest anyone forget that the composer of the world's favorite arias was born here, the Lucchese pay homage at every turn to hometown hero Giacomo Puccini (1858–1924), who spent his first 30 years in Lucca and composed most of his oeuvre in nearby Torre del Lago. Most hotels in town have at least a few rooms named after his masterpieces—*La Bohème, Madama Butterfly,* and *Tosca.* No one's more energetic about the composer than **Puccini e la sua Lucca** (Puccini and his Lucca), a group that puts on highlights of his operas, or the entire works, many nights of the week throughout the year in the church of San Giovanni. Hearing soaring arias like "Nessun Dorma" (from *Turandot*) or "Che Gelida Manina" (from *Bohème*) here on Puccini's native turf is enough to send chills down your spine. For schedules, see www.puccinielasualucca.com, or call ☎ 0583-492229, or stop in at the tourist information office in Piazza Santa Maria. Tickets start at 15€.

anise and raisins isn't for everyone, but they also make all manner of sweet treats and wonderful *caffè.* Piazza San Michele 34. Via S. Giustina. ☎ 0583-494933. $.

8 ★★ **Torre Guinigi.** Topped with an unlikely mini-grove of ilex trees, this 44m (146 ft.) tower was built by the powerful ruling family of Lucca in the 15th century. Climb its 230 steps and you'll be rewarded with wonderful panoramas of the city and surrounding green hills. ⏱ 20 min. Via Sant'Andrea (at Via Chiave d'Oro). ☎ 0583-48524. Admission 3.50€. Mar–May daily 9am–7:30pm; June–Sept 15 daily 9am–midnight; Sept 16–Oct daily 9:30am–8pm; Nov–Feb daily 9:30am–5:30pm.

9 ★★ kids **Amedeo Giusti.** Follow the aroma of freshly baked bread to this *forno a vapore* (steam oven). Line up at the street-facing counter for one of their focaccias (the onion-topped ones are particularly addictive). A local institution. ⏱ 10 min. Via S. Lucia 18/20 (off Via Buia). ☎ 0583-496285. Daily 7am–1pm, 4:30–7:45pm. Closed Wed afternoon Nov–Mar and Sat afternoon Jun–Aug. Closed Sun Jun–Aug. No credit cards.

Where to Stay & Dine

★★ **Buca di Sant'Antonio** CENTRO STORICO
TUSCAN While it's not the perfect dining experience some guidebooks would have you believe, this is nevertheless Lucca's most reliable "fine" restaurant. The excellent waitstaff is very informative about *cucina lucchese*. The folksy street-level dining room is far preferable to the stuffier downstairs. Via della Cervia 3 (off Piazza San Michele). ☎ 0583-55881. Entrees 9€–18€. AE, DC, MC, V. Lunch & dinner Tues–Sun.

★ **Da Giulio in Pelleria** CENTRO STORICO
LUCCHESE/MEAT There's no more authentic Lucchese dining within the city walls. Local specialties include horse tartare, veal snout, and tripe. Less adventurous dishes are also served. Via delle Conce 45 (off Via S. Giorgio). ☎ 0583-55948. Entrees 6€–10€. AE, MC, V. Lunch & dinner Tues–Sat. Closed Aug 1–21.

★ **Gigi** CENTRO STORICO *TUSCAN/LUCCHESE*
This casual trattoria has some of the best-tasting food in town, though portions are smallish. Try the exquisite *gnudi* with a delicate Gorgonzola sauce or the sublimely juicy *petto di pollo al mattone* (chicken breast roasted under a brick). Piazza del Carmine 7. ☎ 0583-467266. www.gigitrattoria.it. Entrees 7–14€. AE, DC, MC, V. Lunch & dinner Tues–Sat.

★★ **Ilaria** CENTRO STORICO
This modern hotel, within the city walls, sits along pretty gardens. The generically furnished rooms are immaculate and bright, and bikes are available for free. Via del Fosso 25 (off Via Elisa). ☎ 0583-47615. www.hotelilaria.com. 41 units. Doubles 110€–130€; suites 200€–230€ w/buffet breakfast.

★★ **Palazzo Alexander** CENTRO STORICO
Lucca's top boutique hotel, in a 12th century palazzo, has plenty of historic charm. Via S. Giustina 48 (off Via Gallitassi). ☎ 0583-583571. www.palazzo-alexander.it. 12 units. Doubles from 200€; suites from 300€ w/buffet breakfast. AE, DC, MC, V.

> *Venerable Buca di Sant'Antonio is Lucca's best restaurant.*

★ **Relais San Lorenzo** CENTRO STORICO
The units at this B&B are comfortable and quiet. The *Madama Butterfly* suite, though not palatial, has an outdoor deck. Via Cesare Battisti 15 (at Via San Giorgio). ☎ 0583-1990191. www.san lorenzorelais.it. 15 units. Doubles 75€–140€; suites 130€–190€ w/buffet breakfast. AE, DC, MC, V.

Lucca After Dark

There isn't much nightlife in Lucca, but **Stella Polare** (Via Vittorio Veneto 21; ☎ 0583-496332) draws a lively crowd before and after dinner. The current hot spot/meat market for young Lucchesi is **Zero Bar** (Via San Paolino, no phone), where drinks are cheap and conversations loud.

Montalcino

Once called "city of honey" for its apicultural prowess, Montalcino is now known to wine lovers the world over as home of the mighty Brunello di Montalcino (see p 240). The international industry surrounding Brunello gives the handsome hill town a sophisticated feel, yet Montalcino remains authentically Tuscan.

> *The vineyards of Montalcino produce award-winning Brunello wines.*

START From Florence, take the A1 south to the Valdichiana exit, then head west, through Montepulciano, following blue signs to Montalcino. From Siena, head south on the SR2 (Via Cassia) past Buonconvento, then follow blue signs to Montalcino. There are also buses from Siena. Trip length: 140km (87 miles) from Florence; 44km (27 miles) from Siena.

❶ ★★ **Enoteca La Fortezza.** It's easy to while away an afternoon getting to know Brunello wine at this atmospheric and energetic tasting room and gourmet shop inside one corner of the old fortress. A limited menu of typical Tuscan fare is also served. ⏱ 15 min.-2 hr. Piazzale Fortezza. ☎ 0577-849211. Tastings from 5€. Apr–Oct daily 9am–8pm; Nov–Mar Tues–Sun 9am–6pm. AE, DC, MC, V.

❷ ★★★ **Abbazia di Sant'Antimo.** The star attraction of Montalcino, besides the wine, is

this 12th-century abbey 10km (6 miles) to the south. A postcard-perfect, cypress-filled valley frames the Romanesque church, where monks sing the masses and hours in Gregorian chant, a goosebump-inducing experience. ⏱ 1 hr. Castelnuovo dell'Abate (follow SP55 to Abbazia S. Antimo). ☎ 0577-835659. www.antimo.it. Free admission. Mon–Sat 10:15am–12:30pm, 3–6:30pm; Sun 9:15am–10:45am, 3–6pm. Religious services in Gregorian chant: Daily 9am, 12:45pm, 2:45pm; Mon–Sat also 9:15am; Sun also 11am.

❸ ★ **Piazza del Popolo.** Back in town, head to Montalcino's central square for some wine (or coffee) and a snack at either ★ **Fiaschetteria Italiana** (☎ 0577-849043; closed Thurs), a 19th-century cafe/*enoteca*, or ★★ **Bar Alle Logge** (☎ 0577-848057; closed Wed), a more modern spot with terrific valley views. The piazza is the focal point of the evening *passeggiata* (collective town stroll). ⏱ 1 hr.

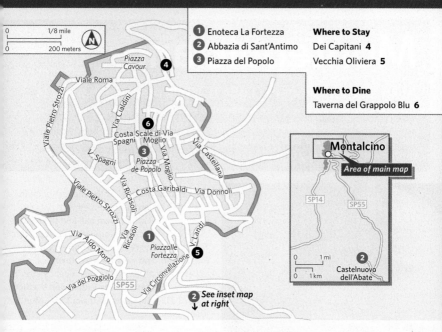

1. Enoteca La Fortezza
2. Abbazia di Sant'Antimo
3. Piazza del Popolo

Where to Stay
Dei Capitani 4
Vecchia Oliviera 5

Where to Dine
Taverna del Grappolo Blu 6

Where to Stay & Dine

★ Dei Capitani CENTRO STORICO
The best traditional hotel in town is this government-rated four-star. Rooms tend to be small and decor bland, but the views are spectacular, and there's a panoramic swimming pool. Via Lapini 6. ☎ 0577-847227. www.deicapitani.it. 29 units. Doubles from 140€ w/buffet breakfast. AE, DC, MC, V.

★★ Taverna del Grappolo Blu CENTRO STORICO
TUSCAN The most consistently enjoyable meals in town are at the bare wooden tables of this two-room, family-run restaurant. Try the *pinci* (hand-rolled spaghetti) with mushroom *ragù* or the sublimely flavorful rabbit in Brunello sauce. Scale di Via Moglio. ☎ 0577-847150. Entrees 10€–20€. Lunch & dinner Sat–Thurs. AE, DC, MC, V.

★★ Vecchia Oliviera CENTRO STORICO
This converted olive mill, built into the city walls, is a relaxing and well-appointed B&B with a country feel and great views from its hillside terrace and small swimming pool. Porta Cerbaia (at Via Landi). ☎ 0577-846028. www.vecchiaoliviera.com. 13 units. Doubles 120€–190€ w/buffet breakfast. AE, DC, MC, V.

> Meat and cheese platters make a perfect, value accompaniment to a wine tasting.

Montepulciano

At an altitude of 605m (1,985 ft.), this medieval hamlet is
Tuscany's loftiest hill town, with remarkable views over the nearby vineyards.
Before checking out individual sites, climb the steeply serpentine main street—
the "Corso"—to Piazza Grande. Montepulciano is heavily touristed, but it's a
convenient base for day trips in southern and western Tuscany, and even Umbria.

> *Sweeping views can be enjoyed from the top of Montepulciano's Palazzo Comunale.*

START From Florence, take the A1 south to the
Chianciano Terme exit, then SS146 toward
Chianciano for 18km (11 miles). From Siena,
head south on the SS2 to San Quirico d'Orcia,
then follow SS146 through Pienza to Montepulciano. Trip length: 124km (74 miles) from
Florence, 67km (40 miles) from Siena.

① ★ **Piazza Grande.** At the highest point in
town, this square is enveloped with palazzi,
including the Gothic town hall and the austere,
15th-century Palazzo Comunale. Palazzo Nobili-
Tarugi, with its great portico and loggia, faces
the Duomo. The view from the town hall clock
tower is one of the most magnificent vistas in
Tuscany. ⏱ 20 min. Piazza Grande (off Via Ricci).
☎ 0578-7121. Admission to tower 1.55€. Mon–Sat
10am–5pm.

② 🍴 ★★ **Antico Caffè Poliziano.** This cafe,
which opened in 1868, has bounced back
after decades of slumber, since the days
when Pirandello and Fellini quaffed here.
Restored to some of its former glory, it
is the center of sleepy Montepulciano's
cultural life and nighttime activities. Via
Voltaia nel Corso (off Via di San Donato).
☎ 0578-758615. Closed Nov 15–30 and Feb.

③ ★★ **Tempio di San Biagio.** This 1529 masterpiece of High Renaissance architecture was
the greatest achievement of architect Antonio
da Sangallo, who was inspired by Bramante's
work on St. Peter's in Rome. ⏱ 20 min. Via di
San Biagio (1km/¾ mile) west of city below the
town walls. No phone. Free admission. Daily 9am–
12:30pm, 3:30–7:30pm.

④ **Vino Nobile.** Montepulciano's vintners have
organized a showroom, Consorzio del Vino Nobile di Montepulciano, at the Palazzo del Capitano
on Piazza Grande, where you can sample their
wines. Montepulciano is riddled with *enoteche*
and *cantine* (wine cellars) where you can sample
or purchase the local goods. See "Montepulciano's Best Winery Tours & Tastings," p 255, for
more information. ⏱ 15 min. Palazzo del Capitano,
Piazza Grande. ☎ 0578-757812. Mon–Fri 10am–1pm,
4–7pm; Sat 11am–3pm.

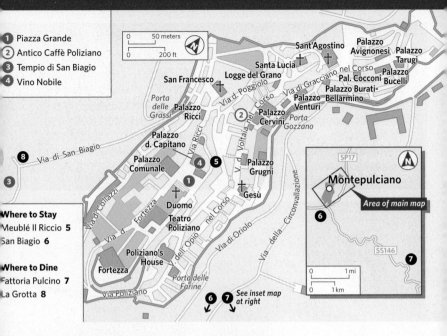

1 Piazza Grande
2 Antico Caffè Poliziano
3 Tempio di San Biagio
4 Vino Nobile

Where to Stay
Meublé Il Riccio 5
San Biagio 6

Where to Dine
Fattoria Pulcino 7
La Grotta 8

Where to Stay & Dine

★ **Fattoria Pulcino** TOWARD CHIANCIANO
TUSCAN Southwest of town, this restaurant serves the regional food and wine at communal tables in a 16th-century farmhouse. SS146 per Chianciano 35 (on the road to Chianciano). ☎ 0578-758711. Entrees 12€–22€. AE, DC, MC, V. Lunch & dinner daily. Closed Jan–Easter.

★★ **La Grotta** SAN BIAGIO *ITALIAN*
Across the street from San Biagio, this tavern with a pretty garden serves tasty specialties, most of them recently harvested from the countryside. Località San Biagio 15 (1km/⅔ miles west of center). ☎ 0578-757479. Entrees 10€–20€. AE, MC, V. Lunch & dinner Thurs–Tues. Closed Jan 10–Mar 10.

★ **Meublé Il Riccio** CENTRO STORICO
The "Porcupine Inn" has lovely rooms that have been recently refurbished without stripping them of their old-style character and quirks. Owners Gio and Ivana are superb hosts. Via di Talosa 21. ☎ 0578-757713. www.ilriccio.net. 6 units. Doubles 100€, breakfast not included. AE, DC, MC, V.

★ **San Biagio** SAN BIAGIO
In a restored nobleman's house outside the city walls, rooms have spare but comfortable "hotel" decor and balconies with postcard views. Via San Bartolomeo 2. ☎ 0578-717233. www.albergosanbiagio.it. 27 units. Doubles 95€–105€ w/buffet breakfast. MC, V.

> The "noble wine" of Montepulciano is the regional specialty.

Perugia

A college town in medieval-city clothing, the capital of
Umbria is a vibrant place with a diverse population and impressive art and
architecture. Perugia also has several good hotels, stylish restaurants, and
nightlife galore, as well as a convenient position that makes it a good base
for exploring Umbria. It's also one of the most underrated, and undervisited
midsize cities in Italy.

> At its northern end, stately Corso Vannucci opens into showpiece Piazza IV Novembre and its Fontana
Maggiore, overlooked by the Palazzo dei Priori.

START From Florence, take the A1 autostrada
south to Bettolle, then head east on the Raccordo Autostradale (150km/93 miles). From
Siena, take the Raccordo Siena-A1 to Bettolle,
then the Raccordo A1-Perugia. Follow signs
for Perugia *centro* (108km/67 miles).

❶ ★★ **Corso Vannucci.** It might just be the
best main drag in all of Italy. Life in Perugia
revolves around this 400m-long (1,300-ft.)
promenade, which runs between Piazza Italia and the Duomo. It's lined with boutiques
and the impressive Palazzo dei Priori (home
to several museums; see ❸ and ❹ below).

Above all, the Corso becomes the stage for the
see-and-be-seen *passeggiata* in the evening.
At its north end, the 13th-century ★★ **Fontana
Maggiore** is one of the city's most beloved
monuments, with intricate sculptural scenes,
by Giovanni and Nicola Pisano, of daily life in
medieval Perugia. ⏱ 30 min.

② 🍫 kids **Perugina Chocolate Shop.** Stock
up on the world famous Baci chocolates,
made right here in Perugia. If time
permits, inquire about touring the
Perugina factory in the western suburbs.
Piazza Italia. $.

> The vaults are all that remain of a hated symbol of papal oppression, Perugia's Rocca Paolina.

3 ★★★ **Galleria Nazionale.** Far and away the best art museum in Umbria, Perugia's National Gallery boasts important 16th-century ★★ **altarpieces** by Perugino (a native son of Perugia, born Pietro Vannucci), though the most celebrated piece here is Piero della Francesca's ★★★ **polyptych of Sant'Antonio,** painted in the 1460s. ⏱ 1 hr. Palazzo dei Priori, Corso Vannucci 19. ☎ 075-5741247. Admission 6.50€. Tues–Sun 8:30am–7:30pm.

4 ★★ **Collegio del Cambio.** Instead of dreary cubicles, employees at Perugia's Exchange Guild sat amid beautiful wood paneling and resplendent frescoes by Perugino. In this 15th-century "office suite," pay attention to the realistic portraiture of the figures, and especially the fantastic detail in the clothing. The ★ **Collegio della Mercanzia,** or Merchants' Guild, has a glorious, vaulted audience hall bedecked with inlaid wood—unusual for Italy. ⏱ 30 min. Palazzo dei Priori, Corso Vannucci 25. ☎ 075-5728599. Admission 2.60€ for Collegio del Cambio; 3.10€ includes Collegio della Mercanzia. Collegio del Cambio: Mar–Oct and Dec 20–Jan 6 Mon–Sat 9am–12:30pm, 2:30–5:30pm, Sun 9am–1pm; Nov–Dec 19 and Jan 7–Feb 28 Tues–Sat 8am–2pm, Sun 9am–12:30pm. Collegio della Mercanzia: Mar–Oct 9am–12:30pm, 2:30–5:30pm; Nov–Feb Tues–Sun 9am–2pm.

> *The steps opposite the Fontana Maggiore are a popular gathering spot for young locals and tourists.*

Italian Classes for Foreigners

Language study programs abound throughout Italy, but the full-immersion courses at Perugia's venerable **Università per Stranieri** (University for Foreigners) are where you'll achieve real results in the least amount of time. If you're serious about learning Italian and can spare the time away from home to study here, Perugia is the place to be. Courses start at a very reasonable 300€ for a 1-month program, and they'll even help you arrange housing. Piazza Fortebraccio 4. ☎ 075-57461. www. unistrapg.it.

5 ★ **La Rocca Paolina.** In 1540, the hated ruling pope, Paul III Farnese, ordered a new fortress built in the heart of Perugia. Instead of destroying wholesale the houses and shops in the area, architect Antonio da Sangallo incorporated the existing medieval buildings into the fortress substructure. The odious fortress was dismantled in 1860, when Perugia finally cast off the papal yoke, but the ★★ **vaults of the Rocca** remain. In this "medieval Pompeii," you can walk the empty streets and enter the doorways of houses and shops that were buried under the fortress. Almost none of this underground maze is off limits, so bring a flashlight and wander at will, imagining the sights, sounds, and smells of medieval Perugia. So why was Paul III so hated? He imposed an onerous salt tax on Perugia; in rebellion, the *perugini* stopped using salt altogether, a custom that continues to this day in their almost saltless bread. ⏱ 30 min. Entrances via the escalators at the Prefettura on Piazza Italia, the Porta Marzia on Via Marzia, or escalators from Piazza Partigiani . No phone. Free admission. Daily 8am–7pm.

6 ★ **San Pietro.** This Benedictine monastery and church has beautiful frescoes from the 14th to 16th centuries—including some small paintings of saints by Perugino that were stolen in 1916 but returned in 1993—and fine inlaid (intarsia) woodwork in the choir stalls. ⏱ 30 min. Borgo XX Giugno (take Corso Cavour all the way past Porta San Pietro). ☎ 075-30482. Free admission. Daily 8am–noon, 4pm–sunset.

Where to Stay & Dine

> *Perugians enjoy drinks and jazz at Caffè Morlacchi.*

★ **Alter Ego** CENTRO STORICO *CREATIVE ITALIAN*
Perugia shows off its cosmopolitan side at this
sexy subterranean joint. The menu makes tantalizing use of all kinds of cheeses, meats, and
earthy vegetables. **Via Floramonti 2a.** ☎ 075-572
9527. www.ristorantealterego.it. Entrees 8€–16€.
AE, DC, MC, V. Mon–Fri lunch & dinner; Sat dinner.

★★ **Brufani Palace** CENTRO STORICO
The top address in town has the perfect location at the foot of Corso Vannucci. Large guest
rooms are appointed with old-fashioned Italian
flair—sumptuous fabrics and tassels. **Piazza
Italia 12.** N075-5732541. www.brufanipalace.com.
94 units. Doubles from 250€ w/buffet breakfast.
AE, DC, MC, V.

★★ **Da Cesarino** CENTRO STORICO *UMBRIAN*
Expect strictly traditional regional fare—pastas
with wild boar *ragù*, roasted meats—at this
Slow Food establishment. **Piazza IV Novembre.**
☎ 075-5728974. Entrees 8.50€–14€. AE, DC, MC,
V. Lunch & dinner Thurs–Tues.

★ **Fortuna** CENTRO STORICO
Rooms are gracious at this moderately priced inn,
popular with older travelers. The location, value,
and old-world bones make it a great bet for those
who don't demand luxury amenities. **Via Bonazzi
9.** ☎ 075-5722845. www.umbriahotels.com. 51
units. Doubles 100€–130€. AE, DC, MC, V.

★★ **Osteria Il Gufo** CENTRO STORICO *CREATIVE
UMBRIAN* At this buzzy spot, *primi* are mostly
traditional, while more unusual *secondi* include a
veal *cotoletta* with apple and ginger chutney. **Via
della Viola 18.** ☎ 075-5734126. www.osteriailgufo.
it. Entrees 7€–10€. AE, DC, MC, V. Tues–Sat dinner only. Reservations recommended.

★★ **Sangallo Palace** CENTRO STORICO
Rooms at this 20th-century structure are spacious and immaculate, with a blend of modern
comforts and antique touches. While its location opposite the bus station isn't quite as ideal
as the Brufani Palace, it's just a short escalator
ride up from here to Piazza Italia. **Via Masi 9 (Piazza Partigiani).** ☎ 075-5730202. www.sangallo.
it. 100 units. Doubles 110€–170€. AE, DC, MC, V.

Perugia Nightlife

If you came to party in Perugia, you're in luck.
The fun-loving town has bars down every medieval alleyway, but the evening always kicks
off with a stroll down Corso Vannucci, which
is lined with cafes. After dark, try ★★ **Buskers,**
Corso Cavour 46 (☎ 075-5729202), a vibrant
pub with frequent live acts. For something
mellower, ★★ **Caffè Morlacchi,** Piazza Morlacchi 6/8 (☎ 075-5721760), is an old standby
where people gather for drinks and jazz.

Pienza

This tiny model Renaissance town was the creation of Pope Pius II, who wanted to transform his modest native village of Corsignano into a town that would glorify his name ("Pienza" means city of Pius, but also city of piety). The pope's envisioned city never grew beyond a few blocks, but what a masterpiece it remains! Zeffirelli recognized it for the stage setting it was, filming his *Romeo and Juliet* here. Give it at least a morning or afternoon.

> *Pienza is one of the most charming towns of the region.*

START From Siena, take the SS2 south to SS146 and follow the signs to Pienza. Trip length: from Siena 55km (33 miles).

1 Piazza Pio II. The square is flanked by the Duomo, Palazzo Piccolomini (papal palace), and the Museo Diocesano, with its collection of Sienese art.

The Palazzo Comunale, home to the town hall, was begun in 1462. The bell tower, added later, was made lower than the Duomo's to emphasize the power of the church over civil authority. ⏱ 30 min. Museo Diocesano: Corso Il Rossellino 30. ☎ 0578-749905. Admission 5€. Mar 15–Nov 1 Wed–Mon 10am–1pm, 3–6:30pm; Nov–mid-Mar Sat–Sun only 10am–1pm, 3–6pm.

2 ★★ Duomo. The Renaissance facade (1462) conceals a restored Gothic interior flooded with natural light. The five-moon crest throughout is the pope's family coat-of-arms. ⏱ 30 min. Piazza Pio II (off Corso Il Rossellino). No phone. Free admission. Daily 7am–1pm and 2:30–7pm.

3 ★ Palazzo Piccolomini. The papal home of Pius II is the masterpiece of Bernardo Rossellino (1409–64). In the pope's private apartments is his original baroque bed. Descendants of Pius II lived here until 1968. ⏱ 40 min. Piazza Pio II (off Corso Il Rossellino). ☎ 0578-748503. Admission 3€ adults, 2€ ages 17 and under. Tues–Sun 10am–12:30pm and 3–6pm.

4 ★ Via dell'Amore. Pienza's de rigueur photo op is in front of the marble sign for "Love Street," with honey-colored medieval walls, cypresses, and a church spire in the background. ⏱ 15 min.

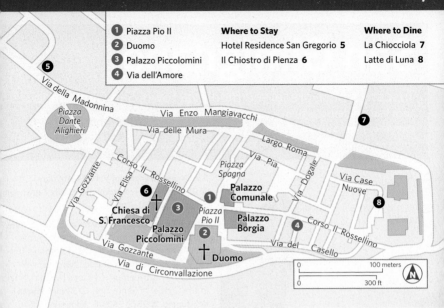

1 Piazza Pio II
2 Duomo
3 Palazzo Piccolomini
4 Via dell'Amore

Where to Stay
Hotel Residence San Gregorio **5**
Il Chiostro di Pienza **6**

Where to Dine
La Chiocciola **7**
Latte di Luna **8**

Where to Stay & Dine

★★ Hotel Residence San Gregorio OUTSIDE CENTRO Set in a former cultural center bombed in World War II, standard doubles and suites are elegant and comfortable. Via della Madonnina 4. ☎ 0578-748175. 19 units. Doubles 80€–120€ w/breakfast. AE, MC, V.

★★ Il Chiostro di Pienza CENTRO STORICO Converted to a hotel in 2005, this 15th-century convent is the best choice within city walls, with a pool overlooking the lush Val d'Orcia. Corso Il Rossellino 26. ☎ 0578-748400. www.relaisilchiostrodipienza.com. 37 units. Doubles 120€–220€; suites 220€–280€ w/buffet breakfast. AE, DC, MC, V.

La Chiocciola OUTSIDE CENTRO *TUSCAN* Dishes at this rustic tavern with outdoor tables have stood the test of time. Try the pappardelle with wild boar or the ravioli stuffed with local pecorino. Viale Mencattelli 4. ☎ 0578-748683. Entrees 7€–15€. AE, MC, V. Lunch & dinner Thurs-Tues. Closed 2 weeks in Jan.

★ kids **Latte di Luna** CENTRO STORICO This laid-back trattoria, serving southern Tuscan cuisine, draws a diverse regular crowd—

from foreign exchange students to local *cara-binieri.* Via San Carlo 2–4. ☎ 0578-748606. Main courses 6€–13€. MC, V. Wed-Mon 12:20–2:20pm and 7:30–9:20pm. Closed Feb-Mar 15 and July.

A Local Treat

Don't leave Pienza without picking up some *pecorino di Pienza,* Italy's best sheep's-milk cheese. It's sold plain or flavored with herbs and vegetables. Fancier varieties are soaked in wine (*ubriaco* or "drunk") or dusted with truffles (*tartufato*).

San Gimignano

Tuscany's best-preserved medieval town, San Gimignano once had a defense system encompassing more than 70 towers, and no fewer than 13 of them survive, earning it the nickname "medieval Manhattan." In summer, it's the real-life setting for open-air operas in Piazza del Duomo.

> *San Gimignano's 70 towers were powerful symbols of clan and family rivalry.*

START San Gimignano is northwest of Siena and southwest of Florence. From either city take the Florence-Siena autostrada to Poggibonsi, and cut west for 12km (8 miles) on S324 into San Gimignano. Parking lots are outside the city walls. Trip length: 40km (24 miles) from Siena, 52km (32 miles) from Florence.

1 ★ **Church of Sant'Agostino.** This Romanesque-Gothic church from 1290, on the north side of town, houses 17 famous frescoes by Benozzo Gozzoli from 1464. ⏱ 20 min. Piazza Sant'Agostino (north of Via 20 Settembre). ☎ 0577-907012. Free admission. Daily 7am–noon, 3–7pm (6pm Oct–Apr).

2 ★★ **Collegiata.** The city's main church dates from the 11th century, but its present look is mostly from the 1400s. Inside, it's among Tuscany's most richly decorated churches, with wonderful 15th-century frescoes by Ghirlandaio in the Chapel of Santa Fina. ⏱ 30 min. Piazza del Duomo. ☎ 0577-940316. Admission 3.50€. Mar–Oct daily 9:30am–7pm; Nov–Feb Mon–Sat 9:30am–5pm, Sun 1–5pm.

3 ★ **Museo Civico & Torre Grossa.** Climb 54m (175 ft.) for one of Tuscany's best panoramic views. Post-descent, take in the art at the 13th-century Palazzo del Popolo (town hall). ⏱ 40 min. Piazza del Duomo 1 (off Vicolo Santa). ☎ 0577-990312. Admission 5€. Nov–Feb daily 10am–6pm; Mar–Oct daily 9:30am–7:30pm.

4 kids **Museo della Tortura.** Housed in the Torre del Diavolo (Devil's Tower), this museum of medieval torture devices features cast-iron chastity belts, bone-crunching manacles, and other gruesome implements. ⏱ 30 min. Via del Castello 1. ☎ 0577-942243. Admission 8€. Apr–Oct daily 10am–8pm; Nov–Mar daily 10am–6pm.

Two Beautiful Squares & Market Days

Piazza del Duomo and **Piazza della Cisterna,** side by side in the heart of town, are two of Tuscany's loveliest town squares. On Thursday and Saturday mornings, country vendors hawk their wares along the ancient town streets and disappear by afternoon. Sit, sip, and people-watch at the gift shops, churches, and cafes in these public spaces.

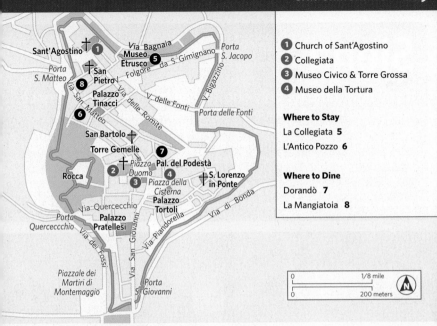

1 Church of Sant'Agostino
2 Collegiata
3 Museo Civico & Torre Grossa
4 Museo della Tortura

Where to Stay
La Collegiata **5**
L'Antico Pozzo **6**

Where to Dine
Dorandò **7**
La Mangiatoia **8**

Where to Stay & Dine

★★★ **Dorandò** CENTRO STORICO *TUSCAN*
The city's top restaurant, with stone walls and a vaulted roof, serves creative, light seasonal dishes from medieval and Etruscan recipes. Vicolo dell'Oro 2. ☎ 0577-941862. Entrees 12€–23€; fixed-price menu 47€. AE, DC, MC, V. Lunch & dinner daily; Nov–Easter closed Mon.

★★★ **La Collegiata** NORTH SAN GIMIGNANO
One of the town's top two hotels, this Relais & Châteaux property in a 16th-century convent amid centuries-old cypresses has tasteful rooms. Località Strada 27. ☎ 0577-943201. www.lacollegiata.it/indexe.html. 19 units. Doubles 210€–520€; suites 600€–1,050€. AE, MC, V.

★★ **L'Antico Pozzo** CENTRO STORICO
Dante slept in this 15th-century palazzo (the old town's best) with rooms of varying size, many with antiques and some with frescoes. Via San Matteo 87. ☎ 0577-942014. www.anticopozzo.com. 18 units. Doubles 110€–135€; triples 150€–180€ w/breakfast. AE, DC, MC, V.

★★ **La Mangiatoia** CENTRO STORICO *TUSCAN*
Many dishes at this fine old-town restaurant—like venison with pine nuts, raisins, vinegar, and chocolate—derive from old San Gimignanese recipes. Via Mainardi 5. ☎ 0577-941528. Entrees 8.50€–18€. MC, V. Lunch & dinner Wed–Mon. Nov, Jan, and June–Sept closed Sun.

> There's a Slow Food ethos behind every bite at Dorandò.

Siena

If you have time for only one Tuscan town besides Florence, make it Siena. Dominating the medieval trade routes between France and Rome, the city in its day had Italy's richest banks, Gothic architecture, a quasi-democratic government, and its own constitution. Once Florence's rival in might and arts patronage, Siena never fully recovered from the Black Death, which mowed down the population from 100,000 to 30,000 in 1348. Now, the medieval character of its public features is frozen in time—a sort of living museum for art, architecture, and history buffs.

> *Whether you're dining, drinking, or enjoying a gelato, you'll wind up in the Campo in the evening.*

START From Florence, Siena is southeast along the Firenze-Siena autostrada. Trip length: from Florence, 75km (47 miles).

① ★★★ **Piazza del Campo.** The most beautiful piazza in Italy is Siena's. First laid out in the early 12th century on the site of a Roman forum, it is dramatically shaped like a sloping scallop shell or fan.

By 1340, the town leaders had paved the square in brick and divided it into nine sections in honor of the Council of Nine, who ruled Siena during its golden age. Today the biggest festival in Italy, the **Palio,** takes place here; see p 293.

At the upper end of the square stands the **Fonte Gaia** (Fountain of Joy), created from 1408 to 1419 by Jacopo della Quercia, Siena's

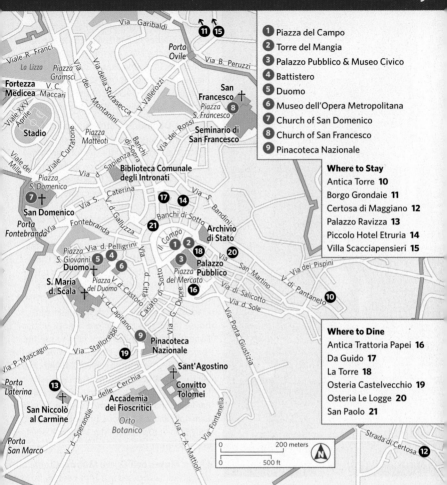

1	Piazza del Campo
2	Torre del Mangia
3	Palazzo Pubblico & Museo Civico
4	Battistero
5	Duomo
6	Museo dell'Opera Metropolitana
7	Church of San Domenico
8	Church of San Francesco
9	Pinacoteca Nazionale

Where to Stay

Antica Torre **10**
Borgo Grondaie **11**
Certosa di Maggiano **12**
Palazzo Ravizza **13**
Piccolo Hotel Etruria **14**
Villa Scacciapensieri **15**

Where to Dine

Antica Trattoria Papei **16**
Da Guido **17**
La Torre **18**
Osteria Castelvecchio **19**
Osteria Le Logge **20**
San Paolo **21**

greatest sculptor. Regrettably, what you see today is an inferior copy from 1868. The eroded remains of the original panels for the fountain can be seen on the loggia of the Palazzo Pubblico (see below). ⏱ 30 min.

2 ★★ kids **Torre del Mangia.** Looming 102m (331 ft.) over Il Campo—and looking entirely too slender for its stratospheric stature—the Torre del Mangia is the Goodyear blimp of medieval Italian towers. Look straight down, and the crowds in the shell-shaped piazza are mere ants. ⏱ 20 min. At the Palazzo Pubblico, Piazza del Campo. ☎ 0577-292262. Admission 6€. Mar 16-Oct daily 10am-7pm; Nov-Mar 15 daily 10am-4pm.

3 ★★★ **Palazzo Pubblico & Museo Civico.** The major rooms of Palazzo Pubblico, the finest Gothic structure in Siena, have been frescoed with themes of secular life in medieval Siena, creating one of Tuscany's grandest and most unusual museums. The Sala dei Priori was frescoed by Spinello Aretino in 1476 with episodes from the life of Pope Alexander III. The Sala del Risorgimento boasts 19 murals illustrating the life of Vittorio Emanuele, who unified the country.

In the Sala della Pace or "peace room" are the badly damaged but still-celebrated frescoes, *The Effects of Good and Bad Government* by Ambrogio Lorenzetti (1335-40). This is the greatest secular medieval fresco

> *Over 40 Sienese artists created the Duomo's marble intarsia floor designs.*

cycle in Europe. ⏱ 90 min. In the Palazzo Pubblico, Piazza del Campo. ☎ 0577-292263. Admission 6.50€, 4€ students; free ages 10 and under. Mar–Oct daily 10am–7pm; Nov–Feb daily 10am–5:30pm.

❹ ★ Battistero. The 14th-century baptistery stands on its own little square on top of a steep flight of steps. It contains some remarkable art, its crown jewel being a baptismal font embellished with some of the finest sculpture of the *quattrocento* (1300s). The hexagonal marble font (1411–30) is a masterpiece by Jacopo della Quercia in the Gothic-Renaissance style. The two statues around the basin, *Faith* and *Hope,* are by Donatello. Panels on the font include Ghiberti's *Baptism of Christ* and *John in Prison,* and the even greater *Herod's Feast* by Donatello. ⏱ 30 min. Piazza San Giovanni (off Piazza del Duomo). ☎ 0577-283048. Admission 3€. Apr–Sept daily 9am–7:30pm; Oct daily 9am–6pm; Nov–Mar daily 10:30am–1pm and 2–5pm.

❺ ★★★ Duomo. The architectural highlight of Siena's golden age is the cathedral of Santa Maria dell'Assunta (its formal name). Beginning in the 12th century, architects set out to create a dramatic facade with colored bands of marble in a Romanesque and Italian Gothic style. Between 1369 and 1547, some 40 leading Sienese artists created the 56 designs on the floor.

The sober campanile (bell tower) dates from 1513. The 13th-century pulpit is the creation of Nicola Pisano (Giovanni's father). The architectural highlight is the Libreria Piccolomini, constructed in 1485 by Cardinal Francesco Piccolomini (later Pope Pius III), to house the library of his more famous uncle, Pope Pius II. Art lovers flock here to see the remarkable early-16th-century frescoes by the Umbrian master Pinturicchio. ⏱ 45 min. Piazza del Duomo. ☎ 0577-283048. Free admission to Duomo; library 3€. Duomo: Mar 16–Oct daily 8am–1pm and 2:30–7:30pm. Nov–Mar 15 daily 8am–1pm and 2:30–5pm. Library: Mar 15–Oct daily 9am–7:30pm; Nov–Mar 14 daily 10am–1pm and 2:30–5pm.

❻ ★★ Museo dell'Opera Metropolitana. This art museum is housed in a 14th-century building originally designed to be the transept of a grand new cathedral until the plague of 1348 descended. Many of the cathedral's masterpieces are now sheltered here, including Giovanni Pisano's statues that originally adorned the facade of the Duomo. The museum's greatest treasure is Duccio's *Maestà* (Virgin in Majesty) on the second floor. This double-sided altarpiece from 1311 is hailed as one of the greatest late medieval paintings in Europe. Climb up to the walkway for Siena's grandest panorama (even better than the view from Torre del Mangia, ❷). ⏱ 1 hr. Piazza del Duomo 8. ☎ 0577-42309. Admission 6€. Mar 16–Sept daily 9am–7:30pm; Oct daily 9am–6pm; Nov–Mar 15 daily 9am–1:30pm.

> *First horse to cross the line wins the palio ("banner"), whether the jockey's still astride or not.*

7 ★ **Church of San Domenico.** This severe-looking church in the monastic Gothic style was founded in 1125 and closely linked with St. Catherine, who is said to have had her visions here. Inside you can see a portrait of her by her contemporary Andrea Vanni. This is the only known portrait by someone who actually knew her. Ask a church official for the exact spot where Catherine is said to have received her stigmata. ⏲ 20 min. Piazza San Domenico (off Via Curtatone). No phone. Free admission. Apr–Oct 7am–1pm and 3–6:30pm; Nov–Mar 9am–1pm and 3–6pm.

8 **Church of San Francesco.** This late Gothic church was begun in 1326 and reconstructed in the 1880s. The cavernous interior has frescoes from the 1330s by the brothers Ambrogio and Pietro Lorenzetti. Time has been cruel to these works, but their beauty survives. ⏲ 20 min. Piazza San Francesco (off Via dei Baroncelli). No phone. Daily 7:30am–noon and 3:30–7pm.

9 ★ **Pinacoteca Nazionale.** Regrettably, the greatest works by Sienese masters are found elsewhere, often in Florence, but this is still an impressive and representative showcase of the city's greatest artists. Of exceptional interest are the cartoons of the Mannerist master Beccafumi, from which many of the panels in the Duomo floor were created. ⏲ 90 min. Via San Pietro 29 (off Via del Capitano). ☎ 0577-281161. Admission 4€ Sun–Mon 8:30am–1:30pm, Tues–Sat 8:30am–7pm.

Bareback Anarchy & Royal Pomp

Two times a year, on July 2 and August 16, Europe's most daring horse race takes place on Siena's main square. Jockeys fly around the dirt-filled square three times with one aim: winning. Forget sportsmanship. "The rule of the barbarian prevails," says a parade marshal. The single rule is that no jockey can grab another horse's reins. But you *can* drug an opponent the morning of the race, kidnap him the night before or, as he rides by, "whip him with a leather belt made from the skin of the bull's penis, which leaves the deepest welts and lasting scars," as recounted by a parade marshal. All this is in tribute to the Virgin Mary, in whose honor the Palio has taken place since 1310.

Where to Stay

> Tranquil gardens at the Palazzo Ravizza.

★ **Antica Torre** CENTRO STORICO
The rooms in this 16th-century tower are mid-size with travertine floors, antique prints, and wrought-iron beds. The top level has panoramic views. Via di Fiera Vecchia 7. ☎ 0577-222255. www.anticatorresiena.it. 8 units. Doubles 90€–115€. AE, DC, MC, V.

★★ **Borgo Grondaie** NORTH SIENA
Combining country charm with a view of the city, this converted farm offers rooms and apartments (ideal for families) in a private mini-village setting. The 1.6 hectare (4-acre) grounds include a saltwater pool and wine cellar. Enthusiastic staff is top notch. Strada delle Grondaie. ☎ 0577-332539. www.borgogrondaie.com. 14 units. Double-occupancy apartments 80€–155€; quadruple-occupancy apartments 94–260€. AE, DC, MC, V.

★★ **Certosa di Maggiano** PORTA ROMANA
Siena's most luxurious hotel is in a 14th-century monastery rife with antiques. Half-board required in summer. No kids under 12. Strada di Certosa 82. ☎ 0577-288180. www.certosadimaggiano.com. 17 units. Doubles 400€–620€; suites from 680€ w/breakfast. AE, MC, V.

★★ **Palazzo Ravizza** CENTRO STORICO
It's not a luxury place, but Siena's best *pensione* is a time warp back to what travel must have been like in the old days. The Renaissance palazzo has original frescoes and large, high-ceilinged, and modernized rooms. There are elegant parlors with card tables off the lobby and a large garden out back. Staff is wonderful, and the on-site restaurant is excellent. Pian dei Mantellini 34. ☎ 0577-280462. www.palazzoravizza.it. 38 units. Doubles 115€–230€. AE, DC, MC, V.

Piccolo Hotel Etruria CENTRO STORICO
Rooms in the main building of this small, immaculate, welcoming family-run hotel are largest, with the most character. Via Donzelle 3. ☎ 0577-288088. www.hoteletruria.com. 13 units. Doubles 86€. AE, DC, MC, V.

★ **Villa Scacciapensieri** NORTH SIENA
Amid a large park, with a pool, tennis court, and terraces, the 19th-century "Villa Troubles-Be-Gone" has medium to large rooms (some facing the Chianti hills), though decor is a tad grandmotherly. Via di Scacciapensieri 10. ☎ 0577-41441. www.villascacciapensieri.it. 31 units. Doubles 130€–265€; suites 250€–330€. AE, DC, MC, V.

Where to Dine

> *Antica Trattoria Papei serves simple, traditional Sienese cuisine in a friendly setting.*

★ **Antica Trattoria Papei** CENTRO STORICO
SIENESE This family-run trattoria serves simple
but well-prepared Sienese fare such as rabbit
in white wine with rosemary and sage or wide
noodles in wild boar sauce. **Piazza del Mercato
6.** ☎ 0577-280894. Entrees 6.50€–11€. AE, MC, V.
Lunch & dinner Tues–Sun.

Da Guido CENTRO STORICO *SIENESE/
INTERNATIONAL* Modern cuisine—among
Siena's best grilled meats and antipasti tables—
is served under old beams, arched ceilings,
and brick walls. **Vicolo Pier Pettinaio 7 (Via della
Galluzza).** ☎ 0577-280042. Entrees 7€–17€. AE,
DC, MC, V. Lunch & dinner daily.

La Torre CENTRO STORICO *TUSCAN*
This mamma and papa operation enjoys a loyal
clientele. Try the delectable homemade pastas,
the perfectly cooked meats, and a few exotic
dishes such as *piccione al forno* (oven-baked
pigeon). **Via Salicotto 7–9 (off Piazza del Campo).**
☎ 0577-287548. Entrees 6€–11€. AE. Lunch &
dinner Fri–Wed. Closed Aug 17–Sept 1.

★ **Osteria Castelvecchio** CENTRO STORICO
TUSCAN/VEGETARIAN This ancient building,
convenient to all the major monuments,
including the Duomo, is the best place in town
for fresh vegetables. You can order meat and

poultry dishes, but the rich harvest of the Tuscan
countryside is given special attention. The menu
changes daily. **Via Castelvecchio 65 (off Via San
Pietro).** ☎ 0577-49586. Entrees 7.50€–12€. AE, DC,
MC, V. Lunch & dinner Mon–Sat.

★★★ **Osteria Le Logge** CENTRO STORICO
SIENESE/TUSCAN This tranquil trattoria
serves the freshest cuisine in a refined but
old-fashioned atmosphere where you'll feel
comfortable whiling away several hours (but try
to get a table downstairs, where the action is).
The tender veal steaks are the best in town, and
the pastas are the most memorable we had on
our last trip to Tuscany. **Via del Porrione 33 (off
Via del Rialto).** ☎ 0577-48013. Entrees 12€–18€.
AE, DC, MC, V. Lunch & dinner Mon–Sat.

★ **San Paolo** CENTRO STORICO *SANDWICHES/
PUB* Choose from over 50 sandwiches and
meal-size salads at this cozy, casual pub right
off Il Campo. It's perfect for when you and your
wallet need a break from typical restaurant
meals, and when the weather's nice, you can
sit on a small balcony with a prime view of
the piazza. **Vicolo San Paolo 2 (off Piazza del
Campo).** ☎ 0577-226622. Sandwiches and salads
3.50€–7€. AE, DC, MC, V. Lunch & dinner daily
(open until 2am).

Tuscany & Umbria Fast Facts

Accommodations Booking Services

The rental agencies listed in the "Renting a Villa" box on p 233 can assist with short-term holiday rental properties (from villas to apartments) as well as hotels and B&Bs around Tuscany and Umbria. Tourist info points at the major train stations and airports can also assist with last-minute hotel bookings.

American Express

The nearest American Express office is in Florence, in Piazza Cimatori (Via Dante Alighieri 22R, ☎ 055-50981; Mon–Fri 9am–5:30pm, Sat 9am–12:30pm; no travel services on Sat; closed Sun).

ATMs

Every town in Tuscany and Umbria has at least one bank with a cash machine (*bancomat*). To find a bank, look for signs saying *banca, banco, credito,* or *cassa.* Italy generally uses 4-digit PINs; if you have a 6-digit number, check with your bank before you leave.

Dentists & Doctors

If you have a mild medical issue or dental problems while traveling in Tuscany, most hotels will be able to refer you to a local doctor (*medico*) or dentist (*dentista*) who speaks English. If you are staying at a rental villa or apartment, ask your rental agent in advance to provide you with a list of local medical contacts. Fees are generally between 50€ and 100€ for a routine visit. Otherwise, go to the *pronto soccorso* (emergency room) at the nearest hospital, where they'll treat your immediate problem (for example, a sprained ankle) for free and give you a short course of prescription drugs if necessary.

Emergencies

For general emergencies, call ☎ **112** for the Carabinieri or ☎ **113** for the Polizia. Call ☎ **114** for an ambulance and ☎ **115** for the fire department. For a medical emergency that doesn't require an ambulance, see "Dentists & Doctors," above. To report lost or stolen items, see "Police," p 297.

Getting There

Florence and Pisa are Tuscany's main airports, though neither one is a major international hub.

Delta flies to Pisa from JFK; for flights into Florence, you'll have to connect through another European airport. For less hassle, many international travelers choose to fly into Rome's Leonardo da Vinci (Fiumicino) airport, which is only a 2-hour drive from southern Tuscany. Few Tuscan and Umbrian towns listed in this chapter are well served by train.

Getting Around

Tuscany and Umbria are best explored by car. Driving is a pleasure in these scenic regions, and it's the only way to get to small towns and wineries off the beaten path. Be aware that the main highway through the Chianti, as well as lesser roads there, are often slow-going. Always allow double the time you think is necessary to get where you're going. Fuel is expensive in Tuscany (as in all of Italy), though the only toll road is the A1 autostrada (running north-south between Tuscany and Umbria). A detailed road map, such as Touring Club Italiano's Toscana map, is essential, and available at airport bookshops and most newsstands.

Renting a car in Italy is never a bargain. However, **AutoEuropa** (www.autoeuropa.it) and **Maggiore** (www.maggiore.it), both with offices at Pisa, Florence, and Rome airports and downtown locations in Florence and Rome, consistently have the best rental rates (expect to pay about 45€ per day, including all taxes and unlimited mileage, for an economy car). International agencies like Hertz and Avis also have offices in Tuscany where you may be able to use travel rewards points toward your rental.

Though a car gives you more freedom and flexibility, the main towns and cities of Tuscany and Umbria can also be toured by regional buses and—depending on your route—by train. Both trains and buses are an economical way to get around, but you are at the mercy of their schedules and time-consuming stops along the way.

For train timetables and ticket prices, visit www.trenitalia.com.

SITA (☎ 800-373760; www.sitabus.it) runs the frequent bus connections between Florence and Siena (6.50€; 1 hr. 15 min.). Siena-based

Train (☎ 0577-204111; www.trainspa.it) offers regional bus service around the Chianti and southern Tuscany. **Lazzi** (☎ 055-363041; www.lazzi.it) is the main company for bus travel in northern and eastern Tuscany. For bus travel around Umbria, Perugia-based **Sulga** (☎ 075-5009641; www.sulga.it) offers fairly comprehensive service, including routes to and from Rome's Fiumicino airport.

Internet Access

Almost all hotels now have a public terminal where guests can sign on, though there may be a small fee; many nicer hotels also have Wi-Fi and/or broadband, which may be free or may carry a reasonable to astronomical daily or hourly charge. Few rental villas have Internet access, but most towns have at least a cafe or other shop where you can log on for about 4€ to 5€ an hour. Italian law requires you show identification to use public Internet terminals. Don't expect fast connections anywhere in Italy.

Pharmacies

Italian *farmacie* will fill foreign prescriptions with little or no hassle. They're also where you buy over-the-counter medicines like ibuprofen or cough syrup, feminine hygiene products, and even sunblock. *Farmacie* are recognizable by a neon green or red cross and are usually open 8am to 1:30pm and 3:30 to 8pm.

For optical care (glasses repair, contact lens solution), go to an *ottica*, which are everywhere in Italy.

Police

To report a lost or stolen article, such as a wallet or passport, visit the local police *questura* or Carabinieri *caserma* in your location. See also "Emergencies," p 296.

Post Office

Stamps *(francobolli)* can be purchased at most *tabacchi* (tobacco stores), and postcards and letters can be mailed from either your hotel or the red letterboxes mounted on walls around town. Note that mail service is notoriously slow throughout Italy.

Safety

Tuscany and Umbria are some of the safest Italian regions for tourists. Petty theft is virtually unheard of, though the one area where you should keep your wits about you is around the bus station in Perugia, where gypsies and pickpockets are sometimes known to lurk.

Visitor Information

For **Tuscany,** the official tourism board's website, www.turismo.toscana.it, is an excellent place to go for general information about what types of activities and attractions you can find in the various areas of the region. Larger individual cities also have their own sites and brick-and-mortar information in offices. In **Siena,** the office is at Piazza del Campo 56 (☎ 0577-280551; www.terresiena.it). In **Lucca,** go to Piazza Guidiccioni 2 (☎ 0583-919920; www.luccaturismo.it). **Pisa** has an information office at Via P. Nenni 24 (☎ 050-929777; www.pisa.turismo.toscana.it).

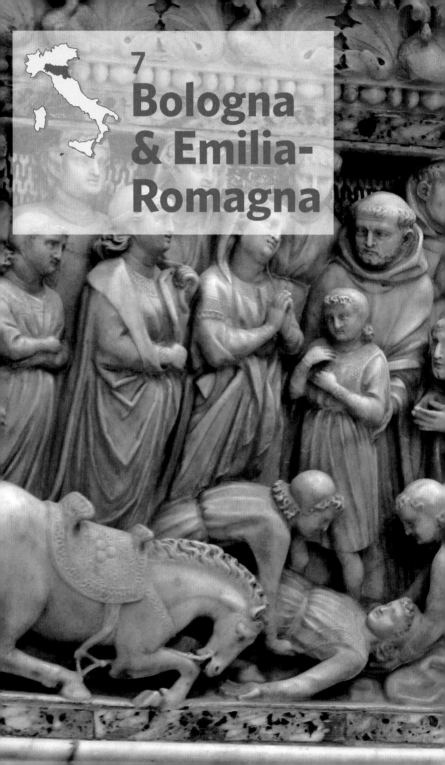

The Best of Emilia-Romagna in 3 Days

The Via Emilia, the road that Roman emperor Marcus

Aemilius Lepidus began in 187 B.C. to connect Piacenza (p 316) with Rimini on the Adriatic coast (p 307), was straight and ensured rapid travel for the legions. The train routes that parallel the old road do the same for travelers today. Three days in Emilia-Romagna allow you time to enjoy the art and architecture of Bologna and Parma, two of the great cities along the Via Emilia, and to make a quick excursion to Ravenna, the final capital of the Western Empire, where brilliant mosaics evoke Byzantium.

> PREVIOUS PAGE The Tomb of St. Dominic in Bologna is decorated with carved reliefs showing episodes from the saint's life. THIS PAGE Mosaics from Ravenna's mausoleum of Galla Placidia, the most powerful woman of the 5th-century Roman world.

START Bologna. Trip length: 265km (165 miles).

① **Bologna.** One of Italy's best-preserved medieval cities was already a great center of culture by the 13th century, when its university, the oldest in Europe, was founded. The city's 34km (21 miles) of arcaded streets were designed to accommodate easy strolling and intellectual discourse, and today these attractive walkways make it a pleasure to traverse the old city in search of its many treasures.

Sturdy medieval palaces and the Gothic **Basilica di San Petronio** (p 318, ①) surround Piazza Maggiore. The elegant 1566 bronze **Fountain of Neptune,** the work of Flemish sculptor Jean Boulogne (Giambologna), splashes to one side of the

1 Bologna
2 Parma
3 Ravenna

> Giambologna, who sculpted some of Florence's most-photographed statues, also cast Bologna's bronze Neptune.

Travel Tip

It is easiest, and preferable, to travel around Emilia-Romagna by train. Most of the sights are in major cities, and train service between them is fast and frequent. Parking in cities, especially Bologna and Parma, is extremely limited. For more information on transportation in the region, see "Getting There & Around," on p 342.

piazza, and in nearby Piazza di Porta Ravegnana rise the **Due Torri** (p 320, ❹), two sturdy but precariously leaning medieval towers.

Just beyond, on Via Zambione, are three more of Bologna's architectural landmarks: the **Church of San Giacomo Maggiore** (p 320, ❺), where the chapel of the Bentivoglio family is decorated with frescoes by Lorenzo Costa that vividly depict a day in the life of a Renaissance court; the **Teatro Comunale,** a baroque theater (p 323); and the **Pinacoteca Nazionale** (p 321, ❻), a vast repository of works by Bolognese artists and other masters.

The **Basilica di San Domenico** (p 322, ❽), to the south of Piazza Maggiore, houses a stunning medieval and Renaissance work, the Tomb of St. Dominic. Two of the first artists to work on the tomb were Nicola Pisano (c. 1220–84)

> Parma's Romanesque Battistero is easily recognized by its octagonal shape and soft pink hue.

and Arnolfo di Cambio (c. 1240–1300). Two centuries later Niccolò da Bari carved the exquisite canopy, and when he died, a young Michelangelo continued the work. Bologna-born Guido Reni added the final baroque touch—a magical ceiling fresco above the tomb.

From Bologna, it is just 95km (57 miles) northwest to Parma, less than an hour by one of the trains that run at least every half-hour.

2 Parma. Like many Italian cities, Parma owes its good fortune and handsome appearance of avenues and piazzas to one family, the Farneses. When the Farneses abandoned the city in the 18th century, Marie-Louise, wife of Emperor Napoleon, stepped in to fill the void.

Parma's greatest architectural works were gracing the city center long before the Farneses arrived. The Romanesque **Duomo** (p 327, **2**) and its pink octagonal **Battistero** (baptistery, p 326, **1**) date from the 12th century, while Parma's greatest artist, Antonio da Correggio, worked in the early 16th century, covering the Duomo's cupola, the walls and ceiling of the **Camera di San Paolo** (p 328, **4**), and the **Church of San Giovanni Evangelista** (p 327, **3**) with his transporting frescoes.

Marie-Louise assembled the remarkable collection in the city's **Galleria Nazionale** (p 328, **6**) in part from convents and villas throughout Italy when the French marched down the peninsula at the end of the 18th century. This museum, one of Italy's finest, occupies a wing of the Farnese's Palazzo Pilotta and includes more works by Correggio, along with those by Anthony Van Dyck and Leonardo da Vinci. Also in the palace is one of Italy's earliest stages, **Teatro Farnese** (p 328, **6**), commissioned by the family for their personal entertainment.

One of the great pleasures of wandering through Parma is to sample the city's famous *prosciutto di Parma* and the local cheese, Parmigiano-Reggiano. These ingredients and the produce of the surrounding farmlands appear in the dishes of the city's legendary restaurants. For more on Parma's pork products and cheese see p 303 and p 306.

Ravenna is just 75km (45 miles) southeast of Bologna, about an hour by one of the trains that run about every hour. From Parma, the best strategy is to backtrack through Bologna.

3 Ravenna. For two brief centuries, before the Lombards invaded in 750, Ravenna flourished as the western seat of the Byzantine Empire. The most striking evidence of the city's former power is the brilliant mosaics that shine within its churches and other landmarks.

A Different Kind of Fizz

The initial taste of Lambrusco—to Emilia-Romagna what Chianti is to Tuscany—may well take the uninitiated by surprise: it's dry, red, sparkling, and served slightly chilled. Lambrusco is a wine that grows on you with each sip, and quite quickly at that. The plains of coastal Romagna yield a pale, dry Trebbiano that, chilled and a bit *frizzante* (sparkling), nicely takes the edge off on a hot afternoon.

More Information

For detailed coverage of sights, hotels, restaurants, shops, and nightlife in Bologna, see p 318; for Parma, see p 326; for Ravenna, see p 336.

> *Parma's 17th-century, wood-and-stucco Teatro Farnese is still used for performances.*

Many of these are quite near Piazza del Popolo, an elegant 16th-century square from the city's days under Venetian rule that is the focal point of the town. The Basilica di San Vitale and Mausoleo di Galla Placidia are a few blocks to the north of the square, and the Basilica di Sant'Apollinare Nuovo is a few blocks to the south.

The greatest show of pomp is in the octagonal **Basilica di San Vitale** (p 336, ❶), completed by Emperor Justinian in 540 (it's the only known church from the period to have survived virtually intact). Byzantine mosaics in the apse depict a seated Christ and next to him is Justinian, endowed with a halo and a crown to indicate his role as head of church and state.

The **Mausoleo di Galla Placidia** (p 338, ❷), the tomb of the sister of the Roman emperor Honorius, is far more humble, and its glittering mosaics are bathed in ethereal light (though, ironically, her remains may not be in the tomb—the contents of the sarcophagus alleged to be her final resting place were burned in the 16th c.).

In the **Basilica di Sant'Apollinare Nuovo** (p 338, ❸), processions of virgins and martyrs proceed toward an enthroned Christ surrounded by angels, caught in midstep for all eternity. Some of Ravenna's most impressive yet charming mosaics adorn the otherwise austere **Chiesa di Sant'Apollinare in Classe** (p 340, ❼), in a landlocked suburb that was once the city's busy port. Lord Byron, the British poet, used to ride in the nearby pine forests when he lived in Ravenna briefly in 1820, and another poet, the great Dante Alighieri, is buried in a **marble tomb** (p 339, ❻) in Ravenna, where he died in 1321.

Where Pigs Rule

Ham, you'll discover quickly enough, is the mainstay of serious gastronomy in Emilia-Romagna. But it's hardly as simple as that. Which cut of the pig? At which altitude was the animal raised? The Roman legions brought pork with them when they settled the region, and this staple shows up on almost any menu in all its manifestations, in sausages, salamis, and, of course, in its most elegant transformation, as wafer-thin *prosciutto crudo*. The best *prosciutto crudo* comes from pigs raised around the town of Langhirano, where the climatic conditions are said to be ideal for curing. But many gourmands of the region, especially those in Parma, would never settle for prosciutto, but insist instead on *culatello*. This cut comes from the leanest part of the *right* hind leg—the leg that receives less weight when the animal is sitting and thus builds up less muscle and is less sinewy.

While Parma fusses over *culatello*, Bologna concerns itself with *mortadella*, an almost sensual pork sausage (often made using the liver) and an aromatic blend of spices and pistachios, and Modena works on perfecting *zamponi* (stuffed pig's feet).

The Best of Emilia-Romagna in 1 Week

A full week in Emilia-Romagna allows more of a chance to see the art and architectural treasures along the Via Emilia, as well as to spend more time in coastal Romagna. You can follow the Roman road to its end, at Rimini, a worldly beach town where a triumphal arch and theater are reminders of the Roman presence.

> Like many Emilia-Romagna markets, Bologna's Mercato delle Erbe is known for the quality of the fresh produce and other foodstuffs.

START Bologna. Trip length: 336km (209 miles).

❶ Bologna. For your first very fulfilling day of sightseeing, see my suggestions on p 300, ❶. On your second day, explore the city in a bit more depth, beginning the morning as many Bolognese do, in one of two bustling markets near Piazza Maggiore, the **Pescherie Vecchie** and the **Mercato delle Erbe.**

The oldest place of worship in Bologna is the **Basilica di Santo Stefano** (p 321, ❼), a remarkable assemblage of four sanctuaries that surround a cloister and together comprise the fifth-largest church in the world. The oldest, **San Vitale e Agricola,** dates to the 5th century and incorporates a Roman temple, while **San Sepolcro** is a replica of the church of the Holy Sepulcher in Jerusalem and houses the tomb of St. Petronius, the 5th-century bishop of Bologna.

At the **Museo Civico Archeologico** (p 322, ❾), artifacts left behind by Etruscan settlers

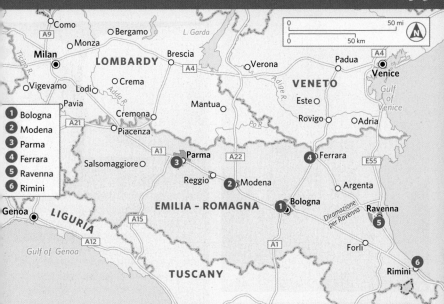

Bologna ❶
Modena ❷
Parma ❸
Ferrara ❹
Ravenna ❺
Rimini ❻

and mileposts from the Via Emilia also evoke the city's beginnings. Though a Roman wall runs through the courtyard of the **Museo Civico Medievale** (p 323, ⓫), the collections are medieval and include the sepulchers of early professors at the university. You can step into one of the old halls of the university in **Palazzo di Archiginnasio** (p 321), where the wooden benches of the **anatomical theater** surround a much-used marble slab.

From Via Saragozza, a portico of 666 arches leads uphill to the church of Madonna di San Luca, a perfect place to end the day while enjoying stunning views of the city and the surrounding Apennine mountains.

After a second night in Bologna, and a morning coffee in one of the cafes on Piazza Maggiore, make the short trip to Modena, just 40km (25 miles) northwest of Bologna and less than half an hour away by frequent train service.

❷ **Modena.** Via Emilia has run right through the center of this town since the Romans founded a colony here in 183 B.C. In recent years the elegant little city has given us opera stars Luciano Pavarotti and Mirelli Freni, Ferraris, and an elixir known as *aceto balsamico*. Here in Modena, balsamic vinegar is made only

> *Bologna's ancient university has one of the earliest known anatomical theaters, shown here.*

> *Modena's Romanesque cathedral campanile towers above a prosperous, largely baroque city center.*

The Big Cheese

In Emilia-Romagna, cheese is synonymous with Parmigiano-Reggiano, made by hand from the milk of cows raised on the flat lands outside Parma and aged for at least 12 months. Parmigiano is often grated over pasta, but that is only the beginning of its appearance on the region's tables. A meal might begin with fresh asparagus tips over which parmigiano has been grated along with melted butter and a chopped egg, include delicate little crepes stuffed with parmigiano, and end with a small wedge of an especially aged parmigiano, to be savored in all its refined simplicity. The cows that provide the milk that goes into parmigiano also provide the butter and cream that appear in the region's pasta sauces.

If you're a cheese lover, a gourmet tour of Emilia-Romagna should include a stop in Parma at the **Consorzio del Parmigiano Reggiano,** Via Gramsci 26 (☎ 0521-2927000). This factory (pictured above) offers tours that extol the wonders of the cheese for which the region is famous.

from the juice of local Trebbiano grapes, aged in a succession of barrels made from different kinds of wood for 12 years, and must pass muster with the city's hallowed consortium of tasters. A few drops, dribbled perhaps over a wedge of parmigiano, is all it takes to prove that the result is worth the effort.

A day and evening allows you time to enjoy the city at leisure. The 12th-century **Duomo** and 87m-tall (285-ft.) **campanile**—the latter known as the Ghirlandina, for the bronze on its weather vane—are some of the great masterpieces of the European Romanesque, but much of the city is baroque, built by the Este family when they came to town at the end of the 16th century. Their enormous **Palazzo Ducale** dominates the city center, the **Galleria Estense** is filled with

the works of Velázquez, Cosimo Tura, and other artists they commissioned, and their precious manuscripts are on display in the **Biblioteca Estense.** For more on Modena, see p 315.

As many as 35 trains a day run between Modena and Parma, located just 56km (24 miles) to the northwest.

❸ **Parma.** A morning arrival gives you a nice amount of time to explore another sophisticated city on the Via Emilia, following my recommendations for Parma on p 302 (❷). Begin your evening with a glass of *frizzante* in one of the cafes on busy Piazza Garibaldi, then enjoy a meal at one of the city's excellent restaurants (p 329).

Ferrara by Bike

Bicycle is the preferred mode of transport in Ferrara, where a spin around the top of the medieval walls, massive enough to be topped by trees and lawns, affords wonderful views of the city. Most hotels provide guests with the free use of bicycles, or you can rent one from the stand in front of the train station for about 8€ a day.

▶ *Bicycles outnumber cars on the streets of Ferrara—unusual for an Italian city.*

The easiest way to reach Ferrara from Parma is to backtrack through Bologna. The total distance is 135km (81 miles) and the trip can take well under 2 hours by the region's frequent train service.

④ **Ferrara.** An easy morning train trip from Parma brings you to another delightful city, the domain of the Este clan from 1200 to 1600. Their massive castle, **Castello Estense,** (p 332, ❶), a center of Renaissance culture as well as the setting for the dastardly deeds of Niccolò d'Este and other members of the family, still dominates the city center. The Estes' palaces line the city's handsome streets and squares, which residents of all ages navigate by bicycle. Several of these palaces deserve special attention, in part for the collections the city now houses in them. **Palazzo dei Diamanti,** Corso Ercole d'Este (☎ 532-244949; 5€, daily 10am–7pm), is named for the 9,000 pointed marble blocks that cover its facade, and the city's *pinacoteca* (picture gallery) occupies many of its salons. **Palazzo Ludovico il Moro** (p 334, ❹) is built around a lovely rose garden and contains the Etruscan and Greek finds of the Museo Archeologico, and the **Casa Romei** (p 334) is an airy villa filled with frescoes and statuary rescued from Ferrara's deconsecrated churches. **Palazzo Schifanoia** (p 334, ❸) is graced with one of the most delightful frescoes to come down from the Renaissance, a cycle of the months that portrays life at the Este Court.

Ravenna is 75km (45 miles) southeast of Ferrara, less than an hour away by train.

❺ **Ravenna.** A short trip across the Romagna plain the next morning brings you to Ravenna, the city of dazzling mosaics that you can explore following my suggestions on p 302, ❸ . You can also take a plunge in the sea at one the small beach towns nestled in pine groves along the Adriatic just east of the city, and on some evenings view the mosaics at night (p 337).

Rimini is just 30km (20 miles) southeast along the coast from Ravenna, reached in about 20 minutes by train.

❻ kids **Rimini.** Italy's most popular beach town is these days a long stretch of hotels fronting the Adriatic and a white-sand beach that is chockablock with bathing huts and umbrella-shaded lounges. Contrary to first impressions, the resort also has a remarkably rich history, evidenced by several well-preserved monuments. Two are Roman, from the days when Rimini was an important crossroads at the juncture of Via Emilia and Via Flaminia: the **Arch of Augustus** and the **Bridge of Tiberius.** One is from the Renaissance, the **Malatesta Temple,** built as a tomb for the city's ruling family. See p 309 for more on all of these Rimini sights.

Into the Riviera Romagnola

The ancient Roman territory of Romagna spreads across the coastal plains to the south and east of Bologna. Much of the land was malarial and untrodden until the 1950s, when the little beach town of Rimini began luring visitors to its beaches. Nearby Pesaro, in the adjoining Marches region, followed suit, and today these are two of Italy's most popular resorts. A visit to the coast affords the chance to dip your toes in the Adriatic, to observe Italians in their rituals of leisure, even to see great Roman monuments in Rimini. Then, it's time to head inland again, to one of the greatest of all Renaissance cities, Urbino.

> The sandy beaches of Rimini and Pesaro draw their biggest crowds in August, Italy's traditional vacation month.

START Rimini. Hourly train service connects Bologna and Rimini, barely an hour apart. Trip length: 2 days, with an overnight in any of the three major towns on the tour. Urbino is by far the most atmospheric.

1 **kids** **Rimini.** This haunt of urbanites on their August holidays, tourists from the north, and barefoot Lotharios is Italy's number-one beach resort, famous for its long stretches of sand. In August, when all of Italy goes on vacation, it can actually be difficult to see the sand, so crowded are the beaches with sun beds, bathing cabanas, and beachgoers who rarely go near the water but spend their time on dry land engaging in that most popular of Italian pastimes, socializing. As in many Italian cities, it is not difficult to come upon a long and

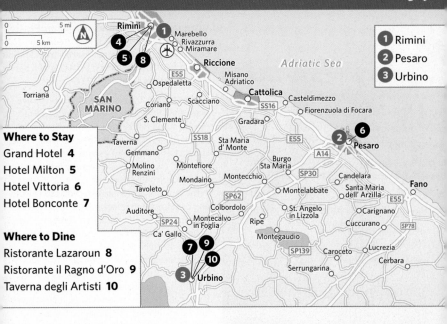

storied past in Rimini. Behind the beachfront promenades are two great monuments from the Romans who founded the city: the **Arch of Augustus,** built in 27 B.C. to commemorate the completion of the Via Flaminia, the road linking the coast to the Via Emilia; and the **Bridge of Tiberius,** completed under its namesake emperor in A.D. 21.

The Renaissance is evoked in the **Malatesta Temple,** commissioned by the powerful Malatesta family. This elegant church by the great architect Leon Battista Alberti (1404–72) reveals only the cultured side of the clan who ruled the city from the 13th through 16th centuries. Like the Estes in Ferrara, the Malatestas are better known for their misdeeds than for their accomplishments. Dante refers to them as "mastiffs" in his *Divine Comedy*, where he tells the story of Francesca da Rimini, murdered in 1285 by her husband, Gianciotto Malatesta, along with her lover, Gianciotto's brother Paolo. Sigismondo Malatesta, who commissioned the church, allegedly strangled his first three wives and built this church as a mausoleum for his mistress and final spouse. Malatesta Temple: Via IV Novembre 35. ☎ 0541-51130. Free admission. Mon–Fri 8am–12:30pm, 3:30–7pm, Sat–Sun 9am–1pm, 3:30–7pm.

> *Leon Battista Alberti's Franciscan church in Rimini is more commonly known as the Malatesta Temple, after its patron family.*

> *The stately city of Urbino, birthplace of Raphael and the setting for some of Piero della Francesca's best work.*

Pesaro is 20 minutes south of Rimini, easily reached by frequent train service.

2 kids **Pesaro.** Just down the coast from Rimini but across the border in the Marches region, this city was also founded by the Romans and was another stronghold of the Malatestas. A ducal palace and several other medieval houses line the cobblestone streets of the old town, but the most popular monument is **Casa Rossini,** 34 Via Rossini (4€, Apr–Oct Tues–Sun 10am–noon and 2–6pm), the birthplace of Gioachino Rossini, who was born here in 1792. The childhood home of the composer of such popular works as *The Barber of Seville* and *William Tell* is now a memento-filled museum, and Pesaro hosts the **Rossini Opera Festival** every August (for information, go to www.rossinioperafestival.it).

Pesaro, too, faces a long beach and is also a resort, though smaller, quieter, and more family-oriented than Rimini.

Urbino is 25km (15 miles) inland from Pesaro. Adriabus (☎ 722-376748; http://adriabus.eu) buses make the trip from Pesaro's train station almost hourly, and tickets, available at a bar next to the bus stop, are 2.75€.

3 kids **Urbino.** Travelers are often awestruck when they first come upon this mirage-like medieval and Renaissance city that straddles a pair of ridges in the foothills of the Apennines. Urbino has always lent itself to a streak of idealism, ever since wise, worldly 15th-century duke Federico da Montefeltro (1422–82) sat in the study of his remarkable **Palazzo Ducale** and contemplated *sprezzatura,* a Renaissance concept attributed to him that combines the notions of grace under pressure and making the difficult seem easy.

The duke and his son, Guidobaldo, oversaw one of Italy's most enlightened courts, so accomplished that Baldassare Castiglione set his *Book of the Courtier,* a series of dialogues revealing the qualities of the ideal courtier and the *Miss Manners* of its chivalrous day, in Urbino.

Federico and Guidobaldo were also great patrons of the arts, and many of the elegant, harmonious rooms of his palace are given over to the **Galleria Nazionale delle Marche.** A stunning collection that includes Paolo Uccello's *Profanation of the Host* and Piero della Francesca's *Flagellation* makes this one of Italy's most outstanding small art museums. Raphael was born in Urbino in 1483 and by the time of his early death at age 37 had achieved a grace in his paintings, including his Vatican frescoes, that makes him one of the great artistic triumvirate of the High Renaissance, along with Michelangelo and Leonardo da Vinci. His *Portrait of a Lady* hangs near some works by his lesser-known father, Giovanni Santi. In **Raphael's Birthplace** on Via Raffaello, a fresco of the Madonna that the artist did as a boy still covers one of the walls. Palazzo Ducale di Urbino/Galleria Nazionale delle Marche: ⏱ 2 hr. Piazza Duca Federico. ☎ 0722-322625. www.galleriaborghese.it/nuove/einfourbino.html. Admission 4€. Mon 8:30am–2pm, Tues–Sun 8:30am–7:15pm, 2–6:30pm. The museum accepts reservations online and by phone for a fee of .50€; during the summer season and on holidays it's a good idea to reserve. Raphael's Birthplace: ⏱ 30 min. Via Raffaello 57. Admission 2.60€. Mar–Jan daily 9am–1pm, 3–7pm.

Where to Stay & Dine

> The glamorous Grand Hotel, set on Rimini's beachfront.

★★★ **Grand Hotel** RIMINI

Federico Fellini, a Rimini native, pays homage to the most glamorous hotel in town in his autobiographical film *Amarcord*, and the elegant salons, gardens, beachfront, and sumptuous accommodations make any guest feel like a star. Parco Federico Fellini. ☎ 0541-56000. www.grandhotelrimini.com. 168 units. Doubles from 350€. AE, DC, MC, V.

★★★ **Hotel Bonconte** URBINO

An old villa next to the city walls is a pleasant retreat just steps from the city center, with large nicely furnished rooms overlooking a garden or the countryside. Via delle Mura 28. ☎ 0722-2463. viphotels.it. 30 units. Doubles 81€–132€. AE, DC, MC, V.

★★★ **Hotel Milton** RIMINI

This pink, Byzantine palace rises from a lush garden near the sea. The older parts were once the home of 19th-century playwright Ermete Novelli, and most of the spacious rooms have water views. Viale Cristoforo Colombo. ☎ 0541-54600. www.bestwesternpremier.com. 88 units. Doubles 150€–160€. AE, DC, MC, V.

★★ **Hotel Vittoria** PESARO

This fine old hotel on Pesaro's waterfront is a favorite beach retreat of Italian celebrities (it was much loved by Luciano Pavarotti) who relish a subdued old-world atmosphere and excellent service, large rooms, and sea views. Piazzale Libertà 2. ☎ 0721-34343. viphotels.it. 74 units. Doubles 116€–304€. AE, DC, MC, V.

★★ **Ristorante il Ragno d'Oro** URBINO

ITALIAN/PIZZA A popular gathering spot since the 1940s serves excellent pasta, pizza, and a popular local snack, *crescia sfogliata,* a crepe stuffed with ham, cheese, and other fillings. Viale Don Minzoni 2. ☎ 0722-327705. Entrees 10€–18€. MC, V. Lunch & dinner daily in summer; hours vary in winter.

★★ **Ristorante Lazaroun** RIMINI *ITALIAN*

A quiet retreat in the old quarter away from the beach scene is one of Rimini's classic favorites, serving homemade tagliatelle and other pastas, as well as steaks from local producers. Via del Platano 21. ☎ 0541-624417. Entrees 8€–18€. MC, V. Lunch & dinner daily.

★★★ **Taverna degli Artisti** URBINO *ITALIAN/PIZZA*

A favorite with locals and their many visitors serves heaping plates of pasta and such hearty fare as *coniglio con porchetta* (rabbit roasted with ham) beneath a lavishly frescoed ceiling. Via Bramante 52. ☎ 0722-2722. Entrees 8€–15€. MC, V. Lunch & dinner daily in summer; hours vary in winter.

Art & Architecture in Emilia-Romagna

The cities of Emilia-Romagna, many of them stretching out along the Romans' Via Emilia, are not far from one another, so in the Middle Ages and Renaissance, artists and artisans could easily travel wherever a commission called them. Often it was the region's ruling families who did the bidding, so much of the appearance of Parma can be credited to the Farneses, and the streets and palaces of Modena to the Estes (who left an even greater mark on Ferrara, p 332). The same proximity makes it easy to witness the artistic fervor that gripped the region from the early Middle Ages through the baroque period.

START Bologna. Trip length: 2 days. The total distance covered, assuming you return to Bologna for departure, is 302km (181 miles).

❶ Bologna. One of the great pleasures of Bologna is to walk across the **Piazza Maggiore,** a lively and beautiful square that has been the city center since the 12th century. One of the square's greatest assets is a relatively recent addition, the bronze **Fountain of Neptune** that Flemish sculptor Jean Boulogne (Giambologna) was commissioned to create in the 16th century. Whether or not it was the sculptor's intention, the presence of a virile water god surrounded by sensual nymphs imparts the square with much welcomed levity to lift the somber mood of its heavy medieval palaces and formidable **Basilica di San Petronio** (p 318, ❶).

While that church certainly warrants a stop, if only to see the marble entranceway carved by Jacopo della Quercia and depicting the Madonna and Child and scenes from the Bible, another nearby church, the **Basilica di San Domenico** (p 322, ❽), yields the city's greatest artistic achievement of the Middle Ages and Renaissance. The **Tomb of St. Dominic** (1170–1221), who founded his teaching order in Bologna, is the work of several artists. Nicola Pisano designed the shrine in 1264, soon after Dominic's death, and he oversaw the work of

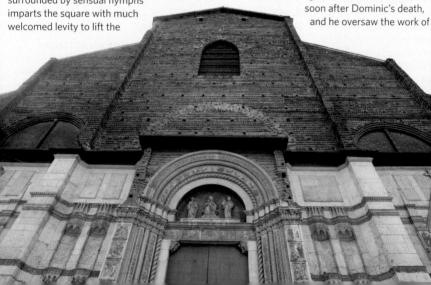

1	Bologna
2	Modena
3	Parma
4	Piacenza

Where to Stay
Canalgrande Hotel **5**

Where to Dine
Fini **6**
Hostaria Giusti **7**

Arnolfo di Cambio, who carved the wonderfully engaging scenes from the saint's life.

Two centuries later Niccolò da Bari was called in to create a canopy, an exquisitely delicate work that depicts the saints and evangelists, and of which the artist was so proud that he changed his name to Niccolò dell'Arca. When Niccolò died in 1492, Michelangelo, still young and untried, came to Bologna to carve translucent images of two of the city's other saints, St. Proculus and St. Petronius, as well as an angel that looks like it might float away into the lofty recesses of the church at any moment. Guido Reni, the master of the high baroque who was born in Bologna and spent most of career in the city, worked on the tomb, too. In 1615 he completed a ceiling fresco showing St. Dominic meeting his heavenly reward amid a swirl of saints.

A walk up Via Zamboni leads past the **Teatro Comunale,** a gift of Bologna's Bibienas. This family of noted theater designers traveled through Europe building theaters for the royal courts of the 16th and 17th centuries, and left

> *OPPOSITE PAGE Bologna's unfinished Basilica di San Petronio was intended to outsize St. Peter's in Rome. THIS PAGE Many artists, including a young Michelangelo, worked on the Tomb of St. Dominic.*

More Information

For detailed information on the sights, recommended hotels, and restaurants in Bologna, see p 318; for Parma, see p 326.

> *The patronage of Bologna's Bentivoglio family ensured that the Church of San Giacomo Maggiore was richly decorated.*

their legacy in their native city with this gem.

Across the street, in the chapel of the wealthy 15th-century Bentivoglio family in the **Church of San Giacomo Maggiore** (p 320, ❺), you encounter two masters of the Renaissance, Bologna's own Francesco Francia (1450–1517) and Lorenzo Costa (1460–1535). The latter came from Ferrara to paint *Triumph of Death* and *Triumph of Fame*, two frescoes that among their complex religious symbolism also provide illuminating scenes of life in a Renaissance household. Given the Bentivoglios' reputation for simony and thuggery, the mannerly lords and ladies are an extremely idealized portrayal.

Another Ferrarese painter, also much favored by the patronage of the Bentivoglios, was Francesco Cossa (1430–77). His *Madonna with Saints Petronius and John* is one of the highlights in Bologna's enormous **Pinacoteca Nazionale** (p 321, ❻). This collection was pulled together hurriedly in 1797, often from churches and convents, just after Napoleon's troops marched down the peninsula. The idea was to get the paintings into a safe place protected by city administrators before the French could cart them off.

A walk through the galleries is an introduction to Bolognese painting, as well as to the works of others who worked in the city. The masterpiece, in fact, is by an outsider. Raphael painted his *St. Cecilia in Ecstasy* on a visit to Bologna in 1515, when he accompanied Pope Leo X to meet Francis I of France.

From Bologna, you can be in the center of Modena, just 40km (25 miles) north, in less than half an hour by train.

❷ **Modena.** The Este family, who you'll encounter in Ferrara (p 332), arrived in Modena at the end of the 16th century. They quickly went to work remodeling the medieval town to a baroque ideal, creating avenues, squares, and a massive palace (the Palazzo Ducale) for themselves. They left the Romanesque **Duomo** and **campanile** intact, so the carved facade depicting scenes from the Old Testament still presents a good show for anyone enjoying a glass of wine in one of the cafes in **Piazza**

> *The Pinacoteca Nazionale in Bologna, largely dedicated to Bolognese painters, also houses Raphael's* St. Cecilia in Ecstasy.

> *The carved facade of Modena's Duomo, one of the few Romanesque structures still standing in the city.*

Grande. Most of these exquisite carvings are the work of Modena's own Wiligelmo, whose *Creation of Adam and Eve* (c. 1110) on the west facade has earned him fame as the first great star of Italian sculpture. He was succeeded in Modena by Anselmo da Campione, whose work graces the stark interior.

When the Estes were not building, they were acquiring, filling their palace with works by Tintoretto, Guardi, Velázquez and most of the other great European artists of the 16th and 17th centuries, and they hung these alongside paintings by Cosimo Tura and other Ferrarese artists they brought to Modena with them. This stunning collection is still in their palace, in the **Galleria Estense,** Piazza Sant'Agostino (☎ 059-4395711; 4€; Tues–Sun 9:30am–7:30pm). Downstairs, the **Biblioteca Estense** (free admission; Mon–Thurs 8:30am–7:15pm, Fri 8:30am–3:45pm, Sat 8:30am–1:45pm) preserves the more than 60,000 books and 15,000 rare manuscripts the family collected. The prizes have been relegated to one room, and among them is

the 1,200-page illuminated Bible of Borso d'Este, considered to one of the finest manuscripts of the Italian Renaissance.

Spending the Night

You can continue from Modena to Parma and spend the night there (for hotel and restaurant choices in Parma, see p 329), but you may well not want to rush away from atmospheric, elegant Modena too quickly. An overnight in Modena allows you the opportunity to see the carved facade of its cathedral under dramatic lighting and to enjoy another taste of the city's famous cuisine. That said, given the good train connections, you could also return to Bologna for the evening and make the trip to Parma from there the next morning.

> *The understated city of Piacenza was once a powerful member of the medieval Lombard League, an alliance of northern cities.*

As many as 35 trains a day run between Modena and Parma, which is just 56km (24 miles) to the north west.

3 Parma. Another family, the Farneses, built much of this gracious city, where you can spend the good part of a day. When the duchy came into the Farnese's hands in the middle of the 16th century, Parma had already benefited from the creative outpourings of Correggio, named for the small town nearby where he was born. Beginning in 1520, the painter was kept busy with commissions that included dome frescoes in the **Duomo** (p 327, **2**) and **Church of San Giovanni Evangelista** (p 327, **3**), as well as the dining salon of the **Camera di San Paolo** (p 328, **4**). These, of course, are mandatory stops of an art tour of Parma, as are the sculptural friezes of Benedetto Antelami in the **Battistero** (p 326, **1**) and Duomo .

Marie-Louise, the second wife of Napoleon, was awarded the duchy of Parma when her husband occupied Italy, and she made it her business to safeguard the city's art treasures. Paintings from throughout Parma and the region were brought to the safety of the palace the Farneses left empty when the last of them, Isabella, married King Ferdinand of Spain and moved her court to Madrid.

The palace is now home to the **Galleria Nazionale** (p 328, **6**). Marie-Louise was Austrian and an artist herself with a wide-ranging eye for genius, so it is not surprising that works by such northern Europeans as Hans Holbein, Brueghel, and Van Dyck hang alongside Correggio's *St. Jerome with the Madonna and the Child* and Parmigianino's *Marriage of St. Catherine.* Among the possessions the Farneses' left behind in the palace is the **Teatro Farnese,** a wooden theater built for them in 1618 by Giambattista Aleotti (1546–1636), a student of Palladio, and modeled on the master's Teatro Olimpico in Vicenza.

From Parma, you can be in Piacenza, just 55km (34 miles) north, in half an hour by trains that run at least every 30 minutes. You can easily fit a side trip up to Piacenza into your day in Parma.

4 Piacenza. This city at the end of the Via Emilia was founded by the Romans and thrived under them as an agricultural center on the River Po. Piacenza flourished throughout the Middle Ages as a member of the powerful Lombard League, the alliance of northern Italian cities that effectively countered the efforts of Frederick I and Frederick II and their Holy Roman Empire to gain control of Italy.

Today the rather forbidding city of heavy brick is still dominated by some of Italy's finest medieval masterpieces. The **Palazzo del Comune** is best known as *Il Gotico,* for its stunning Lombardian Gothic appearance. A marble arcade with five arches faces the **Piazza dei Cavalli** (Horses), named for the two dramatically baroque equestrian statues by Francesco Mochi of Alessandro and Ranuccio Farnese. With much sculpted flourish, these late-16th- and early-17th-century dukes of Piacenza ride across the stony expanse for eternity.

Their palace, just to the north on Piazza Cittadella, was never completed and lies behind massive walls of unadorned brick. Many of the salons house the Roman mosaics, Renaissance paintings, and other varied collections of the **Museo Civico,** Piazza Cittadella (☎ 053-49662; 4.80€; Tues–Thurs 8:45am–1pm, Fri–Sun 8:45am–1pm, 3–6pm), and the most celebrated object is the bronze "Liver of Piacenza." Crafted by Roman settlers in the 1st century B.C., the heavily inscribed organ was probably a prop used to teach the art of *haruspicy,* or divining entrails.

The **Duomo,** Piazza Duomo (☎ 053-335154; free admission; daily 7:30am–12:30pm, 4–7:30pm), completed in 1233, is considered to be one of Italy's great Romanesque masterworks. A striking marble facade, a long nave divided by 25 pillars, and a tall brick campanile contribute to the church's powerful presence.

Piacenza is also the somewhat unlikely home of one of Italy's finest small museums of modern art, the **Galleria d'Arte Moderna Ricci-Oddi,** Via San Siro 13 (☎ 0523-20742; 5€; May–Sept Tues–Sun 10am–noon, 3–6pm; Oct–Apr 10am–noon, 2–4pm). Local collector and nobleman Giuseppe Ricci-Oddi donated his collection to the city in 1924 and oversaw the construction of the handsome galleries around the cloisters of the former monastery of San Siro. Many of the painters, with the exception of Giorgio de Chirico, may not be familiar, but the works provide a wonderful glimpse into 19th- and 20th-century Italian art.

Where to Stay & Dine

> *The garden of the Canalgrande Hotel in Modena.*

★★ **Canalgrande Hotel** MODENA
This 17th-century villa retains its terra-cotta floors, frescoes, and beautifully planted gardens—and houses guests in atmospheric but up-to-date style. Corso Canalgrande 6. ☎ 051-217160. www.canalgrandehotel.it. 74 units. Doubles 176€. AE, DC, MC, V.

★★★ **Fini** MODENA *EMILIA-ROMAGNAN*
One of Italy's most noted restaurants (a favorite of the late Luciano Pavarotti, Modena's native son) produces its own salamis, hams, and other ingredients for the house specialties, accompanied by wine from Fini's own vineyards. Rua Frati Minori 24. 059-223314. **Entrees 15€–40€. AE, DC, MC, V. Lunch & dinner Wed–Sun; closed 3 weeks in Aug.**

Hostaria Giusti MODENA *EMILIA-ROMAGNAN*
A place in this four-table restaurant is one of the region's most highly prized commodities. The adjoining 400-year-old *salumeria* sells the choicest balsamic vinegars, parmigianos, prosciuttos, and homemade jams. 46 Vicolo Squallore. ☎ 059-222533. **Entrees 15€–30€. AE, MC, V. Lunch Tues–Sat; closed Aug.**

Bologna

Bologna is the seat of Europe's oldest university, and a youthful exuberance still pervades this handsome city of ocher-hued buildings and red-tiled roofs. You can easily follow Bologna's long history in visits to the many churches and museums, most of them an easy walk from the Piazza Maggiore.

> The eclectic facade of the Palazzo Comunale on the Piazza Maggiore betrays its origin as several palaces joined together.

START Piazza Maggiore. You can reach this square on foot from the train station in about 10 minutes, on a walk down Via dell'Indipendenza beneath a long swath of the city's famous arcades. Buses 11, 17, 25, 27, and 30 run from the station to the square.

① **Basilica di San Petronio.** Piazza Maggiore, the city's central square, is flanked by medieval palazzi and enlivened with a virile, 16th-century bronze statue of Neptune, rising from an ornate fountain inhabited by sirens. Pride of place belongs to San Petronio, the city's 12th-century bishop, whose namesake basilica (first begun in 1390) was intended to be larger than St. Peter's. Rome got wind of the scheme and cut off the funds for the Gothic structure, but not before the exterior was partially clad in red and white striped marble and Jacopo della Quercia had carved the marble doorway. Frescoes cover much of the massive interior, where Charles V was crowned Holy Roman Emperor in 1530. ⏱ 30 min. Piazza Maggiore. ☎ 051-225-442. Free admission. Daily 7:30am–1pm, 2–6:30pm. Bus 11, 17, 25, 27, 30.

1. Basilica di San Petronio
2. Palazzo Comunale
3. Bar Giuseppe
4. Due Torri
5. Church of San Giacomo Maggiore
6. Pinacoteca Nazionale
7. Basilica di Santo Stefano
8. Basilica di San Domenico
9. Museo Civico Archeologico
10. Caffè Pasticceria Zanarini
11. Museo Civico Medievale

Where to Stay

Albergo delle Drapperie **21**

Grand Hotel Baglioni **15**

Hotel dei Commercianti **20**

Hotel Orologio **14**

Hotel Roma **19**

Hotel Touring **22**

Where to Dine

Olindo Faccioli **16**

Ristorante al Montegrappa
   da Nello **13**

Trattoria Anna Maria **18**

Trattoria Fantoni **12**

Trattoria-Pizzeria Belle Arti **17**

2 Palazzo Comunale. *Madonna and Child*, a terra-cotta statue by Niccolò dell'Arca on the facade of this massive palazzo (comprising several different palaces from the 13th–16th c.), hints at the treasures found within. Tucked away at the top of grand stairways are elegant salons hung with the holdings of the **Collezione Comunali d'Arte,** a showcase for the artists who were commissioned during the Renaissance and baroque periods to decorate Bologna's churches and palaces. Tintoretto's *Old Man* and Donato Creti's *Deeds of Achilles* are among the many treasures. The adjoining **Museo di Giorgio Morandi** is filled with the works of the most famous 20th-century Bolognese artist, whose still lives and

landscapes reflect his simple wish "to reflect what is in nature, in the visual world." ⏱ 1 hr. Piazza Maggiore. ☎ 051-2031111. Free admission. Tues–Sun 10am–6pm. Bus 11, 17, 25, 27, 30.

Getting Around Bologna

In Bologna, the train station and sights are within easy walking distance of one another, so you'll only need to use the city's bus system sparingly; if you are carting luggage from the station to a hotel in the old center, hop on bus 25 or 30 toward Piazza Maggiore. City buses are operated by **ATC** (☎ 051-290290), and the fare is 1€.

> *The main doorway of the Basilica di San Petronio is adorned with sculptures by Jacopo della Quercia.*

Prisoner in a Palace

The medieval heaviness that permeates the Piazza Maggiore is made no lighter by the tale of Enzo (1218–72), king of Sardinia and the illegitimate son of German emperor Frederick II. Enzo was a student at the University of Bologna in the 13th century, when the ongoing wars for control of the Italian peninsula between the Ghibellines (supporters of the league of northern European empires known as the Holy Roman Empire), and the Guelphs (the papal faction) were in full swing. In Bologna the Guelphs won a decisive victory, and the young king, whose heritage put him securely in the Ghibelline camp, was imprisoned, in great comfort, in the palace that has come to be known as Palazzo di Rei Enzo. He languished there until his death 23 years later.

③ 🍨 **Bar Giuseppe.** A table here, beneath the arcades facing Piazza Maggiore, is the perfect place to watch the human comedy that transpires in one of Italy's most enchanting squares. The gelato is the best in town. Piazza Maggiore 1. ☎ 051-264444. $

④ kids **Due Torri.** More than 200 towers once rose above Bologna, built by noble families in the 12th century to show off their wealth and prestige. The two most famous of the very few that remain lean precariously but are the city's tallest landmarks. **Torre degli Garisenda** is the smaller of the two at 49m (162 ft.) and had its top lopped off in 1360 because its precarious lean was viewed as a threat to public safety. Torre degli Asinelli is 102m (334 ft.) and can be climbed; the reward for an ascent up its 500 steps is a stunning view of the city and the Apennines. ⏱ 45 min. (with climb). Piazza di Porta Ravegnana. Admission 3€. Daily 9am–6pm (to 5pm in winter). Bus: 13, 14, 19, 25, 27.

⑤ **Church of San Giacomo Maggiore.** The Bentivoglios, one of Bologna's most prominent and despised medieval and Renaissance families, commissioned a lavish chapel in this 13th-century Gothic church and hired Lorenzo Costa to paint a fresco cycle that depicts a day in the life of a noble court. An underground passageway once connected the chapel to the Bentivoglios' palace, which was burned by an angry mob in the 16th century. ⏱ 15 min. Piazza Rossini, ☎ 051-225970. Free admission. Daily 7am–12:30pm, 3:30–6:30pm Bus 11, 17.

>*Bologna's Due Torri lean almost as much as a more famous structure in Pisa.*

Heads of Their Class

Even in the 13th century Bologna was a bustling university town, with more than 10,000 students from across Europe flooding the arcaded streets. Dante, Petrarch, and Thomas Becket were among the medieval scholars who flocked to the city's famed university. Among visiting lecturers and students of the 16th and 17th centuries were the Dutch astronomer Nicolaus Copernicus and German engraver and painter Albrecht Dürer. Law and medicine were two of the university's earliest specialties, and one of the earliest **anatomical theaters** (detail, pictured above), in the baroque **Palazzo di Archiginnasio** on Piazza Galvani, can be visited (Mon–Sat 9am–1pm; free admission). The University of Bologna is now considered to be the oldest university in the Western world (opened around 1088), and is still one of the finest.

6 Pinacoteca Nazionale. Throughout the Renaissance, artists from all over Italy came to Bologna to decorate churches and palaces. By the 16th century, the city gave rise to a school of baroque painters who included the Carracci brothers and Guido Reni (1575–1642). The work of many of these Bolognese artists, as well as others who worked in the city, hang in the city's principal art gallery. Standouts include Reni's *St. Sebastian* and *Pietà*; Vitale da Bologna's (1330-61) rendition of St. George slaying the dragon; and a polyptych attributed to Giotto. ⏱ 2 hr. Via delle Belle Arti 56. ☎ 051-4211984. Admission 5€. Tues–Sun 9am–7pm. Bus 20, 28, 36, 37, 89, 93.

More on Bologna

For more about Bologna's collections, see "Art & Architecture in Emilia-Romagna" on p 312.

7 Basilica di Santo Stefano. The basilica is actually an assemblage of four churches, standing on the site of both a 4th-century Roman temple to Isis and a 5th-century early Christian church where Charlemagne once stopped to worship. San Petronio, Bologna's patron saint, lies in one of them, the 12th-century **Church of San Sepolcro**—a polygon modeled after the Church of the Holy Sepulcher in Jerusalem. The basin in the adjoining courtyard is said to be the one in which Pontius Pilate absolved himself after condemning Christ, but it is actually a Lombardian piece from the 8th century. A Romanesque cloisters dating to the 11th and 12th centuries is one of Bologna's most charming retreats. ⏱ 30 min. Via Santo Stefano 24. ☎ 051-223256. Free. Daily 9am–noon, 3:30–6:30pm. Bus 11, 13, 19, 25, 27, 29, 30.

> *Lorenzo Costa was summoned from Ferrara to paint a fresco cycle in San Giacomo Maggiore.*

⑧ Basilica di San Domenico. The founder of the priestly Dominican order devoted to study and teaching lies in a chapel that is the greatest treasure of this vast church. Arriving in Bologna in 1218, Dominic soon decided that the vibrant city filled with scholars was well suited to his dedication to intellectual pursuits. He moved his order of brothers into a simple church that was expanded after his death into this basilica that retains some of Bologna's finest Renaissance works. Best of all of them is St. Dominic's shrine, begun in 1264 and not completed until 1492, when a young Michelangelo added delicate carvings of saints and angels as a finishing touch. **Piazza San Domenico.** ⏱ 30 min. ☎ 051-6400411. Free admission. Daily 8am–1pm, 3:30–6:30pm. Bus 16, 30, 38, 39, 52

⑨ Museo Civico Archeologico. In the five centuries before the birth of Christ, Bologna was founded by the Etruscans, invaded by the Gauls, and settled by the Romans. This rich and long history is well preserved in what is considered to be one of Italy's most important collections of antiquities. From the Egyptians come mummies, sarcophagi, and most impressive, bas-reliefs from the tomb of Horemheb, the pharaoh (1319–1292 B.C.) who allegedly murdered the young Tutankhamun to assure his own ascendancy to the throne. Finds from Bologna's beginnings as the Etruscan Felsina include a bronze urn elaborately decorated with a depiction of a funeral procession and, most touchingly, small alabaster and marble sarcophagi with mismatched lids that bear haunting portraits of the interred. The Greeks and Romans are well represented with a parade of statuary; the prize here is a bust of Athena Lemnia from the school of the greatest Greek sculptor of them all, Phidias. ⏱ 1 hr. Via Archiginnasio 2. ☎ 051-2757211. Admission 5€. Tues–Sat 9am–6:30pm; Sun 10am–6:30pm. Bus A, B, 11, 13, 14.

---

⑩ 🍽 **Caffè Pasticceria Zanarini.** One of Bologna's oldest cafes has been serving brioche and other fine pastries since 1924, and for a splurge of decadence they can be accompanied by a cup of the house's famously thick hot chocolate. **Piazza Galvani 1.** ☎ 051-275-0041. $.

⑪ Museo Civico Medievale. A magnificent gold and copper statue of Pope Bonifacio VIII (1235–1303) and many of the artifacts in this museum of medieval history reflect a fine artistic tradition that was well underway before the Renaissance took hold. The pope's presence in these collections reflects the fact that Bologna became a papal holding in the ongoing battles between the Guelphs and Ghibellines, and the museum's many well-worn suits of armor indicate that the Middle Ages were by no means a time of peace for Bologna. Life at the university is wryly reflected in several sepulchers of professors who are depicted for eternity lecturing to dozing and mocking students. The building itself is noteworthy—though it was built as a palazzo in the 15th century, it is set atop a part of the city that is loaded with medieval ruins and artifacts. ⏲ 45 min. Via Manzoni 4. ☎ 051-203903. Free admission. Tues–Fri 9am–3pm, Sat–Sun 10am–6:30pm. Bus 11, 20, 27, 28.

Bologna by Night

The delightfully baroque **Teatro Comunale,** Largo Respighi (☎ 199-107070), is a 1763 landmark and stages Bologna's opera, orchestra, and ballet seasons. Once night falls, the city's many students take to such atmospheric old streets as Via del Pratello and Via de' Poeti, lined with simple *osterie*. At one of the oldest, the 16th-century **Poeti,** Via de' Poeti 1 (☎ 051-236166), jazz and folk music enhance the atmosphere. **Cantina Bentivoglio,** Via Mascarella 4B (☎ 051-265416), is the city's most popular jazz club, and **Cassaro,** Piazza Porta Saragozza 2 (☎ 051-6446902), is the best-known gay club, tucked into one of the old city gates and topped with an open-air dance floor. On evenings in July and August, the parks at the north end of the city are the setting for outdoor concerts and alfresco meals provided by food and wine vendors.

> *Vitale da Bologna's 14th-century frescoes rank among the highlights of the Pinacoteca Nazionale.*

Where to Stay

> *The Albergo delle Drapperie melds traditional elements with chic, contemporary decor.*

★★ **Albergo delle Drapperie** NEAR PIAZZA MAGGIORE Market stalls and food shops surround the entrance to this smart bed and breakfast. Frescoes, twisting hallways, beams and other charms of the old hotel remain, now enhanced with a chic blend of traditional and contemporary decor. Via delle Drapperie 5. ☎ 051-223955. www.albergodrapperie.com. 21 units. Double 75€–140€. AE, MC, V.

★★★ **Grand Hotel Baglioni** NEAR PIAZZA MAGGIORE Bologna's grandest hotel occupies an old palazzo and is suitably awash in grand staircases and frescoed salons. Guest accommodations are well oriented to creature comforts, with antique reproduction furnishings and lavish marble bathrooms. Via dell'Indipendenza 8. ☎ 051-225445. www.baglionihotels.com. 125 units. Double 340€–480€. AE, DC, MC, V.

★★ **Hotel dei Commercianti** NEAR PIAZZA MAGGIORE Few hotels can claim a longer lineage than this one, occupying 12th-century quarters that were the city's first seat of government. Original beams and vaulting, polished woodwork, richly tiled floors, and handsome antiques and fabrics provide suitably atmospheric surroundings. Via de' Pignattari 11. ☎ 051-7457511. http://commercianti.hotelsbologna.it. 34 units. Doubles from 200€. AE, DC, MC, V.

★★ **Hotel Orologio** NEAR PIAZZA MAGGIORE The clock tower of the Palazzo Comunale across a narrow street lends its name to this pleasant small hotel off Piazza Maggiore. A second-floor lounge and many of the tastefully decorated guest rooms overlook the square and its landmarks. Via IV Novembre 10. ☎ 051-745-7411. www.art-hotel-orologio.it. 29 units. Doubles from 140€. AE, DC, MC, V.

★★★ **Hotel Roma** NEAR PIAZZA MAGGIORE A wonderful location just steps off Piazza Maggiore is one of the many charms of this gracious old hotel, where amenities include a pleasant bar off the lobby and a fleet of bicycles at the ready for guests' use. Rooms and bathrooms are unusually commodious and nicely furnished; those on the top floor open to terraces. Via Massimo d'Azeglio 9. ☎ 051-226322. www.hotelroma.biz. 86 units. Doubles 150€. AE, DC, MC, V.

★★ **Hotel Touring** NEAR SAN DOMENICO A location at the edge of the *centro storico* (historic center) adds a relaxing air to this pleasant, newly renovated hotel. The best of the large, sleekly contemporary rooms are those with balconies, and all have access to an airy roof terrace. Via de' Mattulani 1. ☎ 051-584305. www.hoteltouring.it. 36 units. Doubles 120€–240€. AE, MC, V.

Where to Dine

> *Ristorante al Montegrappa da Nello serves Bologna's traditional rich cuisine.*

★ Olindo Faccioli PIAZZA MAGGIORE
Small *botteghe* serving wine by the glass and light meals are very popular in Bologna, but few are better than this small brick-walled room. Daily offerings are posted on the blackboard and almost always include homemade pastas topped with pesto and other fresh ingredients. Via Altabella 15B. ☎ 051-223171. Entrees around 5€. No credit cards. Dinner Mon–Sun. Closed Aug.

★★★ Ristorante al Montegrappa da Nello
NEAR PIAZZA MAGGIORE *BOLOGNESE*
This venerable Bolognese institution spreads across a cavernous cellarlike room and serves the city's traditional cuisine, using cream unabashedly in such presentations as *tortellina Montegrappa* (little homemade tortellini with cream and pork). Salads of locally grown greens are richly embellished with truffles and *funghi porcini.* Via Montegrappa 2. ☎ 051-236331. Entrees 8€–20€. AE, DC, MC, V. Lunch & dinner Tues–Sun. Closed Aug.

★ Trattoria Anna Maria NEAR THE UNIVERSITY
BOLOGNESE What might be the friendliest restaurant in Bologna is a favorite of students, business people, and patrons of the nearby Teatro Comunale. Old photos of stars of that theater line the walls, and the kitchen sends out delicious pasta dishes and such homey favorites as *trippa con fagioli* (tripe and beans). Via delle Belle Arti 17A. ☎ 051-266894. Entrees 7€–13€. AE, MC, V. Lunch & dinner Tues–Sun.

★ Trattoria Fantoni EDGE OF CENTRO STORICO
BOLOGNESE Via del Pratello is lined with simple restaurants popular with students and workers from the neighborhood, and these two simple dining rooms are the most popular of all. Specialties include *bistecca cavallo* (horsemeat steak), but grilled sausages, baked eggplant, and other basics are also available. Via del Pratello 11A. ☎ 051-236358. Entrees 5€–8€. No credit cards. Lunch & dinner Mon–Fri.

★ Trattoria-Pizzeria Belle Arti NEAR THE UNIVERSITY *PIZZERIA/MEDITERRANEAN*
Theatergoers flock here after performances to enjoy such homey pasta dishes as *tortellini alla panna* (homemade tortellini in cream sauce) and *tagliatelle con funghi porcini* (flat noodles with wild mushrooms). A huge selection of pizzas emerge from the wood-burning ovens. Via delle Belle Arti 14. ☎ 051-225581. Entrees 7€–12€. AE, MC, V. Lunch & dinner Thurs–Tues. Closed Aug and part of Jan.

Parma

Today's residents of Parma live in one of Italy's most prosperous cities, surrounded by churches, palaces, and artworks that generations of benefactors have bestowed upon them over the years. The Farneses made the city one of the great centers of the Renaissance, and when the last of them, Isabella, left to assume the throne of Spain in the early 18th century, the French Bourbons were awarded the duchy. Marie-Louise (1791–1847), widow of Napoleon and niece of Marie Antoinette, brought her love of art and music to Parma, and the city soon produced musicians worthy of the opera house she built, among them Giuseppe Verdi and Arturo Toscanini.

> *Christ at the apex of Correggio's* Vision of St. John the Evangelist, *in the Church of San Giovanni Evangelista.*

START Piazza del Duomo. Trains make the hour-long trip between Bologna and Parma almost every half-hour. From Parma's station, the stunning Piazza del Duomo is less than a 10-minute walk along Via Garibaldi.

1 kids **Battistero.** This remarkable octagon, clad in pink marble and rising in five graceful tiers from an airy piazza, is unquestionably the greatest work of the Italian Romanesque. Benedetto Antelami (1150–1230) was both architect and sculptor for the baptistery's

tower, commissioned in 1196. Around the portals are his carvings of a solemn procession of characters and allegorical friezes of plants and animals; inside is his 14-statue cycle depicting the 12 months of the year as well as winter and spring. Frescoes depicting the lives of the apostles by an unknown artist complement the statuary with a stunning display of visual storytelling. ⏱ 30 min. Piazza del Duomo, ☎ 0521-235866. Admission 5€. Daily 9am–12:30pm, 3–6:30pm. Bus 11.

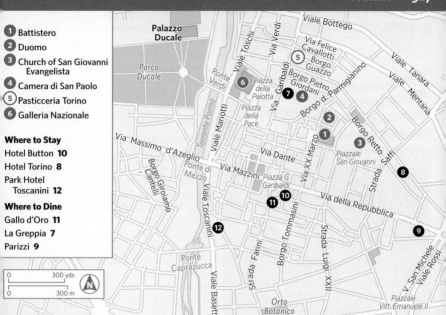

2 Duomo. Antelami also turned his attention to the Romanesque Duomo, whose pink facade is embellished with three tiers of loggias, a perfect counterpart to the tiered baptistery across the way. Even with the presence of Antelami's *Deposition* in the south transept, the interior of the 12th-century church would still be locked in medieval gloominess were it not for the arrival of Correggio (1494–1534) in Parma around 1516. He created in the cupola one of his great masterpieces, the *Assumption of the Virgin,* in which Mary and her entourage seem to be floating right through the top of the church into an Easter-egg-blue Heaven, captured in three-dimensional depth. ☉ 30 min. Piazza del Duomo. ☎ 0521-235886. Free admission. Daily, 9am–12:30pm, 3–7pm. Bus 11.

3 Church of San Giovanni Evangelista. Another Correggio dome painting depicts the *Vision of St. John the Evangelist,* in which Christ seems to be descending to earth amid a swirl of apostles. The artist captured the saint with pen in hand, writing down his vision, in a fresco next to the main altar. Parma's other famous artist, Parmigianino (1503–40), executed some his earliest frescoes in the side chapels, foretelling his mastery of Mannerism and—if you care to read a certain

> Leave yourself at least an hour to soak up the art and architecture of Piazza del Duomo; left to right: the Duomo, campanile, and baptistery.

High Notes for Music Lovers

The **Teatro di Regio** (pictured above), the opera house that Marie-Louise built in Parma, is considered to be one of the world's finest, and the city enjoys an opera season that rivals the one at Milan's La Scala (p 460, ❸). Many opera buffs make a pilgrimage to the little village of Roncole, where composer Giuseppe Verdi was born in 1813. The modest **Verdi childhood home** (☎ 0524-922339) is now a museum crammed with his scores and personal effects. The **Villa Verdi di Sant'Agata** (☎ 0523-830210), a retreat the composer built just outside nearby Busseto in 1849 to share with the soprano Giuseppina Strepponi, is filled with mementos and a reconstruction of the hotel room in Milan where the composer died after suffering a stroke in 1901.

You needn't leave Parma to visit a shrine to the city's other great musical hero, the **Arturo Toscanini childhood home** (☎ 0521-285499), on Via Rodolfo Tanzi. The conductor was born in the rooms that are now filled with his scores and recordings in 1867.

Busseto is about 32km (20 miles) northwest of Parma, via route S9, and served by eight buses a day to and from Parma. The Verdi childhood museum and villa are open Tuesday to Sunday 9am to noon and 3 to 6:30pm; admission to both is 6€. The Toscanini birthplace is open Tuesday to Saturday 9am to 1pm and 2 to 6pm, and Sunday 9am to 1pm; admission is 2€.

gravity into his work—a difficult life that would end in prosecution, imprisonment, and an early death. San Giovanni retains its lovely cloister, where shelves of the pharmacy are still lined with the medieval monks' medicine jars and mortars. ⏱ 30 min. Piazzale San Giovanni. ☎ 0521-235592. Free admission to church; admission to pharmacy 4€ Daily 9am–12:30pm, 3–7pm. Bus 11.

❹ **Camera di San Paolo.** You'll next encounter Correggio in the dining room of one of the convents in which worldly Parma women who for various reasons could not marry led comfortable and not particularly pious lives. When the abbess of San Paolo wanted to fresco her dining room in 1519, she had the means to hire the best and went to Correggio. The artist covered the room with enchanting mythological scenes that include a depiction of the abbess as Diana, goddess of the hunt. ⏱ 15 min. Via Melloni 3. Admission 2€ (includes admission to Teatro Farnese, below). Daily 9am–1:45pm. Bus 11.

⑤ 🍮 **Pasticceria Torino.** At this elegant old coffeehouse you can enjoy some of the city's finest pastries and sample Parma violets, a prissy local delicacy of violets coated in sugar. Strada Garibaldi 61. ☎ 0521-235689. Daily 7:30am–1pm and 3:30–8pm. $.

❻ **Galleria Nazionale.** Under the guidance of Marie-Louise, the Hapsburg wife of Napoleon who ruled the duchy of Parma in the early 19th century, paintings were brought from throughout the domain to fill the rooms of the Palazzo di Pilotta, built for the Farneses in 1583. Much of the palace was blown off the face of the earth during World War II bombings. The paintings had been hidden away, and the Pilotta has been reconstructed to show off works by two Parma masters, Correggio and Il Parmigianino, as well as Leonardo da Vinci and such northern European artists as Van Dyck. The **Teatro Farnese,** the Farneses' little jewel box of a theater, remains, too, and is still used for concerts. A few rooms of the palace are given over to Parma's small Museo Archeologico Nazionale, where the Roman finds from Emilia-Romagna include a bronze engraved tablet from the rule of Trajan. ⏱ 1 hr. Piazza della Pace. ☎ 0521-233309. Admission 6€ museums, 2€ theater (includes admission to Camera San Paolo). Tues–Sun 9am–2pm. Bus 11.

Where to Stay & Dine

> *The finest ingredients are the key to the memorable cooking at La Greppia.*

★★ **Gallo d'Oro** CENTRO STORICO *ITALIAN*
Movie posters, antique toys, and casks of the house Lambrusco line the walls of this trattoria, and the menu sticks to local favorites: platters of prosciutto and salamis, *tortellini di zucca* (stuffed with pumpkin), and chicken breast rolled with prosciutto and parmigiano. **Borgo della Salina 3.** ☎ 0521-208846. **Entrees 7€–15€.** AE, DC, MC, V. Lunch & dinner Mon–Sat.

★★ **Hotel Button** CENTRO STORICO
Simple but comfortable guest rooms and a central location make this family-run inn a longtime favorite. The best rooms are those that open to balconies overlooking a small *piazzetta* on the side of the hotel. **Strada San Vitale.** ☎ 0521-208039. 40 units. Doubles 113€. AE, DC, MC, V.

★★ **Hotel Torino** NEAR THE DUOMO
This modern and stylish hotel is in the middle of the city's central pedestrian zone, an easy walk from most of the major sights. A courtyard provides a perfect retreat. **Via A. Mazza 7.** ☎ 0521-281046. www.hotel-torino.it. 33 units. Doubles 135€. AE, DC, MC, V. Closed Aug 1–21.

★★ **La Greppia** NEAR THE DUOMO *ITALIAN*
Many of the exciting dishes here rely on the city's famous ham and cheese as well as the freshest vegetables. Such Parma favorites as asparagus topped with prosciutto and tortellini in a cream sauce garnished with shaved Parmigiano-Reggiano are in themselves a filling and memorable meal. **Strada Garibaldi 39A.** ☎ 0521-233686. **Entrees 15€–30€.** AE, DC, MC, V. Lunch & dinner Wed–Sun. Closed July.

★★★ **Parizzi** CENTRO STORICO *ITALIAN*
The covered skylit patio at this 50-year-old favorite is Parma's first choice for ham and charcuterie, as well as such local specialties as veal scaloppine filled with the ham and cheese that makes the city so famous in culinary circles. **Strada della Repubblica 71.** ☎ 0521-285952. **Entrees 12€–25€.** AE, DC, MC, V. Lunch & dinner Tues–Sun. Closed 3 weeks in Aug.

★★ **Park Hotel Toscanini** ON THE RIVERFRONT
Large, soothingly contemporary rooms at this modern business-oriented hotel are enlivened with reproductions by the city's masters; the best rooms have views of the River Parma and the riverside quays. **Viale Toscanini.** ☎ 0521-289141. www.hoteltoscanini.com. 48 units. Doubles 185€. AE, DC, MC, V.

MEET THE BORGIAS

The Sopranos of the Renaissance

BY STEPHEN BREWER

WITH THEIR THIRST FOR POWER, penchant for poisoning, and taste for adultery, incest, and corruption, it's little wonder the Borgias are history's favorite criminal clan of the Italian Renaissance (the illustration shows the accidental poisoning of Cesare Borgia and his father, Pope Alexander VI). While much of the family legacy is myth—it's unlikely Lucrezia got rid of tiresome lovers with poison she secreted in her ring—the truth is juicy enough. As popes and cardinals (with strings of mistresses and illegitimate offspring), and through marriage into Europe's ruling houses, the Borgias became enormously wealthy and powerful, infamously dispatching anyone who got in their way—the preferred method was arsenic, released from a secret compartment in a golden wine goblet known as the Borgia cup. The clan has appeared in works from Machiavelli's treatise *The Prince* (1513) to Donizetti's opera *Lucrezia Borgia* (1834); the Borgia name still evokes misdeeds more than 500 years after the family's heyday.

Rodrigo

(1431–1503)
Spanish-born Rodrigo bought his way into the papacy, allegedly with four mule loads of gold, to become Pope Alexander VI. He soon became enormously wealthy, in part by poisoning his enemies and confiscating their lands, but he was also a capable administrator and a great patron of the arts.

Cesare

(1475–1507)
The bad boy of the Renaissance is suspected of murdering his brother and brother-in-law and plenty of nonfamily members who stood in his way. His sadism came in handy in the battles he waged for his father, Pope Alexander VI. One of his more respectable associates was Leonardo da Vinci, whom Cesare hired as a military engineer.

Lucrezia

(1480–1519)
By the time the beautiful blonde was 20 she had been through

two husbands—one was murdered and the other fled for his life—and a string of lovers (see p 334). She then married Alfonso d'Este, prince of Ferrara, and as duchess she established one of Europe's most civilized courts and enjoyed the amorous attentions of the poet Pietro Bembo and other suitors.

Francisco

(1510–1572)
The great-grandson of Pope Alexander VI was an official in the court of Spanish King Charles V and

the father of eight children when he found religion at the age of 28. He became a priest and devoted the rest of his life to converting infidels and helping the sick. He made the family name respectable when he was canonized St. Francis Borgia in 1670.

Alfonso

(1378–1458)
He set in motion the family's rise to power when he became Pope Callistus III, appointing two of his Borgia nephews as cardinals and acquir-

ing massive landholdings throughout Italy.

Catherine of Braganza

(1638–1705)
A great-granddaughter of St. Francis Borgia, she married King Charles II of England. She was maligned for

her Roman Catholicism and overshadowed by Charles's many infidelities, but is credited with introducing England to one of its most beloved traditions—tea drinking.

Ferrara

One family, the Estes, accounts for much of what you will find in this enchanting city on the plains of Romagna. From 1200 to 1600, the Estes ruled and ranted from their imposing palace-cum-fortress that is still the centerpiece of the city. They endowed Ferrara with palaces, gardens, and intrigues, including those of their most famous duchess, Lucrezia Borgia (p 334). After the Estes left (when Rome refused to recognize the last of the line as a legitimate duke) the city fell victim to neglect and, during World War II, to bombing raids. Much of the Renaissance center remains and has been restored, and this city of rose-colored brick is one of the most beautiful in all of Italy.

> *The Este dynasty oversaw the building of most of Renaissance Ferrara, including their fortress, the Castello Estense.*

START Largo Castello, a walk of about 15 minutes down Via Cavour from the train station. Ferrara is just 45 minutes from Bologna on the trains that run every half-hour.

1 **Kids** **Castello Estense.** The moat-encircled domain of the Este family is forever associated with villainy. Most infamous of all is 15th-century duke Niccolò III d'Este (1383–1441), who used mirrors to catch his young wife, Parisina

Malatesta, *in flagrante delicto* with his son, Ugo, and had them both beheaded in the dungeons. Robert Browning recounted the event in his poem, "My Last Duchess." Not to be overlooked is the fact the Estes also made Ferrara a center of art and learning. Niccolò was a Greek scholar, and another duke, Ercole I (1431–1505), laid out this elegant Renaissance city of wide streets lined with palaces and gardens. The unjustly maligned Lucrezia Borgia (who mar-

ried Ercole's son, Alfonso) entertained poets and artists in the finest orangery in Europe. The Estes' enlightenment shines through in what remains of their grand salons—the **Sala dell'Aurora** and **Sala dei Giochi** (Game Room), both lavishly frescoed—their famous hanging gardens, and the marble chapel built for Renata di Francia, the daughter of French king Louis XII who married Ercole II d'Este in 1528. ⏱1 hr. Largo Castello. ☎ 0532-299233. Admission 8€. Tues–Sun 9:30am–5:30pm. Bus 1, 2, 4, 9.

2 **Duomo.** Ferrara's 12th-century cathedral, an elegant assemblage of Romanesque and Gothic styles, is all the more evocative of the city's role as a medieval trading center because of the market stalls that still operate under the merchants' loggia along one side. The dark and baroque interior was shed of many of its artworks during an 18th-century renovation. These are now in the Duomo museum, where the pride of the collection is a rendering of St. George slaying the dragon by Cosimo Tura, Ferrara's 15th-century master. In Jacopo della Quercia's *Madonna of the Pomegranate,* Mary seems to balance the fruit in one hand and the infant Jesus in the other. A relief showing the 12 months of the year was a calendar that once hung in the cathedral for the benefit of the mostly illiterate faithful. ⏱ 30 min. Piazza Cattedrale. ☎ 0532-207449. Free admission to Duomo;

> *The Palazzo dei Diamanti is named for the 9,000 diamond-shaped stones on its facade.*

museum 5€. Duomo: Mon–Sat 7:30am–noon, 3–6:30pm; Sun 7:30am–1pm, 4–7:30pm. Museum: Tues–Sun 9am–1pm, 3–6pm. Bus 2, 3.

③ Palazzo Schifanoia and Museo Civico d'Arte Antica. One of the most enlightened Estes was Borso (1413–71), one of the few legitimate heirs among the dozens of offspring sired by the ill-famed Niccolò. Borso's support of the arts came to fruition in this palace he built near the city walls and decorated with one of the most delightful fresco cycles of the Renaissance, a cycle of the months that is in essence a wall calendar, enriched with signs of the zodiac and figures from classical mythology, as well as scenes of life and leisure at the Este court. The work is a composite of the geniuses of the Ferrara school of painting who came to prominence in the 15th century: Francesco del Cossa (1430–77) painted the March, April, and May scenes; Ercole de' Roberti (1451–96) and other court painters executed the rest; and Cosimo Tura (1430–95), the official painter of the Este court, oversaw the project. Other works of this threesome hang in the *pinacoteca* (painting gallery) in the **Palazzo dei Diamanti** (p 307, ④), though few compare

with these frescoes or the paintings by Cosimo Tura in the Duomo Museum (②). A room in the Palazzo Schifanoia is devoted to ancient art, displaying coins, bronzes, and other artifacts unearthed on the plains around Ferrara. ⏱ 1 hr. Via Scandiana 23. ☎ 0532-64178. Admission 5€. Tues–Sun 9:30am–6pm. Bus 1, 9.

④ Palazzo Ludovico il Moro. Yet another Este palace was commissioned by Ludovico il Moro (1452–1508), duke of Milan, who married Beatrice d'Este. Both were patrons of the arts, and among Beatrice's protégés was Leonardo da Vinci. The two built this palace as a refuge from court life; it surrounds a rose garden, and the airy rooms are filled with their furnishings. A few house the collections of the Museo Archeologico, with Etruscan and Greek finds unearthed near Ferrara at Spina. Sadly, Beatrice died young and Ludovico spent his last years as a prisoner of the French. ⏱ 30 min. Via XX Settembre. ☎ 0532-64178. Admission 5€. Tues–Sun 9am–6pm. Bus 1, 9.

A Woman Misjudged?

Few historical characters have been as infamous as Lucrezia Borgia, the wife of Alfonso d'Este, prince of Ferrara. By the time the beautiful daughter of Pope Alexander VI arrived in Ferrara at the age of 20, she had been married twice—once to Giovanni Sforza, who fled for his life when the pope decided he no longer needed the connection with Giovanni's powerful Milanese family; then to Alfonso of Aragon, who was murdered by Lucrezia's brother Cesare. With such a bad marital record and a family famous for poisonings and intrigue, it is little wonder the Ferrarese gave Lucrezia the cold shoulder at first. But she soon earned a reputation for warmth, sophistication, and patronage of the arts. She died in 1519 at age 39, giving birth to her eighth child. Lucrezia liked to retreat from court life at **Casa Romei,** Via Savanarola 30 (☎ 0532-240341), a villa where paintings and sculptures from churches around Ferrara now fill the airy rooms that wrap around two peaceful courtyards. Admission to the villa is 2€; it's open Tuesday to Sunday 8:30am to 7:30pm (take bus 1 or 9).

Where to Stay & Dine

> *The peaceful garden of B&B Locanda Borgonuovo.*

★ **Al Brindisi** CENTRO *WINE BAR*
The self-proclaimed oldest wine bar in the
world, serving since 1435, dishes up a great
deal of timbered atmosphere with a fine selection from the cellars and excellent light meals
of savory pies or pastas. Via degli Adelardi 11.
☎ 0532-209142. Entrees 6€–10€. MC, V. Lunch &
dinner Tues–Sun. Closed mid-July to mid-Aug.

★★★ **B&B Locanda Borgonuovo** CENTRO
A stylish apartment in an old building around
the corner from Castello Estense provides Ferrara's most charming accommodations, stylishly furnished with Art Deco pieces and other
antiques. Signora Adele Orlandini serves breakfast in a pleasant salon or, weather permitting,
a rear garden, and is on hand with advice on
how to enjoy her native Ferrara and to lend
bicycles for a spin around the city walls. Via
Cairoli 29. ☎ 0532-211100. www.borgonuovo.com.
4 units. Double 85€–95€. AE, MC, V. Bus 1, 2, 3, 9.

★ **Hotel Europa** NEAR CASTELLO ESTENSE
The best rooms in this converted palazzo have
been fashioned from the frescoed grand salons
and are enormous, high-ceilinged, and overlook
the *castello*. All accommodations are gracious

and large. Corso della Giovecca 49. ☎ 0523-
205456. www.hoteleuropaferrara.com. 43 units.
Double 90€–115€. AE, DC, MC, V. Bus 1, 2, 3, 9.

★ **La Provvidenza** NEAR CITY WALLS *ITALIAN*
A rustic dining room and garden are the
perfect settings for hearty Ferrara fare, such as
tortellini stuffed with Gorgonzola and walnuts
and *misto di carne* (mixed grill). Corso Ercole
d'Este 92. ☎ 0532-205187. Entrees 10€–20€. AE,
DC, MC, V. Lunch & dinner Tues–Sun. Bus 3, 9.

★★ **La Romantica** CENTRO *ITALIAN*
A meal in this 17th-century stable block is an introduction to age-old Ferrara dishes that include
walnut flavored pasta sauces and flavorful handmade sausages, *salama da sugo*. Via Ripagrande
36. ☎ 0521-285952. Entrees 8€–15€. MC, V. Lunch
& dinner Thurs–Tues. Bus 2, 3, 6, 9, 11.

★★★ kids **Ripagrande Hotel** CENTRO
A vaulted lobby, cloisters, a garden, and multilevel guest quarters with sitting rooms and
loftlike bedrooms all make a stay at this converted Renaissance palazzo quite extraordinary.
Via Ripagrande 21. ☎ 0532-765250. www.
ferrarahotelripagrande.it. 40 units. Double 155€–
175€. AE, DC, MC, V. Bus 2, 3, 6, 9, 11.

Ravenna

Ravenna has long been a strategically important spot:

Caesar marshaled his forces on the site of Ravenna before crossing the Rubicon in 49 B.C. Shortly afterward, Emperor Augustus oversaw the construction of the Roman Empire's most important Adriatic port at nearby Classe, and Honorius moved the capital of the Western Roman Empire here in A.D. 402. Then, before the Lombards invaded in A.D. 750, Ravenna flourished as the Western seat of the Byzantine Empire. The most striking reminders of the city's one-time Byzantine prominence are the brilliant mosaics that shine within churches and other landmarks.

> Among the figures in the 6th-century mosaics of San Vitale is Emperor Justinian, placed at Christ's side.

START From Ravenna's train and bus stations, it is about a 10-minute walk down Via Farini to the Piazza del Popolo; the Basilica di San Vitale is a few blocks north of the square. Ravenna is 75km (45 miles) east of Bologna, only an hour away by hourly train service. Ferrara is the same distance to the north, also connected with hourly train service.

1 ★★★ **Basilica di San Vitale.** The octagonal church that the Emperor Justinian completed in A.D. 540 as a symbol of his earthly might is covered in mosaics that say much about the power structure of the 6th century. Christ oversees his earthly creatures from his perch on a celestial orb and next to him are Justinian, endowed with a halo and a crown to indicate his role as head of church and state. His two most important mortal adjuncts, Theodora, his empress, and a bald Maximian, bishop of Ravenna, look on. Theodora's presence in these imperial portraits is very much a rags-

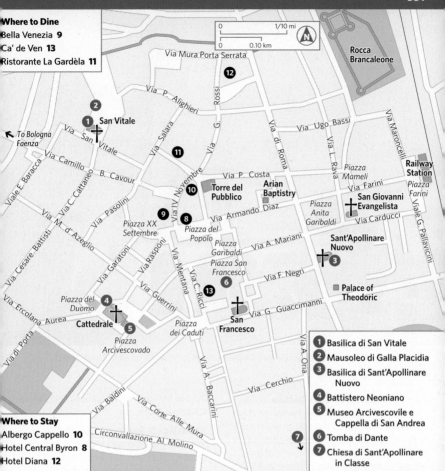

Where to Dine
Bella Venezia 9
Ca' de Ven 13
Ristorante La Gardèla 11

Where to Stay
Albergo Cappello 10
Hotel Central Byron 8
Hotel Diana 12

1 Basilica di San Vitale
2 Mausoleo di Galla Placidia
3 Basilica di Sant'Apollinare Nuovo
4 Battistero Neoniano
5 Museo Arcivescovile e Cappella di San Andrea
6 Tomba di Dante
7 Chiesa di Sant'Apollinare in Classe

o-riches story. Born into the circus, Theodora was an actress and courtesan when she caught the eye of Justinian. As his wife, she was a competent advisor who counseled her husband on all matters of church and state. n fact, it is said she was behind the orders to kill more than 30,000 rebels who gathered n Constantinople's hippodrome in 532 and threatened to overthrow her husband's rule. Given the sheer force of this remarkable woman's character, it is little wonder her countenance here is so severe. ⏱ 30 min. Via San Vitale. Admission via Visit Card (see box, right). ☎ 0544-219518. Apr–Sept daily 10am–7pm; Oct and Mar daily 10am–5:30pm; Nov–Feb daily 9:30am–4:30pm.

The Visit Card

In order to obtain admission to the Basilica di San Vitale, Mausoleo di Galla Placidia, and Basilica di Sant'Apollinare Nuovo, you must purchase a Visit Card (9.50€ March to mid-June, 7.50€ other times). You can purchase the card at any of the above sites, but you cannot pay for separate admissions to them. From July through September, these monuments are open until 10pm several nights a week and blessedly uncrowded; ask for a current schedule of nighttime openings at any of them.

> *Sant'Apollinare Nuovo was originally built for the followers of Arianism, an early Christian sect.*

② ★★★ **Mausoleo di Galla Placidia.** Galla Placidia was the sister of the Roman emperor Honorius, who moved the capital to Ravenna in A.D. 402. Her royal connections did not end there. Captured by Alaric, king of the Visigoths, during the sack of Rome in 410, she married his successor, Ataulf, and later the Emperor Constantius III. With Constantius she had a son, Valentinian III, for whom she acted as regent when he became emperor at age six. In effect, Galla Placidia ably ran the Western Empire for 20 years. The mosaics that commemorate this complex and deeply religious woman are all the more moving for their simplicity and touching symbolism. Doves drink from fountains, as the faithful are nourished by God, and Christ is clad in a brilliant purple robe and surrounded by lambs (the heavenly king surrounded by the faithful). Soft light, filtering through alabaster panels, bathes the depictions in an otherworldly glow. ⏰ 30 min. Via San Vitale, next to Basilica di San Vitale. ☎ 0544-541688. Admission via Visit Card (see p 337). Apr–Sept daily 10am–7pm;

Oct and Mar daily 10am–5:30pm; Nov–Feb daily 9:30am–4:30pm.

③ **Basilica di Sant'Apollinare Nuovo.** In this simple 6th-century church, built by the Emperor Theodoric for the followers of an early Christian sect known as Arianism, lustrous mosaics preserve a swirl of motion for the ages. On the left side the church, once reserved for women, 22 virgins approach Mary and the Christ child with gifts; on the right side, 26 martyrs proceed toward an enthroned Christ surrounded by angels. The mosaics near the door depict the 6th-century city, a postcard from the past: One on the right shows the major monuments, including Theodoric's palace, and one on the left shows the port city of Classe. ⏰ 30 min. Via di Roma. ☎ 0544-219518. Admission via Visit Card (see p 337). May–Sept daily 10am–7pm; Oct–Apr daily 10am–5pm.

④ **Battistero Neoniano.** The small, enchanting octagonal baptistery built in the early 6th century to serve an early Christian church that no longer stands was decorated with mosaics some 50 years later under the orders of Bishop Neon. A sea of intensely colored blue and gold mosaics on the dome depict the baptism of Christ by John the Baptist, while the 12 apostles, carrying crowns as a sign of celestial glory, look on. The prophets make an appearance on reliefs on the arches supporting the rotunda. The 18th-century cathedral next to the baptistery is unremarkable, except for the round, 10th-century campanile that rises to one side. ⏱ 30 min. Piazza del Duomo. ☎ 0544-215201. Admission 7.50€ (includes admission to the Museo Arcivescovile ⑤). Apr–Sept daily 9am–7pm; Mar and Oct daily 9am–5:30pm; Nov–Feb daily 9:30am–4:30pm.

⑤ **Museo Arcivescovile e Cappella di San Andrea.** Ravenna's 6th-century Archbishop's Palace, itself a monument, houses another 6th-century treasure, the ivory throne of Maximian, a bishop of Ravenna during the reign of Justinian. The emperor, it is believed, sent the bishop the throne as a gift from Constantinople, and a debate continues whether it was carved there or in Alexandria, or perhaps both. The most charming images among the rich depictions of Christ and saints are the panels of little animals nibbling the fruit of a vine. Adjoining the museum is a small chapel built in the shape of a cross and dedicated to St. Andrea, every inch of which is emblazoned with dazzling mosaics. The most remarkable scene depicts a haloed but warlike Christ, wearing partial armor and stepping on a serpent and the head of a lion. ⏱ 30 min. Piazza Arcivescovado. ☎ 0544-215201. Admission 7.50€ (includes admission to the Battistero Neoniano ④). Apr–Sept daily 9am–7pm; Mar and Oct, daily 9am–5:30pm; Nov–Feb daily 9:30am–4:30pm.

⑥ **Tomba di Dante.** The author of the *Divine Comedy* died in Ravenna of marsh fever in 1321. Falling out of favor with his native Florence when the White Guelphs, the political faction with which he allied himself, were usurped, the poet traveled restlessly throughout Italy and settled in Ravenna in 1318 as the guest of Prince Guido Novello da Polenta. Dante's native Florence has been clamoring for the remains of the greatest mind of the early Renaissance for centuries, but for the time being visitors to Ravenna can pay homage at his simple

> *The richly decorated apse of the Basilica di San Vitale.*

Another Artistic Tradition

The little city of **Faenza** has been famous as a crafts center since the 16th century, when artisans began applying new firing techniques to the production of majolica-style pottery. Faience ware soon became the rage throughout Europe. The Istituto d'Arte per la Ceramica is a major international center for ceramicists, and artisans sell their wares throughout the town. The **Museo Internazionale delle Ceramiche,** Via Campidori 2 (☎ 0546-21240), provides an overview of the craft and shows off works by Etruscans, Chinese masters, such artists as Matisse and Chagall, and local artists as well. Faenza is half an hour from Ravenna by trains that run about every hour throughout the day. The museum is open daily from 9:30am to 7pm, and admission is 8€.

> TOP Twenty-six arches support the massive nave of Sant'Apollinare in Classe. BOTTOM Sant'Apollinare's apse mosaics depict the eponymous saint, Ravenna's first bishop.

domed tomb and a small museum, where the Dante memorabilia includes a manuscript of the *Divine Comedy*. Ravenna makes use of

an inscription on the tomb to chastise the Florentines with the inscription, "Here in this corner lies Dante, exiled from his native land, born to Florence, an unloving mother." ⏱ 20 min. Via Dante Alighieri. ☎ 0544-30252. Free admission. Tomb daily 9am–noon, 2–5pm; museum Tues–Sun 9am–noon.

❼ Chiesa di Sant'Apollinare in Classe. The size of this austere church bespeaks its former dominance at the center of Classe. What is now a landlocked suburb surrounded by stands of pines was once the busy port for what was briefly the most important city in the Western world. The plain exterior belies the splendors that lie within. A double row of marble columns supports 26 arches, leading past side chapels lined with early Christian sarcophagi to the apse, ablaze with golden mosaics. The main image depicts Christ in Judgment and Sant'Apollinare, a bishop of Ravenna, but most engaging is a Transfiguration set against a field of brilliant green grass where colorful flowers bloom and charming animals roam. Around the church are the pinewoods where Lord Byron, who shared a palace in Ravenna with his mistress, Teresa Guiccioli, and her complacent husband, used to ride. ⏱ 30 min. Via Romea Sud, Classe, about 5km (3 miles) south of city center. ☎ 0544-473569. Admission 2€. Daily 9am–5:30pm. From the train station and Piazza Cadutti (near Dante's tomb), take bus 4 or 44 (1.10€).

Where to Stay & Dine

> *Locals and visitors alike savor tasty snacks and fine wine at the Ca' de Ven.*

★★★ **Albergo Cappello** CENTRO STORICO
A 14th-century palazzo retains its frescoes
and beamed ceilings while providing chic and
comfortable lodgings with contemporary flair.
Via IV Novembre 24. ☎ 0544-219813. www.
albergocappello.it. 7 units. Double 150€–200€.
AE, MC, V. Bus 1, 2, 3, 9.

★★ **Bella Venezia** CENTRO STORICO *ITALIAN/
SEAFOOD* You can eat like a Venetian, enjoying
a *fritto misto* or risotto with shrimp, or venture
into a wide range of handmade pastas topped
with fresh vegetables or rich sauces. All can be
washed down with a Trebbiano from one of the
local vineyards. Via IV Novembre 16. ☎ 0544-
212746. Entrees 10€–15€. AE, DC, MC, V. Lunch &
dinner Mon–Sat.

★ kids **Ca' de Ven** CENTRO STORICO *WINE
CELLAR* Almost as enticing as the city's
mosaics is this atmospheric 16th-century wine
cellar just off Piazza del Popolo. Patrons sit at
long communal tables to enjoy *piadina* (a local
flat bread), served with cheese and prosciutto
and washed down with white wine. The *torta al
marzipane,* a house specialty, is a memorable
dessert. Via C. Ricci, ☎ 0544-30163. Entrees
5€–15€. AE, MC, V. Lunch & dinner Tues–Sun.

★★ **Hotel Central Byron** CENTRO STORICO
Part of this hotel's name refers to its wonderful
location just off the Piazza del Popolo, the other
to Lord Byron, who spent his time in Ravenna
in an adjoining palazzo. Despite the latter
association, rooms are modern and serviceable
rather than atmospheric. Via IV Novembre 14.
☎ 0544-212225. www.hotelbyron.com. 54 units.
Double 80€–110€. AE, DC, MC, V.

★★ **Hotel Diana** JUST OUTSIDE CENTRO
Though the *centro storico* is a short walk away,
this stylish retreat resembles a country house
hotel, with a sunny breakfast room and large,
handsomely decorated guest quarters. Via G.
Rossi 47. ☎ 0544-39164. www.hoteldiana.ra.it. 33
units. Double 75€–90€. AE, MC, V.

★★ **Ristorante La Gardèla** CENTRO STORICO
ITALIAN/SEAFOOD Ravenna's covered market,
just down the street from this restaurant, supplies the freshest ingredients for the specialties served on its two floors of dining rooms.
Tagliatelle smothered in wild mushrooms and
other savory pasta dishes are often paired with
fresh seafood from the Adriatic. Via Ponte Marino 3. ☎ 0544-217147. Entrees 5€–15€. AE, DC,
MC, V. Lunch & dinner Fri–Wed.

Bologna & Emilia-Romagna Fast Facts

Accommodations Booking Services
Bigtours, Piazza Cavour 2, Bologna (☎ 051-272549), is a full-service travel agency that can reserve hotels throughout Emilia-Romagna.

American Express
The closest American Express office is in Milan, Via Brera 3 (☎ 02-7200-3693). It's open Monday to Friday 9am to 5:30pm and Saturday 9am to 5pm.

ATMs
You'll find cash machines (*bancomat*) in every city, town, and village throughout Emilia-Romagna. Italy generally uses 4-digit PINs; if you have a 6-digit number, check with your bank before you leave.

Dentists & Doctors
For emergency medical or dental attention, go to the *pronto soccorso* (emergency room) of the nearest hospital (ask at your hotel). Non-EU residents can consult national health service doctors for a relatively small fee; most good hotels will have a list of doctors and will help with arrangements.

Emergencies
For general emergencies, call ☎ **112** for the Carabinieri or ☎ **113** for the Polizia. Call ☎ **114** for an ambulance and ☎ **115** for the fire department. For a medical emergency that doesn't require an ambulance, see "Dentists & Doctors," above. To report lost or stolen items, see "Police,"p 343.

Getting There & Around
BY PLANE The region's air hub is Bologna's Aeroporto Guglielmo Marconi (☎ 051-647-9615; www.bologna-airport.it), 6km (3¾ miles) north of the town center. Alitalia, Meridiana, British Airways, Air France, and other European carriers serve the airport with connections to and from most major European airports. From within Italy you can fly to Bologna from Milan, Rome, and other Italian cities, but unless you are traveling to Bologna from Naples or Palermo, you'll probably find it just as quick and easy to take the train.

Aerobus runs about every 20 minutes between the airport and Bologna's rail station; cost is 5€. BY TRAIN Excellent rail connections throughout the region make trains the easiest way to get around Emilia-Romagna; most of the sights you'll want to see are in cities on major rail lines. Bologna is on a main line from Rome (about 3½ hr.), Florence (about 1 hr.), and Milan (about 1½ hr.). Parma and Ferrara are about 45 minutes from Bologna by train, and Ravenna is only about an hour away. BY BUS Excellent bus service links the major cities with outlying towns and villages; check with the tourist office for route information and schedules. The popular trip from Pesaro on the coast to Urbino is on **Adriabus** (☎ 722-376748; http://adriabus.eu). The trip takes about an hour and costs 2.75€. BY CAR Bologna, Modena, Parma, and Piacenza are on the busy **A1** autostrada corridor between Rome and Milan. Major roads also link the rest of the province: **A13** heads northeast from Bologna toward Ferrara, and from there to Venice, and **A14** heads southeast toward Ravenna and Rimini. A car is a great inconvenience in Bologna, where most of the central city is closed to vehicles without special permit; if you are staying in the city center and arriving by car, notify your hotel, which will arrange a special permit and provide details on the nearest available parking.

Internet Access
Wi-Fi has become a common amenity in most hotels throughout Emilia-Romagna. Many hotels that do not have Wi-Fi or other in-room Internet connections provide access through a public computer. Internet cafes are also fairly common, especially in student-oriented Bologna. Italian law requires that all patrons provide a passport or another form of identification and fees are usually around 5€ an hour. A handy Internet cafe in Bologna is **Retro,** Via de' Chiari 5b (off Piazza Santo Stefano), that's open Monday to Friday 9am to 11pm, and Saturday 1 to 7pm.

Pharmacies
Farmacie are recognizable by a neon green or

ed cross and are usually open 8am to 1:30pm and 3:30 to 8pm; in any city or town, at least one pharmacy is required to remain open 24 hours on a rotating basis, and the name and location of the designated pharmacy is posted at all others. In Bologna, you'll find a 24-hour pharmacy at Piazza Maggiore 6.

Police

To report a lost or stolen article, such as a wallet or passport, visit the local police *questura* or Carabinieri *caserma* in your location. See also "Emergencies," p 342.

Post Office

Post offices are generally open Monday to Friday 8:15am to 6:30pm and Saturday 8:15am to 12:20pm. The main post office in Bologna is on Piazza Minghetti (☎ 051-223598). Note that *francobolli* (stamps) can be purchased at most *tabacchi* (tobacco stores).

Safety

The cities in the region are quite safe, though pickpockets operate around train stations, especially the one in Bologna. Women should feel comfortable traveling alone just about anywhere in the region, especially among Bologna's large female student population. Rimini has earned a bit of a reputation for gigolos who work their charms on single women.

Visitor Information

An excellent online source for information about events and essential services in Bologna and the surrounding region is **Bologna Inside** (www. iwfbologna.com/bolognainside). **Centro Servizi per I Turisti (CST)** provides accommodations-booking services for Bologna and the rest of Emilia-Romagna online at www.cst.bo.it. The main tourist information office in Bologna is at Piazza Maggiore 1. It's open daily 9:30am to 7:30pm, with a branch in the train station that's open Monday to Saturday from 9am to 7pm, Sunday 9am to 3pm; call ☎ 051-239660, or head online to www.ezilon.com for both.

In **Ferrara,** the IAT tourist information office is in Castello Estense (☎ 0532-209370; http://suv.comune.fe.it); it's open Monday to Saturday 9am to 1pm and 2 to 5:30pm, Sunday 9:30am to 1pm and 2 to 5:30pm. The tourism office in **Parma,** Via Melloni 1A (☎ 0521-218889; http://turismo.comune.parma.it), is open Monday to Saturday 9am to 7pm, Sunday 9am to 1pm. The IAT office in **Ravenna,** Via Salara 8 (☎ 0544-35404; www.turismo.ra.it), is open Monday to Saturday 8:30am to 6pm, Sunday 10am to 6pm.

The tourism office in **Rimini,** Piazzale Cesare Battisti 1 (☎ 0541-51331; www.turismo.provincia.rimini.it), is open May to September, Monday to Saturday 8:15am to 7:15pm, October to April, Monday to Saturday 8:30am to 6:30pm. In **Urbino** the tourism office, Piazza Duca Federico (☎ 0722-2613; www.turismo.pesarourbino.it), is open Monday to Saturday 9am to 1pm and 3 to 7pm.

8
Venice

10 Favorite Moments

Venice, city of visual delights, fires up the imagination.
The colors, the many exotic domes and mosaics, the omnipresence of water, the rich history that's almost palpable in the streets and squares—it's best simply to let yourself be overwhelmed by it all. If you have to choose, though, you can't miss with the activities below.

> PREVIOUS PAGE *There's no shortage of takers for a gondola ride, but Venetians and canny visitors take the vaporetto.* THIS PAGE *Napoleon once called Piazza San Marco the "drawing room of Europe."*

1 Cruising on the Grand Canal. Even though the craft is a humble *vaporetto* (one of the city's boat buses) and the trip is an everyday routine for many Venetians, the experience never fails to be exhilarating. No matter how many times I've taken to the canal here, I'm still in awe of the dreamy water world that is Venice. See p 352.

2 Savoring the Piazza San Marco. This civilized square is, as Napoleon called it, the "drawing room" of Europe. The Piazza, as it's simply known, is where Venetians and their visitors converge to sip a cappuccino or cocktail on the outdoor terraces of some of Europe's grandest cafes. See p 350, **5**.

3 Being dazzled by the mosaics in the Basilica di San Marco. Step into this cathedral and let the shimmering brilliance of thousands of mosaics sweep you away. Then take a close look at the glass tiles that cover the floors, walls, and domes. Saints, sinners, angels, and mere mortals have been touchingly and painstakingly depicted here. See p 368, **3**.

4 Sipping a cappuccino in Campo Santi Giovanni e Paolo. Grab an outdoor table at **Rosa Salva** (p 376, **6**), a venerable cafe, and soak in the scene. Verrocchio's equestrian statue of Bartolomeo Colleoni stands guard over the neighborhood, and the formidable facade

> *The meandering Grand Canal slices Venice into two unequal segments.*

of the Church of Santi Giovanni e Paolo hints at the treasures that await you. See p 358, ❶.

❺ **Strolling through the Rialto markets.** Exotic sea creatures from the Adriatic, artichokes from the island of Sant'Erasmo in the lagoon, and freshly picked pears from the Veneto seem especially appetizing with the Grand Canal flowing past. The sheer bustle of this place, the commercial heart of Venice for more than 1,000 years, brings to mind old Shylock's oft-quoted question in *The Merchant of Venice:* "What news on the Rialto?" See p 361, ❺.

❻ **Standing in front of your favorite painting in the Accademia (or in any other museum or *scuola*, for that matter).** You'll soon find the canvas that captivates you. Some worthy candidates are Giorgione's mysterious *Tempest* or Carpaccio's rich *Story of St. Ursula* and *Miracle of the Relic of the True Cross.* If you're anything like me, you'll find yourself mesmerized by more than one. See p 370, ❾.

❼ **Looking over the Grand Canal and Bacino di San Marco from the Dogana da Mar, the Customs house.** On this point of land where ships once moored to be inspected, with the sea lanes stretching in front of you, it's easy to imagine Venice as a seafaring power and the crossroads between East and West. Magnificent relics of the trading wealth that once

poured into the city—in the form of palazzi (palaces) lining the banks—complete the view. See p 354, ❷.

❽ **Crossing the lagoon to Torcello.** Part of the charm of Torcello is the ghostlike presence of the 20,000 souls who once inhabited this all-but-deserted little island; they left behind the glorious, mosaic-paved Basilica di Santa Maria Assunta, one of the few remaining signs of civilization. Past grandeur aside, Torcello is also a perfectly nice place to escape from the bustle of Venice for an afternoon. See p 384, ❹.

❾ **Taking a *passeggiata* on the Zattere.** Many Venetians couldn't imagine ending a day without an "evening stroll" on this broad promenade along the Giudecca Canal, and you should join them. Ocher-colored houses capture the last rays of the sun, a tangy sea breeze stirs the air, and the church of Il Redentore across the canal provides a stage-set backdrop. See p 381, ⓯.

❿ **Standing on the Ponte di Rialto at night.** Who cares if the gondolas slipping beneath your feet are laden with sightseers and the strains of "'O Sole Mio" are taped? Fall under the spell of the shimmering reflections of the palazzi and imagine a time when the likes of Lord Byron and Casanova glided up the canal in the dark of a Venetian night. See p 358, ❸.

10 Favorite Moments

S. Maria d. Misericordia

Cappella d. Volto Santo

S. Marziale

Pal. Diedo
La Maddalena

Scuola Vecchia
d. Misericordia

Pal. Labia

S. Marcuola

Pal. Zeno

S. Geremia

Pal.
Flangini

Pal. Vendramin
Calergi

S. Fosca

Pal.
Giovanelli

Riva da
Biásio

Pal. Calbo-
Crotta

Pal.
Boldù

S. Felice

Gli Scalzi

Fónd. d.
Turchi

Ca'
Tron

S. Stae

S. Zan
Degola

Ca'
d'Oro

Strada
Nuova

S. Simeòn
Grande

S. Stae

Ca' Pesaro

Ca'
d'Oro

S. Giacomo
dell'Orio

Palazzo
Mocenígo

S. Maria
Máter
Domini

Pal.
Mangilli

Palazzo
Brandolin

S. Simeòn
Piccolo

Palazzo
Gradenigo

Pal. Zane

Pescaria

Ca' da
Mosto

Palazzo
Emo-Diedo

SANTA
CROCE

Pal.
Grioni

S. Cassiano

Fábbriche
Nuove

Scuola Grande
di S. Giovanni

Pal. Muti
Baglioni

Istit. Univ. di
Architettura

S. Giovanni
Evangelista

Pal. Zane
Collalto

Pal. Albrizzi

SAN POLO

Pal. Muti
Cappello

Palazzo
Dieci Savi

5

Ponte
di Rialto

10

Ex Convento
dei Frari

Palazzo
Zen

Campo
S. Polo

S. Aponál

S. Silvestro

S. Bartolomeo

Palazzo
Marcello

S. Polo

Palazzo
Dolfin-
Manin

Campo
dei Frari

S. Silvestro

Rialto

S. Rocco

S. Maria G.
dei Frari

Pal.
Centani

Palazzo
Grimani

Canal Grande

Pal. Dándolo

Palazzo
Dolfin-
Manin

Scuola Grande
di San Rocco

S. Pantalòn

Ca' Farsetti

Pal.
Loredan

Calle dei Fábri

S. Tomà

S. Ángelo

Pal.
Volpi

Cinema
Rossini

Pal. Cornèr
d. Frescada

Pal.
Balbi

S. Tomà

Palazzo
Mocenígo

Palazzo
Corner
Spinelli

Palazzo
Fortuny

Pal. Contarini
del Bovolo

Campo
S. Margherita

Ca' Foscari

Campo
S. Ángelo

S. Gallo

Ca' Rezzonico

S. Samuele

S. Stefano

Ateneo Véneto

Museo
Correr

Calle lunga S. Bárnaba

S. Bárnaba

Ca' del Duca

Teatro
La Fenice

S. Fantin

Ex Convento
delle Eremite

Palazzo
Brandolin

Ca' Rezzonico

Pal. Falièr

S. Maurízio

Palazzo
Morosini

S. Maria
d. Gíglio

S. Moisè

Ospedale
G. B. Giustiniàn

Accademia

Palazzo
Pisani

Palazzo
Corner della
Ca' Grande

Pal.
Gritti

Pal. Ferro
Fini

Palazzo
Tiépolo

Pal.
Giustiniàn

DORSODURO

Ponte
dell'Accademia

1

S. Maria
d. Gíglio

Pal.
Clary

S. Trovaso

6

Gallerie
dell'Accademia

Pal. Venièr
dei Leoni
(Guggenheim)

Pal.
Genovese

Salute

Dogana
da Mar

7

Zattere

S. Agnese

S. Maria
d. Salute

9

Gesuati

Ex Ospízio

Spírito
Santo

Fondam. Zattere ai Saloni

Canale della Giudecca

0   1/8 mile
0   200 meters

Fondamenta Nuove

Ex Convento
e Chiesa di
S. Caterina

Pal. Donà
Gesuiti

Fond. Nove

Ex Convento

Pal. Seriman

CANNAREGIO

Canale delle Fondamente Nove

Ss. Apóstoli

Pal. Widman

S. Canciano

Ospedale Civile

Ospedale

S. Maria dei Miracoli

Pal. Soranzo-Van Axel

Ss. Giovanni e Paolo (S. Zanipolo)

S. Maria d. Pianto

Teatro Málibran

Pal. Pisani

Fóndaco d. Tedeschi

Convento dei Minori Osservanti

Celestia

Palazzo Ruzzini

Palazzo Dona

Pal. Vitturi

Pal. Cappello

Pal. Gritti

S. Francesca della Vigna

Palazzo Gussoni

S. Maria Formosa

Pal. Contarini

Pal. Tasca Papafáva

S. Lorenzo

S. Salvador

Pal. Querini Stampalia

Questura

San Giovanni d. Cavalieri di Malta

Pal. Magno

S. Zulian

Palazzo Soranzo

S. Giovanni Novo

San Giógio dei Greci

SAN MARCO

Palazzo Patriarcale

S. Zaccaria

Arsenal

Basilica di San Marco

Pal. d. Prigioni

Palazzo Dándolo

La Pietá

S. Giovanni in Bragora

S. Martino

Piazza San Marco

Palazzo Ducale

Riva

degli

Schiavoni

S. Zaccaria

Casa Navagero

Giardini ex Reali

Ponte di Sospiri (Bridge of Sighs)

Arsenale

Museo Storico Navale

S. Marco

Bacino di San Marco

Canale di San Marco

S. Giógio

S. Giorgio Maggiore

Ex Magazzini e Dogana di S. Giórgio

Fondazione Cini

1 Grand Canal
2 Piazza San Marco
3 Basilica di San Marco
4 Campo Santi Giovanni e Paolo
5 Rialto markets
6 Gallerie dell'Accademia
7 Dogana da Mar
8 Torcello
9 The Zattere
10 Ponte di Rialto

The Best of Venice in 1 Day

The French novelist Marcel Proust said of his first trip to Venice, "My dream became my address." You may feel the same way as you begin to explore the city. Start in the San Marco section, not far from the Piazza San Marco, and take in the uniquely Venetian palaces and churches. Top off your tour with a cruise along one of the world's most storied waterways, the Grand Canal.

> *The vaporetto is the most efficient way to negotiate the sights of Venice, including the Palazzo Grassi, shown here.*

START Vaporetto to Santa Maria del Giglio.

① ★★ **La Fenice.** The aptly named opera house (*fenice* means "phoenix") has burned several times, most recently in 1996, and risen from the ashes looking just as it has for centuries. Several Verdi operas, including *Rigoletto* and *La Traviata,* premiered in the sumptuous, newly restored house, and Maria Callas is among the stars who have graced the stage. ⊕ 15 min. See p 411.

② ★ **San Moisè.** In a city of beautiful churches, this baroque extravagance stands out as one of the ugliest. ⊕ 15 min. Campo San Moisè. ☎ 041-5285840. Daily 9:30am–12:30pm. Vaporetto: San Marco/Vallaresso.

③ ★★ **Bacino Orseolo.** One of the city's 11 gondola stands is a good place to get a close look at these uniquely Venetian craft—or to

board one. ⊕ 15 min. Fondamenta Orseolo. Vaporetto: San Marco/Vallaresso.

④ 🍴 **Caffè Florian.** You'll pay dearly for your cappuccino on the terrace here, but you'll never sip coffee in more atmospheric surroundings. Piazza San Marco. ☎ 041-5205641. $$ See p 409.

⑤ ★★★ kids **Piazza San Marco.** This square, the heart of the city for more than 1,000 years, combines the very old (the Basilica) with the relatively new (the 16th- and 17th-c. Procuratie Vecchie and Procuratie Nuove buildings on the north and south sides of the square), yet still manages to be harmonious.

SITE GUIDE PAGE 352

1. La Fenice
2. San Moisè
3. Bacino Orseolo
4. Caffè Florian
5. Piazza San Marco
6. Santo Stefano
7. Palazzo Grassi
8. Palazzo Mocenigo
9. Palazzo Fortuny
10. Scala Contarini del Bovolo
11. Grand Canal

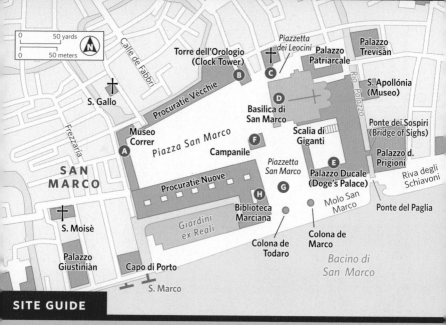

Map labels:
- 0 50 yards / 0 50 meters
- Calle de Fabbri
- Torre dell'Orologio (Clock Tower) **B**
- Piazzetta dei Leocini
- Palazzo Patriarcale **C**
- Palazzo Trevisàn
- S. Apollónia (Museo)
- S. Gallo
- Procuratie Vecchie
- Rio Palazzo
- Frezzeria
- Museo Correr **A**
- Piazza San Marco
- Basilica di San Marco **D**
- Scalia di Giganti
- Ponte dei Sospiri (Bridge of Sighs)
- Palazzo d. Prigioni
- SAN MARCO
- Campanile **F**
- Piazzetta San Marco
- Palazzo Ducale (Doge's Palace) **E**
- Riva degli Schiavoni
- Procuratie Nuove
- **H** **G**
- Biblioteca Marciana
- Molo San Marco
- Ponte del Paglia
- S. Moisè
- Giardini ex Reali
- Colona de Todaro
- Colona de Marco
- Bacino di San Marco
- Palazzo Giustiniàn
- Capo di Porto
- S. Marco

SITE GUIDE

➎ Piazza San Marco

The Piazza San Marco contains many of Venice's major attractions: In the **A** **Museo Correr,** the Museum of the City and Civilization of Venice, maps, coins, costumes, and, best of all, paintings by Jacopo Bellini (Room 36) and Vittore Carpaccio (Room 38) recall the days of the republic. In Carpaccio's *Two Venetian Ladies,* the bored subjects wait for their husbands to return from hunting. Among the other curiosities is a pair of sandals with 2-foot-tall heels upon which women of fashion once tottered. Across the square, bronze Moors strike the bells of the **B** **Torre dell'Orologio** to mark the time. During the feasts of the Ascension and Epiphany, statues of the Magi appear out of the clock on the hour, accompanied by a procession of angels. Below, in the **C** **Piazzetta dei Leoncini,** marble lions stand guard over what was once a marketplace. Next to this plaza is the **D** **Basilica di San Marco** (p 368, ➌), which inspired 19th-century man of letters John Ruskin to exhale into his journals, "The crests of the arches break into a marble foam, and toss themselves into the blue sky in flashes and wreaths of sculpted spray"; less poetical observers will be moved by its ornate Byzantine architecture and the bronze horses (pictured)

overlooking the scene. The adjacent **E** **Palazzo Ducale,** the palace where the doges lived and ruled, is majestic but has a touch of whimsy as well. The city's tallest structure, the **F** **Campanile** (bell tower) of the Basilica, in the center of the piazza, affords stunning views. Two columns, one topped by a winged lion and the other by St. Theodore, frame **G** **Piazzetta San Marco** (p 362, ➋), the seaside extension of Piazza San Marco. Finally, don't miss one of Venice's great Renaissance monuments, the **H** ★ **Biblioteca Marciana,** completed in the 16th century to house a precious hoard of Greek and Latin manuscripts. ⊕ 4–5 hr. San Marco. Vaporetto: San Marco.

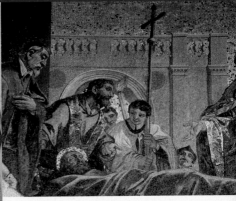

> *The mosaics of San Marco were inlaid over several centuries.*

> *The Scala Contarini del Bovolo mimics the shape of a snail shell, or bovolo.*

⑥ ★ **Santo Stefano.** Beyond this church's 15th-century sculpted portal by Bartolomeo Bon is a wooden ceiling whose shape resembles the inverted hull of a ship, as well as two works by Tintoretto in the sacristy. ⏱ 30 min. Campo Santo Stefano. ☎ 041-5225061. Sacristy 3€. Church daily 9am–7pm; sacristy Mon–Sat 10am–5pm. Vaporetto: San Samuele.

⑦ ★★ **Palazzo Grassi.** One of the last of the great palaces to be built in Venice dates from 1749 and was stunningly converted in 2006 to house the contemporary art collections of French magnate François Pinault. ⏱ 45 min. San Marco 3231, San Samuele. ☎ 041-5231680. www.palazzograssi.it. Admission 10€. Daily 10am–7pm. Vaporetto: San Samuele.

⑧ ★ **Palazzo Mocenigo.** One of the largest and grandest houses in Venice is actually four palaces that a succession of prominent residents combined over the centuries. Lord Byron lived here from 1818 to 1819—with enough pets to populate a small zoo, an army of servants, and his mistress. He often swam home across the lagoon from outings on the Lido. ⏱ 10 min. Calle Mocenigo. Not open to the public. Vaporetto: San Stae.

⑨ ★ **Palazzo Fortuny.** The last resident of this 15th-century palazzo was textile designer and photographer Mariano Fortuny. The mansion now displays his distinctive work. ⏱ 1 hr. Campo San Beneto. ☎ 041-5200995. Admission 8€. Wed–Mon 10am–6pm. Vaporetto: Sant'Angelo.

⑩ ★★ **Scala Contarini del Bovolo.** The beautiful spiral staircase (*bovolo*, or snail, in Venetian dialect) that this palazzo is named for climbs five stories from a lovely courtyard. Until lengthy restoration work is completed (it was ongoing at press time), the staircase can be admired only from below in the courtyard; a reward for a climb to the top is a panoramic view over the rooftops of Venice. ⏱ 15 min. Corte di Contarini del Bovolo. ☎ 041-5322920. Vaporetto: Rialto.

⑪ ★★★ kids **Grand Canal.** A cruise up one of the world's most beautiful waterways is the ideal way to end a long day of touring. Get off at the Ferrovia stop for the return trip. See p 362. For details on the vaporetto, see p 420.

The Best of Venice in 2 Days

Strolling through the Dorsoduro, the quarters across the Grand Canal from San Marco, is not a quiet neighborhood amble: Some of Venice's greatest masterpieces are here, and you'll discover one remarkable church and treasure-filled museum after another.

> The domes of Santa Maria della Salute watch over the southern entrance to the Grand Canal.

START Vaporetto to Salute.

1 ★★ Santa Maria della Salute. The church of "St. Mary of Health" was built in 1630, an offering to the Virgin for bringing an end to a plague outbreak. The massive white-marble cathedral by architect Baldassare Longhena commands the entrance to the Grand Canal, and its domes, suggestive of the Madonna's crown, mimic those of the Basilica di San Marco across the water. An impressive collection of paintings includes Tintoretto's *Wedding Feast at Cana*. The Virgin is honored on the high altar with a wonderfully dramatic marble sculptural group by Giusto Le Corte—an old hag representing the plague flees from a torch-bearing angel as the Virgin and a noblewoman, in the role of Venice, look on. ⊙ 30 min. Campo della Salute. ☎ 041-5225558. Sacristy 2€. Apr–Sept daily 9am–noon, 3–6:30pm; Oct–Mar daily 9am–noon, 3–5:30pm. Vaporetto: Salute.

2 ★★ kids La Dogana da Mar. The 17th-century Customs house at the tip of the Dorsoduro resembles the hull of a ship. On the roof, a statue of Fortune stands over a gold globe, and looking out to sea from the landing stage, it's easy to imagine the time when Venetians felt they were indeed the lucky rulers of the waves. The **Centro d'Arte Contemporanea de Punta della Dogana,** which will house works from the Palazzo Grassi (p 353, **7**), will open here in mid-2009. ⊙ 30 min. Fondamenta Dogana alla Salute. Vaporetto: Salute.

3 ★★★ Peggy Guggenheim Collection. The American heiress (1898–1979) spent her life collecting contemporary art, living up to her pledge to "buy a picture a day." In 1949, she found a home for herself and her paintings, the **Palazzo Venier dei Leoni.** Only the ground floor of the 18th-century palace was completed, providing surreal surroundings for Giorgio

GHETTO

Cappella d. Volto Santo
S. Marziale
S. Maria d. Misericordia

Ponte d. Gúglie
Pal. Diedo

La Maddalena
Scuola Vecchia d. Misericordia

S. Marcuola
S. Fosca

S. Marcuola
Palazzo Vendramin-Calergi
Pal. Giovanelli

Fónd. d. Turchi
Ca' tron
Pal. Boldù
S. Felice

S. Zan Degolà
S. Stae
Ca' d' Oro
Ca' Strada Nova

S. Stae
Ca' Pesaro
Ca' d' Oro

S. Giacomo dell'Orio
S. Maria Máter Domini
Pal. Mangilli

Pal. Zane
Pescaria

SANTA CROCE
Pal. Grioni
S. Cassiano

Pal. Muti Baglioni
Fábbriche Nuove

Pal. Zane Collalto
Pal. Albrizzi
Pal. Molin-Cappello
Palazzo Dieci Savi

SAN POLO
S. Aponàl
S. Bartolomeo

Palazzo Zen
Campo S. Polo
S. Silvestro
Rialto

Ex Convento dei Frari
S. Polo
Pal. Muti Papadópoli
Pal. Dolfin-Manin

S. Rocco
S. Maria G. dei Frari
Palazzo Grimani
S. Silvestro

Istit. Univ. di Architettura
S. Giovanni Evangelista

Palazzo Marcello
Scuola grande di San Rocco
S. Tomà
Pal. Barbarigo
Ca' Farsetti

Casa Tórres
Pal. Corner Spinelli
Cinema Rossini

S. Tomà
Pal. Balbi
S. Ángelo
SAN MARCO

Pal. Cornèr d. Frescada
S. Pantalon
Palazzo Mocenigo
Palazzo Fortuny
Pal. Contarini del Bovolo

Campo S. Margherita
Ca' Foscari
Palazzo Moro-lin
Ateneo Véneto

Pal. Nani
S. Stefano
Campo S. Ángelo
S. Fantin

Cármini
Ca' Rezzonico
S. Samuele
Campo S. Stefano
S. Maurízio
La Fenice

S. Bárnaba
Pal. Stern
Ca' Rezzonico
Ca' del duca
S. Maria d. Giglio
S. Moisè

DORSODURO
Palazzo Pisani
Palazzo Tiépolo

Ospedale G. B. Giustiniàn
Palazzo Brandolin
Accademia
Ponte dell'Accademia
Pal. Corner d. Ca' Grande

Pal. Molin
S. Trovaso
Gallerie dell'Accademia
S. Maria d. Giglio
Salute

Pal. Giustinàn
Pal. Clary
S. Maria d. Visitaz.
S. Agnese
Pal. Venièr dei Leoni (Guggenheim)
Pal. Genovese
Dogana da Mar

Zattere
Gesuati
Ex Ospízio

Fond. Zattere ai Gesuati
Spírito Santo
Fond. Zattere ai Saloni

Canale della Giudecca

0 ____ 1/8 mile
0 ____ 200 meters

de Chirico's *The Red Tower,* René Magritte's *Empire of Light,* and works by Jackson Pollock (whom Guggenheim discovered), Max Ernst (whom she married), and many others. ⏱ 1 hr. Palazzo Venier dei Leoni. ☎ 041-2405411. www.guggenheim-venice.it. Admission 10€. Wed–Mon 10am–6pm. Vaporetto: Accademia.

④ ★★ **Palazzo Cini.** Industrialist Vittorio Cini (1885–1977) spent much of his fortune collecting religious art, and his intimate palace, open only for special events and exhibitions, is filled with works by Sandro Botticelli, Piero della Francesca, and others. ⏱ 45 min. Campo della Carità. ☎ 041-5222247. Open only for special events and exhibitions; prices and times vary. Vaporetto: Accademia.

⑤ ★★★ **Gallerie dell'Accademia.** The galleries here can take the good part of a day. If time is tight, at least see the works by Titian, Tintoretto, and Veronese, and Carpaccio's *Story of St. Ursula* cycle. See p 370, ⑨.

⑥ 🍷 **Da Gino.** Take an outdoor table at this handy stop on the well-worn path between the Guggenheim and the Accademia, and linger over a glass of wine and one of the delicious panini. Calle Nuova Sant'Agnese, Dorsoduro. ☎ 041-5285276. $$

⑦ ★★ **Campo San Barnaba.** The 14th-century campanile of the namesake church rises above the houses on this square; a boat moored alongside a quay serves as the neighborhood greengrocer; and just downstream is the pic-turesquely arched **Ponte dei Pugni** (Bridge of the Punches), where rival clans once slugged out their differences. ⏱ 15 min. Dorsoduro. Vaporetto: Ca' Rezzonico.

⑧ ★★ **Ca' Rezzonico.** The sweeping staircases and flamboyant salons in the onetime home of poets Robert Browning and Elizabeth Barrett Browning are now the backdrop for the **Museo del Settecento Veneziano.** The 18th-century art here includes Pietro Longhi's scenes of everyday Venetian life. ⏱ 1 hr. Fondamenta Rezzonico. ☎ 041-2410100. Admission 6.50€. Apr–Oct Wed–Mon 10am–6pm; Nov–Mar Wed–Mon 10am–5pm Vaporetto: Ca' Rezzonico.

⑨ ★★★ **Campo Santa Margherita.** Churches and *scuole* share this square with cafes, market stalls, and, on a fine day, what seems to be most of the population of Venice stealing a moment in the sun. The eponymous saint, patron of expectant mothers, is remembered twice: A dragon, her symbol, embellishes a niche on the north end and the base of the truncated campanile of her namesake church. ⏱ 30 min. Dorsoduro. Vaporetto: Ca' Rezzonico.

⑩ ★★ **Scuola Grande dei Carmini.** The Carmelite order founded this *scuola* in the 17th century in association with the guild of dyers and hired Baldassare Longhena to build it. See p 370, ⑪.

⑪ ★★★ **Scuola Grande di San Rocco.** San Rocco, the patron saint of the sick, was especially popular for his alleged prowess at curing the plague. A *scuola* was begun in the

> *Works from the Peggy Guggenheim Collection are displayed both inside the Palazzo Venier dei Leoni and out in its garden.*

> *"The Meeting with the Pope,"* one panel from Carpaccio's Story of St. Ursula, *in the Accademia.*

early 16th century to house the saint's relics; it was lavishly decorated by Tintoretto. **See p 372, ⑫.**

⑫ ★★★ **Santa Maria Gloriosa dei Frari.** One of the largest churches in Venice is also one of the city's great treasure troves of art, with masterworks by Titian and Giovanni Bellini. **See p 372, ⑬.**

⑬ 🍴 **Tonolo.** Venetians go out of their way to visit this legendary pastry shop for a buttery croissant and what many claim is the best cappuccino in all the Veneto. Calle San Pantalon. ☎ 041-5224410. $

⑭ ★★ **Campo San Polo.** *Bull Baiting in the Campo San Polo,* a 17th-century painting by German artist Joseph Heintz in the Museo Correr (p 352, Ⓐ), provides a telling glimpse of the colorful past of this square, still the

lively heart of its namesake neighborhood. These days, though, the top spectacle is a summertime outdoor cinema. ⏱ 15 min. San Polo. Vaporetto: San Tomà.

Back to *Scuola*

Founded in the Middle Ages, the Venetian *scuole* (schools) were guilds that brought together merchants and craftspeople from certain trades (for example, the dyers of Scuola dei Carmini), as well as those who shared similar religious devotions. The guilds were social clubs, credit unions, and sources of spiritual guidance. Many commissioned elaborate headquarters and hired the best artists of the day to decorate them; today they house some of the city's finest art treasures.

The Best of Venice in 3 Days

Everyday life in Venice revolves around the busy market-place, the Rialto, so this walk will, too. Start in the historic *sestiere* (district) of San Polo, continuing through the Rialto and into Cannaregio. Along this route you'll also find a few more of the notable churches, palaces, galleries, and monuments with which the city is so liberally laced.

START Vaporetto to Fondamenta Nuove.

1 ★★ **Campo Santi Giovanni e Paolo.** Bartolomeo Colleoni, a 15th-century mercenary, rides across one of Venice's most beautiful squares astride an equestrian monument by Verrocchio. The namesake basilica here (known as **San Zanipòlo** in Venetian dialect) is the final resting place of 25 doges, entombed in marble splendor. ⏱ 45 min. Castello. Vaporetto: Fondamenta Nuove.

2 ★★★ **Santa Maria dei Miracoli.** This small, beautiful church, inconspicuously tucked away on a small campo next to a canal, seems almost like an apparition. See p 374, **4**.

3 ★★ kids **Ponte di Rialto.** A nonstop water show takes place beneath the most monumental of the spans across the Grand Canal: Gondolas, garbage scows, police launches, and all manner of other craft ply the crowded waterway. Also in close view: the centuries-old commercial heart of the city, the **Fondaco dei Tedeschi,** built in 1508 as a warehouse and now the city's main post office; the **Palazzo dei Camerlenghi,** built in 1525 and the world's first-known office building; and two of the city's first palaces, the **Palazzo Loredan** and **Palazzo Farsetti,** which now jointly house city hall. ⏱ 30 min. San Polo. Vaporetto: Rialto.

4 🍷 **Naranzaria.** Set your sights on the Grand Canal while enjoying a glass of wine and a sandwich at a table on the *fondamenta* (walkway) just beneath the Rialto Bridge. Ruga d'Orifici, San Polo. ☎ 041-7241035. $

> *The basilica in Campo Santi Giovanni e Paolo is known as San Zanipòlo in Venetian dialect.*

1 Campo Santi Giovanni e Paolo
2 Santa Maria dei Miracoli
3 Ponte di Rialto
4 Naranzaria
5 Rialto
6 Traghetto
7 Santi Apostoli
8 Strada Nuova
9 Ca' d' Oro/Galleria Franchetti
10 Campo di Ghetto Nuovo
11 Palazzo Labia

SITE GUIDE
PAGE 361

⑤ ★★ Rialto. The name of this marketplace comes from *rivoaltus,* or "high bank," a geographic asset when settlers in the early 9th century were searching for dry ground to establish the city's first bazaar. (The Rialto has been a commercial center ever since.) Ships from around the globe once docked at the Fondaco dei Tedeschi—the Renaissance-style structure that now houses the main post office—and other neighborhood warehouses, and it was here that the Grand Canal was first spanned.

⑥ ★ kids Traghetto. Having already enjoyed a walk over the Ponte di Rialto, return across the canal in one of the *traghetti* that run between the banks. A *traghetto*—basically, a large, plain gondola—provides a poor man's gondola ride (one-way passage is just .50€), but comes with a challenge: By tradition, passengers remain standing during the ride. ⏱ **10 min.** Near the Rialto; traghetti run from Fondamenta del Vin to Riva del Carbòn (Mon–Sat 8am–2pm) and the Pescaria to Santa Sofia (Mon–Sat 7:30am–8:30pm; Sun 8am–7pm). Vaporetto: Rialto.

⑦ ★ Santi Apostoli. Venetian legend has it that the 12 apostles appeared to St. Magnus and told him to build a church where he saw 12 cranes. The church's bell tower, a 17th-century addition, is topped with an onion dome and is a much-beloved landmark. Giambattista Tiepolo's rendering of St. Lucy near the altar is eye-catching indeed—the martyr's eyes lie on the floor next to her, but she seems to be smiling all the same. ⏱ **30 min.** Campo Santi Apostoli. ☎ 041-5238297. Mon–Sat 8:30–noon, 5–7pm; Sun 4–7pm. Vaporetto: Ca' d'Oro.

⑧ ★ Strada Nuova. One of the few straight paths in Venice (**Via Garibaldi,** p 377, ⑯ is another), this street was laid out in the 1860s to facilitate foot traffic to and from the then-new railway station.

⑨ ★★★ Ca' d'Oro/Galleria Franchetti. This 15th-century palazzo just off the Strada Nuova still bears the trappings of a cushy Renaissance lifestyle and is filled with works by Venetian masters. See p 372, ⑭.

⑩ ★★ Campo di Ghetto Nuovo. The Ghetto was once the only part of Venice where Jews

> *The Ca' d'Oro, like most of the palaces along the Grand Canal, was designed to be admired from the water.*

were allowed to live. This large square and surrounding neighborhood occupy an island that was closed off at dusk and still feels remote. The houses on the square are higher than most in Venice, as stories were added to accommodate a population that expanded as the Jewish community prospered in trade and banking. ⏱ **15 min.** Ghetto Nuovo, Cannaregio. Vaporetto: Ponte de Guglie.

⑪ ★★ Palazzo Labia. One of the grandest palaces in Venice is set back from the Grand Canal—a sign that the Labias, a clan of Spanish traders, were never accepted by Venetian nobility. Giambattista Tiepolo painted a magnificent fresco of Anthony and Cleopatra for the Banqueting Hall in honor of the marriage of Maria Labia. ⏱ **30 min.** Fondamenta Labia. ☎ 041-5242812. Closed for restoration; normally open Wed–Fri 3–4pm, by appointment only (call or ask your hotel to make arrangements). Vaporetto: San Marcuola/Ponte de Guglie.

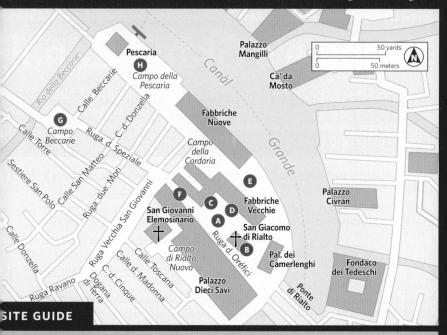

SITE GUIDE

5 The Rialto

The Rialto is centered around the **Ⓐ Campo San Giacomo di Rialto,** a sea of fruit and vegetable stalls above which rise the facade and campanile of the oldest church in Venice, **Ⓑ ★ San Giacomo di Rialto,** founded the same year as the city, 421, and restored in the 11th century. It retains the shape of a Greek cross and other telltale Byzantine elements. The **Ⓒ Gobbo di Rialto,** the "Hunchback of the Rialto," crouches on one side of the campo beneath a rostrum from which proclamations were read. For some Venetians, the humble figure was a welcome sight—he marked the end of a "walk of shame" that those found guilty of petty crimes were forced to make naked from San Marco. **Ⓓ Calle de Banco Giro** is a covered passageway that may have been the world's first banking premises: Merchants and moneylenders once gathered here to take advantage of the city's *"giro"* system, a paperless transfer of funds from one party to another. In **Ⓔ Campo Erberia,** stalls piled high with fresh fruit and vegetables stand in the shadow of the Fabbriche Nuove and the Fabbriche Vecchie, 16th-century warehouses. **Ⓕ Ruga degli Orefici,** the "Passageway of the Goldsmiths," still

> Antonio da Ponte's design for the Ponte di Rialto beat out competing options from such luminaries as Michelangelo and Palladio.

houses a few shops selling gold and silver, as it has since the 14th century. In **Ⓖ Campo Beccarie,** market stalls selling meat maintain a long-standing tradition—the city's abattoir once stood here. In **Ⓗ Campo della Pescaria,** the porticos of a neo-Gothic hall shelter a daily fish market. Alleyways leading off the square likewise bear the telltale names of the tradesmen who once set up shop in the environs (Casaria, "Cheese") and of the taverns that served them (Due Mori, the "Two Moors"). ⏱ 30 min. San Polo. Daily 7am–1pm. Vaporetto: Rialto.

Venice's Grand Canal

Main Street for Venetians is the Grand Canal, a 3.2km-
long (2-mile) stretch of waterway between San Marco and the train station.
A half-hour vaporetto trip up the canal not only reveals the city's past grandeur,
but also provides a look at life in present-day Venice.

START Vaporetto from San Marco/Vallaresso toward Piazzale Roma.

1 ★★ **Ponte dei Sospiri.** Legend has it that the **Bridge of Sighs** takes its name from the sighs of prisoners stealing their last glimpses of freedom on the way to a cell or the executioner's block. In truth, the handsome span connects the Palazzo Ducale with a prison constructed in the late 1500s to house petty criminals, just about all of whom saw the light of day again. ⏱ 15 min. San Marco. Vaporetto: San Zaccaria.

2 ★ **Piazzetta San Marco.** No other Venetian view imparts a greater sense of the city as a maritime republic. Two columns (one dedicated to San Marco, one to San Teodoro, the city's other patron saint) frame a flotilla of gondolas. ⏱ 15 min. San Marco. Vaporetto: San Marco/Vallaresso.

3 ★★★ **San Giorgio Maggiore.** See p 384, **8**.

4 ★★ kids **La Dogana da Mar.** The Customs house recalls the days when Venice strove to master the seven seas. See p 354, **2**.

5 ★★ **Santa Maria della Salute.** This baroque fantasy in white marble hints at the architectural wonders that line the canal ahead. See p 354, **1**.

6 ★ **Ca' Dario.** A long roster of former residents died under mysterious circumstances, endowing this small, 15th-century palazzo with a reputation of being cursed. Vaporetto: Salute.

7 ★★★ **Palazzo Venier dei Leoni.** The Venier clan ran into fiscal straits while building their palazzo, but the ground floor—the only part completed—was suited to the tastes of heiress Peggy Guggenheim. Today the palazzo shows off the **Peggy Guggenheim Collection** of modern art. See p 354, **3**.

8 ★ **Palazzo Corner della Ca' Grande.** The police department is headquartered in this elegant Renaissance palazzo built in the 1590s. Vaporetto: Santa Maria del Giglio.

> *The Grand Canal snakes through the city for 3.2km (2 miles).*

CONTINENTAL

12 ★ **Ca' Rezzonico.** The home of the Museum of 18th-Century Venice has also been home to the poets Robert Browning and Elizabeth Barrett Browning, Cole Porter, and James McNeill Whistler. See p 356, **8**.

13 ★ **Ca' Foscari.** This residence of a 15th-century doge houses the **Università Ca' Foscari Venezia** (University of Venice). Vaporetto: Ca' Rezzonico.

14 ★ **Palazzo Balbi.** Napoleon is among the spectators who have sat on the balcony here to watch the regattas that, since 1315, have crossed the finish line in front of the palazzo. Vaporetto: San Tomà.

15 ★ **Palazzo Mocenigo.** The Mocenigo clan produced seven doges; it also connected four adjacent palaces to create this grand home. In the early 19th century, one wing accommodated Lord Byron. Vaporetto: San Stae.

16 ★ **Campiello del Remer.** No small part of this little square's charm is the Grand Canal, lapping against one side. Byzantine arches gracing an adjoining palazzo and an ornately decorated well provide a picturesque backdrop. ⏱ 15 min. Castello. Vaporetto: Rialto.

17 ★ **Palazzo Loredan/Palazzo Farsetti.** Two of the first palazzi on the canal, from the 13th century, now serve as the city hall. Loredan was home to the first woman to ever earn a college degree (at the University of Padua in 1678). Vaporetto: Rialto.

(18) 🍷 **All'Arco.** Almost as much a part of the Rialto as the markets, this old-fashioned *bacaro* (wine bar) serves tasty *cicchetti* (bar snacks). Calle dell'Ochialar, San Polo. ☎ 041-5205666. $$

19 ★★★ **Ponte di Rialto.** See p 358, **3**.

20 ★ **Fondaco dei Tedeschi.** Built in 1508 as a multipurpose warehouse, office space, and a hostelry for *Tedeschi* (Germans) working in Venice, this Renaissance structure is now the post office. Vaporetto: Rialto.

21 ★ **Palazzo dei Camerlenghi.** The world's first-known office building was completed in 1528 for Venice's financial magistrates—and it still serves as the headquarters of the financial court. Vaporetto: Rialto.

> The 98m (321-ft.) campanile in Piazza San Marco was rebuilt after it collapsed in 1902.

9 ★ **Ponte dell'Accademia.** This prosaic wooden bridge dates from 1934—until then, the Ponte di Rialto was the only span across the canal. Vaporetto: Accademia.

10 ★★★ **Gallerie dell'Accademia.** See p 370, **9**.

11 ★ **Palazzo Grassi.** The last palazzo to be built on the Grand Canal dates from 1749. The salons filled with contemporary art surround a beautiful courtyard and frescoed staircase. See p 353, **7**.

22 ★ **Fabbriche Vecchie/Fabbriche Nuove.** Both these elegant structures were actually built in the 15th century as warehouses. Vaporetto: Rialto.

23 ★ **Ca' da Mosto.** The oldest palace on the Grand Canal was completed in the 13th century for the family of Alvise da Mosto, the 15th-century navigator who discovered the Cape Verde Islands. **Vaporetto: Ca d'Oro.**

24 ★ **Pescaria.** Venetians have bought their fish from this spot since the 14th century; the neo-Gothic market hall dates from the early 20th. Vaporetto: Rialto.

25 ★★ **Ca' d'Oro.** Even without the gold leaf that once graced the facade and lent the palazzo its name, this is a glittering example of early-15th-century Venetian Gothic architecture. See p 372, **14**.

26 ★ **Ca' Pesaro.** The Pesaro family combined three Gothic houses to create one of Venice's largest palaces, now housing Asian **(Museo d'Arte Orientale)** and modern art **(Galleria Internazionale d'Arte Moderna).** ⏱ 1 hr. ☎ 041-5240662. Admission 5.50€. Apr–Oct Tues–Sun 10am–6pm; Nov–Mar Tues–Sun 10am–5pm. Vaporetto: San Stae.

27 ★ **Palazzo Vendramin Calergi.** Richard Wagner completed *Tristan und Isolde* here in 1859, and the Renaissance palazzo is now the winter home of the city-operated casino. Vaporetto: Santa Marcuola.

28 ★★ **Palazzo Labia.** The Labia clan left behind tales of legendary pretension—at their lavish galas, they would hurl gold dinnerware into the canal. The 17th-century home now houses RAI, the Italian television network. See p 360, **11**.

29 ★★★ **Ponte Calatrava.** Venetians are still arguing about the aggressive modernity of Spanish architect Santiago Calatrava's graceful arc of steel and glass, but they agree that its arrival in the city in early 2008, when it was floated up the Grand Canal and barely squeaked under the Ponte di Rialto, was a memorable spectacle. ⏱ 15 min. Santa Croce. Vaporetto: Piazzale Roma.

> *Contrary to myth, few of the prisoners that crossed the Bridge of Sighs were ever executed.*

> *The Ponte Calatrava is the newest way to cross the Grand Canal.*

IS VENICE SINKING?

Saving the City of Water from the Sea

BY STEPHEN BREWER

BLARING SIRENS often compete with church bells in Venice, a warning to residents of this waterlogged city built on 117 low-lying, marshy islands to prepare for *acqua alta*—literally, high water. The waters of the lagoon lap over the quays to fill streets and ground floors with inches, even feet of water. Venetians pull on Wellingtons, get out buckets and pumps to bail water out of their homes and shops, and go about their business, moving around the city on elevated wooden planks. No one, though, takes *acqua alta* in stride. Tides are becoming higher and flooding more frequent all the time—the floods of December 2008 were the worst in 22 years, with the *acqua alta* reaching 156cm (more than 5 ft.). The question "Is Venice sinking?" looms larger all the time. The answer is yes and no—yes, because sea levels are rising and the city is sinking, and no, because Venetians are fighting back the sea, as they have for more than a thousand years.

A City Submerged

RISING WATERS

Why is Venice sinking beneath the waves? The natural movement of geological plates beneath Europe is causing coastal regions around Venice to sink by as much as half an inch a century. Industries on the marshy mainland around Venice accelerated the rate drastically in the 1950s and 1960s by pumping groundwater and causing the city to sink by a foot in 20 years. Meanwhile, silt continues to build up in the Venetian lagoon, raising sea levels, and global warming is causing sea levels to rise as well. Without intervention the city could be underwater by the end of the 21st century.

SQUARE OR LAKE?

It is symbolic that Piazza San Marco, the beautiful square that is the heart of the city for Venetians and their visitors alike, is especially prone to flooding. The low-lying square sits just 5cm (2 in.) above the level of an average high tide. Any above-normal tide fills the piazza with salt water, an event that occurs at least a hundred times a year.

A CITY BUILT ON STILTS

As the city we know today began to take shape in the 9th century, early Venetians drove wooden pilings through the muddy soil into an underlying layer of firmer clay and erected wooden platforms atop them. Brick structures were then built on top of these platforms and faced with waterproof stone. Wood petrifies in mineral-rich water, so these wooden foundations have become solid as bedrock as the years have passed. Unfortunately, the very ground upon which the pilings rest is sinking.

Protecting the City

INFLATABLE PROTECTION

MOSE, the Italian acronym for Experimental Electromechanical Module and a reference to the biblical figure who parted the Red Sea, is building 78 floodgates at the three inlets that connect the Venetian lagoon with the open seas of the Adriatic. Each gate is an inflatable barrier that is 28m (92 ft.) long and 20m (65 ft.) wide, weighs 300 tons, and rests on the seafloor when not in use. When tides begin to rise, the barriers are filled with air to expand and prevent water from entering the lagoon. MOSE is expected to be in operation by 2012.

lagoon

OTHER WAYS TO KEEP THE WATERS AT BAY

To prevent wave damage that boats cause with their wakes and propeller action, water traffic on many waterways has been slowed to 5 to 7km per hour (3 to 4mph). Another ongoing scheme is raising the level of pavement in low-lying parts of the city, and new plans are proposed all the time. One calls for pumping carbon dioxide or seawater into the layer of clay beneath the city to lift it by as much as 30cm (1 ft.) within 10 years, enough to counter the effects of rising sea levels.

The Best Art & Architecture in Venice

Can you actually see the great works of Venetian art in a day or two? If you're ambitious and pressed for time, yes. But it's hard to resist the temptation to linger for hours in any number of the city's fine museums and churches. If you're on a more leisurely trip, you can do this tour over the course of several days.

> *Carpaccio's* Conversion of Matthew *is just one of the artist's great works in the Scuola di San Giorgio degli Schiavoni.*

START Piazza San Marco.

1 ★★ **Scuola di San Giorgio degli Schiavoni.** Carpaccio spent 5 years painting his *Cycle of St. George,* an homage to the patron saint of the Slavic members of this *scuola.* The painter's lush colors and flair for storytelling bring dragon-slaying to vivid life. ⏱ 30 min. Calle dei Furlani. ☎ 041-2750642. Admission 3€. Mon 2:45–6pm; Tues-Sat 9:15am–1pm, 2:45–6pm; Sun 9:15am–1pm. Vaporetto: San Zaccaria.

2 ★★★ kids **Palazzo Ducale.** Doges ruled the Venetian republic from this suitably grandiose palace, built and rebuilt many times from the 7th to the 18th centuries. In the vast **Sala del Maggior Consiglio,** portraits of 76 of these officials line the walls beneath a ceiling painting of *Paradise* by Jacopo and Domenico Tintoretto; a likeness of doge Marino Faller, beheaded in the 14th century for betraying the senate, is painted over. The **Sala dello Scudo** houses the globes and maps that kept track of the trade routes of Marco Polo. ⏱ 1 hr. Piazzetta San Marco. ☎ 041-5224951. Single ticket not available; 12€ for entry to all civic museums. Easter–Nov daily 9am–7pm; Nov–Easter daily 9am–5pm. Vaporetto: San Marco/Vallaresso.

SITE GUIDE
PAGE 371

3 ★★★ **Basilica di San Marco.** Venice's Byzantine extravaganza is a shrine to the city's patron saint. Sometime around A.D. 800, Venetian traders stole Mark's body from Alexandria, where he had been bishop, wrapped the remains

Ospedale Civile
Convento dei Minori osservanti
S. Maria D. Pianto
Pal. Gritti
Pal. Contarini
CASTELLO
San Giovanni d. Cavalieri di Malta
S. Giovanni in Bragora
Casa Navagero
Pal. Gabrielli
Ca' di Dio
Arsenale

Ospedale
Ss. Giovanni e Paolo (S. Zanipolo)
Pal. Cappello
S. Lorenzo
S. Giorgio dei Greci
S. Zaccaria
La Pietà
Schiavoni
S. Zaccaria
Canale di San Marco

Pal.
Widman
Ss. Apostoli
S. Maria dei Miracoli
Teatro Malibran
Canciano
Pal. Soranzo Van Axel
S. Maria Formosa
Pal. Querini Stampalia
S. Giovanni Novo
Questura
Pal. D. Prigioni
Ponte d. Sospiri (Bridge of Sighs)
Riva

Bacino di San Marco

Canale di San Marco
Ex Magazzini e Dogana di S. Giorgio
Isola di S. Giorgio Maggiore
Teatro Verde

Bacino
S. Giorgio Maggiore
Fondazione Cini

Strada Nova
Ca' d'Oro
Pal. Mangilli
Ca' da Mosto
Fondaco d. Tedeschi
Pal. Ruzzini
Pal. Dona
S. Salvador
S. Lio
Pal. Tasca Papafava
Pal. Soranzo
Basilica di San Marco
Piazza San Marco
Giardini ex Reali
S. Marco

Canal Grande
Pescaria
Fabbriche Nuove
S. Cassiano
Pal. Molin
Pal. Cappello
S. Bartolomeo
Ca' Farsetti
Museo Correr
S. Gallo
S. Maria d. Salute
Dogana da Mar
Salute

Pal. Pesaro
Pal. Zane
Pal. Grioni
S. Maria Mater domini
Pal. Muti Baglioni
S. Aponal
S. Silvestro
Pal. Dieci Savi
Rialto
Pal. Dolfin
Ateneo Veneto
S. Fantin
La Fenice
S. Moisè
S. Maria d. Giglio

SANTA CROCE
S. Stae
Pal. Zane Collalto
Pal. Albrizzi
Campo S. Polo
SAN POLO
Pal. Corner Spinelli
Cinema Rossini
Campo S. Angelo
S. Stefano
S. Maurizio

S. Simeón Grande
Scuola Grande di S. Giovanni Evangelista
S. Nicolò di Tolentino
S. Rocco
Scuola Grande di San Rocco
S. Maria G. dei Frari
S. Tomà
Barbarigo
S. Angelo
Palazzo Fortuny

Campo S. Samuele
Ca' Rezzonico
Gallerie dell'Accademia
S. Maria d. Visitaz.

Pal. Venier dei Leoni (Guggenheim)
Spirito Santo
Ex Ospizio
S. Maria d. Salute
Dogana da Mar
Santa Maria d. Salute

Canale della Giudecca
Il Redentore
Convento del Redentore
Redentore

Zitelle
Quartiere Campo di Marte

SAN MARCO

SAN POLO

SANTA CROCE

DORSODURO

Piazzale Roma
Stazione Autobus
Ponte Calatrava
Manifattura Tabacchi
S. Nome di Gesù
S. Teresa
S. Nicolò dei Mendicoli
Ex Chiesa di S. M. Maggiore
Angelo Raffaele
S. Sebastiano
Pal. Zenobia
Stazione Marittima
S. Basilio

Carmini
Ca' Rezzonico
S. Barnaba
S. Margherita
Ospedale G. B. Giustinian
Palazzo Brandolin
Pal. Trovaso
Pal. Giustinian
Accademia
Zattere

N
1/4 mi
0.25 km

Legend

1. Scuola di San Giorgio degli Schiavoni
2. Palazzo Ducale
3. Basilica di San Marco
4. San Giorgio Maggiore
5. Il Redentore
6. Santa Maria della Salute
7. Peggy Guggenheim Collection
8. Il Chioschetto
9. Gallerie dell'Accademia
10. San Sebastiano
11. Scuola Grande dei Carmini
12. Scuola Grande di San Rocco
13. Santa Maria Gloriosa dei Frari
14. Ca' d'Oro
15. Santa Maria Assunta

in pork to deter Muslim guards from prying, and smuggled the prize back home. The saint soon became a symbol of the city's power—and the multidomed, mosaic-paved Basilica built in the 11th century as his resting place still evokes the might of the Venetian republic.

④ ★★★ San Giorgio Maggiore. The **Fondazione Cini,** founded by industrialist Vittorio Cini to support cultural causes, shares the premises with a small community of monks and occasionally hosts conferences and art exhibitions. See p 385, **⑧**.

⑤ ★★ Il Redentore. Built to assuage the plague of 1576, this graceful church is a stately presence on the Giudecca. More than a third of the city succumbed to the disease, but work on the church continued for 2 decades, and it's now an elegant showcase for the restrained classicism of architect Andrea Palladio. ⏱ 30 min. Giudecca. Admission 3€. ☎ 041-2750642. Mon–Sat 10am–5pm. Vaporetto: Redentore, Giudecca.

⑥ ★★ Santa Maria della Salute. Turn your back on the water views and walk up the majestic staircase of this baroque church to admire Titian's *St. Mark Enthroned with Saints* and other masterworks. See p 354, **①**.

⑦ ★★★ Peggy Guggenheim Collection. Picassos, Klees, and Miròs hang in airy, light-filled galleries along the Grand Canal—all of it a refreshing antidote to the religious fervor that permeates most Venetian art. See p 354, **③**.

⑧ 🍴 Il Chioschetto. At this outdoor cafe, a panino and a glass of wine, well deserved after a morning of viewing art, come with a view of the Giudecca Canal. Zattere Ponte Luongo. ☎ 338-1174077. $$

⑨ ★★★ Gallerie dell'Accademia. Venice's largest museum was founded in the 19th century to house art from churches and convents suppressed by Napoleon. Today's galleries occupy a complex including the monastery of the Lateran Canons, the church of La Carità, and the Scuola Santa Maria della Carità. A visit is a stroll through the great periods of Venetian art.

SITE GUIDE PAGE 373

⑩ ★★ San Sebastiano. Paolo Veronese's frescoes of the church's namesake saint cover the walls, ceilings, even the organ doors. More striking than the saint's gruesome martyrdom, perhaps, is the artist's fascination with sumptuous colors. ⏱ 30 min. Fondamenta di San Sebastiano. ☎ 041-2750642. Admission 3€. Mon–Sat 10am–5pm. Vaporetto: San Basilio.

⑪ ★★ Scuola Grande dei Carmini. In this remarkably well-preserved *scuola,* one of Giambattista Tiepolo's great masterpieces, *The Virgin in Glory Appearing to the Blessed Simon Stock,* flows across the ceiling of the upper salon. Mirrors provided to view the painting help visitors capture the drama of the Virgin handing the saint a scapular, a length of cloth draped over the shoulders as a sign of servitude. ⏱ 30 min. Campo dei Carmini. ☎ 041-5289420. Admission 5€. Daily 10am–4pm. Vaporetto: San Basilio.

> The monumental church of San Giorgio Maggiore was designed by influential Vicentine architect Andrea Palladio.

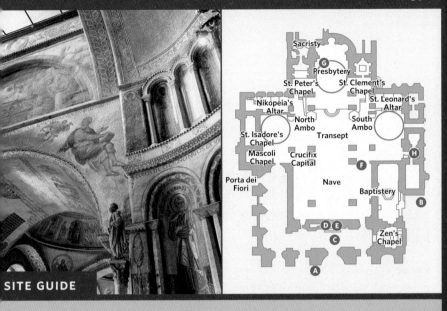

SITE GUIDE

③ Basilica di San Marco

The combined effect of glittering mosaics, domes, and arches on the **Ⓐ main facade** of the Basilica di San Marco is best appreciated from the center of the piazza. Some claim that the **Ⓑ Tetrarchs,** four figures depicting Byzantine emperors, are actually infidels turned to stone while pilfering church treasures. In the **Ⓒ atrium,** illiterate believers boned up on the Old Testament with these lively mosaic depictions of the story of the creation, Noah and the flood, and other biblical narratives. In the **Ⓓ galleria,** make the climb for a close-up look at the atrium's ceiling mosaics; for the view of the piazza from the loggia; and to see the gilded bronze horses, loot from the 4th Crusade, in the **Ⓔ Museo Marciano.** More than 3.8 sq. km (1½ sq. miles) of colorful glass-tile **Ⓕ mosaics** sparkle and bedazzle with rich renditions of an ascending Christ, saints, the apostles, and other religious rank and file. Byzantine goldsmiths fashioned the **Ⓖ Pala d'Oro** (Golden Altar), St. Mark's final resting place, in the 10th century. Among the glittering prizes brought back from the Crusades now on view in the **Ⓗ tesoro** (treasury) are icons, censers (incense containers), and a relic of the true cross. 🕐 2–3 hr. Piazza San Marco. ☎ 041-5225205. Basilica: Mon–Sat 9:45am–5pm; Sun 2–5pm (until 4pm Nov–Easter). Museo Mar-

> Mosaics like those decorating the interior of San Marco helped the illiterate masses to understand biblical teachings.

ciano: Admission 3€. Daily 9:45am–5pm (until 4:30pm Oct–Mar). Pala d'Oro and Tesoro: Admission 2.50€ Pala; 3€ Tesoro. Mon–Sat 9:45am–5pm; Sun 2–5pm (2–4pm Nov–Easter). Vaporetto: San Marco/Vallaresso.

> *Palladio's magnificently proportioned Il Redentore (The Redeemer), on the Giudecca, was offered in thanks for Venice's deliverance from plague.*

⑫ ★★ **Scuola Grande di San Rocco.** When the affluent school dedicated to San Rocco wanted to entrust an artist with its decoration, Tintoretto one-upped the competition and presented a completed painting rather than a sketch as a sample design. He spent the next 23 years filling the interior with depictions of the saint and his heavenly consorts. ⊕ 30 min. Campo San Rocco. ☎ 041-5234864. Admission 5.50€. Apr–Oct daily 9am–5:30pm; Nov–Mar daily 10am–5pm. Vaporetto: San Tomà.

⑬ ★★ **Santa Maria Gloriosa dei Frari.** By the time this Italian-Gothic edifice was completed around 1440, it was one of the largest churches in Venice, and Titian bathed much of the interior in bold colors. His *Assumption of the Virgin,* in which Mary ascends from a crowd of awe-struck apostles amid a swirl of *putti* (cherubs), is especially powerful. Equally moving is the *Monument to Doge Foscari,* who died of a broken heart when his son Jacopo was exiled in 1547. ⊕ 1 hr. Campo dei Frari. ☎ 041-5222637. Admission 1.55€. Mon–Sat 9am–6pm; Sun 1–6pm. Vaporetto: San Tomà.

⑭ ★ **Ca' d'Oro.** This palace's **Galleria Franchetti** houses many treasures, including *St. Sebastian,* by Andrea Mantegna, the artist's last painting and often considered his best. A transcendent *Annunciation* by Carpaccio makes a good showing, too. ⊕ 1 hr. Calle Ca' d'Oro. ☎ 041-5200345. Admission 5€. Mon 8:15am–2pm; Tues–Sun 8:15am–7:15pm. Vaporetto: Ca d'Oro.

⑮ ★★★ **Santa Maria Assunta.** The oldest building in the Venetian lagoon, on the island of Torcello, dates from the 7th century, but its Byzantine splendors—the campanile, paintings, and mosaics—remain intact. At the far end of the church, a fear-invoking mosaic cycle portrays the Last Judgment—with lurid images of sinners burning as Lucifer watches. ⊕ 1 hr. Campo San Donato, Torcello. ☎ 041-730084. Church: 3€. Mar–Oct daily 10:30am–6pm; Nov–Feb daily 10am–5pm. Campanile: Admission 3€. Mar–Oct daily 10:30am–5:30pm (4:30pm Nov–Feb). Vaporetto: No. 12 from Murano to Torcello.

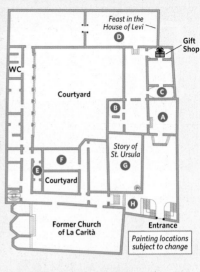

9 Gallerie dell'Accademia

> The rooms of the Gallerie dell'Accademia exhibit works by Veronese, Tintoretto, Titian, and others, including Giorgione's The Tempest (top).

In **A** **Room 2** of the Accademia is Giovanni Bellini's *Virgin and Child with Saints*, often known as the ★★★ *Pala di San Giobbe* (for the Venetian church that commissioned it). ★★ *The Tempest* by Giorgione, found in **B** **Room 5,** portrays a woman suckling her infant in an eerie cast of green light; its meaning has evaded scholars for centuries. Lorenzo Lotto's bold, stark ★★ *Portrait of a Young Gentleman in His Study* in **C** **Room 7** suggests that moodiness, self-absorption, and psychic unrest are not uniquely modern-day preoccupations. Three great 16th-century masters convene in

D **Room 10:** Veronese painted his ★★ *Feast in the House of Levi* as a *Last Supper,* but church authorities found the ribaldry heretical, so he changed the name. Titian, at 90, painted the ★ *Pietà* for his tomb but died before finishing it. Tintoretto's ★★ *St. Mark* cycle illustrates, among other moments, the theft of the saint's body. Canaletto's views of the Grand Canal and Francesco Guardi's *Isola di San Giorgio* in **E** **Room 17** may be familiar; what you may not have seen before are the works of a female artist, Rosalba Carriera. Carpaccio's *Miracle of the Relic of the True Cross* in **F** **Room 20** is a fascinatingly detailed look at Venice in that distant past. **G** **Room 21** contains Carpaccio's ★★ *Story of St. Ursula,* a color-saturated, action-packed medieval travelogue in which the Breton princess and her English betrothed, Hereus, travel to Rome so the groom-to-be can be converted to the true faith. Finally, **H** **Room 24:** Titian painted his *Presentation of the Virgin to the Temple* for this room, the former *albergo* (hostel) of the Scuola della Carità. This elegant rendering is a graceful endnote to our visit. ⊙ 2–3 hr. Campo della Carità. ☎ 041-5222247. Admission 6.50€. Mon 8:15am–2pm; Tues–Sun 8:15am–7:15pm. Vaporetto: Accademia.

Cannaregio & Castello

Venice gets down to everyday business in these sprawling neighborhoods, which stretch north from the Grand Canal to the lagoon. You'll discover quiet squares and one splendid art-filled church after another.

> *The back alleys and canals of Castello offer a welcome escape from Venice's crowds.*

START Campo di Ghetto Nuovo. Take vaporetto 41, 42, 51, or 52 to the Ponte Guglie stop. From there, the Sottoportego di Ghetto Vecchio leads northeast through the Campo delle Scuole to the Campo di Ghetto Nuovo.

1 ★ **The Ghetto.** Until Napoleon conquered Venice in 1797, Jews were allowed to live only here. The extraordinary height of the houses here testifies to the overcrowded conditions that once prevailed; prevented from expanding into other parts of the city, residents could only build up. ⏱ 15 min. Vaporetto: Ponte de Guglie.

2 ★ **Museo Ebraico.** The most memorable part of this museum celebrating Venetian Judaism is the guided tour of three synagogues

that occupy the top floors of nearby houses. ⏱ 1 hr. Campo di Ghetto Nuovo. ☎ 041-715359. www.museoebraico.it. Admission 3€ museum, 8€ museum and synagogue tour. June–Sept Sun–Fri 10–7pm; Oct–May Sun 10am–6pm, Mon–Fri 10am–5:30pm. Vaporetto: Ponte de Guglie.

3 ★★ **Madonna dell'Orto.** Tintoretto is buried in this neighborhood church, surrounded by several of his works, including *Beheading of St. Christopher.* ⏱ 30 min. Campo Madonna dell'Orto. ☎ 041-2750642. 3€. Mon–Sat 10am–5pm. Vaporetto: Madonna dell'Orto.

4 ★★★ **Santa Maria dei Miracoli.** A top contender for the most beautiful church in Venice. Sheathed in gleaming white marble, it's

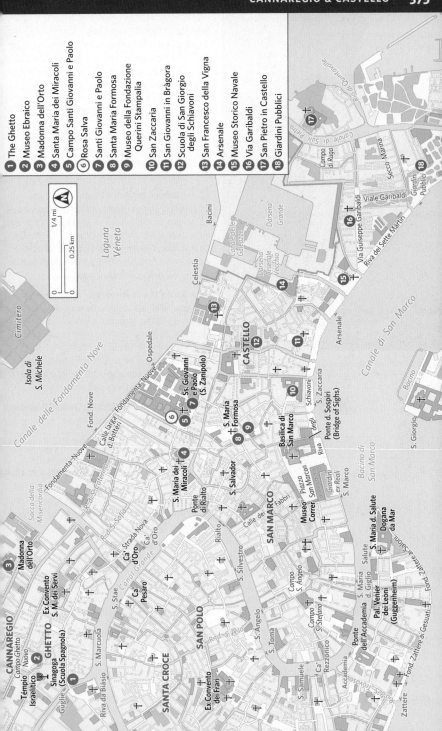

1 The Ghetto
2 Museo Ebraico
3 Madonna dell'Orto
4 Santa Maria dei Miracoli
5 Campo Santi Giovanni e Paolo
6 Rosa Salva
7 Santi Giovanni e Paolo
8 Santa Maria Formosa
9 Museo della Fondazione
   Querini Stampalia
10 San Zaccaria
11 San Giovanni in Bràgora
12 Scuola di San Giorgio
   degli Schiavoni
13 San Francesco della Vigna
14 Arsenale
15 Museo Storico Navale
16 Via Garibaldi
17 San Pietro in Castello
18 Giardini Pubblici

> A canal-level glimpse at Santa Maria dei Miracoli.

> The word "ghetto," for an area where Jews are forced to live, is derived from Venetian dialect.

especially stunning at night. Painted panels on the barrel-vaulted ceiling depict the prophets. ⏲ 30 min. Campo Santa Maria dei Miracoli. ☎ 041-2750462. Admission 3€. Mon–Sat 10am–5pm. Vaporetto: Rialto.

⑤ ★★★ **Campo Santi Giovanni e Paolo.** Pride of place in this square (aka **San Zanipòlo**)

belongs to Bartolomeo Colleoni, a 15th-century mercenary who asked that a statue be erected in his honor. The doges obliged with an equestrian monument by Verrocchio, but they deceived the old soldier—behind him is the Scuola Grande di San Marco, not the San Marco he requested. See p 358, ❶.

⑥ 🍴 **Rosa Salva.** Linger over a pastry and cappuccino while admiring San Zanipòlo at this venerable old cafe. Campo Santi Giovanni e Paolo. ☎ 041-5227949. $

❼ ★★ **Santi Giovanni e Paolo.** One of the largest churches in Venice holds the remains of numerous doges, whose marble tombs line the lofty nave in a show of dusty pomp. ⏲ 30 min. Campo Santi Giovanni e Paolo. ☎ 041-5235913. Admission 2.50€. Mon–Sat 9:30am–6pm; Sun 1–6pm. Vaporetto: Fondamenta Nuove.

❽ ★ **Santa Maria Formosa.** *Formosa* means "buxom," and this 15th-century church honors the image of the Virgin as a fulsome mother. Near the altar is a rare Venetian masterpieces by a woman, *Allegory of the Foundation of the Church* by Giulia Lama. ⏲ 15 min. Campo Santa Maria Formosa. Admission 3€. ☎ 041-2750462. Mon–Sat 10am–5pm. Vaporetto: Rialto.

❾ ★ **Museo della Fondazione Querini Stampalia.** This Renaissance palazzo houses a stunning collection of artwork by Pietro Longhi, Bellini, and others. The library is a haven for night owls, who are allowed to linger until midnight. ⏲ 45 min. Campo Santa Maria Formosa. ☎ 041-2711411. www.querinistampalia.it. Museum: Admission 8€. Tues–Sat 10am–8pm; Sun 10am–7pm. Library: Free admission. Tues–Sat 10pm–midnight; Sun 10–7pm. Vaporetto: Rialto.

❿ ★★ **San Zaccaria.** This Renaissance/Gothic church just behind San Marco has souvenir stands outside and the tombs of several doges inside. ⏲ 30 min. Campo San Zaccaria. ☎ 041-5221257. Mon–Sat 10am–noon, 4–6pm; Sun 4–6pm. Vaporetto: San Zaccaria.

⓫ ★ **San Giovanni in Bràgora.** Composer Antonio Vivaldi was baptized here in 1678. Behind the altar there's a *Baptism of Christ* by Cima da Conegliano; the detailed backdrop was inspired by the artist's namesake birthplace. ⏲ 15 min. Campo Bandiera e Moro. ☎ 041-2702464. Mon–Sat 9am–noon, 3:30–5:30pm. Vaporetto: Arsenale.

> *Rosa Salva is an old-time Venetian pastry shop.*

12 ★★★ **Scuola di San Giorgio degli Schiavoni.** *Schiavoni,* or Slavs from Dalmatia, prospered in Venice; by the 15th century, they had acquired the riches to build this *scuola* and commission Carpaccio to paint it. ☉ 30 min. Calle dei Furlani. ☎ 041-2750642. Admission 3€. Mon 2:45–6pm; Tues–Sat 9:15am–1pm, 2:45–6pm; Sun 9:15am–1pm. Vaporetto: San Zaccaria.

13 ★ **San Francesco della Vigna.** This stately church's 15th-century facade is by Palladio; Pietro Lombardo sculptures and paintings by Bellini grace the simple interior. To clear your head of these depictions of saints and sinners, spend a few minutes in the cloisters. ☉ 30 min. Campo San Francesco della Vigna. ☎ 041-5206102. Mon–Sat 8am–12:30pm, 3–6:30pm; Sun 3–6:30pm. Vaporetto: Celestia.

14 ★ kids **Arsenale.** The shipyards here once equipped the republic's navy, employing some 16,000 shipbuilders who could assemble a galley in a few hours. ☉ 15 min. Campo dell'Arsenale. Vaporetto: Arsenale.

15 ★ **Museo Storico Navale.** On display here are elaborate centuries-old models of Venetian ships and doges' barges, crafted by shipbuilders to show off their designs. Full-scale boats include Peggy Guggenheim's private gondola. ☉ 1 hr. Campo San Biago. ☎ 041-5200276. Admission 1.55€. Mon–Fri 8:45am–1:30pm; Sat 8:45am–1pm. Vaporetto: Arsenale.

16 **Via Garibaldi.** Head inland on this broad avenue, named for the hero of Italian

> *San Zaccaria houses a famous Madonna and Child altarpiece by Giovanni Bellini.*

unification. You'll encounter a boisterous floating market as you continue to the **Fondamenta Sant'Ana.** ☉ 15 min. Castello. Vaporetto: Arsenale.

17 ★ **San Pietro in Castello.** Before San Marco, this neglected-looking basilica was the official cathedral of Venice. In June, the waterside lawns beneath the leaning campanile are filled with revelers celebrating the Feast of San Pietro. ☉ 45 min. Campo San Pietro. ☎ 041-2750642. Admission 2.50€. Mon–Sat 10am–5pm. Vaporetto: San Pietro.

18 ★ **Giardini Pubblici.** Crowds descend upon these pavilions to attend the **Biennale d'Arte Contemporanea e Architettura,** an exhibition of art and architecture. At other times, only birdsong intrudes on the tranquillity. ☉ 15 min. Sant'Elena. Vaporetto: Giardini Esposizione.

Santa Croce, San Polo & Dorsoduro

These neighborhoods surround some of the city's greatest treasure houses, including the Gallerie dell'Accademia and the Peggy Guggenheim Collection—all reason enough for a visit, of course. But you'll also be enchanted by the area's pleasant squares and little alleyways.

> Until 1700, rival gangs were allowed to brawl legally on the Ponte dei Pugni in Rio San Barnaba.

START Piazzale Roma. Take vaporetto 1, 41, 42, 51, 52, 61, 62, or 82 to the Piazzale Roma stop. Follow the Fondamenta Santa Chiara east to Giardini Papadopoli.

① ★ **Giardini Papadopoli.** Many Venetians only know this garden atop the remains of a convent as a quick route to Piazzale Roma. You might want to linger a bit, though, especially on the Esplanade—it's one of the few public spaces on the banks of the Grand Canal. ⏱ 30 min. Santa Croce. Vaporetto: Piazzale Roma.

② ★ **San Nicola da Tolentino.** Behind the unfinished facade and portico of this church are paintings awash in a swirl of *putti* (pink-cheeked cherubs) and saints. Frescoes in the third chapel provide a vivid and gory lesson in the life of St. Cecilia. ⏱ 20 min. Campo dei Tolentini. ☎ 041-710806. Mon–Sat 8:30am–noon, 4:30–6:30pm; Sun 4:30–6:30pm. Vaporetto: Piazzale Roma.

③ ★ **San Giacomo dell'Orio.** The campanile of this 10th-century church rises above a sleepy square. Inside are a 16th-century altarpiece of the *Madonna and Saints* by Lorenzo Lotto and ceiling paintings by Veronese. ⏱ 30 min. Campo San Giacomo dell'Orio. ☎ 041-2750462. Admission 3€. Mon–Sat 10am–5pm. Vaporetto: Riva di Biasio.

④ 🍷 **Al Prosecco.** This landmark *enoteca* (wine shop) serves the namesake sparkling white as well as many other wines by the glass. Campo San Giacomo dell'Orio, Santa Croce. ☎ 041-5240222. $$

⑤ ★★ **Santa Maria Gloriosa dei Frari.** The saints and sinners of Titian and Bellini inhabit this solid Italian Gothic edifice. See p 372, **⑬**.

⑥ ★★ **Scuola Grande di San Rocco.** Tintoretto was entrusted with decorating this school dedicated to the patron saint of the sick, and some of his greatest works are here. See p 372, **⑫**.

7 ★★ **San Pantalon.** More than 60 ceiling paintings by Gian Antonio Fumiani illustrate *The Martyrdom and Apotheosis of St. Pantalon,* a physician who was beheaded by Diocletian. Fumiani's story is no less fervent than the saint's—the artist lay on his back for 24 years to execute these masterpieces, then fell from a scaffold to his death as he applied the last brush strokes. ⏱ 20 min. Campo San Pantalon. ☎ 041-5235893. Admission 2€. Mon–Sat 8-10am, 4–6pm. Vaporetto: San Tomà.

8 ★★ **Campo Santa Margherita.** One of the most appealing squares in Venice is a stage set for market stalls, shops, and cafes. ⏱ 15 min. Dorsoduro. Vaporetto: Ca' Rezzonico.

9 🍴 **Gelateria il Doge/Gelateria Causin.** Campo Santa Margherita is Venice's ground zero for gelato. You decide: Is Il Doge the best in town, or will you cast your vote with Causin? Campo Santa Margherita. Doge: ☎ 041-5234607. Causin: ☎ 041-523-6091. $

10 ★★★ **Scuola Grande dei Carmini.** In this perfectly preserved 17th-century *scuola,* Tiepolo steals the show with magnificent ceiling paintings. See p 370, **11**.

11 ★ **Rio San Barnaba.** Follow this street past lovely houses and a floating market to the **Ponte dei Pugni** (Bridge of the Punches), so-called because rival neighborhood factions were allowed to brawl publicly on the span, until the practice was banned around 1700. ⏱ 15 min. Dorsoduro. Vaporetto: San Basilio.

12 ★★ **San Sebastiano.** Paolo Veronese spent most of his career painting a luridly colorful fresco cycle in this 16th-century church: Queen Esther is opulently clad, and Sebastian is theatrically pierced with arrows. The artist is buried here amid his creations. See p 370, **10**.

13 ★ **Angelo Raffaele.** A gripping story unfolds in the organ loft, where Antonio Guardi's sumptuous paintings relate the archangel's travels in human form. The elaborately carved well behind the church was the gift of a plague-stricken 14th-century merchant who mistakenly believed that contaminated water was the cause of his demise. ⏱ 15 min. Campo dell'Angelo Raffaele. ☎ 041-5228548. Admission 2€. Mon–Sat 8am–noon, 3–5pm; Sun 9am–noon. Vaporetto: San Basilio.

14 ★ **San Nicolò dei Mendicoli.** *Mendicoli* (beggars) once took shelter under the portico of this 7th-century church—the second-oldest in Venice. ⏱ 20 min. San Nicolò dei Mendicoli. ☎ 041-2750382. Mon–Sat 10am–noon, 4–6pm; Sun 4–6pm. Vaporetto: San Basilio.

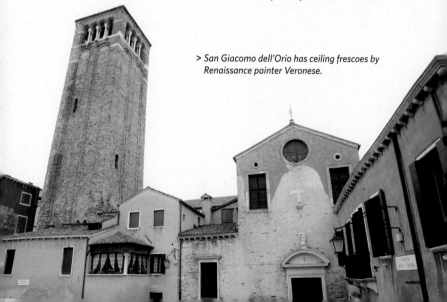

> *San Giacomo dell'Orio has ceiling frescoes by Renaissance painter Veronese.*

> *A walk along the Zattere quayside is rewarded with views across the water to Giudecca.*

15 ★ **Zattere.** This busy quay is named for the rafts that arrived here during the days of the republic, laden with wood to build ships and palaces. Across the canal is **Il Redentore** (p 370, **5**), the impressive dome-topped church. ⏱ 15 min. Dorsoduro. Vaporetto: Zattere.

16 ★ **Squero San Trovaso.** This shipyard builds and repairs gondolas—a uniquely Venetian operation. A stroll along **Fondamenta Nani** affords an excellent view of the goings-on. ⏱ 15 min. Dorsoduro. Vaporetto: Zattere.

17 ★ **San Trovaso.** Dedicated to two saints, Gervasius and Protasius, this elegant 17th-century church has dual facades, an arrangement allegedly made so that members of two warring factions who worshipped here could enter and leave the church without bloodshed. ⏱ 20 min. Campo San Trovaso. ☎ 041-2702464. Mon–Sat 2:30–5:30pm. Vaporetto: Zattere.

18 ★ **Santa Maria del Rosario ai Gesuati.** When the Dominican order took over this waterfront church in the 18th century, they commissioned a series of colorful ceiling panels of St. Dominic by Giambattista Tiepolo. ⏱ 20 min. Fondamenta Zattere ai Gesuati. ☎ 041-2750642. Admission 3€. Mon–Sat 10am–5pm. Vaporetto: Zattere.

19 ★ **Rio Terrá Antonio Foscarini.** This shop-lined street leads north from the Zattere to the Accademia Bridge. Wander off into some of the adjoining alleys to get a sense of the quiet neighborhood. ⏱ 15 min. Dorsoduro. Vaporetto: Zattere or Accademia.

20 ★★★ **Gallerie dell'Accademia.** Viewing Gentile Bellini's *Procession in St. Mark's Square* cycle is like gazing up at the Milky Way: Another splendid detail emerges with every blink of the eye. See p 370, **9** .

21 ★★ **Santa Maria della Salute/Dogana da Mar.** The remarkable church and Customs house supply a dramatic ending to your walk. See p 354, **1** and **2** .

Islands of the Venetian Lagoon

In Venice, an island escape is only a short vaporetto ride away, and the retreat usually comes with a nice smattering of art, architecture, beachgoing, and shopping.

> *Venetian glass, especially that made on the island of Murano, is prized all over the world.*

START Fondamenta Nuove, to catch the vaporetto for Cimitero, the only stop on San Michele.

1 ★★ **San Michele.** Your first stop is the last stop for many Venetians: the cypress-studded island that has served as the city cemetery since the late 18th century. San Michele is the resting place of many distinguished expatriates—among them Ezra Pound, Igor Stravinsky, and Serge Diaghilev, whose grave is usually strewn with dance slippers. Gondoliers are as lively a presence in death as they were in life, and lie beneath elaborately carved models of the crafts they so deftly maneuvered. Venice's first Renaissance church, **San Michele in Isola,** stands at the entrance to this enchanting island of the dead. ⏱ 1 hr. Apr–Sept daily 7:30am–6pm; Oct–Mar daily 7:30am–4pm. Vaporetto: Cimitero.

2 ★★ **Murano.** The glassmakers' island is not always mellow, especially when shills swoop upon passengers disembarking from the vaporetto like pigeons on bread crumbs in San Marco and try to whisk them off to studios and shops along the Fondamenta dei Vetrai. Even so, many of the glass pieces fashioned in the island furnaces are temptingly attractive. For those who seek a respite from shopping, two beautiful churches provide welcome refuge. ⏱ 3–4 hr. Vaporetto: No. 12 from Fondamenta Nuove to Murano (Colonna stop).

Tesséra

✈ **Venice (Marco Polo)**

Palude del Monte

Palude della Rosa

Torcello **4**

I. Buèl del Lovo

Punta Lunga

Mazzorbo

Burano **3**

I. Carbonera

I. Madonna del Monte

Laguna Véneta

San Francisco del Deserto ■

I. di Tesséra

I. San Giacomo in Palude

I. di Campalto

Ca' la Vela

Sacca Serenella

2

Murano

Sant'Erasmo

Ca' Carara

Canale di Treporti

1 *I. S. Michele*

le Vignole

Stazione Santa Lucia ■

Idroscalo S. Andrea

Punta Sabbioni

Venice

Piazza San Marco ■

I. di S. Pietro

la Certosa

Biennale ■

Canale d. Giudecca

Canale di San Marco

I. di S. Élena

San Nicolò

7

8

I. S. Giorgio Maggiore

6

La Giudecca

Porto di Lido

I. la Grázia

I. S. Sérvolo

Lido

I. S. Clemente

I. S. Lázzaro degli Armeni

5

Sacca Séssoa

I. Lazzaretto Vécchio

Casino Municipale

Città Giardino

Palazzo del Cínema

I. S. Spírito

Ca' Bianca

La Rotunda

Litorale di Lido

I. Povéglia

Adriatic Sea

Malamocco

Instituto Marino San Marco ■

0		1 mi
0	1 km	

1 San Michele

2 Murano

3 Burano

4 Torcello

5 The Lido

6 Giudecca

7 Bar San Giorgio

8 San Giorgio Maggiore

> *Murano has been home to Venice's glassmakers since the 13th century.*

> *The simple lanes of Giudecca seem far removed from the crowds and chaos of Piazza San Marco.*

❸ ★★ **Burano.** The most cheerful patch of land in the lagoon is home to lace makers and fishermen. Houses are painted in bright colors, allegedly so they can be spotted from boats at sea. A pleasant scene unfolds on almost any street on the island, where women fashion pieces of lace in the doorways and men mend fishing nets. The island's lively gathering spots are the Piazza Galuppi and the fish market along Fondamenta Pescheria. Burano has been known for its lace making since the 15th century, when young women in Venice and the islands on the lagoon were encouraged to learn the craft—a genteel pastime, and a lucrative export business. ⊕ 2 hr. Vaporetto: No. 12 from Fondamenta Nuove or Murano to Burano.

❹ ★★ **Torcello.** The 7th-century **Santa Maria Assunta** church (p 372, ❶❺) is the oldest building on the lagoon. Until Torcello was abandoned 1,000 years ago, the basilica served a population of 20,000. Elsewhere on the island, a pentagonal portico supported by elegant columns surrounds the small and sparsely elegant church of **Santa Fosca,** built to house the body of its namesake saint, brought to Torcello in the 11th century. ⊕ 90 min. Vaporetto: No. 12 from Murano to Torcello.

❺ ★★ **The Lido.** This stretch of sand, 12km (7½ miles) long and barely 1km (½ mile) wide, separates the Adriatic from the lagoon. It's where Venetians come to swim, golf, ride bikes, and just lie on the beach. Some *fin de siècle* luxury, a la Thomas Mann's novella *Death in Venice*, is in evidence around the extravagant Hotel des Bains and the Excelsior Palace, while at Alberoni, the southernmost settlement on the Lido, beaches are backed by dunes, pine forests, and the greens of the only golf course in Venice. ⏱ 2 hr. Vaporetto: Nos. 1, 41, 42, 51, 52, or 53 to Lido.

6 ★★ **Giudecca.** Once a bucolic getaway for wealthy Venetians, this string of eight connected islands still seems far removed from the bustle of the city. Walks through quiet neighborhoods and visits to three famous churches are the pastimes here. **Il Redentore** (p 370, **5**), the grandest, was begun as an offering to the Redeemer in the midst of a plague outbreak, in 1576. Work on the church continued for 2 decades, and it's now an elegant showcase for the restrained classicism of architect Andrea Palladio. **La Zitelle,** the "church of the spinsters," is so named because young women whose families could not afford a dowry were once sent to the adjoining convent to learn lace making; exile here is a privilege now that the premises house an outpost of the posh Hotel Bauer. The church of **Santa Eufemia** is much older than its Palladian neighbors. It was founded in the 9th century and rebuilt in the 11th century to a Byzantine design. ⏱ 2 hr. Il Redentore: Admission 3€. ☎ 041-2750642. Mon–Sat 10am–5pm. Vaporetto: Redentore.

⑦ 🍴 **Bar San Giorgio.** The view from this waterside terrace, with San Marco across the basin and the lagoon shimmering before you, is almost as captivating as the outlook from the campanile. Isola di San Giorgio Maggiore. ☎ 041-5227827. $

8 ★★★ **San Giorgio Maggiore.** Benedictine monks have inhabited this island across the lagoon from San Marco for more than 1,000 years. They still impose a veil of tranquillity on a stunning complex that includes a church by Andrea Palladio, two cloisters, and a bell tower with heart-stopping city views. The **Fondazione Cini** shares the premises. ⏱ 2 hr. ☎ 041-5227827. Campanile: Admission 3€. Campanile and church: May–Sept Mon–Sat 9am–12:30pm, 2:30–6:30pm; Sun 9:30–10:30am, 2:30–6pm; Oct–Apr daily 9:30am–12:30pm, 2:30–4:30pm. Guided tours of the foundation, including the art collection, baroque staircase by Baldassare Longhena, and cloisters: 12€; Sat–Sun 10am–4:30pm. Vaporetto: San Giorgio.

> *The former fishing and lacemaking community of Burano is instantly identifiable by its colorful houses.*

Getting Active on the Lido

The terrain of the Lido lends itself to outdoor activities. In addition to swimming and relaxing at the beach, you can golf, bike, play tennis, jog, and so on. The 18-hole, par-72 **golf course,** Strada Vecchia 1, Alberoni (☎ 041-7313333; www.circologolfvenezia.it), is the only place to play golf in Venice, and is one of Italy's top courses. It's open April to September Tuesday to Sunday 8am to 8pm; October to March Tuesday to Sunday 8:30am to 6pm. It costs 55€ Monday to Friday, 70€ Saturday and Sunday; cart rental is 35€ for 18 holes.

For **bicycle rentals,** try Gardin Anna Valli, Piazzale Santa Maria Elisabetta (☎ 041-2760005), open May to October 8am to 8pm. Bikes are 2.60€ an hour, 8€ a day.

One of the Lido's best public **tennis** facilities, the Tennis Club Ca' del Moro, Via Ferrucio Parri 6 (☎ 041-770965), is open Monday to Saturday 8:30am to 8:30pm, and Sunday 8:30am to 8pm, and costs 8.50€ per hour.

Venice Shopping Best Bets

Best Silk Ties That Look Like Paper
Alberto Valese-Ebrû, Campo Santo Stefano, San Marco (p 393)

Best Goblets with a Pedigree
Barovier and Toso, Fondamenta dei Vetrai 28, Murano (p 392)

Most Aromatic Shopping Experience
Drogheria Mascari, Calle degli Spezieri, San Polo (p 392)

Best Views of the Grand Canal from a Shop
Genninger Studio, Calle del Traghetto, Dorsoduro (p 388)

Best Source for Announcing Yourself in Style
Gianni Basso, Calle del Fumo, Cannaregio (p 393)

Best Place to Pretend to Be a Gondolier
Gilberto Penzo, Calle Saoneri, San Polo (p 390)

Best Gloves in Town
J. B. Guanti, Calle de l'Ovo, San Marco (p 390)

Best Stop for Exquisite Lace
Jesurum Outlet, Fondamenta della Sensa, Cannaregio (p 390)

Best Stationery That's Sure to Impress
Legatoria Piazzesi, Campiello Feltrina, San Marco (p 393)

Best Handmade Leather Goods North of Florence
Mazzon le Borse, Campiello San Tomà, San Polo (p 390)

Best Place to Hide Behind a Mask
MondoNovo Maschere, Rio Terrà Canal, Dorsoduro (p 391)

Best Place to Look Glamorous on a Budget
Ser Angiù, Piscina del Forner, Dorsoduro (p 390)

Best Paperweights
Sergio Tiozzo, Fondamenta Manin, Murano (p 392)

Best Place to Dip Your Oar in the Water
Spazio Legno, Fondamenta San Giacomo, Giudecca (p 391)

Best Place to Channel Fortuny
Venetia Studium, Calle Larga XXII San Marco (p 392)

Best Place to Fill Your Own Container with Decent Cheap Wine
Vineria Dai Do Cancari, Calle delle Botteghe, San Marco (p 392)

Best Recordings of Baroque Music
Vivaldi Store, Salizzada del Fontego dei Tedeschi, San Marco (p 390)

> *MondoNovo is the best place to buy a Carnevale mask.*

Cannaregio, San Polo & Santa Croce Shopping

Venice Shopping A to Z

Art

★ Cartoleria Accademia DORSODURO
Has Venice inspired you to pick up a brush? This well-stocked shop has been supplying artists for almost 200 years. **Campiello Calbo.** ☎ 041-5207086. AE, MC, V. Vaporetto: Accademia. Map p 389.

★★ Galleria Traghetto SAN MARCO
One of Venice's most respected galleries is well known for showing works by the city's sizable community of painters and sculptors, with an emphasis on abstract painting. **Calle di Piovan.** ☎ 041-5221188. AE, DC, MC, V. Vaporetto: Santa Maria del Giglio. Map p 389.

★★★ Genninger Studio DORSODURO
A salon overlooking the Grand Canal is a showcase for Byzantine-style oil lamps, goblets, jewelry embellished with silver and gold, and other glass creations by American Leslie Ann Genninger. **Calle del Traghetto.** ☎ 041-5225565. www.genningerstudio.com. AE, DC, MC, V. Vaporetto: Ca' Rezzonico. Map p 389.

★★ Schola San Zaccaria SAN MARCO
Venice-born architect and artist Gianfranco Missiaja fills his small gallery with his delightful variations of traditional themes—harlequins here morph into a swirl of sinuous lines. **Gallery: Campo San Maurizio.** ☎ 041-5221209. MC, V. Vaporetto: Santa Maria del Guglio. **Studio: Salizzada dei Greci, Castello.** ☎ 041-5234343. Vaporetto: Arsenale. Map p 389.

★★ Venezia, Le Stampe SAN MARCO
One of the city's best sources for antique prints is filled with a beautiful sampling of their output. **Calle Teatro Goldoni.** ☎ 041-5234318. AE, MC, V. Vaporetto: Rialto. Map p 389.

Books & Music

★ Ca' Foscarina DORSODURO
The bookstore of the University of Venice carries the city's largest selection of books in English, on a wide variety of subjects. **Campiello degli Squellini.** ☎ 041-5229602. AE, DC, MC, V. Vaporetto: San Tomà. Map p 389.

★★ Venice Pavilion Bookshop SAN MARCO
The bookshop of the Venice tourism office is amply stocked with English-language guidebooks and maps, as well as handsome volumes on Venetian art and architecture. **Giardinetti Reali.** ☎ 041-5226356. AE, DC, MC, V. Vaporetto: San Marco. Map p 389.

> *Fortuny lampshades on sale at Venetia Studium.*

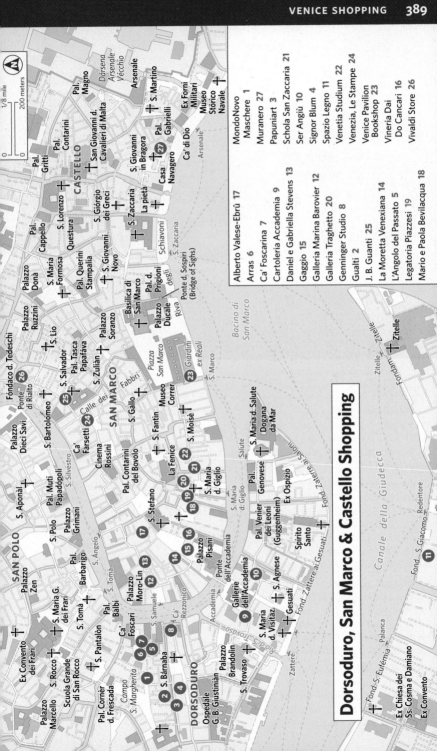

Dorsoduro, San Marco & Castello Shopping

Alberto Valese-Ebrù 17
Arras 6
Ca' Foscarina 7
Cartoleria Accademia 9
Daniele Gabriella Stevens 13
Gaggio 15
Galleria Marina Barovier 12
Galleria Traghetto 20
Genninger Studio 8
Gualti 2
J. B. Guanti 25
La Moretta Venexiana 14
L'Angolo del Passato 5
Legatoria Piazzesi 19
Mario e Paola Bevilacqua 18

MondoNovo
Maschere 1
Muranero 27
Papuniart 3
Schola San Zaccaria 21
Ser Angiù 10
Signor Blum 4
Spazio Legno 11
Venetia Studium 22
Venezia, Le Stampe 24
Venice Pavilion
Bookshop 23
Vineria Dai
Do Cancari 16
Vivaldi Store 26

> *La Cantina sells wines from across the Veneto region.*

★★ Vivaldi Store SAN MARCO
Works by the eponymous composer and other masters line the shelves. Salizzada del Fontego dei Tedeschi. ☎ 041-522-1343. MC, V. Vaporetto: Rialto. Map p 389.

Clothing & Accessories

★ Arras DORSODURO
Woolens and silks, sold by the yard and fashioned into scarves and garments, are woven by a cooperative that employs people with disabilities. Campiello degli Squellini. ☎ 041-5226460. AE, DC, MC, V. Map p 389.

★★★ Gaggio SAN MARCO
Sumptuous, hand-blocked textiles based on old Venetian designs are fashioned into cushions, scarves, and other elegant goods, or sold by the meter. Calle delle Botteghe. ☎ 041-5228574. Vaporetto: San Samuele. Map p 389.

★★★ J. B. Guanti SAN MARCO
Gloves have never looked as appealing as they do here—embellished with sequins, trimmed with fur, and just plain, in sumptuous leather of every shade imaginable. Calle de l'Ovo.

☎ 041-5228633. AE, MC, V. Vaporetto: Rialto. Map p 389.

★★ Mazzon le Borse SAN POLO
Any Venetian can lead you to this store, a well-known local favorite for high-quality, handmade leather goods. Campiello San Tomà. ☎ 041-5203421. AE, DC, MC, V. Vaporetto: San Tomà. Map p 387.

★ Ser Angiù DORSODURO
Designer labels at discounted prices—a winning formula that draws crowds of local shoppers. Piscina del Forner. ☎ 041-5231149. MC, V. Vaporetto: Accademia. Map p 389.

Crafts

★★★ kids Gilberto Penzo SAN POLO
If you marveled over the models of doges' craft in the **Museo Storico Navale** (p 377, **15**), you'll be charmed by these wooden replicas of gondolas and other boats. Calle Saoneri. ☎ 041-719372. MC, V. Vaporetto: San Tomà. Map p 387.

★★★ Jesurum Outlet CANNAREGIO
Venice's most renowned purveyor of lace

> *Davide Penso, on the island of Murano, specializes in glass jewelry.*

traces its origins to Burano almost 150 years ago. Don't let the prices put you off: Affordable items on offer include linen coasters and napkins. Fondamenta della Sensa. ☎ 041-5242540. www.jesurum.it. AE, DC, MC, V. Vaporetto: San'Alvise. Map p 387.

★★ kids **La Bottega dei Mascareri** SAN POLO
The Boldrin brothers sell an amazing variety of masks from their crowded shop at the end of the Rialto Bridge. Calle de Cristo. ☎ 041-5223857. AE, MC, V. Vaporetto: Rialto. Map p 387.

★★★ **La Moretta Venexiana** SAN MARCO
In case you didn't know just how tasteful a *carnevale* mask can be, step into this lovely little shop to see glorious creations crafted in nearby workshops. Calle delle Botteghe. ☎ 041-5228244. MC, V. Vaporetto: San Samuele. Map p 389.

★★★ **MondoNovo Maschere** DORSODURO
Venice's most noted provider of Carnevale masks offers creations in papier-mâché that transform the wearer into just about any conceivable persona, from Renaissance dandy

to mythological beast. Rio Terrà Canal. ☎ 041-5287344. www.mondonovomaschere.it. AE, DC, MC, V. Vaporetto: Ca' Rezzonico. Map p 389.

★★ **Sabbie e Nebbie** SAN POLO
The beautiful pottery and ceramics are from Japan and Italy. Calle dei Nomboli. ☎ 041-719073. MC, V. Vaporetto: San Tomà. Map p 387.

★★ **Signor Blum** DORSODURO
A group of local women fashion wonderful wood models and painted panels of Venetian monuments and scenes, as well as fairy-tale castles and palaces. Campo San Barnaba. ☎ 041-5211399. www.signorblum.com. MC, V. Vaporetto: Ca' Rezzonico. Map p 389.

★★★ **Spazio Legno** GIUDECCA
The business here is making oars, *forcoli* (oar rests), and other wooden components for gondolas. Visitors can walk away with wooden bookmarks shaped like *forcoli* or other small objects made from leftover materials. Fondamenta San Giacomo. ☎ 041-2775505. AE, DC, MC, V. Vaporetto: Redentore. Map p 389.

> *Gaggio is known especially for its textile goods.*

★★ Venetia Studium SAN MARCO

Fortuny-style designs are the distinctive hallmarks of the stunning silk and glass lamps here; they also find their way onto everything from scarves to pillows. Calle Larga XXII (other branches around the city). ☎ 041-5229281. www. venetiastudium.com. AE, DC, MC, V. Vaporetto: Santa Maria del Giglio. Map p 389.

Food & Wine

★★★ Drogheria Mascari SAN POLO

Step in to savor the aromas of spices, coffees, and teas. Huge jars are filled with dried fruits, nuts, and sweets. The selection of olive oil, vinegar, and wine from throughout Italy is probably the best in the city. Calle degli Spezieri. ☎ 041-5229762. No credit cards. Vaporetto: San Silvestro. Map p 387.

★ La Cantina SAN POLO

Bring your own bottle and take your choice: Wines from throughout the Veneto are dispensed from huge vats. Ruga Rialto. ☎ 041-5235042. Vaporetto: Rialto. Map p 387.

★★ Vineria Dai Do Cancari SAN MARCO

A welcoming shop just off Campo Santo

Stefano sells the output of many small vintners and dispenses some excellent local wines from large vats. Calle delle Botteghe. ☎ 041-2410634. MC, V. Vaporetto: San Samuele. Map p 389.

Glass

★★ Amadi SAN POLO

Glass becomes whimsical as it is fashioned into tiny, enchanting animals and sea creatures— the perfect easy-to-carry memento. Calle Saoneri. ☎ 041-5238089. MC, V. Vaporetto: San Silvestro. Map p 387.

★★★ Barovier and Toso MURANO

The most prestigious glass shop in Venice traces its roots to the 13th century, and its creations are regarded as museum pieces. Fondamenta dei Vetrai 28. ☎ 041-739049. www.barovier.com. AE, DC, MC, V. Vaporetto: Colonna. Map p 387.

★★ Galleria Marina Barovier SAN MARCO

One of the city's top showplaces for contemporary designers, run by a member of a distinguished line of glass crafters. Salizzada San Samuele. ☎ 041-5226102. www.barovier.it. No credit cards. Vaporetto: San Samuele. Map p 389.

★★ L'Angolo del Passato DORSODURO

The superb collections of vintage glass here include 19th- and 20th-century Murano pieces rarely on offer. Calle del Capeller. ☎ 041-5287896. AE, DC, MC, V. Vaporetto: Ca' Rezzonico. Map p 389.

★★ Sergio Tiozzo MURANO

The specialty of the house is *murrine,* a technique in which glass flowers are melted together to form colorful mosaic patterns. The designs are well suited to plates, glassware, and vases. Fondamenta Manin. ☎ 041-5274155. AE, MC, V. Vaporetto: Faro. Map p 387.

Jewelry

★★ Daniel e Gabriella Stevens SAN MARCO

Daniel fashions colorful glass and Gabriella creates beautiful traditional and contemporary designs for necklaces and other pieces. Calle delle Carrozze. ☎ 041-5227563. MC, V. Vaporetto: San Samuele. Map p 389.

★★★ Davide Penso MURANO

A top contender for some of Murano's most beautiful jewelry creates stunning contemporary pieces. Fondamenta Riva Longa 48. ☎ 041-5274634. AE, MC, V. Vaporetto: Colonna. Map p 387.

> *Legatoria Piazzesi has been in the paper business for 150 years.*

★★★ **Gualti** DORSODURO
The distinctive contemporary jewelry, each a work of art in bursts of colorful glass, is made on the premises by one of the city's artisans. Rio Terrà Canal. ☎ 041-5201731. www.gualti.it. AE, DC, MC, V. Vaporetto: Ca' Rezzonico. Map p 389.

★★★ **Muranero** CASTELLO
Niang Moulaye combines the art of his native Senegal with Venetian traditions to create exotic pieces in glass. Calle Crosera. ☎ 041-277829. Vaporetto: San Zaccaria. Map p 389.

★★★ **Papuniart** DORSODURO
Ninfa Salerno decided to break away from traditional Venetian glass designs and turned to stones and even PVC for her whimsical and beautiful creations. Ponte dei Pugni. ☎ 041-2410434. MC, V. Vaporetto: Ca' Rezzonico. Map p 389.

Paper & Textiles
★★ **Alberto Valese-Ebrû** SAN MARCO
Aficionados of marbled papers will be delighted to see the technique creatively applied to silk scarves and ties, and to a wide range of paper products. Campo Santo Stefano. ☎ 041-5238830.

AE, DC, MC, V. Vaporetto: San Samuele. Map p 389.

★★ **Gianni Basso** CANNAREGIO
Beautiful papers are personalized with your choice of name and illustration and presented as bookplates, note cards, and stationery. Calle del Fumo. ☎ 041-5234681. MC, V. Vaporetto: Fondamenta Nuove. Map p 387.

★★★ **Legatoria Piazzesi** SAN MARCO
At this 150-year-old shop, frequented by the likes of Ernest Hemingway, handmade papers are sold by the piece and fashioned into boxes, address books, and other enticing items. Campiello Feltrina. ☎ 041-5221202. www.legatoriapiazzesi.it. AE, MC, V. Vaporetto: Santa Maria del Giglio. Map p 389.

★★★ **Mario e Paola Bevilacqua** SAN MARCO
Fine weaving is a time-honored Venetian tradition, and some of the highest quality work emanates from this distinguished shop founded in 1700, which sells brocade, braid work, and fabrics. Campo Santa Maria del Giglio. ☎ 041-2415133. AE, MC, V. Vaporetto: Santa Maria del Giglio. Map p 389.

Venice Restaurant Best Bets

Best Deep-Dish Pizza
Acqua Pazza $$–$$$ Campo Sant'Angelo, San Marco (p 395)

Best Panino with a View
Algiubagiò $ Fondamenta Nuove, Cannaregio (p 395)

Best Place for a Meal on an Out-of-the-Way Square
Alla Frasca $ Corte de la Carità, Cannaregio (p 395)

Best Vegetarian Meal
Alla Zucca $ Ponte del Megio, Santa Croce (p 396)

Best Value for an Excellent Meal
Bea Vita $$ Fondamenta delle Cappuccine (p 398)

Best Place to Get a Whiff of Student Life
Caffè dei Frari $ Fondamenta dei Frari, San Polo (p 398)

Best Panini & Crostini in Town
Cantinone Già Schiavi $ Ponte San Trovaso (p 398)

Best Stop for Carnivores
Dalla Marisa $ Fondamenta San Giobbe, Cannaregio (p 399)

Best Atmosphere for a Quick Bite
Do Mori $ Calle dei Do Mori, San Polo (p 399)

Best Thin-Crust Pizza
Il Refolo $$–$$$ Campiello del Piovan, Santa Croce (p 399)

Best Place to Enjoy Renaissance Recipes & Rare Wines
Le Bistrot de Venise $$$ Calle dei Fabbri, San Marco (p 399)

Best Place to Propose Marriage
Locanda Cipriani $$$$ Piazza Santa Fosca 29, Torcello (p 400)

Best Meal in Town
Osteria da Fiore $$$$ Calle delle Scaleter, San Polo (p 400)

Best Place to Have a Pastry & a Cappuccino
Rosa Salva $ Campo Santi Giovanni e Paolo, Castello (p 376)

> Crostini and panini are popular choices at Cantinone Già Schiavi.

Venice Restaurants A to Z

★★ **Acqua Pazza** SAN MARCO *NEAPOLITAN*
This perennially busy indoor-outdoor pizzeria
is a good place to come with companions with
varying appetites and bankrolls: You can dine
simply and moderately on the delicious, deep-
dish Neapolitan pies or sample one of the many
fish and seafood dishes. Campo Sant'Angelo.
☎ 041-2770688. Entrees 9€–25€. AE, DC, MC, V.
Lunch & dinner Tues–Sun. Vaporetto: Sant'Angelo.
Map p 396.

★★★ **Al Gatto Nero** BURANO *VENETIAN/
SEAFOOD* A delicious meal of fresh fish or
seafood pasta comes with a view of Burano's
fish market across the canal by day and quiet
island life in the evening. Fondamenta della
Giudecca. ☎ 041-730120. Entrees 19€–35€. AE,
DC, MC, V. Lunch & dinner Tues–Sun. Vaporetto:
Burano. Map p 397.

★★ **Algiubagiò** CANNAREGIO *CAFE*
The terrace provides a view of the busy
vaporetto stop, the departure point for the
islands. Before boarding, fortify yourself with
a sandwich or grab a slice of pizza from the

adjoining counter to take with you; by night, a
dining room is the setting for excellent pastas
and seafood. Fondamenta Nuove. ☎ 041-5227949.
Entrees 3€–8€; at night 14€–22€. AE, DC, MC,
V. Breakfast, lunch & dinner daily. Vaporetto:
Fondamenta Nuove. Map p 397.

★★ **Alla Frasca** CANNAREGIO *VENETIAN*
You'll feel you've been transported to a village
square at this simple, out-of-the-way place
that dispenses deliciously fresh seafood and
hearty pastas on a vine-covered terrace and
in an unfussy room. Corte de la Carità. ☎ 041-
5285433. Entrees 10€–15€. No credit cards. Lunch
& dinner Mon–Sat. Closed 1 week in Aug, 2 weeks
Dec–Jan. Vaporetto: Fondamenta Nuove. Map
p 397.

★★★ **Alla Madonna** SAN POLO *VENETIAN/
SEAFOOD* As befits a location near the Rialto
fish market, this clamorous, charming trattoria
serves the freshest fish and seafood available,
in such classic Venetian preparations as rich
zuppa di pesce (fish soup) and *vermicelli al nero
di seppia* (vermicelli with a sauce of cuttlefish

> *The menu at Anticolo Dolo relies on nearby fresh produce markets.*

San Marco & Dorsoduro Restaurants

Acqua Pazza 6
Alla Madonna 2
Alle Testiere 4
Ca é dei Frari 1
Cantinone Già Schiavi 7
Le Bistrot de Venise 5
Lineadombra 9
Osteria I Rusteghi 3
Terrazza del Casin del Nobili 8

ink). Calle della Madonna. ☎ 041-5223824. Entrees 9€–15€. AE, MC, V. Lunch & dinner Thurs–Tues. Closed Jan, 2 weeks in Aug. Vaporetto: Rialto. Map p 396.

★★ **Alla Zucca** SANTA CROCE ITALIAN/ VEGETARIAN The emphasis here is on vegetarian cooking, which, given the bounty of the Veneto, is not to be overlooked. But deftly prepared fish and lamb dishes also appear on the menu. Ponte del Megio. ☎ 041-5241570. Entrees 9€–17€. AE, DC, MC, V. Lunch & dinner Mon–Sat. Vaporetto: San Stae. Map p 397.

★★★ **Alle Testiere** CASTELLO VENETIAN/ SEAFOOD One of Venice's trendiest and most hyped restaurants well deserves its fame, serving aromatic seafood dishes, fine wines, and excellent cheeses in causal-chic surroundings. Calle del Mondo Novo. ☎ 041-5227220. Entrees 19€–30€. MC, V. Lunch & dinner Tues–Sun. Vaporetto: Rialto. Map p 396.

★★★ **Anice Stellato** CANNAREGIO VENETIAN The pleasant ambience of the small beamed rooms is complemented with exceptionally good preparations of fish and such classics

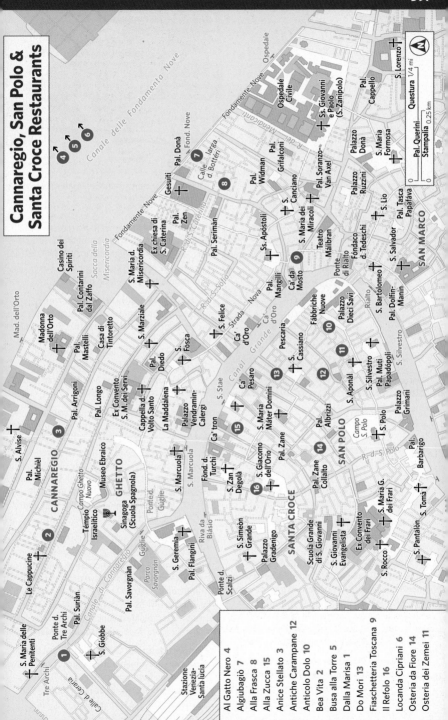

Cannaregio, San Polo & Santa Croce Restaurants

Al Gatto Nero 4
Algiubagiò 7
Alla Frasca 8
Alla Zucca 15
Anice Stellato 3
Antiche Carampane 12
Anticolo Dolo 10
Bea Vita 2
Busa alla Torre 5
Dalla Marisa 1
Do Mori 13
Fiaschetteria Toscana 9
Il Refolo 16
Locanda Cipriani 6
Osteria da Fiore 14
Osteria dei Zemei 11

> Venice's best seafood eateries buy their catch daily at the renowned Rialto markets.

> Your evening at Bea Vita starts with a complimentary glass of sparkling Prosecco.

as *fegato alla veneziana* (calf's liver, Venetian style, sautéed with onions). Fondamenta della Sensa. ☎ 041-5238153. Entrees 14€–24€. MC, V. Lunch & dinner Wed–Sun. Closed 3 weeks in Aug. Vaporetto: Fondamenta Nuove. Map p 397.

★★★ **Antiche Carampane** SAN POLO *VENETIAN/SEAFOOD* The place is almost impossible to find, and a sign announcing "NO PIZZA. NO LASAGNA. NO TELEPHONE. NO TOURIST MENU" is less than welcoming—but persevere: The excellent and exotic seafood pastas and sophisticated fish preparations will win you over. Rio Terà della Carampane. ☎ 041-5240165. Entrees 19€–26€. MC, V. Lunch & dinner Tues–Sat. Vaporetto: San Silvestro. Map p 397.

★★★ **Anticolo Dolo** SAN POLO *VENETIAN/SEAFOOD* The nearby fruit and vegetable markets supply the freshest ingredients for homemade pastas with seafood and perfectly prepared

fish, served in a cramped narrow room hung with brass pots and old photographs. Ruga Vecchia San Giovanni (Ruga Rialto). ☎ 041-5226546. Entrees 19€–26€. AE, DC, V. Lunch & dinner Tues–Sun. Vaporetto: Rialto. Map p 397.

★★★ **Bea Vita** CANNAREGIO *VENETIAN* A complimentary glass of Prosecco sets the tone for an amiable meal that features homemade pastas and fresh fish and meat in innovative preparations. Fondamenta delle Cappuccine. ☎ 041-2759347. Entrees 18€–23€. AE, MC, V. Lunch & dinner Mon–Sat. Vaporetto: Fondamenta Nuove. Map p 397.

★★★ **Busa alla Torre** MURANO *VENETIAN/SEAFOOD* Escape the island's glass-shop craze and take a seat in the pleasant dining room or on the terrace beneath the bell tower—the welcome respite includes an excellent meal of such specialties as *ravioli di pesce*. Campo Santo Stefano. ☎ 041-739662. Entrees 13.50€–20€. AE, MC, V. Lunch & dinner Mon–Sat. Vaporetto: Colonna. Map p 397.

★★ **Caffè dei Frari** SAN POLO *CAFE* This cozy nook is popular with students from the university and provides a nice refuge for weary visitors to the nearby Frari and Scuola Grande di San Rocco (p 372, ⑫). Fondamenta dei Frari. ☎ 041-5241877. Entrees 3€–6€. No credit cards. Breakfast, lunch & dinner Mon–Fri; dinner Sat–Sun. Vaporetto: San Tomà. Map p 396.

★★★ kids **Cantinone Già Schiavi** DORSODURO *WINE BAR* This neighborhood institution draws large crowds for its delicious panini, along with a tempting array of crostini topped with cheeses, vegetables, or smoked fish. They

> *The dining room at Le Bistrot de Venise.*

> *Terrace dining and tasty pizzas are a hit at Il Refolo.*

should be accompanied by a glass of one of the many house wines. Ponte San Trovaso. ☎ 041-5230034. Entrees 4€–7€. No credit cards. Breakfast, lunch & dinner Mon–Sat; breakfast & lunch Sun. Vaporetto: Accademia. Map p 396.

★★★ **Dalla Marisa** CANNAREGIO ITALIAN No serious carnivore should leave Venice without enjoying at least one meal at this simple and inexpensive *osteria* near the Ponte di Tre Archi. Old-fashioned ways still hold sway in the kitchen, which sends out traditional preparations of *osso buco* (braised veal shanks), *trippa* (tripe), and other classics. Fondamenta San Giobbe. ☎ 041-720-211. Entrees 9€–14€. No credit cards. Lunch & dinner Tues, Thurs–Fri; lunch Sat–Mon. Closed Aug. Vaporetto: Tre Archi. Map p 397.

★★ **Do Mori** SAN POLO VENETIAN/WINE BAR This dark, battered-looking place situated in the midst of the Rialto markets has been

dispensing wine and tidbits of fish, meats, and cheeses for some 6 centuries; it still packs in an appreciative crowd of regulars. Calle dei Do Mori. ☎ 041-5225401. Entrees 2€–3€. No credit cards. Breakfast, lunch & dinner Mon–Sat. Vaporetto: Rialto. Map p 397.

★★ **Fiaschetteria Toscana** CANNAREGIO VENETIAN/ITALIAN The name refers to the Tuscan wines and oils once stored and sold from the elegant premises. These days the offerings are such Venetian specialties as grilled sardines and *fegato alla veneziana* (calf's liver). Salizzada San Giovanni Grisostomo. ☎ 041-5285281. Entrees 18€–40€. AE, DC, MC, V. Dinner Mon; lunch & dinner Wed–Sun. Vaporetto: Rialto. Map p 397.

★★★ **kids** **Il Refolo** SANTA CROCE PIZZA/ MEDITERRANEAN Venetians arrive at the canal-side tables in droves for the excellent pizzas with such exotic toppings as roasted figs. This warm-weather-only hit was established by the clan that operates Osteria da Fiore (see below). Campiello del Piovan. ☎ 041-5240016. Entrees 15€–30€. AE, MC, V. Lunch & dinner Wed–Sun; dinner Tues. Closed Nov–Mar. Vaporetto: Riva di Biasio. Map p 397.

★★★ **Le Bistrot de Venise** SAN MARCO VENETIAN Ages-old Venetian recipes and rare, special-production wines are paired for a memorable dining experience in sophisticated surroundings. Calle dei Fabbri. ☎ 041-5236651. Entrees 14€–28€. AE, MC, V. Lunch & dinner daily. Vaporetto: Rialto. Map p 396.

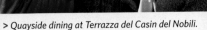

> *Quayside dining at Terrazza del Casin del Nobili.*

> *The chic interior of Lineadombra.*

★★★ **Lineadombra** DORSODURO *VENETIAN*
The sleek dining room and sporty waterside terrace seem ready-made for patrons of the new contemporary art museum next door, and add zest to such innovative pairings as tuna tartare and sea bass. Ponte dell'Umiltà. ☎ 041-2411881. Entrees 15€–25€. AE, DC, MC, V. Lunch & dinner daily. Closed Jan–Feb. Vaporetto: Salute. Map p 396.

★★★ **Locanda Cipriani** TORCELLO *VENETIAN/ SEAFOOD* For many devotees, the sole purpose of a trip to this enchanting island in the lagoon is a meal on the shady terrace of this sophisticated, rustic hotel. To add one more ingredient to a romantic evening here, arrange for transport in the hotel's private launch (about 20€ a person). Piazza Santa Fosca 29. ☎ 041-730150. Entrees 25€–40€. AE, DC, MC, V. Lunch & dinner Wed–Mon. Closed Jan. Vaporetto: Torcello. Map p 397.

★★★ **Osteria da Fiore** SAN POLO *VENETIAN/ SEAFOOD* The Martin family has earned a Michelin star along with a reputation for serving the best food in Venice, for offerings that include a vast selection of seafood antipasti, elegant pasta dishes, and such flavorful entrees as sea bass in balsamic vinegar. Calle delle Scaleter. ☎ 041-721308. Entrees 20€–40€. AE, DC, MC, V. Lunch & dinner Tues–Sat. Closed Aug. Vaporetto: San Stae. Map p 397.

★★ **Osteria dei Zemei** SAN POLO *ITALIAN/ WINE BAR* This neighborhood favorite on a delightful little square makes tempting crostini, *paninetti* (single-bite sandwiches), and a few choice pasta dishes. Rughetta del Ravano. ☎ 041-5208546. Entrees 10€–15€. MC, V. Lunch & dinner daily. Vaporetto: Rialto. Map p 397.

★★ **Osteria I Rusteghi** RIALTO/SAN MARCO *WINE BAR* A secluded courtyard is a quiet setting for a platter of cheese and salami or one of the 28 kinds of bite-size *paninetti* sandwiches on offer here. Corte del Tentor. ☎ 041-5232205. Entrees 5€–8€. Lunch & dinner Mon–Sat. Vaporetto: Rialto. Map p 396.

★★ **Terrazza del Casin del Nobili** DORSODURO *VENETIAN* An outpost of the popular trattoria of the same name near Campo San Barnaba adds views over the Giudecca Canal from an airy dining room and a summertime terrace. Deft preparations of traditional favorites such as *schie* (tiny shrimp) on a bed of polenta, zucchini flowers, and roast rabbit prove that there's more to this place than a great setting. Zattere. ☎ 041-5206895. Entrees 12€–22€. AE, MC, V. Lunch & dinner Tues–Sun. Vaporetto: Zattere. Map p 396.

Venice Hotel Best Bets

Most Hospitable Innkeepers
Al Ponte Mocenigo $$ Fondamenta Rimpetto Mocenigo, San Polo (p 402)

Best Place to Feel You're Staying in an Elegant Venetian Home
Ca' della Corte $$ Corte Surion, Dorsoduro (p 402)

Hippest Hotel
Ca' Pisani $$$ Rio Terrà Antonio Foscarini, Dorsoduro (p 403)

Best Lobby
Danieli $$$$ Riva degli Schiavoni, Castello (p 403)

Most Stylish Small Inn
DD.724 $$$ Rio Terrà Antonio Foscarini, Dorsoduro (p 405)

Best Place to Be Pampered in Luxury
Gritti Palace $$$$ Campo Santa Maria del Giglio, San Marco (p 405)

Best Place to Hang Out by the Pool
Hotel Cipriani $$$$ Giudecca 10, Giudecca (p 405)

Best Palace Hotel for the Money
La Residenza $-$$ Campo Bandiera e Moro, Castello (p 406)

Best Medieval Garret Experience
La Villeggiatura $$-$$$ Calle dei Botteri, San Polo (p 406)

Best Place to Get Away from It All
Locanda Cipriani $$$-$$$$ Piazza Santa Fosca 29, Torcello (p 406)

Best Value Family Suites
Locanda San Barnaba $$ Calle del Traghetto, Dorsoduro (p 406)

Best Romantic Hideaway
Oltre il Giardino $$-$$$ Fondamenta Contarini, San Polo (p 407)

Best Hotel Garden
Pensione Accademia/Villa Maravege $$-$$$ Fondamenta Bollani, Dorsoduro (p 407)

Best Old-Fashioned *Pensione* Experience
Pensione Seguso $$ Fondamenta Zattere ai Gesuati, Dorsoduro (p 407)

> *The Danieli has the grandest lobby in Venice.*

Venice Hotels A to Z

★★★ Al Ponte Mocenigo SAN POLO
In this enchanting palazzo behind a pretty canalside courtyard, large and atmospheric rooms are complemented by modern amenities, including a steam room—as well as a great deal of old-fashioned hospitality from the owners. Fondamenta Rimpetto Mocenigo. ☎ 041-5244797. www.alpontemocenigo.com. 10 units. Doubles 95€–145€. AE, MC, V. Vaporetto: San Stae. Map p 403.

★ Antica Locanda Montin DORSODURO
A pretty garden; a homey, low-key atmosphere; a downstairs trattoria; and even views of a small canal—along with bargain prices for the location—compensate for the worn decor and fairly spartan amenities. Fondamenta Eremite. ☎ 041-5227151. www.locandamontin.com. 12 units. Doubles 85€–110€. AE, MC, V. Vaporetto: Accademia. Map p 404.

★★ Bauer/Bauer Il Palazzo/Bauer Palladio
SAN MARCO/GIUDECCA Choose between an 18th-century palazzo on the Grand Canal, a 1950s addition, or the converted convent of La Zitelle on Giudecca. Rooms vary from grandiose antique-filled suites to some that look like Hollywood movie sets from the 1930s. Guests in San Marco enjoy a stunning rooftop terrace, while the Giudecca outpost is backed by an enormous and luxuriant garden. A solar-powered craft ferries guests between the San Marco and Giudecca properties. Campo San Moisè, San Marco; or Fondamenta delle Zitelle, Giudecca. ☎ 041-5207022. www.bauervenezia.it. 227 units. Doubles 400€–550€. MC, V. Vaporetto: San Marco/Vallaresso or Zitelle. Map p 403 and p 404.

★★★ kids Ca' della Corte DORSODURO
Behind a welcoming entrance court is one of Venice's most charming small inns, with extremely comfortable character-filled rooms, a roof terrace, and a garden. Several apartments are also available. Corte Surian. ☎ 041-715877. www.cadellacorte.com. 7 units. Doubles 110€–125€. MC, V. Vaporetto: Piazzale Roma. Map p 403.

★★★ Ca' Maria Adele DORSODURO
Hip has arrived in Venice with a bang—a taste-

> *The grounds at the Bauer Palladio on the Giudecca.*

Santa Croce, San Polo & San Marco Hotels

ul bang. Be it contemporary or antique, 1950s style or Moroccan, the eclectic decor in the public spaces and themed guest rooms here is elegant and rather exciting, sometimes over the top, but always with an eye toward comfort. Rio Terà dei Catacumeni. ☎ 041-5203078. www. camariaadele.it. 12 units. Doubles 250€–450€. MC, V. Vaporetto: Salute. Map p 404.

★★ Ca' Pisani DORSODURO

A 16th-century palazzo, art moderne furnishings, and wonderful contemporary paintings blend harmoniously in this high-

design, high-chic, and extremely comfortable hostelry. But some traditional elements, such as the quiet neighborhood and proximity to the Accademia, are also part of the appeal. Rio Terrà Antonio Foscarini 979A. ☎ 041-2401411. www.capisanihotel.it. 29 units. Doubles 213€– 435€. MC, V. Vaporetto: Accademia. Map p 404.

★★★ Danieli SAN MARCO

A marble-clad entrance to a 13th-century doge's palace wins the prize for the best lobby in Venice, and the rooms upstairs in what is one of the finest hotels anywhere are no less

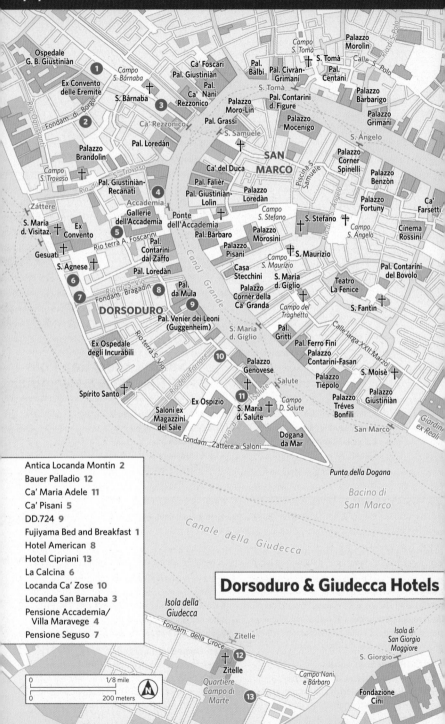

Ospedale
G. B. Giustiniàn

Ex Convento
delle Eremite

Campo
S. Bárnaba

Ca' Foscari
Pal. Giustiniàn

Pal. Balbi

Campo
S. Tomà

Pal. Civràn-
Grimani

S. Tomà

Calle S. Polo

Palazzo
Morolin

Palazzo
Morolin

Pal.
Centani

S. Bárnaba

Ca' Nani
Rezzonico

Pal.

S. Tomà

Pal. Contarini
d. Figure

Palazzo
Barbarigo

Ca' Rezzonico

Palazzo
Moro-Lin

Palazzo
Mocenigo

Palazzo
Grimani

Pal. Grassi

S. Samuèle

S. Ángelo

Pal. Loredàn

Palazzo
Brandolin

Campo
S. Trovaso

Pal. Giustiniàn-
Recanati

Ca' del Duca

Pal. Falièr

Pal. Giustiniàn-
Lolin

SAN
MARCO

Palazzo
Corner
Spinelli

Palazzo
Benzòn

Palazzo
Fortuny

Ca'
Farsetti

Záttere

Accademia

Gallerie
dell'Accademia

Ponte
dell'Accademia

Palazzo
Loredàn

Campo
S. Stefano

S. Stefano

Cínema
Rossini

S. Maria
d. Visitaz.

Ex
Convento

Rio terrà A. Foscarini

Pal.
Contarini
dal Zaffo

Pal. Bárbaro

Campo
S. Ángelo

Gesuati

Palazzo
Morosini

Palazzo
Pisani

Campo
S. Maurízio

S. Maurízio

Pal. Contarini
del Bovolo

S. Agnese

Casa
Stecchini

S. Maria
d. Gíglio

Teatro
La Fenice

Pal. Loredàn

Palazzo
Corner della
Ca' Granda

Campo del
Traghetto

S. Fantin

DORSODURO

Pal.
da Mula

Pal. Venier dei Leoni
(Guggenheim)

S. Maria
d. Gíglio

Pal.
Gritti

Calle larga XXII Marzo

Ex Ospedale
degli Incurábili

Canal Grande

Pal. Ferro Fini

Palazzo
Contarini-Fasan

S. Moisè

Spírito Santo

Palazzo
Genovese

Salute

Palazzo
Tiépolo

Palazzo
Giustiniàn

Giardini
ex Reáli

Saloni ex
Magazzini
del Sale

Ex Ospizio

S. Maria
d. Salute

Campo
D. Salute

Palazzo
Tréves
Bonfili

San Marco

Fondam. Zattere ai Saloni

Dogana
da Mar

Punta della Dogana

Bacino di
San Marco

Canale della Giudecca

Isola della
Giudecca

Fondam. della Croce

Zitelle

Dorsoduro & Giudecca Hotels

Isola di
San Giorgio
Maggiore

S. Giorgio

Zitelle

Quartiere
Campo di
Marte

Campo Nani
e Bárbaro

Fondazione
Cini

0   1/8 mile

0   200 meters

pulent. Riva degli Schiavoni. ☎ 041-5226480. www.starwood.com/luxury. 235 units. Doubles 10€–650€. AE, D, MC, V. Vaporetto: San Zaccaria. Map p 403.

★★ DD.724 DORSODURO

A contemporary, sophisticated style pervades this chic little inn, tucked away near the museums, Salute, and other prime Dorsoduro sights. Rio Terrà Antonio Foscarini. ☎ 041-770262. www.dd724.it. 8 units. Doubles 280€–00€. MC, V. Vaporetto: Accademia. Map p 404.

★★ Domus Ciliota SAN MARCO

The modern rooms in this former monastery are small and utilitarian, but they surround a flower-filled cloister and are an extremely good value. Calle delle Muneghe. ☎ 041-5204989. www.ciliota.it. 51 units. Doubles 90€–140€. MC, . Vaporetto: San Samuele. Map p 403.

Fujiyama Bed and Breakfast DORSODURO

An air of calm pervades these four attractive rooms, each named after the well-traveled owners' favorite cities (Tokyo, Harbin, Shanghai, and Paris). Venice's only Japanese tea room is downstairs, along with a lovely rear garden. Calle Lunga San Barnaba. ☎ 041-241042. www.bedandbreakfast-fujiyama.it. 4 units. Doubles 72€–160€. AE, MC, V. Vaporetto: Ferrovia. Map p 404.

★★ Gritti Palace SAN MARCO

Doge Andrea Gritti built this palazzo on the Grand Canal in 1525, and the sheen of luxury hasn't faded since—the Gritti is a top choice for guests who expect to be pampered amid all the trappings of grandeur. Campo Santa Maria del Giglio. ☎ 041-794611. www.starwood.com/luxury. units. Doubles 550€–850€. AE, DC, MC, V. aporetto: San Zaccaria. Map p 403.

★★ Hotel American DORSODURO

Large rooms furnished in antique Venetian style provide just the right atmosphere for a retreat in this quiet corner of the Dorsoduro neighborhood. In some rooms, flower-filled balconies overlooking a small canal add an extra dose of charm. Fondamenta Bragadin. 041-5204733. www.hotelamerican.com. 30 units. Doubles 80€–310€. AE, MC, V. Vaporetto: Accademia. Map p 404.

★★ Hotel Cipriani GIUDECCA

This getaway reached by private launch pam-

> *Ca' della Corte offers charming rooms as well as apartments.*

pers guests with luxurious accommodations in a cluster of centuries-old buildings. Amenities include a gorgeous swimming pool, a spa, tennis courts, lush gardens, and waterside bars and restaurants. Giudecca 10. ☎ 041-5207744. www.hotelcipriani.it. 96 units. Doubles 625€–815€. MC, V. Closed Nov–Mar. Vaporetto: Zitelle. Map p 404.

★★★ Hotel Saturnia and International

SAN MARCO It looks like another standard big hotel on the well-trodden path between San Marco and the Rialto—but this 14th-century palazzo houses a delightful warren of large and individually decorated rooms that blend traditional Venetian, Art Deco, and contemporary decor. A garden and roof terrace are welcome retreats from the busy neighborhood. Via XXII Marzo. ☎ 041-5208377. www.hotelsaturnia.it. 93 units. Doubles:

> *DD.724 packs a high style quotient.*

140€–240€. AE, MC, V. Vaporetto: San Marco/
Vallaresso. Map p 403.

★★★ La Calcina DORSODURO
British essayist John Ruskin wrote part of *The
Stones of Venice* here, and the years have been
kind to this pleasantly old-fashioned hotel
overlooking the Giudecca Canal. Fondamenta
Zattere ai Gesuati. ☎ 041-5206466. www.
lacalcina.com. 29 units. Doubles 99€–158€. MC,
V. Vaporetto: Zattere or Accademia. Map p 404.

★★ La Fenice et des Artistes SAN MARCO
This favorite with opera buffs and stars from
the nearby Fenice theater encompasses
two 19th-century palaces and offers homey,
comfortable rooms (all with new bathrooms),
rather grand public areas, and even a pretty
little garden. Campiello della Fenice. ☎ 041-
5232333. www.fenicehotels.it. 70 units. Doubles
150€–280€. AE, D, MC, V. Vaporetto: Santa Maria
del Giglio. Map p 403.

★★★ La Residenza CASTELLO
Top prize for palatial and atmospheric lodgings
at a good price goes to this old-fashioned
pensione that occupies the 15th-century Palazzo
Gritti Badoer. The lobby is a period piece of
polished wood, chandeliers, and oil paintings,
while the large high-ceiling guest rooms
have all been beautifully refurbished with
reproduction antiques. Campo Bandiera e Moro.
☎ 041-5285315. www.veniceларesidenza.com. 14
units. Doubles 80€–180€. AE, MC, V. Vaporetto:
Arsenale. Map p 403.

★★ La Villeggiatura SAN POLO
At the top of a series of external staircases, a
wonderfully airy and stylish retreat is tucked
under the heavily beamed ceilings of the top
floors of a medieval palace. Calle dei Botteri.
☎ 041-5244673. www.lavilleggiatura.com. 6 units.
Doubles 140€–180€. MC, V. Vaporetto: Rialto.
Map p 403.

★★ Locanda Ca' Zose DORSODURO
A quiet and sunny corner just steps from
Salute, the Centro d'Arte Contemporeana,
and the Guggenheim offers a pretty lounge/
breakfast room, large attractive guest rooms,
and attentive service from the charming
Campanati sisters. Calle del Bastion. ☎ 041-
5226635. www.hotelcazose.com. 12 units.
Doubles 85€–155€. MC, V. Vaporetto: Salute. Map
p 404.

★★★ Locanda Cipriani TORCELLO
A much-touted celebrity retreat—which
includes a lovely garden and a noted restaurant
(p 400)—lives up to its rep as a haven of
casual elegance. Best of all, guests have the
enchanting island almost to themselves when
the day-trippers leave. Piazza Santa Fosca 29.
☎ 041-730150. www.locandacipriani.com. 6 units.
Doubles 240€–340€. AE, DC, MC, V. Vaporetto:
Torcello. Map p 403.

★★★ kids Locanda San Barnaba DORSODURO
The pretty garden and sunny roof terrace make
it difficult to spend too much time indoors, but
the guest rooms in this fine old palazzo are
delightful—crisscrossed by ancient timbers and
nicely done up with Turkish carpets, painted
bureaus, and plump armchairs. The two-level
junior suites are handy for travelers with kids
in tow. Calle del Traghetto. ☎ 041-2411233. www.
locanda-sanbarnaba.com. 13 units. Doubles

> *Bedrooms are large at Al Ponte Mocenigo.*

120€–170€. AE, MC, V. Vaporetto: Ca' Rezzonico. Map p 404.

★★ Oltre il Giardino SAN POLO
The former home of Gustav Mahler's widow is tucked into a luxuriant garden next to a canal and provides the aura of a country retreat—not dispelled by the handsome and beautifully furnished rooms and suites and excellent service. Fondamenta Contarini. ☎ 041-2750015. www.oltreilgiardino-venezia.com. 9 units. Doubles 150€–250€. AE, MC, V. Vaporetto: San Tomà. Map p 403.

★★★ Pensione Accademia/Villa Maravege
DORSODURO A patrician villa that served as the Russian consulate until the 1930s still exudes the air of a private home, with antique-filled rooms and two large gardens. If the place looks familiar, there's good reason: It's the charming spot where Katharine Hepburn's character stayed in the David Lean movie *Summertime.*

> *The garden at Oltre il Giardino.*

Fondamenta Bollani. ☎ 041-5210188. www.pensioneaccademia.it. 27 units. Doubles 140€–250€. AE, MC, V. Vaporetto: Accademia. Map p 404.

★★★ Pensione Seguso DORSODURO
Many of the guests have stayed here many times before, and it's easy to see the appeal of the homey, old-fashioned ambience, stunning views of the Giudecca Canal, and waterside terrace. Fondamenta Zattere ai Gesuati. ☎ 041-5222340. www.pensionesegusovenice.com. 34 units. Doubles 124€–180€. AE, MC, V. Vaporetto: Zattere or Accademia. Map p 404.

Venice Nightlife & Entertainment Best Bets

Best Place to Watch a Movie under the Stars
Arena di Campo San Polo, Campo San Polo
(p 410)

Best Place to Hear an Organ Recital
Santa Maria Gloriosa dei Frari, Campo dei Frari,
San Polo (p 411)

Best Place to Lose Your Fortune
Casino Municipale, Palazzo Vendramin Calergi,
Fondamenta Vendramin, Cannaregio (p 410)

Best British Pub
Devil's Forest, Calle Stagneri, San Marco
(p 409)

**Best Place to See the Rich & Famous, and the
Rich & Not So Famous**
Harry's Bar, Calle Vallaresso, San Marco (p 409)

Best Place to See an Opera
La Fenice, Campo San Fantin, San Marco (p 411)

**Best Place to See Young Venetians Peacocking
Around in the Wee Hours**
Margaret Duchamp, Campo Santa Margherita,
Dorsoduro (p 409)

Best Place to Hear Early Music
Museo della Fondazione Querini Stampalia,
Campo Santa Maria Formosa, Castello (p 410)

Best Place to Bump into Venetian Youth
Piccolo Mondo, Calle Contarini Corfù, Dorsoduro
(p 409)

Best Latin Sounds
Round Midnight, Fondamenta dei Pugni,
Dorsoduro (p 409)

Best View of Venice
Skyline Bar, Hilton Molino Stucky, Giudecca 810,
Giudecca (p 410)

Best Place to Hear a Symphony
Teatro Malibran, Calle del Milion, Cannaregio
(p 411)

> *La Fenice is one of Italy's great opera houses.*

Venice Nightlife & Entertainment A to Z

Bars & Clubs

★★ Bar al Teatro SAN MARCO
Venice's favorite hangout for theatergoers is situated next door to La Fenice. **Campo San Fantin.** ☎ 041-5221052. Vaporetto: Sant'Angelo. Map p 410.

★★★ Caffè Florian SAN MARCO
What is probably Venice's most famous cafe—the Gran Caffè Quadri, across the square, comes in at a close second—has lost none of its allure since its doors opened in 1720. **Piazza San Marco.** ☎ 041-5205641. www.caffeflorian.com. Vaporetto: San Marco/Vallaresso. Map p 410.

★ Devil's Forest SAN MARCO
The dartboard, London phone box, and afternoon teas are a hit with Anglophiles. **Calle Stagneri.** ☎ 041-5200623. Vaporetto: Rialto. Map p 410.

★★★ Harry's Bar SAN MARCO
Two reasons to make a stop at this Venetian institution: The Bellini (the sparkling wine/peach-juice concoction that's become a brunch-time staple) was invented here, and Hemingway, along with legions of other celebs, drank here. **Calle Vallaresso.** ☎ 041-5285777. www.cipriani.com. Vaporetto: San Marco/Vallaresso. Map p 410.

★★ Margaret Duchamp DORSODURO
One of Venice's most popular hangouts keeps the *campo* animated well into the wee hours. **Campo Santa Margherita.** ☎ 041-286255. Vaporetto: Ca' Rezzonico. Map p 410.

★ Piccolo Mondo DORSODURO
Students from the nearby university get their local disco fix at this small, intimate club, one of very few places in town where you can dance the night away. **Calle Contarini Corfù.** ☎ 041-5200371. Vaporetto: Accademia. Map p 410.

★ Round Midnight DORSODURO
Latin sounds prevail on a tiny, cramped dance floor near the university. **Fondamenta dei Pugni.** ☎ 041-5232056. Vaporetto: Accademia. Map p 410.

> *Venetians parade in* maschera *at Carnevale and in various outdoor performances.*

Venice Nightlife & Entertainment

Arena di Campo San Polo 11
Bar al Teatro 10
Caffè Florian 7
Casino Municipale 1
Devil's Forest 4
Harry's Bar 8
La Fenice 9
Margaret Duchamp 13

Museo della Fondazione Querini Stampalia 6
Piccolo Mondo 15
Round Midnight 14
Santa Maria Formosa 5
Santa Maria Gloriosa dei Frari 12
Skyline Bar 16
Teatro Fondamenta Nuove 2
Teatro Malibran 3

★★ Skyline Bar GIUDECCA

The lights of La Serenissima twinkle at your feet from this perch high atop the Hilton Hotel. Hilton Molino Stucky, Giudecca 810. ☎ 041-272331. Vaporetto: Palanca. Map p 410.

Casinos

★★★ Casino Municipale CANNAREGIO

The surroundings, a 15th-century palace on the Grand Canal, can soften a loss. Palazzo Vendramin Calergi, Fondamenta Vendramin. ☎ 041-5297111. Vaporetto: San Marcuola. No admission without passport; jacket for men required. Map p 410.

Cinema

★★ Arena di Campo San Polo SAN POLO

The square becomes a free outdoor cinema for 6 weeks every summer. Campo San Polo. www.venicebanana.com. Late July to early Sept 9:30pm. Vaporetto: San Tomà. Map p 410.

Classical Music

★★ Museo della Fondazione Querini Stampalia CASTELLO Half-hour recitals of Renaissance and baroque music at the museum-palazzo are a nice appetizer for an evening in Venice. Campo Santa Maria Formosa. ☎ 041-2711411. www.querinistampalia.it. Recitals: Fri–Sat 5 & 8:30pm. Vaporetto: Rialto. Map p 410.

> *The rooftop Skyline Bar at Venice's Hilton.*

★★ **Santa Maria Formosa** CASTELLO
Collegium Ducale, a baroque ensemble,
performs 3 or 4 nights a week throughout the
year in this 15th-century church (for details,
see p 376, ⑧), which also hosts many visiting
choirs. Campo Santa Maria Formosa. Church:
☎ 041-2750462. Admission 3€. Mon–Sat
10am–5pm. Collegium: ☎ 041-984252. www.
collegiumducale.com. Tickets 20€–25€. Box office
open from 10:30am on days of performance.
Vaporetto: Rialto. Map p 410.

★ **Santa Maria Gloriosa dei Frari** SAN POLO
This massive, art-filled church hosts a fall and
spring series of church music and recitals on
the church's organs. Campo dei Frari. ☎ 041-
719308. Vaporetto: San Tomà. Map p 410.

★★★ **Teatro Malibran** CANNAREGIO
This 17th-century theater is often the venue for
concerts by the orchestra of La Fenice, and also
hosts other concerts and dance performances.
Calle del Milion. ☎ 899-909090. www.
teatrolafenice.it. Vaporetto: Rialto. Map p 410.

Opera
★★★ **La Fenice** SAN MARCO
The November-to-June season at the opera
house includes a roster of classic and
contemporary operas performed by some of
the world's greatest voices. Campo San Fantin.
☎ 041-786575. www.teatrolafenice.it. Tickets
35€–200€. Vaporetto: Santa Maria del Giglio.
Map p 410.

The Performing Arts
★ **Teatro Fondamenta Nuove** CANNAREGIO
The repertoire includes experimental drama,
dance, readings, and performance art. The
singers of **Musica in Maschera** perform here
throughout the year, delivering famous opera
arias while attired in 18th-century costumes
and elaborate masks. Fondamenta Nuove.
☎ 041-5224498. www.musicainmaschera.it.
Ticket prices vary. Vaporetto: Fondamenta
Nuove. Map p 410.

Padua

Padua (Padova) seems content to take a backseat to Venice, though it has plenty of treasures of its own. These include one of Europe's oldest universities, a stunning fresco cycle by Giotto, and a medieval botanical garden.

> The Cappella degli Scrovegni interior was one of the few works actually signed by the "Father of Western Art," Giotto.

START Padua is only 30 minutes from Venice by train, with departures about every 15 minutes. By car, take the A4 autostrada. The tourist information office in the Padua train station dispenses maps and other information. From the train station, follow Corso del Popolo and Corso Garibaldi toward Piazza Eremitani and the city center; the route will take you to all the major sights. You can easily tour the city on foot, and buses from the station go to the sites as well.

① ★★★ **Cappella degli Scrovegni.** One of the world's great painting cycles, by Giotto (1267–1337), covers the walls of what was once the chapel of the Scrovegni family palace. The magnificent frescoes are, in effect, atonement for the ill-gotten gains the family acquired through usury. The frescoes have been restored and are painstakingly maintained—visitors enter through a decontamination chamber. Giotto painted the frescoes from 1303 to 1305, and in these scenes of the life of the Virgin

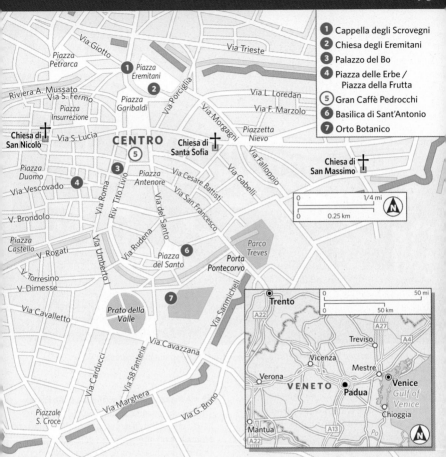

1 Cappella degli Scrovegni
2 Chiesa degli Eremitani
3 Palazzo del Bo
4 Piazza delle Erbe / Piazza della Frutta
5 Gran Caffè Pedrocchi
6 Basilica di Sant'Antonio
7 Orto Botanico

Mary and Christ he introduced the concept of naturalism to Western painting. Off the adjacent cloisters, the **Museo Civico Eremitani** houses ancient artifacts, as well works by Tintoretto and other Venetian artists. ⏰ Visits to chapel restricted to 15 min. Piazza Eremitani 8, off Corso Garibaldi. ☎ 049-2010020. www.cappelladegliscrovegni.it. Admission 11€ plus 1.15€ booking fee. Tickets must be booked in advance by going online, calling the number above, or at Padua tourist offices. Mon–Fri 9am–7pm; Sat 9am–1pm. Bus: 3, 8, 10, or 12 from train station.

2 ★★ **Chiesa degli Eremitani.** What's most moving about this beautifully restored 13th-century Romanesque Church of the Hermits is what's missing—the bulk of a fresco cycle, *Life and Martyrdom of St. James and St. Christopher,*

> *Joachim and Anne embrace, in Giotto's* Meeting at the Golden Gate.

> *Piazza delle Erbe and Piazza della Frutta host one of Italy's largest outdoor markets.*

painted by Padua-born Andrea Mantegna from 1454 to 1457. The church was leveled in an Allied air raid in 1944; fortunately, two of the panels had been removed for safekeeping and two others were salvaged from the rubble. ⏱ 15 min. Piazza Eremitani. ☎ 049-8756410. Daily 8:30am–12:30pm, 4:30–7pm. Bus: 3, 8, 10, or 12 from train station.

③ ★★ **Palazzo del Bo.** Italy's second-oldest university, founded in 1222, has drawn such scholars as Dante, Copernicus, and Oliver Goldsmith, and was Europe's first institution of higher learning to graduate a female, Elena Lucrezia Corner Piscopia (in 1678). Guided tours of the palazzo, named for a medieval inn frequented by students and now the center of the university, show off such features as the anatomical theater from 1594 and the battered lectern from which Galileo Galilei lectured from 1592 to 1610. ⏱ 1 hr. Via VIII Febbraio. ☎ 049-8275111. Admission 3€. Open by guided tour Mar–Oct Mon, Wed, and Fri 3, 4, and 5pm; Tues and Thurs, Sat 9, 10, and 11am. Nov–Feb Mon, Wed, and Fri 3 and 4pm; Tues, Thurs, and Sat 10 and 11am. Bus: 3, 8, or 12 from train station.

④ ★★ **Piazza delle Erbe/Piazza della Frutta.** These two adjoining squares in the city center house one of Italy's largest and liveliest markets; produce is on offer in Piazza delle Erbe, and clothing and housewares in Piazza della Frutta. The building with the loggia rising above market stalls is the Palazzo della Ragione, once housing the law courts. ⏱ 30 min. Piazza delle Erbe and Piazza della Frutta. Market Mon–Sat 8am–1:30pm. Bus: 3, 5, 8, 9, 10, 11, or 12 from train station.

⑤ 🍴 **Gran Caffè Pedrocchi.** One of Europe's legendary grand cafes, recently restored to its 19th-century grandeur, is almost a mandatory stop for a cup of coffee and panino or pastry. For an extra 3€, you can step upstairs to tour the bizarre theme rooms—but spend the euros on another cappuccino instead. Piazzetta Pedrocchi. ☎ 049-8781231. Sun–Tues 9am–9pm; Wed–Sat 9am–midnight. Bus: 3, 8, 12, 16, 18, or 22 from train station.

> *ABOVE Palazzo del Bo is the centerpiece of Padua's ancient and prestigious university. RIGHT The Orto Botanico was founded in the 1540s.*

6 ★★ **Basilica di Sant'Antonio.** The faithful flock to "Il Santo," this 13th-century church honoring Anthony, a Portuguese Franciscan friar who came to Padua around 1230 to preach against usury. Anthony's body rests in the Capella d'Arca, surrounded by nine marble bas-reliefs depicting scenes from his life by Renaissance artists. The saint's tongue is housed separately, in the reliquary, and has been all the more appreciated since its recent theft and recovery. ⏱ 45 min. Piazza del Santo. ☎ 049-8789722. www.basilicadelsanto.org. Late Oct–Apr daily 9am–1pm, 2–6pm; May–late Oct daily 8:30am–1pm, 2–6:30pm. Bus: 3, 8, 12, or 18 from train station.

7 ★★ **Orto Botanico.** The oldest botanical garden in Europe was founded in 1545 to provide medicinal herbs and plants to the university. At the center of the garden, the original design remains: Beds are planted in a circle, representing the earth, surrounded by water. ⏱ 30 min. Via Orto Botanico 15. ☎ 049-656614. Apr–Oct daily 9am–1pm, 3–6pm. Bus: 3, 8, 12, or 18 from train station.

Verona

This handsome city on the River Adige was founded by the Romans in the 1st century A.D., flourished in the Middle Ages, and was a part of the Venetian empire. Traces of its long history are much in evidence in the Roman arena, fine churches, and piazzas and palazzi, and no small part of the city's allure is the star-crossed romance of its two most famous citizens, Romeo and Juliet.

> *Verona's 1st-century arena hosts 21st-century performances on summer evenings.*

START Verona is about 1½ to 2 hours from Venice by train, with departures about every hour. By car, take the A4 autostrada. The tourist information office near the arena in Piazza Bra dispenses maps and other information. From Verona's train station, it is about a 10-minute walk down Corso Porta Nuova to Piazza Bra and the arena, and from there Via Mazzini leads the short distance to Piazza delle Erbe and the other sites of the old city.

1 ★★ kids **Arena.** The best-preserved Roman arena in the world still commands the center of town. When the arena was built in the 1st century A.D., the entire population of Verona could squeeze in for gladiator shows and mock naval battles. The amphitheater is still filled to its 20,000-person capacity when operas are performed on summer evenings—a must-do experience for anyone visiting Verona at this time. ⏱ 30 min. Piazza Bra. ☎ 045-8003204. www.arena.it. Admission 3.10€. Mon 1:45-7:30pm, Tues-Sun 8:30am-7:30pm. Opera performances: ☎ 045-8077500. Tickets 20€-150€. Bus: 11, 12, or 13 from train station.

2 ★★ kids **Castelvecchio.** The castle of the Della Scala family, medieval rulers of Verona, looms over the River Adige. The interior was rebuilt in the 1960s by Venetian architect Carlo Scarpa, and stunning galleries house a collection of paintings by Tintoretto, Tiepolo, Guardi, and

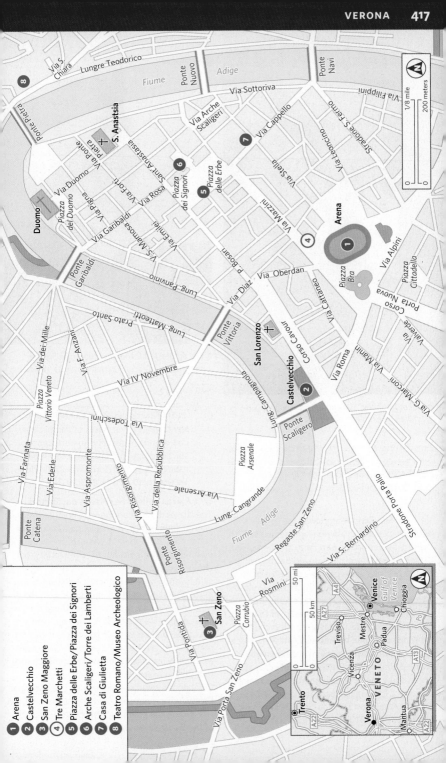

0 1/8 mile
0 200 meters

Via S. Chiara
Lungre Teodorico
Fiume
Ponte Nuovo
Adige
Ponte Navi

Via Sottoriva
Via Filippini
Stradone S. Fermo

Ponte Pietra
Via Arche Scaligeri
Via Cappello

S. Anastsia
Via Ponte Pietra
Sant'Anastasia
Via Leoncino

Via Duomo
Piazza del Duomo
Via Pietra
Via Forti
Via Rosa
Piazza del Signori
Piazza delle Erbe
Via Stella

Duomo
Via Garibaldi
Via Emilei
V. S. Mamosa
P. Bosari
Via Mazzini
Arena

Ponte Garibaldi
Lung. Panvinio
Via Diaz
Via Oberdan
Piazza Bra
Via Cattaneo
Via Alpini
Piazza Cittadella

Prato Santo
Lung. Matteotti
Ponte Vittoria
San Lorenzo
Castelvecchio
Corso Cavour
Via Roma
Corso Porta Nuova
Via Valverde
Via G. Marconi
Via Manin

Via dei Mille
Via F. Anzani
Via IV Novembre
Lung. Campagnola
Ponte Scaligero
Piazza Arsenale

Piazza Vittorio Veneto
Via Todeschini
Via della Repubblica
Via Risorgimento
Via Arsenale
Lung. Cangrande
Fiume Adige
Regaste San Zeno

Via Farinata
Via Ederle
Via Aspromonte
Ponte Catena
Ponte Risorgimento
Via S. Bernardino

Via Rosmini
Piazza Corrubio
San Zeno
Via Pontida
Via Porta San Zeno
Stradone di Porta Palio

Sights

1. Arena
2. Castelvecchio
3. San Zeno Maggiore
4. Tre Marchetti
5. Piazza delle Erbe/Piazza dei Signori
6. Arche Scaligeri/Torre dei Lamberti
7. Casa di Giulietta
8. Teatro Romano/Museo Archeologico

0 50 mi
0 50 km

Trento
A22
A4
Venice
Gulf of Venice
Chioggia
Treviso
A27
Mestre
Padua
Vicenza
VENETO
Verona
Mantua
A13
A22

> *"Juliet's Balcony" is a shameless though much-visited fake, built in the 1920s.*

> *The ornate gothic tombs of the Arche Scaligeri predate the city's long period of rule by Venice.*

other artists whose works are usually associated with Venice. ⏱ 1 hr. Corso Castelvecchio 2. ☎ 045-594734. Admission 3.10€. Mon 1:45–7:30pm, Tues–Sun 8:30am–7:30pm. Bus: 11, 12, or 13 from train station.

❸ ★★★ San Zeno Maggiore. One of Italy's finest Romanesque churches was built in the 12th century as a shrine to San Zeno, the first bishop of Verona and the city's beloved patron saint. Zeno's remains are enshrined behind a magnificent facade on which 12th-century sculptors Niccolò and Guglielmo portray scenes from the Bible, a theme that is carried over to the church's bronze doors. Inside, a triptych of the *Madonna and Child* by Andrea Mantegna graces the altar, and Zeno comes to life in a marble likeness that breaks the mold of religious statuary to show the famously good-natured saint chuckling. ⏱ 45 min. Piazza San Zeno. ☎ 045-592813. Admission 3€. Mon–Sat 8:30am–6pm; Sun 1–6pm. Bus: 31 or 32 from train station.

④ 🍽 Tre Marchetti. Before heading to other sights, linger over pasta or *baccala* (salt cod, a house specialty) in atmospheric surroundings that are truly old—meals have been served here since 1291. Vicolo Tre Marchetti. ☎ 045-8030463.

❺ ★ Piazza delle Erbe/Piazza dei Signori. The site of the Roman forum is now Verona's central square, surrounded by palazzi and the venue for a daily market. Many of the wares on offer are of the ho-hum T-shirt variety, but enough fresh produce from the Veneto is on sale to lend an air of authenticity to the marketplace. Standing amid the hubbub is a statue of Madonna Verona, presiding over these scenes of workaday life since 1368. The adjoining Piazza dei Signori is more somber and was for many centuries the scene of such civic affairs as assemblies of the medieval citizens' council that played a large part in the city government. In the middle of the square is a **statue of Dante,** who spent part of his years in exile from Florence in the beautiful 13th-century palazzo of the Scaligeri family, which faces the piazza.

> *The Teatro Romano looks out over the whole city from its perch across the Adige.*

Walking between these two beautiful squares involves a risk, but only to the truly honest—a whalebone suspended in the Arco della Costa (Arch of the Rib) will fall on the first person to walk beneath it who has never told a lie. ⏱ 30 min. Market: Mon–Sun 8:30am–7:30pm. Bus: 11, 12, 13 from train station.

6 ★★ **Arche Scaligeri/Torre dei Lamberti.** The tombs of the Della Scala family that ruled Verona for most of the 13th and 14th centuries are masterpieces of medieval stone work. What also becomes apparent is the family's taste for bestowing canine names on its members, from Mastino I (Big Mastiff, founder of the dynasty) to Cansignorio (Lord Dog, one of the last of the clan). Cangrande (Big Dog) was a patron and protector of Dante. You can see the tombs at any time through the fence without paying admission, but if you do pay for a close-up look, the same ticket allows you to ascend the nearby Tower of the Lamberti, a medieval hulk that rises 84m (275 ft.) and affords stunning views. ⏱ 30 min. Via Santa Maria in Chiavica. Admission 2.60€ for tombs and tower (elevator); 2.10€ for tombs and tower (stairs). Courtyard open for close-up viewing June–Aug Mon 1:45–7:30pm, Tues–Sun 8:30am–7:30pm. Bus: 11, 12, or 13 from train station.

7 ★ **Casa di Giulietta.** Juliet's House, Verona's shrine to love, is a lovely medieval home—and there any authentic association with Shakespeare's heroine ends. Most shameless is the balcony from which the doomed maiden allegedly hailed Romeo, but don't be swayed—it's a 1920s addition built to capitalize on romantic appeal. The Capulet and Montague families did exist, but they lived in nearby Vicenza and were on undramatically friendly terms. ⏱ 15 min. Via Cappello 23. ☎ 045-8034303. Admission 3.10€. Mon 1:30–7:30pm; Tues–Sun 8:30am–7:30pm. Bus: 11, 12, or 13 from train station.

8 ★★ kids **Teatro Romano/Museo Archeologico.** Verona's Roman theater dates from the 1st century B.C., when the outpost was an important crossroads between Rome and the northern colonies. The stone seats are built into the side of a hill, and the old city across the River Adige provides a stunning backdrop for Verona's summer festival of drama, music, and dance. An elevator ascends from the theater grounds to the cliff-top monastery that now houses the archaeological museum's small collection of statuary and other artifacts; the real draw, though, is the view over the city. ⏱ 45 min. Rigaste Redentore 2. ☎ 045-8000360 Admission 2.60€. Theater Tues–Sun 9am–7pm; museum Mon 1:30–6:45pm, Tues–Sun 8:30am–6:45pm. Festival: ☎ 045-8066485. www.estateteatraleveronese.it. Tickets 8€–36€. Bus: 31, 32, 33, or 73 from train station.

Venice Fast Facts

Accommodations Booking Services
Your best bet is to contact the Venice tourist office; see "Visitor Information," below.

American Express
The main office is on Salizzada San Moisè, just west of Piazza San Marco (☎ 041-5200844). Summer hours are Monday to Saturday 8am to 8pm for banking, 9am to 5:30pm for other services; in winter, all services are Monday to Friday 9am to 5:30pm and Saturday 9am to noon.

Arriving in Venice
BY BUS Buses arrive at the Piazzale Roma station. For schedules, call ☎ 041-5287886.
BY CAR Large car parks at the entrance to the city include the **Garage San Marco,** Piazzale Roma (☎ 041-5232213), about 26€ for 24 hours, and Isola del Tronchetto (☎ 041-5207555), about 18€ a day. It is less expensive to park on the mainland at Mestre for about 4.50€ a day, where options include **Parking Stazione** (☎ 041-938021), and take the train from there. BY PLANE Venice's **Marco Polo airport** is 10km (6½ miles) north of the city on the mainland. The ATVO airport shuttle bus (☎ 042-1383671; www.atvo.it) connects Marco Polo airport with Piazzale Roma, not far from Venice's Santa Lucia train station. Buses leave from the airport about every half hour, and the trip costs 3€ and takes 20 minutes. Buy tickets at the newsstand just inside the terminal. You can get to other parts of Venice by vaporetto from the Piazzale Roma stop. Taxis are also available in front of the terminal building, and the trip to Piazzale Roma costs about 30€. The Cooperative San Marco/Alilaguna (☎ 041-5235775; www.alilaguna.it) operates a large *motoscafo* (shuttle-boat) service from the airport with stops at Murano and the Lido before arriving after about 1 hour in Piazza San Marco; the trip costs 10€. The fee for a private water taxi is a legal minimum of 55€, but the fare is usually closer to 75€ for two to four passengers with a few bags; water taxis are usually available at the landing outside the airport, or contact the Corsorzio Motoscafi Venezia (☎ 041-5222303; www.motoscafivenezia.it).
BY TRAIN **Stazione Venezia–Santa Lucia,** Ven-
ice's train station, is on the Grand Canal; the Ferrovia vaporetto stop is in front of the station.

ATMs
Automated teller machines (*bancomat*) are located throughout the city. Italy generally uses 4-digit PINs; if you have a 6-digit number, check with your bank before you leave.

Dentists, Doctors & Hospitals
Ospedale Civile Santi Giovanni e Paolo, on Campo Santi Giovanni e Paolo, has English-speaking staff and provides emergency service 24 hours a day (☎ 041-785111; vaporetto: San Tomà). Most hotels will have a list of dentists and doctors and will help with arrangements.

Emergencies
Dial ☎ 113 to reach the police, ☎ 112 to reach the carabinieri, ☎ 115 to report a fire, and ☎ 118 to summon emergency medical assistance.

Getting Around Venice
BY GONDOLA On a gondola ride, expect to pay 80€ for up to 40 minutes (100€ between 8pm and 8am), with up to six passengers, and 40€ for each additional 20 minutes (50€, 8pm–8am). But you should negotiate a fee before you step into the craft. There are 11 gondola stations around the city, including those at Piazzale Roma, the train station, the Rialto Bridge, and Piazza San Marco. Gondolas are regulated by the Ente Gondola (☎ 041-5285075; www.gondolavenezia.it).
BY TRAGHETTO *Traghetti* are large, unadorned gondolas rowed by standing gondoliers across the Grand Canal. The ride is reasonably priced at .50€. Some popular traghetto crossings are between Fondamenta del Vin to Riva del Carbòn (Mon–Sat 8am–2pm) and the Pescaria and Santa Sofia (Mon–Sat 7:30am–8:30pm; Sun 8am–7pm), both near the Rialto. An especially scenic ride is that between San Marco and the Dogana (daily 9am–noon, 2–6pm). BY VAPORETTO *Vaporetti* (water buses) connect points along the Grand Canal, other areas of the city, and islands. Boats run every 10 or 15 minutes from 7am to midnight, and once an hour after midnight until morning. An *accelerato* makes every stop; a *diretto* makes express stops. A single fare is 6.50€ and is

valid for 60 minutes. You must stamp your ticket in one of the machines at each stop. Travel cards are available for 12 hours for 14€, 24 hours for 16€, 36 hours for 21€, 48 hours for 26€, and 72 hours for 31€. Tickets are available at stops; travel cards are sold at the tourist offices (see "Visitor Information," below); you may also purchase single fares on the boat. If you're caught without a ticket, the fine is a steep 21€. **BY WATER TAXI** *Taxi acquei* (water taxis) are expensive: 8.70€ fixed rate from departure and 1.30€ for each 60-second period thereafter. Each bag over 50cm (20 in.) long costs 1.50€, plus there's a 5.50€ supplement for service from 10pm to 7am and a 5.90€ surcharge for travel on holidays. These rates are for four people; add 1.60€ for each extra passenger. You'll find water-taxi stations at the Ferrovia; Piazzale Roma; the Rialto Bridge; Piazza San Marco; the Lido; and Marco Polo airport. Call Radio Taxi (☎ 041-5222303 or 041-723112) for a pickup anywhere in the city; a surcharge of 4.15€ is added.

Internet Access

Internet access can be difficult in Venice; some Internet cafes include **Internet Point,** Calle della Sacrista (☎ 041-5284871; daily 10am–11pm; 6€ an hour; vaporetto: San Zaccaria); and **Venetian Navigator,** Calle delle Bande, between San Marco and Campo Santa Maria Formosa (☎ 041-5226084; May–Oct daily 10am–10pm; Nov–Apr daily 10am–1pm, 2:30–8:30pm; 6€ an hour; vaporetto: Rialto).

Post Office

The central post office is on the San Marco side of the Rialto Bridge at Rialto in the Fondaco dei Tedeschi building (☎ 041-2717111 or 041-5285813; stamps available Mon–Sat 8:30am–6:30pm, other services Mon–Sat 8:10am–1:30pm; vaporetto: Rialto). Postal services are also available near Piazza San Marco on Calle Larga dell'Ascensione and near Piazzale Roma on Fondamenta Santa Chiara (Mon–Fri 8:30am–2pm; Sat 8:30am–1pm). You can buy *francobolli* (stamps) at *tabacchi* (tobacconists).

Pharmacies

Regular hours at *farmacie* (look for the neon green or red cross) are Monday to Friday 9am to 12:30pm and 3:45 to 7:30pm; Saturday 9am to 12:45pm. At least one pharmacy in each *sestiere* (district) is open all night on a rotating basis; the tourist office (see "Visitor Information," below) keeps a list, and a sign posted outside all pharmacies indicates which pharmacy is currently remaining open.

Police

To report a lost or stolen article, such as a wallet or passport, visit the local police *questura* or Carabinieri *caserma*. See also "Emergencies," p 420.

Safety

Beware of pickpockets in crowds in the streets or on the vaporetti, and of occasional thievery at night in the dark back streets. As is the case anywhere, common sense is your best protection.

Telephones

Most public phones in Venice require that you use a *scheda telefonica* (phone card), available at newsstands, bars, and elsewhere. Even when calling within Venice, you will need to dial the prefix 041.

Toilets

Public toilets are marked by blue and green wc signs. There is a fee of about .50€ to 1€. *Signori* means men; *signore,* women; when looking for a toilet, ask for "*il bagno.*"

Visitor Information

The government-run tourist bureau, Piazza San Marco (☎ 041-5298711), supplies free maps and information on sights, concerts, exhibitions, and hotels. Offices are in the Piazza San Marco, Giardinetti Reali, the train station, the arrival halls at the airport, Piazzale Roma, on the Lido at GranViale 6A (high season only), and in Mestre at Corso del Popolo 65. Hours vary (and are subject to change): The San Marco office is open daily 9am to 3:30pm, and the offices around the corner in the Giardinetti and in the train station are open daily 8am to 6:30pm (vaporetto for the two San Marco offices: San Marco/Vallaresso). See also the tourism board website, www.turismovenezia.it/eng.

9
Milan, Lombardy & the Lakes

The Best of Lombardy in 3 Days

Often compared unfavorably and unfairly to Rome and other Italian cities, Milan is nonetheless well endowed with monuments, museums, and diversions—many of which can be explored in 3 days. Break up your city tour with half-day jaunts to two nearby art- and monument-filled cities on the Lombardy plains: Bergamo and Pavia.

> PREVIOUS PAGE *Northeast of the lakes, the breathtaking pinnacles of the Dolomites are home to a unique culture that's part German and part Italian.* THIS PAGE *Milan's Duomo is one of the largest and most complex Gothic structures ever built.*

START **Milan. Trip length: Total distance traveled, with the 2 day trips to Bergamo and Pavia, is 175km (105 miles).**

① **Milan.** Italy's largest city and financial center is drably unattractive in some places, but soon reveals an energetic and sophisticated buzz, along with many other charms—not just in its many museums and churches, but also on the cobbled streets of the Brera and along the canals of the Navigli neighborhood. As sprawling as the metropolis is, much of what you'll want to see and do is concentrated in a relatively small area within walking distance of the Piazza del Duomo. Here, at the city's heart, the fourth-

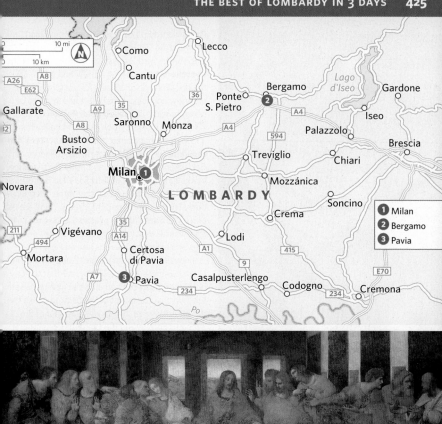

Book a slot far in advance if you want to see Leonardo da Vinci's *The Last Supper*.

largest cathedral in the world (the Cathedral of Seville is the largest) commands center stage, just as its medieval planners intended it to do. In *Innocents Abroad,* even the usually terse Mark Twain was moved to hyperbole by the spectacle of the immense **Duomo** (p 456, ❶), "What a wonder it is! So grand, so solemn, so vast! And yet so delicate, so airy, so graceful! A very world of solid weight, and yet it seems . . . a delusion of frostwork that might vanish with a breath!"

The exterior, adorned with more than 2,000 statues, and the vast interior were more than 5 centuries in the making, inspiring a much-used phrase in Milan, "*fabbrica del Duomo,*" a refer-

Travel Tip

If you plan to see Leonardo da Vinci's *The Last Supper,* arrive in town with a reservation in hand (p 462, ❼). Opera lovers should procure tickets for La Scala well in advance, too (p 469).

ence to a long and complicated undertaking. Inside, amid a colorful blaze from acres of stained glass and Marco d'Agrate's remarkable statue of St. Bartholomew, is a movingly simple relic: A roughly hewn nail said to be from the cross on

> The ancient church of San Lorenzo Maggiore houses the tomb of St. Aquilino, the patron saint of porters.

which Christ was crucified is stored in a niche in the dome above the apse and brought down for a procession and display every September. A similarly modest monument commands pride of place on the roof: the **Madonnina** (Little Madonna), a golden statue that is only 4m (13 ft.) tall but a mighty symbol of the city and inspiration for the schmaltzy and popular 1930s song, "O Mia Bela Madonna," by Giovanni d'Anzi.

Nearby sights to include on your first day in Milan are the church of **Santa Maria delle Grazie** (p 462, **7**), where Leonardo da Vinci's *The Last Supper* graces an interior by Donato Bramante that is in itself a marvel; the **Pinacoteca di Brera** (p 461, **5**), the city's finest art gallery; **La Scala** (p 460, **3**), the world's most famous opera house; and the **Galleria Vittorio Emanuele II** (p 457, **2**), the glass-enclosed shopping arcade

that Milanese proudly refer to as the *"Salotto di Milano"* (the "Living Room of Milan").

Over the next 2 days, take in the sights of the **Castello Sforzesco** (p 448, **6**, and p 461, **6**), the ducal palace of Milan's Renaissance rulers that now houses a remarkable assemblage of seven museums; **Museo Poldi Pezzoli** (p 460, **4**), where works by Botticelli and Bellini hang in a 19th-century palazzo; and the **Pinacoteca Ambrosiana** (p 463, **12**), an enticing collection of Caravaggios, Brueghels, and other Renaissance works gathered by Cardinal Federico Borromeo. Of the dozens of churches that rather incongruously line the city's modern streets, none are as playful as **Santa Maria presso San Satiro** (p 465, **13**), where Donato Bramante's trompe l'oeil creates an illusion of columns and arches.

Even in 3 days it's possible to appreciate Milan's quirkiness, especially the fact that the city is both immensely old and also a stylish trendsetter. Two churches west of the Duomo evoke the 4th century, when Milan was a capital of the Western Empire and the Emperor Constantine adapted Christianity. Milan's first bishop and patron saint founded his **Basilica di Sant'Ambrogio** (p 462, **9**) in 379. Expanded and rebuilt over the centuries, the church still shows its Byzantine origins. Ambrose's likeness appears amid the 5th-century gold mosaics in the chapel of San Vittore in Ciel d'Oro, and mosaics in the apse recount scenes from his life.

Nearby **San Lorenzo Maggiore** (p 463, **11**) is the oldest church in Milan, and the vast, round basilica is said to have grown up around a chapel in the Roman imperial palace. Sixteen columns from a Roman temple flank the entrance, stones from an amphitheater litter the crypt and underground passageways, and 4th-century mosaics pave the walls of the Cappella di Sant'Aquilino, possibly built as a Roman mausoleum.

The epicenter of world fashion is the **Quadrilatero della Moda** (Fashion Rectangle), the boutique-filled blocks between Via della Spiga, Via Montenapoleone, Via Manzoni, and Via Sant'Andrea. A walk past the flagship shops of Italian and other European designers provides a peek at what styles will soon be in vogue and explains why Italians, and the Milanese especially, are so well dressed. It could be argued that even in its pursuit of contemporary design Milan is falling back to tradition because the

> *A funicular railway traverses the split-level hilltop town of Bergamo.*

city was a thriving center of haberdashery and goldsmithing even during the Middle Ages. See p 456 for more on Milan.

On Day 2, take a day trip in the afternoon to Bergamo, 47km (28 miles) east of Milan. Trains run every hour and the trip takes less than 45 minutes each way. To reach the Città Alta from the train station, take bus 1 or 3 (1.20€; tickets available at newsstands, tobacco shops, and machines) to the terminus of the Funicolare Bergamo Alta and make the free transfer.

② **Bergamo.** The centuries slip away in Bergamo's hilltop old town, the Città Alta (literally, "High City"), where medieval houses line the streets and the many monuments that the Venetians left behind during their centuries of rule surround the **Piazza Vecchia** (p 476, ①) and **Piazza del Duomo** (p 476, ②). It should come as no surprise that this terribly romantic town, with its Renaissance loggias and mountain views, inspired the operas of a native son, Gaetano Donizetti, and Italy's popular form of theater, Commedia dell'Arte. Down in the newer Città Bassa ("Low City") is one of Italy's finest art museums, the **Galleria dell'Accademia Carrara** (p 477, ④). ⊙ 4 hr. See p 476.

Return to Milan (①) for the rest of Day 2. On the morning of Day 3, take a train from Milano Centrale to Pavia; they run about every 30 minutes and the trip takes 35 minutes. Buses leave for the Certosa from Pavia's station (1€),

and taxis are also readily available.

③ **Pavia.** Once as important as Milan, a Roman military outpost and capital of the Lombards from the 8th through 12th centuries, this little city on the Ticino River near its confluence with the Po owes its appearance to medieval and Renaissance Visconti rulers. They built the magnificent **Certosa,** a monastery and family pantheon, and a **Castello,** that was one of the great courts of Europe. Petrarch and Christopher Columbus studied at Pavia's university, as did Alessandro Volta, who invented the electric cell in 1800, and the **Duomo,** designed by Donato Bramante and Leonardo da Vinci, is one of the great accomplishments of the Lombardian Renaissance.

A surprising presence in Pavia is that of St. Augustine of Hippo, who is interred in the church of ★★ **San Pietro in Ciel d'Oro.** The North African came to Milan with his mother, St. Monica, in 383 to take up a teaching post at the Roman court, and once there he decided to give up his worldly ways. (On the prospect of leaving his concubine, he famously uttered, "God grant me chastity and continence, but not yet.") Baptized by Ambrose, bishop of Milan, in 387, Augustine returned to Africa, and with his preaching there he influenced Western Christianity perhaps more than any other early thinker. ⊙ 4 hr. For more on all of these Pavia sights see p 448, ⑦.

Return to Milan (①) to finish up your last day in Lombardy.

HITTING THE HIGH NOTES

The Best of Italian Opera BY STEPHEN BREWER

Since *Dafne*, the world's first opera, was performed in Venice in 1598, Italians have been giving us some of the most divine operas ever sung. Tickets for the late-fall through spring seasons of opera houses around the country and summertime performances in outdoor venues are hot commodities; to try your luck, visit the theater websites below or a booking agency such as VivaTicket (www.vivaticket.it) or Select Italy (www.selectitaly.com).

The Great Composers

The 19th century saw a groundswell of operatic genius in Italy, leaving us with classics that are still the mainstays of opera houses around the world.

GIOACHINO ROSSINI (1792–1868) wrote 39 operas including *The Barber of Seville*, *William Tell*, and *Moise et Pharaon* (pictured).

VINCENZO BELLINI (1801–1835) is still the pride of his native Sicily, and though he died young, he left us much immortal works as *Norma*.

GAETANO DONIZETTI (1797–1848) went insane and met a tragic ending worthy of many of his 75 operas, of which *Lucia di Lammermoor* is the enduring classic.

GIUSEPPE VERDI (1813–1901) gave us *La Traviata*, *Rigoletto*, and dozens of other favorites; plus, *"The Chorus of the Hebrew Slaves"* from *Nabucco* and other segments stand alone as wildly popular songs.

GIACOMO PUCCINI (1858–1924), with a flair for great drama, left us some of our most enduring operatic favorites, among them *Tosca*, *La Bohème*, and *Madama Butterfly*.

Where the Fat Ladies Sing

LA SCALA The most famous opera house in the world has been drawing musical talent to Milan since 1778. www.teatroallascala.org

LA FENICE Venice's jewel burned in 1996 and reopened in 2004 with a production of *La Traviata*, which premiered here in 1853. www.teatrolafenice.it

ARENA DI VERONA A remarkably well-preserved Roman monument from A.D. 30 is the evocative setting for June–August operatic productions. www.arena.it

TEATRO REGIO An annual October Verdi festival honors the local son who staged many of his works in Parma's handsome hall, open since 1829. www.teatroregioparma.org

Meet the Stars

MARIA CALLAS
From her Italian debut at the Arena di Verona to stardom at La Scala, Maria Callas captured the world's notice with her talent, earning the title "La Divina" (the Divine).

RENATA TEBALDI
The great conductor Arturo Toscanini called Renata Tebaldi *"voce d'angelo"* (angel voice), and thousands of fans who fell under the spell of her star turns at Milan's La Scala would not quibble.

LUCIANO PAVAROTTI
From his beginnings in provincial Italian opera houses to the world's most famous stages, Luciano Pavarotti earned eternal stardom as one of the finest classical singers of the 20th century.

ENRICO CARUSO
sang at La Scala and the world's other great stages, but the great tenor was immortalized by the 260 recordings he made in the early 20th century.

The Best of Lombardy & the Lakes in 1 Week

For all of its factories and economic muscle, Lombardy is also terrifically scenic. The lakes, most famously, are among Italy's treasured beauties, and the region's hills and plains are liberally dotted with history-rich towns where visitors virtually step back in time. It is easy to dip your toes in lake waters, cruise past magnificent scenery, and witness wonders dating from the Roman era through the Middle Ages and the Renaissance all in the course of a week.

> *Isola Bella, in Lago Maggiore, was embellished with a baroque palazzo and gardens in the 17th century.*

START Milan. Unless you drove into town, do not rent a car until you're ready to leave Milan on Day 3. Trip length: 525km (315 miles) total for the loop.

1 **Milan.** ⏱ 2 days. See p 424, **1**, but do not do the day trips.

On Day 3, head west out of Milan and follow autostrada E62 for the 80-km (48-mile) trip to Stresa on Lago Maggiore, where you should check into a hotel (p 443).

2 **Stresa.** With its lakeside promenades, this pretty town would be a pleasant retreat even

1 Milan
2 Stresa
3 Bellagio
4 Bergamo
5 Sirmione
6 Mantua

without the offshore presence of the **Isole Borromee.** These three craggy outcroppings are named for Milan's most powerful Renaissance family, the Borromeos, who built one of Europe's most lavish pleasure palaces and gardens on one of them, the **Isola Bella.** The boat trip out to Isola Bella is not a solitary experience (most visitors have the same idea). More restful trips are those by ferry to the Borromeo's medieval fortress in Angera, the **Rocca Borromeo** (p 444, 2); the wonderfully atmospheric, 12th-century hermitage of **Santa Caterina del Sasso Ballaro** (p 440, 2), on a lakeside perch near Leggiuno; and the **Giardini Botanici Villa Taranto** (p 442), a landscape of exotic flora outside Verbania. If you still have

More on the Lakes

For more information on visiting Stresa, Bellagio, Sirmione, and other lakeside towns, see p 438 and p 444.

time, you might make the short and scenic excursion from Stresa across the mountains through the village of Mottarone to Orta San Giulio, on Lago d'Orta (see p 439 for details on the scenic drive between the two). ⏱ 1 day.

On Day 4, make the move to Lago di Como. The easiest route drops down on autostrada A26 to E35 then follows the A9 back up to Como. From there, route S583 follows the

> *Bellagio's location, on a promontory where Como's three arms meet, makes it the favorite spot for a lakeside panorama.*

eastern shore to Bellagio. The total distance is about 100km (60 miles).

3 Bellagio. A promontory at the juncture of the three basins of Lago di Como provides Bellagio with one of the world's most beautiful locations, a fact not lost on centuries'-worth of travelers. The gardens of the **Villa Melzi** and **Villa Serbelloni** cover the point in a profusion of greenery. Napoleon was a visitor to Villa Melzi, built by his friend Francesco Melzi d'Eryl, and he, too, was enchanted with Bellagio. Villa Serbelloni: Piazza della Chiesa. ☎ 031-951555. Admission 7€. Apr–Oct Tues–Sun 11am–4pm. Villa Meizi: Lungoiario Marconi. ☎ 031-950204. Admission 6€. Mid-Mar to Oct daily 9am–6pm. ⏱ 1 day. See p 440, **3**.

On Day 5, make the short trip to Bergamo, where you'll overnight. Follow the lake to Lecco, and from there SP72 leads to Bergamo. Total distance is about 65km (40 miles).

4 Bergamo. A perch high on a bluff above the busy plain below and a dense jumble of medieval and Renaissance monuments set Bergamo's Città Alta apart from the modern world in both place and time. To wander through the **Piazza Vecchia** (p 476, **1**) and the **Piazza del Duomo** (p 476, **2**) is to lose yourself in centuries past, and the effect is often nicely accompanied by tolling church bells. The **Duomo** is the least impressive of the three monuments on Piazza del Duomo—the **Cappella Colleoni** and the **Basilica di Santa Maria Maggiore** are not only more graceful, but inside each are exquisite works by Lorenzo Lotto, Tiepolo, and other renowned artists. The sturdy walls the Venetians built to defend the city are now parklike overlooks, and views are especially impressive from the far edge of town at the Castello, reached via a funicular or a climb of about 15 minutes. A descent to the

Città Bassa via old streets lined with villas and churches leads to one of Italy's finest painting galleries, the **Galleria dell'Accademia Carrara** (p 477, ④). ⏱1 day.

On Day 6, follow the A4 autostrada for the trip to Sirmione on Lago di Garda, where you'll spend the night. The trip is only 75km (45 miles) and takes under an hour, leaving plenty of time to get to Sirmione and to cruise up the lake.

⑤ **Sirmione.** It's never been proven that the poet Cattulus (84–54 B.C.) built the **Grotte di Catullo** (☎ 030-916157; 5€; Apr–Sept Tues–Sun 8:30am–7pm; Oct–Mar Mon–Sat 8:30am–4:30pm, Sun 9:30am–4:30pm). Sirmione's Roman villa and baths bear his name, and it's unlikely he could have afforded such extravagance. But whoever planned the site at the edge of the water had a poet's eye for beauty. Sirmione is even more beautiful with the addition of a magnificent waterside medieval castle, the **Rocca Scaligera** (☎ 030-916148; 5€; Mar to mid-Oct daily 8:30am–7pm; mid-Oct to Feb daily 8:30am–5pm), which stands guard over this lively and atmospheric resort at the tip of a long promontory jutting into the southern end of the lake. Ferries pull into docks on the lakeside promenades of one pretty town after another. Salò, settled by the Romans, is surrounded by hillside villas; the poet Gabriele D'Annunzio lived at one of them, **Il Vittoriale degli Italiani** (p 445, ⑥). **Gargnano** is a picturesque medieval fishing port that was home to both D. H. Lawrence and Benito Mussolini. Lemon have been cultivated around **Limone sul Garda** since the 13th century; and in **Riva del Garda,** at the northern end of the lake, medieval porticos surround old piazzas and the cliff faces of Monte Rochetta loom to the west. ⏱1 day.

On Day 7, take the A4 east from Sirmione toward Verona, and then head south on the A22 to Mantua. Total distance is only about 50km (30 miles), and the drive takes less than an hour.

Lake Logistics

Getting around all the lakes is easy by boat. Once you arrive at the lakeside towns where you'll be staying, stash your car and hop aboard. On Lago d'Orta, check with **Navigazione Lago d'Orta** (☎ 0322-844862) for schedules; a full day's ticket is 6.50€. On Lago Maggiore, check with **Navigazione Lago Maggiore** (☎ 0322-46651; www.navigazionelaghi.it). On Lago di Como, check with **Navigazione Lago di Como** (☎ 031-579211; same website as Maggiore). For the extensive boat service on **Lago di Garda**, check with **Navigazione sul Lago di Garda** (☎ 030-2889911; same website as Maggiore). All companies have ticket offices near the docks in larger towns.

⑥ **Mantua.** If the River Mincio didn't curve quite as often as it does and wreak havoc with tidy regional boundaries, Mantua wouldn't be in Lombardy at all: Its nearest neighbors are Parma (p 326) in Emilia-Romagna and Verona (p 416) and Padua (p 412) in the Veneto. Surrounded by the sweeping, lake-like curve of the Mincio and built around three beautiful piazzas, Mantua is remote and rather dreamy—locked in a Renaissance world of its own. Like the towns of Emilia-Romagna, Mantua owes its appearance to one family, the Gonzagas. They took Mantua from the Bonacolsi clan in 1328 and proved themselves to be able administers over the next 3 centuries, leaving their legacy in the enormous **Palazzo Ducale** (p 472, ❶), the **Palazzo del Tè** (p 474, ❸), the **Basilica di Sant'Andrea** (p 473, ❷), and other monuments. ⏱1 day.

From Mantua, it is 155km (95 miles) to Milan via autostradas A22 and A4.

More on Bergamo & Mantua

For detailed coverage of sights, hotels, and restaurants in Bergamo, see p 476; for Mantua, see p 472.

Into the Mountains

North of the lakes rises the mountainous realm of the
Alps and Dolomites. It's not just the chill in the air that signals a change from
the rest of La Bella Italia—German is the preferred tongue in many places, the
cuisine takes on the taste of the north, and a Teutonic crispness comes into play.

> *The jagged peaks of the Dolomites punctuate the landscape in Italy's northeastern Trentino–Alto Adige region.*

START Bolzano, about 100km (60 miles) north of Sirmione on Lago di Garda. A car is the most convenient way to see this region, and the A22, the north–south autostrada, leads from Verona to Bolzano. Trip length: 3 days, with a day each in Bolzano, Bressanone, and Cortina d'Ampezzo. Total distance covered on the circuit to and from Bolzano is 300km (180 miles).

1 **kids** **Bolzano (Bozen).** This attractive and sophisticated city at the confluence of the Talvera and Isarco rivers has long been a crossroads between north and south. Bolzano and much of the South Tyrol was ceded from Austria to Italy

at the end of World War I, and tall gabled houses, snatches of German dialect, the presence of *canederli* (dumplings) on menus, and a chill off the surrounding glaciers reflect an influence that is more northern than Italian.

Most noticeable of all, perhaps, is a certain romantic charm that is often the hallmark of alpine cities. The airy **Piazza Walther** at the heart of Bolzano is named for Walther von der Vogelweide (1170–1230), a wandering minstrel of the Middle Ages. **Piazza delle Erbe,** actually a long street that winds past a statue of Neptune through the city's old town, is lined

1 Bolzano (Bozen)
2 Bressanone (Brixen)
3 Strada delle Dolomiti
4 Cortina d'Ampezzo

Where to Stay
Hotel Elephant 7
Hotel Menardi 9
Stadt Hotel Città 5

Where to Dine
Finsterwirt 8
Vogele 6

with shops selling the region's hearty bread, mountain cheeses, and strudels. The adjoining **Via dei Portici** is named for the overhanging porticos on the street's 15th-century houses.

Bolzano's Hapsburg-era churches and medieval castles are awash in frescos. A religious cycle in the **Church of the Domenicani** (☎ 0471-973133; open Mon–Fri 9:30am–5:30pm, Sat 9am–12:30pm) is attributed to the school of Giotto and includes a chilling, skeleton-filled *Triumph of Death* painted during 14th-century plague years as a terrifying reminder of earthly mortality. Scenes that are more convivial unfold on the walls of the 13th-century **Castel Roncolo,** Via Sant'Antonio (☎ 0471-2608; 6€; Tues–Sat 10am–6pm; bus 12 and a free shuttle run to the castle from Piazza Walther), tucked beneath a cliff face at the northern edge of the city and reached on a footpath from the riverbank. Frescoes in the stone-floored rooms reveal the medieval preoccupation with the story of *Tristan and Isolde* and other tales of romance, chivalry, and courtly routines.

The mummified remains of a very early inhabitant of the region, **Ötzi the Iceman,** are in the South Tyrol Museum of Archaeology, Via Museo (☎ 0471-320100; 8€; Tues–Sun 10am–5:30pm). Ötzi was discovered in an ice field north of Bolzano in 1991, and scientific analysis

> *Like much of Trentino, Bressanone was part of Austria until World War I.*

has revealed a wealth of information about him: He lived 5,300 years ago, died at age 45, ate meals of chamois and deer meat and grains, wore a cloak woven from grass, suffered from arthritis, and was the victim of an assault or ritual murder. Seeing this resident of such a distant time is a touching experience.

On Day 2, make the trip up to Bressanone, 40km (25 miles) north of Bolzano, half an hour by car on the A22. You can easily do this as a day trip from Bolzano but, with its cozy inns and restaurants, Bressanone is a pleasant spot for an overnight.

2 Bressanone (Brixen). The bishop princes of Bressanone ruled the South Tyrol for 8 centuries, until 1803, when the town was ceded to Austria. These religious leaders were often at odds with the secular counts of Tyrol, mandating the moat and thick walls that surround the 13th-century **Palazzo dei Principi Vescovi** (Bishop's Palace), Piazza Vescovile (☎ 0472-830505; 5€; mid-Mar to Oct Mon–Sat 10am–5pm). While the massive and somber palace exudes medieval heaviness, several salons of its Museo Diocesano are charmingly filled with painted wood religious statues and carved nativity scenes. The 14th- to 16th-century cloisters of the **Duomo,** Piazza Duomo (Apr–Oct Mon–Sat 10am–noon and 2–5pm) are frescoed with touching religious scenes that for many centuries served as a visual catechism for the faithful who could not read or afford bibles.

On Day 3, follow the Strada delle Dolomiti to Cortina d'Ampezzo. If you've spent the night in Bressanone, return to Bolzano to pick up the route below.

3 kids Strada delle Dolomiti. One of Europe's most scenic drives rises and falls through the mountains for 110km (66 miles) between Bolzano and Cortina. Along the way spindly, snow-capped peaks rise more than 3,000m (10,000 ft.). The views along the route are so impressive that the Strada Delle Dolomiti was named a UNESCO World Heritage Site in 2009. Given the road's many curves and steep ascents and descents, allow at least 2 hours for a one-way trip.

4 Cortina d'Ampezzo. Italy's most famous ski resort hosted the 1956 Winter Olympics and was known among alpine enthusiasts a hundred years before that. Challenging ski runs crisscross the surrounding slopes, but many visitors never strap on a pair of skis. The sight of the stunning Dolomite peaks is reason enough to spend time in Cortina; the scenery is especially appealing at dawn and dusk, when the ring of surrounding mountains reflects the light to wrap white timbered houses and alpine meadows in a warm rosy glow.

Hitting the Slopes

Cortina is surrounded by 140km (87 miles) of downhill ski runs, and 118km (73 miles) of cross-country trails. A network of 51 lifts and funiculars climbs the slopes. The **Freccia nel Cielo** (Arrow of the Sky) departs from a terminus near the Stadio Olimpico del Giacchio (Olympic Ice Skating Stadium) and ascends first to Ra Valles, at 2,500m (8,500 ft.), then Tafano di Mezzo at 3,050m (10,543 ft.). The **Funivia Faloria** arrives and departs from a terminus on the southeast side of town and floats over forests and meadows, then past a sheer rock face to Faloria, at 2,100m (7,000 ft.). The **Dolomiti Superski Pass** covers unlimited skiing and lift and funicular fees at all Cortina ski areas and those in many outlying resorts. Prices begin at 39€ a day during high season, with discounts for longer periods. For more information, go to www.dolomitisuperski.com.

Flights & Heights

The foothills just south of Bolzano produce a notable Pinot Grigio and Vernatsch, the extremely drinkable red wine of the South Tyrol. The **Strada di Vino** (Weinstrasse) twists and turns through the vineyards, and many tasting rooms are open to the public. Some of the most dramatic landscapes around Bolzano are those of the **Altopiano del Renon,** a 1,000m-high (3,000-ft.) mountain plateau. A funicular makes the climb from Bolzano to Soprabolzano, a little hamlet noted for its refreshing air and dizzying views. An electric tram chugs through a landscape of rocky spires from Soprabolzano to the village of Collabo.

> *Onion domes, like this one in the fashionable resort of Cortina, are a common sight in the Dolomites.*

Where to Stay & Dine

★★ **Finsterwirt** BRESSANONE *TYROLEAN/ WINE BAR* Cozy nooks and a warm-weather garden are perfect settings for creamy polentas and platters of smoked meats and mountain cheeses. Vicolo del Duomo 3. ☎ 0472-835343. Entrees 8€–15€. AE, MC, V.

★★★ **Hotel Elephant** BRESSANONE A fresco of the namesake pachyderm, who stopped in Bressanone on a trek from the port of Genoa to the royal zoo in Vienna, graces the front of this historic inn, where the delightful rooms are filled with nooks and crannies, as well as Tyrolean antiques. Via Rio Bianco 3. ☎ 0472-832750. www. hotelelephant.com. 44 units. Doubles 140€–190€. AE, MC, V.

★★★ **Hotel Menardi** CORTINA D'AMPEZZO A former inn for wagon drivers provides atmospheric and extremely comfortable lodgings overlooking the mountains and alpine pastures. Via Majon 10. ☎ 0436-4778. www. hotelmenardi.it. 51 units. Doubles 110€–230€. AE, MC, V.

★★ **Stadt Hotel Città** BOLZANO Many of the large, bright guest quarters have terraces overlooking the city's main square, and the cafe downstairs is one of Bolzano's favorite gathering spots. Piazza Walther 21. ☎ 0471-975221. www.hotelcitta.info. 100 units. Doubles 136€–180€. AE, MC, V.

★★ **Vogele** BOLZANO *TYROLEAN* Vaulted rooms housing a *weinstube* and a woody dining room serve many different kinds of *canederli* (meat and vegetable–stuffed dumplings) and other hearty fare. Goethestrasse 3. ☎ 0471-973938. Entrees 12€–20€. MC, V.

The Lakes at Their Scenic Best

The lakes offer many diversions, from hobnobbing with the rich and famous to boating and sailing, but none is as pervasive and readily available as simply enjoying the region's scenic beauty, which is often accompanied by manmade marvels. This tour takes in the beauty spots of the four major lakes. Ferries ply the waters of all the lakes and connect many of the towns, so stash your car upon arrival and enjoy cruising across the lake waters (see p 433 for more on ferry information).

> *The cableway from Laveno-Mombello, opposite Stresa, affords spectacular views across Lago Maggiore.*

START Orta San Giulio, Lago d'Orta. Trip length: 4 days on a lake-a-day itinerary. The total distance from Orta San Giulio to Sirmione is 175km (105 miles). Orta San Giulio is about an hour from Milan on autostrada A8 and its continuation, A26; near Comignano, follow exit signs from A26 for Lago d'Orta, which will lead via routes 32 and 229 to Orta San Giulio. Total distance is about 100km (60 miles) and, the trip takes about 1½ hours.

1 Lago d'Orta. Orta is much appreciated for its tranquility, backdrop of gentle hills, and green shorelines. Clustered around the loggia-lined **Piazza Motto,** the lakeside town of **Orta San Giulio** is such a romantic little place that it's easy to fall for the legend that San Giulio spread his cape on the water and floated across the lake to banish a dragon and build a 4th-century basilica on the Isola San Giulio. From the edge of Orta San Giulio a path climbs the hillsides into the **Sacro Monte**

☎ 0322-90149; free admission [donations accepted]; May–Sept daily 9:30am–6:30pm; Oct–Apr daily 9am–4:30pm), where 20 chapels are the setting for tableaux of painted terracotta figures that are set against painted murals and depict scenes from the life of St. Francis. ⏱ **1 day.**

A spectacularly scenic route connects Orta San Giulio and Stresa, on Lago Maggiore. Follow signs for Armeno, then begin the climb into the Mottarone, a narrow spur of mountains that separates the two lakes; from the summit, the view takes in the western Alps, the two lakes, and much of the Po Valley. The road then descends toward Stresa. The total distance is only about 25km (15 miles), but allow at least an hour to negotiate the twists and turns—and to make stops to enjoy the views.

> *The waterfront town of Orta San Giulio makes the best base for exploring Lago d'Orta.*

> *Sirmione's crenellated and moated castle, the Rocca Scaligera, was built for a Verona family in the 13th century.*

② **Lago Maggiore. Stresa** (p 430, **②**) has long been the favored town on Italy's second-largest lake—Garda is bigger—with a string of grand hotels that have hosted generations of travelers on the Grand Tour. Lord Byron, Charles Dickens, Flaubert, Goethe, and Hemingway all rhapsodized about the deep waters backed by the Alps, and the lake's villas, gardens, and monasteries still inspire many a breathtaking postcard. Milan's Borromeo family began snapping up lakefront property in the 17th century, when Carlo Borromeo III decided to build the baroque **Palazzo Borromeo** (☎ 0323-31261; 11€, 5€ children 6–15, children 5 and under free; mid-Mar to mid-Oct daily 9am–5:30pm) and its gardens (p 442) just offshore on Isola Bella. It's not by chance that Napoleon and Josephine spent their first, post-conquest night on Italian soil here in 1797. Boats of Navigazione Lago Maggiore (☎ 0322-233200) make frequent crossings to the island from Stresa. Nearby **Isola dei Pescatore** retains the feel of the quaint fishing village it once was.

The hermitage of **Santa Caterina del Sasso Ballaro** (☎ 0332-647172; free admission; daily 8:30am–noon, 2–6pm) is perched enchantingly on a rock high above the shoreline across the lake from Stresa, outside the village of Leggiuno, and reached by ferry. A 12th-century merchant built the religious redoubt in answer to his prayers for rescue after a shipwreck in the deep waters of the lake, and the place is richly frescoed and full of nooks and crannies to explore. ⏱ 1 day.

The easiest route to Lago di Como from Lago Maggiore drops down on autostrada A26 to E35 then follows the A9 back up to Como. From there, route S583 follows the eastern shore to Bellagio. The total distance is about 100km (60 miles).

③ **Lago di Como.** With its villas and convents, lakeside hamlets clinging to the shores, and the curtain of the Alps plunging into the deep waters, Lake Como is the most romantic of the Italian lakes. For many visitors it is romance-inducing enough to know that actor George Clooney retreats to a villa on the lake. Looking back a bit, Vincenzo Bellini, Gioachino Rossini, and Giuseppe Verdi all wrote operas while staying on Como, Stendhal set the opening scenes of the *Charterhouse of Parma* on the lakeshores, Franz Liszt and Richard Wagner were admirers, and long before any of them came on the scene, Pliny the Younger was raving about his lakeside villas.

The full beauty of the lake comes into play around **Bellagio,** where the three arms of Como flow into one another. One basin extends southwest toward the town of Como, famous for silk-making and as the birthplace of Pliny the Elder and Pliny the Younger, and one southeast toward **Lecco,** a stop for literary pilgrims who know Alessandro Manzoni's *I Promessi Sposi (The Betrothed)*—much of the highly acclaimed novel is set here. Most scenically, the northern basin stretches enticingly into the Alps. Bellagio is an intriguing warren of stepped alleyways, lakeside squares, and outlying villas surrounded by gardens, including **Villa Serbelloni,** Piazza della Chiesa (☎ 031-951555; 7€; Apr–Oct Tues–Sun 11am–4pm) and **Villa Melzi,** Lungo Lario Marconi (☎ 031-950204; 6€; mid-Mar to Oct daily 9am–6pm). Just a short and breathtaking boat ride away across the lake are **Tremezzo,** where the **Villa Carlotta** (p 442) looms above the shoreline; **Menaggio,** clustered along a lakeside promenade beneath the ruins of a medieval castle; and **Varenna,** a medieval fishing village. ⏱ 1 day.

To reach Lago di Garda from Lago di Como, take autostrada A9 from Como down to the A4 and follow that east to Sirmione. Total distance is about 150km (90 miles).

④ **Lago di Garda.** Italy's largest lake is one of the country's most popular getaways, as it has been since the Romans built a huge villa, the **Grotte di Catullo,** on the shores of Sirmione. This lovely town hugging the tip of a long promontory at the lake's southern end was also home to 13th-century lords of Verona, who built the remarkably picturesque **Rocca Scaligera.**

Garda's shores are lined with many other beautiful and legendary spots. It's about 2 hours up the lake from Sirmione by public boat to Malcesine, a medieval town hugging a rocky headland beneath **Castello Scaligero,** Via Castello (☎ 045-6570333; 4€; Apr–Oct daily 9:30am–6:30pm; Dec–Mar Sat–Sun 10am–4pm), built by Verona's Scaligero family. The

> *The idyllic lanes of Bellagio have enchanted emperor Napoleon, composer Franz Liszt, and countless others.*

drafty castle chambers are an evocative setting for the Museo di Storia Naturale del Monte Baldo e del Garda, a small natural history museum. A **cable car** (14€ round-trip) ascends from the town to the top of Monte Baldo, affording breathtaking views in all directions.

The poet Gabriele D'Annunzio (1863–1938) lived in **Il Vittoriale** (p 445, ⑥), a hillside villa above Salò. Here he balanced complicated relationships with some of the most famous women of his time, one of whom was the actress Eleanora Duse and another was his wife, the duchess of Gallese. Mussolini spent the final years of the war at **Villa Feltrinelli,** in Gargnano; he and his mistress were making a run for Switzerland when partisans captured and executed them on Lake Como.

The northern end of the lake is especially scenic, with the Alps looming in the background and lemon groves surrounding **Riva del Garda** and other atmospheric old towns. ⏱ 1 day.

Gardens of the Lakes

A gentle climate and, in many cases, lavish tastes accompanied by unlimited funds have endowed the lakeshores with some of the world's most spectacular gardens. The gates of many of these enchanted bowers are open to the public (though hours and opening times throughout the year can vary; call before you go).

The aristocratic Borromeo family didn't skimp when laying out the terraces and parterres at **Palazzo Borromeo,** Lago Maggiore (☎ 0323-31261; 11€ adults, 5€ kids 6–15). Work began in 1632 (it went on for 40 years), and the resulting extravagance of marble and rich vegetation is a marvel to behold. Boats of Navigazione Lago Maggiore (☎ 0322-233200) make frequent crossings to the island from Stresa.

A Scot, Captain Neil McEachern, laid out the **Giardini Botanici Villa Taranto** (pictured above), Verbania, Lago Maggiore (☎ 0323-556667; www.villataranto.it; 9€ adults, 5.50€ kids 6–14), between 1931 and 1940, importing more than 20,000 plant varieties that flourish amid waterfalls, fountains, and lily ponds on terraced landscapes poised between the lake and the mountains. The overall effect is just what the captain had in mind: the wild look of his native Scotland softened by Italy.

Princess Charlotte of Nassau, a granddaughter of the king of the Netherlands, received **Villa Carlotta,** Via Regina, Lago di Como (☎ 344-4405; www.villacarlotta.it; 8€), as a wedding gift in 1843. The 18th-century building was already in noble-worthy shape, so the newlyweds enthusiastically turned their attention to the gardens. Five terraces that ascend from the lake are planted with azaleas and rhododendrons, as well as ferns and many tropical species, and paths lead to bamboo forests, rock gardens, and groves of majestic cedars.

Tolomeo Gallio built the lakeside **Villa d'Este,** Via Regina, Cernobbio (☎ 031-3481), when he became cardinal in 1565, and wealthy and titled residents have been lavishing care on the house and gardens ever since. Among them was Caroline of Brunswick, the wife of King George IV of England; she bought the villa in 1815 after more or less being run out of England for adultery. The villa has been a hotel, one of Europe's finest, since 1873, and the amenities include gardens that retain much of their Renaissance plan.

The emphasis at **Giardino Botanico Hruska,** Gardone Riviera, Lago di Garda (☎ 0336-410877; www.hellergarden.com; 9€ adults, 5€ kids 6–11), is not on grandeur but on a pleasing display of natural beauty, the creation of Austrian dentist Arturo Hruska. Hruska gathered more than 2,000 species native to the Alps and Dolomites during the first part of the 20th century and lovingly nurtured them among clefts, gullies, ponds, and brooks.

Where to Stay & Dine

★★★ **Albergo Milano** LAGO DI COMO
Most of the view-filled rooms in this old house hanging over the waterfront have balconies— and are much in demand, so reserve well in advance. Via XX Settembre 35, Varenna. ☎ 0341-830061. www.varenna.net. 12 units. Doubles 140€–160€. AE, MC, V. Closed late Nov to mid-Mar.

★★ **Hotel Eden** LAGO DI GARDA
The poet Ezra Pound lived briefly at this pink-stuccoed waterside villa, nicely tucked away from the crowds and now nattily done up in an airy, contemporary style. Piazza Carducci 19, Sirmione. ☎ 030-916481. www.cerinihotelsgarda. com. 33 units. Doubles 110€–160€. AE, MC, V. Closed late Nov to Mar.

★★★ **Hotel Florence** LAGO DI COMO
The Ketzlar family's centuries-old hotel on the waterfront offers handsome lounges, an atmospheric bar, stylish and comfortable guest rooms, and a shady terrace. Piazza Mazzini 46, Bellagio. ☎ 031-950342. www. hotelflorencebellagio.it. 36 units. Doubles 140€– 200€. AE, MC, V. Closed late Nov to Mar.

★★ **Hotel Garni Riviera** LAGO DI GARDA
Pleasant old-fashioned rooms face the lake or mountains, and breakfast is served on a shaded lakeside terrace. Via Roma 1, Gargnano. ☎ 0365-72292. www.garniriviera.it. 20 units. Doubles 58€–90€. AE, MC, V. Closed late Oct to mid-Mar.

★★ **Hotel la Palma** LAGO MAGGIORE
This luxurious lair is a fine retreat, with a lakeside garden and pool and pleasantly decorated guest rooms. Corso Umberto 133, Stresa. ☎ 0323-32401. www.hlapalma.it. 128 units. Doubles 240€–350€. AE, MC, V.

★★★ **Ristorante Barchetta** LAGO DI COMO
ITALIAN/SEAFOOD In all but the coldest weather, rich, fresh lake fish and pasta dishes infused with mountain herbs are served on a delightful enclosed terrace. Salita Mella 13, Bellagio. ☎ 031-951389. Entrees 12€–25€. AE, MC, V. Lunch & dinner Wed–Mon. Closed Dec–Feb.

> Dine right on Lago di Como at Vecchia Varenna.

★★ **Trattoria San Carlo** LAGO DI GARDA
ITALIAN Its cozily beamed dining rooms are off the beaten tourist track in a little hamlet between Gargnano and Salò, but it's well worth seeking them out for the seafood risottos, grilled steaks, and other deftly prepared fare. Via Trento 200, Toscolano-Maderno. 0365-641529. Entrees 9€–18€. AE, MC, V. Lunch & dinner Tues–Sun.

★★ **Vecchia Varenna** LAGO DI COMO *ITALIAN/ SEAFOOD* A stone-floored dining room or lakeside terrace are the romantic settings for a memorable meal of pastas laden with wild mushrooms and grilled lake trout. Contrada Scoscesa 10, Varenna. ☎ 0341-830793. Entrees 15€–25€. AE, MC, V. May–Oct lunch & dinner Tues–Sun; Nov–Dec and Feb–Apr lunch & dinner Wed–Sun.

The Lakes with Kids

While the lakes are often associated with royalty, writers, composers, and wealthy swells, these balmy waters and verdant shores are also playgrounds where young travelers can be amply rewarded for their patient trudges through endless museums.

> *The Sea Life Aquarium is just one of the child-friendly attractions at Gardaland.*

START Stresa. Trip length: 4 days. Total distance traveled by car is about 250km (150 miles).

① **Stresa (Lago Maggiore).** The legendary playground of worldly adults on Lago Maggiore also enthralls young visitors, who will probably delight in the lakeside promenades, the cable-car ride up Montagna Mottarone, and the perennial crowd pleaser, the boat trip out to the **Isole Borromee** (p 431). Encourage older kids to bury their

noses in Ernest Hemingway's *A Farewell to Arms,* parts of which are set in and around Stresa. ⏱ 1 day, including visit to Isole Borromee.

Board a ferry for the 45-minute trip up the lake from Stresa to Angera; see p 443 for boat information.

② **Rocca Borromeo (Angera).** This clifftop medieval fortress was the stronghold of the Borromeo family before they built their extravagant villa on the Isole Borromee (**①**). Behind sturdy crenellated walls is the **Museo della Bambola** (Doll Museum), filled with dolls, dollhouses, and children's toys. ⏱ 1 hr. Via Rocca. ☎ 0331-931300. www.borromeoturismo.it. Admission 7.50€ adults, 6€ kids 6–15, kids 5 and under free. Mid-Mar to mid-Oct daily 9am–5pm.

The easiest way to reach Lago di Como from Lago Maggiore is to drop down from Stresa on autostrada A26 to E35 then follow the A9 back up to Como. From there, route S583 follows the eastern shore to Bellagio. The total distance is about 100km (60 miles).

③ **Lago di Como.** Youngsters can work off energy climbing pretty **Bellagio's** labyrinth of stepped alleyways, and they will enjoy boating across Lake Como to nearby ports. ⏱ 1 day. See also "Gardens of the Lakes," p 442.

To reach Lago di Garda from Lago di Como, take autostrada A9 from Como down to the A4 and follow that east to Sirmione. Total distance is about 150km (90 miles).

④ **Sirmione (Lago di Garda).** As if to heighten a Disney-esque ambience, the streets of this town, magically entrenched in yesteryear, are paved in pink marble. Youngsters can clamor over the Roman ruins of the **Grotte di Catullo,** then climb the battlements of the **Rocca Scaligera,** a lakeside castle from the 13th century.

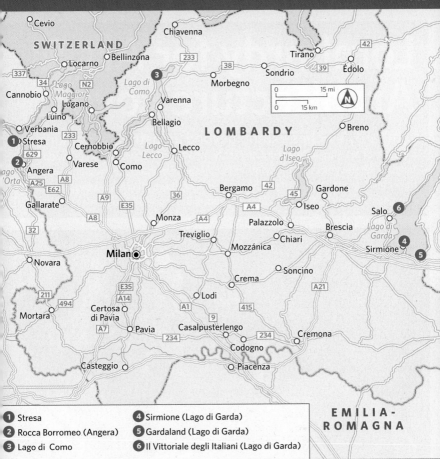

1 Stresa

2 Rocca Borromeo (Angera)

3 Lago di Como

4 Sirmione (Lago di Garda)

5 Gardaland (Lago di Garda)

6 Il Vittoriale degli Italiani (Lago di Garda)

A beach in the shadow of the castle, the **Lido delle Bionde** is popular with families. ⏱ 2 days, including excursions. See also p 441, 4.

Gardaland is about 8km (5 miles) east of Sirmione, reached by following the lake along SR11.

5 Gardaland (Lago di Garda). Young travelers might consider this huge theme park on the shores of Lake Garda just east of Sirmione to be the highlight of a trip to Italy. Flume rides, roller coasters, and dolphin shows are among the attractions. ⏱ 4–6 hr. Peschiera del Garda. ☎ 045-644-9777. www.gardaland.it. 22€ adults, 19€ kids 1–10, kids under 1 free. Late Mar to mid-June and mid-Sept to mid-Oct daily 9:30am–6pm; mid-June to mid-Sept daily 9:30–midnight; Dec to early Jan daily 10am–6:30pm.

Board a ferry for the trip of about an hour up the lake to Gardone Riviera and walk to Il Vittoriale from the dock.

6 Il Vittoriale degli Italiani (Lago di Garda). A visit to the grounds of the hillside estate of the poet and daredevil Gabriele D'Annunzio is a little like a treasure hunt, as each turn in the garden path reveals another fascinating oddity. A favorite is the light cruiser *Puglia*, berthed permanently on a lawn as a reminder of d'Annunzio's World War I–era exploits. See p 441, 4. ⏱ 2 hr. ☎ 0365-296511. www.vittoriale. it. Admission 7€ gardens, 11€ gardens and villa. Gardens: Apr–Sept daily 8:30am–8pm. Villa: Apr–Sept Tues-Sun 9:30am–7pm; Oct–Mar Tues-Sun 9am–5pm.

Lombardy for Art & Architecture Lovers

Lombardy's riches extend beyond industry and banking to a wealth of art and architecture. In fact, with a bounty of works by Leonardo da Vinci, Michelangelo, and many other Renaissance masters, the region is one of the world's great centers of art. Much of this heritage fills Milan's museums and churches, as well as those in Pavia, Bergamo, Brescia, and Mantua.

> Supper at Emmaus, *in Milan's Brera, exhibits Caravaggio's extreme chiaroscuro (light and shade).*

START Milan. Trip length: 5 days.

① ★★★ kids **Santa Maria delle Grazie (Milan).** The church that travelers come to Milan to see is this one, home to the city's most famous piece of art: Leonardo da Vinci painted his *Last Supper* on the refectory wall. Don't even think about arriving in town without a reservation to see it. See p 462, **⑦**, and "Leonardo's *Last Supper*," on p 22.

② ★★ **Sant'Ambrogio (Milan).** This church (built mostly in the 11th c.) with columned porticos, loggias, and a brick facade set the standard for Romanesque architecture in Lombardy. Inside, a few 12th-century mosaics and other bits and pieces from the church's past have survived; the gold and silver altar is by Wolvinus, an artisan from the court of

1. Santa Maria delle Grazie (Milan)
2. Sant'Ambrogio (Milan)
3. Museo Nazionale della Scienza e della Tecnologia Leonardo da Vinci (Milan)
4. Pinacoteca di Brera (Milan)
5. Pinacoteca Ambrosiana (Milan)
6. Castello Sforzesco (Milan)
7. Pavia
8. Galleria dell'Accademia Carrara (Bergamo)
9. Brescia
10. Mantua

Charlemagne, who claimed Milan for the Holy Roman Empire in 774. See p 462, ⑨.

③ kids Museo Nazionale della Scienza e della Tecnologia Leonardo da Vinci (Milan). Come here for the room filled with models of airplanes, helicopters, and other modern conveyances invented by Leonardo da Vinci, who lends true meaning to the term Renaissance man. Leonardo's passion lay with inventing, and he painted as a way to make money, but given the sublime brilliance of *The Last Supper* and his other paintings, who knows what we would have had it been the other way around and painting was his real avocation? Leonardo once wrote, "In painting I can do as much as anyone, whoever he may be." The great sculptor Verrocchio learned just what an

understatement that was. When Verrocchio was a still a painter, young Leonardo was his apprentice. One day the master asked his student to paint an angel's hand in his *Baptism*. Verrocchio took one look at Leonardo's work, put down his brushes forever, and devoted himself to sculpture for the rest of his life. See p 462, ⑧.

④ Pinacoteca di Brera (Milan). Though the collection at the finest of Milan's major painting galleries is relatively small, each of its 38 rooms shines with masterpieces of Italian art from the 13th through 20th centuries. The Renaissance masters of the 15th and 16th centuries take best in show: the *Montefeltro Altarpiece,* painted by Piero della Francesca for the Duke of Urbino in 1475; Andrea Mantegna's *Dead Christ* (1480),

> *Caravaggio's* Basket of Fruit, *in Milan's Pinacoteca Ambrosiana, was the first Italian still-life painting.*

an eerie study in foreshortening; *Marriage of the Virgin* (1504), by Raphael, who signed his name on the frieze of the temple in the background and included a self-portrait in the foreground; and *Finding the Body of St. Mark* (1562–66) by Tintoretto, infused with a supernatural light. This is not to say that many later artists, from Caravaggio (*Supper at Emmaus;* 1606) to Modigliani (*Portrait of Moise Kisling;* 1915), are not given their due. *The Kiss* (1859), by Francesco Hayez, is the favorite work of Italian Romanticism, and prints and postcards of the allegorical scene are perennial bestsellers in the museum gift shop. See p 461, ❺.

❺ Pinacoteca Ambrosiana (Milan). Titian's *Adoration of the Magi,* Caravaggio's *Basket of Fruit,* and Raphael's *Cartoon for the School of Athens* are among the works that the wealthy, learned, and well-connected Cardinal Federico Borromeo acquired and put on display to inspire emerging artists, who were not in short supply in the flourishing culture of 17th-century Milan. Over the years patrons have donated many other works, including Sandro Botticelli's *Madonna del Padiglione; Portrait of a Musician,* a wood panel painting by Leonardo da Vinci; and Guido Reni's *Penitent Magdalena.* Scientific instruments, magnificent gilded bronze objects, and even a lock of Lucrezia Borgia's hair are

also part of the Ambrosiana's fascinating holdings. See p 463, ⓬.

❻ kids Castello Sforzesco (Milan). If the Duomo, on the opposite end of the Via Dante, represents the spiritual might of the generations of Viscontis and Sforzas who ruled Milan from 1277 to 1535, this castle complex shows off their temporal power.

SITE GUIDE PAGE 449

On the afternoon of Day 2, take a train from Milano Centrale to Pavia; they run about every 30 minutes and the trip takes 35 minutes. Buses leave for the Certosa from Pavia's station (1€), and taxis are readily available.

❼ Pavia. Galeazzo Visconti, duke of Milan, had just commissioned Milan's Duomo in 1396 when he turned his attention to a church, monastery, and family mausoleum outside this city 38km (22 miles) south of Milan. Pavia was a court for the Viscontis and then the Sforzas, and the ★★ kids **Certosa di Pavia,** Via Togliatti 12 (☎ 0382-936911; free admission; daily 9–11am and 2:30–4pm, though hours are extended in summer), would become a pantheon for both families. They are entombed behind a facade of richly colored marble amid frescoes, paintings, and elaborate funerary statuary. Among the

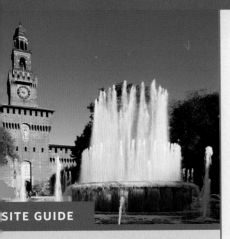

6 Castello Sforzesco

Even on a quick visit a must-see list of the Castello's major attractions includes the **A Mausoleum of Bernabo Visconti,** a delicately carved tribute by Bonino da Campione to a particularly brutish 14th-century lord of Milan who once made emissaries sent by the Pope to excommunicate him eat the incriminating documents; the **B Capella Ducale,** frescoed by Stefano de Fedeli and Bonifacio Bembo for Duke Galeazzo Maria Sforza shortly before his assassination in 1476; the **C Salle delle Asse,** Milan's *other* fresco by Leonardo da Vinci; the **D** *Rondanini Pietà,* on which Michelangelo was working up until days before his death in 1564 (nearby is a remarkable marble head of Byzantine empress Theodora); a satisfying clutch of paintings in the **E Pinacoteca de Castello,** among them Andrea Mantegna's *Madonna in Glory and Saints,* Giovanni Bellini's *Madonna and Child,* Correggio's *Portrait of Giulio Zandemaria,* and Lorenzo Lotto's *Young Man;* and the **F 12 Trivulzio Tapestries,** one of the great Italian textiles, designed by Bramantino in 1503 for General Gian Giacomo Trivulzio and depicting the months and signs of the zodiac. The corridors and salons of the Castello Sforzesco also house civic museums covering a variety of subjects, including **G Civiche Raccolte d'Arte Applicata,** where furniture by Carlo Mollino and other modern designers hold their own against lavishly baroque pieces; and the **H Museo degli Strumenti Musicali,** one of Europe's largest. ⏱ 2 hr. See p 461, 6.

First Floor

Cortile della Roccetta

Cortile Ducale

D **C**
B
A

Biglietteria Ingresso

Piazza d'Armi

Second Floor

Cortile della Roccetta

Ingresso Cortile Ducale **E**

Piazza d'Armi

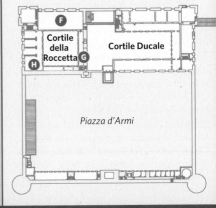

Third Floor

F
Cortile della Roccetta **G**
H

Cortile Ducale

Piazza d'Armi

> *The Certosa is just one among many architectural wonders of oft-missed Pavia.*

many beautiful monuments are graceful effigies of Ludovico "Il Moro" Sforza, by Cristoforo Solari, part of the tomb that Ludovico commissioned for Santa Maria delle Grazie in Milan, where he put Leonardo da Vinci to work on *The Last Supper.* By the 16th century that church's resident Dominicans were in need of cash and sold the tomb to the Certosa. The paintings to take note of here are those by Ambrogio Bergognone (c. 1470s–1524), who worked for 8 years on altarpieces and designs for choir stalls.

A small community of Cistercian monks lives at the Certosa. They reap the benefits of the Renaissance ideal of communal living and reside in two-story cottages, each with its own garden plot, that surround the enormous cloister.

The temptation is to rush through Pavia on the way to and from the Certosa, but that would be a shame, filled as the town is with monumental architecture. Galeazzo Visconti made Pavia's ★★ **Castello** one of the grandest dwellings in Europe and installed a library that in its time was one of the finest in the world (the holdings are now in the Bibliotheque Nationale in Paris). The place is a bit forlorn these days, but in rooms surrounding a handsomely arcaded courtyard, the **Musei Civici,** Viale XI Febbraio 35 (☎ 0382-33853; www.museicivici.pavia.it; 6€; Mon, Wed, and Fri 8:30am–1:30pm, Tues and Thurs 8:30am–

1pm and 2–5pm), brings together some fascinating mosaics, statuary, and paintings by Correggio and others.

Leonardo da Vinci and Bramante worked on Pavia's ★★ **Duomo,** Piazza Duomo (free admission; daily 7am–noon and 3–7pm), and for the **Church of San Michele Maggiore,** San Michele (☎ 0382-26063; free admission; Mon-Sat 8am–noon and 3–7pm, Sun 8am–noon and 3–5pm), medieval artisans achieved what is considered to be the height of Lombardian Romanesque style. They completed the sandstone facade just in time for Frederick Barbarossa to be crowned Holy Roman Emperor in the apse in 1155.

The remains of St. Augustine of Hippo were brought to Pavia in the 8th century, and 4 centuries later the saint was interred in the splendid Arca di Sant'Agostino in the church of ★★ **San Pietro in Ciel d'Oro,** Via Matteotti (☎ 0382-303040; free admission; daily 7am–noon and 3–7pm). The name of the Romanesque church (St. Peter in the Golden Sky) refers to the gold mosaics that once adorned the church's ceilings.

On the morning of Day 3, take a train from Milan's Stazione Centrale (they run hourly) to Bergamo; the trip takes about an hour. Settle into the Città Alta (p 476) and enjoy the sights there, but also leave several hours to enjoy the city's superb art gallery.

❽ ★★★ Galleria dell'Accademia Carrara (Bergamo). A walk through the galleries of the Accademia Carrara is a survey of the great Italian masterpieces, as Botticellis, Bellinis, Mantegnas, Titians, and Tiepolos appear one after another. It is no accident that the paintings here are of such high quality. Count Giacomo Carrara, who began the collection in 1795, had a good eye and unlimited funds— and the many paintings that Napoleon was systematically removing from deconsecrated churches across Italy were his for the bidding. The collection was embellished in the 19th century by Count Guglielmo Lochis and Giovanni Morelli; the latter established the Morellian technique, a systematic method to identify painters and sculptors by analyzing brushstrokes, the way body parts are executed, and other details. Morelli sent American Bernard Berenson (1865–1959) to Bergamo to

> *Lorenzo Lotto painted his* Holy Family with St. Catherine of Alexandria *in 1533; it now resides in Bergamo's Accademia Carrara.*

classify the collection in 1890, and the young art historian soon wrote a book on Lorenzo Lotto that helped earn his reputation as a connoisseur of Renaissance art and established him as an adviser to many of the world's wealthiest collectors.

Lotto, of course, is very well represented in the galleries, with such works as the *Mystic Marriage of St. Catherine* and the *Portrait of Lucina Brembate,* rife with the obscure symbolism that fascinated the painter. Many of the paintings are from the 15th century, the so-called Golden Age of the Early Renaissance. This is when Sandro Botticelli painted the Carrara's arresting portrait of Giuliano de' Medici, one of his patrons in Florence; Pisanello was at the court of the Estes in Ferrara, kept busy with family portraits that includes the one of Lionello d'Este hanging here; and Giovanni Bellini was executing his soft and sensual Madonnas, none as engaging as the Carrara's *Madonna of the Pear,* set against a landscape

that invites the viewer to step into the canvas. See p 474, **4**.

On the morning of Day 4, travel on to Mantua, with a stopover in Brescia. Trains between Bergamo and Brescia run at least every half-hour, and the trip takes less than 30 minutes. Leave your bags at the station while you explore the city.

9 Brescia. Visitors might be tempted to bypass Lombardy's second-largest city—to most travelers just a station stop on the way to Verona and Venice. To put things in historical context, the surrounding industrial area has been turning out arms since the Middle Ages, and military engineer Giovanni Maggi wrote

More on Bergamo & Mantua

For detailed coverage of sights, hotels, and restaurants in Bergamo, see p 476; for Mantua, see p 472.

> *Brescia's Romanesque Rotonda, or Duomo Vecchio, was the Lombard city's first cathedral.*

in the 16th century that "Brescia has almost always been the armory of all Italy."

But there's more to Brescia than bullets. In the old city center, streets and piazzas are lined with Roman ruins, medieval churches, and Renaissance palaces. Founded by the Etruscans and invaded by the Gauls, Brescia was the Roman colony of Brixa by 225 B.C. and was soon graced with three temples, a forum, an aqueduct, and baths. The ruins of the ★★ **Tempio Capitolino** rise along the Via dei Musei, and many of the Roman finds, including the famous bronze *Victory of Brescia*, are displayed in the ★★ **Santa Giulia Museo della Città,** Via Musei 81/b (☎ 030-2977833; www. bresciamusei.com; 8€; Mon–Thurs and Sun 9am–7pm, Fri–Sat 9am–8pm). Celtic helmets, Roman portraits, and Renaissance frescoes almost pale in comparison to the remarkable assemblage of convents, cloisters, and churches that house them. The surroundings incorporate several Roman townhouses unearthed from beneath the monks' vegetable gardens, with their mosaics, frescoes, and heating systems intact.

Nearby on the warren of medieval lanes is the ★★ **Pinacoteca Tosio Martinengo,**
Piazza Moretto 4 (☎ 030-377-4999; www. bresciamusei.com; 5€; Mar to mid-Oct Tues–Sun 9:30am–5pm; mid-Oct to Feb daily 9am–7pm), where the emphasis is on the religious paintings of Moretto, Il Romanino, and other High Renaissance followers of the School of Brescia. A later Bergamese painter, Giacomo Ceruti (1698–1767), dramatically departs from these transcendent scenes with his depictions of vagabonds in tatters and filthy rags that earned him the moniker "*il pitocchetto*" (beggar painter).

Two large squares adjoin each other at the very center of the city. Graceful loggias, porticoed palazzi, and a clock tower left over from the several centuries that Venice ruled Brescia surround the Renaissance-style ★★ **Piazza della Loggia.** In contrast, most of the monuments around ★★ **Piazza Paolo VI** are medieval. These include the city's first cathedral, the domed, 12th-century **Rotonda;** the 13th-century **Broletto,** the town hall; and the **Torre del Popolo,** a formidably tall structure that afforded refuge at a time when citizens were required to build their houses of stone to deflect the torches of the armies of Frederick Barbarossa and other invaders.

A City of Music

If Milan's La Scala is a veritable cathedral for opera-worshippers, then **Cremona** is a pilgrimage site for fans of that most beloved of musical instruments, the violin. An agricultural town that's a bit dusty and out of the way, it is nonetheless forever linked with music because of the violins its world-famous craftsmen have been turning out since the 17th century. If your artistic interests incline toward music, it's a worthwhile short excursion.

Andrea Amati (1505–78) created the first modern violin in Cremona in 1564. Crafting the increasingly popular instruments became a family business, and within a century Cremona's violin school was famous throughout Europe. Among the young craftsmen who honed their skill in 17th-century Cremona were Andrea Guarneri (1626–98), and Antonio Stradivari (1644–1737), and both brought the instrument to new levels of perfection. Though Stradivarius (the Latinized version of the name) is certainly the most famous name in violins today, the instruments made by Guarneri's grandson Bartolomeo Giuseppe (aka Guarneri del Gesù) are said by many music aficionados to be superior. Famed violinist Niccolò Paganini (1782–1840) certainly thought so—his Guarneri del Gesù was his favorite violin.

It is often said in one breath that Stradivari made only 16 violins a year, and in the next that he lived to be 93. More than 500 Stradivarius violins are floating around the world today—many commanding prices in the millions—and some of these precious instruments, along with those of Guarneri and other Cremona violin-makers, are displayed in the civic collection's **Museo Stradivariano** (pictured above), Ugolani Dati 4 (☎ 0372-31222). Tribute is also paid here to two Cremona-born operatic composers: Claudio Monteverdi is credited with writing the first opera, *L'Orfeo,* first performed in 1607, and Amilcare Ponchielli's best-known work, *Il Gioconda,* premiered at Milan's La Scala (p 460, ❸) in 1876. The museum is open daily from 9am to 6pm and admission costs 7€.

If you're in the market for a stringed instrument at prices less stratospheric than the historic names command, you'll certainly find plenty of places in town to acquire one; it is still home to many skilled craftsmen—inquire at the city's tourist office if you're interested.

Cremona is about 70km (42 miles) south of Milan. Trains depart hourly out of Stazione Centrale, the trip takes about an hour, and the round-trip fare is about 10€. Cremona is also often a stop on trains from Brescia to Mantua. The Cremona APT Tourist Office (☎ 0372-23233; www.aptcremona.it) is at Piazza del Comune 5; check the website for the most current operating hours.

> *Giulio Romano's Palazzo del Tè is one of the most important (and whimsical) works of Italian Mannerism.*

Take a late-afternoon train from Brescia to Mantua. Check into your hotel and rest up for Day 5. Trains run about every hour; the trip takes a little less than 2 hours and usually requires a change in Piadena or Verona.

🔟 **Mantua.** Many visitors may come to Mantua with at least a passing familiarity with the great works of art that the Gonzaga family commissioned during their 2 centuries of rule. One of the great surprises at Hampton Court Palace outside London, for example, is the spectacular *Triumphs of Caesar* that Andrea Mantegna painted for the Gonzagas's palace in Mantua. The family's sad end resulted in that fresco cycle making its way to London (and is why their other great paintings are now among the prizes of museums around the world), but the pleasure of being in Mantua is to witness the Gonzagas' heydays, in the late 15th and early 16th centuries, when their court was one of the great centers of Renaissance culture.

Ludovico Gonzaga lured Andrea Mantegna to Mantua as court painter in 1460 and kept the artist busy for 9 years painting an audience chamber in the kids **Palazzo Ducale** (p 472, ①) that has come to be known as the ★★★ **Camera degli Sposi.** This is not only one of the greatest fresco cycles of the Renaissance but also an almost photographic record of life at a Renaissance court and one of the few fresco cycles that Mantegna painted to come through the ages intact. (In Padua, only four panels of his cycle *Life and Martyrdom of St. James and St. Christopher* survived a direct hit by Allied bombs in World War II and are in the Chiesa degli Eremitani; see p 413, ②.) Ludovico intended the cycle to celebrate the elevation of one of his sons, Francesco, to cardinal, but as Mantegna painted he added events as they transpired, such as the visits of kings and other royal visitors. He worked in a wonderfully playful trompe l'oeil effect in which ladies of the court and a peacock peer down into the room from a parapet, and he shows the family in unflinching realism, with wrinkles and hunchbacks and at ease with dogs under their chairs and children standing about.

The Gonzagas also brought Pisanello (c. 1395–1455) to Mantua. He painted the palazzo's

> Mantegna's 1474 frescoed Camera degli Sposi, in Mantua, includes this ring of curious onlookers.

other most noted frescoes, those in the ★★★ **Sala del Pisanello,** where a magical landscape of castles and towers unfolds behind scenes of a battle tournament. These and other works in the sprawling palace, including Lorenzo Costa's mysterious ceiling frescoes for the **Sala dello Zodiaco** and paintings by Tintoretto and Rubens, are just a small sampling of the vast collections the Gonzagas had amassed by the early 17th century. By then the family was broke, and Duke Vincenzo Gonzaga sold hundreds of his best paintings to Charles I of England. Charles wasn't really in a position to be spending that kind of money, and he was soon ousted and then executed during England's Civil War. The paintings went up for auction again, and this time the buyers were France and Spain. That's why today many of the Gonzaga treasures are the crème de la crème of the collections of the Louvre and the Prado.

Work on the ★★★ **Palazzo del Tè** (p 474, ❸), the pleasure palace of Federico II Gonzaga on the outskirts of town, began in 1534. By the time the job was completed 10 years later, every nook and cranny had been covered with frescoes and stuccos; the monumental archway at the entrance, in which the keystone appears to be falling out of place, foreshadows the whimsy that lies beyond. The palace is the masterwork of architect and painter Giulio Romano (c. 1499–1546) and one of the great accomplishments of Mannerism, but this does not diminish the fact that the portraits of horses in the **Sala dei Cavalli** and scenes of giants hurtling thunderbolts across the **Sala dei Giganti** are also just plain fun.

Milan

Italy's largest city is all about business, or so popular perception has it. But come prepared to discover just how untrue that is. The magnificent Duomo at the city's heart and the Leonardo da Vinci masterpiece tucked away in the church of Santa Maria delle Grazie are just the start—from masterpiece-filled small museums to fashion-setting boutiques to cozy trattorias, Milan soon reveals its many charms. You'll need about 3 days to have ample time to see the best of Milan.

> It took a mere 500 years to apply the finishing touches to Milan's Duomo, now a lively people-watching spot.

START Duomo.

1 ★★★ kids **Duomo.** The legacy of the Visconti family, who ruled Milan through the 13th and 14th centuries, was commissioned in 1387 by Count Gian Galeazzo Visconti as an offering that he might produce a male heir. His prayer was answered within a year after construction began, but the magnificent marble-clad cathedral was the better part of this deal. Galeazzo was a shrewd conniver who poisoned his uncle, Bernabò, to gain control of Milan. His cathedral, however, was a great example of

Gothic architecture, one of the largest churches in Christendom, and a work in progress for the next 5 centuries.

The facade, with its 140 pinnacles and many tiers of statuary, was not completed until the 19th century, under orders of Napoleon when he marched into town in 1805 and had himself crowned king of Italy on the high altar. The vast, uncluttered interior is largely the work of St. Carlo Borromeo (1538–84), a 16th-century cardinal of Milan who ordered that monuments, memorials, and other ornamentation be cleared

> *Opening night at the Teatro alla Scala is the pinnacle of the Italian opera world.*

away to demonstrate his intention to restore dignity to the Catholic church; ironically, one of the crypts that remains amid the sea of five aisles and 52 columns is his.

The view from the rooftop promenade extends to the solid curtain of the Alps rising just to the north of the sprawling city, while a descent into the creepy crypt includes a look at the gem-encrusted gold and silver chalices and other pieces in the Treasury. ⏱ 1 hr. Piazza del Duomo. ☎ 02-8646-3456. Church: Free admission. Daily 6:45am–6:45pm. Treasury and crypt: Admission 1€. Mon–Fri 9:30am–12:30pm, 2–6pm; Sat 9:30am–12:30pm, 2–5pm; Sun 1–3:30pm. Bus 50, 54; tram 1, 2, 3, 12, 14, 15, 23, 24, 27.

② ★★★ Kids **Galleria Vittorio Emanuele II.** Giuseppe Mengoni (1829–77) is a man to be cursed or praised, depending on one's views of consumerism. The glass-covered shopping arcade he built in the center of Milan—inaugurated in 1867—is the prototype for shopping malls around the world, but none that have been built since can match this one for grandeur, elegance, or style. Milanese are proud to refer to their landmark as the *"Salotto di Milano"* (the "Living Room of Milan"). Alas, Mengoni never knew how successful his venture would be: He fell to his death from a girder a few days before the Galleria opened. ⏱ 30 min. Between Piazza del Duomo & Piazza della Scala. Daily 24 hr. Metro: Duomo. Bus: 50, 54, 65. Tram: 2, 12, 15, 23, 27.

Getting Around Milan

Buses, trams, and the metro (underground) in Milan are operated by **Azienda Trasporti Milanesi** (☎ 800-808181; www.atm-mi.it, with extensive information in English). Fares are 1€. Bus and tram tickets must be purchased in advance, at newsstands, tobacco shops, and ticket vending machines at stops and in metro stations; tickets must be validated by stamping them in machines on all buses and trams—failure to do so can result in a hefty fine. Milan's metro system has three lines and is fairly extensive; trains run from 6am to 12:30am.

Milan

PORTA VOLTA

CENTRO DIREZIONALE

PORTA NUOVA

PORTA TENAGLIA

BRERA

QUADRILATERO DELLA MODA

MAGENTA

Piazzale Cimitero Monumentale

Stazione Porta Garibaldi

Garibaldi F.S.

Gioia

Piazza Baiamonti

Piazza 25 Aprile

Piazza Lega Lombardo

Moscova

Repubblica

Turati

Arena

PARCO SEMPIONE

GIARDINI PUBBLICI

Piazza Cavour

Arch of Porto Nuova

Lanza

Castello Sforzesco

Piazza Castello

Monte Napoleone

Cairoli

Cadorna

Foro Buonaparte

Magenta

Cordusio

Piazza della Scala

San Babila

Duomo

Piazza del Duomo

Piazza Fontana

Piazza Diaz

Piazza Francesco Sforza

Via De Castillia

Via De Cristoforis

Via Melchiorre Gioia

Viale della Liberazione di Savoia

Via Adda

Via Gen. G. Fara

Via Fabio Filzi

Via C. Farini

Via Ceresio

Via Quadrio

Viale Montello

Viale Pasubio

Viale Crispi

Viale Monte

Bastioni di Porta Nuova

Via Galilei

Viale Monte Santo

Bastioni di Porta Volta

Via A. Volta

Via Marsala

Via Castelfidardo

Via Appiani

Via Parini

Corso di Porta Nuova

Via Solferino

Via Statuto

San Marco

Via Moscova

Via Manin

Via Palermo

Via Montebello

Via Legnano

Via

V. M. De Marchi

Via Pontaccio

Via Fatebenefratelli

Via Palestro

Via Gadio

Via dei Giardini

Via Borgonuova

Via Senato

Via Borgospesso

Via della Spiga

Via Brera

V. d. Carmine

Via Monte di Pietà

Via Montenapoleone

Via S. Andrea

Via dell'Orso

Via G. Verdi

Via Manzoni

Via Dante

Via Broletto

Via Filodrammatici

Via Verri

C. Matteotti

Foro Buonaparte

V.S.G. sul Muro

Via Meravigli

Via Negri

Via Agnello

Pattari

Corso V. Em. II

Corso Europa

Magenta

Via Cappuccio

V. S. M. Fulcorino

Via Orefici

Via Marconi

Via Larga

Via Verziere

Via S. Maurillo

Via Torino

Via Francesco Sforza

1 Duomo
2 Galleria Vittorio Emanuele II
3 La Scala
4 Museo Poldi Pezzoli
5 Pinacoteca di Brera
6 Castello Sforzesco
7 Santa Maria delle Grazie
8 Museo Nazionale della Scienza e della Tecnologia Leonardo da Vinci
9 Basilica di Sant'Ambrogio
10 Civico Museo Archeologico
11 San Lorenzo Maggiore
12 Pinacoteca Ambrosiana
13 Santa Maria presso San Satiro
14 Santa Maria della Passione
15 Museo dell'Ottocento

Where to Shop
Alessi **32**
B & B Italia **33**
Fabriano **31**
Il Salvagente **39**
Peck **36**

Where to Dine
Biffi **37**
Centro Ittico **22**
Da Giannnino L'Angolo d'Abruzzo **24**
Joia **23**
La Latteria **18**
La Trattoria Milanese **35**
Premiata Pizzeria **34**

Where to Stay
Antica Locanda Solferino **17**
Doria Grand Hotel **21**
Grand Hotel et de Milan **30**
Hotel Ariosto **16**
Hotel Giulio Cesare **28**
Hotel London **27**

Nightlife & Entertainment
Auditorium di Milano **25**
Blue Note **19**
Café Atlantique **40**
Le Banque **29**
Le Scimmie **26**
Nuova Idea **20**
Odeon **38**
Teatro alla Scala **3**

> *The glass-roofed 1867 Galleria Vittorio Emanuele II became a model for shopping malls worldwide.*

❸ ★★★ La Scala. Milan's world-famous opera house opened on August 3, 1778, taking its name from the church pulled down to make room for the theater, Santa Maria della Scala. For many decades La Scala was the place to gossip, gamble, and engage in intrigue, and the machinations behind the stage on which many of the world's most beloved operas premiered have been no less riveting. For a long time Giuseppe Verdi did not allow La Scala to perform his works, claiming that the orchestra corrupted his scores. The rivalry between La Scala's two great stars of the 1950s, Maria Callas and Renata Tebaldi, kept the opera world waiting breathlessly for the next exchange of barbs. Callas was once quoted as saying that comparing her to Tebaldi was like "comparing champagne with Cognac, no, with Coca Cola," and Tebaldi once famously hissed, "I have one thing that Callas doesn't have: a heart." More recently, Riccardo Muti was forced to resign as conductor in 2005 after disagreements with the orchestra that even Italy's cultural minister couldn't help resolve.

The theater's long history comes to life in the fascinating **Museo Teatrale,** crammed with scores, news clippings, and other memorabilia, and a visit comes with the chance to step into a box and admire the view of the stage. Seats are one of Milan's most precious commodities; for information on obtaining one, see p 469. ⏱ 2 hr. Piazza della Scala. ☎ 02-720-0374. www.teatroallascala.org. Museum: Admission 5€. Daily 9am–12:30pm, 1–5:30pm. Metro: Duomo. Bus: 61. Tram 1, 2.

❹ ★★★ Museo Poldi Pezzoli. Gian Giacomo Poldi Pezzoli spent most of his life traveling around Europe snapping up items that caught his eye. When Poldi Pezzoli died at age 57, he left his distinguished collection of armor, jewels, carpets, glass, bronzes, porcelain, and many invaluable paintings—along with the family palace—to the city as a museum that opened to the public in 1881. Though World War II bombings made reconstruction necessary, visitors today will encounter Sandro Botticelli's *Madonna del Libro,* Andrea

Mantegna's *Madonna and Child*, Francesco Guardi's *Grey Lagoon,* and Lucas Cranach's portrait of Martin Luther and his wife in rooms arranged much as the collector left them. ⏱ 2 hr. Via Manzoni 12. ☎ 02-794889. www. museopoldipezzoli.it. Admission 8€. Tues–Sun 10am–6pm. Metro: Duomo, Montenapoleone. Bus: 61, 94. Tram 1, 2.

5 ★★★ **Pinacoteca di Brera.** Milan's largest gallery was founded in the 18th century as a small collection of plaster casts for the benefit of art students. The holdings were greatly expanded in the early 19th century when the museum became a repository for the paintings and sculptures that Napoleon carted off from churches and monasteries across Italy and brought to Milan and other cities for safekeeping. Over the years the gallery has continued to acquire some of Italy's greatest masterpieces, with a heavy leaning toward Renaissance works from northern and central Italy. The neoclassical palace that houses them is in part the work of Giuseppe Piermarini (1734–1808), Milan's leading architect and urban planner of the late 18th century. Maria Theresa of Austria established the **Orto Botanico** behind the Pinacoteca in 1774 for the benefit of medical and pharmacological students, and the palazzo has also been home to a flourishing art academy since 1776. Italy's greatest astronomer, Giovanni Schiaparelli (uncle of Elsa, the famed couturiere) oversaw the adjoining **Brera Observatory** in the late 19th and early 20th centuries. For information on the gallery's collections, see p 447, **4**. ⏱ 3 hr. Via Brera 28. ☎ 02-722631. www.brera.beniculturali.it. Admission 5€. Tues–Sun 8:30am–7:30pm. Metro: Lanza, Montenapoleone. Bus 61. Tram 1, 2, 3, 12, 14.

6 ★★ kids **Castello Sforzesco.** When the last of the male Viscontis, Filippo, died in 1447, the lordship of Milan passed to his son-in-law, Francesco Sforza. One of the first things Francesco did was to rebuild the Visconti stronghold as this proper castle from which he ably ruled his holdings and established a court that was a center of Renaissance culture. When Francesco died in 1466, his son Galeazzo—whose passions were music and sadism—became lord of Milan, but he lasted only a decade before he was assassinated. His brother, Ludovico "Il Moro" Sforza, and Ludovico's young

> *A panel from Piero della Francesca's* Montefeltro Altarpiece *in the Brera includes a kneeling Federico da Montefeltro.*

wife, Beatrice d'Este, were soon presiding over one of Europe's most enlightened courts, giving their patronage to the young artists of Italy's Renaissance; a fresco that transforms one of the salons into a leafy bower is Milan's other, less famous work by Leonardo da Vinci. Beatrice died young and Ludovico was driven from Milan by Louis XII of France and spent his last years in the damp dungeons of the castle of Loches in the Loire Valley. Their royal apartments are part of the **Musei del Castello Sforzesco,** a collection of museums that fills the castle with the last work by a 90-year-old Michelangelo, his *Rondanini Pietà;* a 6th-century marble head of the Byzantine empress Theodora; and many of Italy's other great art treasures. For more on this remarkable collection, see p 448, **6**. ⏱ 4 hr. Piazza Castello. ☎ 02-8846-3700. www. milanocastello.it. Admission 3€. Grounds daily 8am–6pm; museums Tues–Sun 9:30am–5:30pm. Bus 43, 57, 61, 70, 94. Tram 1, 3, 4, 12, 14, 27.

> *San Lorenzo Maggiore owes its octagonal shape to ancient roots in the 4th century A.D.*

7 ★★★ kids **Santa Maria delle Grazie.** In the 1490s, Ludovico "Il Moro" Sforza (1452–1508), who would soon inherit the dukedom of Milan, decided to transform the church and convent of Santa Maria delle Grazie into his family pantheon. Only the best would do, so he hired architect Donato Bramante to build a new apse to accommodate the tombs and one of his favored court painters—a young Leonardo da Vinci—to paint **The Last Supper** on a wall of the refectory. Leonardo spent 4 years on the painting, rendering the scene in an entirely new way, using perspective to create the illusion that the refectory extends right into the painting. Unfortunately, among his innovations was the use of fragile tempera paint, and as early as 1517 observers were commenting on deterioration. Centuries of neglect made necessary a delicate, 20-year-long restoration completed in 1999. For more on the painting,

see "Leonardo's *Last Supper*," on p 22. ⏲ 45 min. Piazza Santa Maria delle Grazie. ☎ 02-8942-1146. www.cenacolovinciano.org. Admission 6.50€ plus 1.50€ reservation fee. Reservations to see *The Last Supper* are mandatory and should be made online or by phone as far in advance as possible. Tues–Sun 8:15am–7pm. Metro: Cadorna. Tram: 16, 18.

8 ★★ kids **Museo Nazionale della Scienza e della Tecnologia Leonardo da Vinci.** A 16th-century monastery is now Italy's largest science museum. The second floor is filled with wooden mockups of the airplanes, helicopters, submarines, and other machines that Leonardo da Vinci invented, bringing the imagination of the great artist and engineer to life. Other rooms surrounding two cloisters pay homage to the scientific wizardry of Guglielmo Marconi and other Italian inventors. ⏲ 1 hr. Via San Vittore 21. ☎ 02-485-551. www.museoscienza.org. Admission 8€. Tues–Fri 9:30am–5pm; Sat–Sun 9:30am–6:30pm. Metro: Sant'Ambrogio. Bus 50, 54, 58, 94.

9 ★★ **Basilica di Sant'Ambrogio.** In the 4th century St. Ambrose embraced Christianity and replaced the city's pagan temples with a basilica. Today's sturdy, plain Romanesque edifice, with double bell towers and an atrium once used as a place of refuge, dating largely from the 9th and 11th centuries, was built on the plan of Ambrose's church. The elegant portico in the cloisters is the 14th-century contribution of Donato Bramante (1444–1514), the brilliant architect who helped usher in the Renaissance. Though its medieval altar was intended to house Ambrose's remains, the saint's body is on view in the crypt near those of early martyred Saints Gervasius and Protasius. ⏲ 30 min. Piazza Sant'Ambrogio. Free admission. ☎ 02-8645-0895. Mon–Sat 7:15am–noon, 2:30–7pm; Sun 7:15am–1:15pm, 3–7:45pm. Metro: Sant'Ambrogio. Bus: 50, 54, 59.

10 ★★ **Civico Museo Archeologico.** Romans established Mediolanum, the settlement that would become Milan, in 222 B.C., and in A.D. 293 the outpost became capital of the Western Roman Empire. The emperor Maximian built a circus, baths, and imperial palaces, but all for naught: The Goths invaded a century later, and the capital moved to Ravenna. A 16th-century Benedictine monastery is the atmospheric re-

> *The Basilica di Sant'Ambrogio was built to honor the remains of Milan's patron saint, Ambrose.*

pository of tools, jewelry, and other everyday items from this ancient past. A Roman tower rises in the garden, and a Roman wall provides a backdrop for floor mosaics. Most evocative of all is the delicate 4th-century glass Trivulzio cup, inscribed with the motto, "Drink to Enjoy Long Life." ⏱ 1 hr. Corso Magenta 15. ☎ 02-8645-0011. Admission 3€. Tues–Sun 9am–1pm, 2–5:30pm. Metro: Cadorna. Bus: 18, 50. Tram: 19, 24, 27.

⑪ ★★ **San Lorenzo Maggiore.** The oldest church in Milan is another monument to the city's short reign as a capital of the Western Roman Empire. Roman columns and a statue of the Emperor Constantine stand outside the octagon-shaped structure, one of the largest buildings in the world in its time. The highest dome in Milan is among the many subsequent additions, but the **Cappella di Sant'Aquilino** is delightfully Byzantine, dazzling with 4th-century mosaics and two sarcophagi. One was crafted for Galla Placidia, who as regent for her son, Valentinian III, was ruler of the Western Roman Empire for 20 years. (Her mausoleum is one of the great monuments of Ravenna; see p 338, ⑥.) Another tomb holds the remains of **St. Aquilino,** a wandering preacher from

Germany who was famous for his miraculous ability to cure cholera. He was stabbed to death in 1015, and men who found him carried his body through the fog to San Lorenzo; for this cartage the saint has ever since been considered to be the patron of porters. ⏱ 30 min. Corso di Porta Ticinese 39. ☎ 02-8940-4129. Admission 2€. Mon–Sat 7:30am–12:30pm, 2:30–6:30pm; Sun 7:30am–6:30pm. Metro: Sant'Ambrogio. Tram: 3. Bus: 94.

⑫ ★★★ **Pinacoteca Ambrosiana.** Cardinal Federico Borromeo (1564–1631) was barely 30 when he became archbishop of Milan in 1595, and he devoted much of the rest of his life to creating one of Europe's great centers of art and learning. The cardinal was also a tireless proponent for the city's poor and partly at his own expense saw the city through the famine of 1627 to 1628. Francesco Maria Ricchini (1584–1658), Milan's greatest baroque architect, designed a building to house the cardinal's collection of works by Titian, Caravaggio, Raphael, and other masters, now shown off to great advantage in the museum's intimate spaces. The cardinal's 15,000 manuscripts and 30,000 books—among them Leonardo da Vin-

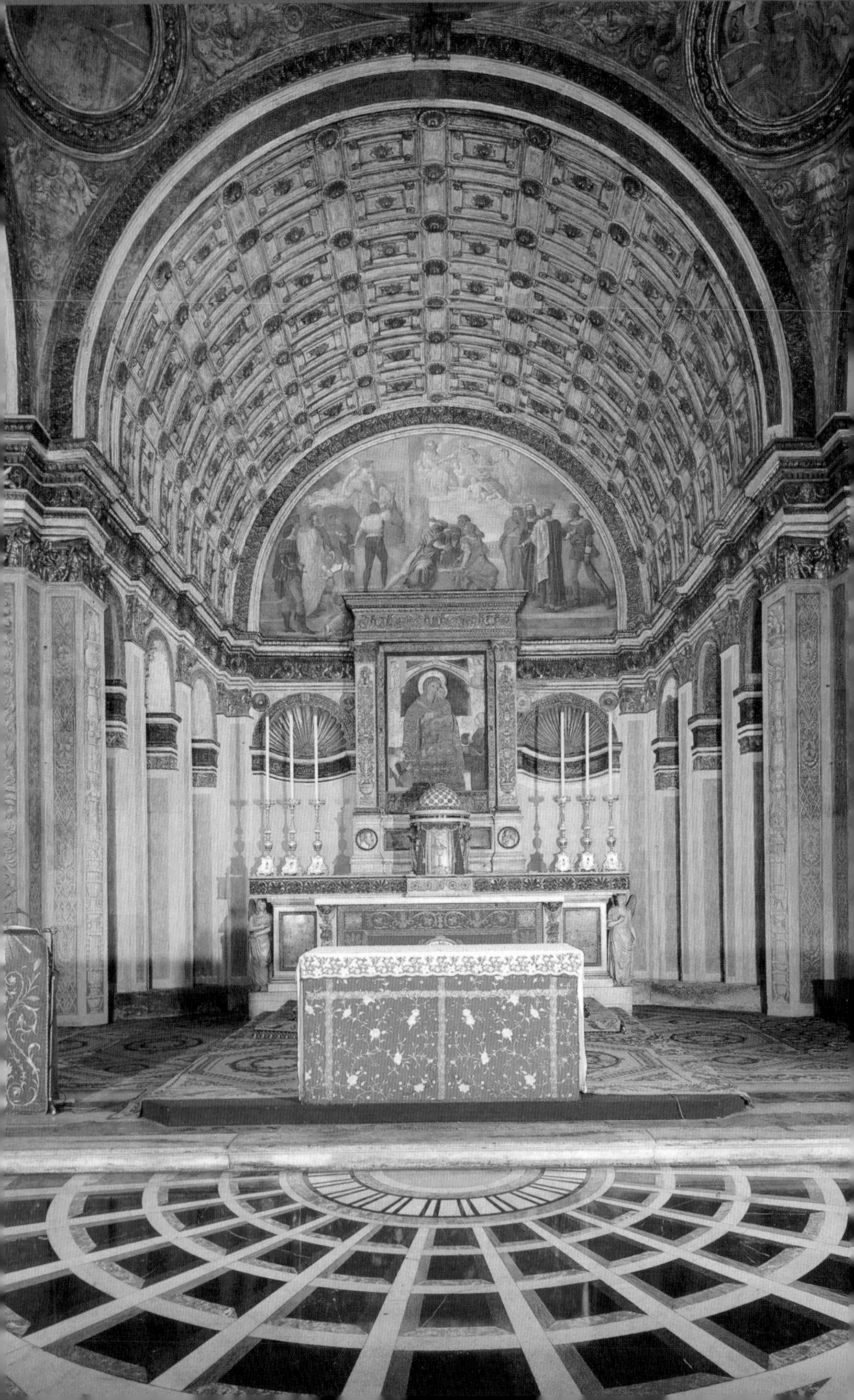

ci's *Codice Atlantico*—once comprised Europe's second-largest public library and are preserved in the adjoining **Biblioteca Ambrosiana,** open only to scholars with credentials. Lord Byron visited the library in 1815 and immersed himself in the love letters of Lucrezia Borgia and Pietro Bembo; he stole a strand of Lucrezia's hair, now encased under glass. For more on the painting collection, see p 448, **5**. ⏱ 2 hr. Piazza Pio XI 2. ☎ 02-806921. www.ambrosiana.it. Admission 7.50€. Tues–Sun 10am–5:30pm. Metro: Cordusio. Bus: 50. Tram: 2, 3, 4, 12, 14, 19, 24, 27.

13 ★★★ **Santa Maria presso San Satiro.** Antonio Amadeo, the sculptor whose work for Milan's Duomo (**1**) kept him busy for many years, designed the beautiful facade of this church that rises above a 9th-century shrine to San Satiro, brother of Milan's patron saint, Ambrose. Donato Bramante, who would later design the church of Santa Maria delle Grazie (**7**), tackled the problematic interior. A road passing behind the site made it impossible to expand the T-shaped apse to classical cross-shaped proportions. Bramante's solution was to create a relief behind the high altar, a trompe l'oeil illusion of columns and arches that seems to lengthen the apse to monumental proportions. Satiro's little shrine is incorporated into the **Cappella della Pietà,** named for the 15th-century terra-cotta *Pietà* it now houses, and graced by lovely Byzantine frescoes and Romanesque columns. ⏱ 30 min. Via Speronari 3. ☎ 02-874683. Mon–Fri 7:30–11:30am, 3:30–6.30pm; Sat–Sun 9:30am–noon, 3:30–7pm. Metro: Duomo. Bus: 54, 60. Tram: 2, 3, 12, 14, 15, 24.

14 ★★ **Santa Maria della Passione.** Milan's finest painter of the 17th century was Daniele Crespi (1590–1630), and the best place to see his work is this church where pillars, chapels, and organ enclosures are awash in his colorful, passionate paintings. Crespi's *San Carlo Borromeo Fasting* is one of Milan's most noted works of art, just as Carlo was one of 16th-century Milan's most celebrated citizens—an archbishop and later a powerful cardinal whose many accomplishments included the founding of the concept of Sunday school. ⏱ 30 min. Via Bellini 2. ☎ 02-7602-1370. Free admission. Mon–Fri 7am–noon, 3:30–6:15pm; Sat–Sun 9am–12:30pm, 3:30–6:30pm. Metro: San Babila. Bus: 54, 61.

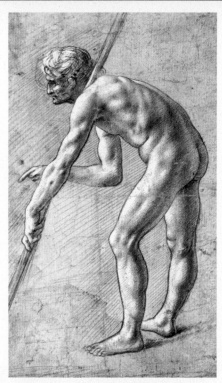

> *OPPOSITE PAGE The trompe l'oeil "apse" of San Satiro reveals architect Donato Bramante as a master of illusion. THIS PAGE Leonardo da Vinci's pencil drawing,* Study of a Man, *in the Biblioteca Ambrosiana.*

15 ★★ **Museo dell'Ottocento.** It is only fitting that Milan's museum for modern art ("modern" as in 19th century and later) is installed in the Villa Belgiojoso Bonaparte, once known as the Villa Reale and a building that has always represented a new order in Milan. Spanish, Austrian, and Bourbon governors administered Milan and northern Italy from its airy apartments, and Napoleon and his stepson, Eugene de Beauharnais, took up residence in 1802. The city's considerable collection of French impressionism resides comfortably here, along with works by such well-known Italians as Giorgio Morandi and Giorgio de Chirico. ⏱ 2 hr. Via Palestro 16. ☎ 02-760028. Free admission. Tues–Sun 9am–1pm, 2–5:30pm. Metro: Palestro. Bus: 94.

Where to Shop

★★ Alessi EAST OF THE DUOMO

Stylish yet utilitarian wares for the kitchen and bathroom, from teapots to toilet brushes, by the world's top designers. Corso Matteotti 9. ☎ 02-795-726. www.alessi.com. AE, DC, MC, V. Metro: San Babila. Bus: 54, 60, 65. Tram: 12, 27.

★★ B & B Italia EAST OF THE DUOMO

More like a museum of modern design than a store, the cavernous space displays vases, tableware, and everything else for the home, all of it pleasing to the eye and functional, too. Via Durini 14. ☎ 02-764441. www.bebitalia.it. AE, MC, V. Metro: San Babila. Bus: 54, 60, 65. Tram: 12, 27.

★★★ Fabriano NORTH OF THE DUOMO

Italy's oldest paper-maker has been in business since 1264, long enough to perfect the craft of making exquisite writing papers and sketch pads. Via Verri 3. ☎ 02-7631-8754. AE, DC, MC, V. Metro: San Babila. Bus: 54, 60, 65. Tram: 12, 27.

★★★ Il Salvagente PORTA VICTORIA

Milan's temple of designer discounts is stacked high with last season's styles, seconds, returns, and other fashionable discards. Via Fratelli Bronzetti 16. ☎ 02-7611-0328. www.salvagentemilano.it. No credit cards. Metro: Porta Venezia. Bus: 54, 60, 61, 62. Tram: 12, 27.

★★★ Peck DUOMO

Humble butcher Franz Peck founded an empire in 1883 that sets the gold standard for Milanese food shoppers. Cheeses, meats, wines, baked goods, and imported delicacies are shown off in elegant surroundings. Via Spadari 9. ☎ 02-802-316. www.peck.it. AE, DC, MC, V. Metro: Duomo. Bus: 54, 60, 65. Tram: 12, 27.

The Big Names

Fashion, ever so famously, is Milan's stock in trade, and all the big fashion names reside in the **Quadrilatero della Moda** (Fashion Rectangle). This little patch of designer heaven is a few blocks northeast of the Duomo between Via della Spiga, Via Montenapoleone, Via Manzoni, and Via Sant'Andrea. Most shops are open Monday to Saturday 10am to 7pm, and many are fashion statements in themselves, as **Viktor & Rolf,** Via Sant'Andrea 14 (☎ 02-796091), so aptly demonstrates with an upside-down look in which chandeliers rise from the floor and chairs hang from the ceiling.

A very short list of top shops in the Rectangle includes: **Giorgio Armani,** Via Sant'Andrea 9 (☎ 02-7600-3234); **Cacharel,** Via San Paolo 1 (☎ 02-8901-1127); **Chanel,** Via Sant'Andrea 8 (☎ 02-782-514); **Fendi,** Via Sant'Andrea 16 (☎ 02-7602-1617); **Gucci,** Via Montenapoleone 5–7 (☎ 02-771271); **Hermès,** Via Sant'Andrea 21 (☎ 02-7600-3495); **Prada,** Via Montenapo-

leone 8 (☎ 02-777-1771); and **Gianni Versace** (pictured), Via Montenapoleone 11 (☎ 02-7600-8528). The city also fulfills every other consumer fancy.

Where to Dine

Biffi DUOMO *MILANESE*
The tourist trail leads right to the terrace of this grand cafe, which has been serving beneath the glass vaults of the Galleria since 1867. Such classics as *cotoletta alla Milanese* do justice to the surroundings. **Galleria Vittorio Emanuele II.** ☎ 02-8057-9611. Entrees 20€–35€. AE, DC, MC, V. Lunch & dinner daily. Closed part of Aug. Metro: Duomo. Bus: 54, 60, 65. Tram: 12, 23, 27.

★★ **Centro Ittico** STAZIONE CENTRALE
SEAFOOD A location near the fish market ensures that the offerings are always fresh at Milan's most popular seafood eatery, where the kitchen cooks the catch of the day to order. **Via Martiri Oscuri 19.** ☎ 02-2804-0396. Entrees 25€–45€. AE, DC, MC, V. Lunch & dinner Mon–Sat. Closed Aug. Metro: Pasteur. Bus: 199. Tram: 1.

★ **Da Giannino L'Angolo d'Abruzzo** PORTA VENEZIA *MILANESE* Leave caloric and cholesterol concerns at the door for a step back to yesteryear, where the homey decor is complemented by creamy pasta sauces and grilled steaks and sausages. **Via Rosolino Pilo 20.** ☎ 02-2940-6526. Entrees 12€–15€. MC, V. Lunch & dinner Tues–Sun. Metro: Porta Venezia. Tram: 5, 11.

★★★ **Joia** PORTA VENEZIA *VEGETARIAN*
The soothing blonde wood ambience sets the mood for the sublime vegetarian creations of Swiss chef Pietro Lemman, whose pasta dishes are especially deft. **Via Panfilo Castaldi 18.** ☎ 02-2952-2124. Entrees 20€–40€. AE, DC, MC, V. Lunch & dinner Mon–Fri. Closed Aug, late Dec to early Jan. Metro: Republica. Tram: 29, 30.

★★ **La Latteria** BRERA *MILANESE*
The emphasis is on careful preparations of risottos and other Milanese staples, and the formula works—come very early or very late to get a table in the elbow-to-elbow space. **Via San Marco 24.** ☎ 02-659-7653. Entrees 9€–13€. No credit cards. Lunch & dinner daily. Closed Aug. Metro: Moscova.

> Biffi has been the Galleria Vittorio Emanuele II's cafe of choice since both opened in 1867.

★★★ **La Trattoria Milanese** WEST OF THE DUOMO *MILANESE* A warren of crooked lanes just west of the Duomo is the atmospheric setting for this decades-old Milanese institution, where diners tuck into generous servings of minestrone, risotto, tripe stew, and other old-fashioned favorites. **Via Santa Marta 11.** ☎ 02-8645-1991. Entrees 15€–30€. AE, DC, MC, V. Lunch & dinner Wed–Mon. Closed mid-July to Aug. Metro: Cordusio. Tram: 2, 3, 14.

★★ **Premiata Pizzeria** NAVIGLI *PIZZA*
The surrounding canals, courtyard patio, and what many regulars claim is the best pizza in Milan compensate for the waits and crowded communal tables here. **Via Alzaia Naviglio Grande 2.** ☎ 02-8940-0648. Entrees 8€–12€. AE, MC, V. Lunch & dinner daily. Metro: Porta Genova. Bus: 47. Tram: 2, 9, 29, 30.

Where to Stay

> A high-style junior suite at the Grand Hotel et de Milan.

★★ **Antica Locanda Solferino** BRERA

This homey old haunt of writers, painters, and actors is so comfortably stylish that no one seems to mind the lack of lounges (breakfast is served in the smallish rooms) or the tiny bathrooms. Via Castelfidardo 2. ☎ 02-657-0129. www.anticalocandasolferino.it. 11 units. Doubles 180€–300€. AE, MC, V. Metro: Moscova. Bus: 41, 43, or 94.

★★ **Doria Grand Hotel** NEAR STAZIONE CENTRALE

One of the many business-oriented hotels near the train station stands out with handsome appointments, luxurious linens and baths, a sumptuous breakfast buffet, and excellent-value rates. Viale Andrea Doria 22. ☎ 02-6741-1411. www.adihotels.com. 112 units. Doubles 100€–185€. AE, DC, MC, V. Metro: Loreto or Stazione Centrale.

★★★ **Grand Hotel et de Milan** NEAR LA SCALA

A 19th-century palazzo is Milan's final word in style and pedigree; Giuseppe Verdi not only slept here, but he also died here. Discretion, marble, antiques, and a fine location make the Grand about as grand as it gets. Via Manzoni 29. ☎ 02-723141. www.grandhoteletdemilan. it. Doubles 580€–680€. AE, DC, MC, V. Metro: Montenapoleone. Bus: 61, 94. Tram: 1 or 2.

★★ **Hotel Ariosto** MAGENTA

At this Art Nouveau lair just around the corner from Santa Maria delle Grazie, a flowery garden, double-glazed windows, and Jacuzzis in many of the rooms create a getaway ambience. Via Ariosto 22. ☎ 02-481-7844. www.hotelariosto.com. 53 units. Doubles 180€–360€. AE, DC, MC, V. Metro: Conciliazione. Bus: 68. Tram: 29 or 30.

★★ **Hotel Giulio Cesare** CASTELLO

An answer to many travelers' prayers: Moderately priced accommodations in the city center. The modern surroundings are spartan yet comfortable, and the Duomo and other attractions are a stone's throw away. Via Rovello 10. ☎ 02-7200-2179. www.giuliocesarehotel.it. 25 units. Doubles 89€–153€. MC, V. Metro: Carioli. Bus: 61. Tram: 1, 3, 4, 7, 12, 14, or 27.

★★ **Hotel London** CASTELLO

Old-fashioned ways prevail at this long-standing favorite of opera- and museum-goers, who can get just about anywhere they want to go on foot. The lobby and bar are cozy gathering places, and the decidedly un-modern quarters upstairs are quiet and comfortable. Via Rovello 3. ☎ 02-7202-0166. www.hotel-london-milan. com. 29 units. Doubles 130€–170€. MC, V. Metro: Carioli. Bus: 61. Tram: 1, 3, 4, 7, 12, 14, or 27.

Nightlife & Entertainment

> *The Blue Note is Milan's leading jazz venue.*

Clubs

★★ **Café Atlantique** SOUTHEAST OF CENTRO
Milan's epicenter of chic, where the focus is on being seen, seeing, and sipping cocktails at the round bar or in the garden. Viale Umbria 42. ☎ 199-111111. www.cafeatlantique.it. 10€–25€ cover. Tues–Sat 9pm–4am; Sun 7:30pm–4am. Closed July–Aug. Bus 90, 91, or 92.

★★ **Le Banque** DUOMO
Where the well-attired business and fashion set hangs out. Via Bassano Porrone 6. ☎ 340-282-3830. www.lebanque.it. 13€–16€ cover. AE, MC, V. Daily 6pm–5am. Closed Aug. Metro: Cadorna.

★★ **Nuova Idea** NORTH OF CENTRO
Milan's oldest gay club, with disco and ballroom dancing. Via de Castilla 30. ☎ 333-481-6780. www.lanuovaidea.it. 10€–16€ cover. Metro: Gioia. Bus: 42, 82, or 83. Tram: 30 or 33.

Film

★ **Odeon** DUOMO
The largest Cineplex in town shows many American hits, in English. Via Santa Radegonda 8. ☎ 199-757757. 5.50€ cover until 5:45pm, 7.80€ after. Metro: Duomo. Bus: 50 or 54. Tram: 1, 2, 12, 14, or 27.

Classical Music

★★ **Auditorium di Milano** SOUTH OF CENTRO
Classical music performed in a beautiful contemporary hall. Largo Mahler 1. ☎ 02-833891. Tickets 10€–50€. Bus 59 or 71. Tram: 3 or 15.

★★★ **Teatro alla Scala** DUOMO
The world's favorite opera house, and the city's toughest ticket. It's always worth checking with the box office—140 balcony seats go on sale 2 hours before a performance, and last-minute tickets go on sale 1 hour before. Tickets are available on the Internet, on an automated telephone booking service (☎ 02-860-775), in Italian, with a 20% booking fee; and through authorized sales agents, who generally charge a hefty fee—see www.vivaticket.it for a list. Piazza della Scala. ☎ 02-88791. www.teatroallascala.org. Tickets 25€–150€. Box office open daily, noon–6pm or until performance. Closed Aug. Metro: Duomo. Bus: 61. Tram: 1 or 2.

Blues & Jazz

★★ **Blue Note** PORTA GARIBALDI
Milan's largest jazz venue, with two shows nightly. Via Borsieri 37. ☎ 02-6901-6888. www.bluenotemilano.com. 25€–30€ cover. Tues–Sat 8:30pm–1am; Sun 8:30pm–11pm. Metro: Porto Garibaldi. Bus: 82 or 83. Tram: 4, 7, or 11.

★★ **Le Scimmie** SOUTH OF CENTRO
This nice jazz venue also hosts stand-up comedy, in English. Via Ascanio Sforza 49. ☎ 02-8940-2874. www.scimmie.it. 8€–15€ cover. Mon–Sat 7pm–3am. Metro: Porta Genova. Tram: 3 or 15.

LA MODA

The Superstars of Italian Fashion

BY SYLVIE HOGG

Milan, the fashion and design capital of Italy, if not the world, has been the headquarters of *la moda italiana* for more than a century. All the top Italian designers have showrooms and design studios here, and twice a year they parade their collections up and down runways all over town during Milan's *Settimana della Moda* (Fashion Week).

DESIGNER PROFILES

DOLCE & GABBANA When Hollywood stars and other glamazons really want to turn on the sex appeal, they come to Dolce & Gabbana. Raised in hot-blooded Sicily, Domenico Dolce and Stefano Gabbana showed their first women's collection in Milan in 1986. The pair has always embraced voluptuous, va-va-voom female beauty and is famous for corset-style dresses and leopard prints.

VERSACE The most glamorous label in Milan was begun by Gianni Versace in 1978. After his murder in 1997, his tanned and platinum-tressed sister Donatella took over the company as head designer. Though the decadent image seen in count-less magazine ads has been played down lately, Versace is still a beacon of look-at-me sexiness.

GIORGIO ARMANI When it comes to mens-wear, *non c'è paragone* (there's no comparison). Most any Italian man, given 1,000€ to spend at any of the high-fashion boutiques, would use it to buy an Armani suit. The impeccably tailored, clean-silhouetted creations are the pinnacle of sophistication. A former med student, Giorgio Armani worked as a department store window-dresser before founding his own design shop in the 1970s.

ROBERTO CAVALLI The Florentine designer's bold, rock-inspired signature style includes flamboyant floral and animal motifs, rich and rebellious textures like embossed leather and ripped denim, and sultry flair. A darling of the European jet set for decades, Cavalli has risen to broad international fame relatively recently.

PRADA Founded in 1913 by Mario Prada and now run by his granddaughter, Miuccia, Prada offers intellectual, avant-garde fashions that tread the fine line between innovation and wearability. This fashion house is always the first to play with new silhouettes or fabric, and the Prada label is espe-cially coveted on shoes and handbags.

WHERE TO OGLE

Milan is so small and chock-full of chic people that it's not hard to find places where you can mix with the *modaioli*. And during Fashion Week (once in Feb, once in Sept/Oct), just about every moderately hip cafe is swarming with style mavens.

A perennial favorite is cafe/gallery/book-shop **10 Corso Como** (Corso Como 10). Or try the Milanese outpost of **Nobu**, above the Armani store at Via Pisoni 1. The **Just Cavalli Café** (Viale Camoens, in Parco Sempione) is a must for its over-the-top, fashion amuse-ment park feel. **Il Girarrosto** (Corso Venezia 31) and **Giulio Pane e Ojo** (Via L. Muratori) may look like regular trattorias, but they're always packed with über-fab fashion types.

Mantua

Set off at the far eastern edge of Lombardy, Mantua
(Màntova, in Italian) is a land apart in time—a city of medieval and Renaissance
squares and palaces. Observers as diverse as the poet Virgil, a native son, and
Aldous Huxley have commented on a certain melancholy to the city, but this
moodiness, like the mists rising off the River Mincio, shrouds Mantua in that
much more atmosphere.

> *Mantua owes its artistic and architectural riches, including the Palazzo Ducale, to the egotism and largesse
of the Gonzaga family.*

START **Palazzo Ducale. Mantua is 158km (95
miles) east of Milan, about 2 hours by train;
the trip usually requires a change in Verona
or Piadena.**

1 ★★★ kids **Palazzo Ducale di Màntova.** The
story of the Gonzaga dynasty unfolds behind
the walls of this huge, brooding palace. Though
they were of humble origins and famously
unattractive, by the 15th century the Gonzagas
had married into some of the most powerful
families in Europe. The most beneficial of
these unions, in terms of the family's artistic
legacy, was the marriage of Isabella d'Este

(sister-in-law of Lucrezia Borgia, her rival in
patronizing the great artists and thinkers of
the Renaissance) to Francesco Gonzaga in
1490. Andrea Mantegna (1431–1506) was
their preferred artist, and he painted Isabella's
private apartments with the remarkable
Parnassus (now in the Louvre), as well as a
magnificent fresco cycle for the **Camera degli
Sposi** (it took 9 years to complete). Isabella's
son Federico and later generations were
collectors, too, and by the 1620s it is estimated
the family had amassed more than 2,000
pieces for this palace alone. Among them are

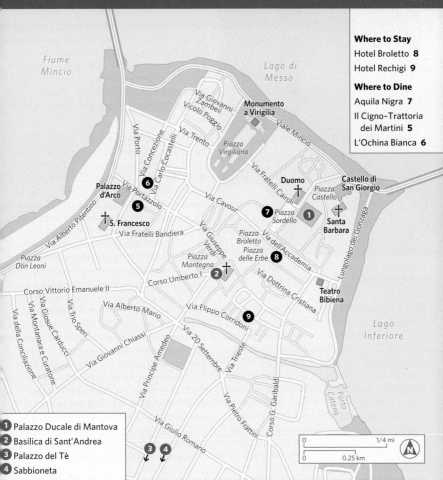

Fiume
Mincio

Lago di
Messo

Via Giovanni
Zambeii

Vicolo Poggio

Monumento
a Virigilia

Viale Mincio

Via Trento

Piazza
Virgiliana

Via Fratelli Cairoli

Via Porto

Via Concezione

Via Carlo Cocastelli

Via Cavour

Duomo

Piazza
Castello

Castello di
San Giorgio

Palazzo
d'Arco **6**

Via Portazzolo

5

† S. Francesco

Via Alberto Pietrino

Via Fratelli Bandiera

Piazza
Don Leoni

Via Giuseppe
Verdi

Piazza
Mantegna

7 Piazza
Sordello

1

Santa
Barbara

Piazza
Broletto

Via dell'Accademia

Piazza
delle Erbe **8**

Corso Umberto I

2 †

Via Dottrina Cristiana

Lungolago dei Gonzaga

Teatro
Bibiena

Corso Vittorio Emanuele II

Via Alberto Mario

Via Giosue Carducci

Via Trio Speri

Via Montanara e Curatone

Via della Conciliazione

Via Flippo Corridoni

9

Via Giovanni Chiassi

Via Principe Amedeo

Via 20 Settembre

Via Trieste

Lago
Inferiore

Via Pietro Frattini

Corso G. Garibaldi

Porto
Catena

Via Giulio Romano

0 | 1/4 mi

0 | 0.25 km

N

1 Palazzo Ducale di Mantova

2 Basilica di Sant'Andrea

3 Palazzo del Tè

4 Sabbioneta

works by Titian, Tintoretto, and Rubens, and
they hang one after another in the palace's 500
rooms. For more on the collections, see p 454,
10. ☾ 2 hr. Piazza Sordello 40. ☎ 0376-320283.
www.mantovaducale.beniculturali.it. Admission
10€. Tues–Sun 8:30am–7pm.

2 ★★ **Basilica di Sant'Andrea.** The largest
church in Mantua is the work of Leon Battista
Alberti (1404–72), whose trademark, a classical triumphal arch, shows up on the facade just
as it does in his church of Santa Maria Novella
in Florence (p 173, **12**) and the Malatesta
Temple in Rimini (p 309). Ludovico Gonzaga
commissioned the church in 1472 to provide
suitable surroundings for one of the most important relics of the Renaissance: a vial said

to contain the *Preziosissimo Sangue di Cristo,*
the most precious blood of Christ, which the
Roman centurion Longinus allegedly obtained
when he thrust his spear into the side of Christ.
Pilgrims still come from all over Europe to be
present on Good Friday, when the relic is paraded through the streets, and again on the feast
of the Ascension, when the vial is raised from
a crypt into the church to symbolize Christ's
ascension into Heaven. The church is also the
final resting place of Andrea Mantegna, who
probably had a hand in the design of his funerary chapel. ☾ 30 min. Piazza Mantegna. ☎ 0376-
328253. Free admission. Daily 7:30am–noon,
3:30–7:30pm.

> Mantua's Rotonda di San Lorenzo is an ancient church with roots in the 11th century.

❸ ★★★ Palazzo del Tè. Federico Gonzaga, son of Isabella and Francesco, inherited his mother's taste for art, and from his father, the congenital syphilis that rendered him a semi-invalid for much of his life and killed him at the age of 40. As a retreat from the rigors of court life, he and his mistress, Isabella Boschetti, converted royal stables near the marshes at the edge of town to a *villa suburbana* where Federico could indulge in his great passion, breeding horses. The architect was Giulio Romano (1499–1546), a pupil of Raphael, and he constructed an airy, low square villa surrounding a courtyard and opening onto formal gardens. Guests were feted in salons remarkably frescoed and stuccoed with horses, giants, astrological figures, and even a bit of pornography in the guise of scenes from classical mythology. For more on the palazzo, see p 455. Viale Tè. ☎ 0376-323266. Admission 8€. Tues–Sun 9am–6pm.

❹ ★★ kids Sabbioneta. In the middle of the 16th century, Vespasiano Gonzaga set out to build the ideal Renaissance city on the plains about 30km (18 miles) southwest of Mantua. Using as his model the concepts of urban planning set down by the Roman architect and engineer Vitruvius, Vespasiano commissioned straight, wide streets, and star-shaped walls breached by two gates. Sabbioneta was soon known as "Little Athens" for its elegant proportions and Vespasiano's high-minded court. It wasn't too long, though, before the Gonzagas were gone from the scene altogether, and Sabbioneta languished for several centuries as a ghost town. In recent years the Palazzo Ducale, the Teatro Olimpico, and palaces have been repaired and the place brought back to life. The buildings can be visited on guided tour (in Italian) only; for more information, contact the tourist office, Via Vespasiano Gonzaga 31. ☎ 0375-52039. Tours 10€ per person. Apr–Oct Tues–Fri 9:30am–1pm, 2:30–6pm, Sat 2:30pm–6:30pm; Nov–Mar Tues–Fri 9:30am–1pm, 2:30–5pm, Sat 2:30–6pm. 7 buses a day serve Sabbioneta from Mantua's train station (4€).

Stage-Set Surroundings

The River Mincio makes a wide loop around Mantua, surrounding the city with smooth waters that moodily reflect the ducal palace and other monuments. Medieval and Renaissance travelers used to arrive in Mantua by barge, which is how Isabella d'Este came up from Ferrara to marry Ludovico Gonzaga. The city center is strung out along three adjoining piazzas that are surrounded by medieval houses and Renaissance churches and palaces. The southernmost, the **Piazza delle Erbe,** is named for the food and vegetable markets that transpire on one side, and for 7 centuries Mantua's civic affairs have been attended to in the medieval and Renaissance **Palazzo della Ragione** (Palace of Justice) and **Palazzo del Podestà** (Mayor's Palace) that overshadow the stalls. The **Torre dell'Orologio,** with a 14th-century astrological clock, rises above the **Rotonda di San Lorenzo,** a round church from the 11th century. In the **Piazza Broletto,** a statue of Virgil commemorates the poet who was born near Mantua in 70 B.C. and celebrated the Mincio and the flat, melancholy countryside that surrounds it in his *Bucolics.* The last square is the enormous **Piazza Sordello**—somber, medieval, and flanked on one side by the overwhelming presence of the Palazzo Ducale.

Where to Stay & Dine

★★ **Aquila Nigra** CENTRO *MANTOVIAN*
A Renaissance feast, served in a fresco-
bedecked convent, includes such local
delicacies as eel and pike from the Mincio,
bathed in delicate sauces. Vicolo Bonacolsi.
☎ 0376-327180. Entrees 25€–35€. AE, MC, V.
Lunch & dinner Tues–Sat; lunch Sun Apr–May &
Sept–Oct. Closed Aug.

★★ **Hotel Broletto** CENTRO
The simple but comfortable accommodations
are enlivened by beams and other medieval
details, and Mantua's piazzas and monuments
are just outside the door. Via dell'Accademia 1.
☎ 0376-326784. www.hotelbroletto.com. 16 units.
Doubles 90€–120€. AE, MC, V.

★★ **Hotel Rechigi** CENTRO
The pleasant, contemporary surroundings
of this business-oriented hotel near the city
center include a courtyard patio. Via P. F. Calvi
30. ☎ 0376-320781. www.rechigi.com. 60 units.
Doubles 110€–190€. AE, MC, V.

> Risotto is a staple of northern Italian cooking.

Dining Tip

Piazza delle Erbe is the scene of a bustling
food market Monday to Saturday from 8am
to 1pm. Another place to find a meal on the
go is the Via Pescherie, just south of the
city center, where stalls sell fresh and fried
fish from the River Mincio and the Adriatic.

★★ **Il Cigno–Trattoria dei Martini** CENTRO
MANTOVIAN An old palazzo is the setting for
specialties—many based on Renaissance recipes—that would please a Gonzaga. Piazza Carlo
d'Arco. ☎ 0376-327101. Entrees 20€–30€. AE, DC,
MC, V. Lunch & dinner Wed–Sun. Closed Aug.

★★ **L'Ochina Bianca** CENTRO *MANTOVIAN*
Simple, contemporary surroundings set the stage
for elegant seafood risottos and such innovations
as *peperoni ripieni di pesce di fiume* (peppers filled
with smoked fish and topped with a fresh tomato
sauce). Via Finzi 2. ☎ 0376-323700. Entrees 10€–
15€. MC, V. Dinner Tues; lunch & dinner Wed–Sun.

A Little Night Music

The Austrians stepped in to administer
Mantua when the Gonzaga line died out in
the early 18th century, and from them comes
the magnificent baroque Teatro Scientifico
dell'Accademia, better known today as the
Teatro Bibiena. The name is a tribute to
Viennese-trained but Italian-born architect
Antonio Galli Bibiena (1697–1774), the leading
theater designer of his day. Wolfgang Ama-
deus Mozart, only 13 at the time, performed
at the theater's inauguration on January 16,
1770. The theater still hosts concerts and
operas, so by all means check with the tourist
office for schedules and tickets. The theater,
at Via dell'Accademia 47 (☎ 0376-220097),
is also open for visits Monday to Saturday
from 9am to noon and 3:30 to 6pm.

Bergamo

Just an hour east of Milan, Bergamo is not only a bucolic retreat from the big city, but is also a seriously well-endowed monument of the Middle Ages and Renaissance—the Città Alta (upper city) is filled with beautiful houses, squares, and churches.

> The Cappella Colleoni honors a mercenary turned governor of Bergamo.

START Piazza Vecchia, in the Città Alta. To reach the Città Alta from the train station and the modern Città Bassa, take bus 1 or 3 (1€), then make the free transfer to the Funicolare Bergamo Alta, which runs every 7 minutes, 6:30am–12:30am, to connect the old city with the new city.

① ★★★ **kids** **Piazza Vecchia.** The Venetians ruled Bergamo from 1428 until Napoleon arrived in the late 18th century, and they left their mark on one of Italy's most beautiful squares, or, in the opinion of the French writer Stendhal, the "most beautiful place on earth." It is easy to imagine how such an evocative assemblage of fountains, arcades, and loggias may have inspired Bergamo-born Gaetano Donizetti (1797–1848) to compose operas as romantic as *Lucia di Lammermoor*. Stone lions, symbols of the Venetian Republic, are much in evidence around the square's fountain. ◷ 10 min.

② ★★★ **Piazza del Duomo.** Bergamo's most important religious monuments surround a square just beyond the arcades of the Palazzo della Ragione. The **Cappella Colleoni** (free admission; Apr–Sept Tues–Sun 9am–noon, 2:30–5:30pm; Oct–Mar Tues–Sun 9am–noon, 2:30–4:40pm) houses the funerary chapel of Bartolomeo Colleoni (c. 1400–75), the *condottiero* (mercenary) who, on behalf of the Venetians, fought off an attack by the Visconti of Milan and in return was rewarded with the governorship of Bergamo. Here, Colleoni rides a gilded wooden horse beneath ceiling frescoes by Tiepolo and against a backdrop of the elaborate relief that Giovanni Amadeo sculpted for Colleoni's tomb and that of his favorite daughter, Medea. The adjoining **Basilica di Santa Maria Maggiore** (free admission; May–Sept 8am–12:30pm, 3–7pm; Oct–Apr 8am–noon, 3–6pm) is the final resting place of Gaetano Donizetti and also a museumlike repository of paintings, tapestries, frescoes, and stucco work. Many of the paintings are by Lorenzo Lotto, who lived in Bergamo from 1513 to 1525 and whose work appears in churches throughout the city. Here he designed the intricate intarsia panels that surround the choir stalls. ◷ 30 min.

③ ★ **Museo Donizettiano.** The composer Gaetano Donizetti was born in 1797 in the cellar of a little house on a street that descends the hillside from Bergamo's Città Alta. In his lifetime, he wrote 75 operas, as well as symphonies and other musical works. He was living in Paris when he fell ill in his mid-40s, and friends (among them Giuseppe Verdi) brought Donizetti back to Bergamo, where he slipped into madness and died in 1848. This small museum dedicated to Donizetti displays sheet music and other memorabilia, including the composer's piano and deathbed. ◷ 30 min. Via Borgo Canale 14. ☎ 035-

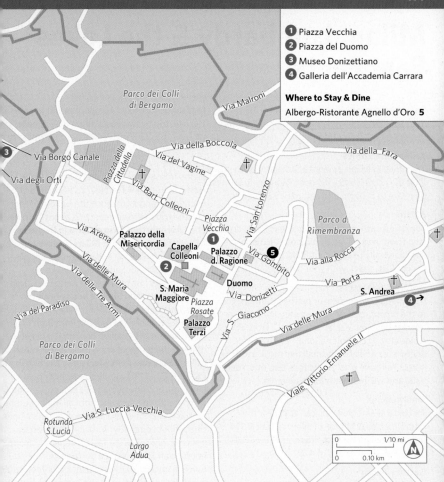

1 Piazza Vecchia
2 Piazza del Duomo
3 Museo Donizettiano
4 Galleria dell'Accademia Carrara

Where to Stay & Dine
Albergo-Ristorante Agnello d'Oro **5**

244483. Free admission. Apr–Sept Tues–Sat 9am–noon, 2:30pm–5pm; Oct–Mar Tues–Sat 9am–noon.

4 ★★★ **Galleria dell'Accademia Carrara.** One of Italy's finest galleries is all the more rewarding because it is small enough not to overwhelm. Instead, as visitors walk along the galleries of a neoclassical palace at the foot of the hill in the Città Bassa, one masterpiece after another shines from the walls: Raphael's *St. Sebastian*, Titian and Giovanni Bellini Madonnas, Venetian scenes by Canaletto. At press time, the museum is closed for renovations; it's tentatively scheduled to reopen in mid-2011. ⏱ 2–3 hr. Piazza Giacomo Carrara 22. ☎ 035-399677. Admission 2.60€. Tues–Sun 10am–1pm, 2:30pm–5:30pm.

Where to Stay & Dine

★★★ **Albergo-Ristorante Agnello d'Oro**
CITTA ALTA *NORTHERN ITALIAN* It is impossible to stay or dine more conveniently or atmospherically in Bergamo than in these natty little rooms overlooking a piazza, and in the paneled dining room downstairs. Via Gombito 22. ☎ 035-249883. Doubles 90€. Entrees 15€–20€. AE, MC, V.

Milan, Lombardy & the Lakes Fast Facts

Accommodations Booking Services
Your best bet is to work with one of the tourist centers (see "Visitor Information," below).

American Express
The office in Milan is near La Scala at Via Brera 3 (☎ 02-7200-3693). It's open Monday to Friday 9am to 5:30pm and Saturday 9am to 5pm.

ATMs
You'll find cash machines (*bancomat*) in every city, town, and village throughout the region. Italy generally uses 4-digit PINs; if you have a 6-digit PIN, check with your bank.

Dentists & Doctors
For emergency medical or dental attention, go to the *pronto soccorso* (emergency room) of the nearest hospital (ask at your hotel). Non–EU residents can consult national health service doctors for a relatively small fee; most good hotels will have a list of doctors, and often dentists, and will help with arrangements.

Emergencies
For general emergencies, call ☎ 112 for the Carabinieri or ☎ 113 for the Polizia. Call ☎ 114 for an ambulance and ☎ 115 for the fire department. See also "Police," p 479.

Getting There
BY PLANE **Malpensa** (☎ 02-7485-2200; www.sea-aeroportimilano.it), 45km (27 miles) west of Milan, is well served by flights from New York, London, and other international cities. **Malpensa Bus Express** (☎ 02-240-7954) and **Malpensa Shuttle** (☎ 02-5858-3185; www.malpensashuttle.it) run between Stazione Centrale and all Malpensa terminals. Service runs from 5am to 11pm, and the trip takes a little over an hour, depending on traffic; the fare is about 7€, payable on the bus. **Malpensa Express trains** (www.malpensaexpress.it) run every half-hour between 6am and 9pm (9:30pm on Sun); service is between a train terminal at Malpensa and Cardona rail station, where you can easily connect to the city's metro, buses, or

trams. The trip takes 40 minutes and the fare is 11€. The trip by taxi costs about 80€. **Linate** (☎ 02-7485-2200; www.sea-aeroportimilano.it) is much more convenient, only 7km (4 miles) east of the city center, but handles only limited flights from some Italian and European cities. From Linate, city ATM bus 73 (1€) makes connections to and from stops throughout Milan, and the trip to the city center is about 15 minutes. **Aeroporto di Orio al Serio in Bergamo,** 45km (27 miles) east of Milan, is served by RyanAir from London and other discount airlines. From Orio al Serio, you can take a Bergamo city bus to and from Bergamo's train station, or the **Orio Shuttle bus service** (www.orioshuttle.com) to and from Milan's Stazione Centrale, with service running from 8am to 11pm; tickets (8€) can be bought at a ticket office in the terminal or on the bus. BY TRAIN Milan's **Stazione Centrale,** Piazza Duca d'Aosta (☎ 02-6371-2016), is a 1930s architectural landmark and one of Europe's busiest rail hubs, with direct service to and from all major European and Italian cities and connections to stations throughout Lombardy. Eurocity and Intercity trains (p 723) offer the fastest service—about 2 hours to and from Venice or Florence. The station, about 2km (1 mile) northeast of the center is easily connected via metro, tram, and bus. BY CAR Milan is at the northern end of Italy's major north-south highway, autostrada **A1,** and at the junction of a network of other major highways. The trip by car is 3 hours from Florence, 2 hours from Venice, and 6 hours from Rome.

Getting Around
BY TRAIN Given the extent and frequency of service in the region, trains are an easy way to get around the region, and the many bus and boat connections make it possible to tour even the lakes and other remote parts of Lombardy without a car. BY BUS Bus lines serve towns throughout Lombardy, including many resorts on the lakes; lines include **Autostradale Viaggi** (www.autostradale.com); **SGEA Lombardia**

www.sgea.it); **SIA** (www.sia.it); and **STEI** (www.stei.it). The main Milan bus station, Autostazione Garibaldi, is north of the center on Piazza Freud. Though trains are a more convenient method of travel, many smaller towns in Lombardy, including most of those around the lakes, are served only by bus. **BY BOAT** For information on getting around the lakes by boat, see p 433. **BY CAR** A network of super-speedy highways (*autostrade*) crisscross the region, making travel by car quick and easy. Smaller roads around the lakes are extremely crowded in the summer, and you are well advised to park your car and get around on foot and by boat. If you are visiting only cities around Milan, a car is unnecessary as train connections are excellent. You will want a car to travel into the mountains and other remote areas.

Driving in Milan is difficult, traffic is horrendous, much of the city is closed to traffic, and legal street parking is almost impossible to find. If you drive into the city, do yourself a favor and stash the car in a garage; some major hotels have them, and large garages in the center include **Autosilo Diaz,** Piazza Diaz Armando 1 (☎ 02-8646-0077)—expect to pay about 30€ a day.

Internet Access

Wi-Fi is a common amenity in Milan hotels and also in many of the larger hotels around Lombardy and the lakes. A lively spot to use a computer is **FNAC,** the large bookstore near the Duomo at Via della Palla 2 (☎ 02-869541; open Mon–Sat 9am–8pm and Sun 10am–8pm).

Pharmacies

Farmacie (look for a neon green or red cross) are usually open 8am to 1:30pm and 3:30 to 8pm. In any city or town, at least one pharmacy is required to remain open 24 hours on a rotating basis; the name and location of the designated pharmacy is posted at all others. The pharmacy in Milan's Stazione Centrale (☎ 02-669-1739) is open 24 hours.

Police

To report a lost or stolen article, such as a wallet or passport, visit the local police *questura* or Carabinieri *caserma* in your location. See also "Emergencies," p 478.

Post Office

Post offices are generally open Monday to Friday 8:15am to 6:30pm and Saturday 8:15am to 12:20pm. The main post office in Milan is on Via Cordusio 4 (☎ 02-7248-2126) and is open Monday to Saturday 8am to 7pm. *Francobolli* (stamps) can be purchased at most *tabacchi* (tobacco stores).

Safety

Milan is safer than many large cities, but tourists should be wary of pickpockets, especially around Stazione Centrale. Here as elsewhere in Italy, groups of children operate in gangs and surround targets while rifling through their pockets and bags. Crime is less of an issue elsewhere in the region, though pickpockets operate at train stations and other busy public places.

Visitor Information

Province of Milan information offices, with listings of sights, events, hotels, and restaurants, are at Piazza del Duomo 19A (☎ 02-7740-4343; www.provinci.milano.it), and in Stazione Centrale on the departures level (☎ 02-7740-4318). Another good source for updated information on Milan is online at **Ciao Milano** (www.ciaomilano.it). Just about all towns around the region have tourist offices that provide maps, brochures, and in many cases help find accommodations. **Mantua's** tourist office is in Piazza Mantegna (☎ 0376-8254; Mon–Sat 9am–noon, 3–6pm; Sun 9am–noon). **Pavia's** tourist office is at Piazza Petrarca 4 (☎ 0382-597001; Mon–Sat, 8:30am–12:30pm, 2–5pm). The **Brescia** tourist office is at Piazza Loggia 6 (☎ 030-240-0357; June–Sept Mon–Sat 9:30am–6:30pm, Oct–May Mon–Fri 9:30am–12:30pm, 2:30–5:30pm, Sat 9:30am–12:30pm). In **Bergamo,** the tourist office is located in the Città Alta at Via Gombito (☎ 035-242226; www.commune.bergamo.it).

If touring the lakes, make it a point to stop in at tourist offices in the major towns to gather info: **Stresa,** Piazza Marconi 16 (☎ 0323-3150; Apr–Oct daily 10am–12:30pm, 3–6:30pm; Nov–Mar Mon–Fri 10am–12:30pm, 3–6:30pm, Sat 10am–12:30pm); **Bellagio,** Piazza Mazzini (☎ 031-950204; www.bellagiolakecomo.com); and **Sirmione,** Viale Marconi 2 (☎ 030-916114; www.provincia.brescia.it) The tourist office for **Lago d'Orta** is in Omegna at Piazza XXIV Aprile 17 (☎ 0323-61930; www.prolocoomegna.vb.it).

The Best of Turin & Piedmont in 3 Days

Piedmont, *Piemonte* in Italian, means "foot of the mountains," and the snow-capped peaks of the Alps are never far from sight in this province of fields, orchards, and vineyards. The gastronomic riches are especially prominent in the rolling hills around Asti and Alba, whose vineyards yield Barolos and other excellent wines. While Turin (Torino), the region's major city, is often associated with industry, the beautiful, baroque city center has changed very little since it was rebuilt by members of the House of Savoy in the 17th and 18th centuries. This tour offers a brief but satisfying taste of the region.

START **Turin.**

1 **Turin.** Turin is often called, much to the annoyance of the Torinese, "the most French city in Italy," or "the most Italian city in France," or "Little Paris"—references to its boulevards and monuments, which can be more reminiscent of France than of Italy. The city's style is distinctly Torinese and reflects the tastes of members of the House of Savoy, who had a preference for marrying into the French aristocracy and who for many centuries ruled lands that included not just the French Savoie but also the Côte d'Azur and many other parts of present-day France.

Most of old Turin was rebuilt over medieval and Renaissance streets in the 17th and 18th centuries and is largely intact, creating what is today one of the world's great baroque cities. Old Turin is easy to explore on foot and you can do so in a day, following a route along and

> PREVIOUS PAGE *Turin's Palazzo Reale was the headquarters of the House of Savoy, one of Europe's longest-lasting royal dynasties.* THIS PAGE *The Savoys oversaw the remodeling of Piazza San Carlo along French baroque lines.*

0   10 mi
0   10 km

SWITZERLAND

Domodóssola

E62

Vogogna

Matterhorn
(Monte Cervino)

Gran Combin

L. Maggiore

Breuil-
Cervinia

Verbánia

Mont Blanc
(Monte Bianco)

Omegna

Stresa

Courmayeur   SS27

Varallo

Aosta   VALLE D'AOSTA

SS26

L. d'Orta

Pila

A5

Parco Nazionale
del Gran Paradiso

Biella

Salussola

Novara

FRANCE

Ivrea

A4

San
Germano

Castellamonte

Strambino

A26

Vercelli

Caluso

Ceres

SS26

Desana

A5

Lemie

Fiano

Venaria

A4

Stroppiana

Bussoleno

Reale

Chivasso

Po River

Casale
Monferrato

A32

Rivoli

Turin

A26

Avigliana

Chieri

Orbassano

Moncalvo

Valenza

Cumiana

Moncalieri

Castell'Alfero

San Salvatore

Pinerolo

PIEDMONT

A21

Asti

Alessándria

Pellice R.

Tanaro R.

Carmagnola

Cavour

Racconigi

Canale

SS231

Nizza
Monferrato

SP456

SS589

SS20

A6

Acqui
Terme

Cavallermaggiore

Bra

Paesana

Saluzzo

SP662

Savigliano

Alba

Bistagno

Bormida R.

Cherasco

Cortemilia

A26

Costigliole

Fossano

Ovada

SS231

Dogliani

Ellero R.

Stura di Demonte

Cuneo

Bagnasco

Valdieri

SS20

Vernante

❶	Turin
❷	Basilica di Superga
❸	Stupinigi
❹	Asti
❺	Alba

> *Piazza San Carlo is home to Turin's grandest street cafes, including Caffè San Carlo.*

just off the **Via Roma** as it runs from the Piazza Carlo Felice north through the city center to the Piazza Castello and adjoining Piazza Reale.

Even emerging from the **Porta Nuova** train station is a pleasure, because that means admiring both the elegant 19th-century facade and stepping into the **Piazza Carlo Felice,** where well-tended gardens are surrounded by arcades. Turin was the favorite city of Napoleon, a stickler for order, and when looking straight down the Via Roma all the way through the city to **Piazza Reale,** it soon becomes apparent why Turin's gridlike arrangement of streets and squares might have appealed to the emperor.

Before exploring Turin's many museums or churches, stroll along the length of Via Roma. Just north of Piazza Carlo Felice marble arcades that went up during the Mussolini era shelter some of the city's most exclusive shops and emerge into **Piazza San Carlo.** This elegant

square is a pleasant introduction to many facets of Turin: to the Savoys, whose 16th-century duke Emanuele Filiberto rides a bronze horse across the center, to the city's many chocolate shops and cafes (p 512), whose terraces provide an outdoor living room for the Torinese, and to such urbane innovations as the **Galleria San Federico,** a glass-vaulted shopping arcade from 1858.

Emanuele Filiberto makes another appearance, in spirit at least, down the street in **Piazza Castello,** created under his orders when he made Turin the Savoy capital in 1559. This piazza and the adjoining Piazza Reale were the Savoys' imposing epicenter of church and state, surrounded as they are by the **Palazzo Reale** (p 506, ❸), the Savoy royal palace; the **Palazzo Madama** (p 504, ❶), graced with a remarkable facade by the city's great 17th-century architect Filippo Juvarra and home to two French-born Savoy widows who acted as regents for Savoy dukes, Christine Marie and Marie Jeanne Baptiste de Savoie-Nemours; and the **Duomo di San Giovanni** (p 507, ❹), where in the 1660s the architect Guarino Guarini created the visually arresting Cappella della Sacra Sindone to house the **Sacra Sindone,** the **Shroud of Turin.**

Travel Tip

It is relatively easy to get to most towns in Piedmont and the Valle d'Aosta by train and bus, and this tour can be done entirely via public transportation.

A few blocks east of Piazza Castello rises Turin's distinctively idiosyncratic brick tower, the **Mole Antonelliana** (p 508, ⑤), now the dramatic setting for the film props, old sets, antique cameras and other holdings of the **Museo Nazionale del Cinema.** A walk back south along the Via Roma soon brings you to some of Turin's great collections. The **Galleria Sabauda** (p 509, ⑦) houses the artworks amassed by the House of Savoy, much added to over the years and especially well endowed with works by Jan van Eyck and other northern artists, and the holdings of the **Museo Egizio** (p 510, ⑧) are second only to those in Cairo. A close-up look at Italian unification in the **Museo del Risorgimento** (p 508, ⑥) can challenge the most eager museum goer, but Turin's collection is particularly impressive and housed in beautiful surroundings behind the curving facade of the **Palazzo Carignano.** ⏱ 2 days, with outings to Superga and Stupinigi. See p 504.

On the afternoon of Day 1, make an outing to the Basilica di Superga, via bus 79 from the Porta Nuova train station to the rack railway station in the suburb of Sassi. Make the ascent by train from there.

② **Basilica di Superga.** This final resting place of princes and kings is an imposing combination of classical and baroque architecture, and is surrounded by parklands laced with walking trails. ⏱ 3 hr., including travel time. See p 502, ①.

Return by bus to Turin. On the morning or afternoon of Day 2, take bus 41 from Porta Nuova station for the half-hour trip to Stupinigi.

③ kids **Stupinigi.** The hunting lodge of Vittorio Amedeo II is shaped like a St. Andrew's cross, the symbol of the knightly order of St. Maurice, of which the king was grand master. Nature makes a grand showing here, too, in the royal hunting grounds now protected as the Parco Naturale di Stupinigi. ⏱ 2 hr., with travel time. See p 503, ②.

On the morning of Day 3, make the 45-minute trip from Turin down to Asti by train.

④ **Asti.** Renaissance palaces and medieval churches line Asti's busy streets and squares, and are especially lively during the weekly

> *The white truffle, or* tartufo bianco, *is Alba's most precious export.*

markets on Wednesday and Saturday mornings. A sip of Asti Spumante, the town's famous sparkling beverage, captures the effervescence of this prosperous town. ⏱ 1 day, with a side trip to Alba (⑤).

On the afternoon of Day 3, take a train (travel time: 20 minutes) from Asti to Alba.

⑤ **Alba.** When French actor Gérard Depardieu was once invited to appear at Alba's annual **Fiera del Tartufo** (truffle fair, see p 721), he asked in recompense for his weight in Nutella (the delicious chocolate spread manufactured in town) and truffles—and you, too, will be tempted by the gastronomic delights of this mellow old town. The beautiful landscapes of the Langhe hills just to the south of Alba yield Barolo and some of Italy's other best wines—enjoy a glass before boarding your train back to Asti for the evening. ⏱ 2 hr.

More on Asti & Alba

For more on sights, restaurants, and hotels in Asti, see p 516; for Alba, see p 520.

The Best of Turin, Piedmont & Valle d'Aosta in 1 Week

Piedmont and adjoining Valle d'Aosta are relatively small regions, and roads and public transportation are excellent, making it possible to cover quite a bit of ground in a week. From Turin, venture north into the alpine realm of the Valle d'Aosta, with stunning mountain scenery, the wild stretches of Parco Nazionale del Gran Paradiso, and in the town of Aosta, a liberal smattering of Roman ruins and medieval castles and churches. Then travel south, where the rolling hills that surround Asti and Alba are carpeted with vineyards that produce some of Italy's finest wines and topped with castles and villages.

START Turin.

1 Turin. For leisurely sightseeing suggestions in Turin, see p 482, **1**. Two days allow time to indulge in chocolates and pastries from such legendary purveyors as **Fratelli Stratta** (p 511, **9**), and to linger in cafes and enjoy a *bicerin* (a chocolate-espresso elixir). In the evenings, enjoy concerts and other performances at the **Teatro Regio,** dating to 1740, or the **Auditorium Giovanni Agnelli** (p 508), in the refurbished Fiat factory in the Lingotto district. Be sure during your two days to visit **Stupinigi** and **Superga,** the basilica and hunting lodge that architect Filippo Juvarra built for the Savoys (p 502). ⏲ 2 days. See p 504.

> *Castello di Fenis is one of several castles in the Valle d'Aosta built by medieval lords.*

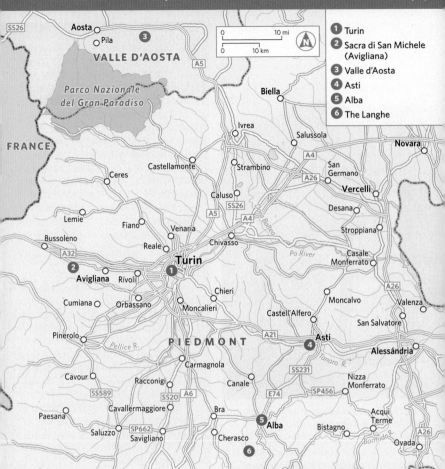

On the morning of Day 3, rent a car and head out of Turin via the A32 to Avigliana and Sacra di San Michele.

2 kids **Sacra di San Michele, Avigliana.** A remarkable monastery from the early middle ages is perched atop Mt. Pirchiriano. Umberto Eco based his accounts of the abbey in his novel *Name of the Rose* on San Michele, and visitors who have read the book will find the dizzying heights and steep staircases and lanes familiar. ⏱ 1 hr. See p 490, **2**.

From Avigliana follow A32 east to A4/A5 for the trip into the Valle d'Aosta and settle into Aosta for two evenings. Total distance from Turin to Aosta, with the stop at Sacra di San Michele, is about 135km (80 miles).

More on the Valle d'Aosta

For more on sights, hotels, and restaurants in the Valle d'Aosta, see p 498.

3 **Valle d'Aosta.** Italy's alpine province follows the fertile valley floor to the base of Monte Bianco (Mont Blanc). The **Castello di Fenis** (p 499, **2**) is the best preserved of the castles that medieval lords built on ridges above the valley as lookouts from which to monitor trade caravans below and extract tolls. In **Aosta,** the so-called Rome of the Alps, the snow-capped peaks provide a dramatic backdrop to a triumphal arch, a theater, and other ruins of the Roman Empire. Just beyond are the

> *Aosta's Roman ruins include an ancient bridge, city gate, theater, and triumphal arch.*

Meet the Savoys

Spending any time at all in Turin or other parts of Piedmont and the Valle d'Aosta means encountering the Savoys, the dukes and kings who left their mark so pervasively with castles, palaces, and monuments. The House of Savoy traces its origins to around 980, when Holy Roman Emperor Conrad II named Umberto I Biancamano (Humbert the White-Handed) a count and awarded him lands in the Alps. Umberto soon came to be known as the count of Savoy, and through marriage into wealthy and powerful French and Italian families and the acquisition of territory, his descendants slowly but steadily became a force on the map of Europe.

By the 11th century the Savoys controlled much of the Valle d'Aosta and parts of Piedmont, including important territory along the European trade routes, and they later expanded west into Genoa and the Côte d'Azur. In 1559 the Savoys made Turin their capital and went on a building spree that hit fever pitch in the 17th and 18th centuries, reshaping the city in a French-influenced baroque style. Turin became a center of the movement for unification and freedom from foreign control that swept over the peninsula in the 19th century, and Savoy duke Vittorio Emanuele was named king of Italy in 1861. The Savoys retained the title until Italy became a republic in 1946, and Europe's longest-reigning dynasty was voted into exile.

70,300 hectares (173,000 acres) of valleys and peaks that rise and fall across former Savoy hunting grounds that now comprise the **Parco Nazionale del Gran Paradiso** (p 500, **4**). One of the Valle d'Aosta's best experiences: a trip across **Monte Bianco** (☎ 0165-89925; www.montebianco.com) by cable car from La Palud, just above Entrèves, to Chamonix, France.

You make the trip in stages—first to Pavillon du Mont Fréty, where you can tour the **Giardino Botanico Alpino Saussurea** (p 500, **5**), and on to Punta Helbronner, a lookout at 3,300m (11,000 ft.) that provides stunning views of the Monte Bianco glaciers and the Matterhorn and other peaks. From Punta Helbronner you board a tiny gondola to swing 2,300m (7,544 ft.) above the Géant Glacier and the Vallée Blanche before descending to Aiguille du Midi in France and from there over more glaciers and valleys to Chamonix. The trip is not inexpensive: expect to pay about 100€ for one-way passage, returning to Palud by bus through the Mont Blanc tunnel, or about 140€ round-trip. ⏱ 2 days.

From Aosta, follow the A5 back to Turin, and from there take A6 south to A21 and head to Asti (overnight here). Distance: 175km (105 miles).

More on Asti & Alba

For more on sights, hotels, and restaurants in Asti, see p 516; for Alba, see p 520; for the Langhe wine region, see p 521, **6**.

> *The wine village of La Morra commands endless views over the hills of Le Langhe.*

4 Asti. Day 6 takes you into the heart of the Piedmont region. Toast your arrival with Asti Spumante, the town's world-famous sparkling beverage. The pleasure of this fine old city is to wander its cobbled medieval streets and lanes, past palaces and churches that include the Romanesque-Gothic **Cattedrale di Santa Maria Assunta** (p 516, **3**) and two places of worship from the Middle Ages, the **Collegiata San Secondo** and **Rotonda di San Pietro** (p 517, **4** and **5**). ⊕ 1 day.

From Asti, it is a short trip of about 30km (18 miles) south along E74 to Alba.

5 Alba. In this mellow old town of rose-colored brick, the past comes forward in Roman gates, fortified towers where residents of the Middle Ages took refuge, and Renaissance palaces and churches. Alba is devoted to the pleasures of the palate, and you'll encounter shop windows laden with velvety red wines, truffles, and chocolates—all local specialties. ⊕ 1 day, including an afternoon drive in the Langhe (**6**).

On the afternoon of Day 7, drive into the Langhe wine country, just south of Alba.

6 The Langhe. One of Italy's most beautiful parcels of countryside is home to vineyards that produce some of the world's finest wines. Three especially rewarding places to get out of your car and stretch your legs are **Grinzane Cavour,** a castle once home to a leading figure in the unification of Italy; **La Morra,** a handsome hilltop village with stunning views across the countryside, and **Barolo,** where the grapes that yield the region's most famous, eponymous wine grow. ⊕ About 3 hr. For more on all of these sites, see p 521, **6**.

From Mountains to Vineyards

In a relatively small area, Piedmont encompasses mountain peaks, rolling hills, and flat agricultural plains, as well as a dizzying wealth of historic towns and monuments. This driving tour introduces you to the region in two days, with an overnight stop in either Alba or Asti. You can reach many of these places by train and/or bus on day trips from Turin (p 504), but you will need a car to follow the length of this tour.

> The dizzying perch of Sacra di San Michele makes it easy to believe the legends that it was built with the assistance of angels.

START Avigliana, 25km (15 miles) west of Turin. Trip length: 2 days. By car from Turin, follow autostrada A32 east for about 20km (12 miles) to Avigliana.

❶ Avigliana. This medieval town was for many years a stronghold of the Savoys and a resting stop on the long route that pilgrims followed all the way from Canterbury, England, to the ports of southern Italy and from there to Jerusalem. Visitors might linger long enough to take a look at the tall old houses surrounding a ruined castle, but most are on their way to swim and bird-watch at two nearby volcanic lakes, **Lago Grande** and **Lago Piccolo;** to head deeper into the **Val Susa,** a narrow, forested cleft wedged between steep Alpine ridges; or to make their way toward one of Europe's most picturesque medieval monasteries, the **Sacra di San Michele (❷).**

Sacra di San Michele is 15km (9 miles) west of Avigliana, off SS25/24 and well marked.

❷ ★★★ kids Sacra di San Michele. The appearance of this monastery dedicated to the archangel MIchael (Michelangelo) and precariously perched atop Mt. Pirchiriano is as magical as many of the stories surrounding its origins. Some legends have it that Michael himself aided the hermit saint Giovanni Vincenzo with its construction in the 10th century by flying the building materials up the mountainside. Other versions lay the founding with a squad of angels who alighted on the peak in the 6th century. What is known for sure is that the monastery, one of 176 such medieval complexes

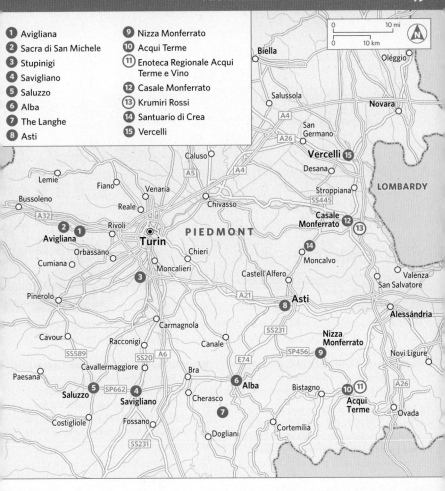

① Avigliana
② Sacra di San Michele
③ Stupinigi
④ Savigliano
⑤ Saluzzo
⑥ Alba
⑦ The Langhe
⑧ Asti
⑨ Nizza Monferrato
⑩ Acqui Terme
⑪ Enoteca Regionale Acqui Terme e Vino
⑫ Casale Monferrato
⑬ Krumiri Rossi
⑭ Santuario di Crea
⑮ Vercelli

dedicated to the archangel who battled Lucifer, was well established by the 11th century.

Piercing the clouds at 960m (3,150 ft.), the many-leveled stone complex is riddled with view-affording terraces, steep staircases and narrow lanes. One of the passageways, the **Scalone dei Morti** (Stairway of the Dead), is lined with niches that until recently were littered with the skeletal remains of deceased monks and at the top is the **Porto dello Zodiaco,** a masterwork of early sculpture carved with astrological imagery. The frescoed Gothic-Romanesque church is built atop several small chapels and a crypt that is the final resting place of 24 early members of the House of Savoy. **Via alla Sacra,** Sant'Ambrogio. ☎ 011-939130. Admission 4€. Mid-Mar to mid-Oct Tues-Sat 9:30am-12:30pm, 2:30-6pm; Sun 9:30am-noon, 2:40-6:30pm; mid-Oct to mid-Mar Tues-Sat 9:30-12:30pm, 2:30-5pm, Sun 9:30am-noon, 2:40-5pm.

From Avigliana A32 heads east for about 10km (6 miles) to A21, the ring road; the exit to Stupinigi is well marked.

③ ★★★ **kids Stupinigi.** South of Avigliana the mountain landscapes give way to rolling hills, and at the Savoys' royal hunting lodge on the outskirts of Turin, the medieval monuments of the mountains are left behind for the cosmopolitan tastes of the 18th century. See p 503, ②.

> *The bronze stag atop the Stupinigi hints at the palace's original use as a royal hunting lodge for the Savoys.*

From Stupinigi, follow A21 to A6, then drop south for about 50km (30 miles) to Savigliano; take the Marene exit and then follow the signs.

④ Savigliano. This old town was a capital of the Savoys. On this brief stop, enjoy a stroll past the Renaissance palaces surrounding the **Piazza Santorre di Santarosa.** A triumphal arch on the square was erected to honor the late-16th-century marriage of duke of Savoy Charles Emanuele I to Infanta Catherine Michelle of Spain.

Saluzzo is about 15km (9 miles) west of Savigliano on SP662.

⑤ Saluzzo. Another short stop introduces you to the quiet pleasures of the medieval upper town, where 14th-century houses climb a hillside to a castle. Several Gothic churches and a cathedral rise above the rooftops, and the

Museo Civico is installed in **Casa Cavassa,** an elegant Renaissance mansion that outshines the fairly dull collection and surrounds a beautiful courtyard. Museo Civico: Via San Giovanni 5. ☎ 0175-41455. Admission 4€. Apr–Sept daily 10am–1pm, 2–6pm; Oct–Mar Thurs–Sun 10am–1pm, 2–5pm.

From Savigliano follow SP662 east to Alba, a distance of about 40km (25 miles).

⑥ Alba. The capital of the beautiful Langhe region is graced with appealing medieval streets and landmarks, and also prospers pleasantly from wine, truffles, and chocolate. These products fill shop windows along Via Vittorio Emanuele II, but Alba's most famous shopping experience is the truffle market on fall weekends that attracts buyers who pay on average around 90€ an ounce.

⑦ The Langhe. From Alba, drop south into one of Italy's most beautiful regions for at least a half-day driving tour. The Barberas, Nebbiolos, Barbarescos, and other wines that local vintners produce are as mellow as the landscapes that nurture them. See p 521, ⑥, for a more detailed itinerary of the Langhe.

More on Asti & Alba

For more on sights, restaurants, and hotels in Asti, see p 516; for Alba, see p 520; for the Langhe wine region, see p 521, ⑥.

From Alba, it is a short trip of about 30km (18 miles) north along E74 to Asti.

8 Asti. For years revelers have celebrated with a glass of the sparkling Asti Spumante that makes the name of this town well known around the world. Asti does justice to this joyously bubbly creation with a romantically medieval assemblage of tall houses on narrow lanes and the brick bell towers of Gothic churches.

From Asti, Nizza Monferrato is about 25km (15 miles) east on well-posted roads.

9 Nizza Monferrato. Legend has it that the boundaries of the Monferrato, the wine and farming region that surrounds Asti, were marked out by a 10th-century nobleman who was given any land he could ride across in three days. His mount was obviously fast, because the Monferrato stretches quite a distance through rolling hills in the south to flat rice fields at the edge of the Lombardian plain to the north and east. Nizza weathered numerous sieges by the French, Spanish, and many other ruling entities before coming under the capable administration of the 18th-century Savoys, who made the town a silk-manufacturing center.

Given the bounty of the region and a location on the banks of the River Belbo along the trade routes between Liguria, Piedmont, and Lombardy, the town has been an important market town since the Middle Ages. Many fine palaces from the 17th and 18th centuries line the Via Carlo Alberto, and a house in the Piazza Dante serves as a museum of rural life, the **Museo Bersano delle Contadinerie e Stampe Antiche sul Vino** (☎ 0141-720211; open by appointment only—inquire at the town hall on Piazza Martiri di Alessandria or the tourist office in the old Foro Boario/Cattle Market); rooms here are filled with historic winemaking equipment and a collection of the wine labels the 20th-century painter Franco Sassi created for his winemaker friends in the region.

Acqui Terme is about 15km (9 miles) southeast of Nizza Monferrato on well-posted roads.

10 Acqui Terme. Roman legionnaires relaxed during their time in the north with a soak in the sulfurous waters of the town that they knew as Acqui Statiellae. Water from bubbling hot springs was channeled through aqueducts to large municipal baths that were so highly reputed that a road was laid from Augusta Taurinorum (Turin) to make it easy to enjoy them. In the 19th century, an attractive marble pavilion was erected over the spring that brought the town fame well into the 20th century and from which a steady stream of water gushes forth at a scalding 167°F (75°C).

The **tourist office,** Via Maggiorino Ferraris 5, (☎ 0144-322142; Mon–Sat 9:30am–12:30pm, 3:30–6:30pm; Sun 10am–1pm), occasionally

> As in Siena, the streets of Asti are the setting for a bareback horserace known as a **palio**.

> *The ridges of Le Langhe (La Morra is shown) provide optimal growing conditions for Piedmont's Nebbiolo, Dolcetto, and Barbera grapes.*

leads tours of ongoing excavations that are unearthing the Roman bath complex, and artifacts are displayed in the **Museo Civico Archeologico** in the Castello dei Paleologi, Via Morelli 2 (☎ 0144-57555; www.acquimusei.it/archeo; 2€; Wed–Sat 9:30am–12:30pm, 3:30–6:30pm; Sun 3:30–6:30pm). This remarkable looking structure and the town's cathedral date from the 11th century. Overall, though, Acqui Terme is a bit faded and shrouded in the melancholy of better days gone by, but a soak in the stylish luxury of the **Grand Hotel Nuove Terme,** Piazza Italia 1 (☎ 0144-58555; 30€ for use of thermal pools), will set things right.

⑪ 🍷 **Enoteca Regionale Acqui Terme e Vino.** The perfect follow-up to a soak is a stop in this pleasant wine bar for a glass of local wine, especially Brachetto d'Acqui, a light red. Piazza Levi 7, ☎ 0144-770273. Tues, Thurs–Sun 9:30am–1pm, 3:30–7pm. $.

The quickest way to reach Casale Monferrato from Acqui Terme is to follow the A26 north; the distance is about 80km (48 miles).

⑫ **Casale Monferrato.** This busy agricultural center on the River Po is built around **Piazza Mazzini,** an animated square on the site of the forum from the town's days as a Roman *municipium.* Streets leading off the piazza are lined with many medieval and Renaissance palazzi, and the town's most famous landmark, the 11th-century, 60m-tall (180-ft.) **Torre Civica,** rises nearby. The Via Roma leads through the Jewish ghetto to the **synagogue**—one of the most beautiful in all of Europe, though by civil order the exterior was made to be completely undistinguished. The women's galleries are now occupied by gilded wood tablets and other treasures of the **Museo d'Arte e Storia Ebraica,** Vicolo Salomone Olper 44 (☎ 0142-71807; www.casalebraica.org; 4.50€; Sun 10am–12:30pm, 3–6pm, other days by request).

Casale Monferrato's great Christian presence is St. Evasius, a 3rd-century bishop of Asti who is beloved throughout Piedmont. When pagans banished Evasius from Asti, he took shelter in a forest near Casale. Exhausted, he stuck his staff into the ground and lay down to sleep, and when he awoke the staff had sprouted into a tree and a spring gushed from the base. Evasius then founded a small church in Casale, but he and 143 of his followers were eventually beheaded by the town's pagan leaders. Casale's 12th-century **Cattedrale di Sant'Evasio,** Piazza Mazzini (☎ 0142-457789; free admission; daily 8am–noon, 2–6pm), is dedicated to the popular martyred saint, whose relics rest within.

Casale also is the birthplace of Leonardo Bistolfi (1859–1933), a sculptor with whom most non-Italians are not familiar but whose busts and murals of kings, politicians, and other notables are ubiquitous throughout Italy. You'll encounter his symbol-laden works in places as far-flung as the Vittorio Emanuele monument in Rome and Cimitero di Staglieno in Genoa, as well as in Casale's **Museo Civico,** Via Cavour 5 (☎ 0142-444309; 3€; Sat–Sun 10:30am–1pm, 3–6pm).

⑬   🍞 **Krumiri Rossi.** One of the most famous bakeries in Piedmont makes the original *krumiro,* a delicate and fragrant biscuit that Domenico Rossi invented in 1870 to assuage a sweet tooth after a night of drinking with the boys. Via Lanza 17. ☎ 0142-453030. Tues–Sat 8am–7pm. $.

The Santuario di Crea is 30km (18 miles) southwest of Casale Monferrato on SS590.

⑭ ★★ kids **Santuario di Crea.** When Vincenzo I, of the Mantua-based Gonzaga family, took control of the Monferrato region in the late 16th century he decided to endow his territories with a *sacro monte,* a collection of little chapels scattered across a hillside. *Sacri monti* were wildly popular in Piedmont and Lombardy at the time, and served as peaceful rustic retreats where pilgrims could enjoy nature while paying homage to a favorite saint or doing the Stations of the Cross. By 1600, 18 chapels and 17 prayer stations were dotting the hillside outside the town of Serralunga di Crea, and others followed; the sanctuary is now littered with 23 chapels, filled with statuary, frescoes, and other artwork. The spirit of a retreat is perpetuated in a 470-sq.-km (181-sq.-mile) nature park that surrounds the chapels and is a haven for many kinds of wildlife. Piazzale Santuario, Serralunga di Crea. ☎ 0142-940109. Free admission. Daily 7am–noon, 2–6pm.

> A plain exterior conceals the beautifully embellished interior of the synagogue in Casale Monferrato.

> Culinarily rich Piedmont was the birthplace of Italy's Slow Food movement.

> *The Torre Civica towers 60m (180 ft.) above the medieval streets of Casale Monferrato.*

From the Santuario di Crea follow SS445 northeast about 20km (12 miles) to Vercelli.

15 **Vercelli.** North of Casale begins the watery province of Vercelli, the rice capital of Europe. Piedmont has been growing rice since the 15th century, but 19th-century engineering propelled the region into large-scale production with the digging of hundreds of miles of canals to flood the Po Valley and create rice paddies. The local output, especially Arborio rice, shows up in the creamy risottos that are a signature dish of the north and on dinner tables all over the world. The eponymous capital of the region is best known architecturally for three churches. The handsomely Gothic **Basilica di Sant'Andrea,** Piazza Roma 35 (☎ 0161-255513; June–Sept daily 7:30–11:45am, 3–7pm; Oct–May daily 7:30–11:45am, 3–6pm), is graced with delightful cloisters. The **Duomo,** Piazza Sant' Eusebio (☎ 0161-252930; daily 7:30–11:45am, 3–6pm), houses the enormous 11th-century crucifix of Bishop Leone, 3.5m (11 ft.) long and one of the great works of early medieval silversmithing. The **Church of San Cristoforo,** Via San Cristoforo (daily 7:30am–noon, 3:30–6:30pm), is decorated with frescoes by Renaissance painter Gaudenzio Ferrari, whose depictions of the shepherds paying homage to the Christ child and other scenes are touchingly pictorial and involving. Among the very rare manuscripts on display in the **Museo del Tesoro del Duomo,** Piazza d'Angennes (☎ 0161-51650; 3€; Wed 9am–noon; Sat 9am–noon, 3–6pm; Sun 3–6pm), is an early English collection of sermons from the 10th century that somehow found its way here and is known as the Vercelli Book.

Piedmont's Gifts to the Taste Buds

It's hard not to fall in love with a place that puts wine, chocolate, cheese, and truffles on the list of top priorities and brings the world such delights as risotto, Barolo, *bicerin,* and Gianduiotto. Little wonder the Slow Food movement took root in the Piedmont town of Bra, just west of Alba, to celebrate local cuisine, promote seasonal ingredients, and turn the world away from fast food.

The composer Rossini called the white truffle the "Mozart of mushrooms," and he was not the first or last to sing the praises of this dirty, smelly little fungus that grows under poplars, oaks, willows, and lindens in the hills around Asti and Alba.

It's said (with a bit of exaggeration) that kings since Charlemagne have enjoyed *Castelmagno,* a creamy but semi-hard cow's-milk cheese that's a close cousin to Gorgonzola. As a filling for *agnolotti* (the region's favorite, ravioli-like pasta) or in any other guise, Castelmagno is simply delicious.

Piedmont's favorite sauce, *bagna cauda,* is a delectable blend of olive oil, garlic, and anchovies; some cooks add butter, others cream, and all serve it warm as a dip for bread and raw, roasted, or boiled vegetables.

Prime minister, count, and reformer Camillo Cavour saw a future in rice back in the 19th century and flooded much of the land around Vercelli to create rice paddies. So it's him we can thank for the creamy risottos that replace pasta in the hearts of many Piedmontese.

From the Piedmontese, we have the *bicerin,* a luscious combination of espresso, chocolate, and cream that is a favorite in Turin cafes; *gianduia,* a mix of chocolate and hazelnut paste that shows up in sweets shops as Gianduiotti, delectable little chocolates shaped like upturned boats; and Nutella, the wildly popular chocolaty, nutty spread made in Alba.

Into the Valle d'Aosta

The travelers who speed up and down the Valle d'Aosta to and from ski resorts in the Alps and France and Switzerland via the Mont Blanc tunnel are following an age-old tradition of travel through the valley. The Romans arrived in A.D. 25 to build roads and forts to establish a hold on the mountain passes, and the verdant valley floor has been a convenient route between the Italian peninsula and northern Europe ever since. Italy's smallest and least populous region is blessed with mountain scenery, Roman ruins, medieval castles, and one of Europe's largest and most beautiful national parks.

> Castles (St. Pierre is shown) pepper the Valle d'Aosta, a favored Alpine pass for invaders since Hannibal and the elephants.

START Ivrea, about 40km (25 miles) north of Turin via autostrada A5 or half-hourly train service. Trip length: 2 days.

❶ Ivrea. In this old town at the foot of the Valle d'Aosta, the Romans built the original Ponte Vecchio across the River Dora Baltea—the current span dates from 1830—and the Savoys erected the **Castello delle Rosse Torri** in the 14th century. These days the turrets and towers are an appealing background for the Olivetti workshops, which opened in 1908 to turn out typewriters and soon became known around the world for office machinery. Forward-thinking management provided ideal working conditions in innovatively designed buildings that are now part of the **Museo al Cielo Aperto dell'Architettura Moderna** (Open Air Museum of Modern Architecture); Via Jervis (☎ 0125-641815; www.maam.ivrea.it). The workers have never been so corporate-minded as not to be swept away by the town's riotous annual pre-Lenten event, **La Battaglia delle Arance** (Battle of the Oranges). Legend has it that in the 12th century, a local duke was in the habit of exercising his right to sleep with any newlywed bride, and one of them, a miller's daughter, did not take keenly to the idea and chopped off his head. To commemorate the event, on Palm Sunday the town squares off into nine teams that over the next 3 days hurl 265,000 kilograms (120,000 lb.) of oranges (filling in for the duke's head) at each other and at gaily decorated carts.

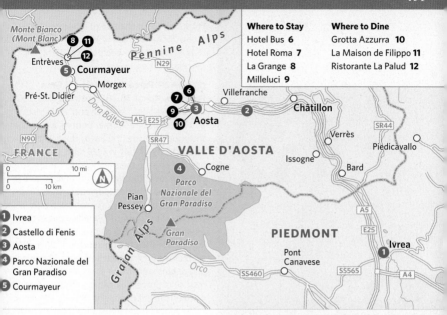

1. Ivrea
2. Castello di Fenis
3. Aosta
4. Parco Nazionale del Gran Paradiso
5. Courmayeur

Fenis is about 40km (25 miles) north of Ivrea on A5.

2 ★★ kids **Castello di Fenis.** Castles all along the Valle d'Aosta once protected holdings in the valley and controlled trade routes with France just across the Alps. The largest and best preserved crowns a small knoll at Fenis. Tall double walls and the many round and square towers lend a satisfyingly storybook appearance to this fortified manor built in the 14th century as the seat of the Challants, local lords who amassed a vast fortune by extracting tolls from merchants passing through the valley. A wooden balcony atop a magnificent curving staircase surrounds an inner courtyard decorated with frescoes depicting St. George slaying the dragon and other mythical scenes. ⏱ 1 hr. ☎ 0165-764263. Admission 5€. Oct–Feb Mon, Wed–Sat 10am–noon, 1:30–4:30pm, Sun 10am–noon, 1:30–5:30pm; Mar–June and Sept daily 9:30am–6:30pm; July–Aug daily 9:30am–7:30pm.

Aosta is about 30km (18 miles) west of Fenis on A5.

3 **Aosta.** The so-called Rome of the Alps was at one time Augusta Praetoria, capital of the province of Alpes Graies (Gray Alps); the **Arco di Augusto** was erected to mark its

> Aosta's 2,000-year-old Arco di Augusto now commands a rather mundane setting.

founding during the reign of Augustus in 25 B.C. Snow-capped peaks provide a dramatic backdrop for walls and the massive eastern gate to the Roman city, the **Porta Praetoria;** the tall windowed facade of the **Teatro Romano;** two bridges; and the forum, much of which was buried beneath Aosta's cathedral in the 11th century. Early Christians worshipped in a primitive church and mausoleum in the northeast corner of the old city as early as the 5th century, and the remnants are part of

> *Courmayeur provides a base for Alpine skiing in the shadow of Monte Bianco.*

the **Church and Priory of San Orso,** Piazzetta Sant'Orso (☎ 0165-262026; free admission; Jan–Feb daily 10am–12:30pm, 1:30–5pm; Mar–June and Sept daily 9am–7pm; July–Aug daily 9am–8pm), where a beautiful cloister is surrounded by 37 marble columns topped with capitals that are among the great masterworks of Romanesque sculpture.

From the Aosta Ovest exit of autostrada A5, follow SS507 and SR47 about 16km (10 miles) to the Parco Nazionale del Gran Paradiso entrance at Cogne.

④ ★★★ kids Parco Nazionale del Gran Paradiso. About 70,300 hectares (173,000 acres) of valleys, plateaus, and peaks rise and fall across the former hunting grounds of Vittorio Emanuele, the Savoy duke who became the first king of Italy in 1861. One of the most popular hikes in the park follows the king's old carriage route through stands of larch and fir to his former hunting lodge at Orvieille and from there to Djouan Lake, where crystal-clear waters reflect the Gran Paradiso peaks that rise as high as 4,000 meters (12,000 ft.). The king established the preserve in 1856 in part to protect the ibex, a mountain goat whose bones and organs were much treasured for their medicinal properties, along with the ability to ward off violent death and provide all sorts of other supernatural assistance. Today some 4,000 ibex, along with chamois, badgers, and other mountain-dwelling creatures, roam the park, as well as the adjoining lands of Vanoise National Park in France. Alpine wildflowers carpet the beautiful Paradisa Alpina botanical gardens, a preserve within the park just outside Cogne. ☎ 0165-749264. Free admission. June and Sept daily 10am–5:30pm; July–Aug daily 10am–6:30pm. Parco Nazionale del Gran Paradiso Cogne Visitor Center: Villaggio Minerario, Cogne. ☎ 0165-749264; for more information on the park go to www.parks.it/parco.nazionale.gran.paradiso

Autrostrada A5 links Aosta and Courmayeur, 35km (21 miles) west.

⑤ Courmayeur. Monte Bianco (Mont Blanc), Europe's tallest mountain, rises to 4,800m (15,781 ft.) above this resort, a haven for alpine enthusiasts who enjoy dozens of ski runs and an abundance of mountain scenery. For a brief period after the snow melts in June the beautiful **Giardino Botanico Alpino Saussurea** (☎ 333-446-2959; www.saussurea.net; 2.50€; late June to Sept daily 9am–5pm) comes into flower on a natural balcony high above the town. For information on a trip by cable car over the flanks of Monte Bianco from a terminus near Courmayeur, see p 488.

Where to Stay & Dine

★ **Grotta Azzurra** AOSTA *PIZZA*
Pasta is on the menu, but the draw at this simple place is the pizza, which can be topped with *fontina,* mountain salamis, and other distinctly local ingredients. Via Croix de Ville 97. ☎ 0165-262474. Entrees 6€–10€. MC, V. Lunch & dinner Thurs–Tues.

★★ **Hotel Bus** AOSTA
Guest rooms are pleasantly decked out in comfortable, contemporary furnishings, and those on the higher floors overlook the peaks, but the best amenity is the center of town location. Via Malherbes 18. ☎ 0165-236958. www.hotelbus.com. 39 units. Doubles 75€–100€. AE, DC, MC, V.

★ **Hotel Roma** AOSTA
This welcoming inn on the pedestrian-only streets of the town center is clean, comfortable, and an excellent value. Via Torino 7. ☎ 0165-40821. 38 units. Doubles 65€–75€. AE, DC, MC, V.

★★★ **La Grange** ENTRÈVES
Many of the rustically furnished rooms of this converted farmstead overlook Monte Bianco, and the stone-floored lobby and bar surrounding a welcoming hearth are popular winter gathering spots. Strada La Brenva 1. ☎ 0165-869733. www.lagrange-it.com. 22 units. Doubles 100€–150€. AE, DC, MC, V.

★★ **La Maison de Filippo** ENTRÈVES
VALDOSTAN A tall wooden barn and warm-weather terrace overlooking Monte Bianco provide suitably alpine settings for a generous fixed menu of cured meats, sausages, local cheeses, and other hearty mountain fare. Near the Mont Blanc tunnel. ☎ 0165-869797. www.lamaison.com. Fixed price 50€. MC, V. Lunch & dinner Wed–Mon. Closed mid-May to mid-July and Nov to late Dec.

★★★ **Milleluci** AOSTA
At this retreat in a garden on a hillside above Aosta, exposed timbers and a glowing hearth provide a rustic ambience in the lounges; the traditionally furnished rooms are welcoming, too, and overlook the surrounding peaks and

> *The manicured gardens of Aosta's Milleluci.*

valley below. Off Via Porossan Roppoz. ☎ 0165-235278. www.hotelmilleluci.com. 31 units. Doubles 140€–240€. AE, DC, MC, V.

★★ **Ristorante La Palud** ENTRÈVES *VALDOSTAN*
The surroundings here are plain, but the cuisine is memorable. Creamy mountain hams, polenta with *fontina* and butter folded into it, and game in season are complemented by seafood on Fridays, when it is trucked in fresh from Liguria. Strada La Palud 17. ☎ 0165-86169. Entrees 12€–20€. AE, MC, V. Lunch & dinner Thurs–Tues.

On the Savoy Trail

Filippo Juvarra (1678–1736) left his native Sicily to work in Rome, designing celebrations and sets for theatrical productions—good training for the work he did in Turin, including his over-the-top facade for the Palazzo Reale (p 506, **3**), as well as the Savoys' greatest monuments, the Basilica di Superga and their hunting lodge at Stupinigi.

> *Juvarra's monumental Basilica de Superga.*

START Superga, above the northern suburb of Sassi, reached from Turin's Porta Nuova station on bus 61, tram 15, or train (see box).

1 ★★★ **Basilica di Superga.** This tall, strikingly attractive church atop a high hill east of Turin is the pantheon of the Savoys, the final resting place of princes and kings. Few visitors, though, come to pay homage at their monumental tombs. Instead they marvel at the fabulous creation of Sicilian architect Filippo Juvarra, an imposing combination of the classical and baroque. Also a set designer, Juvarra clearly had an eye for the dramatic, and for his design he drew upon

Take the Train

The most exciting way to reach Superga is on the **rack railway** (☎ 011-576-4733; www.comune.torino.it/gtt/turismo/sassisup.shtml) that climbs 670m (2,200 ft.) from a terminus in Sassi. To get there, take bus 79 from Porta Nuova station in Turin to the rack railway terminus in Sassi. The rack railway does not operate on Tuesday, when buses run from Sassi to the basilica hourly. Trains generally run from 9am to 5pm (with extra hours on weekends), but call for the most up-to-date schedule. On weekdays, the cost is 4€ round-trip, and it's 5€ on weekends.

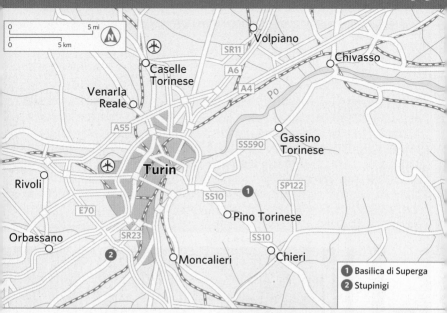

two of the world's greatest landmarks—the temple-like front surrounded by columns recalls the Pantheon, while the dome resembles that of St. Peter's. In the hearts of the Torinese, the Savoy presence is also overshadowed by the tragedy of the Il Grande Torino football team, killed when their plane smashed into the Superga hill while landing at Turin during bad weather in 1949. ⏱ 2 hr., including railway trip. Strada della Basilica di Superga.☎ 011-899-7456. Admission 6€. Apr–Sept Mon–Fri 9:30am–noon, 3–6pm, Sat 9:30am–7pm, Sun 1–7pm; Oct–Mar Mon–Fri 9:30am–noon, 3–5pm, Sat 9:30am–6:15pm, Sun 3–6:15pm.

Return to Turin and board bus 41 from Porta Nuova station for Stupinigi.

2 ★★★ kids **Stupinigi.** Vittorio Amedeo II, the Savoy king of Sardinia, used to ride the 16km (10 miles) from Turin to hunt on lands that are now the beautiful preserves of the Parco Naturale di Stupinigi, an oasis of greenery amid Turin's southern suburbs. In 1729 Vittorio commissioned a hunting lodge from architect Filippo Juvarra, but Juvarra had more than a rustic getaway in mind when he designed Stupinigi. The 137 rooms and 17 galleries, strung out along four angled wings off an oval-shaped main hall topped by a bronze stag, also accommodated family parties and ceremonies. It's little wonder that Paolina Borghese, Napoleon's sister, found the place to

> *A bedroom in the Savoys' Stupinigi hunting lodge.*

be a suitable residence. Her furniture is among the holdings of the Museo dell'Ammobiliamento Artistico, occupying some of the many rooms. ⏱ 1 hr. Piazza Principe Amedeo 7. ☎ 011-358-1220. Admission 7€. Apr–Sept Tues–Sun 10am–6pm; Oct–Mar Tues–Sun 9:30am–5pm. Bus 41 from Porta Nuova station.

Turin

Turin tends to surprise visitors, many of whom expect to find themselves in a smoky industrial center and discover instead one of Europe's largest and best-preserved baroque cities. Fiat and other industries have always been confined to the outskirts, leaving the city center little changed. Many visitors are also unaware that as the seat of the House of Savoy, Turin was the capital of one of Europe's most powerful and longest-standing dynasties for several centuries (and, indeed, the first capital of a united Italy), and has many monuments from this royal past. Arcaded streets, beautiful piazzas, lively cafes, and a backdrop of the Alps add even more sparkle to the city.

> Handsome, sheltering arcades line miles of Turin's streets.

START Piazza Castello.

1 ★★ **Palazzo Madama.** Architect Filippo Juvarra created one of the most elaborate false fronts in the annals of design, what has been called a "facade without a building." Marble, columns, and arched windows create the impression of a vast baroque palace, while what lies within, just beyond Juvarra's monumental staircase, is a medieval castle built around a massive courtyard on the foundations of a Roman gatehouse. "Madama"

is a nod to two powerful women who resided in the palazzo during the 17th century, both widows of Savoy dukes who ably administered the dynasty as regents for their sons. Christine Marie of France, a daughter of King Henry IV who married duke of Savoy Vittorio Amedeo and moved to the palace upon his death, and her daughter in law, Marie Jeanne Baptiste de Savoie-Nemours. Their former salons are filled with collections of the **Museo Civico d'Arte Antica** that are as much of a jigsaw puzzle

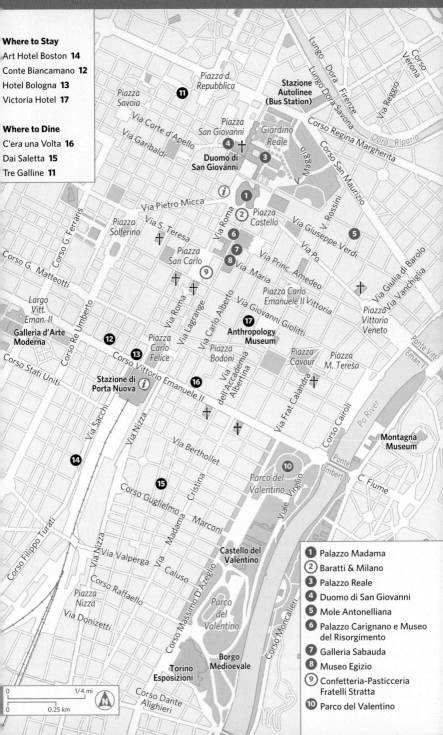

Where to Stay

Art Hotel Boston **14**

Conte Biancamano **12**

Hotel Bologna **13**

Victoria Hotel **17**

Where to Dine

C'era una Volta **16**

Dai Saletta **15**

Tre Galline **11**

1 Palazzo Madama

2 Baratti & Milano

3 Palazzo Reale

4 Duomo di San Giovanni

5 Mole Antonelliana

6 Palazzo Carignano e Museo del Risorgimento

7 Galleria Sabauda

8 Museo Egizio

9 Confetteria-Pasticceria Fratelli Stratta

10 Parco del Valentino

> *The exuberant decoration of the Palazzo Reale reflects the rococo tastes of the royal House of Savoy.*

as the palace itself, ranging from Antonello da Messina's *Portrait of a Man,* to medieval furniture and sculpture to temple art that Italian teams recently excavated at the ancient Indian kingdom of Gandhara. ⏱ 1 hr. Piazza Castello. ☎ 011-443-3501. www.palazzomadamatorino.it. Admission to palace and Museo Civico 7.50€; entrance to staircase and medieval courtyard free. Tues–Fri and Sun 9am–7pm; Sat 9am–8pm. Bus: 11, 12, 51, 55, 56, 61, 68. Tram: 4, 13, 15, 18.

② 🍴 **Baratti & Milano.** Tucked into the Galleria dell'Industria Subalpina, an elegant arcade between Piazza Castello and the much smaller Piazza Carlo Alberto, this bastion of refined elegance has been pairing coffee with chocolates and pastries since 1875. Piazza Castello 27. ☎ 011-440-7138. Tues–Sun 8am–9pm. $.

❸ ★★ **Palazzo Reale.** Over the course of 9 centuries, members of the House of Savoy expanded their rule from a small mountainous territory to all of Italy. When King Umberto II was deposed in 1946 and sent into exile with his family, no European royal house had survived longer. From the early 17th century the Savoy dukes ruled their ever-expanding holdings from this palace, and the carved coffered ceilings, inlaid parquetry floors, and a **remarkable staircase** by Filippo Juvarra reflect the baroque and rococo tastes of their times. Various decoration crazes of the 18th and 19th centuries come to the fore in such rooms as the **Gabinetto Cinese** (Chinese bathroom), paneled in lacquered chinoiserie, and the **Sala da Ballo** (ballroom), with its frescoes in the style of those then being unearthed at Pompeii. Details of court life emerge in the **Camera dell'Alcova,** where courtiers discreetly watched from behind curtains to ensure that royal marriages, often between unwilling partners, were consummated. Visits are by guided tour only, in Italian; English-language cards are placed in the rooms. ⏱ 30 min. Piazzetta Reale. ☎ 011-4361-455. www.ambienteto.arti.beniculturali.it. Admission 6.50€. Tues–Sun 8:30am–7:30pm. Bus: 12, 27, 50, 51, 55. Tram: 11, 13, 15, 18.

Getting Around Turin

It is easy to explore Turin on foot, and rain is not an excuse to abstain from walking—more than 18km (11 miles) of porticoes cover the sidewalks. The Via Roma cuts an elegant swath through the city center, from Piazza Carlo Felice in front of the train station north to Piazza Castello, around which the Palazzo Reale, Duomo, and Palazzo Madama are grouped. Tourist offices are in Piazza Solferino (☎ 011-535901) and the Porta Nuova railway station (☎ 011-531327; www.turismotorino.org).

If you wish to hop on public transport you can choose from trams, buses, and a new and still expanding light-rail system. Tickets (1.20€) can be purchased at *tabacchi* (tobacco shops), newsstands, and from automated vending machines near many stops, and must be validated in one of the machines on board. Transportation is run by **Gruppo Torinese Trasporti** (☎ 800-019152; www.comune.torino.it/gtt). Much of the city center is closed to cars; there are large parking garages on Via Roma near Piazza Carlo Felice and on Piazza Bodoni.

④ **Duomo di San Giovanni.** Turin's Renaissance cathedral is best known for its ★★★ **Cappella della Sacra Sindone,** built to house the Sacra Sindone, the **Shroud of Turin.** The shroud was in Chambéry, France, in 1578, when Duke Emanuele Filiberto got wind that San Carlo Borromeo, archbishop of Milan (p 465, ⑭), had vowed to make a pilgrimage there to give thanks for deliverance from the plague that had ravaged his city. The duke managed to bring the shroud to Turin to make the cardinal's walk shorter, the relic never found its way back to France, and in the 1660s the architect Guarino Guarini oversaw completion

of a magnificent chapel to house it. The walls surrounding the silver altar crafted to contain the shroud are sheathed in black marble and rise to a burst of light in the star-burst-shaped cupola. In one visual sweep the chapel suggests mourning and resurrection. The chapel is closed for restoration after a 1997 fire, with a possible reopening date set for 2010. An exhibit in the cathedral tells the story of the shroud, now stored at a private church museum open only to scholars. ⏱ 30 min. Piazza San Giovanni. ☎ 011-436-1540. Free admission. Mon–Sat 7am–12:30pm, 3–7pm; Sun 8am–12:30pm, 3–7pm. Bus: 12, 27, 50, 51, 55. Tram: 11, 13, 15, 18.

> *The baroque facade of the Palazzo Madama conceals a medieval castle, now a museum.*

> *Turin's Museo Nazionale del Cinema, inside the 167m (548 ft.) Mole Antonelliana, is the tallest museum in the world.*

Stunning Stages

The **Teatro Regio,** Piazza Castello 215 (☎ 011-881-5241; www.teatroregio.torino.it; box office Tues–Fri 10:30am–6pm, Sat 10:30am–4pm, and before performances), dates to 1740, though the elliptical hall within the old facade is from the 1960s. One of the largest stages in Europe hosts highly regarded performances of 19th-century and contemporary operas, as well as dance and orchestral concerts. The **Auditorium Giovanni Agnelli,** Via Nizza 280 (☎ 011-3143190), occupies part of the refurbished Fiat factory in the outlying Lingotto district and is the scene of twice-weekly concerts of the RAI symphony orchestra as well as performances by many visiting companies. The conversion by Genoa-based architect Renzo Piano (p 702) has also created exhibition galleries, a shopping mall, and playful, glass-enclosed halls above Fiat's famous rooftop test track. The **Teatro Carignano,** Piazza Carignano 6 (☎ 011-517-6246; www.teatrostabiletorino.it; box office daily 10:30am–7pm) retains its 18th-century allure, providing lavish boxes from which to enjoy performances by the Teatro Stabile di Torino company.

5 ★ kids **Mole Antonelliana.** What was for many decades the tallest brick structure in the world was intended to be a synagogue when ground was broken in 1864. Costs soared along with the elongated, four-sided dome, and by the time the *mole* was topped off at 167m (548 ft.), it was in the hands of the city of Turin and dedicated as a memorial to the newly appointed first king of a united Italy, Vittorio Emanuele II (1820–78). The charmingly eccentric landmark rises from a neoclassical brick base through several templelike layers to a needlelike spire and is now the setting for the similarly engaging film props, old sets, antique cameras, and other holdings of the **Museo Nazionale del Cinema.** An elevator ascends through the vast interior to an observation platform. ⏱ 1 hr. Via Montebello 20. Elevator: 3.50€. Museo Nazionale del Cinema: ☎ 011-813-8560. www.museonazionaledelcinema. it. Admission 6.50€, 8€ with elevator. Tues–Fri 9am–8pm; Sat 9am–11pm; Sun 9am–8pm. Bus 15, 55, 56, 61, 68, tram 13, 16.

6 ★ **Palazzo Carignano e Museo del Risorgimento.** Any town of any size in Italy has a museum dedicated to the movement that led to the unification of the country, and it is hardly surprising that Turin's is the best. Vittorio Emanuele II of the Turin-based House of Savoy became the first king of Italy, and in 1861 Italy's first parliament convened in the palazzo that houses the museum. Letters and documents trace the Risorgimento (or Revival) and Italy's very long road to unification, but more interesting to visitors not well versed in Italian history are such artifacts as the coach of independence fighter Giuseppe Garibaldi and the wonderfully baroque 1684 palace itself, designed by Guarino Guarini for Savoy prince Emanuele Filiberto Carignano, with a curving facade and gracious elliptical rooms. At press time the museum was closed for renovation and scheduled to reopen in 2010. ⏱ 1 hr. Via Accademia delle Scienze 5. ☎ 011-562-1172. Admission 5€. Tues–Sun 9am–7pm. Bus: 12, 27, 50, 51, 55. Tram: 4, 13, 15, 18.

7 ★★ Galleria Sabauda. The art collection of the House of Savoy, much added to over the years, fills the upper floors of the Palazzo dell'Accademia, once the school for young members of the Savoy court. Many of the finest works are by northern Europeans, both because they were favored by duchess Christine Marie (**1**) and because in the 1820s a good part of the collection was imported in bulk from Genoa, where these northerners were much in demand among the city's wealthy families (p 583, **3**). Jan van Eyck's *Stigmata of St. Francis* and Hans Memling's *Passion of Christ* are among the gallery's prizes. Italians contribute a magnificent *Virgin and Child* by Fra Angelico and a commendable roster of works by Sandro Botticelli, Titian, Tintoretto, and others. ⏱ 2 hr. Via Accademia delle Scienze 6. ☎ 011-440-6903. www.museitorino.it. Admission 4€. Tues 8:30am–2pm, Wed–Thurs 2–7:30pm; Fri–Sun 8:30am–2pm, 3–7pm. Bus: 12, 27, 50, 51, 55. Tram: 4, 13, 15, 18.

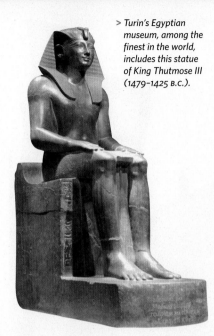

> Turin's Egyptian museum, among the finest in the world, includes this statue of King Thutmose III (1479–1425 B.C.).

Shrouded in Mystery

The legendary linen cloth known as the Sacra Sindone (Holy Shroud) is imprinted with the image of a man just under 2m (6 ft.) tall who has a beard, shoulder-length hair, and wounds, swellings, and other signs of having been whipped and beaten. This image becomes especially noticeable when viewed in a photographic negative. The cloth, by some accounts, was known at least as early as the 10th century as the shroud in which Christ was wrapped when taken from the cross, and by other accounts it was discovered by Crusaders in Constantinople in the 14th century and brought to France. Even modern science has not been able to shed definitive light on how old the cloth is, what its origins might be, and how the haunting image became affixed to it. Radiocarbon dating and chemical analysis puts the manufacture of the cloth around the 13th or 14th centuries, but exposure to fire in the 16th century could affect the readings. Meanwhile, the debate goes on, and the shroud remains a treasured relic of Turin.

> *The Borgo Medievale (or "medieval village") in Parco del Valentino was built for an expo in 1884.*

8 ★★★ **Museo Egizio.** Turin's Egyptian collection is second only to the one in Cairo, and credit for this rests in part with Napoleon. In the wake of his Egyptian campaigns, the emperor named Piedmont-born Bernardino Drovetti (1776–1852) as French consul to Egypt and adviser to ruler Muhammad Ali. The unscrupulous diplomat used his influence to more or less corner the market on the antiquities he plundered from the ancient tombs and monuments that were being explored for the first time. King Carlo Felice (1765–1831) bought up many of Drovetti's most-prized artifacts to flesh out the 300 pieces gathered on a 1753 expedition sponsored by one of his predecessors, Carlo Emanuel. The collections gained even greater stature in the late 19th century, when renowned Egyptologist Ernesto Schiaparelli was director of the museum. His excavations

Gourmet Shopping

A stop in Turin's food shops is a flavor-filled introduction to the gastronomic traditions of the city and the surrounding Piedmont. **Baudracco Gastronomia,** Vittorio Emanuele II 62 (☎ 011-545582; Tues–Sat 9:30am–8pm, Sun 9:30am–1pm), one of the city's great old food emporia, sells fruit, cheeses, breads, and other foodstuffs from throughout Piedmont, as well as wines and many prepared dishes; this an excellent stop before hopping on a train at the station just down the street. All the great wines of Piedmont line the shelves of **Casa del Barolo,** Via Andrea Doria 7 (☎ 011-532038; Mon 3–7:30pm, Tues–Sat 9am–12:30pm, 3–7:30pm; AE, DC, MC, V; closed most of Aug), with special attention to the store's namesake (pictured above). In a city famous for chocolate, the Peyrano family are kings; though **Peyrano,** Corso Vittorio Emanuele II 76 (☎ 011-538765; www.peyrano.com; Tues–Sat 9:30am–8pm, Sun 9:30am–1pm; AE, DC, MC, V), is no longer a strictly family-run affair, the secret, age-old formulas are still made to perfection.

brought the tomb of the royal architect Ka and his bride to Turin, where their funerary chamber is in the good company of a black basalt statue of Rameses II and legions of mummies. ⏱ 2 hr. Via Accademia delle Scienze 6. ☎ 011-561-7776. www.museoegizio.it. Admission 7.50€. Early June to early Sept Tues–Sun 9:30am–8:30pm; early

> *Italy's motor city occasionally rolls out classic models for public viewing, courtesy of the Museo dell'Automobile.*

Sept to early June Tues–Sun 8:30am–7:30pm. Bus: 12, 27, 50, 51, 55. Tram 4, 13, 15, 18.

⑨   🍴 **Confetteria-Pasticceria Fratelli Stratta.** Since 1836, what may be the most famous candy store in Italy has been satisfying sweet tooths with cream-filled chocolates, candied almonds, and other exquisite delicacies. **Piazza San Carlo 191.** ☎ 011-547920. Mon 3–7:30pm; Tues–Sat 9:30am–7:30pm. $$.

⑩ ★★ kids **Parco del Valentino.** Tucked amid the promenades and gardens of this park along the River Po is the lovely **Borgo Medievale,** where quaint houses and cobbled squares surround a castle—all are authentic (if kitschy) reproductions of buildings from throughout Piedmont that were put together for the city's 1884 World Exposition. At one end of the park is a real castle, the beautiful Castello del Valentino, a French château–style assemblage of towers, sloping roofs, and courtyards built over the shell of a medieval fortification and the

summer residence of Christine Marie (1606–63), regent of Savoy. The palace is now used by the University of Turin, but its small botanical garden, much diminished from its original 18th-century plan, can be visited. ⏱ 1 hr. Viale Virgilio, Parco del Valentino. ☎ 011-443-1701. www.borgomedioevaletorino.it. Admission 5€. Apr–Oct 9am–7pm; Nov–Dec 9am–8pm. Garden: Admission 3€. Sat–Sun 9am–1pm, 3–7pm. Bus: 45, 46, 52, 64. Tram: 9, 16.

Museum Tip

Turin's excellent Museo dell'Automobile, a repository of elegant cars of mostly Italian design, is closed indefinitely for renovation. Even so, the museum occasionally rolls out its legendary vehicles for special exhibits at halls around Turin. For current information, check with the tourist office or www. museoauto.it.

Cafe Life

The Torinese are inveterate cafe-goers. Many of the elegant cafes that line the arcades along Via Roma and the piazzas of the *centro storico* (historic center) have been in business since patrons (male ones, that is) showed up in knee breeches and powdered wigs. The coffee, tea, chocolates, and pastries on offer set the gold standard for such fare, and many cafes also serve *tramezzini* (sandwiches) and often more substantial food and are also popular stops for an afternoon ice cream and/or an evening *aperitivo*.

The grandest of all of the city's cafes is the venerable **Caffè San Carlo** (pictured above), Piazza San Carlo 156 (☎ 011-532586), where a sumptuous interior is the setting for excellent pastries and coffee and flawless service. **Caffè Confetteria al Bicerin,** Piazza della Consolata 5 (☎ 011-436-9325),

Turin's oldest cafe, has been in continuous operation since it opened its doors in 1763 and was one of the first of the city's cafes to welcome female patrons, most of whom were communicants at the Santuario della Consolata across the piazza. The house drink is the *bicerin,* a shot of espresso mixed with hot chocolate and cream. Friedrich Nietzsche used to cafe-hop between the Bicerin and **Caffè Elena,** Piazza Vittorio Veneto 5 (☎ 011-812-3341), an atmospheric, far less glamorous old place that's still a favorite with students and bohemians, and popular with night owls who enjoy its late hours. **Caffè Mulassanno,** Piazza Castello 15 (☎ 011-547990), may be Turin's most beautiful cafe and is also exotic, a shrine to 1907 exuberance with elaborately carved wood fittings; the *tramezzini* are also a Torinese institution.

Where to Stay & Dine

> *The Ayrton Senna room at Art Hotel Boston, named after the late Brazilian Formula One driver.*

★★★ Art Hotel Boston NEAR THE STATION
Art Deco details, a stunning art collection, and stylish guest quarters that are an art statement in themselves provide some of the most exciting lodgings in Turin. Via Andrea Massena 20. ☎ 011-500359. www.hotelbostontorino.it. 91 units. Doubles 150€. AE, DC, MC, V. Bus: 12, 14, 63. Tram 15.

★★ C'era una Volta NEAR THE STATION
PIEDMONTESE The menu in the old-fashioned dining room of "Once upon a Time" changes daily but always focuses on Torinese favorites that might include a *bagna cauda* (a blend of olive oil, garlic, and anchovies) and a creamy risotto, offered a la carte or on a tasting menu. Corso Vittorio Emanuele II 41. ☎ 011-655498. Entrees 15€–18€; tasting menu 30€. AE, MC, V. Lunch & dinner Mon–Sat. Bus: 58, 63. Tram: 4, 9.

★★ Conte Biancamano NEAR THE STATION
Grand public salons and plainer guest rooms of varying sizes occupy the second floor of an elegant 19th-century apartment house. Corso Vittorio Emanuele II 73. ☎ 011-562-3281. www.hotelcontebiancamano.it. 24 units. Doubles 100€–145€. AE, DC, MC, V. Bus: 58, 63. Tram 4, 9.

★ Dai Saletta NEAR THE STATION
PIEDMONTESE A family-run trattoria sticks to the old ways, making pastas and sauces from scratch, and following them up with hearty stews and roasted meats. Via Belfiore 37.

☎ 011-668-7867. Entrees 10€–15€. AE, MC, V. Lunch & dinner Mon–Sat. Closed Aug. Bus: 34, 35. Tram: 16.

★★ Hotel Bologna NEAR THE STATION
A rather worn-looking entryway and hallways don't do justice to the very nicely renovated guest rooms spread out over several floors of an old apartment house; some retain frescoes, fireplaces, and other cool details. Corso Vittorio Emanuele II 60. ☎ 011-562-0193. www.hotelbolognasrl.it. 50 units. Doubles 70€–85€. AE, DC, MC, V. Bus 58, 63. Tram 4, 9.

★★★ Tre Galline CENTRO *PIEDMONTESE*
Turin's oldest eatery, in business for over 300 years, specializes in traditional fare as old as the surroundings, from meat-filled *agnolotti* to beef braised in Barolo. Via Gian Francesco Bellezia 37. ☎ 011-436-6553. Entrees 10€–15€. AE, MC, V. Lunch & dinner Tues–Sat; dinner only Mon. Bus 3, 4, 16, 57.

★★★ Victoria Hotel CENTRO
A country-house-style drawing room, with a fire and cozy bar; floral fabrics and wallpapers in the guest rooms; and a garden create a little bit of Anglophile heaven—all beautifully done and just steps from the heart of the city. Via Nino Costa 4. ☎ 011-5611909. www.hotelvictoria-torino.com. 106 units. Doubles 155€–175€. AE, DC, MC, V. Bus: 61, 68. Tram: 18.

CINEMA PARADISO

Italy Goes to the Movies

BY STEPHEN BREWER

ITALY'S FILM INDUSTRY was born at the turn of the 20th century, but the magic of Italian cinema was not unleashed until the dust of World War II began to settle and the cameras started rolling to capture the poverty and hardship of life in postwar Italy. Films from the 1940s through 1960s, the great age of Italian cinema, have been enthralling moviegoers ever since, with themes that range from poverty and loneliness to alienation to the quirkiness of the Italian character to out and out frivolity. A fine Italian film tradition continues to this day. From the war drama *Rome, Open City* (Roberto Rossellini, 1945) to *Cinema Paradiso* (Giuseppe Tornatore, 1988), a sentimental tribute to Italian filmmaking, to *Gomorra* (Matteo Garrone, 2008), a disturbingly realistic look at Naples's Camorra underworld, all reveal a distinctly Italian view of the world.

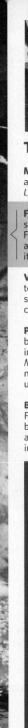

The Great Directors

MICHELANGELO ANTONIONI (1912–2007, above) explored the alienation of modern man in *L'Avventura* (1960) and *The Red Desert* (1964).

FEDERICO FELLINI Fantasy, dreams, and personal memories pervade the works of Federico Fellini (1920–1993), whose *La Dolce Vita* (1960) and other legendary films capture humanity at its most bizarre and endearing.

VITTORIO DE SICA The neorealistic films of Vittorio De Sica (1901–1974) expose the poverty and struggles of post–World War II Italy; a notable classic is *The Bicycle Thief* (1948).

PIER PAOLO PASOLINI Whether shaking up bourgeois values in *Teorema* (1968) or retelling the life of Jesus in *The Gospel According to St. Matthew* (1964), Pier Paolo Pasolini (1922–1975) made films that were often controversial and unfailingly hard-hitting.

BERNARDO BERTOLUCCI (1940–) examined Fascism in *The Conformist* (1970), pushed the boundaries of sexuality in *Last Tango in Paris* (1972), and pursued his favorite themes of sex and politics in *The Dreamers* (2003).

The 1960s and Beyond

Italian cinema took a turn in the 1960s with so-called Spaghetti Westerns. The best of the genre were *A Fistful of Dollars* and other films by director Sergio Leone, starring Clint Eastwood and with memorable soundtracks by Ennio Morricone. In recent years Italian film-

makers have begun to regain the artistic luster of the postwar era. Notably powerful and insightful are Roberto Benigni's *Life Is Beautiful* (1998) and Nanni Moretti's *The Son's Room* (2001).

The Great Stars

SOPHIA LOREN rose out of the slums of Naples to show off her acting talent in such riveting dramas as Vittorio De Sica's *Two Women*, and to charm audiences with her comic side in *Houseboat*, one of her many Hollywood hits.

MARCELLO MASTROIANNI Whether carousing in nighttime Rome in *La Dolce Vita* or soaking in a spa in *8½*, Marcello Mastroianni introduced the world to just how handsome and charming a leading man can be.

GIULIETTA MASINA In *La Strada* and other films by husband Federico Fellini, Giulietta Masina became immortalized as a graceful waif whose good nature never flags in the face of hardship.

Asti

Once a stop on the trade routes between the Ligurian ports and the north, Asti has prospered since its days as a Roman camp. Even during the throes of almost constant siege and warfare during the Middle Ages, the city managed to put up many fine churches and other monuments. In the minds of many, though, Asti's greatest achievement is its eponymous sparkling (*spumante*) beverage, a mainstay at celebrations all over the world.

> A circular baptistery is one of the oldest parts of much-altered San Pietro.

START Asti, 60km (36 miles) southeast of Turin.

❶ ★★★ Corso Vittorio Alfieri. It is only fitting that this lovely and romantic-looking street is named for a native son who spent his life traveling across Europe in search of truth, beauty, and goddesslike women, many of whom were otherwise attached. Count Alfieri (1749–1843) channeled the *Sturm und Drang* of his love life into theatrical tragedies that were wildly popular in late-18th-century Italy. The street and the narrow lanes leading off the cobblestone avenue are lined with many fine Renaissance palaces as well as fortified houses from the early Middle Ages, when Asti was besieged by everyone from Frederick Barbarossa to the Milanese. ⏱ 30 min.

② 🍴 **Pasticceria Giordanino.** Many strollers wouldn't think of walking past the door of Asti's oldest bakery without dropping in for an Amaretto-flavored biscuit *astigiana*, or another pastry baked on the premises. Corso Vittorio Alfieri 254. ☎ 0141-593802. $.

❸ Cattedrale di Santa Maria Assunta. One of the largest cathedrals in Piedmont is also the region's finest example of Romanesque-Gothic architecture, graced with three fine portals

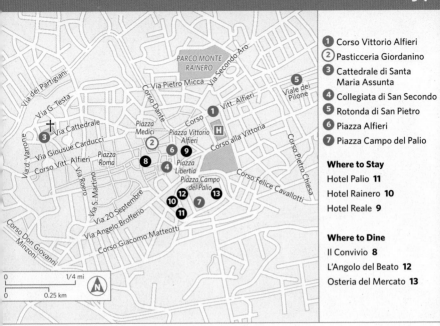

1. Corso Vittorio Alfieri
2. Pasticceria Giordanino
3. Cattedrale di Santa Maria Assunta
4. Collegiata di San Secondo
5. Rotonda di San Pietro
6. Piazza Alfieri
7. Piazza Campo del Palio

Where to Stay

Hotel Palio **11**
Hotel Rainero **10**
Hotel Reale **9**

Where to Dine

Il Convivio **8**
L'Angolo del Beato **12**
Osteria del Mercato **13**

beneath a triplet of rose windows and a tall belfry. Most of the frescoes that wash across the interior are from the 17th century, the work of Asti's own Gandolfino d'Asti. ⏱ 30 min. Piazza Cattedrale. ☎ 0141-592924. Free admission. Daily 8:30am–noon, 3:30–5:30pm.

4 ★ **Collegiata di San Secondo.** Asti's patron saint Secondo was a Roman military officer who was baptized into Christianity in Milan in the early 2nd century and raised the ire of officials when he buried the body of the martyred St. Marcianus, the first bishop of Piedmont. He fled to Asti, where he was tracked down, tortured, and beheaded in A.D. 119. Since the 13th century, the town has paid homage to the saint in a handsome Gothic church that rises above a 6th-century crypt that houses Secondo's relics. The church is also the repository of the coveted Palio Astigiano, the banner awarded to the victor of Asti's annual *palio* (6). ⏱ 30 min. Piazza San Secondo. ☎ 0141-592924. Free admission. Daily 8:30am–noon, 3:30–5:30pm.

5 ★★ **Rotonda di San Pietro.** This solid, octagonal, Romanesque church, completed in 1120, is surrounded by the 15th-century church

Travel Tip

At least two trains an hour run from Turin to Asti and the trip takes about 45 minutes. By car, follow autostrada A21 from Turin to the Asti Ovest exit. Asti's tourist office is at Piazza Vittorio Alfieri 29 (☎ 0141-530357; www.terredasti.it) and is open Monday to Saturday 9am to 1pm and 2:30 to 6:30pm, and Sunday 9am to 1pm.

of San Pietro and a beautiful cloister enclosed by porticoes that once sheltered pilgrims who came to Asti to pay homage to San Secondo. The complex now houses temporary exhibitions of contemporary art, along with a small collection of local Etruscan finds in the Museo Archeologico. ⏱ 30 min. Corso Alfieri. ☎ 0141-353072. Free admission to church and museum. Apr–Sept Tues–Sun 10am–1pm, 4–7pm; Oct–Mar Tues–Sun 10am–1pm, 3–6pm.

6 **Piazza Alfieri.** Like Siena, Asti hosts an annual horse race, this one on the third Sunday of September. Asti's less famous but older *palio* begins with a medieval pageant and, as in Siena, pits contestants from the city's

> *Farmers from the Piedmont hills set up in Asti's Campo del Palio market on Wednesday and Saturday mornings.*

different *roni* (neighborhoods) against one another on a bareback ride around the piazza. The event commemorates a 13th-century victory over Alba, in which Asti besieged Alba and celebrated with a horse race around the conquered city walls. Alba has since staged a *palio* of its own on the first Sunday of October—in theirs the mounts are asses, a comment on Alba's estimation of Asti. ⏲ 15 min.

7 Piazza Campo del Palio. A market takes over this large square on Wednesday and Saturday mornings (7:30am–1pm), and spills over into adjacent Piazza della Libertà and Piazza Alfieri. The stalls provide an excellent introduction to such local specialties as *cardo gobo* (hunchback cardoon) from the fields around nearby Nizza Monferrato (p 493, **9**), an artichoke-like winter vegetable often dipped in *bagna cauda;* the thistle-covered plants grow in a bent fashion and allegedly took their name from the hunched stoop of local gravediggers. Truffles appear in November, when the town hosts its annual truffle fair and exhibition, the Mostra Mercato del Tartufo. ⏲ 1 hr.

Fizz & Funghi

The sparkling wine that has made Asti famous is but one facet of the town's fine winemaking traditions. Moscato grapes from which the bubbling creation known as Asti Spumante is produced also yield refined Moscato dessert wines, and the town's Barbera d'Asti is a memorable red. Oenophiles might turn up their noses at Asti Spumante and dismiss the sweet sparkler as the poor man's Champagne, but frankly, the well-to-do growers around Asti really don't give a damn—they sell 80 million bottles a year. A good place to sample local wines is **Enoteca Boero,** Piazza Astesano 17 (☎ 0141-593365).

Truffles are greeted with all-around high regard, and with the assistance of specially trained sniffer dogs they are dug up from the earth around Asti and Alba from late September into December. It is believed in these parts that a single year rarely yields both good wines and plentiful, high-quality truffles, since what's good for the truffle (lots of rain) tends to be bad for the grape.

Where to Stay & Dine

> *Food comes from the market direct to the plate at the Osteria del Mercato.*

★★ **Hotel Palio** CENTRO

This modern building just down the street from the train station is newer than most of its neighbors, but captures Asti's old-world charms in spacious guest rooms done up in contemporary or traditional style; rooms on the top floor have small balconies. Via Cavour 106. ☎ 0141-34371. www.hotelpalio.com. 37 units. Doubles 100€–130€. AE, DC, MC, V. Closed most of Aug.

★★ **Hotel Rainero** CENTRO

Some of the modern redos of the rooms in this centuries-old house are a bit bland, but the friendly ambience and handy location just off Piazza Campo del Palio more than compensate. Via Cavour 85. ☎ 0141-353866. www.hotelrainero. com. 55 units. Doubles 80€–100€. AE, DC, MC, V.

★★★ **Hotel Reale** CENTRO

The old rooms in a palazzo on a corner of Asti's central piazza have been receiving guests since 1793, and provide a good quotient of charm and comfort—and even an in-house *enoteca.* Piazza Alfieri 6. ☎ 0141-530240. www. hotelristorantereale.it. 23 units. Doubles 100€–130€. AE, DC, MC, V. Closed most of Aug.

★★ **Il Convivio** CENTRO *PIEDMONTESE*

The straightforward contemporary surroundings suggest that food and wine are taken seriously, an impression borne out by the delicious pasta dishes, wine-braised meat preparations, and selections from the extensive wine cellars downstairs. Via G. B. Giuliani 6. ☎ 0141-353866. Entrees 8€–12€. AE, DC, MC, V. Lunch & dinner Mon–Sat. Closed part of Aug.

★★★ **L'Angolo del Beato** CENTRO *PIEDMONTESE* Stepping through the door into this pleasant dining room on the ground floor of a 13th-century palazzo is like walking into a private home, and the welcome and fine renditions of such Piedmontese classics as *agnolotti* stuffed with chicken and rabbit in tuna sauce do nothing to dispel the impression. Via Guttuari 12. ☎ 0141-531668. Entrees 10€–18€. AE, DC, MC, V. Lunch & dinner Mon–Sat.

★ **Osteria del Mercato** CENTRO *PIEDMONTESE*

A plain old room serves only a few dishes at any one meal, varying according to what's available at the market. House wines are available by the glass, and there's also a fine selection of bottles from small winemakers throughout the region. Corso Luigi Einaudi. ☎ 0141-34559. Entrees 5€–8€. No credit cards. Lunch & dinner Mon–Sat.

Alba

A settlement stood here among the Langhe hills as long as 5,000 years ago, and a town flourished under the Romans, then bounced back and forth between Burgundians and Lombards, Gonzagas and Viscontis, and other European powers throughout the Middle Ages before finally coming under the umbrella of the House of Savoy. Alba has long focused on the finer things in life, including velvety red wines, truffles, and chocolate, making a visit here all the more pleasant.

> *Asti's Via Vittorio Emanuele hosts a produce market on Saturday mornings and a buzzing cafe scene at night.*

START Alba, 70km (42 miles) southwest of Turin. From Turin, follow autostrada A6 to the Bra exit and route S231 from there.

① ★★★ **Via Vittorio Emanuele.** Alba's main street crosses the city center to the Piazza Risorgimento, the center of the town Alba Pompeia that the Roman consul Gnaeus Pompeius Strabo founded while he was building a road between Acqui Terme (p 493, ⑩) and Turin. A few sections of the Roman gates and other scant remnants are still scattered about Alba, as are some of the fortified towers from the 14th and 15th centuries that gave Alba the name "Town of the Hundred Towers." ⏱ 1 hr.

② 🍮 **Bar-Pasticceria Cignetti.** A mainstay on Via Vittorio Emanuele since 1878 serves such local creations as homemade *torrone,* nougat laced with hazelnuts. Via Vittorio Emanuele 3. ☎ 0173-440218. $.

③ ★ **Palazzo del Comune.** This solid, old brick structure from the 13th century houses a *Nativity* by Alba's great Renaissance painter, Macrino d'Alba (c. 1465–c. 1528). In the Sala della Resistenza are some fascinating photos of Alba during World War II, when the city was fiercely active in the resistance against German occupying forces and Mussolini's Fascism. Partisans liberated Alba on October 10, 1944, and for 3 weeks the city was the short-lived, independent Republic of Alba. ⏱ 30 min. Piazza Risorgimento. ☎ 0173-292111. Free admission. Mon–Sat 10am–5pm.

④ **Duomo.** Little is left of the 12th-century church built over Roman temples and heavy-handedly restored in the 19th century. The original belfry still stands. ⏱ 15 min. Piazza Risorgimento. ☎ 0173-44000. Free admission. Daily 8am–noon and 3–6:30pm.

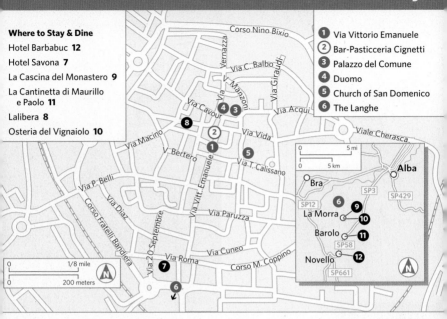

Where to Stay & Dine

Hotel Barbabuc **12**
Hotel Savona **7**
La Cascina del Monastero **9**
La Cantinetta di Maurillo
e Paolo **11**
Lalibera **8**
Osteria del Vignaiolo **10**

1. Via Vittorio Emanuele
2. Bar-Pasticceria Cignetti
3. Palazzo del Comune
4. Duomo
5. Church of San Domenico
6. The Langhe

---

⑤ ★★ Church of San Domenico. One of Piedmont's finest early Gothic churches was built in the 13th century next to a Dominican priory. A few frescoes from the 14th century remain, and a haunting modern monument is a marble Pietà grouping from the early 1920s by Leonardo Bistolfi (1859–1933; see p 495, **⑫**), installed in 1948 to honor the city's World War II resistance movement. ⏱ 30 min. Via Calissano.

⑥ The Langhe. The hills of the Langhe (just outside Alba) are noted for their fine vineyards, castles, and picturesque villages. Full-bodied, velvety Barolo, made from Nebbiolo grapes that grow especially well here, is the best-known wine of the region. You can taste this and other great vintages at the cantinas and *enoteche* in almost every village.

SITE GUIDE PAGE 522

For cycling and hiking tours of the Langhe wine region check with **Consorzio Turistico Langhe Monferrato Roero,** Piazza Risorgimento, Alba (☎ 0173-36328; www.turismodoc.it).

Food Shopping, Alba Style

The flavorful foodstuffs that put Alba on the culinary map are on display during the Saturday morning market along Via Vittorio Emanuele II. Stalls sell hazelnuts, walnuts, apples, and other local produce; truffles; and the many wines of the Langhe region—along with cheese, poultry, household goods, and other items. Every fall, nighttime truffle-hunters prowl secret routes in the company of dogs specially trained to sniff out the prizes. Truffles take center stage in late October and early November when Alba hosts the **Fiera Internazionale del Tartufo Bianco d'Alba** (www.fieradeltartufo.org). At other times, an excellent source for the region's wine and food is **Enoteca Peccati di Gola,** Via Cavour 11 (☎ 0173-361358).

Any time of year, the sweet scent of chocolate wafts through Alba from the Ferrero Rocher confection factory. The most famous output is **Nutella,** the creamy chocolate spread that sweet-toothed Italians have been spreading on bread for more than 4 decades and over the years has gained international acclaim.

BAROLO

SITE GUIDE

6 The Langhe

A **Roddi** is known for truffles, as well for the truffle-sniffing dogs trained in the art at a canine academy since 1880. The castle of **B** **Grinzane Cavour,** Via Cavour (☎ 0173-262159; 3.50€; call for current hours), was once home to Camillo Cavour (1810–61), the Turin-born aristocrat who drafted the nation's constitution, and mementos of his political career and his life are tucked into the stony recesses, along with a small wine museum. **C** **La Morra** (pictured above), is another hilltop village that affords wide-ranging views across the countryside; the Cantina Communale di La Morra, Via Carlo Alberto (☎ 0173-509204), offers tastings from local growers. In the tiny hamlet of **D** **Annunziata,** the Museo Ratti dei Vini d'Alba (☎ 0173-50185; www.renatoratti.com), is the creation of wine scholar Renato Ratti, who developed an excellent Barolo and collected ancient winemaking equipment. **E** **Barolo** is where the noble Falleti family began making the region's most famous wine in the late 17th century; their thousand-year-old **castle,** Piazza Falleti (☎ 0173-56277; 3.50€; Fri–Wed 10am–12:30pm, 3–6pm), stands among the vineyards, and the cellars house a museum and an *enoteca.* **F** **Novello** crowns an adjoining hilltop and was once a summer retreat for Alba's patrician Romans. At **G** **Monforte d'Alba,** members of the Cathar religious sect sought refuge in the castle before they were discovered and burned at the stake. **H** **Serralunga d'Alba** clusters around a beautifully restored 14th-century castle; the village is known for its Serralunga *chinato,* at one time the House of Savoy's favorite cure-all, created by infusing Barolo with herbs to give it medicinal properties. ⏱ **1 day.**

Where to Stay & Dine

> OPPOSITE PAGE, TOP *The village of Barolo is home to Piedmont's iconic red wine.* THIS PAGE *Simple hospitality at La Cascina del Monastero, in La Morra.*

★★★ Hotel Barbabuc NOVELLO

Behind an old facade is a surprising retreat where glass walls and terraces face a beautiful garden and have views beyond of the beautiful country-side; contemporary and traditional pieces fill the guest rooms; an *enoteca* downstairs serves wines from local growers. Via Giordano 35. ☎ 0173-731298. www.barbabuc.it. 9 units. Doubles 75€–90€. AE, DC, MC, V.

★★ Hotel Savona ALBA

Renovations have given this old hotel, overlooking a piazza at the edge of the old town, contemporary comfort, and the pastel-shaded rooms with small balconies are quiet and soothing. Via Roma 1. ☎ 0173-440440. www.hotelsavona.com. 98 units. Doubles 107€. AE, DC, MC, V.

★★★ La Cantinetta di Maurillo e Paolo BAROLO

PIEDMONTESE Two brothers delight their guests with *bagna cauda*, *raviolo* (a plumper pocket, served here with truffle sauce), herb-scented veal roasts, and other excellent preparations, accompanied by wines from the vineyards that run right up to the door. Via Roma. ☎ 0173-56198. Entrees 12€. AE, DC, MC, V. Lunch & dinner Fri–Tues, lunch Wed.

★★ kids La Cascina del Monastero LA MORRA

An old house set amid vineyards and fruit orchards provides attractively rustic and comfortable accommodations, pleasant terraces, and a sumptuous breakfast. Frazione Annunziata. ☎ 0173-509245. www.cascinadelmonastero.it. 5 units. Doubles 85€–100€. AE, MC, V.

★★★ Lalibera ALBA PIEDMONTESE

A contemporary room is the stylish setting for new takes on traditional recipes, such as zucchini flowers stuffed with trout mousse and salads of fresh vegetables and game. Via Elvio Pertinace 24A. ☎ 0173-293155. Entrees 12€–18€. No credit cards. Lunch & dinner Tues–Sat; dinner Mon. Closed part of Aug.

★★ Osteria del Vignaiolo LA MORRA

PIEDMONTESE Innovative fare served in this rustically sophisticated room makes the most of the local bounty, from fresh garden vegetables to wild mushrooms. Frazione Santa Maria. ☎ 0173-50335. Entrees 12€–18€. No credit cards. Lunch & dinner Fri–Tues, dinner Thurs.

Turin & Piedmont Fast Facts

Accommodations Booking Services
Cit Viaggi, Piazza San Carlo 205 (☎ 011-562-5652; www.citonline.it), handles hotel reservations throughout Piedmont.

American Express
The closest American Express office is in Milan, Via Brera 3 (☎ 02-7200-3693). It's open Monday to Friday 9am to 5:30pm and Saturday 9am to 5pm.

ATMs
You'll find 24-hour cash machines (*bancomat*) throughout the region, even in the smallest village. Italy generally uses 4-digit PINs; if you have a 6-digit PIN, check with your bank.

Dentists & Doctors
For emergency medical or dental attention, go to the *pronto soccorso* (emergency room) of the nearest hospital (ask at your hotel). Non-EU residents can consult national health service doctors for a relatively small fee; most goods hotels will have a list of doctors and will help with arrangements.

Emergencies
For general emergencies, call ☎ **112** for the Carabinieri or ☎ **113** for the Polizia. Call ☎ **114** for an ambulance and ☎ **115** for the fire department. For a medical emergency that doesn't require an ambulance, see "Dentists & Doctors," above. To report lost or stolen items, see "Police," p 525.

Getting There & Around
BY PLANE Flights to and from most major European cities serve **Turin Airport** (☎ 011-567-6361; www.aeroportoditorino.it), about 16km (10 miles) north of Turin in Caselle. **Sadem** (☎ 011-300-0611; www.sadem. it) buses connect the international airport with Turin's Porta Nuova train station, with buses running every half-hour from 5am to midnight; buy tickets (5€) from offices at the airport or the train station or at newsstands or ticket machines. The nearest airport handling overseas flights is **Milan Malpensa** (p 478), 130km (80 miles) to the southeast; Sadem buses run between Malpensa and Turin's main bus station on Corso Vittorio Emanuele II

(☎ 011-433-2525) several times a day; the trip costs 17€. BY TRAIN Trains from all over Italy and many European cities arrive at Turin's main station, **Porta Nuova** (☎ 011-532427; www. torinoportanuova.it), on Piazza Carlo Felice, at the edge of the historic center at the end of Via Roma. The trip to and from Milan takes a little under 2 hours; Genoa, 2 hours; Rome, about 6 hours; and Venice, about 4 hours. A smaller station, **Porta Susa,** Piazza XVIII Dicembre 8 (☎ 011-538513), handles some trains, including some to and from Milan, as well as TGV service to and from Paris, with three trains a day making the trip in about 6 hours; the station is at the western edge of the old city and an easy walk to the city center, but Porta Nuova is a little more convenient and many connections will be through there.

Extensive rail links serve towns throughout Piedmont, making it easy to get just about anywhere you want to go by train. Even Parco Nazionale del Gran Paradiso and other remote parts of the Valle d'Aosta are readily accessible by public transportation, via train to Aosta and buses from there. The exception is the Langhe wine region, which can only be easily toured on your own by car. BY CAR Turin is at the hub of an extensive network of super highways. **A4** connects Turin with Milan, a little over an hour away; **A6** drops down toward Bra and Alba and connects Turin with the Ligurian coast (and, from there, with Genoa via **A10,** with a total travel time between the two cities of about 1½ hr.); **A5** connects Turin with Aosta, about an hour away; and **A21** connects Turin with Asti and Piacenza, where you can connect with the **A1** for Florence (about 3½ hr. from Turin) and Rome (about 6½ hr. from Turin).

Internet Access
Wi-Fi is a common amenity in business-oriented and luxury hotels in Turin and in many other towns in the region. Many hotels that do not have Wi-Fi or other in-room Internet connections provide access through a public computer. Internet cafes are fairly common in Turin and most towns of any size; ask at your hotel for the nearest location. Italian law requires that all patrons provide a passport

Don't Light Up

Smoking is illegal in all public places in Italy, though restaurants and other businesses sometimes provide special smoking areas; most patrons congregate on the pavement near the entrance to smoke.

or another form of identification, and fees are usually around 5€ an hour.

Pharmacies

Farmacie are recognizable by a neon green or red cross and are usually open 8am to 1:30pm and 3:30 to 8pm; in any city or town, at least one pharmacy is required to remain open 24 hours on a rotating basis, and the name and location of the designated pharmacy is posted at all others.

Police

To report a lost or stolen article, such as a wallet or passport, visit the local police *questura* or Carabinieri *caserma* in your location. See also "Emergencies," p 524.

Post Office

Turin's main post office is just west of Piazza San Carlo at Via Alfieri 10 (☎ 011-506011); it is open Monday to Friday 8:30am to 7pm and Saturday 8:30am to 1pm. *Francobolli* (stamps) can be purchased at most *tabacchi* (tobacco stores).

Safety

Turin is a pretty safe city, and even the neighborhood around the train station is a lot nicer than such areas tend to be. Even so, be wary of pickpockets, and also keep up your guard when walking on the dark and often-deserted streets near the banks of the River Po at night. Just about all the other parts of this prosperous region are safe, though you will want to stash valuables out of sight and lock your car when parking at resorts and parks in the Valle d'Aosta.

Visitor Information

Turin's tourist offices are in Piazza Solferino (☎ 011-535901) and the Porta Nuova railway station (☎ 011-531327; www.turismotorino. org), and they are open daily 9am to 7pm; an office at the airport is open daily 9am to 10pm.

Other tourist offices around the region are: **Alba,** Piazza Medford 3 (☎ 0173-35833; www. langheroero.it; Mon–Fri 9:30am–12:30pm and 2:30–6:30pm, Sat 9am–12:30pm); **Aosta,** Piazza Chanoux 2 (☎ 0165-33352; www. regione.vda.it/turismo); and **Asti,** Piazza Vittorio Alfieri 29 (☎ 0141-530357; www. terredasti.it; Mon–Sat 9am–1pm and 2:30–6:30pm, Sun 9am–1pm). The tourist office in Aosta can provide information about skiing near Monte Bianco and elsewhere in the region.

11

Liguria

The Best of Liguria in 3 Days

The Ligurian coast arches from the French border to Tuscany, backed by mountains that ensure balmy temperatures year-round and lined with fishing villages and such storied resorts as Santa Margherita and Portofino. Three days allows time to explore the great maritime city in the center of this coast, Genoa, as well as the scenery-filled eastern stretches of Liguria, the so-called Riviera di Levante (Rising Sun), with a day on the Portofino Peninsula and a third day in the Cinque Terre.

> PREVIOUS PAGE Tall, narrow, brightly colored houses appear to rise straight out of the sea at Portovenere, on Liguria's southern coast. THIS PAGE Vernazza and the other Cinque Terre towns can be reached on foot, by train, or by sea.

START Genoa. Trip Length: 100km (60 miles) from Genoa to the Cinque Terre.

① **Genoa.** This ancient city of the sea is as multilayered as the hills it clings to, a place of splendor and squalor, of great piazzas and dark, narrow streets. Phoenicians, Etruscans, Greeks, and Romans all sailed into and out of the ancient port, but it was the navigators of the Renaissance, Christopher Columbus among them, and their banker backers who

made Genoa one of the world's great maritime powers.

A central place to begin a tour of this sprawling, boisterous, and often overwhelming city is **Piazza de Ferrari,** where such landmarks as the Palazzo Ducale, the Opera House, and the church of Sant'Ambrogio surround a splashing fountain. The beautiful little **Piazza San Matteo** (p 548, **④**), just a few steps around the corner, still gives the impression of being the domain of one of the city's most prominent families, the

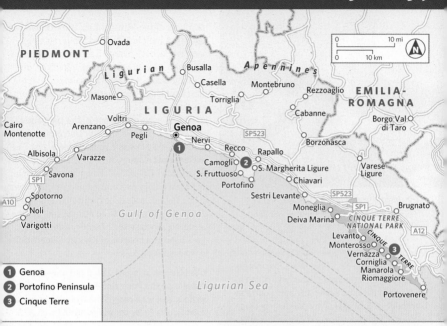

PIEDMONT

Ovada

Busalla

Casella

Montebruno

Rezzoaglio

EMILIA-ROMAGNA

Ligurian

Apennines

Masone

Torriglia

Cabanne

Borgo Val di Taro

LIGURIA

Voltri

Genoa

Cairo Montenotte

Arenzano

Pegli

Nervi

Recco

Rapallo

Borzonasca

SP523

Camogli

S. Margherita Ligure

Varese Ligure

Albisola

Varazze

S. Fruttuoso

Portofino

Chiavari

SP1

Savona

Sestri Levante

SP523

A10

Spotorno

Gulf of Genoa

Moneglia

SP1

Brugnato

Noli

Deiva Marina

CINQUE TERRE NATIONAL PARK

A12

Varigotti

Levanto

Monterosso

Vernazza

Corniglia

Manarola

Riomaggiore

Ligurian Sea

Portovenere

1 Genoa

2 Portofino Peninsula

3 Cinque Terre

Dorias. Their stately palaces and the church they commissioned, San Matteo, line the quiet square that seems light years removed from the modern city that rushes just beyond the stony reaches of this charmingly medieval enclave.

The **Cattedrale di San Lorenzo** (p 548, **5**), just to the south, was the center of the medieval city, commanding the piazza with its black-and-white-striped Romanesque facade and a campanile that rises above the steep, narrow streets and alleyways of the old quarter. This warren of worn-looking houses cascades down the hillside toward the old port and evokes the words of Dylan Thomas, "Dirt and noise and loud wicked alleys with all the washing of the world hanging from the high windows."

This seamier side of Genoa—and even the presence of shrines and statues of the

Traveling by Train

It is easy to travel around Liguria by train. Service between towns is fast and frequent, and the few places that are not served by train, such as Portofino, can easily be reached by bus. Even the Genoese prefer not to hazard their city in a car, and the Cinque Terre is all but off-limits to vehicles.

> Genoa's black-and-white-striped cathedral was consecrated in 1118.

> The upscale resorts of Portofino and Santa Margherita Ligure are linked by a stunning cornice road.

Madonna on every corner don't dispel a sense of unholy doings—is all the more fascinating because of the grandeur that is also much in evidence in the city, especially along the **Via Garibaldi** (p 549, **7**). This grand street was laid out at the top of the old city in the 16th century and soon became the preferred address of the great Genoese trading families. Several of their palaces, including the Palazzo Rosso and Palazzo Bianco, now house some of the city's noted art collections. The most evocative setting for art is the **Palazzo Spinola** (p 550, **11**), around the corner on Piazza Pellicceria. The dim, faded rooms give the appearance that

---

A Medieval Maze

Genoa, like Venice, is a city in which it is easy to lose your bearings, and it can be a pleasure to do so. The characteristic Genoese street, called either a *vicolo* or a *caruggio*, is narrow, dark, and lined with an incongruous jumble of medieval, Renaissance, and baroque houses, churches, palaces, and tenements. Genoa's old quarter, between Piazza de Ferrari and the port, is an intricate labyrinth of these lanes that, as Mark Twain observes in *Innocents Abroad*, are "crooked as corkscrews." The tall old houses, faded now but once painted bright colors so sailors could pick them out from sea, are so close together that a resident need only lean out a window to borrow a cup of sugar from a neighbor across the way.

---

members of the 18th-century Spinola clan have just taken their leave. Amid the furnishings hang works by Giovanni Castiglione and Luca Giordano, as well as Anthony Van Dyck, one of many Dutch and Flemish painters who the merchant kings lured to the city with fat commissions.

As pervasive as a sense of the past and faded glory is in Genoa, the city also embraces the modern world in some remarkable ways. The **ancient port** where Roman galleons docked, Christopher Columbus did an apprenticeship, and Marco Polo was imprisoned, leads the way in this regard, with a striking aquarium that is one of Italy's most-visited attractions. Yet the Lanterna, Genoa's 16th-century lighthouse, rises nearby, a beacon of the city's deep roots in the seafaring past.

From Genoa, it is just 28km (18 miles) to Rapallo on the Portofino Peninsula, less than an hour away on one of the trains that run at least hourly or by car along autostrada A12.

2 Portofino Peninsula. Portofino's enchanting natural harbor has been admired since the Romans named it *Portus Delphini,* Port of the Dolphins, after the creatures that still frolic in the balmy waters. Along with its nearby neighbors, Rapallo and Santa Margherita, the old village of gaily colored houses surrounded by sea pines and olive trees became especially popular with British visitors at the end of the 19th century. Max Beerbohm, D. H. Lawrence, and Ezra Pound were among the many expatriates who have taken up residence on the peninsula, and Friedrich Nietzsche clarified his thoughts for *Thus Spake Zarathustra* while strolling amid the olive groves that carpet the hills. The charms of some of Italy's most scenic seaside retreats have not faded with the decades, and the three towns are surrounded by the protected landscapes of a vast nature preserve.

Rapallo (p 560, **1**) is built around a half circle of a harbor, and the elegant resort of **Santa Margherita Ligure** (p 561, **2**), about 8km (5 miles) south of Rapallo, also stretches along a palm-fringed waterfront. Both towns are protected by formidable 16th-century castles—Rapallo's clings to a rocky outcropping in the harbor—that were built to repel attacks from invaders who have included Saracens, Ottomans, and Barbary pirates.

> *The man-made vine terraces of the Cinque Terre coast yield dry and sweet white wines.*

From Santa Margherita, a stunning cornice road follows the rocky coast to **Portofino** (p 562, ❸), where rows of tall houses surround the horseshoe-shaped harbor. Seaside paths lead to the lighthouse at the peninsula's tip and continue across the coast to such isolated spots as the **Abbey of San Fruttuoso** (p 561).

From Rapallo, it is just 66km (41 miles) south-east to Monterosso, the northernmost town in the Cinque Terre, less than an hour by train (they run at least every hour). Given the ease of getting around, you may want to visit the Cinque Terre as a day trip from the Portofino Peninsula.

❸ kids **Cinque Terre.** The "Five Lands" takes its name from the five hamlets that cling to a ruggedly beautiful coast north of La Spezia.

More Information

For detailed coverage of sights, hotels, restaurants, shops, and nightlife in Genoa, see p 544; on the Portofino Peninsula, see p 560; and in the Cinque Terre, see p 540.

The villagers make their livelihoods in part as they have for centuries, from the sea and from the vineyards that climb impossibly steep hill-sides—and also, these days, by catering to their many visitors. In the absence of easy access by roads, the way to get from one town to the next—**Monterosso al Mare,** the northernmost and most popular of the villages, **Vernazza, Corniglia, Manarola,** and **Riomaggiore**—is by foot along ancient footpaths, by local trains that emerge only occasionally from the tunnels that burrow through the region, or by sea.

The setting, relative isolation, and entic-ing prospect of walking from village to village through vineyards and atop seaside bluffs make the Cinque Terre one of Italy's most appealing regions. Walking and dipping into the sea from one of the Cinque Terre's pebbly beaches or a surf-washed boulder are the major pastimes, and the region has a distinctive gastronomic tradition, too. Small wooden boats set out from the harbors to haul in anchovies, and the ter-raced vineyards yield an excellent white wine and Schiacchetrà, a sweet dessert wine.

The Best of Liguria in 1 Week

A full week allows you time to explore the length of the Ligurian coast, from San Remo near the French border to Lerici and Portovenere, two towns that stand guard over their respective sides of the Gulf of La Spezia on the border with Tuscany. This tour combines the worldly pleasures of 19th-century San Remo and ancient Genoa, as well as stretches of Italy's most beautiful coastline on the Portofino peninsula and the Cinque Terre.

> *The palm-fringed Corso dell'Imperatrice is the site of opulent San Remo's evening passeggiata.*

START San Remo, 140km (81 miles) west of Genoa. Trip length: 250km (144 miles) from San Remo to Lerici.

1 San Remo. The most fabled Ligurian resort retains an onion-domed church, a palm-lined seaside promenade, a glittering casino, and the genteel patina of old-fashioned elegance—all remnants of the 19th century, when San Remo was one of Europe's most fashionable watering holes.

Since the days when Czar Alexander III and Tchaikovsky wintered in San Remo, the custom has been to spend at least part of a day strolling on the **Corso dell'Imperatrice,** a seaside promenade that curves around the bay. Adding to the allure of the old harbor and the many palm-shaded villas is an abundance of flowers, grown in fields and greenhouses up and down the coast.

In the Middle Ages, the ancient port town the Romans founded shifted inland and uphill, onto the slopes of **La Pigna** (the pinecone), so called for its pointed shape. Narrow streets wind up the hill past proud old houses to the church of the

Take the Train

It's easy to do this tour using the trains that run up and down the Ligurian coast with great frequency. A car is a hindrance in Genoa and the Cinque Terre, and the other places on this itinerary are readily accessible without one.

1 San Remo
2 Genoa
3 Portofino Peninsula
4 Cinque Terre

> The art collection at Genoa's Palazzo Bianco is strong on Flemish, Dutch, and Genoese painters.

Madonna della Costa and some breathtaking views. Two of Liguria's most captivating sights are just west of San Remo, practically straddling the French border: the sumptuous seaside **botanical collections of Giardini Hanbury** (p 537, ②) and **Balzi Rossi** (Red Rocks; p 536, ①), seaside caves inhabited by prehistoric humans more than 35,000 years ago.

The trip from San Remo to Genoa takes just under 2 hours by train.

② **Genoa.** Seeing the sights outlined in ① in the "The Best of Liguria in 3 Days" (p 528) will occupy a fulfilling first day. A good part of the second day can be spent at leisure amid the art collections on the Via Garibaldi and the surrounding neighborhood, comparing the Van Dycks in the **Palazzo Bianco** (p 538, ③) and

More Information

For detailed coverage of sights, hotels, and restaurants in and around San Remo, see p 556; in Genoa, see p 544; on the Portofino Peninsula, see p 560; and in the Cinque Terre, see "Hiking in the Cinque Terre," on p 540.

> Outside Portofino, the lonely abbey of San Fruttuoso, founded by Benedictine monks over 1,000 years ago.

the **Palazzo Reale** (p 552, ⑮), and admiring the works by Guido Reni and Caravaggio and other Italian masters in the **Palazzo Rosso** (p 550, ⑩) and **Palazzo Spinola** (p 550, ⑪).

Cinque Terre Travel Tip

Trains run as frequently as every 15 minutes to burrow through tunnels that connect the five villages; each is only a few minutes' travel from the next. Train travel between the towns is included in the fee you pay to visit the Parco Nazionale delle Cinque Terre (see "Visiting the Cinque Terre," on p 542); regular fares are about 1€ from town to town. The Cinque Terre is especially beautiful when viewed from the sea, and boats pull into all the villages except Corniglia; **Consorzio Navigazione,** Golfo dei Poeti (☎ 0187-730336; www.navigazionegolfodeipoeti.it), has four or five sailings a day in between Riomaggiore, Manarola, Vernazza, and Monterosso. Passage is 13€ weekdays and 16€ weekends, or 21€ for a day ticket on weekdays (23€ on weekends), allowing passengers to disembark and embark as they wish.

In the old center, labyrinthine streets and twisting alleyways all seem to lead downhill toward the **old port,** where Phoenicians, Etruscans, and Romans, crusaders and explorers, anchored their vessels. The **Torre della Lanterna** has been guiding ships into the harbor since 1543, making the sturdy tower the oldest working lighthouse in the world. Two other distinctive structures that rise over the port are recent. The ship-shaped **Acquario di Genova** (p 551, ⑬) is Europe's largest aquarium, and **Il Bigo** is a mastlike observation tower built to commemorate the Columbus quincentennial celebrations in 1992.

Genoa is also to be appreciated from the heights of the hills on which the city is built. From the Largo della Zecca downtown, the **Righi funicular** climbs Monte Righi to an overlook 300m (900 ft.) above the city and harbor, making seven stops along the way (1€). The **Ascensore Portello-Castelletto** ascends from the Piazza Castello to the Belvedere Luigi Montaldo, hanging precipitously above the old city.

Frequent train service connects Genoa with Rapallo and Santa Margherita, and buses from there run to Portofino. From Genoa, you can be on the peninsula in well under an hour.

❸ **Portofino Peninsula.** Any one of the peninsula's three resorts—Portofino, Santa Margherita, or Rapallo—provides a pleasant stopover for a night as you follow the coast toward the Cinque Terre. Of the three, Portofino retains the ambience of a quiet port, though this is an expensive and exclusive quaintness—the boats that fill the little harbor are private yachts, not fishing scows. One of the town's most delightful pastimes is free: the popular walk from Portofino on a path that leads through forests and olive groves to the **Abbey of San Fruttuoso** (p 561), a pantheon of Genoa's seafaring Doria clan tucked away on the remote shores.

Monterosso, the largest and northernmost town of the Cinque Terre, is less than an hour from Rapallo by train.

❹ kids **Cinque Terre.** One of Italy's most dramatic coastlines was unknown to outsiders until the fairly recent past and still retains a rugged beauty that is now protected as the **Parco Nazionale delle Cinque Terre** (p 542). Arrive early in the morning, settle into one of

> *Pack sunscreen, plenty of water, and your Cinque Terre card for a summer's day on the coastal trails.*

the villages, and put on sturdy walking shoes to explore the region by foot.

The steep seaside cliffs have defied road builders, and the seaside trail, **Sentiero Azzurro** (Blue Trail; p 540), follows the unspoiled coastline to connect the region's five villages. From Monterosso, the northernmost village, it is 9km (4½ miles) to southernmost Riomaggiore. This 4- to 5-hour walk is at times strenuous enough to be considered a serious hike, and there's certainly no need to rush past the stunning panoramas, fragrant pine groves, and hillsides terraced with vineyards and carpeted in lush Mediterranean flora.

One of the luxuries of a hike in the Cinque Terre is that the return journey can be so easy—via the local train that connects the five villages, or better yet, on one of the boats that connect all the villages with the exception of harbor-less Corniglia.

A second day in the Cinque Terre allows time to relax on one of the beaches, for more walking, and to explore the surrounding region. A short hike from Riomaggiore leads up the mountainside to the 14th-century **Santuario della Madonna di Montenero,** commanding a promontory 300m (1,000 ft.) above the coastline (p 542, **5**). Just south of the Cinque Terre,

Crowds & the Cinque Terre

The beauty and quaint charms of the Cinque Terre are hardly a secret, and troops of hikers clamber along the paths in an almost steady stream from May through September. Many of these visitors are young, and just when it seems as if no creature on the planet could possibly be noisier than an American college boy, his Australian counterpart bellows, "Next pint's on me." The Cinque Terre is also prime turf for walking tours, and large groups weighted down with backpacks and wielding sticks often crowd the paths. To avoid the crush, visit during the week; base yourself in one of the two quietest of the towns, Manarola or Corniglia; and rather than sticking to the popular seaside route between Monterosso and Riomaggiore, go off the beaten path on one of the many trails that traverse the inland forests.

the entrance to the Gulf of La Spezia is guarded by two-storied old fishing villages, **Portovenere** and **Lerici,** both easily reached on a half-day excursion (p 562, **5**).

Liguria's Best Art & Culture

While Liguria is often best appreciated for its scenery, the region shows off a remarkable cultural heritage, too. To say this goes back a long way is an understatement, given that some of Europe's earliest inhabitants left behind traces of their presence on this coast. Just as Englishman Thomas Hanbury was inspired to create splendid gardens, northern artists as well as Italy's own thrived in the creative hothouse of 16th-century Genoa.

> St. Sebastian, *by Guido Reni, in Genoa's Palazzo Rosso.*

START San Remo and environs. Trip length: 2 days, one on the coast west of San Remo, another in the museums of Genoa.

1 ★★★ kids **Balzi Rossi.** Some of the earliest documented Europeans lived in these caves etched into the red rocks ("*baussi russi*" in the local dialect) of a mountainside that plunges into the sea on the border of France and Italy. With the pre-Alps looming as a formidable barrier to the north, the caves were on a well-

trod route along the coast and appear to have been occupied almost continually from the first appearance of humanity. The hipbone of a woman suggests Stone Age humans took up residence in the caves 35,000 years ago. Some 22,000 years ago, a fairly sizable community of early European humans known as Gravettians (so-called for a cave near Gravette, in France's Dordogne, which they also inhabited) were living at Balzi Rossi. They left behind the characteristic pointed stone blades they used to hunt bison, horses, and mammoths, as well as a cache of 15 Venus-like figurines often associated with their culture; these sensual statuettes are fashioned from soft stone or clay, and buttocks and breasts are greatly exaggerated.

Prince Albert I of Monaco, a passionate oceanographer and paleontologist, sponsored an extensive exploration of the caves between 1895 and 1902 and built Monaco's Museum of Prehistoric Anthropology to house the finds. (Monaco is a mere half-hour's drive or short train ride west along the coast.) Sir Thomas Hanbury, who became enchanted with the surrounding Mortola peninsula and built a villa and planted gardens overlooking the sea, also took an interest in the Balzi Rossi excavations. His contributions include the small museum at the entrance to the grottoes, where exhibits provide an excellent introduction to one of Europe's most intriguing archaeological sites. ⏱ 2 hr. Via Balzi Rossi 9 (2km/1 mile west of Giardini Hanbury). ☎ 0184-38113. Admission 2€. Tues–Sun 9am–1pm, 2:30–6pm.

1 Balzi Rossi
2 Giardini Hanbury
3 Genoa

2 ★★★ kids **Giardini Hanbury.** The tea and cloth merchant Sir Thomas Hanbury was still a young man when he first came to the Mortola peninsula outside Ventimiglia in 1867. Struck by the beauty of the mountains and the sea, he bought up 18 hectares (45 acres) on the peninsula. Working with his brother, Daniel, and a team of botanists and landscapers, Hanbury created one of Italy's most noted gardens. He imported tropical and subtropical flora from around the world—more than 5,800 types of ornamental, medicinal, and fruit species. Agave, cacti, and eucalyptus mingle with Mediterranean plants, all benefiting from the warm climate and the shelter of the surrounding mountains. The ruins of a Roman villa, a portion of the Via Postumia, and endless views of the sea add their allure to this retreat, now in the hands of the University of Genoa. Sir Thomas lies in a Moorish-style mausoleum surrounded by the garden he created. ⏱ 2 hr. Corso Monte Carlo 43. ☎ 0184-229507. www. amicihanbury.com. Admission 6€ adults, 15€ for 2 adults and 3 children. Late Mar to mid-June and late Sept to Oct Thurs–Tues 10am–5pm; mid-June to late Sept Thurs–Tues 9am–6pm; Nov to late Mar Thurs–Tues 10am–4pm.

> *Carved figurines found in the Balzi Rossi caves are among Europe's earliest artworks.*

Train Travel

Balzi Rossi and Giardini Hanbury are on the coast just west of Ventimiglia, an ancient town about 20km (12 miles) west of San Remo and less than a half-hour away by frequent train service. Buses from Ventimiglia's train station run to both sites. For more information, see p 558.

> St. Francis, *showing his stigmata, by Bernardo Strozzi, in the Palazzo Bianco, Genoa.*

❸ Genoa. Like many Italian cities, Genoa was emerging from the confinements of the Middle Ages by the 16th century, and the architect Galeazzo Alessi (1512–72) was the man of the hour. Newly arrived in Genoa after showing his talents in his remodeling of the Palazzo dei Priori and other buildings in his native Perugia, Alessi was commissioned to design a new cupola for the cathedral of San Lorenzo and to lay out an entire street, the **Strada Nuova,** to be lined with palaces. Peter Paul Rubens, who arrived in Italy from Antwerp in 1600, was so impressed with the palaces he saw rising around him that he later compiled a book, *The Palaces of Genoa.* The artist also, no doubt, saw the opportunities awaiting him, and he and other northern artists—including Rubens's protégé, Anthony Van Dyck—earned their keep in Genoa painting portraits for the wealthy tenants to hang in their new salons on the monumental street, known since the 19th century as **Via Garibaldi** (p 549, ❼) in honor

More on Genoa

For detailed information on these museums and recommended hotels and restaurants in Genoa, see p 544.

of the Italian freedom fighter.

Ridolfo Brignole Sale commissioned the Palazzo Rosso in 1671, and his last heir, Maria Brignole Sale, duchess of Galliera, donated the palace and its neighbor, Palazzo Bianco, to the city of Genoa in 1884.

The ★★★ **Galleria di Palazzo Rosso** (p 550, ❿) is especially sumptuous with its acres of marble and frescoes. The salons house a good number of northern works, including Van Dyck's portrait of the marchesa Paolina Adorno Brignole Sale. The elegant lady was only 20 at the time of the portrait, yet Van Dyck includes a rose and feathers among his props, popular allegories for decaying beauty. The emphasis, though, is on Italian painters, among them such Genoese artists as Luca Cambiaso (1527–85), who as a teenager got his start as an apprentice working on frescoes for palaces and churches around the city. His *St. Jerome* is wonderfully dark and moody, and the same can be said of one of the museum's great treasures, Caravaggio's *Ecce Homo*. It's a wonder that Caravaggio had time to work on the canvas, in which Pontius Pilate presents Christ to the angry mob, as he was jailed several times for assault during the few months he was executing the work.

The ★★★ **Galleria di Palazzo Bianco** (p 549, ❾), built of white stone for the Grimaldi family in 1565, brings together the works of Flemish and Dutch artists as well as the many Genoese painters who they influenced. Van Dyck's *Portrait of an Unknown Genoese Woman* is one of the many commissions that kept the artist busy while he was in Genoa. Among the Italians is Genoa's own Bernardo Strozzi (1581–1644), whose baroque canvases are filled with color, drama, and dark emotion, as was Strozzi's life. The so-called *prete genovese* (Genoese priest) entered the Capuchin order at age 17, left without permission ten years later to care for his ailing mother, and fled to Venice when the court ordered him to be reconfined to the monastery. Giovanni Castiglione (1609–64)

> Genoa's Via Garibaldi and its palaces were laid out in the 1550s.

is another native son, and he studied both with Van Dyck and Strozzi, but his *Crucifixion,* with its stormy sky and wailing women, is filled with raw emotion that is his alone.

The ★★★ **Galleria Nazionale di Palazzo Spinola** (p 550, ⑪), around the corner from the Palazzo Bianco on Piazza Pelliceria, was also built by the Grimaldi family. The collections owe much of their luster to Maddalena Doria Spinola, an 18th-century marchesa famous for her taste and passion for collecting and for buying up masterpieces from around Europe. Her descendants, Paolo and Franco Spinola, donated the palace and its remarkable contents to the state in 1958. Even the old kitchens can be visited, an antidote to the luxury of the family apartments hung with such masterpieces as Joos van Cleve's *Adoration of the Magi* and Guido Reni's *Sacred and Profane Love.* Castiglione's *Journey of Abraham,* filled with the artist's characteristically detailed renderings of cooking utensils and other everyday objects, fits in especially well among the faience and other belongings the Spinolas left behind.

> The gilded rooms of the Palazzo Spinola in Genoa were inhabited by the patrician family as recently as the 1950s.

Hiking in the Cinque Terre

Hiking is what brings most visitors to the Cinque Terre.
Hikers trek in great numbers along rough paths that for centuries allowed the inhabitants of this once-isolated region to get from one neighboring village to another and to and from their tiny hillside vineyards and orchards. The trails are breathtaking, and the five towns—Monterosso, Vernazza, Corniglia, Manarola, and Riomaggiore—are carved out of one of Europe's most stunning coastlines. Plunging into the warm Mediterranean and enjoying the region's delicious wines and cuisine are other pleasures of the Cinque Terre.

> The coastal path—the Sentiero Azzurro, or Blue Trail—connects all five towns and is the Cinque Terre's most popular hike.

START Monterosso, 93km (56 miles) southeast of Genoa. Trains from Genoa to Monterosso run about every hour, and the trip takes about 1½ hours. The other villages can easily be reached by local train from Monterosso. Trip length: at least 2 days.

① **Monterosso al Mare.** The largest of the Cinque Terre villages is actually two towns. In the old quarter, tall houses surround a harbor

Traveling the Blue Route

The most popular hiking route in the Cinque Terre is the **Sentiero Azzurro** (Blue Trail), the seaside path that connects the five towns and covers a distance of 9km (4½ miles); it takes about 4 to 5 hours to traverse the length of the trail.

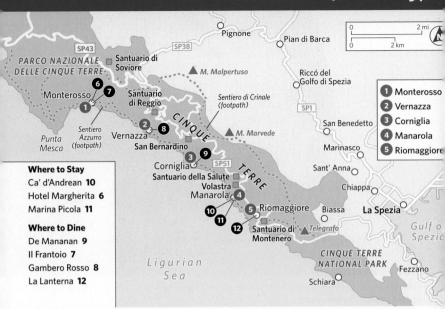

and the ruins of a castle, and on the other side of a seaside promontory a low-key resort stretches along the region's only sand beach, where **Bagni Eden Beach Club** (Via Fegina 7–11; ☎ 0187-818256) and other establishments provide a chaise longue and umbrella for about 16€ a day. Medieval citizens once took refuge from pirates in the towers that still rise above the rooftops, and many of their descendants are fair-haired, a legacy of the Vikings who frequently raided the coast.

With walking sticks at the ready, hikers set out on the most strenuous stretch of the Sentiero Azzurro, the 3km (2 miles) between Monterosso and Vernazza that climb and drop through terraced vineyards from which funicular-like carriages carry grapes down the steep hillsides. Even with a glass of Schiacchetrà, the region's sweet raisin wine, for fortification, a challenging 2 hours are in store for hikers.

2 Vernazza. What was once the most prosperous village in the Cinque Terre is still the prettiest. A *piazzetta* lined with loggias and arcades surrounds the harbor, and a castle of the Doria family rises high above the surf. Stepped streets lead to the church of **Santa Margherita d'Antiochia,** built in the 14th century to house the saint's bones after they allegedly washed ashore during a storm. The next stretch of the Sentiero Azzurro

traverses pine-scented woodlands for 4km (2½ miles) before coming to Corniglia; the hike will take about an hour and a half, including a few stops to admire the views of the coast.

3 Corniglia. Whether arriving on foot or by train, a climb is required to reach this hilltop warren of old stone houses and narrow streets that lead to the handkerchief-sized **Largo Taragio** and open every so often to heart-stopping views up and down the coast. The 377 steps of the **Lardarina staircase** descend from the south end of town to the train station and the next stretch of the Sentiero Azzurro, and from here it is a pleasant seaside amble of a little more than a kilometer (about a mile) to Manarola. Near the foot of the staircase, a disused and gated railway tunnel leads to one of the Cinque Terre's secret getaways, **Guvano Beach.** Ring the buzzer, the gate will open, and an attendant at the other end of the tunnel will collect 5€ for the pleasure of basking on this isolated, pebbly, clothing-optional strand.

4 Manarola. Inhabitants of this village have shown great ingenuity in dealing with the limitations of their natural setting. The small port can accommodate only a few boats at a time, so others are lifted out of the water on winches and dry-docked on the quay; and houses climb the impossibly steep hillsides in piggyback style. The

> *Particularly scenic stretches of the trails, like the Via dell'Amore between Manarola and Riomaggiore, can get crowded in peak season.*

onward journey of about 1km (less than a mile) to Riomaggiore is on a paved walkway that affords many romantic vistas and is aptly known as the **Via dell'Amore.**

5 Riomaggiore. In some ways, life goes on as it has for centuries in this proud-looking town where the River Maior flows into the sea. Fishermen still set to sea from the harbor, and almost everyone tends a patch of grapes and olives in the surrounding hills. The inhabitants are also adept at catering to their many international visitors, who walk up and down the busy Via Colombo and sun themselves on rocky ledges tucked into cliff tops above the surf. The large church of **San Giovanni Battista** looms above the upper town, and the oratory of **San Rocco** was built in honor of the saint who delivered 14th-century inhabitants from an outbreak of the plague. A hillside trail leads through vineyards to the **Santuario della Madonna di Montenero** (free admission; open daily 8am–12:30pm and 2:30–6pm), a frescoed church steeped in legend—in the 8th century an icon depicting the Madonna was hidden on this spot to protect it from invaders; when the icon was recovered years later, a spring miraculously began to gush. A little slip of a crescent-shaped beach skirts a cove next to Riomaggiore's harbor.

Visiting the Cinque Terre

The **Parco Nazionale delle Cinque Terre** comprises 3,860 hectares (9,500 acres) and protects the five villages and the vineyards, forests, and seacoasts that surround them. A Cinque Terre card is required to gain access to the paths during daytime hours and must be presented to sentries at trailheads. The fee for one day is 5€, or 8.50€ with unlimited train travel between the five towns; for 2 days it's 8€, or 15€ with train travel; for 3 days it's 10€, or 20€ with train travel; and for 7 days it's 20€, or 37€ with train travel.

The cards are available at park information centers in or near the train stations in the five villages, as well as at outlets near the parking area in Riomaggiore and on Piazza Garibaldi in Monterosso. The offices provide maps and a wealth of information on hiking and other activities within the park; those in Riomaggiore and Monterosso have large gift shops and Internet cafes as well. The administrative headquarters are at Via Telemaco Signorini 118, Riomaggiore (☎ 0187-76031; www.parconazionale5terre.it).

Where to Stay & Dine

> *The picturesquely rustic dining room at De Mananan in Corniglia.*

★★★ Ca' d'Andrean MANAROLA

A former olive press and wine cellar is now a pleasant little lair where guests can relax in a lemon-scented garden or around a fireplace. Several of the spacious rooms have terraces. Via Discovolo 101. ☎ 0187-920040. www.cadandrean.it. 11 units. Doubles 70€–96€. DC, MC, V.

★★★ De Mananan CORNIGLIA *LIGURIAN*

Vegetables plucked from a garden just outside the village, fresh fish, and homemade pastas appear on an ever-changing menu posted on a blackboard and served in the stone cellars of an old house. Via Fieschi 117. ☎ 0187-821166. Entrees 8€–14€. No credit cards. Lunch & dinner Wed–Mon.

★★★ Gambero Rosso VERNAZZA *SEAFOOD*

A meal at this Cinque Terre landmark comes with a view of Vernazza's harbor. House specialties include a memorable *ravioli di pesce* (homemade ravioli stuffed with fresh fish) and *muscoli ripieni* (mussels stuffed with fresh herbs). Piazza Marconi 7. ☎ 0187-812265. Entrees 10€–18€. MC, V. Lunch & dinner daily; closed Mon in winter.

★ Il Frantoio MONTEROSSO AL MARE *ITALIAN*

The busy counter here dispenses some of the best *focacce* in Liguria, as well as a delicious morning treat—*dolci castagnoni* (pastries laden with raisins, pine nuts, and chestnuts). Via Gioberti 1. ☎ 0187-818333. From 1.50€. No credit cards. Lunch & dinner Fri–Wed.

★★ Hotel Margherita MONTEROSSO AL MARE

Monterosso has always been the village with the most hotels, but none has ever been as stylish as this inn near the beach. Amenities include a chic bar, and all the guest rooms have spiffy bathrooms. Via Roma 72. ☎ 0187-808002. www.hotelmonterosso.it. 25 units. Doubles 80€–150€. MC, V.

★★ La Lanterna RIOMAGGIORE *SEAFOOD*

This perch above Riomaggiore's little harbor specializes in fresh-caught fish and such simple local favorites as *chicche verdi ai frutti di mare,* homemade spinach gnocchi filled with seafood. Via San Giacomo 46. ☎ 0187-920589. Entrees 8€–17€. MC, V. Lunch & dinner daily Apr–Oct.

★ Marina Piccola MANAROLA

The sound of waves breaking against the rocks at the entrance to Manarola's harbor ensures a good night's sleep, and many of the simple, tile-floor rooms have sea views. A fireplace warms the cozy lobby when a chill sets in. Via Birolli 120. ☎ 0187-920103. www.hotelmarinapiccola.com. 9 units. Doubles 115€. DC, MC, V.

Genoa

Founded in the 6th century B.C. and a port for the Etruscans, Greeks, and Romans, Genoa was a major sea power by the 13th century and ruled an empire that stretched across the Mediterranean and Aegean seas. As Genoa's fortunes increased, proud palazzi and churches were built on the slopes of the hills above the port, and artists came from throughout Europe to decorate them, leaving a rich artistic heritage. The former maritime republic is still a city of the sea—a fascinating place, much less visited than other Italian cities, and a place where, as Charles Dickens said, "Things that are picturesque, ugly, mean, magnificent, delightful, and offensive break upon the view at every turn."

> *A former Savoy palace close to Genoa's old port now houses the Galleria di Palazzo Reale art and sculpture collection.*

START Piazza de Ferrari. Allow at least 2 days to see the city in full.

❶ ★★ **Piazza de Ferrari.** The busy hub of Genoa is bordered by banks, the headquarters of shipping companies, and such landmarks as the Teatro Carlo Felice. The columned facade is all that remains of the opera house that the city erected in the early 19th century to host the wildly popular new art form that was burgeoning in Italy at the time. Opened in April 1828 with a performance of Vincenzo Bellini's *Bianca e Fernando,* the hall was all but leveled in World

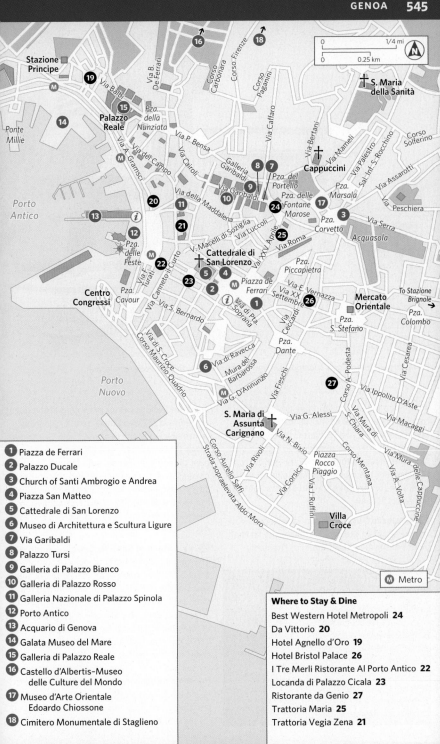

1. Piazza de Ferrari
2. Palazzo Ducale
3. Church of Santi Ambrogio e Andrea
4. Piazza San Matteo
5. Cattedrale di San Lorenzo
6. Museo di Architettura e Scultura Ligure
7. Via Garibaldi
8. Palazzo Tursi
9. Galleria di Palazzo Bianco
10. Galleria di Palazzo Rosso
11. Galleria Nazionale di Palazzo Spinola
12. Porto Antico
13. Acquario di Genova
14. Galata Museo del Mare
15. Galleria di Palazzo Reale
16. Castello d'Albertis–Museo delle Culture del Mondo
17. Museo d'Arte Orientale Edoardo Chiossone
18. Cimitero Monumentale di Staglieno

Ⓜ Metro

Where to Stay & Dine

Best Western Hotel Metropoli **24**
Da Vittorio **20**
Hotel Agnello d'Oro **19**
Hotel Bristol Palace **26**
I Tre Merli Ristorante Al Porto Antico **22**
Locanda di Palazzo Cicala **23**
Ristorante da Genio **27**
Trattoria Maria **25**
Trattoria Vegia Zena **21**

> *The flag of Genoa marks a lamppost in the Piazza de Ferrari, the city's commercial hub.*

War II bombings. The stunning new theater that lies behind the old facade was not completed until 1991. Via XX Settembre and other wide boulevards rush in fairly dull fashion east from the square into the new city, and off to the west are the much more enticing lanes that twist and turn through the old quarter toward the port. ⊙ 15 min.

2 ★ **Palazzo Ducale.** This great palace began to take shape in the early 14th century, at the height of the Genoese Republic. The richly decorated salons became the seat of the doge of Genoa in 1329 and have been extensively refurbished over the centuries. The Grimaldina tower that rises high above the palace is a remnant of medieval Genoa, built by 13th-century citizens as a place of refuge, and one of the city's most beloved landmarks. ⊙ 30 min. Piazza Matteotti 9. ☎ 010-557-4000. Free admission. Tues–Sun 9am–9pm. Bus 17, 18, 19, 31, 33, 37, 39, 40, 41, 47, 49.

3 ★★ **Church of Santi Ambrogio e Andrea.** The vast interior is nothing short of sumptuous, a riot of colored marble, rich stuccowork, and some of the city's finest art. One of the great masterpieces of Guido Reni, an *Assumption,* is in a side chapel. The *Miracles of St. Ignatius* is by Peter Paul Rubens, whose remarkable *Circumcision* is over the high altar. The Flemish painter spent the first decade of the 17th century in Genoa and other Italian cities, and like many travelers, he was overwhelmed by the peninsula. He wrote frequently about returning to Italy, and though he never did, until his death in 1640 he signed his letters "Pietro Paolo Rubens." ⊙ 15

Tourist Info

For information on getting around Genoa, see "Getting There & Around" on p 564. For information on Genoa's tourist offices, see "Visitor Information" on p 565. Available at all tourist offices and at the city's museums is the excellent-value **Genoa museum card,** allowing free entry to most collections; it costs 12€ for 24 hours and 16€ for 48 hours.

Famous Sons & Daughters

Genoa has nurtured many fine citizens during its long history, some very well known, others less so, but all an important part of the colorful story of this very complex city.

Genoa's most famous citizen, of course, is **Christopher Columbus** (1451–1506), depicted above. A ramshackle house on Piazza Dante is said to be his childhood home, but the providence is doubtful. Scholars debate whether or not the explorer was actually born in the city and the veracity of such claims that as a youth he worked in his father's cheese stand. It is fairly widely agreed upon that Columbus went to sea at the age of 10, as a business apprentice for the Spinolas and other influential Genoese families, and that by the 1480s he was planning a voyage to the Indies. Although Columbus spent most of his life at sea and in Spain, he remained loyal to Genoa and donated one-tenth of the income he was awarded by the Spanish crown for the discovery of the Americas to the city to help relieve the taxation on foods.

The Venetian explorer **Marco Polo** (1254–1324) was captured in one of the Republic's frequent clashes with Genoa. He was imprisoned in Genoa's Palazzo San Giorgio in 1298 and spent his months of confinement dictating accounts of his travels in China to his fellow prisoner Rustichello da Pisa. These came to life in a richly illuminated manuscript, *Il Milione,* a wildly popular bestseller in its pre-printing press times.

One of Genoa's most beloved monuments is Francesco Schiaffino's sculpture of Fieschi Adorno in the church of Santissima Annunziata di Portoria on the Via IV Novembre. Fieschi was canonized as **St. Catherine of Genoa** and is a favorite heroine of the city. Born into an aristocratic family in 1447, as a teenager she was married off to a dissolute young nobleman, Giuliano Adorno. She found refuge from her husband's violence and philandering in her faith, dedicating herself to the sick and the poor at the city hospital. Her repentant husband eventually joined her in her good works. She died in 1510.

The violin virtuoso **Niccolò Paganini** was born in Genoa in 1782. A childhood prodigy, he was sent off to Parma to study. By the early 19th century he was celebrated throughout Europe, famous for his performances and compositions, and infamous as a womanizer and gambler. He died in Nice in 1840, and his body was brought back to Genoa and displayed to an adoring public.

> *Gothic stonework on the facade of the Cattedrale di San Lorenzo.*

> *Giovanni Pisano carved this funerary monument for Margherita of Brabant, now in the city's Museo di Architettura e Scultura Ligure.*

min. Piazza Corvetto 3. Free admission. Mon–Sat 8am–noon, 3–6:30pm; Sun noon–6:30pm. Bus 1, 7, 8, 17, 18, 19, 20.

4 ★★ **Piazza San Matteo.** Generations of the mercantile Doria clan amassed their fortunes at sea and from financing the expeditions of Spanish and Portuguese navigators. Their palaces surround this small piazza in a stunning assemblage of facades and loggias, though none is grander than the Romanesque-Gothic **Church of San Matteo,** which they built in the 13th century. Andrea Doria, the swashbuckling imperial admiral who drew up the city's constitution, is buried in the church, and the cloisters are lined with plaques heralding the family's many accomplishments. ⏱ 15 min. Piazza San Matteo. Free admission. Mon–Sat 8am–noon, 3–6:30pm; Sun noon–6:30pm. Bus 1, 7, 8, 17, 18, 19, 20.

5 ★★ **Cattedrale di San Lorenzo.** By the 12th century, Genoese fleets were reaping the riches that could be made from the Crusades, and it seemed only fitting to bestow the city with a grand cathedral. With a facade of striped marble and graced with three elegantly carved doorways, San Lorenzo is one of Italy's great Gothic monuments. The somber stone interior was frescoed over the centuries as benefactors acquired even greater fortunes, and in the **Cappella di San Giovanni,** a 13th-century crypt contains what crusaders returning from the Holy Land claimed to be relics of John the Baptist. John is one of the patrons of Genoa, and these scant remains were at one time frequently paraded through the streets in a silver ark that is among the many fine pieces in the handsome modern galleries of the **Museo del Tesoro del San Lorenzo** beneath the cathedral. Also here is the silver platter on which Salome allegedly presented John's head to her mother, Herodias, and a chalice said to be that from which Christ drank at the Last Supper. ⏱ 1 hr. Piazza San Lorenzo. ☎ 010-296695. Cathedral: Free admission. Mon–Sat 8am–noon, 3–6:30pm; Sun noon–6:30pm. Museum by guided tour only. Admission 5.50€. Mon–Sat 9am–noon, 3–6pm. Bus 1, 7, 8, 17, 18, 19, 20.

6 ★★ **Museo di Architettura e Scultura Ligure.** The grassy cloisters gardens and vaulted halls of the 13th-century church and monastery of Sant'Agostino are the repository for fragments, sculptures, and detached frescoes from Ge-

> *Riches earned from the Crusades helped pay for the arcaded interior of the Cattedrale di San Lorenzo.*

noa's churches and palazzi. The treasures here are the sculptures from a funerary monument to Margherita of Brabant, wife of the German emperor Henry IV. Margherita died in Genoa in 1312 while en route to Rome for her husband's coronation as Holy Roman Emperor, and Henry commissioned the sculptor Giovanni Pisano to carve this graceful monument in her memory. ⏲ 1 hr. Piazza di Sarzano. ☎ 010-2511263. Admission 4€; free with museum card. Tues–Sat 9am–7pm, Sun 9am–12:30pm. Bus 39.

7 ★★★ **Via Garibaldi.** The grandest street in Genoa was laid out in the 1550s by Galeazzo Alessi, who embellished many Renaissance Italian cities with his classically influenced designs. Genoa's leading families commissioned the palaces along the street, and it is only fitting that these landmarks now house some of the city's most stunning art collections. While not all the palaces are so generously filled with art, it's safe to assume that most of the salons

behind the tall windows that face the narrow street sport a fresco or two.

8 ★ **Palazzo Tursi.** It is not surprising that the grandest house on Via Garibaldi was built for the banker Nicola Grimaldi (1673–1732), called the "Monarch" for all the titles bestowed upon him by King Philip III, to whom Grimaldi lent copious sums of money. Genoa's city hall (it has been the seat of Genoa's Commune since 1848—note the city's coat of arms over the entrance portal) now inhabits these sumptuous surroundings, and among the many civic treasures on display are letters from Christopher Columbus and the Guarnieri del Gesù violin that belonged to Niccolò Paganini. ⏲ 30 min. Via Garibaldi 9. ☎ 010-557-2269. www.museopalazzotursi.it. Admission 8€, includes admission to Palazzo Rosso and Palazzo Bianco; free with museum card. Tues–Fri 9am–7pm; Sat–Sun 10am–7pm. Bus 18, 20, 39, 40.

9 ★★★ **Galleria di Palazzo Bianco.** This palazzo built for the Grimaldi family holds paintings

> *Frescoed chambers in the Brignole Sale family home, now the Palazzo Rosso art gallery.*

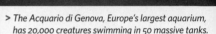

> *The Acquario di Genova, Europe's largest aquarium, has 20,000 creatures swimming in 50 massive tanks.*

of many Flemish and Dutch artists who were lured to Genoa with big commissions, as well as the works of the city's own painters. Few images are more arresting than the fleshy saints and sinners who inhabit the baroque canvases of Bernardo Strozzi. For more on this museum, see p 538. ⏱ 1 hr. Via Garibaldi 11. ☎ 010-557-2269. www.museopalazzobianco.it. Admission 8€, includes admission to Palazzo Rosso and Palazzo Tursi; free with museum card. Tues–Fri 9am–7pm; Sat–Sun 10am–7pm. Bus 18, 20, 39, 40.

⑩ ★★★ **Galleria di Palazzo Rosso.** The salons that were once the home of the Brignole Sale family are still filled with the red velvet furnishings and frescoes that befit the taste of merchant princes, and the rich surroundings are embellished with works by such masters as Guido Reni, Titian, Caravaggio, and Van Dyck. For more on this museum, see p 538. ⏱ 1 hr. Via Garibaldi 18. ☎ 010-557-4973. www.museopalazzorosso.it. Admission 8€, includes admission to Palazzo Bianco and Palazzo Tursi; free with museum card. Tues–Fri 9am–7pm; Sat–Sun 10am–7pm. Bus 18, 20, 39, 40.

⑪ ★★★ **Galleria Nazionale di Palazzo Spinola.** The elaborate palace that the Grimaldis commissioned in 1565 passed through the hands of some of Genoa's wealthiest families. The last owners, the Marquises Spinola, donated the house and its contents to the Italian state in 1958, and the palazzo retains the atmosphere of a private residence, a rather grand one, and a bit dusty and faded at that. Most strikingly, the Guido Renis and Van Dycks the Spinolas bought over the centuries remain just where they hung them. For more on this museum, see p 539. ⏱ 1 hr. Piazza Pellicceria 1. ☎ 010-270-5300. www.palazzospinola.it. Admission 4€; free with museum card. Tues–Sat 8:30am–7:30pm; Sun 1:30–7:30pm.

⑫ ★★ kids **Porto Antico.** Almost a thousand years ago, Genoa's civic leaders set out to create a waterfront that would befit the city's growing stature as a maritime power. For centuries afterward, the city prospered from the seagoing commerce concentrated on this curving stretch between the Mole Vecchio to the east and the Lanterna to the west. Though an elevated roadway, the **Strada Sopralevata,** looms overhead, life on the quays and alleys below is not too far removed from what it was centuries ago. Fishmongers and *frigitorie* (vendors of fried sardines and other seafood) still operate from beneath handsome old porticos along the Via di Sottoripa. Fruit and vegetable markets are clustered around the 16th-century Loggia dei Mercanti in Piazza Banchi, where one of the world's first stock exchanges went into operation in 1858. Marco Polo was held prisoner nearby in Palazzo San Giorgio, on the waterfront Piazza Caricamento. The **Palazzata della Ripa** is a row of tall medieval houses surrounding an airy ellipsis that in medieval times accommodated vendors plying wares that had just arrived from faraway ports. ⊕ 1 hr.

⑬ ★★★ kids **Acquario di Genova.** In stunning surroundings alongside a pier in the harbor, coral reefs, shark tanks, and penguin pens magically recreate life in the seas. The aquarium, one of the largest in Europe, is part of a restoration of the old port that Genoese architect Renzo Piano undertook for the 1992 quincentennial of the voyage of Christopher Columbus. Among Signor Piano's other appealing designs for the port is

> *Genoa's harbor has been the source of its prosperity for almost 1,000 years.*

A City that Inspires

As a port, Genoa has welcomed foreigners for much of its history. While Anthony Van Dyck and Peter Paul Rubens left their many canvases in Genoa, several well-known writers have bestowed their observations upon the city.

John Evelyn, the great 17th-century diarist, wrote, "This beautiful city is more with horrid revenges and murders than any one place in Europe, or haply in the world."

Charles Dickens referred to the city as "a bewildering phantasmagoria, with all the inconsistency of a dream." All in all, he concluded, Genoa is a place that "grows upon you every day."

Dylan Thomas, the Welsh poet, wrote that the "dock-front of Genoa is just marvelous."

Director of Dublin's Abbey Theatre and noted traveler **Walter Starkie,** arriving by ocean liner, rhapsodized in lyrical Irish fashion, "In the clear air the city rises like a gigantic jewel glittering in its rugged Alpine setting. . . . From the boat, it looks like a fantastic city of the Genii, created by magic power."

Il Bigo, an observation platform atop a spiky appendage resembling a ship crane. ⊕ 2–3 hr. Piazza Spinola. ☎ 010-234-5666. www.acquariodigenova. it. Admission 16€ adults, 10€ children 4–12, children under 4 free. Nov–Feb Mon–Fri 9:30am–7:30pm, Sat–Sun 9:30am–8:30pm; Mar–June and Sept–Oct Mon–Fri 9am–7:30pm, Sat–Sun 8:45am–8:30pm; July–Aug daily 8:30am–10pm. Bus 3, 7, 8, 38. Il Bigo: admission 3€ adults, 2.50€ children 4–12, children under 4 free. Jan–Feb Sat–Sun 10am–5pm; Mar–May Mon 2–6pm, Tues–Sun 10am–6pm; June–Aug Mon 4–11pm, Tues–Sun 10am–11pm; Sept–Oct Mon 2–6pm, Tues–Sun 10am–6pm; Nov Sat–Sun 10am–5pm. Bus 12, 13.

> *The city's once-seedy port was overhauled for the Columbus quincentennial in 1992.*

14 ★★ **Galata Museo del Mare.** Glass-enclosed galleries perched over the harbor pay homage to Genoa's long-standing relationship with the sea. A replica of a 17th-century trading ship is the most overwhelming presence, measuring more than 30m (120 ft.) long. Fascinating, too, are the smaller exhibits that trace the growth of the port since ancient times and the days when ocean liners steamed across the harbor to the atmospheric Andrea Doria terminal, just west along the waterfront. ⏱ 2 hr. Calata de Mare. ☎ 010-234-5655. www.galatamuseodelmare. it. Admission 10€ adults (22€ combined ticket with aquarium **13**), 5€ kids 4–12 (12€ combined ticket with aquarium). Mar–Oct Tues–Sun 10am–7:30pm; Nov–Feb Tues–Fri 10am–6pm, Sat–Sun 10am–7:30pm. Bus 12, 13.

15 ★★★ **Galleria di Palazzo Reale.** The Balbis, a fabulously wealthy family of merchants, built their palace just behind the port, and they filled the enormous rooms with baroque furnishings and sculpture and paintings by Anthony Van Dyck and other masters. The House of Savoy bought the palace as one of its many royal residences in the early 19th century, when the family was expanding its hold on the Italian peninsula. As befits a royal palace, the gilded salons include a glittering hall of mirrors, and an extensive formal garden overlooks the port. ⏱ 1 hr. Via Balbi 10. ☎ 010-271-0236. www. palazzorealegenova.it. Admission 6€; free with museum card. Tues–Wed 9am–1:30pm; Thurs–Sun 9am–7pm. Bus 20.

16 ★★ **Castello d'Albertis–Museo delle Culture del Mondo.** Captain Enrico Alberto d'Albertis (1846–1932) carried on the seagoing tradition of his native city and circumnavigated the globe three times. At home in Genoa in the 1890s he built the remarkable neo-Gothic Castello d'Albertis atop medieval fortifications on Montegalletto Hill. Artifacts Captain d'Albertis gathered on his travels fill the imposing rooms, where African spears, New Guinea drums, Turkish tiles, North American tribal clothing, and Aztec relics share space with Genoese nautical instruments. ⏱ 1 hr. Corso Dogali 18. ☎ 010-2723820. www.castellodalbertisgenova.it. Admission 6€; free with museum card. Oct–Mar

Tues–Fri 10am–5pm, Sat–Sun 10am–6pm; Apr–Sept Tues–Fri 10am–6pm, Sat–Sun 10am–7pm. Bus 33, 39, 40.

⑰ ★ Museo d'Arte Orientale Edoardo Chiossone. Among the many surprises of Genoa is this stunning collection of Asian art, shown off to advantage in a contemporary gallery just above the old city in Villetta di Negro park (the views of the city are excellent). Edoardo Chiossone, an Italian banknote maker, was dispatched in 1875 to Japan as an advisor to the Japanese government and helped to produce several versions of the yen (and executed several portraits of royal members of the imperial household, including the official portrait of the Meiji emperor) before he died in Japan in 1898. He bequeathed his vaunted art collection (over 15,000 works) to Italy. Much of the collection is Japanese, and the enamels, ceramics, masks and other artifacts were brought back to Genoa by the city's many navigators. ⊕ 1 hr. Villetta di Negro, Piazzale Mazzini 4. ☎ 010-542285. www.museochiossonegenova.it. Admission 4€; free with museum card. Tues–Fri 9am–1pm; Sat–Sun 10am–7pm. Bus 18, 19, 20.

⑱ ★★★ Cimitero Monumentale di Staglieno. A favorite retreat for the living is this hillside city of the dead where Gothic chapels and sensual marble statuary tumble down a wooded hillside. The most popular monument is the simple tomb of Giuseppe Mazzini (1805–72), a Genoa native who spent much of his life fighting for Italian democracy, often from exile. More than 100,000 Genoese turned out for Mazzini's funeral in 1872, and the patriot is enjoying new recognition as one of the founders of the notion of a united Europe. ⊕ 2 hr. Piazza Manin. ☎ 010-870184. www.cimiterodistaglieno.it. Free admission. Daily 7:30am–5pm; entrance closed at 4:30pm. Bus 12, 14, 34, 48.

> *The cemetery at Staglieno doubles as a gallery of 19th-century funerary sculpture.*

Where to Stay & Dine

> *Ristorante da Genio specializes in Ligurian cuisine, which means plenty of seafood.*

★★ **Best Western Hotel Metropoli** NEAR CENTRO STORICO Some rooms are rather plain, and others are more character-filled, but all share the advantage of being just steps away from Via Garibaldi. Piazza delle Fontane Marose. ☎ 010-246-8888. www.bestwestern.it/metropoli_ge. 48 units. Doubles 100€–180€. AE, DC, MC, V.

★★ **Da Vittorio** PORTO ANTICO *SEAFOOD* In small crowded rooms tucked under 8-century-old arcades alongside the port, fresh seafood makes an appearance in variations from fish-filled omelets to *fritto misto*. Via Sottoripa 59R. ☎ 010-247-2927. Entrees 18€–25€. AE, DC, MC, V. Dinner daily.

Farinata on the Go

The Genoese answer to the sandwich is the *farinata*, and this specialty reaches perfection at unassuming little **Antica Sciamadda**, Via San Giorgio (☎ 010-280843). Specially milled chickpea flour is brushed with olive oil and sprinkled with sea salt, then baked in special steel pans, cut into circles, and filled with spinach ricotta and other stuffings. A *farinata* will run you about 3€, and they don't take credit cards. It's open Monday through Saturday from 9am to 7:30pm.

★★ Hotel Agnello d'Oro NEAR STAZIONE PRINCIPE A converted 16th-century convent retains scant traces of its origins, but such modern additions as balconies off the top-floor rooms overlooking the old city are most welcome. Via Monchette 6. ☎ 010-246-2084. www.hotelagnellodoro.it. 25 units. Doubles 100€. AE, MC, V.

★★★ Hotel Bristol Palace CITY CENTER Art Nouveau style abounds, with a sweeping staircase and grand salons. The guest quarters, some filled with period antiques, others done in "business comfort" style, are an oasis of calm just off Piazza de Ferrari. Via XX Settembre 35. ☎ 010-592541. www.hotelbristolpalace.it. 133 units. Doubles 200€–470€. AE, DC, MC, V.

★ I Tre Merli Ristorante Al Porto Antico PORTO ANTICO *WINE BAR* This enterprise has a couple of restaurants and wine bars around the city; the waterside garden and lofty dining room here serve pastas and seafood, as well as focaccia and other light fare. Calata Mandraccio. ☎ 010-246-4416. Entrees 10€–20€. AE, MC, V. Lunch & dinner daily.

★★★ Locanda di Palazzo Cicala CENTRO STORICO A 16th-century palazzo overlooking the cathedral of San Lorenzo is strikingly appointed in contemporary style, though the views steal the show. Piazza San Lorenzo. ☎ 010-258824. www.palazzocicala.it. 15 units. Doubles 175€–380€. AE, MC, V.

★★ Ristorante da Genio CENTRO STORICO *LIGURIAN* Though plenty of meat and fish dishes fill the menu, it's tempting just to graze through such fare as vegetable and herb *torte*. Salita San Leonardo 61R. ☎ 010-588463. Entrees 7€–11€. AE, MC, V. Lunch & dinner Mon-Sat. Closed Aug.

★★★ Trattoria Maria NEAR CENTRO STORICO *LIGURIAN* As popular with bankers as it is with dock workers, this decades-old institution dishes up delicious risottos and other favorites in plain, boisterous rooms. Via Testadoro 14R. ☎ 010-581080. Entrees 6€–10€. MC, V. Lunch Mon; lunch & dinner Tues-Fri.

Genoa by Night

Much of Genoa's nightlife is concentrated in the historic center near the port—as it has been for centuries, though these days the venues are a bit more respectable than the sailors' lairs of old. Some favorites include **Quaalude,** Piazza di Sarzano 14, with live bands on weekends; **Fellini,** Via XII Ottobre 182R (☎ 010-532713), Genoa's disco heaven with three dance floors, open daily 10pm until very late (check www.teatrofellini.it for what's on); and **DLF,** Via Eustachio Degola (☎ 010-596350), a multilevel dance club that has transformed a former movie theater into a high-tech fantasy world. More sedate but just as popular are **Britannia,** Vico della Casana 76R, off Piazza de Ferrari, popular with expats with a thirst for Guinness; **Le Corbusier,** Via San Donato 36 (☎ 010-246-8652), a coffee bar that serves panini late into the night; and **Le Cantine Squarciafico,** Piazza Invrea 3R (☎ 010-247-0859; daily 12:30pm–2:30pm, 7:30–11pm), maybe the city's most popular wine bar, serving vintages from more than 70 producers, as well as meals.

Genoa's venues for culture are **Teatro Carlo Felice,** Piazza de Ferrari (☎ 010-589-329; www.carlofelice.it), home to the city's opera company and also the stage for concerts and other events; and **Teatro della Corte** (☎ 010-534-2200; www.teatrodellacorte.it), on Piazza Borgo Pila near Stazione Brignole, hosting concerts, dance events, and many visiting companies.

★★★ Trattoria Vegia Zena PORTO ANTICO *LIGURIAN* No fuss, no pretension—just good old-fashioned Genoa classics, such as *fritto misto* and pasta with pesto, served at communal tables. Via del Serriglio 15R. ☎ 010-251-3332. Entrees 8€–14€. MC, V. Lunch Mon; lunch & dinner Tues-Sat.

San Remo & the Riviera di Levante

This flowery city at the western end of the Ligurian coast still glows with a refined shine, though the luster has faded a bit since the late-19th-century days when Russia's Empress Maria Alexandrovna and her royal companions used to stroll down the palm-shaded avenues. Gambling, beach-going, enjoying the year-round balmy climate, and even exploring prehistoric caves at nearby Balzi Rossi are among the many present-day pastimes.

> The best tables at San Remo's elegant Casino still require male gamblers to wear jacket and tie.

START Along the seafront, on Corso dell'Imperatrice.

1 ★★ **The Casino.** San Remo's stylish and legendary casino dates to 1905. The film director Vittorio De Sica thought his image should be emblazoned on the exterior of the Art Nouveau edifice, since his losses more or less kept the place in business. Authors Erika and Klaus Mann once opined that the gaming tables were popular with players who "look as if they want to be ruined by gambling . . . because if you lose in San Remo, you lose it respectably, in an elegant way." Jacket and tie are required at the roulette and card tables, where you may still find yourself in the company of a royal or two, or least those who look like they could be; less formal but respectable attire is required at the slot machines, in the restaurant and bar, and on the roof garden. ⊙ 30 min. (longer if you decide to try your luck). Corso degli Inglesi 18. ☎ 0814-5951. Free admission. Daily 10am–2am (some game rooms from 2:30pm–2am).

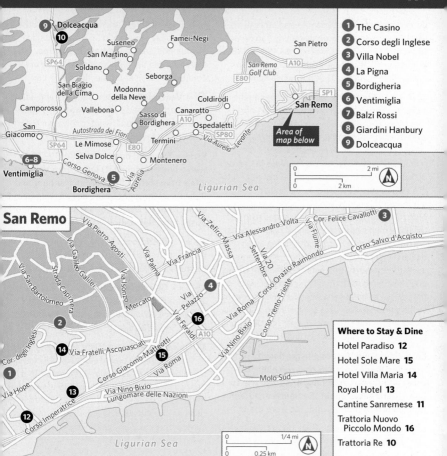

San Remo

1 The Casino
2 Corso degli Inglese
3 Villa Nobel
4 La Pigna
5 Bordigheria
6 Ventimiglia
7 Balzi Rossi
8 Giardini Hanbury
9 Dolceacqua

Where to Stay & Dine

Hotel Paradiso **12**
Hotel Sole Mare **15**
Hotel Villa Maria **14**
Royal Hotel **13**
Cantine Sanremese **11**
Trattoria Nuovo
  Piccolo Mondo **16**
Trattoria Re **10**

2 ★★★ **Corso degli Inglesi.** In the last quarter of the 19th century, titled and wealthy Europeans from the north built more than 200 villas in San Remo, many of them along this shady hillside avenue. It is no accident that the onion-domed Russian Orthodox church rises near one end of the *corso,* as many of the villas were built by Russians who began wintering in San Remo after Czarina Maria Alexandrovna (1824–80) sent back reports of a smashing winter season in 1874. The gracious royal guest showed her gratitude to the municipality by donating the palm trees that still shade San Remo's seaside promenade, the Corso dell'Imperatrice. ⏱ 30 min.

Train Tip

San Remo is 140km (81 miles) west of Genoa, less than 2 hours away by frequent train service.

3 ★ **Villa Nobel.** Alfred Nobel spent the last eight years of his life in San Remo, where he died in 1898. The Swedish chemist left his fortune to the establishment of the Nobel Prize, and his elaborately decorated Belle Epoque villa celebrates his work as well as that of the recipients of the prestigious awards he originated. In the cellar is the laboratory where Nobel carried out

his experiments with dynamite and other explosives he sometimes detonated along San Remo's seafront. ⏱ 1 hr. Corso Cavallotti. ☎ 0184-507380. Admission 3.50€, only by guided tour, usually in Italian. Tues–Sun 11am–12:30pm; Sun 3–4pm.

④ ★★★ **La Pigna.** Old San Remo clings to the sides of a cone-shaped hill above the old port that resembles a pinecone (a *pigna*), creating a labyrinthine stronghold that through many violent centuries provided a safe haven from marauding pirates. From two openings in the medieval walls, the Porto di Santo Stefano and Porto di San Giuseppe (the latter is still equipped with a trapdoor through which boiling oil was poured onto intruders), narrow lanes twist and turn past tall fishermen's houses and proud palaces. Most are now worn and crumbling, emitting an air of benign neglect that suggests their inhabitants leave the modern world behind at the foot of the hill. The church of Nostra Signora della Costa at the top of La Pigna is a beacon for sailors, who by tradition turn to Our Lady for salvation from shipwreck and in the 17th century took up collections to build the baroque sanctuary. ⏱ 1 hr.

Bordighera and Ventimiglia are easy to reach from San Remo on trains that run along the coast about every half-hour or so; the trip to Bordighera takes about 15 minutes, and Ventimiglia is less than 10 minutes from there.

⑤ ★ **Bordighera.** This resort 15km (9 miles) west of San Remo is famous throughout Italy for its palm trees, the fronds of which are har-

vested every spring and sent down to Rome for Palm Sunday services in St. Peter's Basilica. A promenade, the **Lungomare Argentina,** runs along the sea beneath an old town of pastel-colored houses set on the hillside. ⏱ 1 hr.

⑥ ★ **Ventimiglia.** A Roman theater and walls, and a fortified medieval town warrant a quick look around, but you'll want to move on soon to some of the fascinating nearby sights. ⏱ 30 min.

Riviera Trasporti buses (☎ 0184-592706; www.rivieratrasporti.it) leave from Ventimiglia's train station for Giardini Hanbury and Balzi Rossi throughout the day, leaving about every 2 hours. Dolceacqua is served by hourly buses from the station.

⑦ ★★★ **Balzi Rossi.** Stone Age humans were taking shelter in the caves at Balzi Rossi more than 35,000 years ago. ⏱ 1 hr. See p 536, ❶.

⑧ ★★★ **Giardini Hanbury.** One of Europe's largest and most noted botanical gardens thrives just down the coast from Ventimiglia. ⏱ 2 hr. See p 537, ❷.

⑨ **Dolceacqua.** About 10km (6 miles) inland of Ventimiglia is a pretty stone village clustered beneath a castle along the banks of a river spanned by the single arch of a medieval bridge. The painter Claude Monet visited in 1884 and enthused in his diary, "The place is superb; there is a bridge that seems to be a jewel of lightness." ⏱ 1 hr.

> *The remarkable single-arched stone bridge at Dolceacqua dates from the 15th century.*

Where to Stay & Dine

> Local trattorias specialize in traditional recipes, such as the Ligurian green sauce pesto.

★★★ **Cantine Sanremese** SAN REMO LIGURIAN
Tantalizing tidbits—a slice of *torta verde* (a quiche of green vegetables), minestrone topped with pesto—are a tasty introduction to Ligurian cuisine, served in homey old rooms. **Via Vittorio Emanuele 158.** ☎ 0184-2615380. Entrees from 3€. Lunch & dinner Tues–Fri.

★★ kids **Hotel Paradiso** SAN REMO
Many of the bright, spacious guest rooms at this much-enlarged villa set in gardens behind the seafront have balconies facing the sea, and amenities include a swimming pool and a private patch of sand on the nearby beach. **Via Roccasterone.** ☎ 0184-571211. www. paradisohotel.it. 41 units. Doubles 100€–180€. DC, MC, V. Closed early Jan to late Apr.

★★★ **Hotel Sole Mare** SAN REMO
The upper floors of an apartment house near the casino are the setting for airy lounges and spacious, sleekly appointed guest rooms, many of which open onto a wide terrace. **Via Carli 23.** ☎ 0184-532778. www.solemarehotel.com. 21 units. Doubles 60€–100€. AE, DC, MC, V.

★★ **Hotel Villa Maria** SAN REMO
Three adjoining villas on a flowery hillside above the casino are a quiet retreat in pleasantly old-fashioned surroundings, yet the town center and seafront are just a short walk away. **Corso Nuvoloni 30.** ☎ 0184-531422. www. villamariahotel.it. 38 units. Doubles 65€–120€. AE, DC, MC, V.

★★★ **Royal Hotel** SAN REMO
San Remo's grand hotel, set amid palm-shaded lawns above the sea, recalls the town's end-of-the-19th-century heyday, and still pampers guests in style, with lovely gardens, a stunning swimming pool, and luxurious public rooms and guest quarters. **Corso dell'Imperatrice.** ☎ 0184-5391. www.royalhotelsanremo.com. 126 units. Doubles 230€–450€. AE, DC, MC, V. Closed mid-Nov to mid-Dec.

★★★ **Trattoria Nuovo Piccolo Mondo** SAN REMO
LIGURIAN Little has changed here since the kitchen began serving in the 1920s—the service is as attentive as ever and such specialties as *verdure ripiene* (fresh vegetables stuffed with rice and seafood) do justice to age-old local recipes. **Via Piave 7.** ☎ 0184-50912. Entrees 8€–17€. Lunch & dinner Tues–Sat.

★★ **Trattoria Re** DOLCEACQUA LIGURIAN
The pesto that appears atop homemade pastas is typically Ligurian and nothing short of sensual, while mountain herbs flavor dishes that suggest nearby Provence. The views of Dolceacqua's stone bridge are an atmospheric bonus. **Via Maritiri 26.** ☎ 0184-206137. 9€–15€. Lunch & dinner Tues–Sat. Closed Nov to mid-Dec.

The Portofino Peninsula

This dramatic and beautiful peninsula is both civilized and uncivilized. Rapallo, Santa Margherita Ligure, and Portofino are old resorts that were on the fashionable tour circuit as long as a century ago, yet they are surrounded by remote coasts accessible only on foot or by boat and backed by hills carpeted with pines and scented with wild rosemary.

START Rapallo. Trip length: Rapallo is about 37km (24 miles) east of Genoa. More than 30 trains a day run between Genoa and Rapallo, and the trip takes about 30 minutes. From Rapallo, it is about 10 minutes by train to Santa Margherita Ligure, and from there buses travel along the coast road to Portofino. Camogli is another 10 minutes west of Santa Margherita by train.

① **Rapallo.** The old town that in the early part of the 20th century was a favorite stop for well-heeled travelers is clustered around a harbor and a castle crowded onto a tiny islet. Among the expatriates who favored Rapallo were the

American poet Ezra Pound, who wrote part of his most famous work, *The Cantos,* here in the late 1920s and later made many of the pro-Mussolini broadcasts that led the United States to imprison him on charges of treason. He later returned to Rapallo and died here in 1972. A seaside promenade follows the curving waterfront, and a funicular from the edge of town makes the ascent to the 16th-century **Santuario di Montallegro.** The views over the town and surrounding hills are stunning, and inside the frescoed church is a Byzantine icon of the Virgin that is said to have shown up near the altar after flying to Rapallo from Dalmatia on its own. ⏱ 1 hr. Santuario di

> *Rapallo nestles between hills and harbor.*

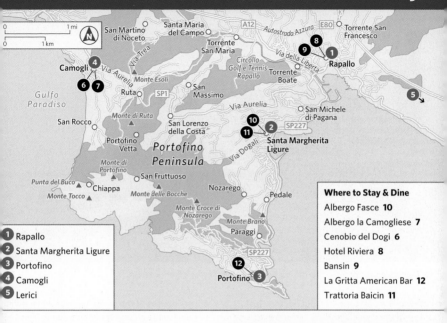

1 Rapallo
2 Santa Margherita Ligure
3 Portofino
4 Camogli
5 Lerici

Where to Stay & Dine
Albergo Fasce **10**
Albergo la Camogliese **7**
Cenobio del Dogi **6**
Hotel Riviera **8**
Bansin **9**
La Gritta American Bar **12**
Trattoria Baicin **11**

Montallegro: Via al Santuario 24. ☎ 0185-239000. Free admission. April–Oct Mon–Sat 7:30am–noon, 4:30–7pm, Sun 7am–noon, 2:30–7pm; Nov–Mar Mon–Sat 8am–noon, 4:30–5pm, Sun 8am–noon, 2:30–4pm. Funicular: ☎ 0185-273444. 5€ round-trip. Operates daily, every half-hour, 9am–6pm.

2 **Santa Margherita Ligure.** Rapallo's neighbor, a popular retreat for the past century or so, has faded a bit, but beaches, marinas, outdoor cafes, and a long, palm-shaded promenade still line its pretty seafront. The Genoese built the sturdy castle that rises above the cobblestone

Portofino Travel Tip

From Santa Margherita Ligure, buses for Portofino run about every 20 minutes. A round-trip ticket, purchased at newsstands or from machines, costs 2€. For information, contact **Tigullio bus** (☎ 0185-288-8334). A pleasant alternative, especially welcome when the coast road is choked with traffic, is by boat; operated by **Servizio Marittimo del Tigullio** (☎ 0185-284670), frequent service runs between Rapallo and Santa Margherita (3.50€) and Santa Margherita and Portofino (5€).

Hiking across the Peninsula

The **Parco Naturale Regionale di Portofino** comprises more than 1,200 hectares (3,954 acres) on the Portofino Peninsula. Hillsides carpeted in oaks, pines, and olive trees drop down to the rocky shoreline, and the countryside is crisscrossed by hiking trails. One of the most popular routes follows the southern end of the peninsula from Portofino to the seaside **Abbey of San Fruttuoso** (☎ 0185-772703; 4€; May–Sept daily 10am–6pm; Oct and Mar–Apr Tues–Sun 10am–4pm; Dec–Feb Sat–Sun 10am–4pm), founded by Benedictine monks at the end of the 10th century. The Dorias, the Genoese seafaring family, offered their protection to the community throughout the Middle Ages, and several members are buried in the handsome stone church. Olive groves the monks cultivated for centuries grow on terraces around the abbey, and a watchtower the Dorias built overlooks the coast. The park headquarters are at Viale Rainusso 1, Santa Margherita Ligure (☎ 0185-289479; www. parks.it/parco.portofino); this office and a visitor center in Portofino distribute maps of hiking routes and other information.

> *The forbidding coastal castle at Lerici inspired Mary Shelley's* Frankenstein.

streets and piazzas of the old quarter. Just beyond the castle a narrow cornice road, one of Italy's most scenic drives, follows the sea around the peninsula to Portofino. ⏱ 2 hr.

❸ Portofino. The town most likely to enchant visitors to the Portofino Peninsula is a colorful stage set of tall pastel-colored houses surrounding a tiny harbor, a fishing port since Roman times. Trails from the town's edge provide lovely hikes along the surrounding coastline and into the herb-scented hillsides, and most of this landscape is protected as **Parco Naturale Regionale di Portofino** (see p 561). A nice escape from the town's often-crowded, boutique-lined quays is the easy walk past Portofino's **castle** to the **lighthouse** at the tip of the peninsula. ⏱ 3 hr.

❹ Camogli. The name of this village on the west side of the Portofino Peninsula is said to derive from old terms for "houses close togeth-

er" or "houses of the wives"—a reference either to the visually arresting arrangement of extremely tall houses crowded around the harbor, or to the fact the women stayed at home while their husbands went to sea. On a rocky promontory at one end of the beach, the 12th-century fishermen's church, **Basilica di Santa Maria Assunta** (open daily, 8am–7pm), rises above the surf and the Castello Dragone houses the small **Acquario Tirrenico** (☎ 0185-773375; 4€; May–Sept daily 10am–noon, 3–7pm; Oct–Apr Fri–Sun 10am–noon, 2:30–6pm), where fascinating representatives of local sea life are on view. ⏱ 1 hr.

Frequent trains make the 45-minute trip from Rapallo south to La Spezia, and from the train station there, bus L continues to Lerici about every 15 minutes (1.20€).

❺ Lerici. Nineteenth-century poets had a penchant for Lerici, straddling the end of a peninsula in the Gulf of La Spezia. Percy Bysshe Shelley lived in a "lonely house close by the seaside surrounded by the soft and serene scenery," and he drowned offshore while sailing up the coast. The dark, forbidding castle that rises above the old lanes inspired his wife, Mary Shelley, to write *Frankenstein*. Lord Byron used to swim across the gulf from Lerici to **Portovenere,** where tall, brightly painted houses surround the fishing harbor. ⏱ 1 hr.

A Big Fish Fry

On the second weekend in May, Camogli hosts the **Sagra del Pesce,** claimed to be the world's biggest fish fry. More than a ton of fish are fried in the world's largest skillet, 4m (12 ft.) in diameter, and served to the entire town. The event honors San Fortunato, Camogli's patron saint.

Where to Stay & Dine

> *Bansin in Rapallo spoils diners with its hearty Ligurian fare.*

★★ **Albergo Fasce** SANTA MARGHERITA LIGURE
To a courtyard garden, sundeck, and bright, spacious rooms add such welcome amenities as the free use of bicycles; and, depending on the length of your stay, free train passes to the Cinque Terre. Via Luigi Bozzo. ☎ 0185-286435. www.hotelfasce.com. 16 units. Doubles 98€–165€. AE, DC, MC, V.

★★ **Albergo la Camogliese** CAMOGLI
Some of the simply furnished rooms here have sea views, but all enjoy the warm hospitality and excellent location near the beach and center of town. Via Garibaldi. ☎ 0185-771402. www.lacamogliese.it. 17 units. Doubles 70€–110€. AE, DC, MC, V.

★★ **Bansin** RAPALLO *LIGURIAN*
Rapallo regulars count on this century-old institution (the quarters aren't original, but they are friendly) for *pasta al pesto* and other nononsense traditional Ligurian fare. Via Venezia 105. ☎ 0185-231119. Entrees 10€–20€. AE, DC, MC, V. Lunch daily; dinner Tues–Sat.

★★★ **Cenobio del Dogi** CAMOGLI
Live like a doge at this seaside retreat where the surroundings include a 16th-century chapel, sprawling swimming pool, and sea-facing rooms complemented by luxurious marble bathrooms. Via Cuneo 34. ☎ 0185-7241. www.cenobio.it. 16 units. Doubles 160€–320€. AE, DC, MC, V.

★★ **Hotel Riviera** RAPALLO
The Gambero family is continually updating their hotel in an old waterfront villa, where most of the attractive and comfortable rooms face the waterfront, and many have small terraces. Piazza 4 Novembre 2. ☎ 0185-50248. www.hotelrivierarapallo.com. 20 units. Doubles 130€. AE, MC, V.

★ **La Gritta American Bar** PORTOFINO *LIGHT FARE* American author James Jones called this legendary lair the "nicest waterfront bar this side of Hong Kong"; hyperbole aside, the floating terrace and snug little barroom are nice places to enjoy a salad, omelet, and a glass of wine or a cocktail. Calata Marconi 20. ☎ 0185-269126. Entrees 10€–15€. MC, V. May–Oct breakfast, lunch & dinner daily; Nov–Apr breakfast, lunch & dinner Wed–Sun.

★★★ **Trattoria Baicin** SANTA MARGHERITA LIGURE *LIGURIAN* Fish caught fresh in the morning and such specialties as *trofie alla Genovese*—a combination of gnocchi, potatoes, fresh vegetables, and pesto—are served in a cheerful dining room or on a terrace a few steps off the seafront. Via Algeria 9. ☎ 0185-286763. 12€–25€. AE, DC, MC, V. Lunch & dinner Tues–Sun. Closed Nov to mid-Dec.

Liguria Fast Facts

Accommodations Booking Services
CTS, Via San Vincenzo 117R (☎ 010-564366; www.cts.it), arranges hotels and tours in Genoa and throughout Liguria. It's open Monday to Friday 9am to 12:30pm and 2 to 6pm.

American Express
The closest American Express office is in Milan, Via Brera 3 (☎ 02-7200-3693). It's open Monday to Friday 9am to 5:30pm and Saturday 9am to 5pm.

ATMs
You'll find 24-hour cash machines (*bancomat*) throughout the region, even in the smallest villages. Italy generally uses 4-digit PINs; if you have a 6-digit PIN, check with your bank.

Dentists & Doctors
For emergency medical or dental attention, go to the *pronto soccorso* (emergency room) of the nearest hospital; ask at your hotel. Non-EU residents can consult national health service doctors for a relatively small fee; most good hotels will have a list of doctors and will help with arrangements.

Emergencies
For general emergencies, call ☎ **112** for the Carabinieri or ☎ **113** for the Polizia. Call ☎ **114** for an ambulance and ☎ **115** for the fire department. For a medical emergency that doesn't require an ambulance, see "Dentists & Doctors," above. To report lost or stolen items, see "Police," p 565.

Getting There & Around
BY PLANE Flights to and from most major European cities serve **Aeroporto Internazionale de Genova Cristoforo Colombo,** just 6.4km (4 miles) west of the city center (☎ 010-601-5410; www.airport.genova.it). **Volabus no. 100** (☎ 010-558-2414) connects the airport with Stazione Principe and Stazione Brignole, with buses running every half-hour from 6am to 10pm; buy tickets on the bus (2€). The nearest airports handling overseas flights are at Nice, 187km (116 miles) west just over the border with France, and Milan,

137km (85 miles) to the north; both cities are well connected to Genoa by superhighways and train service. **BY TRAIN** Genoa is the hub for trains serving the Italian Riviera, with trains arriving and departing for Ventimiglia on the French border about every half-hour, and La Spezia, at the southeastern edge of Liguria, even more frequently, as often as every 15 minutes during peak times between 7am and 7pm. Train lines follow the coast and make local stops at just about all seaside towns and resorts (for towns covered in this section, see individual listings for connections with Genoa). Excellent train service connects Genoa with major Italian cities: Milan (1–3 trains per hour; trip time: about 1½ hr.), Rome (hourly; trip time about 5 hr.), Turin (1 or 2 per hour; trip time: about 1½ hr.); Florence (hourly, but always with a change, usually at Pisa; trip time: 3 hr.).

An important thing train travelers should know about Genoa is that the city has two major train stations, **Stazione Principe** (designated on timetables as Genova P.P.), near the old city on Piazza Acqua Verde, and **Stazione Brignole** (designated on timetables as Genova B.R.), in the modern city on Piazza Verdi. Many trains, especially those on long-distance lines, service both stations; however, many trains stop at only one, making it essential that you know the station at which your train is scheduled to arrive and from which it will depart. Trains connect the two stations in just 5 minutes and run about every 15 minutes. City buses 40 and 37 also run between the two train stations, leaving from the front of each station about every 10 minutes; you must allow at least 20 minutes for the connection on Genoa's crowded streets. **BY CAR** Genoa is linked to other parts of Italy and to France by a convenient network of superhighways. The **A10/A12** follows the coast and passes through dozens of tunnels to link Genoa with France to the west (Nice is less than 2 hr. away) and Pisa, about 1½ hours to the southeast. The **A7** links Genoa with Milan, a little over an hour to the north. Given the convenience of train travel, a car is unnecessary for touring the region and can be a nuisance in such places as the Cinque Terre and Portofino, which are closed to traffic and where parking is limited. Dolceacqua and other inland towns not on rail routes are well served by bus. **BY BUS** The easiest way to get around Genoa is on foot, and most of the sites you will want to visit are within easy reach of one another in and around the old city. If you do take the bus or the city's metro system (now under construction), buy tickets for 1.20€ at newsstands and tobacco shops. Public transport is run by **AMT** (☎ 010-254-3431; www.amt.genova.it). **BY BOAT** Ferries operate up and down the coast of Liguria, and an especially popular route is from towns on the Portofino Peninsula to the Cinque Terre; the major operator is **Tigullio** (☎ 0185-284670; www.traghettiportofino.it). Genoa is also a port for Mediterranean cruises, with ships docking at **Stazione Marittima** (☎ 010-256682).

Internet Access

Wi-Fi has become a common amenity in most hotels throughout Liguria, especially in business-oriented hotels in Genoa and luxury hotels along the coast. Many hotels that do not have Wi-Fi or other in-room Internet connections provide access through a public computer. In the Cinque Terre, Internet connections are available at the national park offices in Riomaggiore and Monterosso (p 542). Internet cafes are also fairly common in Genoa and larger resort towns; Italian law requires that all patrons provide a passport or another form of identification, and fees are usually around 5€ an hour.

Pharmacies

Farmacie are recognizable by a neon green or red cross and are usually open 8am to 1:30pm and 3:30 to 8pm; in any city or town, at least one pharmacy is required to remain open 24 hours on a rotating basis, and the name and location of the designated pharmacy is posted at all others.

Police

To report a lost or stolen article, such as a wallet or passport, visit the local police *questura* or Carabinieri *caserma* in your location. See also "Emergencies," p 564.

Post Office

Genoa's main post office is on Piazza Dante (☎ 010-591762); it's open Monday to Saturday 8:10am to 7:40pm. *Francobolli* (stamps) can be purchased at most *tabacchi* (tobacco stores).

Safety

Caution is in order on Genoa's dark lanes, where purse and jewelry snatchings and even muggings are not uncommon. Avoid deserted streets at night and in the quiet of afternoon siesta, especially those around the port. Women traveling alone will feel decidedly uncomfortable in the old section around the port, still a haunt of sailors and other single men. With its laid-back ambience, the Cinque Terre is especially hospitable to single travelers of both sexes.

Visitor Information

Genoa's tourist office has an office and a kiosk on Piazza Matteotti (☎ 010-542098; www.genova-turismo.it) that's open daily from 9:30am to 7:45pm; there's another branch at Stazione Principe (☎ 010-246-2633), open Tuesday to Saturday from 9am to 1pm and 2:30 to 6:30pm. In **San Remo,** the tourist office is at Largo Nuvoloni 1 (☎ 0184-571571; www.rivieradeifiori.travel), and is open Monday to Saturday 8am to 7pm and Sunday 9am to 1pm. You'll also find tourist offices in **Rapallo,** Lungomare Vittorio Veneto 7 (☎ 0185-230346); **Portofino,** Via Roma 35 (☎ 0185-269024); and **Santa Margherita Ligure,** Via XXV Aprile 2 (☎ 0185-287485)—these are all generally open Monday to Saturday from 9am to 12:30pm, 2:30 to 5:30pm, and Sunday 9am to 12:30pm.

12
Naples &
Campania

The Best of Naples & Campania in 3 Days

Rugged coastlines of staggering dimension, vertiginous views more breathtaking than any photo can convey, and the imposing cone of Mt. Vesuvius make coastal Campania (the region from the Bay of Naples to Amalfi) the most magnificent landscape in Italy—and the area has world-class cultural sites that are equally impressive. Though they'll be packed from morning to evening, 3 days in this region are enough to see and do the highlights, from natural spectacles such as the Blue Grotto on Capri to the transporting ruins of Pompeii. Use the lively resort town and transportation hub of Sorrento as your base for the first 2 nights; spend the third night in Naples.

> PREVIOUS PAGE A hotel terrace with fanfare, at the Caesar Augustus, Anacapri. THIS PAGE In Ravello, Villa Cimbrone's Terrazza dell'Infinito is lined with Roman busts, but no one's looking at the statues.

START Sorrento. Trip length: 3 days. Before you set out on Day 1, find out the afternoon boat schedule from Positano to Sorrento. See "Getting Around" on p 631 for transportation information.

1 Amalfi Coast Drive (Sorrento to Amalfi). The two-lane road that clings to the vertiginous hillside, with nothing but a skilled driver and a pathetically low guardrail standing between you and a 150m (500 ft.) drop to the sea, is the most exciting attraction on the Amalfi Coast. Public transportation (the blue SITA bus) is the classic way to experience the drive (31km/19 miles). From Sorrento's Circumvesuviana train station, catch an Amalfi-bound SITA bus. Get a seat on the right-hand side of the bus for the best view.

There are no sea views for the first 7km (4 miles) of the ride, as you cross the Sorrentine peninsula. But when you bear left past the village of San Pietro, nothing can prepare you for the ★★★ **epic vistas**—grander and more heart-stopping than you could have imagined—that surround you as the bus begins to swing its way around the curves of the SS163 Nastro Azzurro. The mere engineering of the road, regardless of the landscape, is enough to make jaws drop.

After about 11km (7 miles) of this spectacular scenery—forested mountains to the left, plunging cliffs and the azure Mediterranean to the right—you'll reach the nondescript stop for Positano (see p 570, **5**), where you

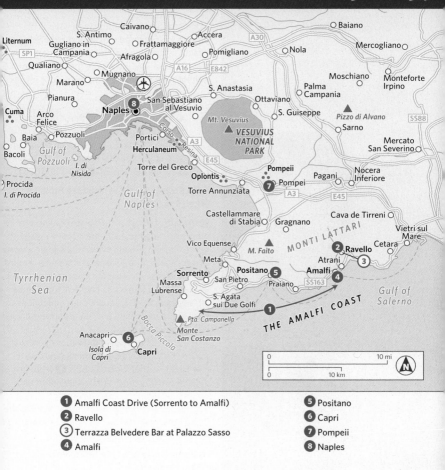

① Amalfi Coast Drive (Sorrento to Amalfi)
② Ravello
③ Terrazza Belvedere Bar at Palazzo Sasso
④ Amalfi
⑤ Positano
⑥ Capri
⑦ Pompeii
⑧ Naples

might wonder what all the fuss over this town is about. Another 20 to 30 minutes down the road, the bus will pull into the terminus of Amalfi, right on the water. Ask one of the drivers there when the SITA bus to Ravello departs to determine whether you have time for a toilet or coffee break nearby. ⏱ 1½ hr.

From Amalfi, take a SITA bus to Ravello (7km/4 miles).

② **Ravello.** Of the actual towns along the Amalfi Coast, Ravello is the one must-see, for its unique position high on a hill, and for the multibillion-euro views in the gardens of Villa Cimbrone.

After navigating the tight hairpin turns up to lofty Ravello, your bus will deposit you in

a panoramic parking lot. You'll want to spend at least a few hours in Ravello, but before you walk through the tunnel into town, read the posted SITA schedule, or ask a driver, and find out exactly when you need to catch the return bus to Amalfi. This will save you a lot of waiting

Travel Tip

As thrilling as it is, the Amalfi Coast drive can pose a problem for serious sufferers of carsickness or vertigo. If you're worried about the S-curves and heights, you can also make the journey from Sorrento to Amalfi by boat. See "Getting Around" on p 631 for transportation details.

> Nobel Prize–winning novelist John Steinbeck was one of many writers to fall for the dramatic scenery of the Amalfi Coast.

around later (and the temptation to take a ridiculously expensive taxi) at the bus terminus.

Though taking in the sublime views while you stand around with a beatific grin is a perfectly valid activity in Ravello, there are also two villas worth visiting: ★★★ **Villa Cimbrone** (p 622, ❸) and ★ **Villa Rufolo** (p 622, ❶). If you have to prioritize and visit only one, make it the far more impressive Villa Cimbrone, which lays claim to perhaps the most beautiful panorama in all of Italy. To reach Villa Cimbrone from Ravello's main piazza, it's a 15- to 20-minute, well-marked walk over 2m-wide (6½-ft.),

sloping back streets. If the walk sounds off-putting, rest assured that the overwhelming beauty of the gardens here, and the rapturous view from its star attraction, the **Belvedere dell'Infinito,** will more than repay your efforts. ◷ At least 2 hr.

③ 🍷 **Terrazza Belvedere Bar at Palazzo Sasso.** If your time and the bus schedule permit, have a drink on the gorgeous terrace of this friendly luxury hotel. Via San Giovanni del Toro 28. ☎ 089-818181. $$$.

From Ravello, take a SITA bus to Amalfi (7km/4 miles).

❹ **Amalfi.** Though Amalfi and Positano are often compared to each other, they're really quite different. Amalfi, which used to be a naval power rivaling Pisa, Genoa, and Venice, is more authentic than its more famous neighbor to the west—though tourism is big here, too—and a bit less expensive. Frequent bus connections to Positano make Amalfi an easy stopover on your way back up the coast.

It takes less than an hour to tour the *centro storico* (historic center) of Amalfi (the only real "sight" is the Duomo; p 628, ❶), but just outside Amalfi proper are two very different, very highly recommended lunch spots. See p 630 for reviews of the Ristorante al Mare at the Santa Caterina hotel and Le Palme in Atrani. ◷ 1 hr. to tour Amalfi plus 1½ hr. for lunch.

From Amalfi, take a SITA bus to Positano (15km/9 miles).

❺ **Positano.** The bus leaves you at the deserted intersection of Via Cristoforo Colombo and the SS163, from which point you might ask yourself, "*This* is Positano?" The actual town is just west and down, down, down (where big buses can't drive) from here. Start walking down Via Cristoforo Colombo, and you'll get a feel for the orientation of the place—Positano is shaped like a theater, and everyone gets a view. Cheaper hotels and rental properties at the top, good hotels and restaurants are in the middle, and a labyrinth of narrow shopping streets fills out the bottom. The "stage" is the town beach and ferry dock. Luckily, this itinerary has you starting at the top and walking only downhill.

Though Positano isn't a particularly authentic Italian town (it blossomed as a resort village after World War II), there's no denying the romance here. Wander down toward the water, and if you're in the market for linen tunics and the like, the endless racks of resort wear along the way will not disappoint. (For everything else, the shops in Sorrento and Naples are better and less expensive.) Take a few minutes to check out the harbor, then board a boat back to Sorrento, and watch the sun as it begins its slow descent over the water.

Get a good night's sleep in Sorrento. In the morning, from Sorrento's Marina Piccola, take a hydrofoil, jet boat, or ferry to Capri (13km/8 miles). Allow 30 minutes to 1 hour crossing time.

⑥ **Capri.** Drop-dead-gorgeous and activity-filled, Capri is a wonderful day trip from Sorrento, with frequent boat connections making getting there and back a breeze. Upon arrival at Capri's Marina Grande, resist the urge to do the Blue Grotto right away. (Save it for later in the day, when the light is better and the cave is less crowded.) Instead, take the **funicular** up to ★ **Capri town,** where you'll find hundreds of day-trippers like you milling around. Push through the tourist crowds in "posh" Capri town and walk out to the end of ★ **Via Tragara** for fabulous views over the southern side of the island and the ★★★ **Faraglioni** (p 612, ③)

> *ABOVE Villa Rufolo's formal gardens host classical concerts during the Ravello Festival. BELOW The town of Amalfi is one of the few on its eponymous coast with a sandy beach.*

> *Mt. Vesuvius forms the backdrop for Roman ruins at Pompeii, which have been preserved since its infamous eruption in the 1st century.*

> *No-frills pizzeria Da Michele is Naples's best.*

outcroppings in the water below. (From the end of Via Tragara, physically fit people in search of a good workout can tackle the strenuous but stunning ★★★ **Via Pizzolungo** trail to the Arco Naturale, but this adds at least another 1½ hr. to your Capri day trip. See p 614, ❼.)

Otherwise, head back to the main piazza of Capri and hop on a bus to ★★ **Anacapri** (see "Getting Around," p 613). In Anacapri, if visibility is good, go for a round-trip chairlift ride to the top of ★★ **Monte Solaro** (p 615, ❿), and then take a bus from Anacapri to Grotta Azzurra (Blue Grotto). Have a late lunch at the delicious and fairly priced ★★ **Add'ò Riccio** (p 617), and then walk down the stairs below to catch one of the rowboats that will take you into the ★★★ **Blue Grotto** (p 614, ❽). By now, it's probably after 3pm, when the light is at its most electric in the grotto, and the crowds are about a tenth of what they were a few hours before. (On occasion—though rarely from May to October—the seas are too rough to permit grotto visits, but it's still worth the trek down here if only for a meal at Add'ò Riccio and to see this more rustic side of the island; it's a world away from the snobby boutiques in Capri town!) After your grotto visit, take the bus back up to Anacapri, and from there a bus to Marina Grande, where you'll catch your boat back to Sorrento. ⊕ **At least 8 hr., including round-trip boat travel.**

On the morning of Day 3, from Sorrento take the Circumvesuviana train to Pompeii–Villa dei Misteri (28km/18 miles). There is an attended luggage deposit service at the ticket office where you can leave your suitcases free of charge while you tour the ruins.

7 kids **Pompeii.** The most famous ancient Roman city besides Rome itself, Pompeii was buried in A.D. 79 by the eruption of Mt. Vesuvius and has risen from the ashes to become the undisputed king of all archaeological sites. A quick survey of the ruins can be done in 2 hours, but you'll need 4 hours or more to see the full range of ancient building types in Pompeii and to explore the site end to end. ⊕ **At least 2 hr. See p 588 for full details on touring Pompeii.**

From Pompeii, take the Circumvesuviana to Napoli–Porta Nolana (25km/16 miles; avoid the much more chaotic Napoli–Piazza Garibaldi, which is under Napoli Centrale train station), or take a private car.

8 **Naples.** Upon arrival in Naples, take a taxi to your hotel. For a stay this brief, it's a good idea to book accommodations in the *città antica* (old city); see p 610 for my recommendations.

After seeing the ruins of Pompeii, the artifacts in the ★★★ **Museo Archeologico Nazionale** (p 605, 10) are not to be missed. The displays include remarkably modern-looking kitchen tools and surgical implements as well as fabulous mosaics recovered from the homes of wealthy Pompeiians.

It would be sacrilegious to spend the night in Naples and not have pizza for dinner, so cap off your whirlwind tour of Campania with the region's official food—*la vera pizza napoletana* (real Neapolitan pizza). My favorite *pizzerie* are ★★★ **Gino Sorbillo** and ★★★ **Da Michele** (see p 605 for reviews of both), both of which are extremely popular, so go early or you're in for a long wait.

Limoncello!

The official liqueur of Naples and the Amalfi Coast is the inimitable and potentially insidious limoncello. If you've never heard of or tasted this thick yellow *digestivo*, it takes only a few days in the region to become a convert and even an aficionado. Most restaurants will offer patrons shots of the house limoncello after dinner—whether or not they show up on your bill depends largely on how enthusiastically you receive the limoncello. You'll know you've made a good impression when your waiter (usually in less touristy restaurants) brings you a bottle of the stuff from which you can pour freely. After a few meals, you'll begin to notice subtle differences between one limoncello and the next. Though the basic recipe is the same throughout the region, there are tricks and variations, many of which have been in a family for generations, that can make limoncello sweeter or more bitter. Some limoncelli are opaque, while others are more transparent. Most have a fluorescent yellow-green hue. It's all a matter of taste, so while you're here, get to know them all. But keep to two or three shots per night: The limoncello hangover does not back down easily.

If, when you return home from your trip, you want to relive the experience, you can make your own limoncello. All it takes are a few simple ingredients—lemons, alcohol, and sugar—and a couple of months to craft a homemade liqueur that will impress friends and family. Ask a local for the basic recipe, or do a search online.

The Best of Naples & Campania in 1 Week

With a full week in Campania, you'll be able to go to all the places on the 3-day tour, plus a few more, with the luxury of more time and more ways to enjoy them. Begin with 2 days and nights on the Amalfi Coast—it doesn't matter whether you stay in Amalfi, Positano, or Ravello—then a day trip to Pompeii and Mt. Vesuvius from Sorrento, followed by a 2-day sojourn to Capri, and finally, 2 nights in Naples.

> *Classic Amalfi Coast views are the biggest tourism draw of the Mezzogiorno, the Italian south.*

START Ravello.

1 Ravello. The aristocrat of Amalfi Coast towns isn't actually on the coast. Perched on a mountainside and set back from the water, Ravello is far from the noise and traffic of Amalfi and Positano. Though its geographical distinction is notable, Ravello also offers something its seaside brethren don't—that is, actual sightseeing beyond scenery gazing. Spend the better part of Day 1 touring and enjoying the air and culture up here.

If you're traveling to Ravello by bus, check the return bus schedule so that you know exactly when you need to be back at the bus terminal. Otherwise, you could be waiting around for more than an hour and find yourself

Getting Around

For detailed information on transportation options in Campania, see "Getting Around," on p 631.

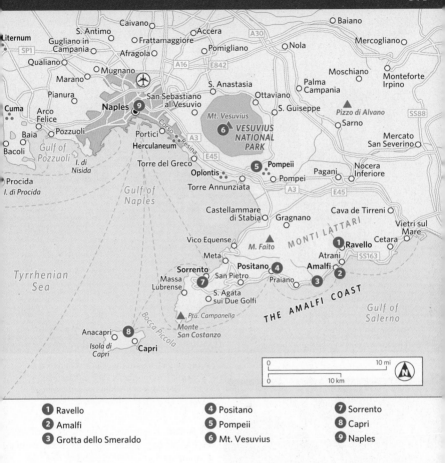

1 Ravello
2 Amalfi
3 Grotta dello Smeraldo
4 Positano
5 Pompeii
6 Mt. Vesuvius
7 Sorrento
8 Capri
9 Naples

tempted to take an astronomically expensive taxi back down the hill.

The main sights to see in Ravello are the Villa Cimbrone, the Villa Rufolo, and the town Duomo. Accessed via a narrow footpath (a gentle, 15-min. climb), the 15th-century ★★★ **Villa Cimbrone** (p 622, ➌) was once the private residence of an eccentric Englishman, Lord Grimthorpe (1856–1917). The property is now a hotel, but what draws most people up here is its gardens and their phenomenal views. Just on the south side of Ravello's main square, the ★★ **Villa Rufolo** (p 622, ➊) is easier to reach. Past the gates is a world of Moorish architecture and sultry gardens. In contrast to Villa Cimbrone's sweeping panora-

mas, the views here come in snatches of coastline and sea between rows of the villa's dense foliage. Richard Wagner composed much of *Parsifal* here. For that reason, you'll find plenty of hotels, restaurants, and shops in the area named after the opera and characters in it. ⏱ 6 hr.

From Ravello, take the SITA bus to Amalfi.

More on the Coast & Capri

For information on hotels, restaurants, and sights in Ravello, see p 622; for Amalfi, see p 628; for Capri, see p 612.

> *ABOVE* Visit the Grotta dello Smeraldo—or Emerald Grotto—for its eerie atmosphere.
> *LEFT* The black-and-white-banded facade of Amalfi's handsome Arab-Norman Duomo.

2 Amalfi. The biggest town on the coast sits on a lovely bay backed by the picturesque rock formations of the Valle dei Mulini. The laid-back but lively waterfront is a world apart from Positano's cafe- and boutique-filled port, and the pastel town has a definite lived-in feeling, despite a high concentration of tourists in high season. Amalfi's **Duomo** (p 628, **1**) is the finest church on the coast, looking for all the world like it was created expressly for a "southern Italy church scene" movie set. Besides the cathedral, Amalfi's must-do is the **panoramic walk up the Valle dei Mulini** (p 629, **2**). ⏱ 3 hr.

To reach **3** from Amalfi, you can take either a boat excursion or a SITA bus to Conca dei Marini.

3 kids Grotta dello Smeraldo. With its eerie light effects and limestone formations, the "Emerald Grotto" is a worthwhile stop between Amalfi and Positano, though the experience

> *The damage Pompeii suffered during an earthquake in A.D. 62 was just a prelude to its devastation 17 years later.*

of going inside is the ultimate in tourist camp. Flat, boxlike rowboats take visitors into the cave, where the boatmen deliver a cacophony of hot-blooded spiels that barely graze the subject of speleology, concentrating instead on the uncanny resemblance of certain stalactites to Benito Mussolini. ⏱ 1 hr. See p 600, ⑤.

Take the SITA bus to Positano (or, if you've taken a round-trip boat excursion to the Grotta from Amalfi, take a boat from Amalfi to Positano).

④ **Positano.** Spend the afternoon and early evening in Italy's number-one honeymoon destination. Go for a swim at Fornillo beach, or stock up on souvenirs at the endless boutiques in town and around the port. Positano really turns on the romance when the sun goes down. Have a sunset *aperitivo* at **Chez Black** (p 621), and then head up to one of the panoramic restaurants in the higher part of town for dinner. ⏱ 4 hr.

On Day 3 I recommend taking the SITA bus from Positano to Sorrento, as the westernmost stretch of the SS163 Amalfi Drive is the most dramatic part of the fabled coast and is best experienced on land. Upon arrival in Sorrento, check into your hotel, and then take the Circumvesuviana train to Pompeii.

⑤ **Pompeii.** Allow several hours to tour the phenomenal ruins of this once-wealthy Roman town that was destroyed by the eruption of Mt.

Vesuvius in A.D. 79. It would take days to see all the unique corners and individual structures of Pompeii, so use this time to see a few typical houses, such as the **House of the Vettii** and the **House of the Faun,** the theaters, the baths, the amphitheater, and the forum. ⏱ At least 3 hr. See p 588.

From Pompeii, take a Trasporti Vesuviani (☎ 081-963420; 3€ each way from Pompeii; 1.70€ from Ercolano) bus to Vesuvio-Cratere.

⑥ kids **Mt. Vesuvius.** After traipsing around Pompeii, take the bus up to Mt. Vesuvius. Buses depart from Pompeii's Piazza Anfiteatro and Piazza Esedra every half-hour or so, stopping in Ercolano (Herculaneum) on the way up to the crater. From the parking lot at 1,000m (3,300 ft.), it's an easy, zigzagging walk, with incredible panoramas and fascinating vegetation along the way, to the very top edge of the *cono grande* ("big cone," or summit of Vesuvius). ⏱ At least 2 hr., including travel time.

From Vesuvius, hop a bus back to Ercolano; then catch the Circumvesuviana back to Sorrento.

⑦ **Sorrento.** When you return to Sorrento in the evening, watch the sun set from the parapets of Piazza Tasso and go for a walk in its dense historic core, which is brimming with souvenir boutiques and lemony-yellow good cheer. Have dinner down by the sea at Marina Grande (see p 627 for my recommendation).

> *The mercantile spirit is alive and thriving in Naples's many back-street markets.*

By midmorning on Day 4, be on a boat from Sorrento to Capri. Crossing time is 20–45 minutes.

8 **Capri.** Upon arrival at Capri's Marina Grande, make your way to your hotel (you'll spend 2 nights here). If you're staying in Capri town, take the funicular. If you're staying in Anacapri, take the bus. (Many hotels offer pick-up service for guests at the port—check to see if yours does before you start schlepping your suitcases.)

Where you stay on the island will affect when, and in what order, you do the recommended activities below. Even if you don't choose to do all of them, you'll find that your 2 days on Capri can be very full, if you want them to be. (Staying put at your hotel pool and admiring the fabulous views might also be equally appealing.) Have a look at p 571, **6**, for a sample itinerary of the island's highlights.

As a rule, Capri town is most crowded between 11am and 4pm, when all the day-trippers are here, so come back later in the evening to explore the quaint streets. Another time-sensitive Capri activity is the ★★★ **Blue Grotto** (p 614, **8**): Most visitors go in the morning, making it very crowded and chaotic (which

is admittedly part of the fun), but the light is actually better, and the cave nearly empty, after 3pm. With that timing in mind, do the 2-hour ★★★ **full-island boat tour,** which takes you to the grotto, no earlier than 2:30pm.

Nature lovers, or anyone in search of a good walk, can embark on a number of hikes on Capri, from the easy ★ **Arco Naturale** loop, to the longer ★★★ **Via Pizzolungo** route, which skirts the southeastern corner of the island, above the ★★★ **Faraglioni** (p 612, **3**). Capri's highest point, ★★ **Monte Solaro,** is accessible via a rickety old chairlift or your own two feet.

The ancient Roman ruins of ★★ **Villa Jovis** (p 582, **4**), one of 12 luxurious retreats built on Capri by Emperor Tiberius, combines archaeology, exercise, and vertiginous views, on the northeastern tip of the island. ☺ 2 days.

By midday on Day 6, take a boat to Naples-

More on Capri

For details on recommended hotels, restaurants, and activities on Capri, see p 612.

Beverello port. Crossing time is 1 hour.

9 Naples. Once you're ashore, find your hotel (you're checking in for 2 nights), freshen up, take a deep breath, and greet this gorgeous and maddening city. (Unless you demand the kind of services and amenities that the large waterfront hotels have, I recommend staying in one of the *centro storico*'s boutique hotels for convenience and authenticity.)

Start with a walk down ★★ **Spaccanapoli** (p 602, **1**), the street that runs arrow-straight across the *centro storico*, "splitting Naples" in half. It changes names along the way but is called Via Benedetto Croce and Via San Biagio dei Librai in its most characteristic stretches. This is the heart of old Naples and the most interesting place to wander aimlessly on a morning or afternoon. (The quieter back streets can feel threatening after dark.)

After that, walk up to the **Museo Archeologico Nazionale** (p 605, **10**), a treasure trove of ancient relics and sculptures, many of which were found in the areas buried by Vesuvius in A.D. 79. Take one of Naples's funiculars up to Vomero hill and back down, just for the fun of riding a "big-city" version of these slanted cable railways. Have an epic seafood dinner, with views of Capri and Vesuvius to match, at **Giuseppone a Mare** in Chiaia (p 611).

The next morning, start your day with a strong Neapolitan cappuccino and a *sfogliatella* pastry at **Caffè Gambrinus** (p 609, **19**). For some local color (bordering on theater), wander over to the wild and boisterous seafood market at **Porta Nolana** (p 604, **7**), near the train station; it's a priceless window onto Naples's deep-seated mercantile tradition. You might even walk away with a bag full of octopus, not quite sure how you were roped into buying it.

The underground tours of Naples's Greek and Roman foundations, offered by **Napoli Sotterranea** (p 605, **8**), are likely to be the highlight of your stay in this endlessly surprising city. Be sure to book in advance, as there are only a few tours in English per day.

On your last night, cap off your time in Naples and the Amalfi Coast with a steaming hot *pizza napoletana.* ⏱ 1½–2 days.

The Best Swimming

After gazing rapturously out over the big blue as you've traveled around Campania, chances are you'll be jonesing for an actual swim in the gorgeous, warm, and caressing waters of the Tyrrhenian Sea.

Fornillo Beach, Positano. With an idyllic natural setting, backed by a verdant rock wall and hemmed in by a limestone promontory, Fornillo (west of the port) is the best place to sun and swim in Positano.

La Gavitella, Praiano. Views of Positano and Capri's Faraglioni and all-day sun are the big selling points at this cerulean cove. The west-facing platform is divided into two small establishments, **La Gavitella** and **One Fire Beach.**

Marina Piccola, Capri. The best place to swim on Capri is on the south side of the island, accessed by bus or Via Krupp, a spectacular footpath with eight hairpin turns against a sheer cliff. See p 614, **6**.

Faraglioni, Capri. Two beach clubs, **La Fontelina** and **Da Luigi** (p 612, **3**), offer access to the glamorous waters beneath Capri's rock formations.

The Blue Grotto, Capri. It's technically illegal but unforgettable—swimming into Capri's famed sea cave is possible only after 5pm and when the sea is utterly still.

The Best Ancient Sites

With its extensive and varied archaeological offerings, Campania is perhaps the richest region in Italy when it comes to ancient sights. Beneath the ominous foothills of Mt. Vesuvius, Pompeii is justly celebrated as the best archaeological site in the world, but the other victims of the A.D. 79 eruption, Herculaneum and Oplontis, are equally fascinating and more manageable. Other must-sees include the thrilling Villa Jovis on Capri; the Doric temples at Paestum; and the under-visited Greek and Roman sites north of Naples. A visit to the Naples Archaeological Museum helps tie it all together.

> The unmistakably Greek temples at Paestum have a history that stretches back to 550 B.C.

START Pompeii. Trip length: 7 days.

1 ★★★ kids **Pompeii.** ⏱ At least 4 hr. See p 588.

Take the Circumvesuviana train from Pompeii to Ercolano.

2 ★★★ kids **Herculaneum (Ercolano).** When Vesuvius erupted, Roman Herculaneum was buried by catastrophic surges of volcanic mud.

Hardening over and around the buildings of Herculaneum like a rock-hard cast, the mud preserved organic aspects of the ancient city, such as wooden doors and clothing, which you won't even find at Pompeii.

Herculaneum's main bath complexes were the ★ **Terme Suburbane** and ★★ **Terme del Foro.** The ★★ *thermopolia* (ancient fast-food

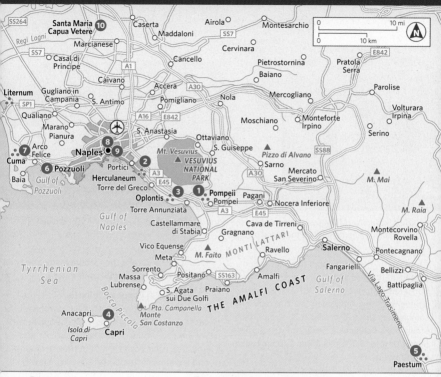

1 Pompeii
2 Herculaneum (Ercolano)
3 Villa di Poppea (Oplontis)
4 Villa Jovis (Capri)
5 Paestum
6 Pozzuoli
7 Cuma
8 Museo Archeologico Nazionale (Naples)
9 Napoli Sotterranea (Naples)
10 Campanian Amphitheater (Santa Maria Capua Vetere)

joints) have huge earthenware *dolia* set into a marble counter—these jars, in which food and mulled wine were kept warm, are so big that kids and small adults can climb in. Herculaneum's ★ **two-story houses** are in better shape than Pompeii's. Seek out the ★★ **Casa del Tramezzo di Legno** (House of the Wooden Partition) for its carbonized wooden partition in the back of the atrium. In the ★★ **Casa di Nettuno e Anfitrite** (House of Neptune and

Travel Tip

Sorrento is the recommended base for 1 to 5; stay in Naples for sites 6 to 10. For detailed information on the transportation options for this tour, see "Getting Around" on p 631.

> Ruined cities with Greek and Roman heritage, including Pompeii, shown here, are within reach of Naples and the major towns of the Amalfi Coast.

> *ABOVE Still active, Mt. Vesuvius looms above the city it destroyed, Pompeii. BELOW Villa Jovis is one of 12 villas Emperor Tiberius built on the island of Capri.*

Amphitrite), there's a gorgeous blue-toned mosaic of the god and his nymph. ⏱ 2–3 hr. Corso Resina 1, Ercolano. ☎ 081-7324311. www.pompeiisites.org. Admission 11€; 20€ for 3-day combination ticket also valid at Pompeii, Oplontis, Stabiae, and Boscoreale. Daily Apr–Oct 8:30am–6pm; Nov–Mar 8:30am–3:30pm. Circumvesuviana: Ercolano.

From Ercolano, take the Circumvesuviana train to Torre Annunziata (15km/9 miles).

❸ ★★ **Villa di Poppea, Oplontis.** Once the fabulous seafront residence of a wealthy 1st-century Roman family, the Villa di Poppea was yet another victim of Vesuvius's A.D. 79 eruption. The ruins aren't vast, but they're charming and wonderfully undervisited—and easy to reach. Below street level of the ugly modern town of Torre Annunziata, you'll enter a world of lush Mediterranean vegetation and follow a path through frescoed walls and suggestive brick-and-marble porticoes immersed in lemon groves. ⏱ 45 min. Via Sepolcri, Torre Annunziata. ☎ 081-8575347. Admission 5.50€; 20€ for 3-day combination ticket also valid at Pompeii, Ercolano, Stabiae, and Boscoreale. Daily Apr–Oct 8:30am–6pm; Nov–Mar 8:30am–3:30pm. Circumvesuviana: Torre Annunziata–Oplonti.

Take the Circumvesuviana train to Sorrento and catch a boat to Capri. On arrival in Capri, take the funicular up to Capri town and then walk 45 minutes east to the ruins of Villa Jovis.

❹ ★★ **Villa Jovis, Capri.** This spectacular cliff-side archaeological site on the northeastern tip of Capri is the best preserved of the 12 lavish retreats Emperor Tiberius built on the island. The ruins are quite extensive and make for adventurous exploration—perched as they are on a vertiginous face of limestone—but only the low masonry outlines are left of the complex structure, making it a bit difficult to picture the former splendor here. Scholars know that Tiberius threw extravagant parties at the Villa Jovis (Villa of Jupiter), and it was here that his most perverse personal habits were recorded by ancient Roman historians—the emperor had a thing for kinky sexual stimulation in the villa's hot tubs. Legend also has it that the capricious and ruthless emperor threw his enemies off a rocky promontory here, the so-called Salto di Tiberio, or Tiberius's Leap, to the sea 334m (1,096 ft.) below. ⏱ 2½ hr., including round-trip walk. Via Tiberio (45-min. walk east of Piazza Umberto I). ☎ 081-8570381. Admission 4.50€. Daily 9am–1 hr. before sunset.

Return to Sorrento by boat. To reach Paestum by public transportation, take the Circumvesuviana to Pompeii–Villa dei Misteri. At the hotel Victoria, hop on bus 4 to the Pompeii FS (national railway) station and catch the train (1 hour) to Paestum. (You can also walk from the Circumvesuviana station to the FS station; allow 20 minutes). To return, take the train back to Pompeii.

⑤ ★★★ Paestum. Travelers who brave the trek to reach Paestum by public transportation are rewarded with an intimate look at three Doric Greek temples. Even though archaeologists disagree on which gods were honored here, the ruins are on a par with the Greek temples in Sicily and a refreshing contrast to all the Roman ruins elsewhere.

The largest and oldest temple (from 550 B.C.) is generally referred to as the ★★ **Temple of Hera,** although a longitudinal partition of the structure remains of mysterious function. The so-called ★★★ **Temple of Neptune** (450 B.C.) is smaller but better preserved, with more perfect architecture (the 6/17 ratio of columns is a clas-

> A classic Doric construction, at Paestum.

sical Greek proportion). The 500 B.C. ★ **Temple of Athena** (or Demeter) still has its pediments. Look for *entesis,* or deliberate bulging in the girth of the columns, a hallmark of Greek temple design. Also, the fact that the temples are peripteral (having columns on all four sides) sets them apart from Roman temples.

The museum is home to the ★★★ **fresco of the diver,** a sweet image of a male figure swandiving into a stream of water, found in a tomb nearby. Other frescoes from the tomb include a ★ **symposium** scene, or Greek drinking party, at which attendees flung their wine around the room in a game called *kottabos.* ⏱ 2½ hr. Via Magna Graecia 919, Capaccio. ☎ 0828-811023. www.infopaestum.it. Admission 4€, or 6.50€ for temples and museum. Daily 9am–5pm.

For sites ⑥ and ⑦, take metro line 2 from Naples's Stazione Centrale or Montesanto to Pozzuoli-Solfatara.

When Vesuvius Erupted

In Pompeii, many survived the initial ash fall on August 24, A.D. 79, only to be asphyxiated by a deadly cloud of volcanic gases that belched from the crater. The Romans of Herculaneum met an even more violent end when rivers of hot volcanic mud surged down the slopes of Vesuvius and breached the walls of their town, sealing them and their buildings in a rock-hard cast when the mud cooled.

> *Pozzuoli's Solfatara volcano emits clouds of sulfurous steam.*

6 ★★ **Pozzuoli.** The main sights in this seaside Naples suburb, the hometown of Sophia Loren, are a 1st-century-A.D. Roman amphitheater, the so-called Temple of Serapis—in reality, it was a covered market—and the crater of the

Discounts & Combination Tickets

Campania's **Artecard** museum and monument passes will save you money on this admission-fee-intensive itinerary. Buy the Artecard at any of the sites included on the circuit, the Naples train station, or newsstands. A number of options are available, some of which offer free admission at certain sites only and discounts at others; some passes include public transportation. Serious culture vultures should invest in the **Artecard 365** (40€, valid for all museums and monuments in Campania for 1 year). For full details, see www.artecard.it.

dormant Solfatara volcano (p 597, **5**. Pozzuoli (ancient Puteoli, from the "putrid" smell of the sulfur-emitting volcano) rose to prominence in antiquity as an import-export center and for its proximity to the Roman naval base at Misenum.

The 20,000-spectator ★★ **Flavian amphitheater,** Via Terracciano 75, was designed by the same architects behind the Colosseum in Rome. The circular ★ **Temple of Serapis,** Via Serapide, is considered the symbol of Pozzuoli. The sunken archaeological site is surrounded by lively cafes. ⏱ 2½ hr. ☎ 081-5266007. Admission 2.50€; includes amphitheater and temple. Wed–Mon 9am–1 hr. before sunset. See also "Discounts & Combination Tickets," left.

A nice spot for lunch after seeing the sights of Pozzuoli, and before heading off to Cuma and Baiae, is ★ **Grottino A'mmare,** Via dell'Emporio 35–37, Pozzuoli port (☎ 081-5262480; reservations recommended on weekends; entrees 9–16€). The restaurant's setting on the water provides an entertaining view of port activities.

From the Pozzuoli-Solfatara metro station, take a SEPSA bus to Cuma (8km/5 miles).

7 ★★ kids **Cuma.** One of the most intriguing ancient sites in the Naples region is the ★★★ **Antro della Sibilla** (Cave of the Sibyl). Carved out of solid rock by the Greeks in the 5th century B.C., the 122m-long (400-ft.) tunnel has an unusual profile—in cross section, it looks like a house with a steep mansard roof. The red-rock tunnel is mysterious and otherworldly, like something out of an Indiana Jones film. According to Virgil's *Aeneid*, it was here in the eerie *antro* that Aeneas consulted the sibyl, or prophetess, of Cuma when he needed directions to the underworld. ⏱ 1 hr. Via Monte di Cuma, Pozzuoli. ☎ 081-8543060. Admission 2.50€. Daily 9am–1 hr. before sunset. See also "Discounts & Combination Tickets," left.

Take metro line 2 from Pozzuoli (the station higher on the hill and not the one by the port) to Napoli–Piazza Cavour.

8 ★★★ **Museo Archeologico Nazionale, Naples.** Thanks to its amazing collection of well-preserved objects—from everyday tools to refined works of art—from Pompeii, as well as magnificent Roman sculptures, this is the richest archaeological museum in Italy. ⏱ 2 hr. For more on the museum, see p 605, **10**. See also "Discounts & Combination Tickets," p 584.

⑨ ★★★ Napoli Sotterranea, Naples. Amazing and atmospheric tours into Naples's underbelly take you to Roman sites most locals don't even know exist. ⏱ 2 hr. See p 605, ⑧.

From Naples's Stazione Centrale (49km/31 miles), take the Napoli-Caserta-Piedimonte metropolitan commuter railway to Santa Maria Capua Vetere–Anfiteatro.

⑩ ★★ kids Campanian Amphitheater, Santa Maria Capua Vetere. Though its exterior has mostly fallen down, the interior and substructures of this 1st-century-B.C. amphitheater are in fantastic condition. The real highlight of this site is that you can walk through the **★★★ subterranean passageways** where animals, gladiators, weapons, props, and scenery were kept and see the elevator shafts where they were sprung up into action on the arena floor. It's haunting and evocative: You need only picture the tense prefight scenes of Ridley Scott's *Gladiator* to imagine what went on down here. Second only to the Colosseum in size, ancient Capua's was likely the first stone amphitheater built in Italy. The small Gladiator Museum here has a diorama depicting the ancient combats, casts of weapons from Pompeii, and reconstructions of parts of the amphitheater. ⏱ 1 hr. Piazza 1 Ottobre. ☎ 0823-798864. Admission 2.50€; includes Gladiator Museum. Tues–Sun 9am–5pm.

> *ABOVE* The Apollo Citaredo *and other Roman-era sculptures are among the fascinating finds displayed at Naples's Museo Archeologico. BELOW The museum's prize mosaic, from Pompeii, showing Alexander the Great and his steed Bucephalus in battle against the Persians.*

A DAY IN THE LIFE OF JULIUS PUBLIUS

From Temple to Triclinium

BY SYLVIE HOGG

WHAT STRIKES many visitors the most about the ruins of Pompeii is just how sophisticated the everyday lives of ancient Romans must have been. With specialized shops, entertainment facilities, and social venues all over town to fill their time (holidays just about every other day), an ancient Roman probably didn't suffer much boredom. Here is the hypothetical day of "Julius Publius," an average Joe who might have lived in Pompeii in A.D. 79 before the eruption of Mount Vesuvius. The lives of Romans in other preserved towns, such as Herculaneum, just north of Pompeii, and Ostia Antica, near Rome, would have been quite similar.

7am

At his *domus* (house), Julius Publius wakes up and makes an offering to the *lares* and *penates* (household gods) at his *lararium* shrine.

8:30am

He makes a sacrifice to

Minerva at the Temple of Jupiter, Juno, and Minerva in the Forum. Minerva was, among other things, a goddess of medicine, and his offering today is intended to safeguard the health of his family.

toured the empire. Exotic beasts from Africa were also imported to fight in the arena. Best of all, admission to the games was free.

4–5pm
He runs some errands, stopping at the *pistrinum* (bakery) and the *macellum* (butcher shop, in the Forum) for tonight's *cena* (dinner), and then at the *fullonica* (cleaner's) to pick up some freshly laundered togas.

6:30pm
Back at home for the evening, he and the family enjoy a meal and conversation in their *triclinium* (dining room).

After Hours
Not that a good family man like Julius Publius would ever stop here, but the centrally located, 10-room brothel, the Lupanare, was open at all hours.

(warm bath), and finally, a plunge in the bracing *frigidarium*.

Noon
He won't be home for lunch today, so he stops by the *thermopolium* (hot food bar) for a midday bite—maybe a protein-rich *merenda* (snack) of lentils and fish soup.

1:30–2:30pm
He catches an afternoon fight—human or animal—at the amphitheater. A prosperous and good-size town, Pompeii drew the well-known gladiators who

9:30–11am
He heads out to meet some friends at the Stabian Baths. They talk about work and town gossip while exercising in the *palestra* (open-air gym). Then they bathe—first the *caldarium* (hot bath), then the *tepidarium*

Pompeii

Barring the invention of a time machine, the best way to transport yourself back to ancient times is to visit Pompeii, the largest Roman town be buried during the devastating eruption of Mt. Vesuvius on August 24, A.D. 79. Though Pompeii is not perfectly preserved, the archaeological site is vast and gives a hauntingly complete picture of what daily life must have been like in this well-to-do town 2,000 years ago. Baths, theaters, taverns, shops, and especially houses—for which Pompeii is so famous—all appear strikingly sophisticated, even 2 millennia later.

> On August 24, A.D. 79, Mt. Vesuvius transformed Pompeii's civic forum into a silent memorial.

START **Take the Circumvesuviana train Pompeii Scavi–Villa dei Misteri. From Naples, make sure you are on the Sorrento line.**

❶ ★ **Porta Marina.** Tickets in hand, trudge up the basalt flagstone road that takes you under the original arched gate that led from Pompeii to the seacoast, and crest the hill that the entire ancient town was built upon. The dark tunnel of the ancient gateway is like a portal in time itself. Emerging into the sunlight on the other side, you officially step back in time to A.D. 79. ⊕ 1 min.

❷ ★★ **Forum.** The first major cluster of buildings you'll come upon are those of the forum—the central public square of a typical Roman city, where civic meetings, judicial proceedings, and most commercial activities took place. The ★ **Temple of Apollo** is off the left side of the road, before you reach the open space of the forum, which had marble porticoes on three sides. The **Temple of Jupite** occupied the northern end. The ★ **Basilica,** a long rectangle with column stumps, off the southwest end of the forum, was where trials

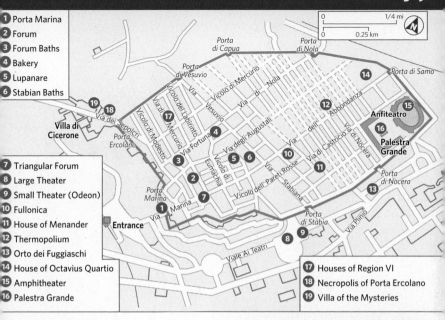

1. Porta Marina
2. Forum
3. Forum Baths
4. Bakery
5. Lupanare
6. Stabian Baths
7. Triangular Forum
8. Large Theater
9. Small Theater (Odeon)
10. Fullonica
11. House of Menander
12. Thermopolium
13. Orto dei Fuggiaschi
14. House of Octavius Quartio
15. Amphitheater
16. Palestra Grande
17. Houses of Region VI
18. Necropolis of Porta Ercolano
19. Villa of the Mysteries

nd other legal activities were held. Along the
astern side of the forum square are several
uildings of note: In the ★ **Macellum,** or food
market, the foundations of a 12-sided seafood
ank are still visible. Next to the Macellum,
he so-called ★ **Building of Eumachia** has
nteresting apses and exedras and was
edicated to the patron goddess of laundry;
nside, you can still see the container where
irty clothes were soaked in urine. The long
hed along the west side of the forum was the
Horrea (granary) and now contains a host
f fascinating ★★ **artifacts**—body casts and
ottery galore—that can be viewed through
arred gates. ⏱ 20 min.

3 ★★ **Forum Baths.** Of Pompeii's two main
athing complexes, these are frequently the
host crowded, but it's well worth braving the
ogjam of tour groups to have a look. In the
epidarium (warm bath chamber), the vaulted
eiling has elaborate stuccoes, and the walls
re lined with niches where patrons could
tore their togas while they bathed in the nude.
he barrel vault of the caldarium (hot bath)
s grooved so that condensation would drain
own the sides and not drip over bathers'
eads. There are also several casts of bodies
ound here. ⏱ 10 min.

4 ★ **Bakery.** This is a great example of a
Roman pistrinum, where flour was milled
and bread baked. Still in place here are the
millstones—the hourglass-shaped grinders
were turned by mules hitched to wooden
beams (the rectangular cutouts on the grinders
are where the beams were fixed in place).
Also visible at this structure are several arched
bread ovens. ⏱ 5 min.

> *TOP Pompeii's baths had separate areas for men and women. BOTTOM A lararium shrine, like this one from the House of the Vettii, honored a household's guardian spirit.*

5 ★★ **Lupanare.** Prostitution was commonplace in ancient Rome, and Pompeii was no exception. But while most "business" was conducted in unremarkable cubicles attached to taverns and private houses around town, the Lupanare was Pompeii's one and only purpose-built brothel. Titillating but by no means luxurious, the brothel consists of ten small client rooms on two floors. Each chamber has a stone bed on which a mattress would have lain, and above the doorway of each room is a faded but still very legible erotic painting of the "specialty" performed by the girl (or boy) there. ⏱ 5 min.

6 ★ **Stabian Baths.** About twice the size of the Forum Baths, these baths have a large grassy *palestra* (exercise area) at the center and remains of an open-air *natatio* (swimming pool). Along the eastern side of the complex were the bathing rooms proper—roughly symmetrical, and strictly separated, sets of cold baths, tepid baths, and hot baths for men and women. The men's *frigidarium* (cold bath) has one of the earliest known examples (from the 1st century B.C.) of a concrete dome. Its underside is painted to mimic a starry night sky. ⏱ 10 min.

7 ★ **Triangular Forum.** Not only is this shady grove a fine place to sit down, get your bearings, and maybe break out some picnic goods, it's also one of Pompeii's oldest religious areas, with remains of an evocative 6th-century-B.C. Doric temple among the trees. ⏱ 10 min.

8 ★★ Large Theater. Entertainment—funded by the ruling class and free for all to attend—was a huge part of Roman daily life. Pompeii's principal venue for highbrow culture (as opposed to the gore of the amphitheater; see **15**) was this semicircular theater that once sat 5,000 spectators and was where Greek tragedies and comedies were staged. ⏱ 10 min.

9 ★★ Small Theater (Odeon). This diminutive auditorium (which had a wooden roof, now lost) was where Pompeiian art patrons came for intimate concerts, poetry readings, and mime shows. Note the colorful marble paving in the orchestra and the elegant masonry of the *cavea* (seating area), which accommodated 1,500. ⏱ 10 min.

10 ★★ Fullonica. Yet another wonderful window onto Roman daily life is this laundry, where Pompeiians brought their dirty togas and household linens to be washed. Several stone washtubs are preserved here. Washing clothes in ancient times was an unsavory affair and involved soaking the soiled items in urine to loosen the dirt, which is why the citizens of Pompeii left the task to the *fullones*. Even having your own family servants do the job would have had the nasty side effect of permeating your lovely residence with the stench of urine. ⏱ 5 min.

Built to Last

Despite a serious earthquake that hit Pompeii in A.D. 62 (and from which the town was still recovering when it was buried by Vesuvius in A.D. 79), many of the structures unearthed at Pompeii can be dated back to several centuries B.C. A far cry from today's tear-down mentality, Roman houses and public buildings were designed to serve many, many generations and even make it through an act of God or two.

11 ★★ House of Menander. Though it's grander than some other houses, the basic design is the same: The first part of a Pompeiian *domus* is an atrium with a water-collecting *impluvium* basin in the center. The rooms along the atrium were *cubiculae* (bedrooms), *oeci* (rooms for receiving guests), and the *tablinum* (office). In the rear of the house, there's a large peristyle garden off of which the *triclinium* (dining room) and other chambers were located. ⏱ 10 min.

12 ★ Thermopolium. This is just one of dozens of ancient "snack bars" that were found all over Pompeii. From the L-shaped counters, which faced the street for quick service, hot food and drinks were served from enormous

> The Small Theater, or Odeon, seated just 1,500 for intimate arts performances.

Picnicking at Pompeii

It's essential to stay fueled and hydrated when touring Pompeii—at the very least, pack a sandwich and water. The site's cafeteria was closed at press time, and the snack stands (pictured above) outside the site are nothing to write home about, though they'll do in a pinch—especially for a cold, post-ruins beer or a cup of fresh-squeezed citrus juice. Inside the site, the best spots to sit down with a picnic are the Triangular Forum (**7**) and the Palestra Grande (**16**) near the Amphitheater, both blessedly shady. You can fill up your water bottle at public fountains throughout the ruins.

If you care to splurge on a serious meal while in the area, ★★★ **Il Principe,** Piazza Bartolo Longo (☎ 081-8505566), is not only modern Pompeii's best restaurant but one of the finest in Campania, period. It serves lunch and dinner Tuesday through Saturday. Reservations are required. Entrees start at 15€, and major credit cards are accepted.

dolia (earthenware jars for hot food and drink)—hence the round cutouts in the marble countertops. ⏱ 5 min.

13 ★ **Orto dei Fuggiaschi.** The "Garden of the Fugitives" is a touching monument to the desperation during the eruption of A.D. 79. Plaster casts of the bodies found here preserve the contorted and anguished positions the victims assumed as poisonous gases descended on Pompeii and asphyxiated so many of the citizens. ⏱ 10 min.

14 ★★ **House of Octavius Quartio.** Another fine example of a Roman domus, this residence is notable for its remarkable peristyle (rectangular garden): With its pergolas, terrace, and water canals, it resembles a country villa. ⏱ 10 min.

15 ★★★ **Amphitheater.** Having made the trek to the eastern end of town, you're rewarded with one of Pompeii's star landmarks: the elliptical arena. Built in the 1st century B.C.—making it the world's oldest-known surviving amphitheater—it's nowhere near as large as the Colosseum in Rome, but it's so perfectly preserved that it's even more evocative of the gladiatorial contests and wild animal fights that took place here. ⏱ 15 min.

16 ★ **Palestra Grande.** This large and grassy rectangle, lined with columns and umbrella pines, was the chief exercise area in Pompeii. It's also a prime shady spot where you can sit and have a picnic, if you've brought one along. ⏱ At least 5 min.

> ▸ OPPOSITE PAGE BOTTOM *Among the eerier sites at Pompeii are plaster casts of the dead.* THIS PAGE *Two-thousand-year-old frescoed walls at the Villa of the Mysteries.*

⑰ ★★★ Houses of Region VI. Region VI, which occupies the far northwestern end of the site, is where some of Pompeii's finest residences were concentrated. Together, the ruins of these opulent dwellings paint a picture of the true luxury patricians lived in. Start at the enormous **★★★ House of the Faun,** which remains impressive though much of it was bombed out during World War II. This is where the celebrated Alexander mosaic, now at the Museo Archeologico in Naples (p 605, ⑩), was found. Next, the **★★★ House of the Vettii** is for many the most memorable house in Pompeii, whether for its eye-popping erotic paintings, its kitchen implements still in situ, or its vivid frescoes. The **★ House of the Golden Cupids** is worth a quick peer for its pretty peristyle. Continue along to the *fauces* (entry hall) of the gated-off **House of the Tragic Poet** to see the oft-reproduced **★ *Cave Canem*** (Beware of Dog) mosaic on the floor. ⏲ 30 min.

⑱ ★★ Necropolis of Porta Ercolano. On your way to the Villa of the Mysteries (a good 10-min. walk from the main site), stop and inspect the funerary monuments of Pompeiians who died years before A.D. 79, oblivious to the wrath that Vesuvius would unleash on their town. As in all Roman cities, Pompeiian tombs had to be placed outside the *pomerium,* or sacred boundary of the city—in this case, the city walls. ⏲ 10 min.

⑲ ★★★ Villa of the Mysteries. With stunning frescoes and a sprawling architectural layout unlike anything else in Pompeii, this suburban villa is a must-see detour away from the main archaeological site. The villa is named for the provocative **★★★ frescoes,** interpreted as scenes of the bizarre and disturbing rites of initiation into the mysterious cult of Dionysus (Bacchus), in one of its salons. ⏲ 15 min.

The Best Outdoor Activities

If you're an adventurous type, there's no shortage of low-key ways to get close to the thrilling natural wonders of the Campania region. From the desolate summit of Mt. Vesuvius to the dizzying hikes across the Amalfi Coast, the beauty is always extreme here, though thankfully your physical efforts don't always have to be.

> Strike out on your own, on foot or by boat, to get a different angle on the coastline and islands.

START Capri. Trip length: 5 days.

1 Capri. The island may not be as well-known for its hikes as for its glamorous hotels and chic boutiques, but Capri boasts a surprising number of easy-to-access, satisfying nature trails that range in difficulty from moderate to strenuous. All are heart-stoppingly panoramic.

The classic trail, if you have to pick just one, is the ★★★ **Via Pizzolungo** (p 614, **7**), which starts at the end of Via Tragara and loops around the southeastern corner of the island, winding up at the Arco Naturale. The sea views along the way are precipitous. Relentless stairs along parts of the route make this a moderately strenuous

hike, especially in hot weather. Have a well-earned meal at **Le Grottelle** (p 617) afterward.

Over in Anacapri, you can also hike up to the top of the island's highest point, ★★ **Monte Solaro** (or hike down after taking the chairlift to the top; p 615, **10**). The most difficult hike here is the ★★★ **Passetiello;** passing through chestnut and pine groves, it was once the old mule path connecting Capri with Anacapri.

When you're finished with the hiking, head down to the water and visit Capri's greatest natural wonder-cum-tourism machine of them all—the ★★★ **Blue Grotto** (p 614, **8**). ⏱ 1 day.

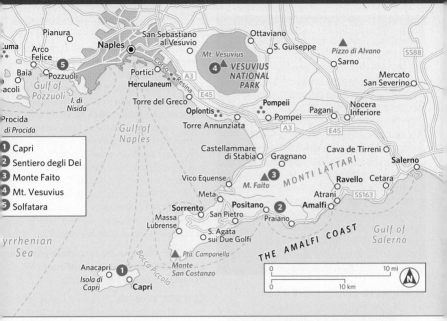

Legend:
1. Capri
2. Sentiero degli Dei
3. Monte Faito
4. Mt. Vesuvius
5. Solfatara

from Capri, take a boat to Positano and then a bus to Agerola or Praiano (18km/ 11 miles total).

2 Sentiero degli Dei. The lofty name of this trail, "Path of the Gods," isn't that much of a stretch. Suspended just below the highest peaks of the Amalfi Coast's interior, the hike between Agerola and Positano is the most peaceful way to experience those epic views over mountain and sea. Best of all, the hike isn't difficult: As long as you start in Bomerano, from which the entire 10km-long (6-mile) *sentiero* is either flat or slightly downhill. (Fitness buffs can start the trek from Praiano, which requires climbing 500m/1,640 ft. of stepped switchbacks.) Just wear comfortable shoes and clothing, and bring water, sunscreen, and steady feet, as parts of the route are extremely vertiginous. Upon completion of the hike in Montepertuso, you can either walk or take a bus down the hill to Positano.

If you'd rather go with a guide, contact **Sul Sentiero degli Dei** (☎ 339-1718194; www. sulsentierodeglidei.it), a Praiano-based outfitter that can tailor excursions to your needs.

from Positano, take a SITA bus to Sorrento and then the Circumvesuviana to Castellammare di Stabia (35km/22 miles total).

> *Via Tragara leads to Via Pizzolungo, one of Capri's many scenic walks.*

More Information

For the best swimming in Campania, see p 579. For hotels, restaurants, and sights in Capri, see p 612; for Sorrento, see p 624. For detailed information on the transportation options in Campania, see "Getting Around," on p 631.

Living in the Shadow of Il Vesuvio

The area around Mt. Vesuvius is the most densely inhabited volcanic region in the world, with a population of over 3 million living within striking distance. On the one hand, modern Neapolitans know full well what Vesuvius is capable of, yet they seem unfazed by the very real prospect that someday the mountain could unleash the same gas clouds and mud flows that wiped out their predecessors. Indeed, people today live closer to the summit than the ancients did, and in far greater numbers. Part of it is that the fertile slopes of Vesuvius are just too lucrative: Vesuvian grapes support a burgeoning wine business, and sweet Vesuvian *pomodorini* (cherry tomatoes) fetch nice prices at the produce market.

3 Monte Faito. Just outside the Castellammare di Stabia Circumvesuviana station is the lower terminus of the ★★ **Monte Faito cableway,** a gondola service that whisks you up the 1,131m-high (3,710-ft.) Monte Faito in 8 minutes. Along the way, there are thrilling views down the steep mountainside and over the Bay of Naples. At the top, a network of trails makes for ★★ **good hiking,** most of it shaded from the beating summer sun. The walks range from easy, level circuits to the long *saliscendi* (up-and-down) to Positano, a spectacular panoramic route that takes about 6 hours. (From Positano, you can take a bus back to Sorrento.) If you decide to embark on a longer hike, be sure to have a detailed trail map with you (available at newsstands and bookshops in Positano) and plenty of water. ⏰ 1 hr.; more for hiking. Cableway: Castellammare di Stabia. ☎ 081-7722444. Admission 7€. Mar 22–June 15 and Sept 1–Oct 31 9:30am–4:25pm; June 16–Aug 31 7:25am–7:15pm. Closed Nov–Mar 21.

From Sorrento, take the Circumvesuviana to Ercolano and then catch a local bus to Mt. Vesuvius (53km/33 miles total).

4 kids Mt. Vesuvius. The most active volcano on mainland Europe, Mt. Vesuvius is best known for the destruction of the Roman towns of Pompeii and Herculaneum, when it erupted on August 24, A.D. 79. The summit of Vesuvius

s well worth a visit. The most common approach is by **Trasporti Vesuviani bus** (☎ 081-9634420; 1.70€ each way) from Ercolano (Herculaneum). The bus takes you to the visitor center at 1,000m (3,300 ft.); from here it's a gentle 1km (about ½-mile) climb on foot to the top. It takes about an hour to walk all the way around the crater. ⏱ 3 hr., including round-trip transportation from Ercolano. Cratere del Vesuvio. ☎ 081-7710911. www.vesuviopark.it. Admission 6.50€. Daily 9am–5pm.

From Ercolano, take the Circumvesuviana to Napoli Centrale–Piazza Garibaldi and then metro line 2 to Pozzuoli-Solfatara (26km/16 miles total).

5 kids **Solfatara.** In the town of Pozzuoli, this is the biggest and most interesting to visit of the 40 dormant volcanoes in the Campi Flegrei (Burning Fields) district north of Naples. Well before you arrive at the gates of the park, you'll be able to smell the volcano: Its name, Solfatara, is derived from *sulpha terra* (land of sulphur), and its rotten egg odor permeates everything in the area. Don't come expecting an ominous, Vesuvius-like cone—the gentle slopes of Solfatara are buried under the modern town; only the crater is a park, and it's without a doubt one of the weirdest, most surprising attractions in southern Italy.

In the volcano park-cum-campground, after following CRATERE signs down some wooded paths, the scenery abruptly morphs into a blindingly white moonscape where mud pools bubble and jets of vapor hiss from fissures in the rock. Solfatara has four "attractions," marked not only by fences but also by huge DANGER signs, adding to the sense of adventure. The ★ **Bubbling Mud Pit** (La Fangaia) is a primordial-looking pool where volcanic gases just beneath the surface cause the mineral-rich clay to simmer at about 392°F (200°C). The 18th-century **Well** (Il Pozzo) marks the spot where Solfatara's characteristic thermal waters, containing alum, sulfur oxide, magnesium, and calcium sulfate and tasting of sour lemons, were tapped for therapeutic purposes. The **Ancient Saunas** (Le Stufe) are two masonry caves carved out of the side of the crater where sufferers of respiratory problems came to breathe the intense mineral vapors that supposedly had curative properties. Where you

> OPPOSITE PAGE *The trail to the summit of Mt. Vesuvius.* THIS PAGE *The Sentieri degli Dei trail is accessible even to inexperienced hikers.*

really get up close and personal with the crater is at the ★★★ **Grand Fumarole** (La Grande Fumarola). Every few seconds, the *bocca grande* (big mouth) belches out thick, sulfurous steam clouds that momentarily envelop anyone standing nearby. By all means, queue up for the chance to get "vaporized" (and have someone snap your picture while you're up there). There are also steaming hot fissures on the ground here, causing you to hop and dance around as you get closer. It's great fun. ⏱ 1 hr. Via Solfatara 151, Pozzuoli. ☎ 081-5262341. www.solfatara.it. Admission 5.50€. Daily 8:30am–sunset.

Volcanic Camping

Can't get enough of that "therapeutic" rotten egg smell? You can spend the night at the Solfatara crater—you and your gear just might reek of sulfur for the next few days. Camping fees are 9.60€ per person, plus applicable tent and car fees (from 6€); there are also bungalows (bedding included) available from 51€ per night. For more information, check out www.solfatara.it.

The Best of the Amalfi Coast

Stretching from the tip of the Sorrentine Peninsula to Salerno, the jagged Amalfi Coast is one of very few destinations in Italy where cultural touring and "sightseeing" aren't the chief attractions. Instead, the 60km-long (38-mile) coast draws lovebirds and relaxation-seekers with its incomparable, epic, way-more-impressive-in-person natural beauty. With the breathtaking Amalfi Drive to connect the dots, here's what you should sample along the coast—if you can be bothered to get out and do anything besides stare at the views, that is.

> If you can afford pricey Positano, you're paying for the best location on the Amalfi Coast.

START Sorrento. Trip length: 5 days.

1 ★★★ **Amalfi Coast Drive.** The Via Amalfitana (SS163) is the most celebrated corniche road in Europe for good reason. Death-defying curves, thrilling precipices, and sublime views in every direction make this engineering marvel the real stand-out attraction on the coast. While it's often convenient to travel up and down the Amalfi Coast by boat, don't miss a chance to do the white-knuckle SITA bus ride from Sorrento to Positano at least once. On the bus, the seat

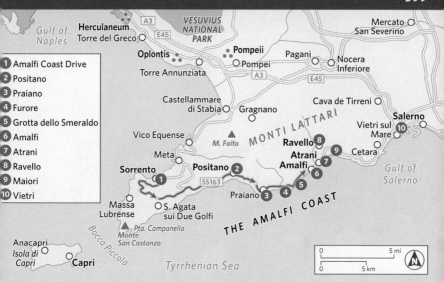

Amalfi Coast map legend:
1. Amalfi Coast Drive
2. Positano
3. Praiano
4. Furore
5. Grotta dello Smeraldo
6. Amalfi
7. Atrani
8. Ravello
9. Maiori
10. Vietri

rmrests are warped and unhinged—some ave even fallen off—from being clenched so ightly over the years. (Show-offs can do the ide standing up in the aisle, though the views ren't as good, and you'll need strong biceps, riceps, and core muscles to maintain your balance.) SITA buses depart Sorrento every half-hour. ⏱ 1 hr.

2 ★★★ **Positano.** The most glamorous (and xpensive) resort town on the Amalfi Coast is he perfect antidote for anyone tired of going o museums and seeing ruins. There's nothing o do here but eat, drink, shop, and absorb the abulous surroundings. The lively port is fun or people-watching, but if you want to go for a swim, the nearby beach of **Fornillo** (p 579) s far preferable to Positano's central *spiaggia grande*. ⏱ At least 4 hr.

3 ★★ **Praiano.** This "suburb" of Positano is a reat place to spend a few hours, away from acationer hordes, absorbing authentic local fe, whether it's a lazy afternoon at Bar del ole or an evening outing at Hotel Le Fioriere.

Getting Around

For detailed information on the transportation options on the Amalfi Coast, see "Getting Around," on p 631.

Praiano's Gavitella shoreline gets the best sun on the coast.

For lunch or dinner in Praiano, the **★★ Ristorante La Brace,** Via Gennaro Capriglione 146 (☎ 089-874226; entrees 10€–20€; lunch & dinner Thurs–Tues), is an old favorite for typical dishes such as spaghetti *alle vongole* (with clams) and fresh pastas with seasonal vegetables, as well as fresh and simple grilled fish. The atmosphere is warm and familial, and it's not unusual to share the dining room with a post-baptism party of 30 people, a priest, and a dolled-up baby making the rounds. ⏱ At least 2 hr. For more on Praiano, see p 620.

4 **Furore.** The viaduct of the SS163 passes high over the gorge of Furore and its tiny village of Marina di Furore. It's worth a quick stop on the way toward Amalfi to admire the limestone chasm, referred to by locals with typical southern Italian hyperbole as *il fiordo* (the fjord). A massive and "furious"—hence the name Furore—rush of water often runs down the gorge in winter (you'll see postcards of this phenomenon all over the area), though there's usually just a trickle in the fissure in summer. There are many, many steps involved from the highway to explore the Amalfi Coast's little corner of Norway properly, so I recommend you snap your photos from the bridge and move on. ⏱ 30 min.

> *The emerald light inside the Grotta dello Smeraldo is best viewed from a rowboat between about noon and 3pm*

5 ★★ kids **Grotta dello Smeraldo.** Billed as a green version of Capri's Blue Grotto, the "Cave of the Emerald" ís the Amalfi Coast's best attempt at a tourist trap (complete with tacky signs). No, it's nowhere near as cool as the whole Blue Grotto experience, but it's still impressive, and it's also half the price. If you've got kids along who are at all into pirates, this will be a huge hit. (Besides, who doesn't love a grotto excursion?) On arrival at the grotto (by land or by sea), smaller rowboats will take you into the cave, which is 45m (148 ft.) long and 32m (105 ft.) wide, with a height of 24m (79 ft.), and has interesting stalactite formations that, as the boatmen will surely point out, can resemble famous statesmen from just about every tourist-supplying country, if you squint hard enough (George Washington for the Americans, Napoleon for the French). The rest of the spiel drones on unintelligibly, so feel free to tune out and marvel at the brilliant green water instead.

More on the Coast

See p 618 for more information on hotels and restaurants in Positano; for Amalfi, see p 628; for Ravello, see p 622.

You can access the grotto by SITA bus (at Conca dei Marini, the driver will announce "Grotta, signori, Grotta") and then descend on the special *grotta* elevator, but the sea route is more fun. At the ports of Amalfi or Positano, there are outfitters offering departures every 30 minutes for the Grotta. ⏱ 1½ hr. Conca dei Marini (SS163). ☎ 089-871107. Grotto admission 5€; transportation from Amalfi or Positano ports 10€. Daily 9am-3:30pm, sea conditions permitting.

6 ★★★ **Amalfi.** The unpretentious charm of Amalfi is infectious. It's less manicured than Positano, but it's also less swarmed, and you get the distinct feeling that real people do real things here—it's not *all* about tourism. Amalfi's bus terminus and port also make it an ideal hub for exploring the coast. The *centro* of sunny Amalfi is surprisingly flat and dominated by its eye-popping Duomo. A few hundred meters inland, the terrain steepens at the ★★ **Valle dei Mulini** (p 629, **2**), an idyllic valley where the ruins of old paper mills can be seen. Amalfi is home to my favorite hotel on the coast, the ★★★ **Santa Caterina** (p 630), whose thatched-roof ★★★ **Ristorante al Mare** (seaside restaurant) makes for an unforgettable meal in a romantic setting overlooking the bay.

7 ★★ **Atrani.** Back in the days of the *Repubblica Marinara,* when Amalfi was a big-time naval power on the Mediterranean stage, this is where the top brass lived. Today, Atrani is a preposterously compact little fishing village whose interesting look is a direct result of the SS163 passing directly over its old buildings. The neighborhood beneath the highway is called the *sopportico,* an intriguing, practically roofed warren of whitewashed streets with a happening central square. A great local place to eat here is ★★ **Le Palme** (p 630).

8 ★★★ **Ravello.** By now you've been on the coast a while. You've seen the swoon-inducing views around every corner. Well, in Ravello, the panoramas are taken to new heights—literally. On the Terrazza dell'Infinito at the ★★★ **Villa Cimbrone** (p 622, **3**), it's not what you see but how you see it—from a platform that juts out over a steep precipice. As you approach the railing, which is lined with Roman marble busts, all you see is the sky behind it. When you reach the railing and look down—390m (1,300 ft.) to the deep blue below—it takes a moment or two to get your heartbeat back. Running from late June to the end of October, the ★★ **Ravello Festival** (☎ 089-858422; www.

ravellofestival.com) is the premiere venue on the coast for open-air concerts and other cultural engagements.

9 ★ kids **Maiori.** The widest sand ★★ **beach** on the coast is Maiori's claim to fame. The long, gently curving *lungomare* is crowded with beach clubs and their color-coordinated lounge beds and umbrellas, but it's the best bet in the area for families to bring their tots to swim. (Most other Amalfi Coast swimming areas are glorified cement platforms not suitable for little ones.) The water is calm, clear, and shallow. The rest of the town is lively but rather blighted by mass tourism.

10 ★ **Vietri.** If you fall in love with the dishes at a restaurant in Praiano or the bathroom tilework at your hotel in Positano and you want to bring some home, the source isn't far away. For Italians in the know, Vietri is synonymous with the Amalfi Coast's signature ceramic production. The sunny painted motifs include periwinkle waves, turquoise florals, and lemony garlands. Vietri's best outlet is ★★★ **Ceramica Solimene,** Via Madonna degli Angeli 7(☎ 089-210243), whose color-washed tiles in beautiful magentas, tangerines, and cobalts adorn many a hotel and restaurant in the region.

> *The gardens of Villa Cimbrone house a famous belvedere for taking in the views, a faux Sicilian-Arabic cloister, and a Gothic-style crypt.*

Naples

Bella Napoli—the birthplace of pizza and Sophia Loren—
is in many ways the Italy of your imagination. It's an exuberant place of musical dialect and vigorous gesturing, of infectious warmth and wit, and yes, of scams and petty theft. Naples has art and history in spades and the intoxicating aroma of pizza on every corner. It's also the most naturally stunning of all Italian cities, with the wide blue bay and the brooding cone of Mt. Vesuvius to frame it. The more time you're able to spend here, the better your chances of seeing past the city's chaotic and dirty veneer and being able to take part in the most authentic and tradition-steeped urban experience left in Italy.

> *Thick crusts and simple flavors entice in the city that pizza calls home.*

START **Naples is 227km (141 miles) south of Rome and 50km (31 miles) north of Sorrento; it can be reached by car or train from both.**

① ★★★ Spaccanapoli. The best place to start exploring is in Naples's most interesting and pedestrian-friendly area—the compact historic core. *Spaccanapoli* means "split Naples" and refers to the dead-straight, east-west-running street that cleaves the *città antica* (old city) in half. (You won't see "Spaccanapoli" written on a map: Look for Via San Biagio dei Librai or Via Benedetto Croce.) This narrow thoroughfare and its lattice of characteristic side streets are filled with wonderful little shops, bakeries, and churches. The once-grand building facades here are tarnished by age and neglect, adding to the authenticity. Come in the morning, when you'll find coffee bars crowded with boisterous locals and the cheery atmosphere of the day's first *buongiorno*s as merchants open their shops. ⏱ 1 hr.

② ★★ Via San Gregorio Armeno. The raison d'être of this Spaccanapoli cross street is its *presepe* (nativity scene) artisans and vendors,

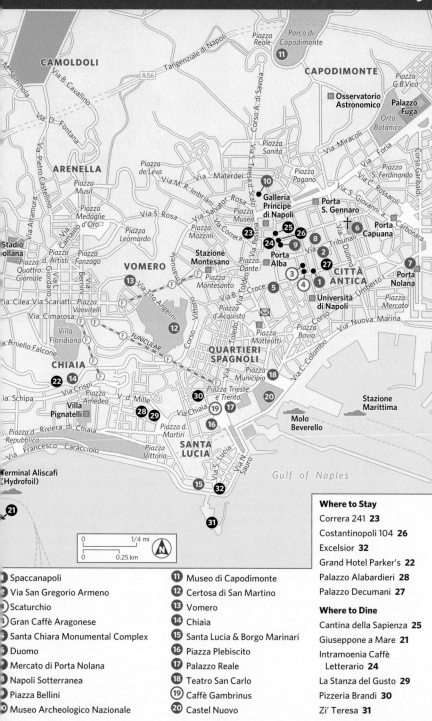

Where to Stay

Correra 241 **23**

Costantinopoli 104 **26**

Excelsior **32**

Grand Hotel Parker's **22**

Palazzo Alabardieri **28**

Palazzo Decumani **27**

Where to Dine

Cantina della Sapienza **25**

Giuseppone a Mare **21**

Intramoenia Caffè
  Letterario **24**

La Stanza del Gusto **29**

Pizzeria Brandi **30**

Zi' Teresa **31**

1 Spaccanapoli

2 Via San Gregorio Armeno

3 Scaturchio

4 Gran Caffè Aragonese

5 Santa Chiara Monumental Complex

6 Duomo

7 Mercato di Porta Nolana

8 Napoli Sotterranea

9 Piazza Bellini

10 Museo Archeologico Nazionale

11 Museo di Capodimonte

12 Certosa di San Martino

13 Vomero

14 Chiaia

15 Santa Lucia & Borgo Marinari

16 Piazza Plebiscito

17 Palazzo Reale

18 Teatro San Carlo

19 Caffè Gambrinus

20 Castel Nuovo

> *At the feast of Naples's patron San Gennaro, in the Duomo, the liquefaction of the saint's blood is followed by a devout procession.*

where you can peruse a mind-boggling range of animatronic Bethlehem folk, farm animals, and landscape features. ⏱ 15 min.

③ 🍴 ★★ **Scaturchio.** Stop in for a *sfogliatella* at Naples's most famous pastry shop. Piazza San Domenico Maggiore 19. ☎ 081-5516944. $.

④ 🍴 ★★ **Gran Caffè Aragonese.** For a longer coffee break take a seat at the alfresco tables here. Piazza San Domenico Maggiore 5/8. ☎ 081-5528740. $$.

❺ ★★ **Santa Chiara Monumental Complex.** The Gothic church is wonderfully light-filled, but it's the cloister, a garden haven done up in exuberant majolica tiles, that makes this one of Naples's signature sights. ⏱ 30 min. Church: Via Benedetto Croce. ☎ 081-5526280. Free admission. Daily 7am–12:30pm, 4:30–8pm. Cloister and museum: Via Santa Chiara 49C. ☎ 081-7971256. Admission 5€. Mon–Sat 9:30am–1pm; 2:30–5:30pm Sun 9am–1pm.

❻ ★ **Duomo.** The Gothic cathedral of Naples—built in the 14th century and tinkered with for the next 500 years—has a sumptuous interior, but it doesn't come close to the grand scale of the cathedrals in other major Italian cities. Naples's Duomo is, however, the site of the miraculous, twice-yearly liquefaction of the blood of San Gennaro (first Sat in May and Sept 19). Most of the year, the blood is locked away in a chest behind the altar. ⏱ 15 min. Via del Duomo 147. ☎ 081-449097. Free admission. Daily 8am–12:30pm, 4:30–7pm.

❼ ★★ **Mercato di Porta Nolana.** The prime spot for witnessing Naples's long history as a port and mercantile city is at the Porta Nolana seafood (and more) market. Just be aware of pickpockets. Open-air stands glisten with anchovies and tuna, wriggly octopus and squid glare at you from ice-packed trays, and fresh mussels huddle together in great watery vats. All around, shouting fishmongers tout the superiority of their offerings, the end of their pitches lilting off in improvised ballads about the catch of the day (invariably, *mamma* is also invoked in their ditties), while Italian radio blares in the background. The quintessentially Neapolitan spirit of the place is so infectious

hat you might end up buying some swordfish
teaks—even though you may have no place to
ook them. ⏱ 45 min. Mon–Sat early morning-
arly afternoon.

③ ★★★ Napoli Sotterranea. Swing back to the
ittà antica and Piazza San Gaetano to see the
ights of the Neapolitan "underworld" (by guided
our only; it's a good idea to book ahead). Plenty
f European cities let visitors peek at antiquities
ınder the modern street level, but Naples's be-
ow-ground showcase—a fascinating 90-minute
tinerary through ancient quarries, a Greco-Ro-
nan theater, cisterns and aqueducts, and caves
hat were used as air-raid shelters in World War
I—is truly unique and surprising. Claustrophobes
hould be aware that several passages are very
ight and low-ceilinged, with candles as your only
ght. Coolest of all, the tour pops out in the back
arden of someone's ground floor apartment,
roving that you never know what lies beneath
he surface in a 3,000-year-old, multilayered city
ke Naples. ⏱ 1½ hr. with guided tour. Piazza San
Saetano 68. ☎ 081-296944. Tour 9.30€: Mon–Fri
oon, 2, and 4pm; Thurs also at 9pm; Sat–Sun
0am, noon, 2, 4, and 6pm.

⑨ ★★ Piazza Bellini. Filled with cafes and
alm trees, this pedestrian-only square con-
ains ruins of a 4th-century-B.C. Greco-Roman
vall and a statue of composer and piazza
amesake Vincenzo Bellini (1801–35). Bellini
tudied at the music conservatory on the south
ide of the square, where the violin and piano
otes of modern students still float out over the
eighborhood. Piazza Bellini is a hive of social
ctivity, with an intellectual vibe at its relaxed
afes and pubs—try Intramoenia (p 611). ⏱ At
east 30 min.

⑩ ★★★ Museo Archeologico Nazionale. The
choey halls of this enormous palazzo house
he **★★★ artifacts from Pompeii** and from
nany other sites buried by the eruption of Mt.
/esuvius. These finds are an astonishing time

Pizza Napoletana

Pizza was invented in Naples, and the particular style of dough, tomato sauce, and mozzarella used here isn't replicated anywhere
else in the world. (It's also dirt cheap.) My
favorite *pizzerie*, below, are both first-come,
first-served establishments and extremely
popular, so go early (around 7pm), or be prepared to wait.

Much of the appeal at ★★★ 🄺🄸🄳🄺 **Da Michele,** Via Sersale 1 (☎ 081-5539204; pizzas
from 3€; AE, DC, MC, V), a tiny pizza joint
(pictured above) widely held to be Naples's
best, is the stripped-down, focus-on-product-
not-frills approach: There's zero decor and
only five items on the menu. Ask about any
extra toppings and you'll get a Neapolitan
earful about how pizza is a food for the simple
folk and additions like mushrooms and seafood are for snobs. Try for a seat in the front
room, where you can watch raw pizzas go into
the wood-fired oven only to reappear, fully
cooked, a mere 20 seconds later.

The pizza is incredible at ★★★ 🄺🄸🄳🄺 **Gino
Sorbillo,** Via dei Tribunali 32 (☎ 081-446643;
closed Sun; pizzas from 3.50€; AE, DC, MC,
V), and the sultry baroque facade and ivy-
framed doorway fully look the part of the
Naples institution that it is. To get your name
down, barge through the crowds outside and
into the dining room, and find the woman with
the clipboard. Though the menu is long and
varied, I always get the *quattro stagioni* (four
seasons), with its quadrants of mushrooms,
prosciutto, *salame*, and plain cheese divided
by a "+" of pizza dough.

Getting Around

In the city of Naples, buses, metros, and
funiculars are a great help when your feet
tire of pounding the hot pavement. Tickets
cost 1.10€ and are valid for 90 minutes. Buy
tickets at *tabacchi* shops or newsstands.

> *Andy Warhol's* Mount Vesuvius *captures the dynamism that is an integral part of the mountain's history (and likely future).*

capsule that must be seen if you're also visiting the sites of Pompeii or Herculaneum. Display cases of ancient baking equipment, surgical instruments, and delicate glasswork bear witness to the sophistication of Roman civilization in the 1st century A.D.

The ★★★ **mosaic collection** includes the famed Alexander the Great mosaic that was recovered from the House of the Faun (p 593, 🔟), as well as charming scenes of groceries that would look fabulous in any kitchen of today. The once off-limits ★★ **Gabinetto Segreto,** which is the museum's trove of erotic art from Pompeii, with eye-popping frescoes and sculptures of amorous acts both tender and (literally) bestial, is now regularly open—to adults only.

The museum's other star attraction is the renowned ★★★ **Farnese collection of ancient sculpture,** which includes the *Farnese Hercules,* a masterful Hellenistic work depicting the hero in a rare moment of rest, and the incredible *Farnese Bull,* which depicts the Punishment of Dirce. This massive marble group (3.7m/12 ft. high and 3m/10 ft. wide), chiseled from one piece of stone, is the largest single sculpture recovered from antiquity. Many of these colossal works came from the Baths of Caracalla in Rome (p 81, 🔟). ⏱ 2 hr. Piazza Museo 19. ☎ 081-440166. Admission 6.50€. Wed–Mon 9am–7:30pm.

🔢 ★★ **Museo di Capodimonte.** The premier art museum in Naples is in a green sanctuary north of the center. The world-class collection in the ★★★ **Galleria Farnese** contains works by Titian, Raphael, El Greco, Parmigianino, Correggio, and Caravaggio. The building was once a royal residence, and much of the original furniture has been preserved in the ★★ **Appartamenti Reali.** The museum's small contemporary section even has a pop-art Mt. Vesuvius by Andy Warhol. ⏱ 1 hr. Via Miano 2. ☎ 081-7499111. Admission 7.50€. Thurs–Tues 8:30am–7:30pm.

🔢 ★★★ **Certosa di San Martino.** From their commanding position atop Vomero hill, the Carthusian Monastery of St. Martin and the fortress of Castel Sant'Elmo behind it are imposing landmarks on the Neapolitan skyline. The entire complex is a palatial trove of Renaissance and baroque art and architecture, with gorgeous cloisters and lush gardens, but it's the postcard panorama of the bay and Capri, Vesuvius, and Sorrento that is the real draw here. ⏱ 1 hr. Largo San Martino 5. ☎ 081-5781769. Admission 6€. Tues–Sat 8:30am–7:30pm; Sun 9am–7:30pm.

🔢 ★★ **Vomero.** It may not have many "sights," but Vomero is a great mainstream neighborhood for shopping, dining, and watching the modern Neapolitan parade. Laid out in the late 19th century, Vomero consists of perpendicula

> *ABOVE The Certosa di San Martino rewards those who ride the funicular up the Vomero hill with baroque architecture and views across the bay. BELOW A famous dog mosaic from Pompeii is preserved in Naples's Museo Archeologico Nazionale.*

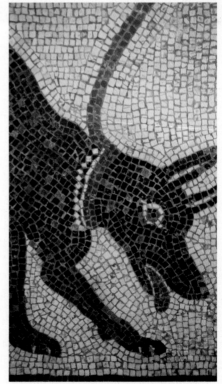

streets and broad sidewalks, which are lined with mostly affordable fashion boutiques (Via Luca Giordano and the pedestrianized Via Scarlatti are the best) and specialty food shops. There's also a welcome "green lung" here in the shady avenues of ★ **Villa Floridiana** park (entrance on Via Cimarosa; open dawn–dusk). Of course, half the fun of Vomero is taking the funicular to get there and back down. ⏰ At least 1 hr. Funicular: Montesanto, Centrale, or Chiaia.

⑭ ★★ kids **Chiaia.** Hop on the Chiaia funicular from Vomero and exit at Piazza Amedeo. Airy and elegant Chiaia occupies the crescent between Piazza Vittoria and Mergellina harbor and enjoys sea views that stretch from Ischia to Capri. Higher on the hill, you'll find gorgeous Art Nouveau villas and gardens, while halfway down, on **Via dei Mille,** is where Naples's luxury boutiques are concentrated. The slender green seaside park, **Villa Comunale,** is great for strolling, especially on summer nights, when it's alive with festivals and concerts. In the middle of the park, the 19th-century **Aquarium** (☎ 081-5833111; 1.55€; Tues–Sun 9am–5pm) has tanks of live local species that will help acquaint you with the menu at seafood restaurants. If possible, visit Chiaia on a Sunday, when busy Via Caracciolo is closed to traffic and the waterfront chalets are a buzz. ⏰ At least 1 hr. Funicular: Chiaia.

> *The Teatro San Carlo's operatically grand setting.*

> *San Francesco di Paola in Piazza Plebiscito bears a striking resemblance to Rome's Pantheon.*

15 ★ **Santa Lucia & Borgo Marinari.** East of Chiaia, the quiet seafront area is called Santa Lucia, where most of the city's luxury hotels are clustered along Via Partenope. The area's biggest attraction is the tiny island that juts into the bay here, ★ **Borgo Marinari.** Accessed from Via Partenope by a short causeway, the old fishing village consists of a picturesque ancient fortress, **Castel dell'Ovo,** a quaint marina, and romantic restaurants with twinkling white lights (see p 611 for recommendations). ⏱ 1 hr.

16 ★★ **Piazza Plebiscito.** The city's grandest open space is this vast U-shaped square. The curved end of the piazza is dominated by the church of San Francesco di Paola (an imitation of Rome's Pantheon) and delineated by colonnades that recall St. Peter's Square in Vatican City. ⏱ 15 min.

17 **Palazzo Reale.** Naples's "Royal Palace" was one of four regal residences used by the Bourbon monarchs during the Kingdom of the Two Sicilies (1730–1860). Go inside the apartments for an eyeful of state decor at its most pompous and lavish. ⏱ 1 hr. Piazza Trieste e Trento. ☎ 081-5808111. Admission 4€. Thurs–Tues 9am–8pm.

18 ★★★ **Teatro San Carlo.** This is one of the grandest opera houses in Europe, with six level f box seating and an enormous stage that can ccommodate live camels and elephants during the production of such operas as *Aïda*. Even if ou can't get tickets, do tour its red-velvet-and-old bedecked interior. ⏱ 1 hr. for tours. Via San arlo 101. ☎ 081-5534565. www.teatrosancarlo. , Tours 5€. Thurs–Mon 9am–5:30pm; Tues–Wed y reservation.

🍺 ★★ **Caffè Gambrinus.** Whenever the *bella gente* of Naples need to make a coffee date, this historic salon is where they go. You'll pay quite a bit more for your cappuccino here, but the people-watching makes it worth the extra euros. Piazza Trieste e Trento, at Via Chiaia. ☎ 081-417582. $$.

★★ kids **Castel Nuovo.** Most Italian castles on't exactly look the part of the European medieval stronghold reproduced in movies and miniature golf courses, but the 13th-century astel Nuovo, with imposing turrets at its corners, crenellated parapets, and a deep moat, is rchetypal. Legend has it that the prisoners in the castle dungeon fell prey to freely roaming rocodiles, brought from Egypt for the express urpose of devouring inmates. ⏱ 45 min. Piazza Municipio. ☎ 081-7955877. Admission 5€. Mon–at 9am–7pm.

Funiculì Funiculà

In Italy, funicular railways are usually found in resort destinations. Tourists love the novelty of these alpine contraptions, but the steep cableways generally aren't made for moving large amounts of people. Not so in Naples. Naples's funiculars are big-city transport—like a New York City bus or a London Underground train that happens to be pitched at a 30-degree angle. The heights of Vomero, one of Naples's nicer neighborhoods, are connected to the "lower" city by three funicular lines, the Montesanto, the Centrale, and the Chiaia. The three swift and smooth lines make going up and down a breeze, and it's a giddy way to feel like a real Neapolitan. Before you go, download the classic Neapolitan folk song "Funiculì Funiculà," which joyously celebrates this wondrous mode of transport. To ride the funiculars, use the UnicoNapoli ticket (1.10€, sold at *tabacchi* shops and newsstands; also valid on buses and metros).

> The incongruous triumphal arch was squeezed in between the 13th-century turrets of the Castel Nuovo in the mid-1400s.

Where to Stay

> *Costantinopoli 104 features chic interiors in an Art Nouveau wrapper.*

Correra 241 CITTÀ ANTICA

Proud to call itself an "art hotel," this funky *pensione* has guest rooms awash in bright colors and pop art—if loud decor isn't your thing, book somewhere else. The hip staff and guests are on the younger side. **Via Correra 241.** ☎ 081-19562842. www.correra.it. 12 units. Doubles 75€–120€. AE, DC, MC, V.

★★★ **Costantinopoli 104** CITTÀ ANTICA

This jewel of an inn occupies an Art Nouveau palazzo at the back of a quiet, private courtyard. Think well-appointed chic guesthouse—not formal luxury—with comfortable rooms, plenty of amenities (there's a small pool!), and a friendly staff. **Via S. Maria di Costantinopoli 104.** ☎ 081-5571015. www.costantinopoli104.it. 19 units. Doubles 170€–220€. AE, DC, MC, V.

★ **Excelsior** SANTA LUCIA

The best of the waterfront grande dames offers sweeping views of the bay and Mt. Vesuvius. The beautiful palazzo has opulent common areas and a gorgeous roof terrace, though the staff can be a bit officious. **Via Partenope 48,** ☎ 081-7643180. www.excelsior.it. 136 units. Doubles 220€–360€. AE, DC, MC, V.

★★ **Grand Hotel Parker's** CHIAIA

This intimate luxury property epitomizes old-world Neapolitan style. The graceful rooms have not been modernized too much over the years, but that's part of the appeal. The wood-paneled bar and rooftop terrace, with dizzying views, are straight out of a James Bond film. **Corso Vittorio Emanuele 135.** ☎ 081-7612474. www.grandhotelparkers.it. 81 units. Doubles 255€–360€. AE, DC, MC, V.

★★ **Palazzo Alabardieri** CHIAIA/SANTA LUCIA

This meticulously restored, early-20th-century-modern hotel is conveniently located and a wonderful place to stay. Architectural flourishes jazz up the room decor and make you feel like a guest in your fabulous Neapolitan aunt's house. **Via Alabardieri 38.** ☎ 081-415278. www.palazzoalabardieri.it. 33 units. Doubles 170€–230€. AE, DC, MC, V.

★★ **Palazzo Decumani** CITTÀ ANTICA

With a prime location and spotless, spacious rooms (with enormous travertine bathrooms), this newcomer is one of my favorite addresses in Naples. Interiors are contemporary and masculine, and the hotel's techie amenities make it highly recommended for business travelers, too. **Piazza Giustino Fortunato 8.** ☎ 081-4201379. www.palazzodecumani.com. 28 units. 130€–220€. AE, DC, MC, V.

Where to Dine

Sandwiches and salads are always tasty at Intramoenia Caffè Letterario.

★ **Cantina della Sapienza** CITTÀ ANTICA NEA-
POLITAN This spot serves the best *parmigiano
melanzane* (eggplant parmesan) I've had in
Naples—it's Neapolitan home-style cooking at
its heartiest. Just about everything comes with
heaps of fresh tomato sauce, and the inexpensive house wine is very drinkable. Via della Sapienza 40. ☎ 081-459078. Entrees 5€–8€. No credit
cards. Lunch Mon–Sat.

★★ **Giuseppone a Mare** POSILLIPO (SOUTH-
WEST OF CHIAIA) SEAFOOD Come here with an
empty stomach and a camera—you dine on a
stunning panoramic terrace. Start with one of
the delectable fresh pastas, and then pick your
main dish from the cart of glistening whole fish
and crustaceans and specify how you want it
cooked—grilled, baked, or fried. Via Ferdinando
Russo 13. ☎ 081-575-6002. Entrees 10€–20€. AE,
DC, MC, V. Lunch & dinner Tues–Sat; lunch Sun.
Reservations required.

Intramoenia Caffè Letterario CITTÀ ANTICA
SNACKS/SANDWICHES When you can't bear to
look at one more pizza or plate of pasta (and it
will happen), grab a light salad or sandwich at
this hip alfresco "literary cafe" on trendy Piazza
Bellini. Piazza Bellini 70. ☎ 081-290988. Entrees
from 5€. AE, DC, MC, V. Lunch & dinner daily.

★★ **La Stanza del Gusto** CHIAIA/SANTA LUCIA
CREATIVE NEAPOLITAN The "Room of Taste"
specializes in cheese and wine and is a great
place to splurge on modern Neapolitan cuisine.
The small restaurant offers a short menu that
strictly utilizes in-season, market-fresh ingredients. Vicoletto Sant'Arpino 21. ☎ 081-401578.
Entrees 10€–18€. AE, DC, MC, V. Dinner Tues–Sat.
Reservations required.

★ kids **Pizzeria Brandi** SANTA LUCIA/CHIAIA
PIZZA/NEAPOLITAN Marketing itself as the
place where the *margherita* (tomato, mozzarella, and basil) pizza was invented (for Queen
Margherita of Savoy in 1889—a reasonable
historic claim), Brandi is one of Naples's most
prominent pizza joints. It's an attractive and fun
spot to dine, with tasty pies. Salita Sant'Anna di
Palazzo 1–2. ☎ 081-416928. Pizzas from 5€. AE,
DC, MC, V. Lunch & dinner daily.

★★ kids **Zi' Teresa** SANTA LUCIA SEAFOOD/
NEAPOLITAN The menu at this standout har-
bor-front restaurant runs the gamut from antipasti of fresh local seafood to entrees piled high
with vegetables and shellfish. It's a Neapolitan
standby for family events, so the best atmosphere is on weekends (book ahead). Borgo
Marinari 1. ☎ 081-7642565. Entrees 13–20€. AE,
DC, MC, V. Lunch & dinner Tues–Sat; lunch Sun.

Capri

If you have a weakness for natural beauty, gorgeous Capri will bring you to your knees. If you like glamour, there's plenty of that here, too, in the island's luxury hotels, boutiques, and see-and-be-seen cafes. And for such a tiny island, there's much to see and do, from the de rigueur Blue Grotto excursion to ancient ruins to spectacular hikes of all difficulty levels. Capri can seem like a tourist machine in high season, but don't let a few pitfalls—like high prices and day-tripping hordes—interfere with your enjoyment of this jewel of the Mediterranean.

> The view of the Faraglione, limestone seastacks, from the Giardini di Augusto.

START Capri is 16km (10 miles) west of Sorrento and 35km (22 miles) south of Naples; access by ferry or hydrofoil. Trip length: from Sorrento about 45 minutes; from Naples about 1 hour.

1 ★ **The Piazzetta.** The island's famed social crossroads is smaller than a basketball court but still Capri's prime spot for people-watching. The four alfresco cafes here are fairly identical, and like all of Capri town, at their best after 5pm, when all the day-trippers have left. If you can't find "La Piazzetta" on a map, it's because the official name is Piazza Umberto I. ⏱ At least 15 min.

2 ★ **Shopping in Capri Town.** Via Camerelle and Via Vittorio Emanuele are lined with luxury boutiques that are happy to take your credit card to the limit. For unique perfumes inspired by the flora and marine climate of Capri (and made right here, too), visit the ★★ **Carthusia Profumi di Capri** shop and factory, Viale Matteotti 2 (☎ 081-8370368). The products make wonderful souvenirs. ⏱ At least 30 min.

3 ★★★ **Faraglioni.** At the end of Via Tragara is a magnificent lookout over the impressive limestone stacks (*Faraglioni*) in the water just off the southeastern tip of the island. If you're

Where to Stay	Where to Dine
Caesar Augustus **15**	Add'ò Riccio **12**
Casa Mariantonia **13**	Aurora **18**
Grand Hotel Quisisana **21**	Barbarossa **14**
J. K. Place **16**	Le Grottelle **19**
La Tosca **20**	Pulalli Wine Bar **17**

1 The Piazzetta
2 Shopping in Capri Town
3 Faraglioni
4 Giardini di Augusto
5 Via Krupp
6 Marina Piccola
7 Arco Naturale & Via Pizzolungo
8 Blue Grotto & Island Tour
9 Villa Jovis
10 Monte Solaro
11 Villa San Michele

Getting Around

Capri's buses and funicular are a convenient way to get around and are run by the private **SIPPIC** (☎ 081-8370429) and **Staiano** (☎ 081-8372422) companies. Single-ride tickets are 1.40€; the hourly (2.10€) and day passes (6.70€) entitle you to only one funicular ride (extra funicular rides cost 1.40€ each, though there's a bus covering the same route that is included in the day pass). Watch out for the packed midday buses between Capri and Anacapri. You can buy tickets on the bus or from the terminal in Capri town.

feeling energetic, there's a path from here down to water level, where you can admire the *Faraglioni* up close and personal, from below. There are also two beach-club-cum-restaurants here—Luigi ai Faraglioni and La Fontelina. ⏱ 15 min., or at least 2 hr. if going to restaurants/ beach clubs. Luigi ai Faraglioni: ☎ 081-8370591. La Fontelina: ☎ 081-8370845. Use of bathing platform and changing rooms is 16€ per person.

4 ★★ **Giardini di Augusto.** This park has blissful views of the Faraglioni. The red-brick paths are lined with geraniums, pines, and manicured lawns. ⏱ 15 min. Via Matteotti.

5 ★★ **Via Krupp.** With its hairpin turns set snug against a sheer rock wall, this spectacular

> *La Piazzetta shows its best side after the day-trippers have left Capri town.*

pedestrian path descends 100m (330 ft.) from the south end of Capri town to the water at Marina Piccola. ⏱ 20 min. Starts at the western end of Via Matteotti.

⑥ ★★ Marina Piccola. The beach here is rocky but scenic, with a beautiful cove of cerulean water. There are beach clubs here where you'll pay upwards of 15€ for a lounger and facilities, or you can just bring a towel and go for a dip in the public central area. ⏱ At least 30 min.

⑦ ★ Arco Naturale & Via Pizzolungo. Nature lovers and fitness freaks can keep busy for days with Capri's rewarding hiking trails (p 594, ❶). The best bet for "amateurs" is the easy trail to the **Arco Naturale** (Natural Arch), a striking rock formation set in the sloping woods. For a calorie-burning outing, extend the hike to the **Grotta di Matermania** and do the length of **Via Pizzolungo.** This challenging but stunningly scenic trail takes you past a Roman cave and around the panoramic southeastern corner of the island, ending up at Via Tragara, overlooking the Faraglioni. (You can also start

the hike from this end, though it involves more stair-climbing.) Bring plenty of water and sunblock. ⏱ 20 min. for Arco Naturale; at least 1 hr. for Pizzolungo.

⑧ ★★★ kids Blue Grotto & Island Tour. Capri's tourist *pièce de résistance* is a rip-off, but it's one of the giddiest things you can do in Italy. The countless postcards you'll see of the Grotta Azzurra do not do even minimal justice to the experience of seeing the electric-blue water in person. Even the process of getting into the grotto is an adventure. Every stage of the Blue Grotto requires cash, so make sure you come prepared.

Most people visit the grotto as part of a boat excursion from Capri's main port (see below), but you can also arrive by land by taking the Grotta Azzurra bus (1.40€) from Anacapri. The light effects are best and the crowds lightest after 3pm.

Upon arrival at the Blue Grotto, you'll board a rowboat that will take you into the cave. The grotto is quite large inside, but the only way to get in is through a tiny sea-level arch in the rock wall—just big enough for your rowboat to pass

> *Visit the Blue Grotto after 3pm to experience the cave's iridescent light at its bluest.*

through, and only when the sea is calm. When the critical time comes to slip into the cave, your trusty boatman will ask you to lie all the way down (noncompliance results in being manhandled into position) so that you don't crack your head open on the low ceiling. Then he'll set down his oars and pull the boat inside with the aid of a chain strung below the vault of the entrance. A few dark and thrillingly bumpy seconds later, you're in, and the full splendor of the Blue Grotto appears as your eyes adjust.

The eerily bright coloring of the Grotta Azzurra is created by sunlight that enters via an underwater arch in the rock wall. The light is filtered by the water, which absorbs the red tones, leaving only the blue ones to pass into the cave. As the boatmen row you around the cave, they sing Neapolitan sea chanties that echo marvelously off the walls.

Amortize some of the expense of seeing the Blue Grotto by making it part of the full-island tour from Marina Grande, which covers every nook and cranny of Capri's dramatic perimeter from an intimate wooden skiff. The cost of the island tour is only 15€, compared with 11€ for the water shuttle service to the Blue Grotto and back. ⏱ 45 min. grotto only; 2 hr. with island tour. No phone. Admission 5€ plus 5€ rowboat fee; transportation (boat or bus) to the grotto is additional. Cash only. Daily 9am–5pm, only when the sea is calm.

9 ★★ **Villa Jovis.** ⏱ 2 hr. See p 582, **4**.

10 ★★ kids **Monte Solaro.** At 589m (2,062 ft.), Capri's highest peak affords top-of-the-world views over the island's craggy topography and the surrounding Mediterranean. From Anacapri, you can ride the rickety old chairlift to the summit or make the trek (on a shady, gradual path) on foot. ⏱ At least 1 hr. No phone. Chairlift 8€ round-trip. Daily 9am–5:30pm.

11 ★★ **Villa San Michele.** Swedish doctor and writer Axel Munthe's (1857–1949) Anacapri manor boasts a wealth of antiquities and objets d'art as well as sultry gardens and sublime cliff-edge views. ⏱ 45 min. Viale Axel Munthe. ☎ 081-8371401. Admission 5€. Daily 9:30am–4:30pm.

Where to Stay

> *The renowned infinity pool at the Caesar Augustus.*

★★★ kids Caesar Augustus ANACAPRI
There are hotels with more obvious glitz on Capri, but for a relaxing retreat, the Caesar Augustus gets my vote. The bright yellow villa is fronted by gardens and backed by terraces (and a famed infinity pool) that hang over sheer cliffs, and it's the vertiginous views that make this place such a showstopper. Via G. Orlandi 4. ☎ 081-8373395. www. caesar-augustus.com. 56 units. Doubles 430€–550€. AE, DC, MC, V.

★★ Casa Mariantonia ANACAPRI
This superstylish guest house makes an ideal base for those wanting to experience the more authentic side of the island. The immaculately restored, peach-toned villa is surrounded by fragrant lemon trees, and the fresh and airy rooms open on to a communal terrace. Proprietress Vivica Canale and her staff will personally help you make the most of your stay. Via G. Orlandi 180. ☎ 081-8372923. www. casamariantonia.com. 9 units. Doubles 140€–220€. AE, DC, MC, V.

★★★ kids Grand Hotel Quisisana CAPRI
Movers and shakers with a taste and budget for luxury need look no further than the historic "Quisi," the apex of classy Caprese hospitality. Each guest room is unique but all are light and airy, with private terraces and great views. Given its snug surroundings (it's in the heart of Capri town), the property is remarkably large, with all the expected amenities. Via Camerelle 2. ☎ 081-8370788. 150 units. Doubles from 400€. AE, DC, MC, V.

★★★ J. K. Place MARINA GRANDE
Practically cantilevered over the water just west of the port, this white mansion is an all-around stunner, with ultrastylish decorative accents in the common areas and cosmopolitan flair and clever design in the guest rooms. Expansive teak terraces, with views over the sea to Vesuvius, wrap around the building. The staff is wonderfully attentive and engaging. Via Provinciale Marina Grande 225. ☎ 081-8384001. www.jkcapri.com. 22 units. Doubles 500€–700€. AE, DC, MC, V.

★★ La Tosca CAPRI
Beloved of island habitues on a budget, this simple inn run by the *gentilissimo* Ettore Castelli is the antithesis of the showy consumerism so prevalent in Capri town. Rooms are basic but immaculate and homey, and you will always feel well taken care of by the reception staff. Always book well in advance. Via Birago 5. ☎ 081-8370989. E-mail: h.tosca@capri.it. 11 units. Doubles 70€–140€. AE, DC, MC, V.

Where to Dine

> *Aurora is the place to spend a little extra on a special dinner.*

★★★ **Add'ò Riccio** GROTTA AZZURRA *CAPRESE/ SEAFOOD* The most down-to-earth, high-quality restaurant on Capri. There are no flights of fancy on the menu, just generous portions of homey Caprese and Neapolitan standards made with the best ingredients. Best for lunch. Località Grotta Azzurra. ☎ 081-8371380. Entrees 8€–18€. AE, DC, MC, V. June–Sept lunch & dinner daily; Mar–May and Oct lunch daily.

★★ **Aurora** CAPRI *CAPRESE*
A great splurge choice in Capri town, the Aurora is a venerable family-run culinary institution that consistently turns out top-notch cuisine with warm, impeccable service to boot. Menu offerings adhere mostly to Caprese tradition, though ingredients are a bit more creative here than anywhere else, and the presentations are gorgeous. Via Fuorlovado 18/22. ☎ 081-8370181. Entrees 10€–20€. AE, DC, MC, V. Apr–Dec lunch & dinner daily.

★ kids **Barbarossa** ANACAPRI *PIZZA/ITALIAN*
There's no cachet or glamour in eating at this bilevel *ristorante-pizzeria,* with TVs that broadcast all the big Italian league soccer games. But it is a comfortable place to watch some sports with animated fellow patrons and fill up for less than 15€ a head. Via Porta 1 (Piazza Vittoria). ☎ 081-8371483. Entrees 5€–10€. AE, DC, MC, V. Lunch & dinner daily.

★ **Le Grottelle** CAPRI/ARCO NATURALE *CAPRESE*
There's no better place to rest your feet and refuel after the Arco Naturale hike than this elegant restaurant. The dining terrace looks out over woods and the steep hillside to the crystalline water far below. Try the homemade ravioli *alla caprese,* perfect pillows with the freshest tomato and ricotta. Via Arco Naturale. ☎ 081-8375719. Entrees 11€–20€. AE, DC, MC, V. Apr–Oct lunch & dinner daily.

★ **Pulalli Wine Bar** CAPRI *WINE BAR/SNACKS*
A mellower and more stylish alternative to the four Piazzetta cafes, this hip little *enoteca* next to the clock tower has a great wine list (by the glass or bottle), appetizers, and small plates. Piazza Umberto I 4. ☎ 081-8374108. Small plates from 6€. AE, DC, MC, V. Lunch & dinner Wed–Mon.

Dining Tip

Most restaurants on Capri are ridiculously overpriced. To offset the expense of eating out, I recommend picking up picnic supplies or pizza by the slice for at least some of your meals. Tucked along the back streets of Capri town, you'll find minimarkets where you can stock up on provisions or have a simple panino made. In Anacapri, **Liberato Pollio's,** Via Trieste e Trento (near the church piazza of Santa Sofia), is a friendly deli/market that sells a full range of cheeses and meats and inexpensive wine.

Positano

It doesn't matter whether you're up close, peering down its narrow back streets, or far away, gazing upon the astonishingly vertical town from offshore, Positano is postcard-perfect any way you look at it. Of the Amalfi Coast towns, it's certainly the most glamorous—though quietly so, so don't come expecting a rollicking nightlife. Positano has a wealth of attractive places to dine and shop, and though there's not much in the way of sightseeing in the town itself, Positano's handy boat and bus connections make it a good base for day trips around the region, whether over to Capri or down the coast to Amalfi and Ravello.

> Impossibly stacked Positano makes a convenient, if crowded, base on the Amalfi Coast.

START Positano is 14km/9 miles east of Sorrento and 17km/11 miles west of Amalfi on the SS163 (via SITA bus). Trip length: from both Sorrento and Amalfi about 30 minutes.

1 Santa Maria Assunta. Positano's one and only proper "sight" is its Duomo, whose Moorish, Vietri-tile-covered dome is the standout feature on the lower town's skyline. The baroque white stucco interior is accented in gold and contains such art treasures as a *Circumcision* by Santafede and the town's most prized religious relic: a 13th-century Byzantine wood panel depicting the Virgin Mary and Child. Legend has it the panel was once stolen by Saracen raiders, but as they tried to sail away with the booty, the seas became angry and a

voice from on high told them *"posa, posa"* ("put it back"), which they did. The *posa* part of the story, locals say, is how Positano got its name. ⏲ 15 min. Via dei Mulini. No phone. Free admission. Daily 7am–8pm.

2 ★★★ Sea Excursions. Positano's busy port is filled with charter outfits that will take you for half- or full-day boat excursions—a must while you're on the Amalfi Coast. The waters are clear, warm, and mostly calm, and trips usually involve an anchor drop where you can dive in for a swim. One of the better companies is **Lucibello,** which organizes group and custom private trips to places such as the Grotta dello Smeraldo and the Li Galli islands that aren't served by regular ferries and hydrofoils. If you're feeling adventurous,

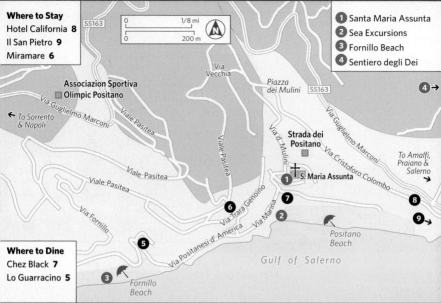

Where to Stay
Hotel California **8**
Il San Pietro **9**
Miramare **6**

SS163
0 ___ 1/8 mi
0 ___ 200 m

1 Santa Maria Assunta
2 Sea Excursions
3 Fornillo Beach
4 Sentiero degli Dei

Via Vecchia

Associazion Sportiva
Olimpic Positano

Via Guglielmo Marconi

← To Sorrento
& Napoli

Viale Pasitea

Piazza
dei Mulini SS163

Via Guglielmo Marconi

Strada dei
Positano

Via di Mulini

Via Cristoforo Colombo

S. Maria Assunta

To Amalfi,
Praiano &
Salerno →

Viale Pasitea

Viale Pasitea

Via Fornillo

Via Trara Genoino

Via Positanesi d' America

Via Marina

Positano
Beach

Where to Dine
Chez Black **7**
Lo Guarracino **5**

Gulf of Salerno

Fornillo
Beach

Getting Around

The local **Flavio Gioia** buses, Via C. Colombo 9, Positano (☎ 089-811895; www.flaviogioia.com), are small orange buses that travel squiggly Viale Pasitea (the main street) and to the nearby town of Praiano, making intermediate stops at certain hotels and restaurants along the way. A one-way ticket costs 1.20€ and can be bought in *tabacchi* shops or on the bus. That said, the only way to get all the way up or down steep Positano is with your own two feet, so plan your outings accordingly—or else just come home with super-toned quads.

> *Chartering a boat allows you to experience parts of the coast that most visitors don't see.*

you can also rent your own boat from Lucibello (highly recommended) and jaunt over to Capri (nothing makes you feel more glamorous than piloting your "own" boat around the island). No skipper ambitions? You can also rent canoes and pedal boats for closer-to-shore exploration. ⏱ At least 2 hr. Lucibello: Via del Brigantino 9. ☎ 089-875032. www.lucibello.it. Excursions from 10€ per person. Self-captained motorboat rentals from 100€ a day, plus fuel (around 50€ for 2 people). Open daily May–Sept.

3 ★ **Fornillo Beach.** If you're looking to swim, skip the crowded and pebbly Spiaggia Grande

in town, and head west of the port to Spiaggia del Fornillo. Fornillo is much more scenic and less crowded—the clear winner if you're considering spending a full day on the sand. ⏱ At least 1 hr. See also p 579.

4 ★★★ **Sentiero degli Dei.** The coast's most spectacular hiking trail can be accessed from the village of Nocelle, a 20-minute ride from central Positano on the Montepertuso-Nocelle bus line operated by Flavio Gioia. ⏱ ½ day or more. See p 595, 2, for details.

Authentic Praiano

Ask any Amalfi Coast hotel staffer, restaurant waiter, or bus driver where they live, and chances are it won't be Positano, Amalfi, or Ravello: Instead, they'll tell you they're from ★★ **Praiano.**

Only 6km (4 miles) south of Positano, Praiano is a bustling village with a position just as spectacular as its more famous neighbors but little of the international hype that's made those other places so touristy. When you've had enough of Positano's identical resort wear shops and 5€ cappuccinos, hop on a bus to Praiano for a real slice of *vita costierina.*

Ground zero of Praiano social life is ★★ **Bar del Sole,** Via G. Capriglione 120, where you can get coffee or a glass of Prosecco and watch local life play out. Just about every resident of Praiano, young and old, passes through here at least once a day. If you see a 40-ish Eric Clapton look-alike, that's Peppe, who restores and sells vintage saxophones on eBay for a living. He speaks some English and will excitedly talk about jazz with you if you've got a few hours to spare. You might also see Gennaro, a 30-ish guy with curly brown hair, who runs the One Fire Beach club in the summer and works for his family's plumbing business in the off season. Gennaro's grandfather is the namesake of the town thoroughfare, Via Gennaro Capriglione. Praiano is a place where everyone really does know everyone else's name, and if you spend just a little time here, you'll find a much more personal experience than anywhere else on the coast.

Praiano also has some of the coast's best and most authentic restaurants and drinking holes. ★ **Ristorante La Brace** (p 599, ❸) is a locals' favorite (and many a hotel concierge's) for exquisite, simple preparations of pasta and seafood. Closer to the water (there are many steps involved), in a cove called Cala Gavitella, is the eponymous ★★ **Ristorante La Gavitella,** Via Gavitella 1 (☎ 089-8131319; lunch & dinner daily May–Oct; entrees 10€–18€; AE, DC, MC, V), a fresh and airy spot with sea breezes and blissful views of the rugged coastline and Positano. The specialties here are seafood pastas with fresh local herbs and vegetables, as well as excellent grilled fish. For after-dinner entertainment, the sidewalk tables of the ★ **cocktail bar at Le Fioriere** hotel, Via G. Capriglione 138 (☎ 089-874203), are where the action is.

To reach Praiano from Positano, take the (local) orange Flavio Gioia bus service or the (regional) blue SITA bus. From Amalfi, take the SITA bus. See p 631 for more details.

Where to Stay & Dine

★ **Chez Black** CENTRO *SOUTHERN ITALIAN*
Of the half-dozen restaurants under the arcades by the port, this is the most stylish choice, with yacht-style decor and the most charming young waitstaff in town. Serving standard regional fare in a lively alfresco setting, it's ideal for lunch or for watching the parade go by over predinner cocktails. Via del Brigantino 19-21. ☎ 089-875036. www.chezblack.it. Entrees 10€–20€. AE, DC, MC, V. Lunch & dinner daily.

★ **Hotel California** CENTRO
For simple accommodations, nothing beats the Hotel California. Rooms in the 18th-century original structure (featured in the movie *Under the Tuscan Sun*) are far preferable to those in the 1968 addition. The hospitality is warm, though proprietress Maria can come on a little strong. Via Cristoforo Colombo 141. ☎ 089-875382. www. hotelcaliforniapositano.com. 15 units. Doubles 150€–185€. AE, DC, MC, V.

★★★ **Il San Pietro** SOUTH OF POSITANO
The San Pietro boasts the most magnificent location (it's set in a cliff) and physical plant of any hotel on the coast, and its relaxed and secluded feel make it popular with honeymooners and older couples. All guest rooms have stunning views from their private terraces. There's free shuttle service to Positano and back at all hours. Via Laurito 2 (2km/1¼ miles from Positano). ☎ 089-875455. www.ilsanpietro.it. 62 units. Doubles 420€–600€. AE, DC, MC, V.

★★ **Lo Guarracino** CENTRO *SOUTHERN ITALIAN*
Overlooking the sand at the Spiaggia del Fornillo, this vine-covered terrace is Positano's best bet for true waterfront dining (and removed from the worst crowds). Be here at sunset for the most romantic experience, and order the house specialty, lemon pasta. Via Positanesi d'America 12. ☎ 089-875794. Entrees 12€–22€. AE, DC, MC, V. Lunch & dinner daily. Reservations recommended.

★★ **Miramare** CENTRO
This lovely inn run by Rosita and Nicola may be Positano's best midrange option. Rooms are classic, with terra-cotta floor tiles and warm antiques, and many have terraces. Try to book

> *A taste of the sea at Lo Guarracino.*

room 215, a corner unit with dazzling views over the town—from the terrace and a huge plate-glass window above the tub. Via Trara Genoino 27. ☎ 089-875002. www.miramarepositano.it. 18 units. Doubles 185€–290€. AE, DC, MC, V.

Dining Tip

Eating all your meals out in Positano gets very expensive very quickly. Luckily, tucked into the narrow streets that descend from Via Cristoforo Colombo to the port there are a number of little markets where you can get simple sandwiches or stock up on picnic supplies.

Ravello

Just when you thought the Amalfi Coast couldn't possibly get any more stunning, along comes Ravello, with views that trump all. And unlike Positano and Amalfi, the town of Ravello actually has a few "sights" worth seeing, first and foremost of which is the impossibly gorgeous Villa Cimbrone gardens. Connected by SITA bus to Amalfi, Ravello works well as a few hours' excursion for those staying elsewhere on the coast or in Sorrento.

> To access all areas at Villa Cimbrone you'll need to stay there, but the gardens are open to all.

START Ravello is east of Sorrento and Amalfi on the SS163 and SS373 (by car or bus). Trip length: from Sorrento (38km/24 miles), about 1 hour; from Amalfi (7km/4 miles), about 15 minutes.

1 ★★ **Villa Rufolo.** Richard Wagner composed part of his opera *Parsifal* here, in the sultry gardens of this Arab-inspired villa just off Ravello's main square. Villa Rufolo was originally built in the 13th century and became a public heritage site in 1975. Each summer, during the Ravello festival, concerts featuring Wagner's music are held here, on a terrace 340m (1,115 ft.) above the sea. ⏱ 45 min. Piazza Duomo. ☎ 089-857657. Admission 5€. Daily 9am–6pm.

2 ★ **Duomo.** Ravello's cathedral is a wonderful example of Romanesque architecture. On the right side of the nave, don't miss the Ambone dell'Epistola, with its adorable ★★ **12th-century mosaics of Jonah and the whale.** ⏱ 1 hr. Piazza Vescovado. ☎ 089-858311. Free admission. Daily 9am–1pm, 4–7pm.

3 ★★★ **Villa Cimbrone.** Dainty majolica signs point the way along a sloping footpath that takes you seemingly farther and farther away from civilization, to the most awesomely romantic gardens in southern Italy. The initial sight of Villa Cimbrone is enchanting enough: medieval cloisters and pavilions are surrounded by lush greens, and charming flower beds, ponds, and patinated statuary are haphazardly dotted here and there among the lawns. But what everyone comes away gasping about is the ★★★ **Terrazza dell'Infinito.** At the far end of the property, this stone parapet, lined with Roman portrait busts, rests on a sheer cliff and offers the most extraordinary, vertigo-inducing views into the great blue of sky and sea beyond. Gore Vidal called it "the most beautiful panorama in the world." ⏱ 1½ hr., including the walk there and back. Via Santa Chiara 26. ☎ 089-857459. www.villacimbrone.com. Admission 6€. Daily 9am–6pm.

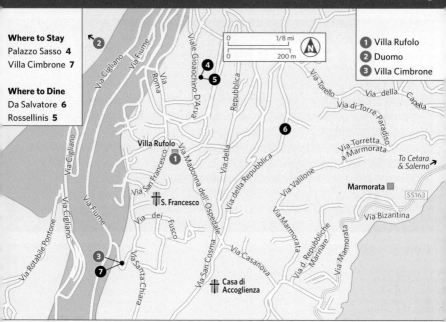

Where to Stay
Palazzo Sasso **4**
Villa Cimbrone **7**

Where to Dine
Da Salvatore **6**
Rossellinis **5**

1 Villa Rufolo
2 Duomo
3 Villa Cimbrone

Where to Stay & Dine

★★ Da Salvatore CENTRO *SOUTHERN ITALIAN*
Ravello's best bet for views and value, this panoramic restaurant offers unfussy but delicious local cuisine such as fresh tomato pastas and grilled fish. The atmosphere is relaxed and the panoramas sublime. Via della Repubblica 2. ☎ 089-857227. Entrees 12€–18€. AE, DC, MC, V. Apr–Oct lunch & dinner daily; Nov–Mar closed Tues.

★★★ Palazzo Sasso CENTRO
Luxurious yet down-to-earth, the Moorish peach palazzo has supremely comfortable and well-appointed rooms; all have mountain or sea views. Staff are bright and responsive. Via San Giovanni del Toro 28. ☎ 089-818181. www.palazzosasso.com. Doubles 320€–650€. AE, DC, MC, V.

★★★ Rossellinis CENTRO *CREATIVE ITALIAN*
The chicest place to dine in Ravello is at this two-Michelin-star restaurant. It's surprisingly unpretentious, and chef Pino Lavarra's amazing food and the views from the terrace justify the

> *All rooms come with a view at Palazzo Sasso.*

splurge. Via San Giovanni del Toro 28, in Palazzo Sasso. ☎ 089-818181. Entrees 16€–30€. AE, DC, MC, V. Apr–Oct dinner daily; closed Nov–Mar. Reservations essential.

★★ Villa Cimbrone CENTRO
Upgrades have made this former aristocratic residence (the estate attached to the gardens of the same name) a wonderful little hotel with historic character. Some rooms have gorgeous vaulted ceilings with original frescoes; all have hydro-massage tubs. It's a pleasant 15-minute walk from central Ravello. Via Santa Chiara 26. ☎ 089-857459. www.villacimbrone.com. 19 units. Doubles 380€–550€. AE, DC, MC, V.

Sorrento

If you want some insight into the sunny personality of this picturesque resort, just ask a local to pronounce the name of the town: What you'll hear is not Soh-*rehn*-toh but Sur-ri-*en*-toh—an enthusiastic utterance that seems to have four or five *R*s in it and makes the speaker smile just to form the sounds. While Sorrento doesn't have any major "sights" apart from its dramatic natural setting, the town's role as a lively nexus where happy holidaymakers constitute the general population is appealing enough. With easy access to Pompeii, Naples, the Amalfi Coast, and Capri, this resort town makes an ideal base for exploring just about everything in this chapter.

> *Etruscans, Greeks, Romans, and now keen shoppers have all colonized this pretty seaside resort, just an hour from Naples.*

START Sorrento is 50km/31 miles south of Naples. Trip length: about 1 hour by car, Circumvesuviana train, or ferry.

1 ★ **Piazza Tasso.** The nerve center of Sorrento is this busy traffic roundabout, where buses stop and taxis line up—anyone staying in Sorrento passes through here at least once a day. Piazza Tasso is lined with bars where you can grab a quick bite or drink; at sunset, don't miss the rapturous view from the terraces facing the sea. ⏲ At least 10 min.

2 ★★ **Vallone dei Mulini.** Just behind Piazza Tasso is an immense gorge, hundreds of feet deep, where dense groves of ilex trees grow alongside the steep rock walls. In the valley, there are also ruins of old stone mills (*mulini*) that used to run off a river here. Stand on the road just past the hotel Antiche Mura for the

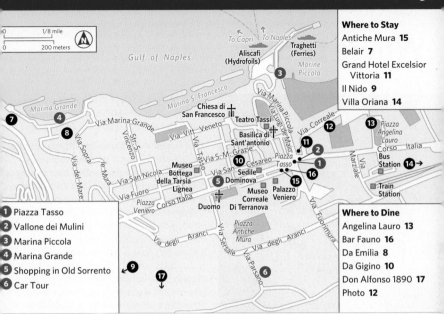

Where to Stay
Antiche Mura **15**
Belair **7**
Grand Hotel Excelsior Vittoria **11**
Il Nido **9**
Villa Oriana **14**

1 Piazza Tasso
2 Vallone dei Mulini
3 Marina Piccola
4 Marina Grande
5 Shopping in Old Sorrento
6 Car Tour

Where to Dine
Angelina Lauro **13**
Bar Fauno **16**
Da Emilia **8**
Da Gigino **10**
Don Alfonso 1890 **17**
Photo **12**

best view. In the early 20th century, the mills became defunct when part of the valley was filled in for the construction of Piazza Tasso. Sorrento's beautiful natural gorge continues on the seaward side of Piazza Tasso down to Marina Piccola. ☉ 15 min.

③ ★ **Marina Piccola.** Sorrento's two ports are confusingly named: Marina Piccola is actually bigger than Marina Grande and where most tourist activity takes place. All the boats for Capri, the Amalfi Coast, and Naples depart from and arrive here. The walk down here from Piazza Tasso is easy enough—allow 15 minutes if you're catching a boat—but you'll save yourself some huffing and puffing on the way back up by hopping on a local orange bus. ☉ At least 10 min. Walk or take the bus from Piazza Tasso.

④ ★ **Marina Grande.** The quieter of the town's two ports is used mostly by fishermen. There are some great restaurants where you can get an authentic seafood meal with locals. (See Da Emilia on p 627.) ☉ At least 10 min. Take a bus from Piazza Tasso.

⑤ ★★ **Shopping in Old Sorrento.** Even if you have no retail agenda, it's hard to resist the tiny boutiques that line the warren of narrow streets in old Sorrento. Lemons—the official fruit of the region—are represented in every form imaginable, and lemon-themed knickknacks make inexpensive souvenirs that will surely always remind you of this part of your trip! High-fashion boutiques can be found along Corso Italia (in either direction from Piazza Tasso), and there's a COIN department store at Via S. Cesareo 39. ☉ At least 1 hr.

⑥ ★ **Take a Car Tour.** If you want to see a lot of Campania in a short amount of time—such as the greatest hits of the Amalfi Coast or a visit to the Paestum temples, otherwise time-consuming to reach by public transportation—your best bet may be to hire a car and driver. Sorrento-based **Autoservizi di Martino** offers private excursions all over the area from 35€ per hour for a midsize sedan, 60€ per hour for a six- to eight-person van, for a minimum of 5 hours. The friendly staff can also help design custom itineraries for you, whether your interests tend toward volcano-trekking on Mt. Vesuvius or exploring under-the-radar towns along the coast. They also offer Naples airport transfers to and from Sorrento (from 80€). ☉ 5 hr. or more. Via Parsano 8D. ☎ 081-8782801. www.autoservizidemartino.com.

Where to Stay

> *Antiche Mura has the best location in town, right on Sorrento's main piazza.*

★★ kids **Antiche Mura** CENTRO

The best midrange choice in central Sorrento is this modern palazzo overlooking Piazza Tasso on one side and the dramatic gorge of the Valle dei Mulini on the other. Rooms are comfortable if a tad bland, and many units have panoramic balconies. **Piazza Tasso 1.** ☎ 081-8073523. www.hotelantichemura.com. 46 units. Doubles 100€–250€. AE, DC, MC, V.

★★ **Belair** WEST OF CENTRO

A bit removed from the bustle of central Sorrento, this somewhat faded beauty is still an excellent hotel with a surprisingly good restaurant, a delightful staff, and stunning views of Vesuvius and the bay from all rooms. **Via Capo 29.** ☎ 081-8071622. www.belair.it. 49 units. Doubles 180€–300€. AE, DC, MC, V.

★★★ **Grand Hotel Excelsior Vittoria** CENTRO

The grandest dame in town occupies real estate so central and prized it's hard to believe it's private property. Rooms are distributed between three 19th-century buildings on a cliff directly above Marina Piccola (which can be accessed by the hotel's private elevator—a major bonus). Each building has unique historic flair (one is Art Nouveau, another is faux Swiss chalet), though amenities are the same throughout. Five acres of verdant grounds, set well back from the street noise, make this a wonderful retreat. **Piazza Tasso 34.** ☎ 081-8777111. www.exvitt.it. 96 units. Doubles 275€–550€. AE, DC, MC, V.

★ **Il Nido** HILLS

These great value accommodations are set in the hills above Sorrento. Many rooms have fabulous views over the cliffs of the peninsula to Mt. Vesuvius, and a free hourly shuttle takes guests to Piazza Tasso and the Circumvesuviana station. **Via Nastro Verde 62.** ☎ 081-8782766. www.ilnido.it. 27 units. Doubles 100€–120€. AE, DC, MC, V.

★★★ **Villa Oriana** SAN'AGNELLO

In all my years of traveling in Italy, I have never met anyone more suited to her vocation than Maria d'Esposito, the hostess at this B&B in the hills just east of Sorrento. A ray of sunshine incarnate, Maria sees to all guests' needs, from breakfast to sunset cocktails, while her trendy son Pasquale handles the business side of things. Come for the splendid, relaxing setting; stay for the sheer charm of the d'Esposito family: This kind of hands-on hospitality is getting harder and harder to find in Italy's mainstream destinations. **Via Rubinacci 1.** ☎ 081-8782468. www.villaoriana.it. 10 units. Doubles from 75€. AE, DC, MC, V.

Where to Dine

★ **Angelina Lauro** CENTRO *SNACKS*
Conveniently located near the Circumvesuviana train station, this *tavola calda* (hot snack bar) has all kinds of pastas, roasted veggies, and pizzas available to go. Piazza Angelina Lauro 39/40. ☎ 081-8074097. Entrees from 3.50€. No credit cards. Daily 10am–8pm.

★ **Bar Fauno** CENTRO *CAFE*
The most venerable watering hole on Piazza Tasso is a great place to rest your feet and watch the parade of Sorrento holidaymakers go by. Piazza Tasso 13–15. ☎ 081-8781135. Drinks and snacks from 3€. AE, DC, MC, V. Daily 7am–midnight or later.

★★ **Da Emilia** MARINA GRANDE *SEAFOOD*
Overlooking the fishing harbor of Marina Grande, this family-run trattoria with checkered tablecloths is southern Italian simplicity at its best. Order one of the pastas with fresh seafood, and you won't come away hungry or disappointed. Via Marina Grande 61. ☎ 081-8072720. Entrees 7€–15€. No credit cards.

★ **Da Gigino** CENTRO *ITALIAN*
For a broad menu of basic but well-executed local fare at a fair price, it's tough to beat centrally located Gigino's. The waiters are especially charming and efficient, and the Neapolitan-style pizzas are some of the best in town. Via degli Archi 15. ☎ 081-8781927. Entrees 6€–16€. AE, DC, MC, V. Lunch & dinner Wed-Mon.

★★ **Don Alfonso 1890** SANT'AGATA SUI DUE GOLFI *ITALIAN* Sorrento's splash-out gourmet experience is a bus ride (or more likely, a cab ride) away in the seaside hamlet of Sant'Agata. The refined Campanian cuisine and service truly wow, though the dining room is rather brightly lit, with a decor more appropriate for brunch than an expensive dinner. Corso Sant'Agata 11/13, Sant'Agata sui Due Golfi. ☎ 081-8780561. www.donalfonso.com. Tasting menus 30€–145€ per person. AE, DC, MC, V. Lunch & dinner daily. Reservations required. SITA bus to Sant'Agata sui Due Golfi.

> *Buffet dining at Angelina Lauro.*

★★ **Photo** CENTRO *ITALIAN*
If the resorty vibe and kitschy lemon paraphernalia in Sorrento get to be too much, head to this bar-cum-restaurant, which also doubles as a photography gallery (hence the name). For all its contemporary trappings, the food here is fairly traditional, though presentation is artful. It's a popular *aperitivo* spot for vacationers and hip locals alike, and small plates and cocktails are served until late. Via Correale 19. ☎ 081-8773686. Entrees from 9€. AE, DC, MC, V. Daily 4pm–late.

Amalfi

If the towns on the Amalfi Coast were sisters, Positano would be the attention-getting, popular younger sibling and Amalfi would be the older one who has more personality. Amalfi is the real working town on the coast, with a busy port and a history as a naval power that far precedes the advent of tourism here. If you want to be enveloped by postcard perfection, stay in Positano, but if you want a dash of real vita costerina ("coastal life") along with your stunning views and sunsets, try Amalfi.

> *The Arab-Norman Duomo is the centerpiece of the atmospheric coastal town of Amalfi.*

START **Amalfi** is east of Sorrento and Positano on the SS163 (via SITA bus) and south and east of Naples on the A3 and SS163 (via SITA bus). Trip length: from Sorrento, 31km/19 miles, about 45 minutes; from Positano, 19km/12 miles, about 30 minutes; from Naples, 72km/45 miles, about 1¼ hour.

➊ ★★ **Duomo.** At the cathedral of Sant'Andrea, a theatrical set of stairs leads up from the main piazza to an Arab-Norman facade done up in striking bands of white and black stone. Inside, the baroque nave is clad with opulent 18th-century marble panels. ⏱ 30 min. Piazza del Duomo. ☎ 089-871324. Free admission to church;

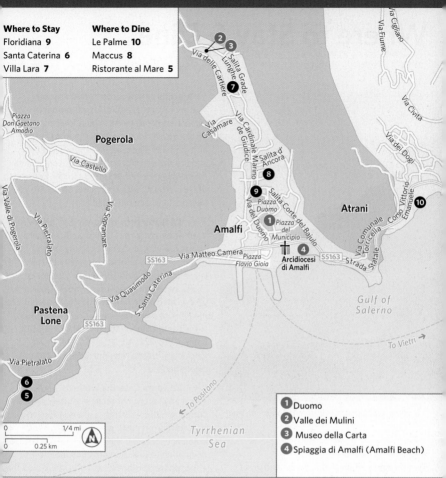

Where to Stay	Where to Dine
Floridiana **9**	Le Palme **10**
Santa Caterina **6**	Maccus **8**
Villa Lara **7**	Ristorante al Mare **5**

1 Duomo
2 Valle dei Mulini
3 Museo della Carta
4 Spiaggia di Amalfi (Amalfi Beach)

crypt and cloister 2.50€. Daily Mar–June and Oct 9am–6:45pm; July–Sept 9am–7:45pm; Nov–Feb 10am–1pm, 2:30–4:30pm.

2 ★★ **Valle dei Mulini.** Amalfi's classic excursion is this scenic walk inland, past the edge of town, and up into the Valley of the Mills. In this tranquil landscape, you'll find shady vegetation, waterfalls, and the ruins of abandoned paper mills. ⏱ 2 hr.

3 ★ **Museo della Carta.** On the way back into town, stop at the Paper Museum, which attests to the area's history of papermaking, with interesting exhibits and demonstrations. Fine paper products are still made in Amalfi and can be purchased here and at several shops in town. ⏱ 1 hr. Via delle Cartiere 24. ☎ 089-8304561. Admission 3.50€; includes guided tour. Daily 10am–6:30pm.

4 ★ **Spiaggia di Amalfi (Amalfi Beach).** The coast isn't known for broad sandy shores, but the gray-sand beach on the east side of the port is perfectly suitable for a dip (it's protected from marina traffic by a jetty), especially late in the afternoon when all you want is a quick cool-down in the Mediterranean. ⏱ 1 hr. Access from Piazza Flavio Gioia.

Where to Stay & Dine

> *Informal glamour at the luxurious Santa Caterina.*

★ **Floridiana** CENTRO
This tiny gem offers great service and great value smack in the heart of town. The modern rooms are bright and clean. Don't miss the amazing 18th-century frescoes and stucco work in the grandiose lounge/breakfast room. Salita Brancia 1. ☎ 089-8736373. www.hotelfloridiana.it. 7 units. Doubles 110€–140€. AE, DC, MC, V.

★★ **Le Palme** ATRANI SOUTHERN ITALIAN
To sample the highest quality, family-style *cucina amalfitana* for a very reasonable tab, head to this casual restaurant in the village of Atrani. Don't even bother with the menu: Instead, just tell your waiter how hungry you are and let the kitchen craft your dinner. Supportico Marinella 10, Atrani. ☎ 089-871495. Entrees 7€–14€. AE, DC, MC, V. Lunch & dinner Thurs–Tues.

★★ **Maccus** CENTRO SOUTHERN ITALIAN
The best place to eat in Amalfi proper is this attractive trattoria, which focuses on prime-quality local ingredients from sea and land. On weekend evenings, live music adds to the warmth and festivity. Largo Santa Maria Maggiore 1/3. ☎ 089-8736385. Entrees 9€–18€. AE, DC, MC, V. Lunch & dinner Fri–Wed. Reservations recommended.

★★★ kids **Ristorante al Mare** WEST OF AMALFI
SOUTHERN ITALIAN This relaxed (kids and shorts are welcome) hotel dining "room" is a bamboo-roofed alfresco terrace with splendid views of Amalfi bay. The menu consists of lovely, barely-dressed-up regional classics, as well as an overflowing antipasto plate that's a meal on its own. Via Mauro Comite 9 (SS163), in the Santa Caterina (below). ☎ 089-871012. Entrees 14€–22€. AE, DC, MC, V. May–Oct lunch daily; closed Nov–Apr. Reservations recommended.

★★★ kids **Santa Caterina** WEST OF AMALFI
This is my favorite hotel in all of Italy, with a stunning natural setting; a glamorous pool; sea views from every guest room; the best breakfast spread in the region; and a heartfelt dedication to real, personal hospitality. The atmosphere is informal, but you still get all the amenities you'd expect of a luxury hotel. Via Mauro Comite 9 (SS163). ☎ 089-871012. www. hotelsantacaterina.it. 66 units. Doubles 240€–710€. AE, DC, MC, V.

★★ **Villa Lara** CENTRO
Practically attached to the side of a cliff, this panoramic and exceptionally sweet little hotel is "in town" but removed from the summer crowds. Rooms are awash in—and named for—bright colors; many have breathtaking views over the rooftops of Amalfi to the sea. Via delle Cartiere 1. ☎ 089-8736358. www.villalara.it. 7 units. Doubles 90€–195€. AE, DC, MC, V.

Naples & Campania Fast Facts

Accommodations Booking Services

The California-based **Amalfi Rentals** (☎ 415/499-9490; www.amalfirentals.com) specializes in villas along the Amalfi Coast and on the islands of Capri and Ischia. Four-person rentals start at $1600 weekly. **Porta Napoli** (www.hotel.portanapoli.com) has a good range of apartment rental listings in the city of Naples and a mostly affordable selection of villas and apartments on the islands, in Sorrento, and on the Amalfi Coast. Two-person units start at 70€ per day.

American Express

There are no American Express offices in Naples or the Amalfi Coast. For information on the office in Rome, see p 148.

ATMs/Cashpoints

You'll have no trouble finding cash machines (bancomat). They're always attached to banks (banca, banco, credito, cassa), which are ubiquitous in Naples and in touristy places such as Capri and Positano. Even small towns off the beaten path have at least one bank with an ATM. Italy generally uses 4-digit PINs; if you have a 6-digit PIN, check with your bank.

Dentists & Doctors

If you have a mild medical issue or dental problem, most hotels will be able to refer you to a local doctor (medico) or dentist (dentista) who speaks English. Fees are generally between 75€ and 100€. Otherwise, go to the pronto soccorso (emergency room) at the nearest hospital, where they'll treat your immediate problem (for example, a sprained ankle) for free and give you a short course of prescription drugs if necessary.

Emergencies

For general emergencies, call ☎ **112** for the Carabinieri or ☎ **113** for the Polizia. Call ☎ **114** for an ambulance and ☎ **115** for the fire department. For a medical emergency that doesn't require an ambulance, see "Dentists & Doctors," above. To report lost or stolen items, see "Police," p 632.

Getting There

BY PLANE Naples's airport, **Capodichino** (☎ 081-7896259; www.gesac.it), is only 10km (6¼ miles) from the city center and served by several daily flights from Rome, Milan, Venice, and other European cities. From May to October, **Eurofly** (☎ 800-459-0581 toll-free in the U.S.; www.euroflyusa.com) also operates several nonstop flights per week between New York's JFK airport and Naples. Naples airport transfers to or from Sorrento start at 80€; to or from Positano or Amalfi, the price jumps to 130€. **BY TRAIN** Naples is easily accessible by train from all over Europe. The main train station is **Napoli Centrale–Piazza Garibaldi** (☎ 081-5543188). For information on train travel in Italy, see p 723.

Getting Around

On the average trip to Campania, you won't need to rent a car. The driving on the Amalfi Coast's magnificent corniche road is best left to someone else, so that you can enjoy the view!

The region's transportation network is efficient, reliable, and generally inexpensive. Nearly all hotels can provide you with up-to-date information about schedules for the various means of transportation, none of which needs to be booked in advance. In high season (June–Sept), the SITA buses that serve the Amalfi Coast are at maximum capacity, which just means you might have to wait an extra half-hour or so to get where you're going. **BY TRAIN** For sites within the crescent-shaped Bay of Naples, the local **Circumvesuviana** train (www.vesuviana.it) provides a convenient link between Naples and Sorrento, with stops at the archaeological areas of Pompeii (Pompei Scavi–Villa dei Misteri) and Herculaneum (Ercolano) along the way. In Naples, make sure you board the "Sorrento" line of the Circumvesuviana train. The trip from Naples to Sorrento takes 1 hour; Pompeii is at the halfway point. Trains run every 30 minutes, and tickets are 4.60€ (valid for 1 day of travel anywhere between Naples and Sorrento). **BY BOAT** Perhaps the most enjoyable way to jaunt around Campania—and the only way to reach Capri, apart from a helicopter—is by ferry (traghetto, nave), or by hydrofoil (aliscafo) or jet boat, which are faster, more expensive, and run more frequently.

Naples and Sorrento are the main ports from which boats to Capri and the Amalfi Coast sail, with dozens of departures daily in high season (the schedule is scaled back considerably Oct–May). Boats are also a fun and convenient way to get around once you're on the Amalfi Coast, but they only serve the ports of Positano and Amalfi. *Tip:* Clever combinations of bus and boat travel will help you minimize uphill walks. For instance, take the bus to Positano, then walk downhill through town, and leave via boat at the port.

Between Naples and Capri it's 45 minutes and 17€ by hydrofoil or jet boat, 1½ hours and 10€ by ferry. Sorrento to Capri is 20 minutes and 15€ by hydrofoil or 45 minutes and 10€ by ferry. Sorrento to Positano is 1 hour and 8.50€ by ferry. Naples to Positano is 2 hours and 13€ by hydrofoil.

Most ferries and jet boats have outside deck space where you can stand, take photographs, and feel the sea spray (or inhale the engine fumes, as the case may be), while hydrofoils have enclosed cabins with windows that are often coated with salt water, limiting passengers' view of the passing scenery.

Hydrofoils and jet boats between Sorrento and Capri are run by **Consorzio LMP** (☎ 081-8781430; www.consorziolmp.it), while **NLG** (☎ 081-5520763; www.navlib.it) and **SNAV** (☎ 081-4285555; www.snav.it) operate the hydrofoils and jets between Naples and Capri. **Caremar** (☎ 081-0171998 or 892123; www.caremar.it) runs ferries on both the Naples–Capri and Sorrento–Capri lines. Boats to the Amalfi Coast (from Naples, Sorrento, or Capri) are run by **Metro del Mare** (☎ 199-600700; www.metrodelmare.com; mid-May to mid-Oct only) and **Coonsorzio LMP** (see above).

BY BUS & FUNICULAR The blue **SITA** buses (www.sitabus.it; in Italian) are the less expensive alternative to boats for traveling between Sorrento and Amalfi Coast towns such as Positano and Amalfi—and the view from the bus, if you've got the stomach to take the right-hand window seat, even trumps the view from the water. Amalfi Coast–bound buses leave from Sorrento's Circumvesuviana station every half-hour, but there's often a queue in high season—meaning you might have to wait up to an hour to board a bus. Not all buses serve all cities on the coast: Many go only as far as Positano, but you can wait there for the next bus to Amalfi, or wherever your plans take you. Unless you're sure you're taking the bus only once per day, buy the 24-hour ticket for 6€; otherwise, a 90-minute ticket (essentially good for one trip only) costs 3.30€. *Tabacchi* shops and many hotels sell SITA tickets; otherwise, you can usually buy them on the bus.

Internet Access

Almost all hotels now have a public terminal where guests can sign on, though there may be a small fee; many nicer hotels also have Wi-Fi, which may be free or carry a daily or hourly charge. In every town listed in this chapter, you'll also find Internet points or copy shop/phone centers with PCs where you can log on for about 5€ to 6€ an hour.

Pharmacies

Italian *farmacie* will fill foreign prescriptions with little or no hassle. They're also where you buy over-the-counter medicines, feminine hygiene products, and even sunblock. *Farmacie* are recognizable by a neon green or red cross and are usually open 8am to 1:30pm and 3:30 to 8pm.

For optical care (glasses repair, contact lens solution), go to an *ottica,* which are everywhere in Italy.

Police

To report a lost or stolen article, such as a wallet or passport, visit the local police *questura* or Carabinieri *caserma* in your location. In Naples, there are police and Carabinieri desks in the train station. See also "Emergencies," p 631.

Post Office

The main post office in Naples is at Piazza Matteotti (☎ 081-5511456) All post offices in Campania are closed Sunday. Note that stamps (*francobolli*) can be purchased at most *tabacchi* (tobacco stores), and postcards and letters can be mailed from either your hotel or the red letterboxes mounted on walls around town. Mail service is notoriously slow throughout the region.

Safety

Be very vigilant about petty theft in Naples, especially at the train station and on crowded streets. Naples's reputation for being the most crime-ridden city in Italy is accurate. However, the only crime that tourists encounter is petty theft—enraging, but not violent. (Your biggest risk for bodily harm is crossing the street!) With some extra vigilance, you and your wallet can make it through Naples in one piece. I don't mean to scare you with this information, just to prepare you.

Do be aware that pickpocketing at the crowded train station and port is rampant, as well as on busier buses and metro trains. When you're in these areas, it pays to be overly cautious. Anyone is a potential perpetrator, from the Neapolitan "gentleman" in the crisp white shirt and linen pants, to the cute gypsy girl with the Hannah Montana backpack. The warnings you may have heard about motorcycle thieves snatching bags off your arm as you're walking down the street are a bit exaggerated, though not totally baseless. Believe it or not, men's trouser pockets are targeted much more than women's shoulder bags. (Just to be safe, always walk with your bag on the building side of the sidewalk.) If you see someone eyeing you shiftily, it's a good bet he's sizing you up for valuables—cross the street or step into a shop. The techniques pickpockets use are creative and numerous, but a commonly employed tactic (against tourist couples) is "accidentally" bumping into the woman so that the accompanying husband or boyfriend is distracted by making sure she's all right or hasn't had anything taken, while the original bumper or a sidekick takes advantage of the jostling and commotion to empty the man's pockets.

On the plus side, it takes only a day or so for that initial threatening feeling of Naples to subside. You'll soon learn how to relax while still playing defense. As far as the scam culture, I've found cab drivers here to be generally more scrupulous than their Roman counterparts, and restaurant tabs on the whole to be fair and square. Much of central Naples is perfectly safe to walk around at night, as Neapolitans of all ages populate the streets well into the evening, but avoid walking alone in any dark or deserted areas.

Visitor Information

For extensive information about all monuments and museums in the Campania region, www.culturacampania.rai.it is an invaluable resource, or you can visit the provincial tourism offices in Naples at **Stazione Centrale** (☎ 081-268799; Mon–Sat 9am–7pm) or at Stazione Mergellina (☎ 081-7612102; Mon–Sat 9am–7pm). For Naples-specific info, visit the info desks at **Piazza Plebiscito** (☎ 081-402394; Mon–Sat 9am–1:30pm, 2:30–7pm) or **Piazza del Gesù** (☎ 081-5512701; Mon–Sat 9am–1:30pm, 2:30–7pm). Online, check www.inaples.it for links to information about transportation, accommodations, and things to do in Naples. For Capri, check out www.capri.net and www.capri.com, or stop by the info kiosks at Capri's **Marina Grande** and in the **Piazzetta**.

13
Sicily

The Best of Sicily in 3 Days

In a place as culturally and topographically varied as Sicily, 3 days will only whet your appetite for more. On this ambitious tour, which starts out in crazy Palermo and winds up in mellow Siracusa, you'll sample a bit of everything Sicily has to offer, from the city to the hills to the sea—with lots of great food along the way.

> PREVIOUS PAGE *The colorful port of Lipari, hub of the Aeolian Islands, is an hour by hydrofoil from the Sicilian mainland.* THIS PAGE *Palermo's sea-facing expanse is known as the Conca d'Oro, or "Golden Shell."*

START **Palermo.**

1 ★★ **Palermo.** Tempting as it may be—especially if you are coming from another busy city—to sidestep the urban chaos of Sicily's capital, taking the time to scratch the surface of chaotic Palermo is well worth the effort. It'll be a busy first day, but to fully experience Sicily, you must soak up at least some of Palermo.

The good news is you needn't worry about making it to any museums; your short stay in this colorful, maddening city should focus on street life and rewarding sights that don't require a huge time commitment. But if you're feeling ambitious, the dazzling mosaics of the **Cappella Palatina**, at the **Palazzo dei Normanni** (p 668, **1**), are the one major at-

More Information

For detailed information on sights and recommended hotels and restaurants, see individual town listings later in this chapter.

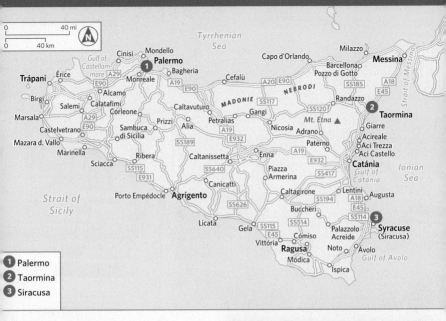

1 Palermo
2 Taormina
3 Siracusa

traction worth squeezing into a 1-day tour.

In the morning, start with a visit to the souklike **Vucciria** market (p 670, ③), where Palermo's rich history as a cultural crossroads between East and West is gloriously apparent, then spend the afternoon walking around the **Kalsa** district (p 671, ⑥)—elegant in places, derelict in others (it was heavily bombed in World War II and much of it never rebuilt),

The Biggest Sicilian Cliché of All

What would a trip to Sicily be without some Cosa Nostra tourism? An easy detour from Palermo, the hill town of **Corleone** is the namesake of *The Godfather* don and a real-life Mafia stronghold since the 1960s. The most egregious and elusive *capo* of the past several decades, Totò Riina, hails from Corleone (he's serving a life sentence in prison now), and as recently as 2006, mob boss Bernardo Provenzano was arrested here. Corleone is proud of its anti-Mafia strides and is totally safe for tourists. It's 1 hour south of Palermo on the SS118. For more about the myths and realities of Italy's storied organized crime syndicates, past and present, see "The Mafia: Myth & Reality" on p 703.

> The Byzantine mosaics of the Cappella Palatina are the highlight of Palermo's Palazzo dei Normanni.

> Taormina's pedestrian Corso Umberto is Sicily's best shopping street.

this is the oldest and most fascinating part of the city. Don't miss the adjacent churches of **San Cataldo & La Martorana** (p671, ⑤) for a low-key primer in Palermo's Arab-Norman architecture, and deeper within the Kalsa district, seek out the romantic ruins of **Santa Maria dello Spasimo,** where trees have grown out of the floor through the church's open brick vaults. For more faded grandeur, check out the façade of the 15th-century **Palazzo Ajutamicristo,** Via Garibaldi 23, once ground zero for Sicilian high society (think Burt Lancaster in *The Leopard*).

After your Kalsa walking tour, rest your feet in the district's garden square, the sultry **Piazza Marina.** There, benches and shade trees (including a huge old ficus tree, with its creepy tangle of gnarled trunks) offer welcome respite from Palermo's heat and traffic.

Later on, duck into the **Oratorio di San Lorenzo** (see "Putti-Palooza: Serpotta's Stuccoed Oratories," p 673, for details) for an eyeful of fabulous baroque stuccoes, then have a snack at **Antica Focacceria San Francesco** (p 674), a Palermo institution with delicious *panelle* (chickpea fritters) and *cannoli,* among other traditional local dishes. Make that snack your dinner, or try one of the restaurants recommended on p 674, then end with a nightcap at the bar of the **Grand Hotel et des Palmes** (p 674), a relic of decadent old Palermo. But don't stay too long—you'll want to hit the road to Taormina relatively early on Day 2.

Taormina is 2½ hours from Palermo. Take the A19 through the interior to Catania, then cut north on the A18 to Taormina. You can also take the A20 from Palermo along the coast to Messina and then cut south on the A18 to Taormina. Both routes are scenic, although the A20 has many long tunnels that can be stressful after a while.

② ★★★ **Taormina.** Day 2 is dedicated to rest, relaxation, and the resort life of Sicily's most breathtaking town. Plan to arrive by noon,

ut don't make a big production of lunch—
aormina's best assets aren't its restaurants.
Grab something quick and easy from a deli or
osticceria, then make your way to the stunning
Teatro Greco-Romano (p 680, **2**), which is
set magnificently against the steep hillside and
has views of Mt. Etna and the sea below. It's
Taormina's one must-do admission-fee attraction. After that, if the weather is warm, hop on
the **funivia** (cableway) down to **Mazzarò beach**
(see "Swimming near Taormina," p 682) for
a refreshing dip in the sparkling water of the
Ionian Sea or a refreshing sip of something by
the shore. There are several beach clubs here
where you can satisfy either need.

After your jaunt down to the beach at
Mazzarò, head back up into town, freshen up at
your hotel, and change into the best outfit you
have in your suitcase (Taormina's dressier than
the rest of Sicily). Before or after dinner, go for
the de rigueur evening stroll along Taormina's
pedestrian main drag, **Corso Umberto,** pausing
to admire the vistas from **Piazza IX Aprile.** If
the crowds on the Corso are too stifling, venture up or down any stepped alleys to hidden
corners and quiet panoramas, where the real
magic of Taormina lies.

The next morning, stretch your legs with
a walk through Taormina's lovely and shady
Giardino Pubblico, and then make your way to
Siracusa.

Siracusa is 1½ hours from Taormina. Take the
A18 autostrada south (toward Catania) for
41km (25 miles), then follow the E45 highway
for 20km (12 miles) around Catania (keep following signs for Siracusa or SS114 from here),
after which continue south on the A18 for
24km (15 miles). Merge onto the SS114, and
then cut east (toward the water) after 23km
(14 miles), following the bull's-eye signs for
Siracusa Centro and Ortigia.

3 ★★★ **Siracusa.** We've saved the most all-
around satisfying and delightful Sicilian town
for last. Ideally, you should arrive in Siracusa
by mid- or late morning so you have time for
an introductory stroll before lunch. Start with
an orientation tour of Siracusa's ancient core,
Ortigia Island, stopping at **Piazza del Duomo,**
one of Italy's most beautiful squares, then find
a place to eat lunch on one of Ortigia's many

> *The back streets of Siracusa are rich in baroque
architectural details.*

atmospheric baroque back alleys.

In the afternoon, go a few kilometers north
of Ortigia to explore Siracusa's fantastic, absolutely not-to-be-missed **Parco Archeologico
della Neapolis** (p 677, **5**), whose extensive grounds include the **Teatro Greco** and
Anfiteatro Romano (Roman Amphitheater),
as well as ancient caves and quarries in a lush,
primeval valley. If you have time, the artifacts
at the adjacent **Museo Archeologico Regionale
Paolo Orsi** (p 678, **6**) are a natural complement to the ruins in the archaeological park.

In the evening, head back to Ortigia and see
how nighttime changes the look and feel of the
magical Piazza del Duomo. Stand at the railing
near romantic **Fonte Aretusa,** gaze out over the
harbor, and savor this quintessentially Sicilian
moment.

The Best of Sicily in 1 Week

Though you're staying overnight in the same cities you'd visit on a 3-day tour (Palermo, Siracusa, and Taormina), 7 full days on Sicily allow you to soak up more local culture in each place—or sun, as the case may be—and pursue some wonderful side trips. The biggest benefit of a weeklong stay, however, is that you'll have time to take a full-day trip to the top of Mt. Etna.

> The sun-kissed produce from a typical Palermitan grocer is among the best buys at Palermo's markets.

START Palermo.

1 ★★ **Palermo.** With 2 days in Palermo, spend the first as you would on Day 1 of the "Best of Sicily in 3 Days" itinerary (p 636, **1**), getting acquainted with the city's personality and seeing characteristic sights as you wander around the **Vucciria** (p 670, **3**) and **Kalsa** areas (p 671, **6**).

On your second, well-organized day (and paying careful attention to opening hours), you can see the rest of Palermo's greatest hits. In the morning, get your fix of over-the-top Byzantine mosaics at the **Cappella Palatina** (part of the

Palazzo dei Normanni—see p 668, **1**) or those at the **Cattedrale di Monreale** (p 646, **1**), a short bus ride out of town. The 12th-century mosaics at these two sites are somewhat redundant (art-historical blasphemy!), so I don't recommend trying to squeeze in both if you have only a few days in Palermo.

Travel Tip

For detailed information on sights and recommended hotels and restaurants, see individual town listings later in this chapter.

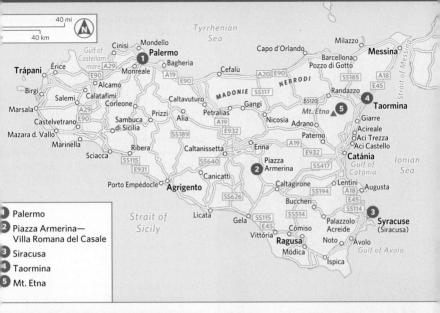

One of the remarkably preserved Roman mosaics at Villa Romana del Casale in Piazza Armerina.

In the afternoon, take a bus or taxi to Palermo's creepy **Catacombe dei Cappuccini** (p 672, 8), where there are whole bodies—flesh, clothing, and all—hanging on the walls. After that, if you aren't beat by the heat and traffic, the **Museo Archeologico Regionale** (p 671, 4) and **Galleria Regionale della Sicilia–Palazzo Abatellis** (p 672, 7) are Palermo's best museums and well worth seeking out. Otherwise, toast the setting of that Sicilian sun with a well-earned *aperitivo* at the splendid seaside **Villa Igiea** hotel (p 675).

Piazza Armerina is 2 hours from Palermo. Take the E90 to the A19 (signs for Catania). About 13km (8 miles) past Enna, exit at Mulinello and follow the blue signs to Piazza Armerina. (You'll be on some dubious-looking country roads, but you're going the right way.) In the town of Piazza Armerina, keep following the brown or yellow signs for Villa Romana del Casale or Mosaici (mosaics). The villa is actually 5km (3 miles) past the town center.

> *Fontane Bianche beach, an easy excursion from ancient Siracusa.*

Is Mt. Etna Dangerous?

Unlike Mt. Vesuvius, which did its worst back in A.D. 79 when it buried ancient Pompeii, Etna is still quite active: It buried half of Catania during a 4-month eruption in 1669 and has spewed lava down its slopes several times in the past decade alone. Its summit crater emits a continuous plume of smoke that's startlingly visible throughout eastern Sicily when the sky is clear. Satellite images frequently show a bright orange, molten center in Etna's cone. Still, locals don't seem too worried about their formidable neighbor. As volcanoes go, Etna is a "friendly giant" that's only registered 77 fatalities in 190 eruptions since 1500 B.C. When she blows, the lava tends to move slowly, allowing plenty of time for evacuation.

② ★★★ kids **Piazza Armerina—Villa Romana del Casale.** Mosaics, mosaics, and more mosaics—the most amazing cycle of them in the Roman world—are the reason to visit the ruins of this 4th-century-A.D. nobleman's country estate. As you walk the labyrinth of catwalks leading through the site, you'll see gory mosaics of wild boars taking lances to the jugular (Room 25), fascinating mosaics of Roman animal traffickers capturing and transporting exotic beasts (like the rhinoceros and ostriches in Room 28, perhaps destined for spectacles in the Colosseum), and cute mosaics of girls in bikinis lifting weights (Room 30).

As this guide went to press, an enormous restoration project is underway at the Villa Romana, which should greatly improve the visitor's experience: Room by room, the mosaics are being cleaned and returned to their original brilliant colors, and the old hamster-cage enclosure of glass and metal—which was insufferably hot in summer and cast irksome shadows on the mosaics—is being completely replaced with an opaque-roofed structure with state-of-the-art illumination. **Strada S161, Contrada Casale (5km/3 miles southwest of Piazza Armerina).** ☎ 0935-680036. www.villaromanadelcasale.it. Admission 3€. Daily 8am–6:30pm.

Siracusa is 2 hours from Piazza Armerina. Return to the A19 and head east, toward Catania. Near Catania, take the E45 south (keep following signs for Siracusa from here), which becomes the A18. Merge onto the SS114, and then cut east (toward the water) after 23km (14 miles), following the bull's-eye signs for Siracusa Centro and Ortigia.

③ ★★★ **Siracusa.** Arriving midafternoon gives you plenty of time to get to know the heart of old Siracusa, Ortigia Island. Wander down any of the criss-crossing streets south of **Piazza Archimede** for a taste of Ortigia's delightful baroque architecture, but make sure you're on **Piazza del Duomo** when the setting sun casts its orange glow on the square. Have an *aperitivo* here or on Piazza San Rocco, and then join the social masses at the lovely **Fonte Aretusa.**

Your second day in Siracusa is for immersing yourself in the ancient world. Start with visits to the enormously atmospheric **Parco Archeologico della Neapolis** (p 677, **⑤**) and comprehensive **Museo Archeologico**

> *Taormina's Teatro Greco-Romano once accommodated 10,000 Greek (later Roman) spectators.*

Regionale Paolo Orsi (p 678, ⑥). Dedicated antiquities enthusiasts should also make it to the **Castello Eurialo** (p 678, ⑦), a fun-to-explore Greek fortress and where Archimedes first uttered "Eureka!"

Later in the afternoon, take a trip on the **Ciane river** (p 678, ⑧), a fluvial time machine of sorts, where small boats ply a shady waterway lined with thick papyrus plants—it's the most extensive papyrus growth in Europe.

The morning of Day 5, go for a few hours' excursion to the 18th-century *centro storico* of **Noto** (p 650, ⑥), whose line-up of ebullient, honey-tinged *palazzi* represent the baroque at its sunniest. In the afternoon, consider hitting the nearby beach of **Fontane Bianche** (p 657, Ⓐ).

Taormina is 1½ hours from Siracusa. Follow highway signs to Catania (the SS114 will become the A18 autostrada after about 20km/12 miles). As you near Catania, follow signs for Messina and the E45 highway around downtown Catania. After about 20km (12 miles) on the E45, you'll rejoin the A18 to Messina. After another 40km (25 miles) on the A18 (for which there's a 3€ toll), take the Taormina exit

and follow the signs leading up the hill to the town. Parking is tricky in Taormina—find out from your hotel if they have parking on-site or the location of the nearest public lot.

④ ★★★ **Taormina.** Once settled in Taormina, where you'll spend 2 nights, visit the **Teatro Greco-Romano** (p 680, ②) and soak up what's left of the day's rays at one of the beaches below town (see "Swimming Near Taormina," p 682). In the evening, join the festive *passeggiata* on Corso Umberto.

On Day 7, set out early in the morning for your day trip to **Mt. Etna** (see p 645, ⑤). Allow 4 to 5 hours round-trip for the excursion from Taormina, and because Etna is such an exhilarating experience, don't plan anything too energy-intensive for the rest of the afternoon. Go shopping, have a drink at the Timeo, and enjoy the last sunset of your week in Sicily.

To reach Etna from Taormina (1 hr.), take the A18 south (toward Catania) and exit just after Giarre, following signs to Zafferana Etnea and Etna. Past Zafferana, keep following the Etna signs to Rifugio la Sapienza, where there's a large parking lot (1€ per day).

★★★ Mt. Etna. Standing atop the desolate landscape of Europe's largest active volcano, as a fierce wind nearly knocks you over, it's hard to believe you're on a Mediterranean island. Yet this 3,324m (10,906 ft.) behemoth is inextricable from Sicily's identity. The ancients explained its belching, rumbling, and molten output quite simply: It was where Hephaestus, god of fire, and his trusty sidekick, the Cyclops, made thunderbolts for Zeus.

Mt. Etna isn't beautiful, per se, but a trip to the top of this awesome peak is a must for nature lovers and a highlight for anyone traveling in Sicily. Conditions at the summit are often extreme, so bring a light jacket, sturdy shoes, sunblock, and water. Visibility is generally better before noon.

By car or bus, ascend Etna from its lava-covered south side to **Rifugio la Sapienza,** the touristy outpost at 1,900m (6,234 ft.) where you'll board the **Funivia dell'Etna** cableway (www.funiviadelletna.com) that takes you to 2,500m (8,202 ft.). At the *funivia* office, you'll pay a steep 46€ for the various transport and guide fees that get you to the top. First, the thrilling cableway climbs to the **Torre del Filosofo** station, where, in winter, you can hop off and ski down the snow-covered volcano. At Torre del Filosofo, you'll transfer to ungainly **all-terrain vehicles.** These "Jeeps" (as locals call them) clamber up another 100m to around 3,000m (10,000 ft.)—not quite the summit, but as close as tourists can safely go—where you're led around on foot by a grizzled old *guida alpina* (mountain guide), who may not speak any English but will manage to explain fumaroles and the like with emphatic gestures and a lit cigarette as prop. There's also a short walk at this point, over exposed and blustery volcanic dunes, to some steaming craters. The extreme wind and sloping terrain make it exhilarating and fun, but anyone with respiratory, heart, or balance problems should skip it. Active types can make the ascent from starting points at 1,900m or 2,500m up to 3,000m (6,234 ft. or 8,202 ft. up to 9,843 ft.) on foot—and it'll knock a bunch of euros off that 46€ fee—but it's a shadeless and wind-beaten climb over a squirrelly footing of loose pumice and an astonishing number of dead ladybugs.

OPPOSITE PAGE Base yourself in Taormina for an assault on the 3,324m (10,906-ft.) peak of Sicily's "friendly giant," Mount Etna.

Several bus companies in Taormina also run a wide range of day tours to Etna, but be sure to get details about what's included before you book: The less expensive tours generally do not take you all the way to the top. There are basic facilities (restrooms, snack bars, gift shops) at Rifugio la Sapienza and the upper station of the cableway, but no real dining to speak of.

Commercial Etnamania is, of course, everywhere on Sicily. Cinnamon-flavored Etna firewaters are sold in kitschy lava-themed bottles, even tackier "Madonna dell'Etna" Virgin Mary statuettes are crafted of Etna lava and blue glitter, and on the mountain's southern side, there's the ★ kids **Etnaland** waterpark, where kids go crazy for the slides and lazy rivers after heavy cultural touring in intense heat—and adults love the priceless Sicilian family-dynamic people-watching! Take the Misterbianco exit off the E45, then follow signs for Valcorrente and Etnaland. ☎ 095-7913333. www.etnaland.eu. Adults 22€; children up to 140cm (55 in.) tall 13€; children up to 100cm (40 in.) free. Late June to early Sept daily 10am–6pm.

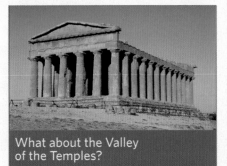

What about the Valley of the Temples?

If you can't fathom coming all the way to Sicily and not seeing the Valley of the Temples in Agrigento—I've left it out of this tour simply because it's a significant detour from everything else, and a one-trick pony—it's easy to make a day trip to Agrigento on Day 2 (in lieu of seeing more of multifaceted Palermo). There are public trains and buses as well as private coach tours between Palermo and Agrigento (2 hr. each way) that depart in the morning, give you time to tour the temples, and have you back by dinnertime. See p 650, ⑦, for more information.

Sicily's Best Art, Architecture & Archaeology

Prepare for a whirlwind of historical eras and cultural aesthetics on this tour of the island's most compelling man-made attractions. From Greek ruins to Roman mosaics to Arab-Norman cathedrals to baroque piazzas, you'll be covering the greatest hits of the Sicilian art history book.

> The cloister at Monreale is just one ingredient in the cathedral's Arab, Norman, and Byzantine mix.

START Monreale, just outside of Palermo. Trip length: 7 days or more.

❶ ★★★ Monreale. The dazzling 12th-century mosaics in the Arab-Norman **Cattedrale** (cathedral) of this hill town are perhaps the greatest artistic treasure in all of Sicily. The debate rages on as to who has the better mosaics—the other contender being the **Cappella Palatina** at the **Palazzo dei Normanni** (p 668, ❶) in Palermo—though it's true that the vast scale of Monreale's mosaics creates the more astonishing impression. The work of Byzantine

artisans commissioned by Norman king Roger II, the mosaics cover 6,000 sq. m (65,000 sq. ft.), culminating in the 13m by 9m (42 by 30 ft.) figure of Christ Pantokrator ("Ruler of All") in the apse. The rest of the mosaics—all of which are set on a glittering background of gold tes-

More Information

For detailed information on sights and recommended hotels and restaurants, see individual town listings later in this chapter.

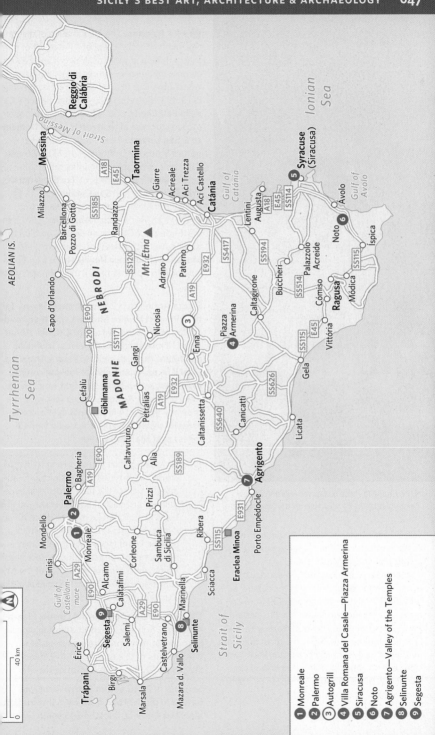

① Monreale
② Palermo
③ Autogrill
④ Villa Romana del Casale—Piazza Armerina
⑤ Siracusa
⑥ Noto
⑦ Agrigento—Valley of the Temples
⑧ Selinunte
⑨ Segesta

> *The Cappella Palatina houses Palermo's finest examples of the Byzantine craft of mosaicwork.*

serae—depict scenes from the Old and New Testaments, though the overall geometry of the architecture has a Muslim feel.

Monreale is an easy and popular day trip from Palermo. ***Note:*** Parking is tricky here, so take the 30-minute ride on bus 389 from Palermo's Piazza Indipendenza. The bus departs every 20 minutes and costs 1€ each way. Just bear in mind that the 389 is the most notorious bus line in Sicily for pickpockets, so keep a very close eye on your valuables. **Piazza Guglielmo Il Buono.** ☎ 091-6404403. Admission 6€. Daily 9am–7pm.

Take the 389 bus to Palermo.

② ★★★ **Palermo.** The combination of distinctive sights in Sicily's capital—the result of more than a thousand years of Western and Eastern cultural influences—simply doesn't exist anywhere else. Not to be missed are the stunning Byzantine mosaics at the Norman Palace's **Cappella Palatina** (p 668, **①**) and the eye-popping rococo stuccoes at the ***oratori* of San Domenico & San Lorenzo** (see "Putti-Palooza: Serpotta's Stuccoed Oratories," p 673). Witness Palermo's striking Islamic-inflected architecture in the bulbous red domes of **San Giovanni degli Eremiti** (p 649) and **San Cataldo** (p 671, **⑤**). In the crumbling, captivating **Kalsa** district (p 671, **⑥**), visit **Palazzo Abatellis** (p 672), the masterpiece of Catalonian-Gothic architecture that houses Sicily's best art museum. Palermo's **Museo Archeologico Regionale** (p 671, **④**) is a helpful complement to all the open-air ruins on Sicily.

Piazza Armerina is 2 hours from Palermo. Take the E90 east toward Messina, and then head southeast on the A19 toward Catania. About 13km (8 miles) past Enna, exit at Mulinello and follow the blue signs to Piazza Armerina. (You'll be on some dubious-looking country roads, but you're going the right way.) In the town of Piazza Armerina, keep following the brown or yellow Villa Romana del Casale or Mosaici signs. The villa is actually 5km (3 miles) past the town center.

③ 🍴 ★**Autogrill.** If you're driving to Piazza Armerina, this rest stop/cafe chain—and integral part of the Italian road-trip experience—just east of Enna (before you exit the A19 at Mulinello to head down toward Piazza Armerina) is *the* place to stock up on lunch stuff (they have great panini and all manner of refreshments) before heading down to see the mosaics. **Exit the A19 autostrada at Area Servizio Sacchitello, 5km (3 miles) east of Enna. $–$$.**

④ ★★★ 🄺🄸🄳🅂 **Villa Romana del Casale, Piazza Armerina.** Some of the most amazing mosaics from the Roman world are preserved, in situ, on the floors of this extensive 4th-century villa. See p 642, **②**, for details on visiting the site.

Siracusa is 2 hours from Piazza Armerina. Return to the A19 and head east, toward Catania. Near Catania, take the E45 south (keep

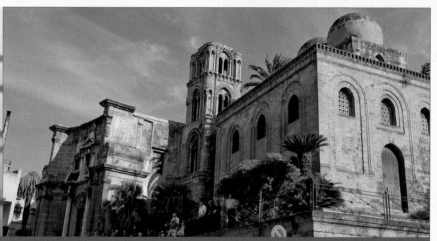

Arab-Norman Architecture in Palermo

The palm trees, the souklike markets, the sand-filled scirocco winds . . . Palermo may strike you more as an exotic trading post caught between continents than just another Italian "art city." Palermo is the most conquered city in the history of the world. For 3 millennia Phoenicians, Greeks, Jews, Turks, Syrians, Spaniards, and, most significantly, Arabs and Normans, have blended cultures (not to mention gene pools).

Palermo reached its heyday under Arab rule in the 9th and 10th centuries, when it was known as the "city of 300 mosques." In 1072, the Normans wrested control of the city—absorbing the best of Arab culture and allowing religious freedom for all. Under this enlightened patronage, Palermo was considered one of the grandest cities in Europe.

Commissioned by Norman kings but executed by Arab or Byzantine engineers and craftsmen, the unique monuments of Arab-Norman Palermo (and Monreale, p 646, **1**, and Cefalù, p 652, **2**) are wonderful reminders of Sicily's cultural cross-pollination.

Palazzo dei Normanni. At the Norman Palace, look for Saracen arches, slit windows, and toothy crenellations on the fortresslike western edge of the building, elements that have traces of both Arab and Norman Gothic style. (The Renaissance main façade was a later addition.) Inside, the **Cappella Palatina** holds phenomenal Byzantine mosaics from 1130. See p 668, **1**.

Cattedrale. Palermo's Duomo was built over the site of a mosque, which in turn was built over an early Christian basilica. Later restoration blurred the original 12th-century architecture, but you can still make out verses from the Koran inscribed in the church's columns. Visit the tomb of Roger II, the Norman king who sponsored so much art during his reign (1130–54). See p 668, **2**.

San Giovanni degli Eremiti. With its pinkish-red domes, this is a prime example of Christian architecture with an Islamic look. The romantic gardens and cloister add to the sense of history. Via dei Benedittini 20. ☎ 091-6515019. Admission 6€. Daily 9am–7pm. Bus: 109 or 318.

San Cataldo & La Martorana. Look for mosquelike red domes and Moorish crenellations on San Cataldo (pictured above) and Byzantine mosaics inside La Martorana, which give the church an Eastern Orthodox aspect. See p 671, **5**.

La Zisa & La Cuba. These two strongly Arab minicastles were built as part of a hunting resort for King William I. Austere and fortress-like even in ruin, they have Saracen arches, prisonlike windows, and Norman-inspired crenellated roof lines. La Zisa: Piazza Zisa. ☎ 091-6520269. Admission 4.50€. Daily 9am–7pm. Bus: 124. La Cuba: Corso Calatafimi 100. ☎ 091-590299. Admission 2€. Daily 9am–7pm. Bus: 105 or 389.

> *The mosaics at Piazza Armerina include a roomful of exercising, bikinied women.*

following signs for Siracusa from here), which becomes the A18. Merge onto the SS114, and then cut east (toward the water) after 23km (14 miles), following the bull's-eye signs for Siracusa Centro and Ortigia.

⑤ ★★★ Siracusa. This cheerful coastal town is a one-two punch of architectural delights from the ancient to the baroque. Ortigia Island is Siracusa's *centro storico,* where narrow alleys lined with romantic 18th-century palazzi spill onto such visual treats as **Piazza del Duomo**—in my opinion, the prettiest square in Sicily.

Among Siracusa's outstanding archaeological offerings, don't miss the gleaming white **Teatro Greco** (Greek theater), which once sat 16,000 and is still used for summer performances, the lush **Latomia del Paradiso** (Quarry of Paradise), and the **Roman amphitheater.**

Noto is 45 minutes from Siracusa. Take the SS115 west, following signs for Noto and Ragusa. As you near the top of Noto's hill, keep following the white signs to the *centro,* not the brown signs for the archaeological site of Noto Antica.

⑥ ★★ Noto. The *centro storico* of this hill town is Sicily's crown jewel of baroque delights. An earthquake leveled most of the town in 1693, clearing the way for the fanciful *barocco* style to establish a foothold in the early 18th century. Noto's pedestrian-only main strip, **Corso Vittorio Emanuele III,** cuts east-west through a stage-set of honey-colored limestone confections, most of which are centered on **Piazza Municipio.** The most photographed spot in Noto, however, is hidden away on Via Corrado Nicolaci (a cross street of Corso Vittorio): About halfway up, on the left, is **Palazzo Nicolaci di Villadorata,** with its diminutive but wonderful balcony supports carved with the heads of cheeky maidens, dwarves, lions, and horses—the individual figures' expressions are fabulous!

Agrigento is 3½ hours from Noto. Take the SS115 west to Agrigento, and follow signs for Valle dei Templi. You can also take the A18 back past Siracusa and up to Catania, head west on the A19 toward Caltanissetta, and cut down on the SS640. The autostrada route is about 30 minutes shorter but is mostly backtracking over roads you'll have driven already.

⑦ ★★★ kids Agrigento—Valley of the Temples. The ruins of ancient Akragas are Sicily's most celebrated archaeological site. The 5th-century-B.C. temples, in various states of ruin, are set on a ridge with olive and almond trees and views of the sea. As you wander the site, imagine the glorious beacon that these temples, embellished with gold sculptural details, must have been for those approaching by sea.

Had the ★ **Temple of Zeus** ever been completed (war with Carthage and an earthquake sealed its unfinished fate), it would have been the largest ever built, with 20m-high (66 ft.) Doric columns. The four extant columns of the ★ **Temple of Castor & Pollux** still carry part of the entablature and pediment, a romantic and oft-photographed sight.

> *The massive 300m (900-ft.) Greek temple at Segesta nestles in the idyllic shadow cast by Monte Barbaro and Monte Bernardo.*

Across Via dei Templi you'll find the eastern zone of the archaeological park. This is a far more complex area, home to the oldest and most impressive of the temples. Indeed, at one time the ★★ **Temple of Hercules** ranked in size with the Temple of Zeus, but today only eight columns stand. The ★★★ **Temple of Concord** is the most impressive temple at the site and is on par, preservation-wise, with the Temple of Hephaestus in Athens. The ★★ **Temple of Juno** has 30 re-erected columns and a romantically skeletal look. An on-site museum has explanations of the many artifacts unearthed in this area. ⏲ At least 3 hr. Via Panoramica dei Templi. ☎ 0922-497226. Admission 6€. Daily 8:30am–7pm. Drive or take a bus from the entrance gate to the temple zone.

Selinunte is 1¾ hours from Agrigento. Continue west on the SS115 (toward Mazara del Vallo and Marsala), and take the exit toward the SP48 (signs for Marinella and Selinunte). From there, follow the brown Selinunte Zona Archeologica signs.

8 ★★ **Selinunte.** Explore the fallen ruins of more Greek temples (one has been reconstructed) in this poignant, peaceful archaeological garden. See p 658, **2**, for details on visiting the site.

Segesta is 1 hr. from Selinunte. Take the A29 north, and follow the SS119 and SS33 toward Calatafimi. From there, follow the brown Area Archeologica di Segesta signs.

9 ★★ **Segesta.** A single, perfectly preserved ★★★ **Greek temple** set in a storybook vale is the reason to make the trip to this site between Palermo and Trapani. ⏲ 2 hr. See p 662, **5**, for details on visiting the site.

A Poignant Scene

An immense heap of fallen columns, now aligned and placed side by side on the ground like fallen soldiers, now having fallen in a chaotic manner.
GUY DE MAUPASSANT (ON SELINUNTE)

The Best Sun & Sea

Sicily has more sandy beaches and dramatic coastline than any other region of Italy (except for maybe Sardinia), and it's warm enough for swimming 6 months of the year (May–Oct). Fantastic shorefront restaurants abound, and there are plenty of ways to get out on the water, whether in a rented *pedalò* at San Vito lo Capo or a beach shuttle boat in the Aeolian Islands. Allow at least a week to visit all the places on this itinerary and to have time to enjoy them at a leisurely pace.

> *The north coast beach of Mondello is a lovely crescent easily accessible from Palermo.*

START Palermo. Trip length: 7 days or more.

① ★ **kids** **Mondello, Palermo.** A crescent bay with shallow water and white sand, an Art Nouveau bathhouse, and a carnivalesque atmosphere make this the quintessential "people's beach" of Palermo, especially for families. Windsurfing and snorkeling are popular here, and the grand ★★ **Stabilimento Balneare** (bathing club), built on a pier in the middle of the bay in 1913, is a fabulous nugget of the old-fashioned European good life. Mondello is an easy 15-minute bus ride from Palermo, so it's best to visit as a day trip from there.

Cefalù is 1 hour from Palermo. Take the A20 east, toward Messina, and exit at Cefalù.

② ★ **Cefalù.** Picturesque Cefalù is where Giuseppe Tornatore shot most of 1988's *Cinema Paradiso* (rent it before you go), and despite a considerable influx of northern European sunseekers in summer, it's still a working fishing village where everyone seems to be named Salvatore.

The swimming- and sunbathing-friendly part of this fishing village is its western, modern end, along Lungomare G. Giardina, where gentle breakers lap at a narrow but well-used strip of white sand. Farther east (closer to the old town),

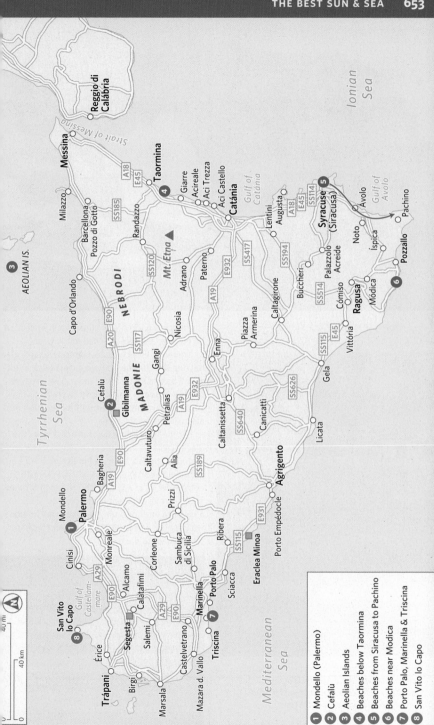

1. Mondello (Palermo)
2. Cefalù
3. Aeolian Islands
4. Beaches below Taormina
5. Beaches from Siracusa to Pachino
6. Beaches near Modica
7. Porto Palo, Marinella & Triscina
8. San Vito lo Capo

the beach is packed with sunseekers, while it's a bit broader and less crowded to the west.

There isn't much to do, sights-wise, in Cefalù beyond the Duomo and *rocca* (fortress), but it's a nice base if sunbathing and a slow pace are of chief interest. **Think Sicily** (www.thinksicily.com) has a number of wonderful vacation rentals in and around Cefalù.

For the best (almost) seafront dining (the places right on the water tend to be lower-quality tourist traps), try ★ **Al Porticciolo,** Via Carlo Ortolani di Bordonaro 66 (☎ 0921-921981; entrees 8€–17€; AE, DC, MC, V; lunch & dinner Thurs–Tues), adjacent to the old port. There's a cavelike interior dining room as well as sidewalk tables. The seafood pastas and Sicilian pastries are to die for.

Dining in Mondello

The best dining in Mondello (it may even top anything in Palermo) is at ★★★ **Charleston Le Terrazze,** the restaurant in the Stabilimento Balneare. The Gilded Age setting alone is enough to charm you, but the food also happens to be glorious, and the prices are reasonable for such a memorable experience. Viale Regina Elena. ☎ 091-450171. Entrees 11€–18€. AE, DC, MC, V. Daily for lunch & dinner. Reservations required.

> *TOP Renting a boat is the best way to see the cerulean coves of the Aeolian Islands.*
> *BOTTOM Cefalù's best strip of sand for sun-worshippers is just west of the town.*

Milazzo, departure point of most ferries and hydrofoils to the Aeolian Islands, is 1¾ hours from Cefalù. Take the A20 east, toward Messina, for 130km (81 miles). Exit when you see signs for Milazzo–Isole Eolie and follow surface roads 6km (3¾ miles) north to the port.

❸ ★★★ Aeolian Islands. If you have the time, it's well worth hopping on a hydrofoil at Milazzo to spend a few days in this archipelago off Sicily's northeast coast. Because they're a bit harder to reach, the Aeolians remain a mostly Italian vacation spot where you can have a truly authentic "native" vacation experience. Each island has its own character—Lipari is the largest with the most services, Salina is the best for nature lovers, and Panarea is for partying with jet-setters and wannabes—but all the Eolie have clear, calm water and paradisical places to swim, though very few sandy beaches. Don't miss a chance to rent a small motorboat and putter around whichever island you choose as your base. It's a fabulously independent way to get out on the water—you can drop anchor and dive in whenever you want. See p 664 for more details on visiting the Aeolians.

Taormina is 1 hour from Milazzo. Take the A20 east, toward Messina, and follow the A18 south toward Catania. Exit at Taormina for the beaches or the hill town.

❹ ★ Beaches below Taormina. See "Swimming near Taormina," p 682.

The beaches below are about 1½ hour from Taormina. Take the A18 south, past Catania to Siracusa. Continue on the A18 past Siracusa (signs for Gela), and exit at Cassibile, Noto, or Pachino.

❺ ★★ Beaches from Siracusa to Pachino. Some of the best unspoiled shoreline in all of Italy is on Sicily's southeastern coast. This is also one of the most popular zones for vacation rentals on the island, thanks to the combination of beaches and cultural offerings nearby.

The beaches in ❻ are about 45 minutes from those in the "Beaches from Siracusa to Pachino" tour. Take the A18 west (toward Gela) to Pozzallo or Modica.

> *Salina is the best of the Aeolian Islands for hiking and seashore relaxation.*

❻ ★ Beaches near Modica. Head west around the point of Pachino, and you find a more windswept coastline. Though the waves are hardly oceanic in scale, there are generally whitecaps and breakers at these beaches. Think less Caribbean, more California. Starting in the town of Santa Maria del Focallo, there's a long stretch of **undeveloped beach** that extends for miles toward **Pozzallo.** If you're looking to get a jog or vigorous walk in while on holiday, this is the place for it.

Farther west, the town beach of **Marina di Modica** is a wide swath of fine beige sand—the kind that sticks to you no matter how many rinse-offs—bordered by low dunes and equipped with a few simple facilities. It faces west, so you can catch a lot of afternoon rays and, of course, the sunset from here. The beach of **Cava d'Aliga** is another charming little town beach with kayaks and *pedalò*s for hire.

Porto Palo is 4 hours from Modica on the SS115. Consider breaking up the trip with a visit to the Valley of the Temples in Agrigento (p 650, **7**), just past the halfway point.

7 ⋆ **Porto Palo, Marinella & Triscina.** With the urban blight of Agrigento in the rearview mirror, it's only another hour and a half until you reach another great stretch of sandy coastline. **Porto Palo** as a town is not particularly attractive, but its beach is a gloriously vast expanse of white sand. A tourist port offers small boat charters. Porto Palo can also lay claim to having one of the best restaurants, **Ristorante da Vittorio** (p 661), on the southern Sicilian coast. A few kilometers farther west is another unspoiled beach, **Marinella,** where there are views of the Selinunte ruins above the dunes (and Malta to the south, when the sky is clear). **Triscina** is a vacation home development with miles of pristine sand and sea.

San Vito lo Capo is 1¾ hours from the beaches in **7**. Take the SS115 to the A29 north (signs for Palermo). Exit at Castellammare del Golfo and follow the SS187 and SP16 to San Vito lo Capo, which is clearly signposted.

Not-So-Ancient History

The quiet and relaxing shores of southeastern Sicily are where Allied troops landed on July 10, 1943, to launch "Operation Husky," which resulted in Sicily's liberation from Axis forces and was a major turning point in World War II. From their beachheads between Siracusa and Licata, and aided by airborne operations, American, British, and Canadian infantry units advanced inland and defeated the German and Italian army divisions that had been dispatched from their stations in the mountains. There are still some Sicilians who remember that campaign (Husky lasted over a month) and greet visitors from those Allied nations with touching warmth and gratitude.

8 ⋆⋆ **San Vito lo Capo.** A glittering sandy beach, irresistible turquoise water, a dramatic mountain at land's end (Monte Monaco), and a funky, Arab-inflected town make this spot between Trapani and Palermo one of Sicily's best up-and-coming resort destinations. See p 663, **6**, for details on visiting San Vito lo Capo.

> Fishing boats bob in the magnificent turquoise waters of San Vito lo Capo's harbor.

ITE GUIDE

5 Beaches from Siracusa to Pachino

he color palette is lighter down here—the
ater is more pastel than cerulean, and the
and is white and sugary. From north to south,
Fontane Bianche (pictured above) is the
assic beach detour for those who stay in
iracusa, 15 minutes away. It's an almost-
quare bay with laid-back beach clubs and
xurious deep sand. **B Lido di Noto,** 15
inutes from the baroque hill town, is a lively
wn beach with great waterfront restaurants.
alf the beach is private beach clubs (where
ou pay around 10€ for day use of a lounge
hair, umbrella, and shower facilities), and

half is free public access. Between Noto and
Pachino is the **Vendicari Nature Reserve,**
where beaches are small and hard to find
but the scenery is beautiful. Thousands of
migratory birds nest here every year. A few
miles south of the autostrada on SP19, park at
the Agriturismo Calamosche to reach the more
alternative **C Calamosche,** favored by local
teens and 20-somethings. After a 15-minute
walk down a nature path you're rewarded with
an intimate cove framed by rock cliffs and sea
caves that feels like a real discovery. The water
is a calm, perfectly dappled teal. **D Isola delle
Correnti,** at the very southeastern tip of the
island, is one of the best beaches on Sicily. It's
a bit wilder, more windswept and wavy than
the other spots, and can be a nice change from
perfectly still turquoise water and searing
sunshine. An abandoned tuna factory at one
end of the beach adds to the atmosphere, and
on a clear day, you can even wave hello to
Malta, which is just 100km (60 miles) south.

The Best of Western Sicily

Concentrating your visit on the less-traveled end of the island (west of the line between Palermo and Agrigento) practically ensures the kind of authentic cultural interaction and discovery that's harder to find in the more well-known destinations of eastern Sicily. It's an itinerary rich in Greek ruins, from the Valley of the Temples to Segesta (though you don't have to do all of them), that also takes you to Sicily's most breathtaking hill town, Erice, and the sparkling beach of San Vito lo Capo, with its neighboring nature reserves.

> *Monte Monaco towers over the town of San Vito lo Capo and its harbor.*

START Agrigento is 127km (79 miles) south of Palermo and 215km (134 miles) west of Siracusa. Trip length: 5 days or more.

1 ★★★ kids **The Valley of the Temples, Agrigento.** See p 650, **7**, for full details on touring the Agrigento archaeological site.

Selinunte is 1¾ hours from Agrigento. Take the SS115 west toward Trapani. A few kilometers after Menfi, exit and follow the brown signs to Selinunte.

2 ★★ **Selinunte.** If the Valley of the Temples was enough to satisfy your hunger for Greek ruins, skip this one—it's more ancient temples—but the archaeological site of Selinus is in a muc more tranquil setting than Agrigento and nicely breaks up the journey to Trapani. Thanks to a lucrative celery export business (the English name of the vegetable in fact derives from "Selinus"), the colony rose to prominence in the 5th century B.C., at which time several grand temple were built here. Only one, the ★ **Temple of Hera,**

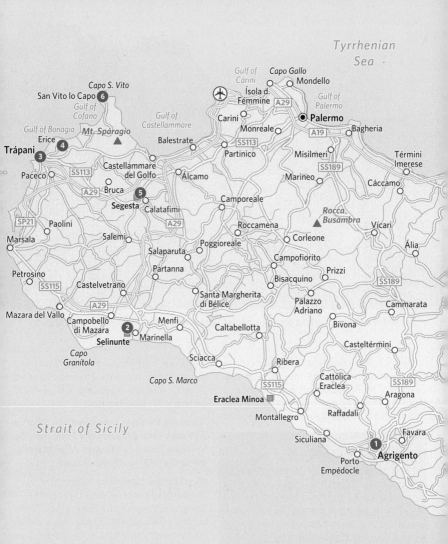

Tyrrhenian Sea

Gulf of Carini

Capo Gallo

Mondello

Capo S. Vito

San Vito lo Capo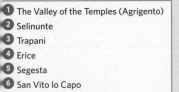

Ísola d. Fémmine

A29

Gulf of Palermo

Gulf of Cofano

Carini

Monreale

Palermo

Bagheria

Gulf of Bonagia

Mt. Spáragio

Gulf of Castellammare

A19

Erice

Balestrate

SS113

Términi Imerese

Trápani

Castellammare del Golfo

Partinico

Misilmeri

Paceco

SS113

Álcamo

SS189

Bruca

A29

Marineo

Cáccamo

Segesta

Calatafimi

Camporeale

Rocca Busambra

SP21

Paolini

A29

Roccamena

Vicari

Marsala

Salemi

Poggioreale

Corleone

Álía

Salaparuta

Campofiorito

Prizzi

SS189

Petrosino

Partanna

Bisacquino

SS115

Castelvetrano

Santa Margherita di Bélice

Palazzo Adriano

Cammarata

Mazara del Vallo

A29

Campobello di Mazara

Menfi

Caltabellotta

Bivona

Casteltérmini

Capo Granítola

Selinunte

Marinella

Sciacca

Ribera

Cattólica Eraclea

Aragona

SS189

Capo S. Marco

SS115

Eraclea Minoa

Montallegro

Raffadali

Favara

Siciliana

Agrigento

Strait of Sicily

Porto Empédocle

0   40 mi

0   40 km

> *The ruins of a Norman castle sit above the cobbled lanes of the precipitously steep hill town of Erice .*

or Temple E, is standing (it was reconstructed by archaeologists). The other temples lie on the ground as if an earthquake has just hit; almost all the pieces are still there. The exquisite marble metopes from Temples E and F, depicting scenes

from Greek mythology, are on display at the archaeological museum in Palermo. ⏱ 2 hr. Via di Selinunte, Marinella di Selinunte. ☎ 0924-46277. Admission 6€. Daily 9am–5pm.

Trapani is 1¾ hours from Selinunte. Take the A29 east toward Mazara del Vallo, then the SS115 northwest to Marsala. After Marsala, follow the SP21 north into Trapani.

❸ ★ Trapani. Some liken the port city of Trapani to a watered-down version of Palermo—in a good way: There's local flavor but less traffic and sketchiness. Allow a few hours to walk the *centro storico,* which occupies the western (seaward) end of Trapani's sickle-

A Winery Detour

A visit to the **Planeta** winery is a fun inland detour on the way from Agrigento to Selinunte. Planeta makes some of the most well-regarded Sicilian wines, including exquisite Chardonnay and Syrah, and their Cantina dell'Ulmo estate in Sambuca di Sicilia has a 16th-century farmhouse set up for tastings and tours (by appointment).

To get there, exit the SS115 a few kilometers east of Menfi and follow the SS624 and SS188 to Sambuca di Sicilia. In Sambuca, follow signs for Azienda Agricola Planeta–Terre Sicane. ☎ 091-327965. www.planeta.it. Tues–Sat 9am–3pm. Book appointments at least 3 days in advance; e-mail visits@planeta.it or fax 091-6124335.

Beach Tip

In warm weather, for an unforgettable only-in-Sicily moment, stop at the crystal-watered beach in **Marinella** around sunset, swim about 50m (164 ft.) offshore, and look to the west—you'll see the Temple of Hera outlined on top of the hill.

shaped bay. The pedestrianized main street in the old town, an ancient Arab *casbah,* is Corso Vittorio Emanuele, also known as Rua Grande. Many elegant baroque buildings are found along this street, which makes for a grand promenade. Via Garibaldi (also known as Rua Nova, or "New Road") is flanked with churches and palaces. Via Torrearsa has the best shopping in town and leads down to a bustling *pescheria* (fish market) where it's all about the *tonno* (tuna), many residents' lifeblood.

If you're in Trapani at dinnertime, your best bet is ★ **Ai Lumi,** Corso Vittorio Emanuele 75 (☎ 0923-872418; entrees 8€–18€; AE, DC, MC, V; dinner Mon–Sat), a rustic-chic *tavernetta* near the Duomo that draws a stylish clientele of actors and politicians.

Erice is 15 minutes from Trapani. Take the SS113 to the SP3, the hairpin road that climbs toward the village. You can also leave your car in Trapani and take the newly opened cable car from Trapani to Erice (see Erice entry below for service information).

④ ★★★ **Erice.** In a Sicilian hill town beauty pageant, the tiara would go to Erice. (Taormina would be first runner-up.) Originally an ancient Elymian settlement, Erice is 751m (2,464 ft.) above sea level, but only about 3km (2 miles) inland, with a wonderfully preserved medieval *centro.* It's one of the highlights of western Sicily to stroll the cobblestoned lanes here, catching glimpses of stunning views in every direction—that is, when Erice isn't engulfed in a misty cloud created by its own microclimate. The Villa Balio gardens, on the southwest side of town, are worth a look, and beyond them, there's a path leading up to the Norman Castello di Venere, ruins of a castle built on the spot where a temple to Venus once stood.

The newly opened ★ **FuniErice** cableway, Piazza Umberto I 3 (☎ 0923-869720; www. funiviaerice.com; Mon 1:10pm–1am, Tues–Fri 7:45am–1am, Sat–Sun 8:45am–2am; 2.70€ one-way, 5€ round-trip), connects Erice with Trapani's Casa Santa neighborhood; the 11-minute ride is a great way to experience the town's thrilling altitude, especially at sunset.

Restaurants in town tend to be rather touristy, but there are a number of renowned pastry shops, including ★ **Pasticceria Michele Il Tulipano,** Via Vittorio Emanuele 10 (☎ 0923-869672; daily 7:30am–9pm), where you can pick up

> The Temple of Castor and Pollux at Agrigento, evidence that long before the rise of Rome, Sicily was an important outpost of ancient Greece.

An Amazing Meal After the Ruins

The best restaurant in the vicinity of Selinunte is on the water at Porto Palo di Menfi, a few kilometers east of Marinella and Selinunte. ★★★ **Ristorante da Vittorio** draws gourmands from all over for its superb seafood-only menu and open-air, family-friendly beachfront locale. The 40€ prix fixe menu (excluding wine) is the best way to sample Vittorio's food. Vittorio and his family also offer overnight accommodations in 12 simple but comfy rooms (75€), all with direct views of the sand and surf. There's even an alfresco nightclub of sorts here in summer, which locals of all ages come out for in droves—yet another great slice of Sicilian community life. Via Friuli Venezia Giulia 9, Porto Palo di Menfi. ☎ 092-578381. www.davittorioristorante.com. Entrees 10€–25€. AE, DC, MC, V. Lunch daily year-round; dinner daily June–Sept; by reservation only Oct–May.

> *Segesta's 36 Doric columns comprise Sicily's best-preserved Greek temple.*

a heavenly *cassatella* (fritter filled with sweet ricotta).

Segesta is 45 minutes from Erice. Head back down the hill on the SP3, then follow the A29 toward Palermo. After 27km (17 miles), exit at Segesta and keep following signs to the archaeological site.

5 ★★ **Segesta.** Segesta's one and only raison d'être on the tourist route is a single, amaz-ing ★★★ **Greek temple.** The setting is unreal: a fairytale landscape of rolling hills, splendidly enveloped by a green valley and framed by the peaks of Monte Barbaro and Monte Bernardo. The 5th-century-B.C. temple at the center of this scene (at 300m/900 ft.) is just as impressive: It's perhaps the best-preserved ancient Greek temple anywhere, with 36 Doric columns sup-porting unadorned entablatures and pediments (scholars say the temple lacks decoration—and a roof—because construction was interrupted, and never resumed, when a war broke out with nearby Selinunte). A short bus ride (1€) far-ther up Monte Barbaro, to 431m (1,414 ft.), is Segesta's ancient ★★ **theater,** hewn straight into the side of the mountain in the 3rd century B.C. Contrada Segesta. ☎ 0924-952356. Admission 6€. Daily 9am–5pm.

San Vito lo Capo is 1 hour from Segesta. Take SS113 to SP57 north (past the A29 highway), then SP44 north through Bruca to SS187 west (signs for Erice and Trapani), then SP16 north to San Vito.

Spending the Night in Erice

Erice is a quiet town that's easily explored in a few hours, so I don't recommend staying more than 1 night here. A good bet, and quite a decent value, is ★★ **Torri Pepoli.** As stun-ning to look at as it is to look out from, this 13th-century Arab-style castle has been refit-ted as a four-star hotel, with large and colorful rooms, modern bathrooms, and neo-Gothic furnishings. Viale Conte Pepoli, Giardini del Balio. ☎ 0923-860117. www.torripepoli.it. 7 units. Doubles 100€–150€. AE, DC, MC, V.

> *San Vito lo Capo's crescent beach is part of the tranquil, authentic Sicilian experience to be found on the western side of the island.*

6 ★★ **San Vito lo Capo.** At first glance, a panorama of this beach town looks like a postcard from Rio de Janeiro—a broad expanse of white sand lines a curving bay, with a massive mountain promontory at one end. But this Sicilian resort is a much smaller, quieter affair (even though San Vito's Monte Monaco stands just as tall as Rio's Sugarloaf). There are no high-rises or wild nightlife here: The mellow *centro* consists of boxy, whitewashed houses with Saracen arch doorways that bear the unmistakable influence of Arabic culture. That influence carries over to the local cuisine as well—couscous is bigger than pasta here, and there's even an international festival for it held in San Vito every September (www.couscousfest.it).

San Vito's gorgeous **beach**—a kilometer-long (¾-mile) stretch of clean, fine sand—makes it a popular summer destination for Italian families and couples. (Singles and party-seekers take note: Go to the more happening, rockier shores of the Aeolian Islands instead.) Swimming in the turquoise waters here, with the imposing contours of Monte Monaco to the east, is an unforgettable experience. Organized boat tours of the nearby **Zingaro** and **Scopello** nature reserves are a great way to access hidden coves and see unspoiled Sicilian flora and marine fauna.

Spending the Night in San Vito

Consider staying in San Vito so you can sample the signature couscous dishes at a local restaurant. At the ★ **Ghibli Hotel,** rooms are tastefully decorated in a North African style. Use of an affiliated beach club, just minutes down the road, is included in the room rate. The hotel's alfresco restaurant, **Profumi di Couscus,** is a perfect foray into *cucina sanvitese* under a canopy of citrus trees. Via Regina Margherita 80. ☎ 0923-974155, www. ghiblihotel.it. Doubles from 85€; AE, DC, MC, V.

The Aeolian Islands

Still wonderfully under the radar of international tourism (though plenty of foreigners do make it here), the Aeolian archipelago off northeastern Sicily is one of the best places in Italy for a laid-back and authentic sea-themed vacation. The islands are small and easy to navigate (though English is not widely spoken), and the views over the sea to the other islands are rapturous. Just don't come expecting sandy beaches—Aeolian shores tend to be pebbly inlets or vertical rock faces, but that's what makes for those perfectly cerulean swimming coves.

> Lava-sand beaches and turquoise water are two of the reasons why Lipari is the most frequented Aeolian island.

START Take a hydrofoil or ferry from Milazzo, on the northern coast of Sicily between Cefalù and Messina. Trip length: at least 1 day, depending on how many islands you decide to explore.

❶ ★★ **Vulcano.** The volcanic summit of Gran Cratere and the Laghetti di Funghi (smelly, sulphury mud baths with supposed therapeutic qualities) are the big draws here and especially popular with northern European holidaymakers. Vulcano's black-sand beach is the finest in the archipelago.

❷ ★★ **Lipari.** With a lively port town and some good lava beaches like the famous Spiaggia Bianca (white-sand beaches are a novelty in this volcanic island chain), this is the most frequented Aeolian, with hotels for all tastes and budgets, good restaurants, and handy connections with the other islands. In addition to being the most bustling of the archipelago, Lipari is the world's biggest exporter of pumice stone.

❸ ★★ **Salina.** Thanks to some hot and hip hotels, a lush interior that's great for hiking, and the fact that the charming 1994 film *Il Postino*

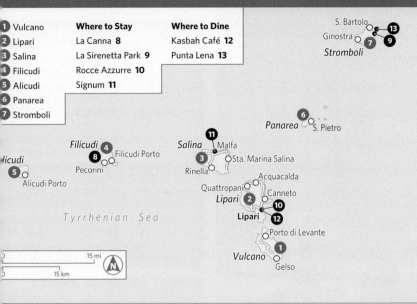

	Where to Stay	Where to Dine
1 Vulcano	La Canna **8**	Kasbah Café **12**
2 Lipari	La Sirenetta Park **9**	Punta Lena **13**
3 Salina	Rocce Azzurre **10**	
4 Filicudi	Signum **11**	
5 Alicudi		
6 Panarea		
7 Stromboli		

Lipari's port is conveniently linked by boat with the rest of the archipelago.

⋯as shot here, Salina has become a sort of "it" ⋯sland of late. Movers and shakers and nightlife-⋯eekers should note that there's not much ⋯action" on relaxing Salina; it's better suited to ⋯ouples and nature lovers.

4 ★ **Filicudi.** It's one of the more remote ⋯eolians (away from the ferry arc between ⋯alina and Stromboli), which makes it perfectly ⋯uited for complete relaxation, unimpeded by ⋯he day-trip traffic of the other islands. There's ⋯ust enough development, in the form of laid-⋯ack hotels and restaurants.

Vacation Rentals

If you can stay several days or a week in the Aeolians, and are traveling with your family or in a group, your best bet (and certainly the most economical option) may be a vacation rental. The website www.eoliando.it lists rental properties on all the islands. Most are (surprisingly affordable) villas and must be booked for at least 3 days. You'll also feel like an insider if you go this route, as vacation rentals are how Italians "do" the Eolie.

> *The island of Stromboli is the cone of a sluggish but active volcano.*

⑤ ★ **Alicudi.** Even more remote and less developed than Filicudi, the westernmost island in the archipelago attracts the yoga-retreat crowd in summer; the rest of the year, it's populated by just over 100 fishermen and goatherds.

⑥ ★★ **Panarea.** This tiny speck is the Aeolians' party isle, where Italian glamazons hit the open-air disco at the Hotel Raya until the wee hours. Avoid August, when the place resembles Spring Break, and you'll enjoy the island's hip, ethnic feel, and of course, its gorgeous swimming coves.

⑦ ★★★ **Stromboli.** The entire island is the cone of an active but sluggish volcano, which emits puffs of smoke all day that are visible throughout the archipelago. The nighttime trek to the summit, where fiery red lava flows can be seen, is the absolute highlight of an adventurous Aeolian holiday. One recommended outfitter for these up-close-and-personal volcanic excursions is **Magmatrek,** Via Vittorio Emanuele (☎ 090-9865768; www.magmatrek.it; tours from 25€ per person).

Travel Tip

Note that from October to April the Aeolians all but shut down; many hotels are closed and boat trips to the islands are drastically reduced. The website www.eoliando.it is an invaluable resource for planning your trip here. To get to the islands, take a hydrofoil or ferry from Milazzo. The main companies are **Siremar** (www.siremar.it), **Ustica Lines** (www.usticalines.it), and **Snav** (www.snav.it).

By ferry, allow 1 hour to reach Lipari from Milazzo and 4 hours to reach the farthest-flung of the chain, Stromboli. The times are halved on the faster hydrofoils. Ferry and hydrofoil fares run from 8€ (for a trip between Salina and Panarea) to 22€ for the long haul between Milazzo and Stromboli.

Cruising the Aeolians, You at the Helm

No matter which island you choose as your base, don't miss out on the most fabulous Aeolian recreational activity—**renting your own motorboat.** Many of the prettiest coves and idyllic swimming areas are not accessible by land, so captaining your own wooden *gozzo* or rubber *gommone* is the only way to go. When you see a spot where you'd like to stop for a swim, just drop anchor and dive in. The camaraderie between fellow boaters out on the water is great—you might even be invited aboard someone's yacht for cheese and Champagne. No experience is necessary to rent, as the boats are small and the waters calm. You'll find rental outfits stationed at the ports of each island. Half-day rates start at 50€ for a 5m (16-ft.) motorboat that will accommodate up to four people.

Where to Stay & Dine

Aeolian-style architecture at La Canna, on sleepy Filicudi.

★ Kasbah Café LIPARI *ITALIAN*

good bet for a fun night out, Kasbah serves elicious pasta and pizza in its alfresco garden f citrus trees below the citadel. There's live music many summer nights. Via Maurolico 25. ☎ 090-981-1075. Entrees 8€–16€. AE, DC, MC, V. pr–Oct lunch & dinner daily. Closed Nov–Mar.

★ La Canna FILICUDI

Carved out of an Aeolian-style house—all whitewashed walls and fat blue columns— very room has a private terrace with sea view, nd the sundrenched swimming pool looks out ver the port. Via Rosa 43. ☎ 090-9889956. www.lacannahotel.it. 14 units. Doubles 70€–140€. AE, DC, MC, V.

★★ kids La Sirenetta Park STROMBOLI

This is the best hotel on Stromboli, with airy guest rooms and common areas that include a nightclub. Via Marina 33. ☎ 090-986025. www.lasirenetta.it. 55 units. Doubles 150€–260€. AE, DC, MC, V.

★★★ Punta Lena STROMBOLI *SEAFOOD*

The best cuisine on Stromboli is served at this beachfront Aeolian house that's been converted into a 17-seat restaurant. Try the *pescato del giorno* (fish of the day) or the *gnocchi alla Saracena* (with whitefish, capers, olives, and tomatoes). The 10-minute walk to this place from town is a good excuse to indulge in dessert, too. Via Marina, Località Ficogrande. ☎ 090-986204. Entrees 10€–18€. AE, DC, MC, V. Apr–Oct lunch & dinner daily. Closed Nov–Mar. Reservations recommended.

★ Rocce Azzurre LIPARI

Staying at this old-fashioned place on a small bay is what a traditional Aeolian vacation is all about. Rooms are done up in an appropriate marine palette of blue and white, with lots of tile throughout. Via Maddalena, Porto delle Genti. ☎ 090-9813248. www.hotelrocceazzurre.it. 33 units. Doubles 150€–220€. AE, DC, MC, V.

★★ Signum SALINA

From the hillside setting of this hip and quiet retreat, 6km (3¾ miles) from the port, an infinity pool offers spectacular views of Panarea and Stromboli. Guest rooms are chic and spare. Via Scalo 15, Malfa di Salina. ☎ 090-9844222. www.hotelsignum.it. 30 units. Doubles from 150€. AE, DC, MC, V. Closed mid-Nov to mid-Mar.

Dining Tip

When deciding where to eat in the Aeolians, it's often best to take the advice of your hotel staff—because they're accustomed to discerning Italian gourmands, they'll rarely point customers to a bad meal. I've also had the best tomato bruschetta of my entire life at a simple beach shack on Panarea.

Palermo

A personal confession: I find Palermo as frustrating and stressful as anyone else, but I can't get enough of it. It's certainly the most challenging city in Italy for visitors, as oppressive heat and constant chaos can hinder your ability to cover itineraries that look easy on a map. For those who brave the madness, the reward is the discovery of artistic gems and memorable vignettes of street life. I can't guarantee you'll love every inch of this city, but if you can get to even two-thirds of the places I list (allowing for some cannoli breaks along the way), you'll get closer to the soul of Sicily.

> Just about anything you could ever want is on sale at Palermo's Ballarò and Vucciria street markets.

START Palermo is accessible by air from all major Italian cities, and by boat from Naples.

① ★★ **Palazzo dei Normanni.** Sumptuous and remarkably evocative of the golden age when Palermo was a splendid court city where West met East, the formidable Arab-Norman palace consists of the **Royal Apartments,** where King Roger II himself slumbered and held court (the apartments are now part of Sicily's regional government offices, so access to those chambers isn't always guaranteed), and the

★★★ **Cappella Palatina,** commissioned by Roger II from 1130 to 1140 and adorned with the most spectacular Byzantine mosaics outside **Monreale** (p 646, **①**), Ravenna, or Istanbul. ⊕ 2–3 hr. Piazza del Parlamento. ☎ 091-7054006. Admission 6€. Mon–Sat 8am–noon, 2–5pm; Sun 8:30am–2:30pm. Bus: 104, 105, 108, 109, 110, 118, 304, 309.

② ★ **Cattedrale.** The Arab-Norman Duomo, a 12th-century structure much reworked and muddled in subsequent eras, with its grassy

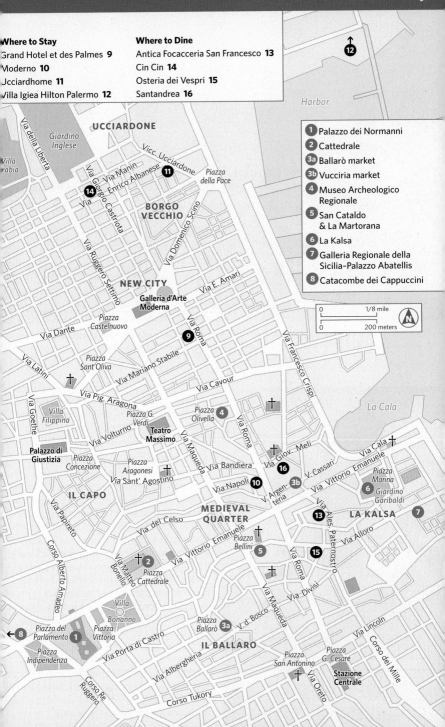

1 Palazzo dei Normanni
2 Cattedrale
3a Ballarò market
3b Vucciria market
4 Museo Archeologico Regionale
5 San Cataldo & La Martorana
6 La Kalsa
7 Galleria Regionale della Sicilia–Palazzo Abatellis
8 Catacombe dei Cappuccini

0   1/8 mile
0   200 meters

> *ABOVE* Palermo's 12th-century Duomo is an architectural jumble of Arab and Norman influences.
> *BELOW* Santa Maria dello Spasimo in La Kalsa is now an atmospheric Gothic shell.

square is a welcome stop along one of the most maniacal roads in the city. ⏱ **30 min.** Piazza Cattedrale. ☎ 091-334373. Duomo: admission free; crypt and treasury: 1€ each. Mon–Sat 9:30am–1:30pm, 2:30–5:30pm. Bus: 101, 104, 105, 107, 139.

③ ★★ Ballarò & Vucciria markets. Nowhere is Palermo's multicultural pedigree more evident than at its boisterous street markets. The stalls at both Ballarò and Vucciria go on for blocks and blocks, hawking everything from spices to seafood to sides of beef to toilet paper to handicrafts to electronics and meat snacks (not sold together) of questionable provenance. **Ballarò,** Piazza del Carmine to Piazza Ballarò (west of the train station toward the Palazzo dei Normanni), is perhaps the more authentic of the two, where more real Palermitans shop. But the twinkling lights of **Vucciria,** Via Argenteria (north of Via Vittorio Emanuele and east of Via Roma),whose name comes from the French *boucherie,* or "butcher shop," and its covered souklike atmosphere is irresistibly charming. The vendors' colorful theatrics are very much for your benefit, so feel free to photograph away as they ham it up with swordfish heads and the like. ⏱ **1 hr. or more.**

> *An anonymous, grisly* Triumph of Death *is the star exhibit at the Galleria Regionale della Sicilia.*

④ ★★★ **Museo Archeologico Regionale.** It's one of Italy's best archaeological museums and a must if you're visiting any of the Greek sites on the island, especially Selinunte: The metopes from several of the temples there are on display here. The museum is a dusty, rambling, and not very well-marked place (a common feature of southern Mediterranean museums with world-class collections), which makes the adventure of "discovering" its treasures all the more fun and Indiana Jones–like. In addition to the native Sicilian artifacts, the Egyptian and Etruscan collections are noteworthy. Eleven thousand works are on display. ⏱ 2 hr. Piazza Olivella 24. ☎ 091-6116805. Admission 6€. Daily 8:30am–2pm; Tues–Fri also 2:30–6:30pm. Bus: 101, 102, 103, 104, 107.

⑤ ★★ **San Cataldo & La Martorana.** These side-by-side medieval churches, separated by a sultry little garden of tropical plants and trees, are more good examples of Palermo's striking Arab-Norman architecture. The bell-towered La Martorana, to the left as you climb the stairs from Piazza Bellini, has sumptuous mosaics, while San Cataldo is more interesting from the outside: It's the one with the red domes that look like worn pencil erasers and lacy Moorish crenellation around the tops of the walls. San Cataldo's opening hours are erratic; if it's closed when you arrive, ask the custodian at La Martorana for the key. ⏱ 45 min. Piazza Bellini. ☎ 091-6161692. Free admission. La Martorana: Mon–Sat 9:30am–1pm, 3:30–6:30pm; Sun 8:30am–1pm. Bus: 101, 102.

⑥ ★★ **La Kalsa.** The key to understanding the contrasts of Palermo—if that's even possible—is this tangle of streets south of the main

> *Many of the mummified corpses in the Catacombe dei Cappuccini remain fully clothed centuries after death.*

harbor. The name is derived from the Arabic *khalisa,* or "pure," which the Kalsa is anything *but.* In the oldest and most intriguing part of the city, tarnished baroque gems like Palazzo Gangi (Piazza Croce dei Vespri), Palazzo Ajutamicristo (Via Garibaldi), and Palazzo Mirto (Piazza Marina) evoke Palermo's princely heyday, while entire blocks of the neighborhood are crumbled, having never been rebuilt after Allied air raids in 1943. Some of the bombed-out buildings are makeshift homes for families (and their livestock), who live together in a few rooms and sleep on simple pallets, while other scarred buildings have been repurposed as avant-garde art exhibition spaces.

Palazzo Abatellis, on Via Alloro, is home to the **Galleria Regionale della Sicilia (7)**. **Santa Maria dello Spasimo** is a swoon-inducing skeleton of a church, where mature trees grow out of broken Gothic vaults into the Palermitan sky. La Kalsa is safe during the day, but don't walk around here alone at night. ⏱ 1 hr. or more.

7 ★★★ **Galleria Regionale della Sicilia–Palazzo Abatellis.** There aren't very many "big names" here, but this is nevertheless one of the most wonderful art museums in Italy. The star work is a 15th-century painting of the *Triumph of Death* (artist unknown), a gory, shrill, and immediately captivating scene of a skeleton on horseback, trampling hapless men and women—their fine clothing and jeweled necklaces notwithstanding. The rest of the collection concentrates on Sicilian art from the 13th to the 18th centuries. ⏱ 1½–2 hr. Via Alloro 4. ☎ 091-6230011. Admission 6€. Daily 9am–1pm; Tues–Fri also 2:30–7pm. Bus: 103, 105, 139.

8 ★★★ **Catacombe dei Cappuccini.** Palermo's "Library of Corpses" is the most bizarre final resting place in Italy, downright creepy to some, oddly clinical to others. Mummified, fully dressed cadavers hang from the walls, cantilevering eerily toward you as you walk the corridors of this ostensibly holy place. From

Putti-Palooza: Serpotta's Stuccoed Oratories

Palermo is justly famous for its fantastic rococo oratories, decorated with delightful and remarkably three-dimensional stuccoes by native son Giacomo Serpotta in the early 18th century. (An *oratorio* is a private place of prayer attached to a church of the same name—and in the case of the three listed below, the attached church is far less interesting than its *oratorio*.)

The ★★★ **Oratorio di San Lorenzo,** Via dell'Immacolatella (☎ 091-332779), was his earliest such work—the walls are filled with playful white *putti* (cherubs) blowing bubbles or kissing over the architectonic elements, which are also in white stucco. The effect is disarmingly dynamic, as if the whole place were inhaling and exhaling around you. At the more polychrome ★★ **Oratorio del Rosario**

0 di San Domenico, Via dei Bambinai (☎ 091-332779), another profusion of charming *putti* frames more introspective statues of the Christian virtues. Admission to both spots is free; they're open Monday 3 to 6pm, Tuesday to Friday 9am to 1pm, and 3 to 5:30pm, and Saturday 9am to 1pm.

The ★★★ **Oratorio di Santa Cita** (pictured above), Via Valverde 3 (☎ 091-332779), is the other great Serpotta masterpiece, another all-white chapel where the cherubs steal the show—romping and climbing over the "architecture," coyly contorting their chubby bodies, they are unself-conscious joy personified, like a day-care center full of the most adorable toddlers imaginable. Admission is free, and it's open Monday to Saturday 9am to 1pm.

the 16th to the 20th centuries, some 8,000 souls were "buried" here, most of them having elected while alive to be displayed thus—in the open and in their Sunday best (though the campy poses of some look more like mortician's license).

Embalming was an experimental science for much of the crypt's history, so some corpses

have held up better than others. The astonishingly well-preserved body of 2-year-old Rosalia Lombardo, who died in 1920, is a particularly successful (and very disturbing) example. ⏱ 30 min. Piazza Cappuccini 1. ☎ 091-212117. Admission 1.50€. Daily 9am–noon, 3–5pm. Bus: 327.

Where to Stay & Dine

★★ kids **Antica Focacceria San Francesco** CENTRO STORICO *PALERMITAN* A casual place in a grand palazzo setting, this famous spot is great for your first primer in typical Palermitan food. From the self-serve area on the left as you walk in, you can assemble a sampler plate of swordfish roulades, various stuffed pizzas and baked pastas, and the delicious *panelle* (chickpea fritters). More "advanced" palates can go to the counter where a taciturn staffer stirs a giant black cauldron full of stewed spleen for the *pane con milza* sandwiches. There's also a proper sit-down restaurant with tables in the lovely piazza out front and a menu of traditional *primi* and *secondi*. Via Paternostro 58. ☎ 091-320264. www.afsf.it. Entrees 8€–16€. AE, DC, MC, V. Lunch & dinner daily. Bus: 101, 103, 104, 107.

★★ kids **Cin Cin** NORTH OF CENTRO STORICO *SICILIAN/CREOLE* The name means "Cheers!" in Italian, and you'll always find a convivial reception at this locally adored Sicilian-Creole spot off Via Libertà, in the new part of town. The succulent seafood pastas are my personal favorite in Palermo—see if you can get them to bring you a sample of several. The chef-owner, Vincenzo Clemente, also does excellent meat entrees as well as a few Cajun-inspired dishes. Via Manin 22. ☎ 091-6124095. Entrees 7.50€–16€. AE, DC, MC, V. Lunch July–Aug Mon–Fri; dinner year-round Mon–Sat. Bus: 101, 107.

★★ **Grand Hotel et des Palmes** CENTRO STORICO The top address for reliving bygone glamour, this was once the city's prime setting for trysts and intrigue. A recent sprucing-up of the property made rooms much more modern and comfortable, but the place is still decadent and sultry, and as one Sicilian friend describes it, *palermitano da morire* ("ridiculously Palermitan"). Via Roma 398. ☎ 091-6028111. www.hotel-despalmes.it. 180 units. Doubles 150€–250€. AE, DC, MC, V.

Moderno CENTRO STORICO
It's been several decades since this budget hotel right off the Quattro Canti was "modern," but the pale pastel walls and simple, homey decor make this a cool and comfortable choice in the most central location possible. Via Roma

> *Stirring the vat for the* pane con milza *(spleen sandwich) at Antica Focacceria San Francesco.*

276. ☎ 091-588683. www.hotelmodernopa.com. 38 units. Doubles 75€. AE, DC, MC, V.

★★ **Osteria dei Vespri** CENTRO STORICO *PALERMITAN* This consistently delicious and atmospheric spot, on the ground floor of the elegant baroque Palazzo Gangi, is where Palermitans take out-of-towners for well-crafted twists on local cuisine in an intimate, old-fashioned setting. Mario Batali loves this place and says that it feels as if "the Corleone family could walk in at any moment." Piazza Croce dei Vespri 6. ☎ 091-6171631. Entrees 10€–16€. AE, DC, MC, V. Lunch & dinner Mon–Sat. Bus: 103, 105.

Street Eats

Are you steely of stomach? Is the phrase "barbecued goat intestines" more appetizing than revolting? If so, you'll definitely want to try out some of the *cibo di strada* (street food) in markets like **Vucciria** and **Ballarò** (p 670, ❸). Real Palermitans go crazy for this stuff, and you'll earn major credit if you step up to the challenge.

Slaughterhouse leftovers play a starring role on the "menu" at these stands, so you might be better off not asking what's in there. No matter what stewed organ they're hawking—all organs and medleys thereof are fair game—Palermo's colorful *cibo di strada* vendors will unfailingly tell you it's the most *pregiato* (prized) piece of the animal. Sure, many of these nondescript meats will tempt you with their aromas, but it's only fair to disclose that *stigghiola* is essentially barbecued goat intestines, and that the *pane con milza* sandwich consists of chopped spleen on a roll. (You go in thinking, "Piece of cake, it's just a modified Sloppy Joe," but those decommissioned red blood cells are an acquired taste.) Still, locals line up all day for the *pane con milza* (with optional cheese on top) at **Antica Focacceria San Francesco** (p 674), where the spleen bits are churned in a huge, ominous-looking cauldron.

On the less daring side, try *sfincione*, a typical Palermitan pizza with tomatoes, anchovies, onion, and grated cheese, but you'll get bonus points for ordering *babaluci*, baby snails with olive oil, garlic, and fennel. Craving stadium food? Have *pane con salsiccia*, an herb-y Sicilian riff on bratwurst on a roll. If you are vegetarian, try a delicious *pane e panelle* sandwich. *Panelle* are disks of fried chickpeas—no weird stuff, I promise—and universally adored by *cibo di strada* newbies. Least bizarre of all, *arancini* are another typical Sicilian snack and easy to eat on the go. These deep-fried rice balls with mozzarella or meat inside will cost you about 1€ each. The best *arancini* in town are at **Antico Caffè Spinnato**, Via Principe di Belmonte 107/115 (☎ 091-329229).

★★ **Santandrea** CENTRO STORICO *SICILIAN*
More chic than the restaurants listed above, this spot has alfresco and inside tables. Thanks to its location in the heart of the Vucciria market, Santandrea features only the freshest vegetables and seafood. Santandrea is beloved by one of our photographers, who calls it "just the place you are always looking for—the right combination of inventive dishes with amazing ingredients and a relaxed, hip setting." Piazza Sant'Andrea 4. ☎ 091-334999. Entrees 8€–18€. AE, DC, MC, V. Dinner Mon–Sat. Bus: 101, 103, 104, 107.

★★ **Ucciardhome** NORTH OF CENTRO STORICO
At Palermo's "it" hotel for modernist aesthetes, dark wenge wood furniture contrasts with ivory fabrics for a masculine and ultra-relaxing feel. Rooms are filled with techno-gadgetry, and the sleek bathrooms are done up in metallic mosaics. Ucciardhome is on the less chaotic modern side of town, across from the Carcere Ucciardone, a prison and the hotel's namesake! Via Enrico Albanese 34–36. ☎ 091-348426. www.hotelucciardhome.com. 14 units. Doubles 120€–200€. AE, DC, MC, V.

★★★ kids **Villa Igiea Hilton Palermo** WATERFRONT Newly acquired by Hilton, this peach-toned castle surrounded by gardens and the sea is the most luxurious place to stay in Palermo. Graceful columns of a Greek temple ruin stand alongside the hotel's kidney-shaped swimming pool, beyond which there's a sheer drop to the sea. The Villa Igiea is not in the center of town; you'll need a car or taxi to go anywhere. Salita Belmonte 43. ☎ 091-6312111. www.hilton.com. 124 units. Doubles 250€–300€. AE, DC, MC, V.

Siracusa

A happy vibe, wonderful baroque architecture, and impressive Greek ruins make it hard not to fall in love with this seaside city. Siracusa's *centro storico* is the island of Ortigia (where you should stay if at all possible), an impossibly picturesque village with sea views down every bewitching alley; the ancient sites are on the mainland. Taking in the sights and local flavor of Siracusa is a breeze and enormously satisfying—no wonder it's so many visitors' favorite destination in Sicily.

> The ornamental Duomo is just one of the theatrical buildings that ring Piazza del Duomo.

START Siracusa is 1½ hours south of Taormina on the A18/E45. It's 3 hours southeast of Palermo on the A19 and A18, and 3 hours east of Agrigento on the SS540, A19, and A18.

① ★★★ **Piazza del Duomo.** The theatrical baroque perfection of Sicily's most beautiful piazza seems the creation of an operatic set designer. Dominating the square is the ★★ **Duomo** (daily 8am–noon, 4–7pm), a sunny baroque cathedral built on top of the ancient Greek Temple of Athena. On the northwest side of the piazza is the striking ★★ **Palazzo Beneventano del Bosco**—with its convex, wrought-iron balconies. On the south side of the square is the sultry-looking church of ★ **Santa Lucia alla Badia.** Also here is an entrance to the ★★ **Hypogeum** (no phone; admission 3€; Tues–Sun 9am–1pm, 4–8pm), a network of underground chambers and corridors dug as air raid shelters in World War II. ⏱ 1 hr.

② ★★ **Fonte Aretusa.** This unique sunken natural fountain near the harbor is one of Siracusa's loveliest sights. Papyrus grows in the shallow pool, and the freshwater spring beneath once served as the city's main water supply. ⏱ 15 min. Passeggio Aretusa.

③ ★ **Jewish Ghetto & Miqwe.** In the ladder of narrow streets between Via della Giudecca and Via Alagona are remnants of the old Jewish Ghetto. The recently unearthed **Miqwe** (mikvah) consists of three freshwater pools, used for ritual bathing, and a private pool for the rabbi. ⏱ 45 min. Miqwe: Via Alagona 52. ☎ 0931-22255. Admission 5€. Daily 10am–7pm.

④ **Temple of Apollo.** The ruins of the oldest Doric temple in Sicily, the 6th-century-B.C. Apollonion, lie near the modern shopfronts of

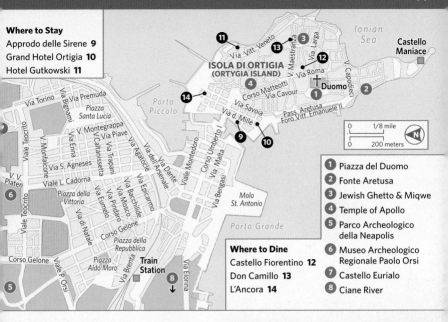

Where to Stay	
Approdo delle Sirene	**9**
Grand Hotel Ortigia	**10**
Hotel Gutkowski	**11**

① Piazza del Duomo
② Fonte Aretusa
③ Jewish Ghetto & Miqwe
④ Temple of Apollo
⑤ Parco Archeologico della Neapolis
⑥ Museo Archeologico Regionale Paolo Orsi
⑦ Castello Eurialo
⑧ Ciane River

Where to Dine	
Castello Fiorentino	**12**
Don Camillo	**13**
L'Ancora	**14**

Piazza Pancali. ⏱ 15 min. Corso Matteotti/Via dell'Apollonion. No access.

⑤ ★★★ 🧒 **Parco Archeologico della Neapolis.** The main draw at Siracusa's wonderfully enjoyable archaeological park is the gigantic **Teatro Greco** (Greek Theater), whose *cavea* (seating area) was hewn right out of bedrock in the 3rd century B.C. This bowl of blazing white stone is a heat trap in summer, but there are some nymphaeums (alcoves with pools—a sort of ancient air conditioner) at the top of the theater where you can splash yourself with water.

The thickly vegetated area below the theater is the **Latomia del Paradiso** (Quarry of Paradise), a lush and primeval garden where a stegosaurus would not look out of place. Down here, follow the tour groups into the **Orecchio di Dionisio** (Ear of Dionysius), a tall and vaguely ear-shaped cave where the Greek tyrant Dionysius supposedly kept and eavesdropped on prisoners. Visitors are welcome to test out the acoustics.

Back across the park entrance road is the 2nd-century-A.D. **Anfiteatro Romano** (Roman Amphitheater), where gladiators fought and mock sea battles were staged. ⏱ 2 hr. Viale Paradiso. ☎ 0931-66206. Admission 6 €; 9 € when combined with Museo Archeologico; 10€ when combined with Museo Archeologico and Castello Eurialo. Daily 9am–1 hr. before sunset.

> Siracusa's patron, Santa Lucia, is often depicted holding her eyes on a plate, in reference to her blinding and martyrdom.

> *Siracusa's Parco Archeologico della Neapolis includes ruins from ancient Greek settlements.*

⑥ ★★ **Museo Archeologico Regionale Paolo Orsi.** Eighteen thousand artifacts cover Sicilian prehistory to the Greek classical period, including some particularly gorgeous Greek archaic terra cottas. Observing the skilled execution and artistic sensitivity of the works here, it's easy to imagine the wealth and sophistication of ancient Siracusa. ⏱ 1 hr. Viale Teocrito 66. ☎ 093-464022. 4€; 9€ when combined with Parco Archeologico; 10€ when combined with Parco Archeologico and Castello Eurialo. Mon 3-5pm; Tues-Sat 9am-1pm, 3-5pm; Sun 9am-1pm.

⑦ ★ **Castello Eurialo.** This 4th-century-B.C. fortress is the best-preserved example of a Greek castle anywhere in the Mediterranean. It's also one of those great, under-visited Italian archaeological sites where you can romp all over everything, from the towers to the tunnels, without getting yelled at. There was yelling in the past, however, for legend has it that Castello Eurialo is where Greek mathematician Archimedes famously cried "Eureka!" upon discovering the law of water displacement while taking a bath. ⏱ 1 hr. Piazza Eurialo 1, in the Belvedere district. ☎ 0931-481111. Admssion 2€; 10€ when combined with Parco Archeologico and Museo Archeologico. Daily 9am-5:30pm.

⑧ ★ **Ciane River.** Just south of Ortigia is a nature reserve where dense papyrus grows along the banks of the Fiume Ciane. Boat tours up this gentle waterway are a rustic and peaceful way to step back in time. You can also walk the path that follows the river course, past an ancient temple. ⏱ 1 hr. or more. Take Via Elorina (SS115) south to the bridge that crosses both the Anapo and Ciane rivers. Boats are usually stationed on the far (Ciane) side. Boat rides are 5€-8€ for 1½ hr., and can also be arranged through tour companies at the marina in Ortigia.

Beach Tip

For recommendations on great beaches within a half-hour drive of Siracusa, see p 655, ⑤.

Where to Stay & Dine

> *Don't be surprised to see sea urchin* (ricci) *and scorpionfish on Sicilian menus.*

★★ **Approdo delle Sirene** ORTIGIA

The "Mermaid's Landing" was opened in 2004 by a mother and son from Rome. The nautical decor features dark wood floors and striped linens. Rooms with water views are considerably more spacious than standards. Riva Garibaldi 15. ☎ 0931-24857. www.apprododellesirene.com. 8 units. Doubles 90€–125€. AE, DC, MC, V. 2-night minimum stay June–Aug.

★★ kids **Castello Fiorentino** ORTIGIA *PIZZA*

You can't get the full Italian dining picture without going to a great pizzeria—and this is one of the best in Sicily. Waits can be long, but the warm, what-can-I-getcha service makes you feel like a regular. Via Crocifisso 6. ☎ 0931-21097. Pizzas from 5€. AE, DC, MC, V. Dinner Tues–Sun.

★★ **Don Camillo** ORTIGIA *SEAFOOD*

This is the place to splurge on the most exquisite, delicate renditions of Sicilian specialties, including spaghetti with *ricci* (sea urchin—trust me, it's wonderful). It's a special night out, where the focus is on the food, not Sicilian theatrics. Via Maestranza 96. ☎ 0931-67133. www.ristorantedoncamillosiracusa.it. Entrees 12€–22€. AE, DC, MC, V. Lunch & dinner Mon–Sat. Reservations recommended.

★ **Grand Hotel Ortigia** ORTIGIA

This Art Nouveau palazzo facing the marina is the best choice for the services and amenities of a larger hotel. It's a dated but comfortable place,

with ample bathrooms. Viale Mazzini 12 (at Via XX Settembre). ☎ 0931-464600. www.grandhotelsr.it. 58 units. Doubles 160€–250€. AE, DC, MC, V.

★ **Hotel Gutkowski** ORTIGIA

On the quieter back side of Ortigia, this robin's-egg-blue palazzo is a haven of minimalist, spalike style, though some rooms are small. Lungomare Vittorini 26. ☎ 0931-465861. www.guthotel.it. 25 units. Doubles 110€. AE, DC, MC, V.

★★ kids **L'Ancora** ORTIGIA *SIRACUSAN/SEAFOOD*

The full bounty of the sea plus lots of fresh local vegetables and herbs are employed at this bustling local favorite near the main post office. Via G. Perno 7. ☎ 0931-462369. www.ristoranteancora.com. Entrees 10€–16€. AE, DC, MC, V. Lunch & dinner Tues–Sun.

Siracusa after Dark

For nightlife with a little more edge than people-watching on Piazza del Duomo, walk 1 minute south to Piazza San Rocco. **San Rocco** (pictured above), Piazza San Rocco 3/5 (☎ 333-9854177), is a sleek indoor/outdoor cocktail bar with a great *aperitivo* spread and a young crowd. Next door, **Doctor Sam,** Piazza San Rocco 4 (☎ 0931-483598), is perfectly friendly but big on tattoos, piercings, and reggae. Down the street, at the English-style **Vecchio Pub,** Via delle Vergini 9 (☎ 0931-464692), tourists and expats of all ages come to tie one on among their own species.

Taormina

Sicily's most breathtaking resort destination is also its most heavily exploited by mass tourism—expect big crowds in July and August. Having said that, Taormina is a must on any first-time itinerary through Sicily. Apart from its astonishing natural beauty—it's set high on a hill that slopes steeply through lush vegetation to the Ionian Sea—Taormina is undeniably jolly. It's also a convenient base for trips to Mt. Etna; numerous agencies in town operate a variety of full-day excursions, or you can do it yourself if you have a car.

> *The Teatro Greco-Romano still hosts theater, 2,300 years after it was built.*

START Taormina is 2½ hours from Palermo. Take the A19 through the interior to Catania, then cut north on the A18 to Taormina. It's 1½ hours north of Siracusa on the A18.

① ★ **Corso Umberto I.** Anyone who visits Taormina will walk the length of this pedestrian thoroughfare at least once. It's the town's retail artery and the de rigueur place in town for tanned vacationers on parade, though it can be a slow-moving and downright claustrophobic parade in summer. The ★★ **shopping** here is the best on Sicily, ranging from high-fashion to high-kitsch, and there are plenty of cafes and bars where you can grab a seat and watch the pageant go by. (As for restaurants, the better tables in Taormina are usually on side streets,

away from the tourist crush.) Halfway down Corso Umberto I is the panoramic ★★ **Piazza IX Aprile,** with its medieval clock tower and wide expanse of checkerboard pavement overlooking the sea. Taormina's fortresslike 15th-century **Duomo** lies near the southern end of Corso Umberto. ⊙ At least 30 min.

② ★★★ kids **Teatro Greco-Romano.** The most spectacular playhouse of the ancient world—known to most locals as the *Teatro Antico*—is precipitously nestled on a promontory with mesmerizing views over the sea and Mt. Etna. Built in the 3rd century B.C., the theater once accommodated 10,000 spectators and is still used today for the **Taormina Arte** summer festival (www.taormina-arte.com); both the

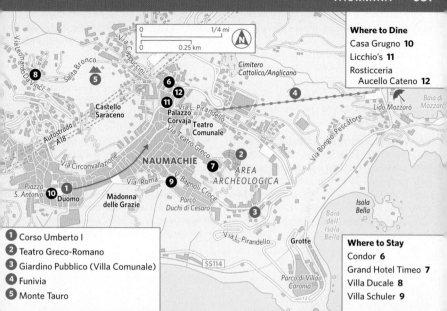

Where to Dine
Casa Grugno **10**
Licchio's **11**
Rosticceria
  Aucello Cateno **12**

① Corso Umberto I
② Teatro Greco-Romano
③ Giardino Pubblico (Villa Comunale)
④ Funivia
⑤ Monte Tauro

Where to Stay
Condor **6**
Grand Hotel Timeo **7**
Villa Ducale **8**
Villa Schuler **9**

> The gardens of the Villa Comunale are a delightful Victorian folly bequeathed by an eccentric Englishwoman.

onstage dramatics and histrionic peanut gallery make for one very memorable evening. (Hot-blooded Sicilians don't withhold audible commentary and wild gesturing when a performance stirs their passions.) The magnificent site also captured the attention of Woody Allen, who set the chorus scenes of *Mighty Aphrodite* here.🕑 1 hr. Via del Teatro Greco 40. ☎ 0942-23220. Admission 6€. Daily 9am–7pm.

③ ★★ kids **Giardino Pubblico (Villa Comunale).** Taormina's quiet and shady municipal park is the perfect antidote to the crowds elsewhere in town. Bring a picnic and snag a spot on one of the benches, or just go for a walk, and you might be lucky enough to see a slice of authentic Taorminese life, such as a young *mamma* pushing a stroller toward the playground, uninfected by

A Toast at the Timeo

One of Taormina's classic experiences is having a drink at the **Grand Hotel Timeo** (p 683), spectacularly located beneath the Teatro, with sumptuous Mediterranean gardens. It's a pricey detour (cocktails are around 15€) but a beautiful and always lively spot that perfectly embodies Taormina's holiday spirit.

tourism. Lower in the park, there's a bizarre cluster of masonry towers and wooden railings—a Victorian folly created by Florence Trevelyan, the noble Englishwoman whose private garden became Taormina's public Villa Comunale in 1927. As with most everything in Taormina, the park has incredible views. ⏱ 45 min. Via Bagnoli Croci. No phone. Free admission.

❹ ★ **Funivia.** Taormina is 200m (650 ft.) above the shore of the Ionian Sea, but the handy *funivia* (cableway) makes it a snap to access the beaches below—for a swim or just a stroll. Right outside the lower station of the cableway is **Mazzarò**, while a few minutes' walk south (to the right as you exit the station) leads to a larger bay and **Isola Bella** (see "Swimming near Taormina,"

below, for information on both beaches). Via Pirandello. Tickets 1.80€ one-way, 3€ round-trip. No credit cards. Daily 9am–1am.

❺ ★★ **Monte Tauro.** One of the best views in all of eastern Sicily is from this high point 3km (2 miles) northwest of Taormina (on the road to Castelmola). Monte Tauro's 390m (1,280 ft.) elevation affords visitors awe-inspiring ★★ **views of Mt. Etna** on clear days. There are also some hiking paths and ancient ruins here, but Monte Tauro is mostly recommended as a panoramic spot—and an escape from the hordes down in town. ⏱ 1 hr. Follow Via Leonardo da Vinci up to Castelmola, then look for signs for Monte Tauro, or take the Castelmola-Monte Tauro bus from Via Pirandello in Taormina town.

Swimming near Taormina

Don't let the town's vertical distance from the water discourage you: It's easy to reach the shore, whether by taking the funivia (❹) or local buses from Via Pirandello. As with the best Italian coastlines, "beaches" tend to be narrow and crowded, with gravelly sand, but the surrounding scenery of forests and rocky cliffs and warm, cerulean water make up for it! Expect to pay 8€ to 10€ for use of a chair and umbrella at any of the beach clubs.

At the bottom of the cableway is **Mazzarò** (pictured), a small bay with several beach clubs and kayak rentals. The larger bay to the south is punctuated in the middle by **Isola Bella,** a gorgeous island and World Wildlife Federation nature reserve that's connected to the beach by a narrow spit of sand (you walk or wade to the *isola*, depending on water level). If you want to see where young Italians party, take a bus to **Giardini-Naxos,** a more modern resort development with budget hotels and thumping nightclubs on the beach.

Where to Stay & Dine

> Request a sea view for your stay at Villa Schuler.

★★ **Casa Grugno** CENTRO *SICILIAN*
The hottest restaurant in town is helmed by an Austrian-born chef who uses strictly fresh local ingredients to prepare traditional island recipes in artful, modern ways. Via Santa Maria dei Greci. ☎ 0942-21208. www.casagrugno.it. Entrees 15€–25€. AE, DC, MC, V. Dinner Thurs–Tues. Reservations essential in high season.

Condor CENTRO
The accommodations at this popular budget choice are spacious but bare-bones basic European. Via Dietro Cappuccini 25. ☎ 0942-23124. www.condorhotel.com. 12 units. Doubles from 80€. AE, DC, MC, V.

★ **Grand Hotel Timeo** CENTRO
If you must indulge in the pseudoglamorous (and overpriced) "grand hotel" experience in Taormina, skip the overly formal San Domenico and book a room instead at the buzzier and more central Timeo. Or just visit the fabulous gardens and happening bar. Via Teatro Greco 59. ☎ 0942-625837. www.framonhotelgroup.com. 83 units. Doubles 380€–500€. AE, DC, MC, V.

★★ kids **Licchio's** CENTRO *SICILIAN*
Ignore the painfully anglicized name, because this is one of local Taorminesi's favorite places to eat, not a tourist trap. You'll dine in a surgically bright and bustling back garden on classic, seafood-focused Sicilian *primi* and *secondi*, plus *antipasti* like tuna burgers and out-of-this-world carpaccio. Via C. Patricio 10.

☎ 0942-625327. Entrees 7€–18€. AE, DC, MC, V. Dinner Fri–Wed. Reservations essential in high season.

★ **Rosticceria Aucello Cateno** CENTRO *SNACKS*
With so many tourist-trap restaurants in Taormina, **take-out** joints are a godsend. My favorite is this jolly place where you can get freshly made lasagne, cannelloni, roast chicken, and *arancini* for a few euros each. Via Cappuccini 8. ☎ 0942-623672. Daily 10am–8pm. No credit cards.

★★★ **Villa Ducale** WEST OF TOWN
My favorite place to stay in Taormina is this sunny boutique inn, serenely perched high above town and decorated with folksy Sicilian flair—no bland bubble of luxury here, though rooms are well appointed. Many units have terraces with jaw-dropping views of Mt. Etna. A free shuttle bus throughout the day makes reaching town a nonissue. Via Leonardo da Vinci 60. ☎ 0942-28153. www.villaducale.com. 16 units. Doubles 130€–260€. AE, DC, MC, V.

★★ kids **Villa Schuler** CENTRO
This pastel palazzo hearkens back to a gentler era of Taormina tourism. Immersed in lush gardens below the madness of Corso Umberto, the family-run hotel is a haven of tranquility with airy rooms (many with dramatic sea views) and huge bathrooms. Via Roma, Piazzetta Bastione. ☎ 0942-23481. www.villaschuler.com. 27 units. Doubles 107€–190€. AE, DC, MC, V.

Sicily Fast Facts

Accommodations Booking Services
Sicily Hotels (www.sicilyhotels.com) is linked in with most of the best properties in each major tourist area and lesser-known spots. They also work with B&Bs, *agriturismi,* and rental villas, but the best source for vacation rentals (especially higher-end properties) is the London-based **Think Sicily** (☎ 44-0207/377-8518; www.thinksicily.com). Tourist info points at the major train stations and airports can also assist with last-minute hotel bookings.

American Express
There are no American Express offices in Sicily. The Italian cities with AmEx offices are Rome, Florence, Venice, and Milan.

ATMs
You'll have no trouble finding cash machines (*bancomat)* in Sicily. They're always attached to banks (*banca, banco, credito, cassa),* which are ubiquitous in touristy places like Taormina, and even small towns off the beaten path have at least one bank with an ATM. Italy generally uses 4-digit PINs; if you have a 6-digit PIN, check with your bank.

Dentists & Doctors
If you have a mild medical issue or dental problem while traveling in Sicily, most hotels will be able to refer you to a local doctor (*medico)* or dentist (*dentista)* who speaks English. Fees are generally between 50€ and 100€. Otherwise, go to the *pronto soccorso* (emergency room) at the nearest hospital, where they'll treat your immediate problem (for example, a sprained ankle) for free and give you a short course of prescription drugs if necessary.

Emergencies
For general emergencies, call ☎ 112 for the Carabinieri or ☎ 113 for the Polizia. Call ☎ 114 for an ambulance and ☎ 115 for the fire department. For a medical emergency that doesn't require an ambulance, see "Dentists & Doctors," above. To report lost or stolen items, see "Police," p 685.

Getting There
Palermo and Catania airports are well-connected with the Italian mainland and other European hubs. From May to October, "low-cost" airline **Eurofly** (www.euroflyusa.com) flies nonstop between New York's JFK and Palermo. You can also take the **overnight train** from Rome or Naples (which crosses into Sicily via ferry over the Strait of Messina) or the **overnight ferry** from Naples to Palermo, operated by **Tirrenia** (www.tirrenia.it) and **SNAV** (www.snav.it).

Getting Around
It's best to explore Sicily by car. Once out of Palermo, it's a pleasurable and hassle-free affair, as the roads are good and traffic is minimal. Do note that fuel is expensive in Sicily (as with all of Italy), and a few of the autostrade are toll roads. A detailed road map, such as Touring Club Italiano's Sicilia map, is essential and available at airport bookshops and most newsstands. **Sicily by Car** (www.sbc.it) and **Maggiore** (www.maggiore.it), both with offices at Palermo and Catania airports and in the major cities, consistently have the best rental rates.

Though a car gives you more freedom and flexibility, Sicily is also well served by trains and comfortable coach buses, which are certainly an economical way to get around. As an example, a bus from Palermo to Siracusa takes 3 hours, 15 minutes and costs 6€ one-way.

For train timetables and ticket prices, visit www.trenitalia.com.

The main bus companies in Sicily are **AST** (www.aziendasicilianatrasporti.it) and **Interbus** (www.interbus.it). **Cuffaro** (www.cuffaro.info) operates buses between Palermo and Agrigento's Valley of the Temples. Palermotourism.com also has a searchable interactive map for bus routes and which company serves them.

To reach the Aeolian islands, all ferries and hydrofoils depart from Milazzo. For fares and schedules, see www.siremar.it, www.usticalines.it, or www.snav.it.

Internet Access
Almost all hotels now have a public terminal where guests can sign on, though there may be a small fee; many nicer hotels also have Wi-Fi, which may be free or carry a daily or hourly

charge. Internet points are not as common in Sicily as in other regions, but well-touristed towns like Taormina, Siracusa, and Palermo have several copy shop/phone centers with PCs where you can log on for about 4€ to 5€ an hour.

Pharmacies

Italian *farmacie* will fill foreign prescriptions with little or no hassle. They're also where you buy over-the-counter medicines like ibuprofen or cough syrup, feminine hygiene products, and even sunblock. *Farmacie* are recognizable by a neon green or red cross and are usually open 8am to 1:30pm and 3:30 to 8pm.

For optical care (glasses repair, contact lens solution), go to an *ottica,* which are everywhere in Italy.

Police

To report a lost or stolen article, such as a wallet or passport, visit the local police *questura* or Carabinieri *caserma* in your location. In Palermo, the most visitor-friendly Carabinieri and Polizia offices are at the train station. See also "Emergencies," p 684.

Post Office

Mail delivery in Sicily can be haphazard at best. The post office for Palermo is at Via Stabile Mariano 273; for Taromina it's at Piazza Bucinì Medaglia d'Oro 1; and in Siracusa it's at Via Taro 4. Note that *francobolli* (stamps) can be purchased at most *tabacchi* (tobacco stores), and postcards and letters can be mailed from either your hotel or the red letterboxes mounted on walls around town.

Safety

Sicily is safer than many people think; most of the warnings concern Palermo: Watch out for pickpockets in crowded tourist areas, markets, or buses. Motorbike pickpockets do occasionally pluck purses off the arms of women walking down the sidewalk, so always walk with your bag on the arm facing the buildings, not the street. Women should not walk around alone after dark in the Kalsa district of Palermo.

Visitor Information

Best of Sicily (www.bestofsicily.com) is a comprehensive and very informative English-language site. Regione Sicilia's tourism site, www.regione.sicilia.it/turismo/web_turismo, is clunkier but has thoughtful write-ups on various aspects of Sicilian culture that are well worth reading. The vacation rental agency **Think Sicily** (www.thinksicily.com) has excellent profiles of the island's regions and culture in their cleanly designed online guide to Sicily.

For Palermo, the tourist board site, www.palermotourism.com, is packed with information—almost too much—but a bit difficult to navigate. Websites dedicated to other individual destinations tend to be Italian-only and unsophisticated, with the exception of the very handy www.eoliando.it, which has great info about the Aeolian Islands.

There are tourist information offices in Palermo at the airport, train station, and in the city center at Piazza Castelnuovo 34, with maps and brochures about the city itself and other popular destinations in Sicily.

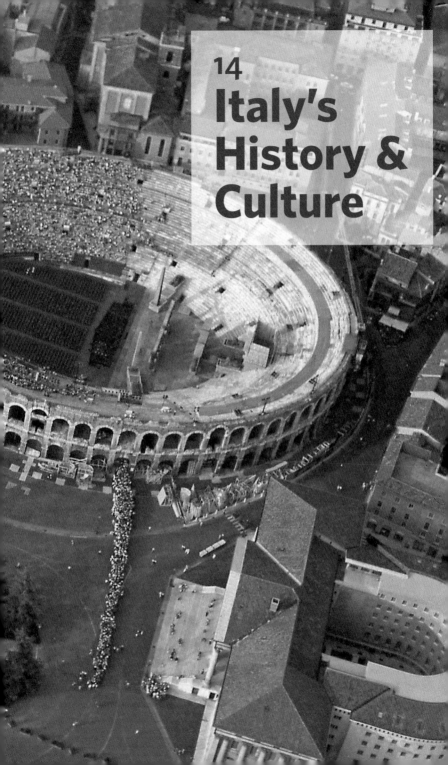

14
Italy's History & Culture

Italy's 10 Greatest Cultural Hits

1 **The Colosseum.** This ancient amphitheater comes to us from the 1st century as a potent symbol of the accomplishments and exoticism of ancient Rome, conjuring up emperors and gladiators, tigers and slaves, and the blood-thirsty roar of the populace. It's the forerunner of today's major sports arenas. See p 80, **8**.

2 **Brunelleschi's Dome.** The dome topping the Duomo has crowned the Florentine skyline since 1436. Filippo Brunelleschi's design for an inner dome nestled within the outer to dis-tribute the weight was thought to be folly, but 6 centuries' passage provide the proof of his genius. See p 179, **2**.

3 **Michelangelo's *David*.** Michelangelo's *David* is perhaps the most famous work of the Renaissance. More than that, thanks to its sheer beauty and the elegant tension of the pose, the statue is a symbol of an age of artistic fervor. See p 159, **8**, and 171.

4 **Caravaggio.** The evocative, and sometimes disturbingly dark, chiaroscuro (blending of shadows and select illumination) style of Italian baroque painter Michelangelo Merisi da Caravaggio (1571–1610) is like no other. His paintings and their dramatic light and perspective provoked strong reaction in his day—and are no less affecting today. Though famous in his lifetime, Caravaggio was relegated to obscurity following his death until the 20th century, when his genius was once again acknowledged. Two places to find Caravaggios are the **Pinacoteca di Brera** in Milan (p 447, **4**) and the **Galleria Borghese** in Rome (p 84, **2**). See also p 701.

5 **Dante.** The *Divine Comedy* made Dante Alighieri (c. 1265–1321) Italy's most celebrated man of letters and ushered in Italy's literary Renaissance. Exiled upon pain of death from his native Florence thanks to a political dust-up in 1301 (it no doubt made great fodder for his masterwork), he died and is buried in Ravenna. So beloved is he now that Florentines decided that they wanted him back and built a grave for him in 1829 that's still waiting to be filled

(Ravenna won't give him up)—though they didn't actually get around to rescinding his death sentence until 2008.

6 Stradivarius. The violins and other stringed instruments crafted by the Stradivari family of Cremona—especially those built by Antonio Stradivari from 1698 to 1720—are considered the finest ever made. Modern science has tried to unlock the magic of these stringed masterpieces, but to no avail—no one has ever been able to replicate a Stradivarius. And you'll need at least a couple of million euros to own an original made by Antonio. See p 453.

7 The Fiat. Italians love to drive, and so it goes that they love their cars: Alfa Romeo, Lamborghini, Maserati, Ferrari, Lancia—these evoke speed and glamour. But most lovable of all is the humble Fiat, and rare indeed is the Italian who has never gotten behind the wheel of one.

8 The Gucci Bag. Jackie Onassis, Audrey Hepburn, and Grace Kelly were all loyal clients, and few other purveyors of leather goods can match the House of Gucci for timeless high style and a spicy dash of Italian temperament. The first iconic Gucci bag was introduced in 1947 and has been a hit ever since. See p 446 for information on designer shopping in Milan.

9 Sophia Loren. An international sex symbol, she introduced Italian va-va-voom to the world, dazzled leading men from Clark Gable to Cary Grant, and showed time and again just how talented she was. Her best-actress Academy Award in 1960 for Vittorio De Sica's *La Ciociara* (*Two Women*) was the first ever awarded for a non-English-speaking role.

10 Seafood Risotto. Italian cooking can be both maddeningly exacting and deeply personal. If one dish captures the complexity of the art, it's this creation native to the north of Italy, an adventure in taste that varies with the seas where the ingredients were netted, the season, and the unique skills of the chef.

A Timeline of Italian History

B.C.

1000–500 B.C. Villanovan and Etruscan culture (pictured left) thrives.

800 B.C. Greeks began forming Magna Graecia, a territory of more than 40 colonies in Sicily and southern Italy. Phoenicians from Carthage (northern Africa) eventually occupy Sardinia and wrest much of Sicily from the Greeks

6TH–5TH C. B.C. Following the expulsion of the seventh king of Rome, the Roman Republic begins. Roman law is codified in 450 B.C.

3RD C. B.C. Rome defeats Carthage in the Punic Wars, opening the way for Mediterranean expansion.

2ND C. B.C. Rome conquers Greece and adopts the Greek gods.

44 B.C. Julius Caesar is assassinated on the Ides of March.

A.D.

A.D. 64 The Great Fire destroys two-thirds of the city of Rome. Universally loathed emperor Nero is blamed for doing nothing to stop it.

A.D. 64 OR 65 St. Peter is crucified, upside down, at the Circus of Nero, on the future site of Vatican City.

A.D. 79 Mt. Vesuvius erupts, burying Pompeii and Herculaneum.

313 Constantine (pictured left) legalizes Christianity.

4TH–5TH C. Rome is fragmented politically, and the empire is besieged by barbarian invaders. Historians cite A.D. 476 as the end of the Western Empire.

800 Charlemagne is crowned Holy Roman Emperor by Pope Leo II. Italy dissolves into a series of small warring kingdoms.

1000

9TH–11TH C. A conflict-ridden "alliance" between the popes and the Holy Roman Empire brings centuries of bloody warfare.

1088 Europe's first university opens in Bologna.

1250–1600 The Humanist era—when intellectual pursuit of knowledge and study of the classical and Arab worlds—takes precedence over blind Christian doctrine and superstition, and lifts Europe out of its medieval stupor.

1271 Seventeen-year-old Venetian Marco Polo (pictured left) leaves on a 24-year-long expedition to the Orient with his father and uncle.

1289 Conflicts between supporters of the Papal States (Guelphs) and those of the Holy Roman Empire (Ghibellines) come to a head; the Guelphs emerge victorious.

1303–1377 The Papal Schism occurs; the pope and his entourage move to Avignon in France for 74 years.

1308–21 Dante writes the *Divine Comedy,* which sets the Tuscan dialect as the predecessor of modern Italian.

1348 The Black Death (pictured left, from Dante's *Divina Commedia*) rips through Italy, killing more than half the population.

1436 Brunelleschi's dome caps the Duomo in Florence as the Renaissance bursts into full bloom in Italy.

1300

1508 Michelangelo begins his frescoes in the Sistine Chapel.

1778 La Scala opens in Milan.

1800–1801 Napoleon conquers Italy, spurring a wave of nationalism.

1861 The Kingdom of Italy is established with a capital in Turin.

1870 Rome becomes the capital of a newly united Italy.

1900

1928 Mussolini (pictured left) becomes the Fascist dictator of Italy.

1929 Vatican City becomes a sovereign state with the signing of the Lateran Treaty.

1940–44 World War II. Fascist Italy participates as an Axis power until surrending to the Allies in 1943.

1945 Mussolini is killed by a mob in Milan; World War II ends.

1946–97 The Republic of Italy is established. Italy averages a new national government every 9 months.

2000

2000 Italy welcomes a massive number of Jubilee visitors in the wake of political discontent.

2001 The richest man in Italy, media tycoon Silvio Berlusconi (pictured left), is elected prime minister for the second time. (He was prime minister very briefly in the 1990s.)

2002 On January 2, Italy and most of western Europe adopt the euro as their currency.

2005 Pope John Paul II dies at the age of 84 after serving for 27 years. He is replaced by Pope Benedict XVI.

2006 Italy defeats France to win the World Cup, touching off nation-wide celebrations.

2008 Berlusconi is voted back in as prime minister, for a third time.

Italy: A Brief History

> PAGE 686 *Verona's 1st-century Roman arena still crams in 20,000 for summer opera.* ABOVE *Much of what we know about Etruscan art and craft has been learned from bronzes.*

The history of Italy, richly loaded as it is with conquering heroes, arch villains, numerous warring factions and families, a good dose of religion, a number of assassinations, quite a few crazy rulers, natural disasters and a plague or two would make even the most creative soap opera writer's head spin. It's the stuff of high drama, that's all the more interesting because of its reality.

Archaeological evidence suggests a human presence on the Italian peninsula going back perhaps 200,000 years. After the 10th century B.C., areas north of Rome were occupied by the Iron Age Villanovan people and then the Etruscans. To this day, nobody knows much about these mysterious people because the Etruscan language has never been deciphered by modern scholars.

We do know that Rome (a sheepherding colony of Latins) remained free of the Etruscans until about 600 B.C., when the locals were swept away by the sophisticated Mesopotamian conquerors. The new overlords introduced some of the best art and culture of Greek and Asia Minor to the area. They also made Rome (from the Etruscan Roma) the governmental seat of all Latium.

Early Rome

The city of Rome was founded in 753 B.C., allegedly by Romulus. Romans established the Law of the Twelve Tables, outlining rights and procedures for civil matters (property, inheritance, marriage, and such) that is still the basis for western legal code today. The stern Roman Republic was characterized by a belief in the gods (adapted from the Greeks), the necessity of learning from the past, the strength of the family, education through reading books and performing public service, and, most important, obedience.

The Roman Republic and the Carthaginian Empire engaged in the three Punic Wars (264–146 B.C.), and despite the success of Hannibal's elephant-driven attack via the Alps, Rome prevailed. Further conquests made Rome the domineering power of the time, and the all-powerful senate presided as Rome grew to rule the Mediterranean.

The Roman Empire

Charismatic Julius Caesar laid

> *The* Prima Porta Augustus *is just one of the finds from antiquity on display in Rome's Vatican Museums.*

the groundwork for an empire when he conquered Gaul, invaded Britain, and defeated the Roman general Pompey. He also proved too popular for his own good and was assassinated on March 15, 44 B.C., shortly after he was named dictator for life. His grandnephew Octavius succeeded him, defeating Cleopatra and Mark Antony (and driving them to suicide) and extending the republic to Egypt. In 27 B.C. Octavius received the title Augustus Caesar and formally established the Roman Empire, which eventually extended from the United Kingdom to northern Africa and Portugal to Mesopotamia. The Pax Romana, a period of peace, extended from the reign of Augustus through that of Marcus Aurelius (A.D. 180). It also marked a period of time when the empire's oft-changing rulers were better known for their bad behavior than their effective leadership. For more on the craziest of the bunch, see the "Roman Emperors' Hall of Infamy" on p 144.

Mother Nature also helped move the Roman Empire along on the road to ruin. Mt. Vesuvius erupted in A.D. 79, destroying the cities of Pompeii and Herculaneum, and a plague swept the empire in 165–180, killing an estimated 5 million people, Marcus Aurelius among them. Emperor Diocletian (244–311) furthered along its demise when he divided the empire into eastern and western halves, with the western capital in

Roman Games

The Romans erected huge arenas for extravagant spectacles and contests. A day's entertainment generally started with exotic animal death matches and hunts. Midday was for executions, usually by crucifixion or wild beast attack. The afternoon saw gladiatorial combat—staged battles between professional fighters, mainly slaves or low-caste volunteers—and bloody recreations of great battles or scenes from mythology.

Ravenna and the eastern capital in Byzantium—and started taxing the population into penury. Emperor Constantine (272–337) recognized Christianity as the official religion of the empire in 313, and then resettled in Byzantium, which he renamed Constantinople in his own honor. Rome was then successively sacked by Visigoths, Vandals, and Ostrogoths. The Western Roman Empire was finally brought to an end by the Goths in 476, but the Eastern (Byzantine) Empire endured for another 1,000 years.

Early Middle Ages

Though the popes did their best to assume imperial power after the fall of the empire, political unity eluded them until around 750, when most of Italy succumbed to Frankish rule under Pepin the Short. Under his son Charlemagne (crowned emperor by the pope in 800 in an event likely orchestrated to boost both their reputations), the Papal States were established in central Italy. German King Otto I took control of Italy and became the first Holy Roman emperor in 962, though Sicily and parts of the south were notably absent from his realm, because they came under Islamic rule in the 9th century, then Norman, and then Spanish. The repressive feudal system put in place in the south during these turbulent times accounts for the economic discrepancies that remain between northern and southern Italy to this day.

Middle Ages

Between 1000 and 1400, various power struggles divided the Italian peninsula and Sicily into several different republics, states, and city-states. During the reigns of Holy Roman Emperors Frederick Barbarossa (1152–90) and Frederick II (1220–52), conflicts in northern Italy between supporters of the Papal States (Guelphs) and those of the empire (Ghibellines) came to a head. The

Frederick II

Although he lived in the 13th century, **Frederick II** (1194–1250) remains one of the most colorful characters in Italian history. His accomplishments were myriad: Holy Roman emperor, king of Germany, Burgundy, Italy, Sicily, Cyprus, and Jerusalem, crusader, patron of the arts, legal reformer, falconer, master of six languages, and noted philanderer. Widely held to be a religious skeptic, he also had a talent for ticking off popes (managing to get himself excommunicated not once, but twice); reportedly got along very well with the Muslim population of Jerusalem (they pretty much handed the city over to him); and was a decidedly enlightened monarch for the Dark Ages, possessing a rather keen interest in scientific experimentation.

> *If you thought David was supposed to be smaller than Goliath, just wait until you see Michelangelo's version.*

Guelphs finally emerged victorious in 1289.

Though the end of the Dark Ages was heralded in the 1300s by the rise of such Italian literary giants as Dante Alighieri and Petrarch, progress was almost derailed when the Black Death —a deadly plague originating in Asia—arrived in Europe in 1347 via a ship harbored in Sicily and wiped out some 75 million people worldwide. Superstition ran rampant in the plague's wake, but eventually reason prevailed.

The Renaissance
The golden age of cultural enlightenment began in Italy in the mid- to late 14th century in Florence under the Medici family. Lorenzo the Magnificent and other family members were generous patrons of, among others, Michelangelo, Botticelli, and da Vinci. Other ruling families that supported the arts included the Gonzagas in Mantua, and the Estes in Ferrara. Meanwhile, the murderous, possibly incestuous, and certainly criminal Borgias (see

"Meet the Borgias," on p 330) became lasting examples of the machinations of the time.

Girolamo Savonarola (1452–98), Dominican friar, doomsday preacher, leader of Florence, and anti-Renaissance activist, did his best to end the era, seizing and publicly burning books, mirrors, fine clothing, musical instruments, paintings, and other "immoral" possessions in the Bonfire of the Vanities. But in 1498 he was charged with numerous crimes, including heresy (the pope was an unforgiving Borgia who didn't care for Savonarola's criticism of Rome), and burned at the stake.

The Italian Wars (1494–1559) drew the peninsula's city-states, France, Spain, England, Scotland, and the Holy Roman and Ottoman empires into a struggle for power and territory, ending with Italy mainly under Spanish control. Toward the end of the 16th century, the Catholic Church launched the Roman Inquisition, unleashing nearly three centuries of prosecutions of Protestants, Jews, philosophers, scientists (including Galileo), and others for such crimes as heresy, blasphemy, and witchcraft.

Napoleon through Risorgimento
The Italian peninsula passed from largely Spanish rule to the Austria-based Habsburgs, who maintained control for most of the 18th century. The turn of the 19th century was dominated by the exploits of Napoleon Bonaparte, who gained control of most of the Continent and redrew virtually all of its political boundaries. In the post-Napoleonic Congress of Vienna, Sicily and southern Italy were united as the King-

dom of the Two Sicilies, and Austria established the Kingdom of Lombardy-Venetia in the north. By 1815, the concept of *risorgimento,* the unification of the states of the peninsula into a single nation of Italy, was spurred by Italian distrust of Austrian control. Most of Italy was finally united under Vittorio Emanuele II of the House of Savoy as the Kingdom of Italy in 1861. The resulting shakeup contributed to the Italian Diaspora, the mass migration of 16 million Italians, many of them to the Americas.

The World Wars
Italy fought World War I on the side of the Allies, and gained new territory in Trento, Trieste,

Galileo

Pisan scientist Galileo Galilei (1564–1642), the "father of modern astronomy" and one of the most famous scientists of his day, was a Renaissance man of the first order, making contributions to the advancement of mathematics, physics, and astronomy. He made notable improvements to the telescope and compass, discovered Jupiter's four largest moons, observed the phases of Venus, and studied sunspots. Unfortunately for him, he was also ahead of his time: He was a proponent of the Copernican theory that Earth orbits the sun, rather than vice versa, and that led the Roman Inquisition to try and convict him for heresy in 1632—he was made to live out the rest of his life under house arrest.

and Istria. After the war, Benito Mussolini formed the National Fascist Party, and took control of the government. By 1928 he was dictator, known as Il Duce (The Duke), and over the next decade extended the Italian empire to Ethiopia and Albania.

In 1940, Italy, Germany, and Japan formed the Axis partnership, and Italy entered World War II in June, sending forces to Africa, the Russian front, the Balkans, and elsewhere. When the Allies took northern Africa and invaded Italy in 1943, the country joined the Allied forces.

> *The fate of Florence's Santa Croce, and especially Cimabue's* Crucifixion, *became a global symbol for the great Arno flood of 1966.*

Garibaldi

As the idea of a unified Italian peninsula began to spread in the 19th century, various factions formed, and revolts and protests grew. While many people and events contributed to the Risorgimento, it was a twice-exiled revolutionary named Giuseppe Garibaldi (1807–82) who closed the deal. With the consent of the first Italian king, Vittorio Emanuele II, Garibaldi led 1,000 "red shirts" to conquer the Kingdom of the Two Sicilies in 1860, effectively completing the reunification.

Modern Italy

The Republic of Italy was formed in 1946, and the U.S. Marshall Plan gave a boost to its postwar recovery. The late '60s were a tumultuous period in Italy, marked by student protests, the *autunno caldo* ("hot autumn") strikes in the industrial north by a largely southern workforce, and a deadly bombing in Milan's Piazza Fontana in 1969, one of many acts of domestic terrorism. Nature wreaked havoc, too: On November 4, 1966, the River Arno rose as much as 6.7m (22 ft.) to flood parts of the center of Florence, destroying or damaging millions of art and literary treasures and killing 100 people.

Things did not calm down in subsequent decades. In 1978 the Red Brigades, a homegrown revolutionary group, kidnapped and killed Prime Minister Aldo Moro. Palestinian terrorism, too, took a toll, with deadly attacks at Rome's Fiumicino airport in 1973 and 1985. Large-scale mafia prosecutions in Sicily in 1986–87 charged 474 defendants and caused lasting damage to the Cosa Nostra (see p 703 for more on the mafia).

In 1993 Italy joined the European Union and in 2002 adopted its currency, the euro. The Christian Democrat party formed coalitions with other parties to dominate postwar Italian politics until 1992, when discontented voters protested the entrenched culture of bribery, corruption, and organized crime. The resulting *mani pulite* ("clean hands") investigation exposed political and business leaders. Media and finance tycoon Silvio Berlusconi formed a new party, Forza Italia (later the Party of Freedom), and was elected Prime Minister in 1994, 2001, and 2008.

Early Art & Architecture

> *The Marriage Sarcophagus is an outstanding example of Etruscan funerary sculpture.*

Etruscans

The Etruscans dominated northern Italy from circa 800 to 396 B.C. from walled and gated cities perched strategically on hilltops. *Necropoli* (burial cities), still in evidence in Volterra, Cerveteri, and Tarquinia, were located far away, to prevent spirits of the dead from interfering with the living. Tombs were supplied with wall murals, gold work, sculpture, even exact reconstructions of the house of the deceased. The Marriage Sarcophagus at the **Etruscan Museum at Villa Giulia** (p 84, ❶) in Rome gives us a poignant look at a couple enjoying the afterlife.

Roman Street Plans

The towns of ancient Rome often grew out of military encampments on a grid structure, with one main street set precisely north–south and a second set east–west. At their intersection was the forum—a large, public space often surrounded by a columned portico and all commercial and political institutions.

Magna Graecia

Sicily and southern Italy, occupied by the Greeks from around 800 B.C., was an important center of Greek life. Mt. Etna was home to the Cyclops, and the entrance to Hades was near Naples. Grand temples and artifacts in **Agrigento** (p 650, ❼) and **Siracusa** (p 676, ❹–❻) in Sicily and **Paestum** (p 583, ❺), south of Amalfi, attest to adaptation of the Greek refined Classical style.

> *The House of the Vettii at Pompeii has taught scholars much about everyday life in the Roman world.*

Ancient & Imperial Rome

Ancient Rome eventually developed its own distinctive art and architecture. Such innovations as vaulted construction and the use of concrete allowed for a new type of scale and spatial design and yielded structures of unsurpassed strength and longevity. Remains of everyday architecture—from the typical Roman atrium house to apartment houses—are preserved in the ancient cities of **Pompeii** (p 588), **Herculaneum** (p 580, ❷), and **Ostia Antica** (p 146).

The development of concrete and vaulting also enabled the Romans to one-up the

> *Agrigento's Valley of the Temples is among the best-preserved Greek complexes in the Mediterranean.*

Greeks in the "bigger is better" department. They proceeded to put up graceful aqueducts (some still in use today) and triumphal arches (the better to stroke an emperor's ego after a victory), as well as mammoth arenas and amphitheaters as gathering places for spectacles. The best known of the latter would be Rome's **Colosseum** (p 80, ❽). But perhaps the most breathtaking example of the era's engineering and construction skills is the **Pantheon** (p 102, ⓫), a temple built in 125. The dome, with its 5,000 tons of unreinforced concrete spanning 142 feet, provides irrefutable proof that the Romans perfected both concrete mixing and the barrel vault system.

Much of the surviving sculpture of the Roman Empire is modeled on Greek bronzes that have long been lost. Among the most impressive of all Roman works are the colossal 2nd-century **Farnese marbles**—*Hercules, Atlas,* and *Bull*—housed in the **Museo Archeologico Nazionale** in Naples (p 605, ❿).

Roman Catacombs

Ancient Roman law forbade burials for all (Jew, Christian, you name it) inside the city walls. The average pagan Roman was cremated and his ashes placed in an above-ground, "extra-mural" necropolis. Early Roman Christians, however, adopted the practice of burying and honoring the deceased in massive networks of underground tunnels—what we now call catacombs—outside the city. The catacombs of Rome were all hand-dug from a volcanic mud that turns to stone, called tufa, when exposed to air. Long before Christianity, Roman builders had exploited this material for construction projects all over the city. Where workers had quarried away significant amounts of tufa, gaping cavities were left in the landscape. The catacombs of San Sebastiano (p 76, ❷), were dug adjacent to one of these quarries. *Kata* was the Greek word for "nearby" and *kymbas* the word for "cavity" or "quarry"; thus, the very word *catacomb* was coined right here.

The first catacombs were dug alongside the Appian Way in the early 2nd century A.D., and eventually all the roads that famously led to Rome had catacombs along them. Of the more than 60 catacombs that have been discovered, only a handful are open to the public. The catacombs of San Callisto (p 74, ❶; pictured above), which were started in the 2nd century and in use until the end of the 5th

century, are the largest known Christian burial complex in Rome (more than 100,000 tombs) and phenomenally impressive.

On a tour of any Roman catacomb, you'll descend through multiple levels of labyrinthine corridors, past a mind-boggling number of tombs. The bodies were wrapped in cloth and placed in niches that were just big enough to hold them. The small niches were children's tombs. Each niche was sealed with a marble or terracotta slab (some are still in place) with endearing Latin or Greek inscriptions indicating the deceased's name, age, and occupation. Most of the slabs were also incised with Christian symbols, such as the XP (Greek letters *chi* and *rho*) epigram for *Christos*, or figures with hands raised in prayer, or fish, anchors, or lambs.

If you're hoping to see bones, however, you'll be disappointed. Because some past visitors felt compelled to liberate them as souvenirs, the bones in the Roman catacombs have all been removed to large ossuaries away from the tour route. For real body parts, go to the Crypt of the Capuchin Monks (see p 97, ❼), a veritable bone-a-palooza where femurs and pelvises form morbid wall art. If you're heading to Sicily, Palermo's catacombs (see p 672, ❽) are even creepier, with entire embalmed bodies—hair, flesh, clothes, and all—hanging from hooks along the corridors.

Medieval Art & Architecture

> San Marco's mosaics reflect Italy's artistic debt to Byzantium and the Near East.

Byzantine (5th–13th c.)
The Byzantine style of painting and mosaic was very stylized and static. Byzantine artists exploited the shimmering metallic effects of mosaics for their haunting depictions of early Christian images. The **Basilica di San Marco** (p 368, ❸) in Venice is awash in glittering mosaics, as are the 4th- to 6th-century mausoleums and churches of **Ravenna** (p 336).

> The archetypal rounded Romanesque arches of San Zeno Maggiore's cloister, in Verona.

Romanesque (11th–13th c.)
Rounded arches, piers in place of columns, and towers are the hallmarks of the Romanesque, heavily influenced by the monuments of ancient Rome. The style comes to the fore with great relish in the churches of **Sant'Ambrogio** in Milan

(p 462, ❾) and **San Zeno Maggiore** in Verona (p 418, ❸), while Pisa's Duomo, baptistery, and **Leaning Tower** (p 228, ❷), built between 1063 and 1173, show off the sheer solidity and mass that is often associated with the style.

> Sicily's position at the crossroads of several Mediterranean cultures explains the city's Islamic domes.

Arab-Norman
In 12th-century Sicily, the Normans drew on the earlier Arab occupation to yield an Eastern-influenced style, best seen in the **Cattedrale di Monreale** (p 646, ❶) and the arched and gilded **Cappella Palatina** (p 668, ❶) in Palermo.

Gothic (13th–15th c.)
By the late 12th century, engineering developments freed architecture from the heavy, thick walls of the Romanesque and allowed ceilings to soar, walls to thin, and windows to proliferate. The Gothic style was characterized by cross vaults, flying buttresses, pointed arches, and stained-glass windows. A prime example of the period is Milan's extravagantly spiny and pinnacled **Duomo** (p 456, ❶).

> In his fresco cycle at Padua's Cappella degli Scrovegni, Giotto gave biblical figures a human face and visible emotions.

Proto-Renaissance Sculpture & Painting
Nicola Pisano, arguably Italy's greatest medieval sculptor and creator of the pulpits in Pisa's **Battistero** (1255–60; see p 228, ❷) and Siena's **Duomo** (1266–68; p 292, ❺), carved figures that hearken back to the Greek and Roman Classical forms and proportions—and as such anticipated the great revival of those ideals in the Renaissance.

Cimabue (1251–1302), a Florentine who left us brilliant but sadly deteriorated frescoes in Assisi, is one of the two best-known 13th-century Italian painters. The other is his student **Giotto** (1267–1337), who in his 1305 frescoes in the **Cappella degli Scrovegni** (p 412, ❶) in Padua displays the telltale attention to composition that gave his paintings a fresh kind of beauty, simplicity, and emotionality.

The Renaissance

> *Bramante, Michelangelo, and Bernini each contributed to the visual experience of St. Peter's.*

Architecture

Renaissance architectural rules from the 15th to the 17th centuries stressed proportion, order, Classical inspiration, and mathematical precision to create unified, balanced structures.

Crowning the **Duomo** (p 178, ❶) in Florence, **Filippo Brunelleschi's** (1377–1476) dome is one of the greatest engineering feats in Western architecture. Brunelleschi solved the twin problems of spanning the 140-foot width and supporting the structure's weight by constructing a two-layer dome, adding 24 support ribs, and topping the whole with a heavy lantern to anchor the ribs properly.

Donato Bramante (1444–1514) hearkened back to Classical Greek and Roman architecture for his elegantly proportioned, columned and domed **Tempietto** (1508;

p 111, ⓫) at Rome's San Pietro in Montorio. Bramante was commissioned to design the new **St. Peter's Basilica** (p 66, ❽), but died before its completion. Several architects succeeded him, most influentially Michelangelo, who kept Bramante's essential plan, added a substantial extension, and redesigned the dome, which remains the world's tallest.

Vicentine architect **Andrea Palladio's** (1508–80) symmetrical, mathematically precise designs, such as that of the **Villa La Rotonda** outside Vicenza, were formal and classical, featuring columned porticoes, domed centers, and great halls—and influenced dozens of other remarkable buildings around the world.

> *Ghiberti's bronze doors for Florence's Battistero took decades to complete.*

Sculpture

Innovative young painters, sculptors, and architects broke with static medieval traditions in pursuit of a greater degree of expressiveness and naturalism.

Lorenzo Ghiberti (1378–1455) began the east doors for the **Battistero** (p 181, ❹)

> *Michelangelo distilled 200 years of experimentation in painting to create his iconic ceiling for the Sistine Chapel.*

in Florence at age 21. In full Renaissance style, they exhibit new techniques of perspective that give the panels—each depicting a biblical story—depth, drama, and action.

Donatello (1386-1466) created a stir with his slender, provocatively posed *David* (c. 1440; p 171, ❺; 172), the first standing, in-the-round male nude since ancient Rome—now in Florence's **Bargello**. The *David* (p 159, ❽) that tops all Davids is, of course, by **Michelangelo**. His conveys dynamism, strength, and godlike youth, while his *Pietà* (p 68) displays an unprecedented empathy and tenderness. Michelangelo believed that he simply provided the tools to help release the figures inside each block of stone—indeed, in his uncompleted *Slaves* in the Accademia (p 159, ❽) in Florence, the figures seem to be flinging off the marble that imprisons them.

> *Raphael's* The School of Athens, *in the Vatican's Stanza della Segnatura, explicitly ties the Renaissance to Classical ideals.*

> *Titian's* Assumption, *painted between 1516 and 1518, shows off the Venetian painter's complete mastery of color.*

Painting

The genius of dozens of painters emerged in the Renaissance—Fra Filippo Lippi, Piero della Francesca, Sandro Botticelli, Ghirlandaio, and Perugino, to name but a few—but the triumvirate of Michelangelo (1475–1564), Leonardo da Vinci (1452–1519), and Raphael (1483–1520) stands above all.

Michelangelo's paintings reflect his belief that human virtue and spirituality are outwardly expressed in the beauty of the human body. His **Sistine Chapel** ceiling is splendidly bedecked with 300 figures, all displaying his signature sculptural solidity. In a stroke of brilliance, the ceiling's focal point is the tiny empty space in the *Creation of Adam* between the vigorously outthrust finger of God and the feebly proffered hand of Adam. The artist's magnificent *Last Judgment* occupies the massive wall behind the altar.

The epitome of the Renaissance man, **Leonardo da Vinci** was noted for his use of innovative techniques, marrying his knowledge of the sciences with tone and composition. He painted two of the world's most famous paintings, *Mona Lisa* (now in the Louvre) and *The Last Supper* (p 462, **7**).

Raphael's unique style displayed a signature beauty and graciousness of line and composition. Murals he painted for the papal apartments in the Vatican (Stanze di Raffaello, p 91, **G**) are his best-known works, most importantly *The School of Athens,* depicting the great thinkers of ancient Greece and tying Renaissance ideals and thought to the Classical age.

Venetian School

Titian (1485–1576) was the most famous of the Renaissance painters north of Rome and Florence. Renowned for landscape and portraiture, he also excelled at the large-scale religious painting, as seen in his *Assumption of the Virgin,* in the church of **Santa Maria Gloriosa dei Frari** (p 372, **13**) in Venice. His **Venus of Urbino** (p 176, **16**, set a template for the reclining female nude that became so prevalent in later schools of painting, and he perfected the technique of using oil paints on canvas still largely employed today.

Fellow Venetian **Tintoretto** (1518–94), one of the last great painters of the Renaissance, painted with a deep perspective and a chiaroscuro style that foresaw the baroque. His *Miracle of the Slave,* in the **Gallerie dell'Accademia** (p 370, **9**) in Venice, displays his high sense of the dramatic.

Other painters of the Venetian school include Vittore Carpaccio, Giovanni and Gentile Bellini, Andrea Mantegna, and Giorgione.

Beyond the Renaissance

Baroque Architecture, Sculpture & Painting

One of the preeminent baroque artists, **Gian Lorenzo Bernini** (1598–1680) was architect of the colonnade and piazza in front of St. Peter's Basilica (p 66, ❽) and the **Baldacchino**—the elaborate canopy—over the main altar. Among his famous sculptures, both in Rome, are the *Fountain of the Four Rivers* in the Piazza Navona (p 100, ❻), and *Apollo and Daphne* in the Galleria Borghese (p 84, ❷), which captures the strange moment when the god touches the nymph and she begins to metamorphose into a tree.

The Italian baroque painter **Caravaggio** (1571–1610) perfected chiaroscuro, the pronounced play of shadow and light. He also set up the drama of his paintings by arranging unusual compositions—for example, showing backs (and backsides) of key figures. *The Conversion of St. Paul on the Road to Damascus* (in Santa Maria del Popolo; p 92, ❸), with an unusual amount of space devoted to the horse's hind end, is distinctly Caravaggian.

18th and 19th Century Painting & Sculpture

The light and delicate rococo style, highly influenced by the French, followed the baroque style, and its best practitioner was Venetian **Tiepolo** (1696–1770), whose exuberant, colorful, and highly decorative frescoes adorn many palazzi,

> TOP *An etching from 1775 shows Bernini's plan for St. Peter's Square.*
> BOTTOM *Canaletto's oil* The Piazzetta from the Molo *is just one of countless cityscapes he painted.*

including the **Palazzo Labia** (p 360, ⓫) in Venice.

Canaletto (1697–1768), another Venetian, cultivated a trend for grand cityscape and landscape paintings, several of them in the **Gallerie dell'Accademia** (p 370, ❾) in Venice. His use of atmosphere and local color arguably presaged Impressionism.

Venetian sculptor **Antonio Canova** (1757–1822), working in the neoclassical style, depicted figures from Greek mythology and contemporary history—and he often combined the two, as in his portrait of Napoleon's sister Pauline as *Venus Victrix* in Rome's **Galleria Borghese** (p 84, ❷).

Modern Art & Design

> Milan's elliptical Pirelli Tower, completed in 1958, is an icon of modern Italian architecture.

Painting

Italy's golden years as an artistic authority ended during the baroque period, but some notable successes have arisen in the modern era, artists who drew from many sources, including their proud national tradition, while breaking new ground.

Best known of the modern Italian painters is probably **Amedeo Modigliani** (1884–1920), whose unique and eclectic style drew inspiration from many global cultures and isn't neatly categorized. **Giorgio de Chirico** (1888–1978) founded the metaphysical art movement in Italy, which seeks to explore the imagined inner life of ordinary objects, and his paintings have a decidedly dreamy quality. So impressive was **Giorgio Morandi** (1890–1964), a still-life artist who was a forerunner of minimalism in Italy, that Federico Fellini chose to feature his work in *La Dolce Vita*.

Architecture

Italy's most revered architecture tends to belong more to the past than the present, though the country has had influential successes in the modern age.

Gio Ponti (1891–1979) designed Milan's 32-story **Pirelli Tower,** which was completed in 1958 and one of the first skyscrapers in the world to abandon the old block format. It is considered the beacon of modern Italian architecture. Ponti was assisted by **Pier Luigi Nervi** (1891–1979), who came to dominate the mid-20th century with his strong, lightweight, steel-reinforced concrete buildings, including Florence's **Giovanni Berta Stadium** (1932), Rome's **Palazzeto dello Sport** (1960), and Turin's **Exposition Hall** (1949).

Among the top architects of the 21st century is Genoa-based **Renzo Piano** (b. 1937), whose stunning work includes his renovation of that city's ancient port.

Fashion

It's no surprise that Italians are tops among the biggest names in fashion and one of the few countries in the world that has the power to set fashion trends worldwide. Italians consider it almost a national duty to put forth *"una bella figura"*—which in essence means, no matter what you are doing, look fantastic doing it. For more information on Italian fashion and the country's top designers, see "La Moda," on p 470.

> This 1965 Vespa was conceived at Piaggio's headquarters in Pontedera, close to Pisa.

Italian by Design

Whether applied to a chair, a car, or a coffeemaker, Italian design is modern and chic, applying style and form to ensure an item is both functional and attractive. Artemide's adjustable desk lamps revolutionized lamp design, and the Olivetti typewriter is a revered classic. The Vespa, epitome of Italian urbanity and insouciance, was actually designed with practicality in mind: The iconic front shield keeps the driver clean and dry, while the seat, which is stepped into rather than straddled, and accompanying legroom accommodate any user, old or young, big or small, dressed in jeans or a skirt and heels.

The Mafia: Myth & Reality

Anyone who's seen *The Godfather* is bound to have some preconceived notions about the most famous and romanticized crime organization in the world—the Mafia. Truth be told, Sicily isn't exactly crawling with Don Corleone types, and Italy's anti-Mafia police forces have made great strides in shutting down Mafia activities. Sicilian organized crime hasn't gone away completely—the majority of Sicilian businesses still pay the *pizzo*, or Mafia protection money—though the atrocities and intrigue that originally won the Cosa Nostra its place in the popular imagination are largely a thing of the past.

Historically, more than 100 clans have been part of the Mafia over the decades. Each family consists of a *capofamiglia*, his *consigliere* (adviser), a *sottocapo* (underboss), a few *caporegimes*, several soldiers, and countless associates, who aren't technically "in the family." All other members of the organization are considered *mafiosi*. The names Mafia and Cosa Nostra ("our thing") refer to the Sicilian mob only, not Italian organized crime in general; in Naples, it's called the Camorra, and in Calabria, the 'Ndrangheta. Mafia "businesses" include drug-trafficking, arms-trafficking, extortion, loan-sharking, and controlling contracts.

Central to every mafioso's honor and safety is *omertà*, the code of silence when dealing with law enforcement. Turncoats and their families are penalized by murder. But during the Maxi-Trial of the 1980s and '90s, several Sicilian bosses turned informant and helped the Italian government convict hundreds of mafiosi and associates. The outcome of the trial was especially crippling to relations between Sicilian and American crime families—a key turning point in debasing Mafia operations. The trial, however, also resulted in the 1992 bombing murders (pictured above) of the Maxi-Trial judges, Giovanni Falcone and Paolo Borsellino (Palermo's airport was renamed Falcone-Borsellino in their memory). A year after the bombings, the truly thuggish *capo di tutti capi* ("boss of all bosses"), Totò Riina, from the Mafia stronghold of Corleone (see p 637), was arrested for plotting the judges' murders and sentenced to life in prison, where he remains today.

These days, the organized crime headlines in Italy aren't about the Sicilian Mafia, but the Neapolitan Camorra. With far-reaching interests that include the fashion industry and a track record for cold-blooded acts of violence, the Camorra is a sinister reality against which authorities have made little headway. In 2006, 27-year-old journalist Roberto Saviano published the Italian bestseller *Gomorra*, a chilling account of his time spent working undercover for *camorristi* in Naples. Saviano lives under 24-hour police protection and regularly receives death threats from Camorra godfathers.

Music & Literature

> *Venetian composer Vivaldi had a sideline career as a priest.*

Classical Music

Music has been an integral part of Italian society for more than a millennium, though despite the old legend, Nero never fiddled as Rome burned—the instrument in question wasn't invented until centuries later. This is the country that gave the world opera, the piano, and the violin, and whose Renaissance- and baroque-era compositions gave birth to many forms of classical music (from the sonata to the concerto) that are still alive today.

Italy's musical history is varied and rich. The most important name in medieval Italian music is **Guido d'Arezzo** (c. 992–c. 1050), a Benedictine monk whose name you might not know, but who perfected the modern system of musical notation when his fellow monks had problems remembering their Gregorian chants.

The Italian composers of the Renaissance era built upon the single-melody-themed religious music of the medieval period, by introducing polyphony, or multiple melodic tones in a single piece. The most important composer of this time

period was **Giovanni Pierluigi da Palestrina** (c. 1525–94).

It was the work of revolutionary composer **Claudio Monteverdi** (1567–1643) that marks the transition from the Renaissance to the baroque (and truly ushered in opera as an art form). He married polyphony with a supporting instrument (known as *basso continuo*) to allow for solos and duets.

Another great composer of the era was **Arcangelo Corelli** (1653–1713), famous for his *concerto grosso,* emphasizing string instruments. But perhaps the most well known Italian baroque composer of all is **Antonio Vivaldi** (1678–1741), whose *Four Seasons* is one of the world's most recognized (and purchased) pieces of classical music.

The emergence of the concerto and the violin (p 453) as a major musical instrument helped drive the career of **Niccolò Paganini** (1782–1840), who is celebrated as much for his skill with the violin, as for his compositions. His *Caprice No. 24 in A Minor* inspired countless other classical composers, from Liszt to Brahms.

The ultimate mix of choral and orchestral music, **opera** dominated the Italian music scene in the 19th and early 20th centuries. For information on this art form and its great composers, see "Hitting the High Notes," on p 428.

But the late 20th and early 21st centuries have not seen a wane in Italy's musical for-

> *Alberto Moravia was one of 20th-century Italy's most influential novelists.*

tunes. In addition to continuing the country's opera tradition, **Luciano Berio** (1925–2003) did pioneering work in electronic music. And several Italian film composers have attracted international fame with their work. It's almost impossible to think of *The Godfather* or Zeffirelli's *Romeo and Juliet* without hearing their famous scores by **Nino Rota** (1911–79). And Sergio Leone's famous spaghetti westerns wouldn't be nearly as memorable if not for Academy Award–winning **Ennio Morricone's** (b. 1928) haunting soundtracks.

Literature

A number of Italian writers hold vaunted positions in the canon of world literature, their work giving readers insight into the lives and issues of their times.

The literary tradition in Italy began with the great classical Roman writers. Among them are such legends as **Virgil** (*Aeneid*, 29–19 B.C.); **Ovid** (*Metamorphoses*, A.D. 8); and **Cicero,** whose prose style influenced many writers, including St. Augustine, who followed him.

Italian literature, however, really did not get off the ground until **Dante** published ***The Divine Comedy*** in 1308 and moved literature out of the Middle Ages and toward the Renaissance. Other notable works of this time include Boccaccio's ***The Decameron*** (1353), a fascinating look into the plague era in Florence; Petrarch's ***Il Canzoniere*** sonnets (1327–74), which demonstrated the writer's humanist leanings; Machiavelli's ***The Prince*** (1513), a treatise that has had a profound effect on political theory in modern times; and Vasari's ***Lives of the Artists*** (1568), which laid the foundation for today's art biographies, as well as first used the term "Renaissance" in print.

In more recent years, writers have explored what it is to be human—and Italian—after war, Fascism, the Holocaust, and other modern realities. Notable authors of the modern period include Alberto Moravia, whose *The Conformist* (1951) explores life under Fascism; his wife Elsa Morante's *La Storia* (1974), detailing life in post–World War II Italy; Holocaust survivor Primo Levi's *If This Is a Man* (1947), influenced by his time

> *Machiavelli's* The Prince *was a no-holds-barred political how-to for the often-ruthless Medici era.*

in Auschwitz; and Carlo Levi's *Christ Stopped at Eboli* (1945), a memoir of a life spent in political exile in the south of Italy. One other notable author of the 20th century with a more philosophical bent—and a fondness for the Middle Ages—is Umberto Eco, whose popular *The Name of the Rose* (1980) is an atmospheric medieval mystery with decidedly postmodern themes.

Two Italians have won the Nobel Prize for Literature in the 20th century: playwright/novelist **Luigi Pirandello** in 1934 and playwright **Dario Fo** in 1997.

The Cinema

For a detailed look at Italy's rich postwar film history, see "Cinema Paradiso," on p 514.

Food & Wine

> *No need to ask for an espresso—simply* "un caffè."

The Italians have blessed us with some of our favorite foods, from a hearty plate of spaghetti with meat sauce, to *osso buco,* risotto, polenta, ravioli, *tiramisù,* gelato, cappuccino, and pizza.

For help in ordering meals and deciphering menus, see "Useful Phrases & Menu Terms," on p 738.

Dining Tip

Traditional foods and wines benefit from strict controls and aging processes in Italy, and there can be no substitution for the real thing, crafted according to centuries-old methods, be it balsamic vinegar from Modena, prosciutto di Parma, or a fine Barolo wine. A "PDO" label (*Denominazione di Origine Protetta*) indicates that a food is made according to established, traditional standards.

Cuisine by Region

Despite the unification of Italy, regional tradition still dominates the various kitchens, from Rome to Lombardy, from the Valle d'Aosta to Sicily. The term "Italian cuisine" has little meaning unless it's more clearly defined as Neapolitan, Roman, Sardinian, Sicilian, Venetian, Piedmontese, Tuscan, or whatever. Each region has a flavor and a taste of its own, as well as a detailed repertoire of local dishes. So what you'll get on your table will often depend on where in Italy you are.

> *Roman* carciofi alla giudia, *or "Jewish artichokes."*

Rome

This is probably the best place to introduce yourself to Italian cuisine because it boasts specialty restaurants representing every region. You'll encounter such specialties as *zuppa di pesce* (a soup or stew of various fish, cooked in white wine and flavored with herbs); cannelloni (tube-shaped pasta baked with any number of stuffings); *riso col gamberi* (rice with shrimp, peas, and mush-

> Porcini, *wild bolete mushrooms gathered between early summer and late autumn, elevate a simple plate of funghi and pasta.*

rooms, flavored with white wine and garlic); *scampi alla griglia* (grilled prawns); *quaglie col risotto e tartufi* (quail with rice and truffles); *lepre alla cacciatora* (hare flavored with tomato sauce and herbs); *zabaglione* (a creamy dessert made with sugar, egg yolks, and Marsala); *gnocchi alla romana* (potato-flour dumplings with a meat sauce, covered with grated cheese); *abbacchio* (baby spring lamb, often roasted over an open fire); *saltimbocca alla romana* (literally "jump-in-your-mouth"—thin slices of veal with sage, ham, and cheese); *fritto alla romana* (a mixed fry likely to include everything from brains to artichokes); *carciofi alla romana* (tender artichokes cooked with herbs such as mint and garlic, flavored with white wine); *fettuccine all'uovo* (egg noodles with butter and cheese); *zuppa di cozze* (a hearty bowl of mussels cooked in broth); *fritto di scampi e calamaretti* (baby squid and prawns, fast-fried); *fragoline* (wild strawberries); and *finocchio* (fennel, a celery-like raw vegetable with the flavor of anise, often eaten as a dessert or in a salad).

Florence & Tuscany

The cuisine of Tuscany is hearty, and the main ingredient for almost any meal is the superb local olive oil, adored for its low acidity and lovely flavor. In Italy's south, the olives are gathered only after they've fallen off the trees, but here they're handpicked off the trees so that they won't get bruised (ensuring lower acidity and milder aroma). Typical Tuscan pastas are *pappardelle* and penne mingled with a variety of sauces, many of which are tomato based. Tuscans are extremely fond of strong cheeses such as Gorgonzola, Fontina, and Parmigiano-Reggiano. Meat and fish are prepared simply and might seem undercooked; locals would argue that it's better to let the inherent flavor of the ingredients survive the cooking process.

Emilia-Romagna

Rich in produce, this gastronomic center's school of cooking produces many notable pastas now common around Italy: tagliatelle, tortellini, and cappelletti (larger than tortellini and made in the form of "lit-

> *Treviso's sought-after radicchio is sold at produce markets all over the Veneto.*

tle hats"). Tagliatelle, of course, are long strips of macaroni, and tortellini are little squares of dough stuffed with chopped pork, veal, or whatever. Equally popular is lasagne, which by now everybody has heard of. In Bologna, it's often made by adding finely shredded spinach to the dough. The best-known sausage of the area is mortadella, and equally famous is a *cotoletta alla bolognese* (veal cutlet fried with a slice of ham or bacon). The distinctive and famous cheese Parmigiano-Reggiano is a product of Parma and also Reggio Emilia. *Zampone* (stuffed pig's foot) is a specialty of Modena. Parma is also known for its ham, which is fashioned into air-cured *prosciutto di Parma*. Served in paper-thin slices, it's deliciously sweet and hailed by gourmets as the finest in the world.

Cheese

In addition to the more obvious cheese options (mozzarella, for example), do try to sample some regional favorites that you may have never encountered before. Just for starters, in the Alps, ask the locals where to get the best fresh *toma;* in Piedmont try a soft-ripened *robiolo;* and in Verona sample both fresh and aged *Monte Veronese.*

> Osso buco with saffron risotto, a typical Lombard secondo.

> The best Neapolitan food, like this shellfish pasta dish, emerges from the sea.

Salumi

You can never go wrong ordering a plate of local or house-made *salumi* (cured meats)—sopressata, pepperoni, mortadella, pancetta, and many kinds of salami—produced all over Italy, often by small and private producers who make their own variations. And ham? The regional varieties of *prosciutto crudo* and *cotto* (ham, cured and cooked) are countless and unvaryingly delicious.

Venice

Two of the most typical dishes are *fegato alla veneziana* (liver and onions) and *risi e bisi* (rice and fresh peas). Seafood figures heavily in the Venetian diet, and grilled fish is often served with the bitter red radicchio, a lettuce that comes from Treviso.

Lombardy

The cuisine in this region tends to be refined and flavorful. No dish here is more famous than *cotoletta alla milanese* (cutlets of tender veal dipped in egg and bread crumbs and fried in olive oil until they're a golden brown). *Osso buco* is the other great dish of Lombardy; this is cooked with the shinbone of veal in a *ragù* sauce and served on rice and peas. *Risotto alla Milanese* is also a classic—rice that can be dressed in almost any way, depending on the chef's imagination. It's often flavored with saffron, butter, and chicken giblets; and it's seemingly always served with heaps of Parmigiano-Reggiano cheese. Polenta, a cornmeal mush that's "more than mush," replaces pasta in some parts of northeastern Italy.

Piedmont

The cooking in Piedmont and the Valle d'Aosta is different from that in the rest of Italy. Cuisine here is said to appeal to strong-hearted men returning from a hard day's work in the mountains. You get such dishes as *bagna cauda*, a sauce made with olive oil, garlic, butter, and anchovies, in which you dip uncooked fresh vegetables. *Fonduta* is also celebrated—made with melted Fontina cheese, butter, milk, egg yolks, and, for an elegant touch, white truffles.

Liguria

The sea is a major source of this region's cuisine, as reflected by its version of bouillabaisse, a *burrida* flavored with spices. But its most famous food item is pesto, a sauce made with fresh basil, garlic, cheese, and walnuts or pine nuts (*pignoli*) that is used to dress pasta, fish, and many other dishes.

Campania

Much of the cookery here (spaghetti with clam sauce, pizzas, and so forth) is already familiar to North Americans

> *Whether it was a Florentine or a Sicilian who first made gelato is a dispute that's never quite been settled.*

> *The bitter aperitivo Campari hails from Lombardy.*

because so many Neapolitans moved to the New World and opened restaurants. *Mozzarella di bufala,* made from buffalo milk, is the classic cheese of this area. Mixed fish fries, done a golden brown, are a staple of nearly every table.

Sicily

The distinctive cuisine features good, strong flavors and aromatic sauces. A staple of the diet is *maccheroni con le sarde* (spaghetti with pine nuts, fennel, spices, chopped sardines, and olive oil). Fish is good and fresh in Sicily. Among meat dishes, you'll see *involtini siciliani* (rolled meat with a stuffing of egg, ham, and cheese cooked in bread crumbs) on the menu. A *caponata* is a flavorful way of cooking eggplant in tomato sauce. The desserts and homemade pastries are excellent, including cannoli, cylindrical pastry cases stuffed with ricotta and candied fruit (or chocolate). The gelato is among the best in Italy.

Pasta

Italians craft myriad shapes of pasta and have a charming custom of naming them after things they look like: *farfalle* (butterflies), *orecchiette* (little ears), *vermicelli* (worms), and more. These come dry and fresh, made with semolina, spelt, buckwheat, or other grains, while gnocchi are plump little dumplings made with potatoes. Italians are very particular about pairings of pastas and sauces and whether or not to add cheese—if in doubt, ask your waitperson to guide you. Among the standouts: *lasagne alla bolognese,* made with only one cheese (Parmigiano-Reggiano), béchamel, and a slow-cooked *ragù*; *pasta con le sarde,* a Sicilian classic with fresh sardines, fennel, and pine nuts; pasta with *prosciutto e piselli* (prosciutto and peas) in cream sauce; and *spaghetti alle vongole,* garlicky noodles with clams.

Wine & Liquor

For information on wine in Italy, see our "Grape Guide" on p 242.

As with wines, Italians are serious about their before- and after-dinner drinks: *aperitivi* and *digestivi.* Individuals and restaurant owners make their own *limoncello* (p 573) and other fruit liqueurs and flavor their own grappa, and they are always eager to have a visitor try their version. There are many commercial brands as well, including Cynar (made from artichokes), Aperol (bitter orange), which is splashed in a glass of sparkling Prosecco to make a spritz, and Campari, the exact ingredients of which are known to only one member of the family who invented it, but include rhubarb, herbs and spices, quinine, and tree bark.

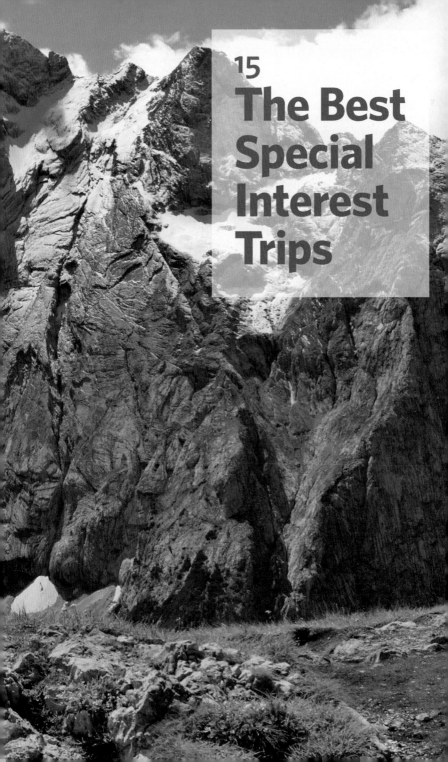

15

The Best Special Interest Trips

Multi-Activity Outfitters

Adults Only

Italy is one of the most popular destinations for **Elderhostel,** the 34-year-old not-for-profit organization for mature adults that combines travel and educational opportunities. Two-week programs that combine lectures and tours in the Italian lakes and Tuscany have been among recent offerings. 11 Avenue de Lafayette, Boston, MA 02111. ☎ 800/454-5768. www.elderhostel.org.

Family Vacations

Family vacations from the **American Museum of Natural History Expeditions** house participants in a medieval Tuscan village, where the young ones learn about the Renaissance, swim, make pizza, and explore Florence. Central Park West at 79th St., New York, NY 10024-5192, ☎ 800/462-8687. www.amnhexpeditions.org.

Inn-to-inn walks, stays at alpine resorts, and holidays in Tuscany from **Inntravel** are geared to kids, with skiing, horseback riding, low-key sightseeing (no slogs through museums), and other kid-friendly activities. Inntravel Ltd, Whitewell Grange, near Castle Howard, York YO60 7JU U.K. ☎ 44-01653/617949. www.inntravel.co.uk.

Outdoor Activities A to Z

Biking

Excellent meals and fine wines come along with the ride on **Chain Gang** tours through Tuscany and Umbria. 30 Prospect Park, Exeter EX4 6NA, U.K. ☎ 44-01392/6622 62. www.thechaingang.co.uk.

On itineraries from **Ciclismo Classico,** you can bike the entire length of the peninsula, explore such relatively untrod turf as the Abruzzi, or enjoy Tuscany, Umbria, and Italy's other most popular regions. Ciclismo also leads tours that traverse Italy on two feet. 30 Marathon St., Arlington, MA 02474. ☎ 800/866-7314 or 781/646-3377. www.ciclismoclassico.com.

All paths lead downhill with **Freewheel** tours, led by experienced mountain cyclists who special in manageable rides through the Dolomites. 8a Milton Court, Ravenshead, Nottingham NG15 9BD, U.K. ☎ 44-0845/372-0315. www.freewheelholidays.co.uk.

VBT Bicycling Vacations, a 38-year-veteran of the bike tour business and a specialist in Italian routes, makes a point of combining a great experience with excellent value. Many of the rides are in Tuscany and Apulia. 614 Monkton Rd., Bristol, VT 05443-0711. ☎ 800/245-3868. www.vbt.com.

Horseback Riding

Tuscany is prime horseback-riding turf, and **Equitours** provides instruction, long rides through the countryside, and stays in atmospheric rural settings. Worldwide Horseback Riding Adventures, P.O. Box 807, 10 Stalnaker St., Dubois, WY 82513. ☎ 800/545-0019 or 307/455-3363. www.ridingtours.com.

Spas

A week at Montecatini Terme in western Tuscany from **Crystal Tours** includes thermal treatments, massages, whirlpools, and even wine tastings. 895 W. 46th St., Miami Beach, FL 33140. ☎ 888/823-0055 or 305/534-5507. www.crystal-tours.com/tours/spa.

Tennis

Seats at the Tennis Masters series in Rome is just part of the package with **Steve Furgal's International Tennis Tours;** also included are court time, luxury accommodations, and sightseeing in the Eternal City. 11305 Rancho Bernardo Rd., Suite 108, San Diego, CA 92127. ☎ 800/258-3664 or 858/675-3555. www.tours4tennis.com.

Kids and adults who love to travel and to play tennis will find their match with **Tuscan Tennis Holidays,** which combines coaching and court time in Florence and Lucca with touring through one of Italy's most beautiful regions. 63 Partickhill Rd., Glasgow G11 5AB, Scotland. ☎ 44-0141/576-7205. www.tuscanytennis.com.

Walking & Hiking

Above the Clouds follows the high routes of the Dolomites, moving from refuge to refuge on weeklong outings. P.O. Box 388, Hinesburg, VT 05461. ☎ 802/482-4848. www.aboveclouds.com.

Arblaster and Clarke combines tours of Italy's most noted wine regions with visits to food markets, nights at the opera, and music festivals. Cedar Court, 5 College St., Petersfield, Hampshire, U.K. GU31 4AE. ☎ 44-01730/263111. www.arblasterandclarke.com.

Bredeson Outdoor Adventures arranges weeklong hikes through the Cinque Terre, the Dolomites, Sicily's Zingaro Nature Preserve, and other Italian regions of great scenic beauty. 14 Cliffview Dr., Norwalk, CT 06850. ☎ 866/533-

> PREVIOUS PAGE *Excursions to the Alps and Dolomites (pictured) provide spectacular views of the region's majestic mountains.* THIS PAGE *More national obsession than national pastime, cycling is a great way to tour Italy, including Tuscany (pictured).*

4361 or 203/840-0295. www.bredeson.com.

Country Walkers follows routes through the Alps around Monte Bianco (Mont Blanc) and along the shores of the Italian lakes and the Mediterranean, including the Cinque Terre and the Amalfi Coast. P.O. Box 180, Waterbury, VT 05676. ☎ 800/464-9255 or 802/244-1387. www.countrywalkers.com.

Mountain Travel Sobek adds Italian flair to outdoor adventures with hikes in the Piedmont that combine treks through vineyards with wine and food tastings, and Dolomite snowshoeing expeditions that come with cozy Tyrolean lodgings and hearty northern Italian cuisine. 1266 66 St., Emeryville, CA 94608. ☎ 888/687-6235 or 510/594-6000. www.mtsobek.com.

Sherpa, an adventure-travel specialist based in the U.K., serves up two types of Italian experiences—self-guided inn-to-inn walks and cycle itineraries along the Amalfi Coast and through Umbria and other scenic regions (with such hindrances as accommodations and baggage transfer taken care of) as well as escorted tours. 131A Heston Rd., Hounslow TW5 0RF, U.K. ☎ 44-020/8577-2717. www.sherpa-walking-holidays.co.uk.

Enjoy Florence helps you do so, with walking tours that might include a stop at designer outlet shops, as well as tours to Chianti vineyards, Siena, and other nearby places. Via Stefano Ussi 2, 50142 Florence. ☎ 055-0515485. www.enjoyflorence.com.

In Venice, some excellent and unusual tours offered through the **Azienda di Promozione Turistica della Provincia di Venezia (APT)** take visitors into private gardens, show off palaces of the Dorsoduro, and in other ways introduce lesser-known aspects of the city. Castello 5050, Venice. ☎ 041-529-8711. www.turismovenezia.it.

When in Rome guides small groups on night-time walks past illuminated fountains and magically lit monuments, shows off the prizes of the Vatican, and in other ways introduces the magic of the Eternal City. Via Varese 34, Rome 00185. ☎ 06-328-895-9571. www.wheninrometours.com.

Ask a Local

Wherever you find yourself in Italy, someone is waiting to show off the local wonders, from monuments to food markets. Check with local tourist boards (listed throughout this guide) for a list of tours of local interest. A small sampling in the major cities is included in the "Walking & Hiking" section (opposite page), but it's just a tiny taste of what's available.

Learning Trips & Language Classes

Archaeology

Barebones specialists lead guided tours of the most exciting archaeological sites in the world, including Sicilian temples, the ruins of Pompeii, and other Italian sites. The Old Barn, Old Road, Alderbury, Salisbury SP5 3AR, U.K. ☎ 44-01722/713800. www.andantetravels.co.uk.

Art Appreciation

What better place to study art history than Florence? The city's **British Institute** offers month-long courses on the dawn of the Renaissance, the Early Italian Renaissance, and the High Renaissance; you can take all three over 12 weeks, attend one for a month, or join any one for 1 to 3 weeks. Piazza Strozzi 2, Florence. ☎ 055-267781. www.britishinstitute.it.

Touring the Uffizi with a Renaissance specialist, cruising down the Grand Canal with a Venetian scholar and author, visiting the Vatican museums with a noted art historian—these are among the many specialized experiences that **Artvia** can arrange. The firm also leads walking tours of Florence, excursions to Pompeii, vineyard visits, and many other uniquely Italian experiences. Via Sassetti 1, Florence. ☎ 055-2645033. www.italy.artviva.com.

Gardens

The gardens of Florence are among stops on the itinerary of **American Horticultural Society Study Travel Program Garden Tours;** destinations change annually. 7931 E. Boulevard Dr., Alexandria, VA 22308. ☎ 800/777-7931 or 703/768-5700. www.ahs.org.

The horticulture experts of **Garden Tours** introduce travelers to the gardens that have flourished in Italy since ancient times near Rome and Pompeii, to medieval botanic gardens in Padua and Florence, and to the great Renaissance and baroque gardens of Lake Como. www.gardenvisit.com.

General Learning Vacations

Orvieto is the setting for hands-on learning with **Adventures in Italy**—from painting to journal keeping—mixed with wine tasting and cultural appreciation. 1 Nob Hill Rd., Columbia, SC 29210. ☎ 803/233-3164. www.adventuresinitaly.net.

Outdoor painting sessions in Tuscany and Campania are interspersed with field trips and lectures during weeklong sessions with **Etruscan Places.** 10 Ashland St., Newburyport, MA 01950. ☎ 212/780-3216. www.etruscan-places.com.

Tuscany, Venice, and Lago di Garda are among the scenic locales for weeklong workshops in painting, photography, fiction writing, cooking, singing, acting, poetry, creativity, and yoga from **Il Chiostro.** Sessions come with atmospheric lodgings, homemade meals, and sightseeing and other experiences. 23 W. 73rd St., Suite 306, New York, NY 10023. ☎ 800/990-3506. www.ilchiostro.com.

Italy Workshops help photographers capture the visual wonders of Italy during weeklong sessions with expert instruction in Tuscany, on the Italian lakes, and on the Italian Riviera. 701 E. South Temple, Salt Lake City, UT 84102. ☎ 801/364-6645.

Language

Società Dante Alighieri in Siena offers Italian-language courses, lasting a week or longer, in group or individual settings, in Italy's most beautiful medieval city, and also has programs in Viterbo and Ischia. Via Tommaso Pendola 37, 53100 Siena. ☎ 0577-49533. www.dantealighieri.com.

A course in beginner's Italian at **Università per Stranieri di Perugia** requires a stay of at

---

One-Stop Shopping

Looking for more things to do in Italy? An excellent overall resource is **ShawGuides,** an online resource to language vacations, cooking schools, art and photography workshops, and much more. Browse through the offerings at www.shawguides.com.

A good overall introduction to Rome, Florence, Milan, Naples, and Palermo is a tour with **City Sightseeing,** the hop-off, hop-on-again bus-tour company that allows 24 hours' worth of transport to major sights around a city, allowing you to get on and off the bus as you wish. The canned, multilingual commentary is not going to enlighten you greatly, but rolling through a strange city is a delight. The best approach is to stay aboard once for the whole route, then redo the circuit making the stops that interest you. Check out routes and prices for the city you are visiting at www.city-sightseeing.com.

> *Learn to make gnocchi the Italian way on a Divina Cucina tour.*

east a month, but you'll get no better education than the one at Italy's oldest and most prestigious language school—and in one of Italy's most beautiful Renaissance cities. Piazza Fortebraccio 4, 06123 Perugia. ☎ 075-57461. www.unistrapg.it/english.

Music
Open-air performances in Rome, a tour of Verdi sites in and around Parma, and an in-depth look at Sicilian music are among the **Allegro** tours geared to fans of opera and classical music. Itineraries include some of Italy's most noted musical events, such as Pesaro's Rossini Opera Festival and the summer season at Verona's arena. ☎ 800/838-6860 or 416/362-5000. www.allegroholidays.com.

Nature
Butterflies of the Dolomites, wildflowers of the Gargano Peninsula, and other flora and fauna throughout Italy are the focus of trips from

Naturetrek, whose naturalists lead weeklong walks through some of Europe's most spectacular scenery. Cheriton Mill, Cheriton, Alresford, Hants S024 ONG, U.K. ☎ 44-01962/733051. www.naturetrek.co.uk.

Hikes through the spectacular scenery and diverse flora of Trentino–Alto Adige (South Tyrol) are a specialty of **Touching Nature Travel.** Alderstrasse 5, 85354 Freising, Germany. ☎ 44-08161/549795. www.touchingnature.co.uk.

Food & Wine Trips

Cooking
Giuliano Bugialli, one of the world's most popular teachers of Italian cookery, welcomes students to his Florence kitchen for weeklong courses. 105 South 12th St., Apt. 205/206, Philadelphia, PA 19107. ☎ 215/922-2086. www.bugialli.com.

Chef Judy Francini of **Divina Cucina** leads students through Florence's central market to buy the ingredients to prepare a meal, and also spices up the menu with wine tastings, cooking tours of Chianti and Sicily, and visits to makers of balsamic vinegar and other Italian specialties. 2130 Comistas Dr., Walnut Creek, CA 94598. ☎ 925/939-6346. www.divinacucina.com.

Live like an Italian in Arcidosso, a medieval village high in the mountains of southern Tuscany, while learning culinary skills from restaurateur and chef **Carlo Innocenti.** c/o Isabel Innocenti, 2829 Bird Ave., Suite 5, PMB 242, Coconut Grove, FL 33133. ☎ 800/766-2390 or 305/598-8368. www.tuscanway.com.

Mama Margaret and Friends claims to put the "mama" feeling into Italian food tours, visiting home and restaurant kitchens and small wineries, and offering small-group instruction from local chefs. 101-1184 Denman St., Suite 310, Vancouver, BC Canada V6G 2M9. ☎ 800/557-0370 or 604/681-4074. www.italycookingschools.com.

Wine
Cellar Tastings pairs wine tastings and vineyard visits with gourmet meals and tours of cheese-making operations and other foodie experiences, along with luxury accommodations and private tours of top sights. C. Infantas, No. 27, 3 Derecha, 28004 Madrid, Spain. ☎ 34-091/521-3939. www.cellartours.com.

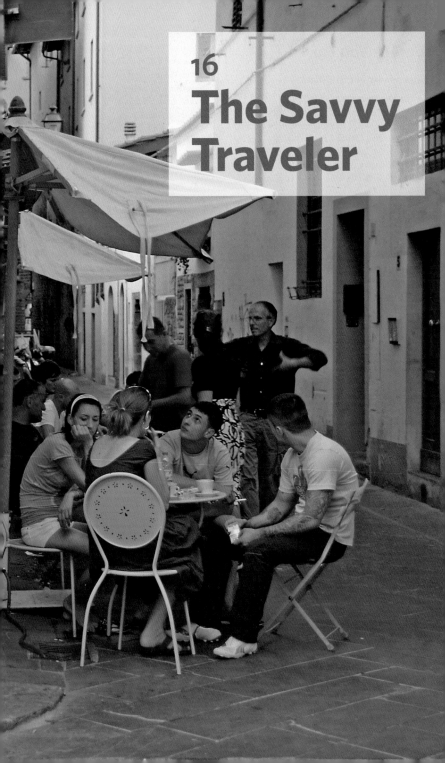

Before You Go

Government Tourist Offices

IN THE UNITED STATES

630 Fifth Ave., Suite 1565, New York, NY 10111 (☎ 212/245-4822; fax 212/586-9249); 500 N. Michigan Ave., Suite 2240, Chicago, IL 60611 (☎ 312/644-0996; fax 312/644-3019); and 12400 Wilshire Blvd., Suite 550, Los Angeles, CA 90025 (☎ 310/820-1898; fax 310/820-6357).

IN CANADA

175 Bloor St. E., South Tower, Suite 907, Toronto, ON M4W 3R8 (☎ 416/925-4882; fax 416/925-4799).

IN THE UNITED KINGDOM

1 Princes St., London W1R 8AY (☎ 020/7408-1254).

Best Times to Go

April to June and late September to October are the best times for traveling in Italy—temperatures are usually mild and the crowds aren't quite so intense. In mid-June, the summer rush begins to pick up, and from July to mid-September the country teems with visitors. August can be uncomfortably hot and muggy, and the entire country goes on vacation from August 15 to the end of the month. Many Italians take off the entire month. Many hotels, restaurants, and shops are closed (except at the spas, beaches, and islands, where many Italians head). From late October to Easter, most attractions go on shorter winter hours. Many hotels and restaurants take a month or two off between November and February, and many resorts become ghost towns.

Festivals & Special Events

For major events for which tickets should be procured well before arriving, contact Keith Prowse (☎ 800/669-8687 in the U.S.; www. keithprowse.com), one of the world's largest independent ticket agencies and packagers; or go to **Culturalitaly.com** (☎ 800/380-0014), a Los Angeles–based Web company specializing in Italy's high-end events, museum reservations, and tours. You get the best seats, and reservations are available for such popular events and attractions as operatic performances at the ancient Baths of Caracalla in Rome and at the arena in Verona, Venice carnival, the Palio in Siena, the Uffizi in Florence and *The Last Supper* in Milan. Most reservations carry a $10 fee, plus the cost of the event.

For an exhaustive list of events beyond those listed here, check http://events.frommers.com, where you'll find a searchable, up-to-the-minute roster of what's happening in cities all over the world.

JANUARY

All cities, towns, and villages in Italy stage **Epiphany observances** on or around January 6. One of the most festive celebrations is the Epiphany Fair at Rome's Piazza Navona. During mid-January's ancient ceremony of **Festa di Sant'Agnese,** at Sant'Agnese Fuori le Mura, Rome, two lambs are blessed and shorn and their wool is used for *palliums* (Roman Catholic vestments). In late January at the **Fiera di Sant'Orso,** Aosta, Valle d'Aosta, artisans from the mountain valleys observe a tradition that has existed for 10 centuries and display wares—often made of wood, lace, wool, or wrought iron—created during the long winter.

FEBRUARY

The **Almond Blossom Festival,** Agrigento, Sicily, held in the first half of February, includes song, dance, costumes, and fireworks (☎ 0922 401352). Theatrical presentations and masked balls take place throughout Venice and on the islands in the lagoon during **Carnevale,** held the week before Ash Wednesday. The balls are by invitation only (except the Doge's Ball), but the street events and fireworks are open to everyone. Contact the Venice Tourist Office, San Marco, Giardinetti Reali, Palazzo Selva, 30124 Venezia (☎ 041-5298711; www.turismovenezia it). Rome's Carnevale, held at the same time, is centered in Piazza Navona.

MARCH

At San Remo's **Festival della Canzone Italiana (Festival of Italian Popular Song)** major artists perform the latest Italian song releases; it takes place in mid-March. During the **Festa di San Giuseppe** (the Trionfale quarter, north of the Vatican, Rome), usually held on March 19, the heavily decorated statue of the saint is brought out at a fair with food stalls, concerts, and sporting events.

APRIL

Holy Week observances start 4 days before Easter Sunday, nationwide. Processions and age-old ceremonies are staged. The most notable procession is led by the pope, passing the Colosseum and the Roman Forum up to the Palatine Hill; a torchlit parade caps the observance. In an event broadcast around the world, the pope gives his blessing from the balcony of St. Peter's on **Easter Sunday (Pasqua),** St. Peter's Square, Rome. Sicily's observances are also noteworthy. Also on Easter Sunday is the **Scoppio del Carro (Explosion of the Cart),** Florence. A cart laden with flowers and fireworks is drawn by three white oxen to the Duomo, where at the noon Mass a mechanical dove detonates it from the altar. At the **Festa della Primavera,** Rome, the Spanish Steps are decked out with banks of azaleas and other flowers; later, orchestral and choral concerts are presented in Trinità dei Monti. Dates vary.

MAY

Italy's oldest and most prestigious music festival, **Maggio Musicale Fiorentino,** Florence, is staged from late April to the end of June. It emphasizes music from the 14th to the 20th centuries but also presents ballet and opera. Some concerts and ballets are presented free in Piazza della Signoria; ticketed events (concerts 20€–30€; operas 25€–85€; ballet 20€–70€) are held at the Teatro Comunale, Corso Italia 16, or the Teatro della Pergola, Via della Pergola 18. For schedules and tickets, contact the Maggio Musicale Fiorentino/Teatro Comunale, Corso Italia 16, 50123 Firenze (☎ 055-277-91245; www.maggiofiorentino.com).

On May 15 at the **Corsa dei Ceri (Race of the Candles),** Gubbio, Umbria, 9m-long (30-ft.) wooden "candles" (ceri) are raced through the streets of this perfectly preserved medieval hill town (☎ 075-92371) to celebrate the feast day of patron saint Ubaldo.

JUNE

The town of Pisa honors its patron saint on June 16 with candlelit parades during **San Ranieri.** That's followed the next day by eight rowing teams competing in 16th-century costumes. For more information, call ☎ 050-42291.

The summer **Festival di Ravenna,** of international renown, draws world-class classical performers. A wide range of performances are staged from mid-June to July, including operas, ballets, theater, symphonic music concerts, solo and chamber pieces, oratorios, and sacred music. Tickets start at 15€, and reservations are needed for the most popular events. For details, call ☎ 0544-249211 (www.ravennafestival.org).

Calcio in Costume (Ancient Football Match in Costume) in Florence is a revival of a raucous 16th-century football match, pitting four teams in medieval costumes against one another. For information, call ☎ 055-23320. There are four matches, usually culminating around June 24, the feast day of San Giovanni.

Dating from 1958, the **Spoleto Festival (Festival dei Due Mondi)** was the artistic creation of maestro and world-class composer Gian Carlo Menotti, who presided over the event until his death at 95 in 2007. International performers convene for 3 weeks (late June to mid-July) of dance, drama, opera, concerts, and art exhibits in this Umbrian hill town. The main focus is to highlight music composed from 1300 to 1799. For tickets and details, check out www.festivaldispoleto.it.

At Pisa's **Gioco del Ponte,** on the last Sunday in June, teams in Renaissance costume take part in a much-contested tug-of-war on the Ponte di Mezzo. The most significant Roman religious festival, **Festa di San Pietro,** is observed at St. Peter's Basilica in Rome on June 29. Also in Rome, the **Son et Lumière,** the Roman Forum and Tivoli areas are dramatically lit at night from early June to the end of September.

In Venice, the **Biennale d'Arte Contemporanea e Architettura,** the international exposition of modern arts and architecture, is one of the most prestigious art events in Europe. The art exhibition takes place during alternate odd-numbered years, architecture in even years, from June to October. Call ☎ 041-521-8711. At Arezzo's **Giostra del Saracino (Joust of the Saracen),** a colorful procession in full historical regalia precedes the tilting contest of the 13th century, with knights in armor in the town's main piazza in mid-June.

JULY

Ballet, drama, and jazz performances are included in the **Shakespearean Festival,** Verona (July 1–July 30), and a few of the performances are in English. Ballet, drama, and jazz performances are included in this festival of the Bard.

ITALY'S AVERAGE DAILY TEMPERATURE & MONTHLY RAINFALL

ROME	JAN	FEB	MAR	APR	MAY	JUNE	JULY	AUG	SEPT	OCT	NOV	DEC
Temp. (°F)	49	52	57	62	72	82	87	86	73	65	56	47
Temp. (°C)	9	11	14	17	22	28	31	30	23	20	13	8
Rainfall (in.)	2.3	1.5	2.9	3.0	2.8	2.9	1.5	1.9	2.8	2.6	3.0	2.1

FLORENCE	JAN	FEB	MAR	APR	MAY	JUNE	JULY	AUG	SEPT	OCT	NOV	DEC
Temp. (°F)	45	47	50	60	67	76	77	70	64	63	55	46
Temp. (°C)	7	8	9	16	19	24	25	21	18	17	13	8
Rainfall (in.)	3	3.3	3.7	2.7	2.2	1.4	1.4	2.7	3.2	4.9	3.8	2.9

VENICE	JAN	FEB	MAR	APR	MAY	JUNE	JULY	AUG	SEPT	OCT	NOV	DEC
Temp (°F)	43	48	53	60	67	72	77	74	68	60	54	44
Temp (°C)	6	9	12	16	19	22	25	23	29	16	12	7
Rainfall (in.)	2.3	1.5	2.9	3	2.8	2.9	1.5	1.9	2.9	2.6	3	2.1

NAPLES	JAN	FEB	MAR	APR	MAY	JUNE	JULY	AUG	SEPT	OCT	NOV	DEC
Temp. (°F)	50	54	58	63	70	78	83	85	75	66	60	52
Temp. (°C)	9	12	14	17	21	26	28	29	24	19	16	11
Rainfall (in.)	4.7	4	3	3.8	2.4	0.8	0.8	2.6	3.5	5.8	5.1	3.7

Palio fever grips Tuscany's Siena on July 2 (and again on Aug 16) for a wild and exciting horse race from the Middle Ages. Pageantry, costumes, and the celebrations of the victorious *contrada* (sort of a neighborhood social club) mark the spectacle in Piazza del Campo. It's a "no rules" event: Even a horse without a rider can win the race. For details, contact the Azienda di Promozione Turistica, Piazza del Campo 56, 53100 Siena (☎ 0577-280551).

From early July to late August, culture buffs flock to the 20,000-seat **Arena di Verona,** one of the world's best-preserved amphitheaters, for the outdoor opera season **(Arena Outdoor Opera Season)**. Call ☎ 045-800-5151 or go to www.arena.it.

Trastevere, the most colorful quarter in Rome, becomes a gigantic outdoor restaurant in mid-July, with tables lining the streets and merrymakers and musicians providing the entertainment at the **Festa di Noantri.** For details, contact the Azienda di Promozione Turistica, Via Parigi 11, 00185 Roma (☎ 06-488911). During the same time period, Perugia in Umbria hosts the country's (and one of Europe's) top jazz festivals, **Umbria Jazz,** featuring world-class artists. Call ☎ 075-573-2432 or go to www.umbriajazz.com.

The **Festa del Redentore (Feast of the Redeemer)** in Venice marks the lifting of the plague in July 1578 with fireworks, pilgrimages, and boating. It takes place the third Saturday and Sunday in July.

In mid-July, international performers converge on Urbino, Raphael's birthplace, for the most important Renaissance and baroque music festival in Italy, the **Festival Internazionale di Musica Antica.** For details, contact the Azienda di Promozione Turistica, Piazza del Rinascimento 1, 61029 Urbino (☎ 0722-2613).

Puccini operas are performed from mid-July to mid-August in Lucca's open-air theater, near the celebrated composer's summertime villa, at the **Festival Puccini.** Call ☎ 0584-350567 or go to www.puccinifestival.it.

AUGUST

The world's top bel canto specialists perform Rossini's operas and choral works during the monthlong **Rossini Opera Festival in Pesaro.** Call ☎ 0721-380-0291 or go to www.rossini operafestival.it.

Ranking only after Cannes in prominence, the **Venice International Film Festival** brings together stars, directors, producers, and filmmakers from all over the world. Films are shown between 9am and 3am in various areas of the

Palazzo del Cinema on the Lido. Although many of the seats are reserved for international jury members, the public can attend when seats are available. Films are also screened to the public in Campo San Polo. For information contact the Venice Film Festival, c/o the La Biennale office, Ca' Giustinian, San Marco 1364A, 30124 Venezia. Call ☎ 041-521-8711 for details on how to acquire tickets, or check out www.labiennale.org. The action happens from August to early September.

SEPTEMBER

Festooned boats with crews in period costumes make their way down Venice's legendary Grand Canal during the **Regata Storica** on the first Sunday in September.

OCTOBER

Alba, Italy's truffle capital, celebrates its prestigious fungus on the first Sunday of October with contests, truffle-hound competitions, and tastings of this ugly but very expensive and delectable fungus at the **Fiera Internazionale del Tartufo Bianco d'Alba.** For details, head online to www.fieradeltartufo.org.

DECEMBER

The **season at La Scala,** one of the world's most prestigious opera houses, opens on December 7, the feast day of Milan's patron, St. Ambrogio, and runs into July, and from September to mid-November. Even though opening-night tickets are close to impossible to get, it's worth a try; call ☎ 02-861827 or visit www.teatroallascala.org for information and reservations.

The pope delivers his **Christmas blessing** from the balcony of St. Peter's Basilica, Rome, at noon on December 25 and it is broadcast around the world.

Weather

It's warm all over Italy in summer, with high temperatures in Rome and the south lasting from May until sometime in October. Temperatures can stay in the 90s°F (30s°C) for days, but nights are most often comfortably cooler. Winters in the north of Italy are cold, with rain and snow, but in the south the weather is warm all year, averaging 50°F (10°C) in winter.

Cellphones (Mobiles)

To use your cellphone in Italy, you must have a GSM (Global System for Mobiles) cellphone with a 900 GSM frequency; this allows you to make calls anywhere in the world, though it can be expensive. It may be less expensive to rent a cellphone from an Italian provider at the airport or to purchase a prepaid phone chip to use in your phone. GSM phones function with a removable plastic SIM card, encoded with your phone number and account information. In Italy, you can purchase a phone and SIM card for about 100€ and buy prepaid minutes in increments of 5€ to 20€. To rent a phone outfitted for use in Italy in advance of your trip, check www.roadpost.com, www.intouchglobal.com, or Cellhire (www.cellhire.com, www.cellhire.co.uk, www.cellhire.com.au).

U.K. mobiles all work in Italy; call your service provider before departing your home country to ensure that the international call bar has been switched off, and to check call charges, which can be extremely high. Remember that you are also charged for calls you *receive* on a U.K. mobile used abroad.

Ecotourism

Italy has one of Europe's worst environmental records and has been slow to embrace concerns that range from air and water pollution to damage inflicted on monuments by vibrations and emissions from automobiles. Recent initiatives of special interest to visitors include turning more lands over to national parks (22 parks now comprise 5% of the total land area) and setting aside coastal waters as protected marine areas. Visits to these protected regions and payment of appropriate fees help fund their ongoing protection.

Interest in *agriturismo,* in which guests stay on farms, vineyards, and other agricultural properties, is increasing. Guests enjoy the rural setting, sometimes partake in farming activities, and enjoy food and wine produced on the properties (p 728).

One of the most noticeable environmental initiatives of recent years is Italy's recent ban on smoking, now prohibited in any public place.

For general ecotourism information, **Responsible Travel** (www.responsibletravel.com) contains a great source of sustainable travel ideas run by a spokesperson for responsible tourism in the travel industry. **Sustainable Travel International** (www.sustainabletravelinternational.org) promotes responsible tourism practices.

You can find ecofriendly travel tips, statistics, and touring companies and associations—listed by destination under "Travel Choice"—at the TIES website, www.ecotourism.org. Ecotravel.com is part online magazine and part ecodirectory that lets you search for touring companies: water-based, land-based, spiritually oriented, and so on.

In the U.K., the **Association of Independent Tour Operators** (**AITO;** www.aito.co.uk) is a group of interesting specialist operators leading the field in making holidays sustainable.

Getting There

By Plane

High season on most airline routes to Italy is usually from June to the beginning of September. This is the most expensive and crowded time to travel. **Shoulder season** is from April to May, early September to October, and December 15 to December 24. **Low season** is from November 1 to December 14 and December 25 to March 31.

Italy's major overseas air gateways are Rome and Milan, though Venice and Pisa are now also served by nonstop flights from the U.S. Flights from within Europe also serve Bologna, Palermo, Verona, and many other smaller Italian airports.

FROM NORTH AMERICA

Most visitors traveling to Italy by air fly into either Rome (p 148) or Milan (p 178). Flying time to Rome from New York, Newark, and Boston is 8 hours; from Chicago, 10 hours; and from Los Angeles, 12½ hours. Flying time to Milan from New York, Newark, and Boston is 8 hours; from Chicago, 9¼ hours; and from Los Angeles, 11½ hours.

American Airlines (☎ 800/433-7300; www.aa.com) offers daily nonstop flights to Rome from Chicago's O'Hare, with flights from all parts of American's vast network making connections into Chicago. **Delta** (☎ 800/221-1212; www.delta.com) flies from New York's JFK Airport and Atlanta to Milan and Rome every evening and has frequent nonstop service from New York to Venice and Pisa. **USAirways** (☎ 800/428-4322; www.usairways.com) offers one flight daily to Rome out of Philadelphia. And **Continental** (☎ 800/231-0856; www.

continental.com) flies several times a week to Rome and Milan from its hub in Newark.

Air Canada (☎ 888/247-2262; www.aircanada.ca) flies daily from Toronto to Rome. Two of the flights are nonstop; the others touch down en route in Montreal, depending on the schedule.

British Airways (☎ 800/AIRWAYS; www.britishairways.com), **Virgin Atlantic Airways** (☎ 800/821-5438; www.virgin-atlantic.com), **Air France** (☎ 800/237-2747; www.airfrance.com), **Northwest/KLM** (☎ 800/225-2525; www.nwa.com), and **Lufthansa** (☎ 800/645-3880; www.lufthansa-usa.com) offer some attractive deals for anyone interested in combining a trip to Italy with a stopover in, say, Britain, Paris, Amsterdam, or Germany.

Alitalia (☎ 800/223-5730; www.alitalia.com) is the Italian national airline, with nonstop flights to Rome from many North American cities, including New York (JFK), Newark, Boston, Chicago, Miami, Washington, and Toronto. Nonstop flights into Milan are from New York (JFK) and Newark. From Milan or Rome, Alitalia can easily book connecting domestic flights if your final destination is elsewhere in Italy.

FROM THE UNITED KINGDOM

Both **British Airways** (☎ 0870/850-9850 in the U.K.; www.britishairways.co.uk) and **Alitalia** (☎ 0870/544-8259; www.alitalia.it) have frequent flights from London's Heathrow to Rome, Milan, Venice, Pisa (the gateway to Florence), and Naples. Flying time from London to these cities is from 2 to 3 hours. British Airways also has direct flights from Manchester to Rome.

Two discount airlines have extensive service to Italy from the U.K. **Ryanair** (☎ 050/503770; www.ryanair.com) flies from London's Stansted airport to many Italian cities, including Milan, Palermo, Parma, Pisa, Rome, Venice, and Verona. It also has some service from London's Luton airport. Ryanair also offers service from Liverpool and Manchester to Milan.

EasyJet (☎ www.easyjet.com) has service from London Gatwick and other London airports to Milan, Pisa, Rome, and Venice.

FROM AUSTRALIA

Qantas (☎ **131313** in Australia; www.qantas.com.au) flies from Sydney and Melbourne to Rome, Milan, and other cities from Sydney, with a change to British Airways in London. The airline also has service from Sydney and Melbourne via Hong Kong to Rome.

Alitalia (☎ 61/29244-2400 in Australia; www.alitalia.com) has limited service from Melbourne to Rome.

FROM NEW ZEALAND

Qantas serves Italian destinations from Auckland and Christchurch through connections in Sydney and Melbourne.

PACKAGE TOURS

One good source of package deals is the airlines themselves. Most major airlines offer air/and packages to Italy, including **American Airlines Vacations** (☎ 800/321-2121; www.aavacations.com), **Delta Vacations** (☎ 800/654-6559; www.deltavacations.com), **Continental Airlines Vacations** (☎ 800/301-3800; www.covacations.com), and **United Vacations** (☎ 888/854-3899; www.unitedvacations.com). Several big **online travel agencies**—Expedia, Travelocity, Orbitz, Site59, and Lastminute.com—also do business in packages.

ESCORTED GENERAL-INTEREST TOURS

Escorted tours are structured group tours, with a group leader. The price usually includes everything from airfare to hotels, meals, tours, admission costs, and local transportation. For information on tours catering to those with special interests, see chapter 15, "The Best Special Interest Trips."

Perillo Tours (☎ 800/431-1515; www.perillotours.com) has been family operated for three generations. A trip with them will cost much less than if you arranged the same thing yourself. Accommodations are in first-class hotels, and guides tend to be well qualified and well informed.

Trafalgar Tours (☎ 866/544-4434; www.trafalgartours.com) is one of Europe's largest tour operators, offering affordable guided tours with lodgings in unpretentious hotels. Check with your travel agent for more information on these tours (Trafalgar takes calls only from agents).

Globus+Cosmos Tours (☎ 800/338-7092; www.globusandcosmos.com) offers first-class escorted coach tours of various regions lasting from 8 to 16 days (for a more in-depth review of a Globus tour in Italy, check our website, Frommers.com). Cosmos, a budget branch of

Globus, sells escorted tours of about the same length.

Insight Vacations (☎ 800/582-8380; www.insightvacations.com) books superior first-class, fully escorted motorcoach tours lasting from 1 week to a 36-day grand tour.

Abercrombie & Kent (☎ 800/554-7016 in the U.S., or 01242/547-700 in the U.K.; www.abercrombiekent.com) offers a variety of luxurious premium packages. Your overnight stays will be in meticulously restored castles and exquisite Italian villas, most of which are government-rated four- and five-star accommodations.

Cox & Kings (☎ 020/7873-5000; www.coxandkings.co.uk) specializes in organized tours through Italian gardens and sites of historical or aesthetic interest, opera tours, pilgrimage-style visits to sites of religious interest, and food- and wine-tasting tours. The staff is noted for their focus on tours of ecological and environmental interest.

By Train

If you plan to travel heavily on the European rails, you'll do well to secure the latest copy of the *Thomas Cook European Timetable of Railroads.* It's available online at www.thomascooktimetables.com.

A fast-train network has made travel to Italy faster and more comfortable than ever. **France's TGVs** travel at speeds of up to 296kmph (185 mph) and have cut travel time between Paris and Turin from 7 to 5½ hours and between Paris and Milan from 7½ to 6¾ hours. **Italy's ETRs** travel at speeds of up to 232kmph (145 mph) and currently run between Milan and Lyon (5 hr.), with a stop in Turin. Tilting **Cisalpino** (*Chee*-sahl-peeno) trains are some of the world's most advanced and speed from northern Italy (primarily Venice, Florence, and Milan) to major cities in Switzerland and Germany. Though aimed mostly at business travelers, they're a great way to get from Switzerland to Italy. There is also direct express service to many major Italian cities from Spain and Austria.

A luxurious **Trenhotel Elipsos** overnight train (the *Salvador Dalí*), connects Milan and Turin with Barcelona in Spain. **Artesia de Nuit** trains connect Paris to various cities in Italy. And **EuroNight (EN)** trains service both international and domestic routes.

Reservations are mandatory on all Artesia, Cisalpino, and night trains. All sleeping accommodations (except for sleeperette seats on many EN trains) require additional supplements in addition to a railpass (if you go the pass route) and must be reserved well in advance. I recommend reserving before you leave home if possible. If you're traveling at night, it's wise to reserve a *couchette,* especially for long distances, such as the train that goes from Paris to Rome or vice versa. A wide variety of sleeping accommodations are available depending on the night trains that you choose.

EURAIL GLOBAL PASS

Many North American travelers to Europe take advantage of one of the greatest travel bargains, the **Eurail Global Pass,** which allows you unlimited travel over a select period of time (from 15 days to 3 months) in 21 Eurail-affiliated countries. Unless you'll be traveling through Europe extensively before arriving in Italy, however, it's not a cost-effective option for you. Prices for first-class adult travel range from $687 for 15 days to $1,926 for 3 months. Children 4 to 11 pay half fare; those 3 and under travel for free. Additional global pass options include the **Eurail Global Pass Saver,** which offers a special deal for two or more people traveling together; and the **Eurail Global Youth Pass** for those age 12 to 25, which allows second-class travel for $446 for 15 days to $1,255 for 3 months.

For those limiting their travel to Italy and the surrounding territory, Eurail does offer a host of discount passes that are cheaper and more flexible than the Eurail Global Pass. Check out www.raileurope.com for details.

WHERE TO BUY A PASS

In **North America,** contact **Rail Europe** (☎ 800/622-8600 in the U.S., 800/361-RAIL in Canada; www.raileurope.com) if you have questions about passes or wish to purchase one. Rail Europe can also provide information on rail/drive versions of the passes. No matter what everyone tells you, you can buy Eurailpasses in Europe as well as in America (at the major train stations), but they're more expensive. You can also buy these passes from travel agents or rail agents in major cities such as New York, Montreal, and Los Angeles.

For details on the rail passes available in the

United Kingdom, stop in at or contact the **National Rail Inquiries,** Victoria Station, London SW1V 1JZ (☎ 08705/848-848). The staff can help you find the best option for the trip you're planning. Some of the most popular are the **Inter-Rail** and **Under 26** passes, entitling you to unlimited second-class travel in 26 European countries.

By Car

Major routes from Western Europe leading into Italy require a toll. These include segments of Europe's superhighway system and the St. Gotthard and Mont Blanc tunnels under the Alps.

The drive from London to Rome covers a distance of 1,810km (1,124 miles), via Calais/Boulogne/Dunkirk, or 1,747km (1,085 miles) via Oostende/Zeebrugge, not counting channel crossings by ferry or the Chunnel. Milan is some 644km (400 miles) closer to Britain than is Rome. Most drivers budget 3 days for the journey. If you don't want to drive such distances, ask a travel agent to book you on a Motorail arrangement where the train carries your car. This service is good only on the Continent, and service within Italy is limited. The most efficient option from the U.K is to pick up a Motorail train in Calais (Motorail trains do not operate in the Channel Tunnel) and travel to Nice, continuing the drive from there. Fares start at about 150€ for car and driver, including a second-class couchette. For more information, go to www.raileurope.co.uk.

Getting Around

By Train

Train travel is reasonably priced and moderately efficient in Italy. Most Italian trains have been integrated into the state system, and are operated by **Ferrovie dello Stato (FS).** Information on the rail network is available online at www.ferrovie.it, but be aware that the website is mainly in Italian.

Many different kinds of trains operate, and fees vary accordingly. **ETR Eurostar Italia (ES)** and **Eurocity (EC)** trains connect major cities, with the fastest service and greatest comfort; seat reservations are required, and holders of rail passes must pay a supplement; **InterCity trains** (**IC** on train schedules) make limited stops, and **InterCity Plus** trains are especially fast and comfortable—seat reservations are required, and holders of rail passes must pay a supplement. Slower trains include: *Espresso,* which stop at main stations; *Diretto,* which stop at most stations; and *Locale,* which stop at all stations (avoid the latter if at all possible—they are very slow). Most trains, except in deep rural areas of the south, are modern and air-conditioned.

As a rule of thumb, second-class travel usually costs about two-thirds the price of an equivalent first-class trip. That said, unless you're riding Eurostar Italia, you're better off opting for first class when traveling by rail in Italy. *Warning:* Theft on some Italian trains is a problem. If you opt for a couchette or sleeperette on an Italian train, make sure your belongings are well secured.

Even though reservations are optional on most rail journeys in Italy, it's still wise to book a ticket and a seat on runs between such major cities as Florence and Venice, Rome and Naples, or Rome and either Florence or Milan. Italian trains are very crowded on public holidays, and reservations might as well be mandatory during these peak periods. Big rail depots, such as the Stazione Termini in Rome, often have separate windows for making reservations—labeled *prenotazioni.* North Americans can reserve seats in advance through Rail Europe (see below) for anywhere from $11 to $30, depending on the train and desired seat.

Eurail Italy Pass covers 3 to 10 days of travel within 2 months. Price for 3 days is $244 in first class, $199 in second class. North Americans can buy these passes from their travel agent or by contacting **Rail Europe** (☎ 800/622-8600 in the U.S., 800/361-RAIL in Canada; www.raileurope.com). In the United Kingdom, contact **National Rail Inquiries,** Victoria Station, London SW1V 1JZ (☎ 08705/848-848). The staff can help you find the best option for the trip you're planning.

By Plane
Italy's domestic air network on **Alitalia** (☎ 800/223-5730 in the U.S., or 0870/544-8259 in the U.K.; www.alitalia.com) is one of the largest and most complete in Europe. Some 40 airports are serviced regularly, and most flights within the country take less than an hour. **Meridiana** and its affiliate **Eurofly** (☎ 892928 in Italy; www.meridiana.com) offers low-cost options on flights within Italy.

By Bus
Italy has an extensive and intricate bus network, covering all regions. Buses serve most towns and villages not served by trains, especially many in the Dolomites and Alps, around the Italian lakes, and in Sicily, where the train network is limited. Buses in general are clean and comfortable, and service is usually frequent.

Most often, buses leave from terminals or well-marked stops near train stations, and in larger towns bus companies maintain ticket offices. Otherwise, buy tickets from tobacco shops or newsstands or on the bus. Information desks in train stations can often also provide bus information or at least direct you to someone who can. Before boarding a bus, make your destination known to the driver and make sure that you are on the right bus; many drivers do not speak English, so be prepared to write out your destination.

One of the leading bus operators is **SITA,** Viale dei Cadorna 105, Florence (☎ 055/47821; www.sita-on-line.it). SITA buses serve most parts of the country, especially the central belt, including Tuscany, but not the far frontiers. Among the largest of the country's other bus companies, with special emphasis on the north and central tiers, is **Autostradale,** Autostazione Garibaldi, Milan (☎ 02/637901; www.autostradale.it). **Lazzi,** Via Mercadante 2, Florence (☎ 055/363041; www.lazzi.it), goes through Tuscany, including Siena, and much of central Italy. Where these services leave off, local bus companies operate in most regions.

By Car
The Italian road network is excellent, and roads are extremely well maintained. Drivers may well be surprised to see that roads in Italy are in much better condition than those at home. Roads are well marked with international signage.

Italy's extensive system of superhighways, or *autostrade,* covers the entire country and makes long-distance travel quick and easy. Travel on these highways requires a toll. Some lanes at toll booths are reserved for "Telepass" and "Viacard" holders. Telepass is a similar to the EZ Pass system in the U.S. and geared to EU residents, but it is a prepaid pass that nonresidents can buy at toll booths and at shops in rest stops along the autostrade. Drivers with the pass can zip through special lines at toll booths, sparing long waits and the need to pay with cash at each stop.

Other primary roads are marked with an S, as in S75, and are often four-lane or two lanes with passing lanes. Roads with SR designations are secondary roads and often only have two lanes.

Speed limits are 50kmph (30 mph) in residential zones, 90kmph (55 mph) on secondary roads, 110kmph (65 mph) on primary roads, and 130kmph (90 mph) on autostrade.

U.S., Canadian, Australian, and New Zealand drivers do not need an International Driver's License (IDL) to drive a rented car in Italy, but do require one if driving a private car. While not required, an IDL provides an internationally recognized form of identification and can help cut through red tape when dealing with authorities.

You can apply for an International Driver's License at any **American Automobile Association (AAA)** branch. You must be at least 18 and have two 2x2-inch photos and a photocopy of your U.S. driver's license with your AAA application form. The actual fee for the license can vary, depending on where it's issued. To find the AAA office nearest you, check the local phone directory or contact AAA's national headquarters (☎ 800/222-4357; www.aaa.com). Remember that an International Driver's License is valid only if physically accompanied by your original driver's license and only if signed on the back. In Canada, contact the **Canadian Automobile Association** (☎ 800/267-8713; www.caa.ca) to find the closest branch office where you can apply. In the U.K., contact the **British Automobile Association** (☎ 0800 085 7240; www.theaa.com). In Australia, contact the **Australian Automobile Association** (☎ 2/6247-7311-216; www.aaa.asn.au); in New Zealand, contact the **New Zealand Automobile Association** (☎ 0800 500 444, www.aa.co.nz).

The **Automobile Club d'Italia (ACI),** Via Marsala 8, 00185 Roma (☎ 06/49981), is open Monday through Friday from 8am to 2pm. The ACI's 24-hour Information and Assistance Center (CAT), providing road information, itineraries, and travel assistance, is at Cristoforo Colombo 261, 00147 Roma (☎ 06/491115).

RENTALS

A valid driver's license and a valid passport are required and (in most cases) the renter must be over 25. Insurance on all vehicles is compulsory. When booking, ask what insurance coverage is included and determine how much additional insurance might be necessary. For instance, some companies charge extra for collision damage waiver (CDW) insurance (which covers the cost of damage to vehicles in case of an accident), personal liability insurance (which covers injuries inflicted on others), and theft-and-break-in insurance. Some of this insurance might be covered in a package price, by your individual auto insurance policy, or by the credit card you use to rent the car. Before signing the rental documents, read them carefully so you understand the terms.

The major rental companies in Italy are **Avis** (☎ 800/331-1084; www.avis.com), **Budget** (☎ 800/472-3325; www.budget.com), and **Hertz** (☎ 800/654-3001; www.hertz.com). U.S.-based companies specializing in European car rentals are **Auto Europe** (☎ 888/223-5555; www.autoeurope.com), **Europe by Car** (☎ 800/223-1516, or 212/581-3040; www.europebycar.com), and **Kemwel Drive Europe** (☎ 877/820-0668; www.kemwel.com).

In some cases, discounts are offered to members of automobile associations outside Italy, such as the American Automobile Association (AAA) and British Automobile Association (AA), and to seniors.

Most rental agreements permit you to drive the car anywhere within the EU, though some companies place limitations of driving in Naples and other areas where the incidence of auto theft is very high.

In general, but not always, you will pay extra to drop a rental car at a location other than the one from which you rented it, and quite a bit more if you drop the car at a location outside Italy.

Italians have truly earned their reputation for being "bad but daring" drivers, so drive defensively.

GASOLINE

Gasoline, or petrol (known as *benzina*), is very expensive in Italy. Be prepared for sticker shock every time you fill up with *super benzina,* which has the octane rating appropriate for most of the cars you'll be able to rent. Gas stations on the autostrade are open 24 hours, but on regular roads gas stations are rarely open on

Sunday; also, many close from noon to 3pm for lunch, and most shut down after 7pm. Make sure the pump registers zero before an attendant starts filling your tank. A popular scam, particularly in the south, is to fill your tank before resetting the meter, so you pay not only your bill but also the charges run up by the previous motorist.

DRIVING RULES

Driving is on the right; passing is on the left. In cities and towns, the speed limit is 50kmph (31 mph). For all cars and motor vehicles on main roads and local roads, the limit is 90kmph (56 mph). For the autostrade, the limit is 130kmph (81 mph). Use the left lane only for passing. If a driver zooms up behind you on the autostrade with his or her lights on, that's your sign to get out of the way! Use of seat belts is compulsory, and cellphones can only be used with earphones or a speaker. The penalties for serious traffic violations are stiff fines and in some cases imprisonment.

BREAKDOWNS & ASSISTANCE

All drivers are required to carry a warning triangle to place next to the car in case of a breakdown and to wear a special reflector when getting out the car on the road (both are provided with rental cars). For highway assistance in case of breakdown, use one of the phones on yellow poles placed every 2km (1¼ miles) along autostrade or call ☎ **116.** This assistance is provided by **The Automobile Club d'Italia (ACI)** and is free for all cars with foreign plates as well as to drivers of rental cars in Italy.

RECOMMENDED MAPS & ATLASES

Touring Club Italiano (TCI) publishes excellent maps of the Italian road network, as well as highly detailed maps of specific regions. These regional maps are available as a set, and TCI also publishes a road atlas and a smaller pocket road atlas. TCI maps and atlases are available at newsstands and bookstores throughout Italy, as well as in many bookstores in the U.S. and U.K. You can also order them from the TCI website, www.touringclub.com.

PARKING

Good luck. Parking is often problematic in Italy, and poses as big a challenge to Italians as it does to foreign drivers. You will find large lots outside the entrances to many towns and in some major cities; use these whenever possible. You can expect to pay about 2€ or more an hour and up to 25€ to 30€ for overnight parking. Car parks are usually well posted with international parking signs, a large P on a blue background; they usually give the distance to the nearest parking facility and an arrow points in the general direction.

Be especially wary of street parking, which is often highly restricted and available only to residents or prohibited altogether at certain times. Read signs carefully. When parking on the street, it is usually necessary to pay in advance (often with a credit or debit card) at a curbside machine, which will issue a ticket that you display in your windshield or on the curbside window.

Car break-ins are common. Leave no valuables in your car, and if possible, take the radio with you. And use a supervised lot when your car is loaded with luggage and other valuables.

Tips on Accommodations

Accommodations in Italy are rated by regional council and awarded one to five stars, depending basically on the amenities offered. In general, the more amenities and stars a hotel has, the more expensive it will be. Overall, accommodations in Italy meet a fairly high standard. Except in some of the more remote rural areas, increasingly rare is the room that does not have a private bathroom, air conditioning, television, and telephone, as well as some type of Internet service, whether it's Wi-Fi, in-room dial-up, or cable connections, or a public computer for guest use in the lobby. As elsewhere in Europe, standard rooms in Italy tend to be rather small, especially in city hotels where space is limited. Single travelers are often relegated to quarters not much larger than the cabins on a ship.

Most hotels include breakfast in the rates, and this can range from a fairly miserly offering of a roll and coffee to a lavish buffet.

Rates can vary widely from season to season, and from place to place, and are usually broken down by: room with or without breakfast (if a hotel charges extra for breakfast, it is almost always cheaper to enjoy a coffee and pastry at a nearby bar); *mezza pensione,* or half-board, which includes breakfast and one other meal, usually dinner (many hotels in resorts require this arrangement during high season); and *pensione completa,* or full board, including breakfast, lunch, and dinner.

Booking in Advance

As a rule of thumb, you should always reserve a room in advance in any Italian city at any time, but always during high seasons—keeping in mind that high seasons vary considerably and include Christmas, New Year's, and Easter in resorts and some cities. August is high season for hotels in the mountains and at the coast, and low season in Bologna and many other cities—even, surprisingly, Venice. The fall is an especially busy time in Milan, when many fashion shows are held, and high seasons can pop up out of the blue and extend for just a week during times when Bologna and other cities host international trade shows. In short, if you wish to travel without making reservations and enjoy the freedom that affords, check to see how busy the regions you will be visiting will be. Hotel websites usually list their seasonal rates and what periods they consider to be high and low.

Checking out the hotel listings in this book is the best place to begin to locate a hotel. Expedia, Travelocity, and Orbitz also offer, in addition to air bookings, reasonably priced hotel rooms, as does Hotels.com. Keep in mind that most of these services require you to pay in full upfront, so you may be stuck with a room you don't like. (But if you don't like it when you arrive, always ask to change rooms.) You should also check with hotels directly to see what sort of special offers they offer on their own. (These usually appear on the hotel's website.) If you see an offer on another website, call or write the hotel, mention the offer you've seen, and ask if the hotel will match it or do better—this way you will be dealing with the hotel, can request the sort of room you want, and won't be locked into a prepaid arrangement. Bargaining is a respected skill in Italy, so never be afraid to ask if a hotel can provide a more favorable rate.

Other good websites that book hotel rooms in Italy include **ItalyBy.com** (it usually has a great selection of photos of a property's individual rooms) and **Venere.com.**

Types of Accommodations

The terms *albergo, locanda,* and *hotel* appear interchangeably in Italy, and don't really designate the character of the hotel—whatever name they go by, these accommodations can include sleek modern hotels and converted seaside villas and mountain castles—the same way that "inn" in English might be used for a business hotel or a quaint country retreat.

Italy offers some of Europe's finest accommodations. These include historic grand hotels around the Italian lakes, spectacular resorts along the Amalfi Coast and on Capri, and large hotels in Florence, Rome, and Venice. Italy also has a fine tradition of small, family-run hotels, and you will find them throughout the countryside and in almost every city as well. Some have been renovated and are now chic inns, while others retain a homey, nonfussy atmosphere. As a center of style, Italy has also seen the emergence of some very chic hotels, especially in Milan, Florence, and Rome. Even traditional Venice has some stunning new contemporary lodgings.

International chains are an increasing presence in Italy, especially in large cities. While the Four Seasons and some others offer atmospheric and distinctively luxurious surroundings, other middle-of-the-road chains rely on the predictability of their offerings and you will usually find more character in locally owned and managed properties.

Alternative Accommodations

AGRITOURISM

Rooms and apartments are available on farms and wine-producing estates throughout Italy, providing a slice of rural life often accompanied by fresh produce and other delicious local cuisine. Many *agriturismo* accommodations are located near cities, allowing you to combine a country vacation with visits to museums and monuments. Sources for information and listings of agriturismo vacations include **Agritourism Italy** (www.agritourismitaly.com) and **Agriturismo Italy** (www.agriturismo.it).

BED-AND-BREAKFAST

This term is not widely used in Italy, where just about any hotel offers this arrangement. However, **Caffelletto** (☎ 049/663980; www.caffelletto.it) lists unusually atmospheric bed-and-breakfasts located in palaces, castles, villas, and farmhouses.

HOUSE-SWAPPING

House-swapping is becoming a more popular and viable means of travel; you stay in their place, they stay in yours, and you both get a more authentic and personal view of a destination. Try **HomeLink International** (www.Homelink.org), the largest and oldest home-swapping organization, founded in 1952, with more than 11,000 listings worldwide, including Italy ($75 yearly membership). **HomeExchange.org** ($50 for 6,000 listings) and **InterVac.com** ($69 for over 10,000 listings) are also reliable.

RELIGIOUS INSTITUTIONS

Convents, monasteries, and other religious institutions throughout Italy offer accommodations. While rooms are sometimes basic and appropriately monastic, others are on par with two- or three-star hotels and offer such amenities as air-conditioning and private bathrooms. Many are also historic and character-filled properties, with cloisters and other welcome features. Some are limited solely to men or to women. Prices are almost always lower than they would be for similar lodgings in a hotel. For more information, contact the government and local tourist boards of the region which you plan to visit.

YOUTH HOSTELS

These standbys for backpackers yield some nice surprises, as many of the dozens of youth hostels throughout Italy now offer private or semi-private rooms and family suites, and are often well located in city centers or in scenic rural locations. A stay requires membership in **Associazone Italiano Alberghi (AIG)** or Hostelling International. For information, including a listing of hostels throughout Italy, contact AIG (☎ 06/487-1152; www.ostellionline.org).

Fast Facts

Apartment, Villa, or Condo Rentals
See "Tips on Accommodations," above.

ATMs/Cashpoints
The easiest way to get euros in Italy is at an ATM (or cashpoint), using your bank or credit card. Keep in mind that credit card companies charge interest from the day of your withdrawal, even if you pay your monthly bill on time. Nearly every small town and village has an **ATM** (*bancomat*), and you'll find numerous ones in the major cities. Note that many ATMs will charge you at least a 3€ fee (in addition to whatever your home bank charges for international withdrawals). Italy generally uses 4-digit PINs; if you have a 6-digit PIN, check with your bank before you leave to ensure that you will be avble to withdraw cash in Italy. See the individual "Fast Facts" in each destination chapter for more on ATMs in each region. Do note that cash tends to run out in some ATMs (especially in Rome) on Saturday night and isn't replenished until Monday afternoon, so think ahead. Also, find out your daily limit before you leave home.

The Cirrus (☎ 800/424-7787; www.mastercard.com) and PLUS (☎ 800/843-7587; www.visa.com) networks span the globe, including Italy. Go to your bank card's website to find ATM locations at your destination.

Banking Hours
Banks are open Monday through Friday from 8:30am to 1pm or 1:30 and 2pm or 2:30pm to 4pm, and are closed all day Saturday, Sunday, and national holidays.

Bike Rentals
Biking is a popular mode of transportation in many parts of Italy, especially in the cities on the flat plains of Emilia-Romagna: the streets of Ferrara, Bologna, Parma, and Ravenna are filled with cyclists of all ages. In cities where cycling is popular, rentals are usually available from stands near train stations and rates are about 10€ a day; many hotels offer bikes for the free use of guests.

Business Hours
Regular business hours are generally Monday through Friday from 9am (sometimes 9:30am) to 1pm and 3:30 (sometimes 4pm) to 7 or 7:30pm. In July and August, offices might not open in the afternoon until 4:30 or 5pm. The *riposo* (midafternoon closing) is often observed in Rome, Naples, and most southern cities; however, in Milan and other northern and central cities, the custom has been abolished by some merchants. Most shops are closed on Sunday, except for certain tourist-oriented stores that are now permitted to remain open on Sunday during the high season.

Customs
Customs (*dogana*) at Italian airports tends to be lax; unless you're carrying a great deal of

luggage or look suspicious, no one will bother to inspect you as you clear the arrivals area. By law, foreign visitors can bring along most items for personal use duty-free, including 400 cigarettes or a quantity of cigars or pipe tobacco not exceeding 500 grams (a little more than 1 lb.). There are strict limits on importing alcoholic beverages. However, for alcohol bought tax-paid, limits are much more liberal than in other countries of the European Union. There are no limits for anyone, foreign nationals included, arriving from another E.U. country. File through the "Blue Exit" lane at Customs.

Rules governing what you can bring back duty-free from Italy vary from country to country and are subject to change, but they're generally posted on the Web.

U.S. CITIZENS For specifics on what you can bring back, download the invaluable free pamphlet *Know Before You Go* online at www.cbp. gov, or contact the U.S. Customs & Border Protection (CBP), 1300 Pennsylvania Ave. NW, Washington, DC 20229 (☎ 877/287-8667; www.cbp.gov) and request the pamphlet.

CANADIAN CITIZENS
For a clear summary of Canadian rules, write for the booklet *I Declare,* issued by the Canada Border Services Agency (☎ 800/461-9999 in Canada, or 204/983-3500; www.cbsa-asfc.gc.ca).

U.K. CITIZENS For information, contact HM Revenue & Customs at ☎ 0845/010-9000 (from outside the U.K., 02920/501-261), or consult their website at www.hmrc.gov.uk.

AUSTRALIAN CITIZENS
A helpful brochure available from Australian consulates or Customs offices is *Know Before You Go.* For more information, call the Australian Customs Service at ☎ 1300/363-263, or log on to www.customs.gov.au.

NEW ZEALAND CITIZENS
Request the free pamphlet *New Zealand Customs Guide for Travellers, Notice no. 4* from New Zealand Customs Service, The Customhouse, 17-21 Whitmore St., Box 2218, Wellington (☎ 04/473-6099 or 0800/428-786; www. customs.govt.nz).

Dining
Most Italians eat a leisurely full meal—appetizer and first and second course—at lunch and dinner. You can, however, find many more casual options.

A full-fledged restaurant will go by the name *osteria, trattoria,* or *ristorante.* Once upon a time, these terms meant something—*osterie* were basic places where you could get a plate of spaghetti and a glass of wine; *trattorie* were casual, serving full meals of filling peasant fare; and *ristoranti* were fancier, with waiters in bow ties, printed menus, wine lists, and hefty prices. Nowadays, fancy restaurants often go by the name of *trattoria* to cash in on the associated charm factor; trendy spots use *osteria* to show they're hip; and simple, inexpensive places sometimes tack on *ristorante* to ennoble themselves.

Pizza al taglio or *pizza rustica* indicates a place where you can order pizza by the slice. A *tavola calda* (literally "hot table") serves ready-made hot foods you can take away or eat at one of the few small tables often available. The food is usually very good. A *rosticceria* is the same type of place, and you'll see chickens roasting on a spit in the window.

The *enoteca* is a popular marriage of a wine bar and an *osteria,* where you can sit and order from a host of local and regional wines by the glass while snacking on finger foods (and usually a number of simple first-course possibilities) that reflect the region's fare. Relaxed and full of ambience and good wine, these are great spots for light and inexpensive lunches—perfect to educate your palate and recharge your batteries.

For a quick bite, go to a bar. Although bars in Italy do serve alcohol, they function mainly as cafes. Prices have a split personality: *al banco* is standing at the bar, while *à tavola* means sitting at a table where you'll be waited on and charged two to four times as much. In bars you can find panino sandwiches on various kinds of rolls and *tramezzini* (giant triangles of white-bread sandwiches with the crusts cut off). These both run about 2€ or 3€.

Most sit-down restaurants charge a *pane e coperto* (bread and cover, at least 1€) that you must pay for the mere privilege of sitting at the table. Many restaurants, especially larger ones and in cities, offer a *menu turistico* (tourist's menu), sometimes called *menu del giorno* (menu of the day). This set-price menu usually covers all meal incidentals—including table wine, cover charge, and 15% service charge—along with a first course (*primo*) and second course (*secondo*). Sometimes a better choice is a *menu à prezzo fisso* (fixed-price menu), which usually offers a wider selection of better dishes, occasionally house specialties and local foods. Ordering a la carte, however, offers you the best chance for a memorable meal. Even better, forego the menu entirely and put yourself in the capable hands of your waiter.

To request the bill, ask *"Il conto, per favore."* A tip of 15% is usually included in the bill these days, but if you're unsure, ask, *"È incluso il servizio?"*

Electricity

Like most of continental Europe, Italy uses the 220-volt system (two round prongs). American (110-volt) electronics with dual voltage (laptops and shavers) can be used with a simple adapter. Other appliances such as hair dryers require a clunky voltage converter; using such appliances with simple adapters (not converters) will most likely fry the appliance and blow fuses. U.K. 240-volt appliances need a continental adaptor, widely available at home but impossible to find in Italy.

Embassies & Consulates

In case of an emergency, embassies have a 24-hour referral service.

The **U.S. Embassy** is in Rome at Via Vittorio Veneto 121 (☎ 06/46741). U.S. consulates are in Florence, at Lungarno Amerigo Vespucci 38 (☎ 055/266951), and in Milan, at Via Principe Amedeo 2-10 (☎ 02/290351). There's also a consulate in Naples on Piazza della Repubblica 1 (☎ 081/583-8111). The consulate in Genoa is at Via Dante 2 (☎ 010/584492). There is also a consulate in Palermo (Sicily) at Via Vaccarini 1 (☎ 091/305857).

The **Canadian Consulate** and passport service is in Rome at Via Zara 30 (☎ 06-445981). The Canadian Embassy in Rome is at Via Salaria 243 (☎ 06/445981). The Canadian Consulate in Milan is at V.V. Pisani 19 (☎ 02/6758-3420).

The **U.K. Embassy** is in Rome at Via XX Settembre 80A (☎ 06/422-00001). The U.K. Consulate in Florence is at Lungarno Corsini 2 (☎ 055/284-133). The Consulate General in Naples is at Via Dei Mille 40 (☎ 081/4238-911). In Milan, contact the office at Via San Paolo 7 (☎ 02/723001).

The **Australian Embassy** is in Rome at Via Antonio Bosio 5 (☎ 06/852-721). The Australian Consulate is in Rome at Corso Trieste 25 (☎ 06/852-721). The Australian Consulate in Milan is at Via Borgogna 2 (☎ 02/777041).

The **New Zealand Embassy** is in Rome at Via Zara 28 (☎ 06/441-7171). The **Irish Embassy** in Rome is at Piazza di Campitelli 3 (☎ 06/697-9121).

Emergencies

Dial ☎ **113** for police, ☎ **114** for an ambulance, or ☎ **115** for a fire. In case of a car breakdown, dial ☎ 803-116; the nearest Automobile Club of Italy (ACI) will be notified to come to your aid.

Etiquette & Customs

Legs and shoulders should be covered when entering churches. Women may want to carry a scarf to cover their heads.

Event Listings

To keep abreast of Italy's many temporary art exhibitions and events such as the Venice Biennale, go to **www.beniculturali.it** (in Italian). Another good Internet source (in English) is the events section of **Italy On-line** (www.initaly.com).

Government tourist offices and local tourist offices are also excellent sources for information on local events (p 718).

Culturalitaly.com (☎ 800/380-0014; www.culturalitaly.com), a Los Angeles–based Web company, specializes in Italy's high-end events, everything from operatic performances at the ancient Baths of Caracalla in Rome to tickets for Venice carnival events.

Family Travel

Most Italian hoteliers will let children 12 and under stay in a room with their parents for free—sometimes after a bit of negotiating at the reception desk. While a kids' menu in a restaurant is a rarity, you can usually order a half portion (*mezza porzione*) for the little ones. At attractions, inquire if a *sconto bambino* (kids' discount) is available. For European Union kids under 18, admission is free to state-run museums.

Gay & Lesbian Travelers

Since 1861, Italy has had liberal legislation regarding homosexuality, but that doesn't mean it is looked on favorably in a Catholic country. Homosexuality is much more accepted in the north than in the south, although Taormina in Sicily has long been a gay mecca and Capri is Italy's leading gay resort. Most major towns and cities have an active gay life, especially Florence, Rome, and Milan. **ARCI Gay** (www. arcigay.it) is the country's leading gay organization.

Health

In general, Italy is viewed as a "safe" destination, although problems, of course, can and do occur anywhere. You don't need to get shots, most foodstuff is safe, and the water in cities and towns potable. It is easy to get a prescription filled in towns and cities, and nearly all places throughout Italy have English-speaking doctors at hospitals with well-trained medical staffs. Any foreign consulate can provide a list of area doctors who speak English. For information on the cost of care and health insurance in Italy, see "Insurance," below.

If you suffer from a chronic illness, consult your doctor before your departure. Pack prescription medications in your carry-on luggage, and carry them in their original containers, with pharmacy labels—otherwise they might not make it through airport security. Carry the generic name of prescription medicines, in case a local pharmacist is unfamiliar with the brand name.

The following government websites offer up-to-date health-related travel advice.

AUSTRALIA www.dfat.gov.au/travel
CANADA www.hc-sc.gc.ca/index_e.html
U.K. www.nhs.uk/nhsengland/Healthcare-abroad
U.S. www.cdc.gov/travel

GENERAL AVAILABILITY OF HEALTHCARE

Contact the **International Association for Medical Assistance to Travelers** (IAMAT; ☎ 716/ 754-4883, or 416/652-0137 in Canada; www.iamat.org) for tips on travel and health concerns in Italy, and for lists of local, English-speaking doctors. The **United States Centers for Disease Control and Prevention** (☎ 800/ 311-3435; www.cdc.gov) provides up-to-date information on health hazards by region or country and offers tips on food safety. **Travel Health Online** (www.tripprep.com), sponsored by a consortium of travel medicine practitioners, may also offer helpful advice on traveling abroad. You can find listings of reliable medical clinics overseas at the **International Society of Travel Medicine** (www.istm.org).

Holidays

Offices and shops in Italy are closed on the following national holidays: January 1 (New Year's Day), Easter Monday, April 25 (Liberation Day), May 1 (Labor Day), August 15 (Assumption of the Virgin), November 1 (All Saints' Day), December 8 (Feast of the Immaculate Conception), December 25 (Christmas Day), and December 26 (Santo Stefano).

Closings are also observed in the following cities on feast days honoring their patron saints: Venice, April 25 (St. Mark); Florence, Genoa, and Turin, June 24 (St. John the Baptist); Rome, June 29 (Sts. Peter and Paul); Palermo, July 15 (St. Rosalia); Naples, September 19 (St. Gennaro); Bologna, October 4 (St. Petronio); Cagliari, October 30 (St. Saturnino); Trieste, November 3 (St. Giusto); Bari, December 6 (St. Nicola); and Milan, December 7 (St. Ambrose).

Insurance

In addition to specific insurers mentioned below, you might want to browse the insurance products of these U.S. based companies: **Travel Insured International** (☎ 800/243-3174; www. travelinsured.com) and **Travelex Insurance Services** (☎ 800/228-9792, 603/328-1965 outside U.S. or Canada; www.travelex-insurance.com). In the U.K. contact **Endsleigh** (☎ 0800/028-3517; www. endsleigh.co.uk); in Australia, contact the **Australian Federation of Travel Agents (AFTA)** (☎ 1300/363-416; www.afta.com.au).

Other good sources for insurance geared to travelers are the automobile associations in your home country; see p 726.

TRAVEL INSURANCE

The cost of travel insurance varies widely, depending on the destination, the cost and length of your trip, your age and health, and the type of trip you're taking. Insist on seeing any policy and reading the fine print before buying. You can get estimates from various providers through **InsureMyTrip.com.** Enter your trip cost and dates, your age, and other information, for prices from more than a dozen companies, or call ☎ 800/487-4722. In the United Kingdom, try **Columbus Direct** (☎ 0870/033-9988; www.columbusdirect.net).

TRIP-CANCELLATION INSURANCE

Trip-cancellation insurance will help retrieve your money if you have to back out of a trip or depart early, or if your travel supplier goes bankrupt. Trip cancellation traditionally covers such events as sickness and natural disasters. The latest news in trip-cancellation insurance is the availability of "any-reason" cancellation coverage—which costs more but covers cancellations made for any reason. You won't get back 100% of your prepaid trip cost, but you'll be refunded a substantial portion. **TravelSafe** (☎ 888/885-7233; www.travelsafe.com) offers both types of coverage. Expedia also offers any-reason cancellation coverage for its air-hotel packages.

LOST-LUGGAGE INSURANCE

On international flights (including U.S. portions of international trips), baggage coverage is limited to approximately $9.07 per pound, up to approximately $635 per checked bag. If you plan to check high-value items, see if your homeowner's policy covers your valuables; if not, purchase baggage insurance as part of your comprehensive travel-insurance package.

If your luggage is lost, immediately file a lost-luggage claim at the airport, detailing the luggage contents. Most airlines require that you report delayed, damaged, or lost baggage within 4 hours of arrival. The airlines are required to deliver luggage, once found, directly to your house or destination free of charge.

MEDICAL INSURANCE

For travel overseas, most U.S. health plans (including Medicare and Medicaid) do not provide coverage, and the ones that do often reimburse you only after you return home.

As a safety net, you may want to buy travel medical insurance. If you require additional medical insurance, try **MEDEX Assistance** (☎ 410/453-6300; www.medexassist.com) or **Travel Assistance International** (☎ 800/821-2828; www.travelassistance.com; for general information on services, call the company's **Worldwide Assistance Services, Inc.,** at ☎ 800/777-8710).

Very few health insurance plans pay for medical evacuation back to the U.S. (which can cost $10,000 and up). A number of companies offer medical evacuation services anywhere in the world. If you're ever hospitalized more than 150 miles from home, **MedjetAssist** (☎ 800/527-7478; www.medjetassistance. com) will pick you up and fly you to the hospital of your choice. Annual memberships are $225 individual, $350 family; you can also purchase short-term memberships.

Canadians should check with their provincial health plan offices or call **Health Canada** (☎ 866/225-0709; www.hc-sc.gc.ca) to find out the extent of their coverage and how to proceed if they are treated in Italy.

U.K. nationals will need a European Health Insurance Card (EHIC) to receive free or reduced-costs health benefits during a visit to a Italy. The European Health Insurance Card replaces the E111 form, which is no longer valid. For advice, ask at your local post office or see www.dh.gov.uk/travellers.

Internet Access

Wi-Fi has become a common amenity in most hotels throughout Italy, especially in business-oriented hotels. Many hotels that do not have Wi-Fi or other in-room Internet connections provide access through a public computer. Internet cafes are common in towns of any size and in resorts. Italian law requires that all patrons provide a passport or another form of identification and fees are usually around 5€ an hour. For a partial list of cybercafes in Italy, check www.cybercafe.com. To find public Wi-Fi hotspots, go to www.jiwire.com.

Language

English is generally understood at most attractions and museums, and at most hotels and restaurants that cater to visitors. As you travel in remote towns and villages, especially in the south, a phrase book is a handy accompaniment. Even attempting a little Italian will go a long way with the natives—consult "Useful Phrases & Menu Terms," p 738.

Legal Aid

The consulate of your country is the place to turn for legal aid, although offices can't interfere in the Italian legal process. They can, however, inform you of your rights and provide a list of attorneys. You'll have to pay for the attorney out of your pocket—there's no free legal assistance. If you're arrested for a drug offense, about all the consulate will do is notify a lawyer about your case and perhaps inform your family.

Lost Property

Alert your credit card companies the minute you discover your wallet has been lost or stolen and file a report at the nearest police precinct. Your credit card company or insurer may require a police report number or record of the loss. Most credit card companies have an emergency toll-free number to call if your card is lost or stolen: Visa (☎ 800/819-014); MasterCard (☎ 800/870-866); and Amex (☎ 06-7220-348). Companies may agree to wire you a cash advance immediately or deliver an emergency credit card in a day or two.

If you lose your passport, immediately report the loss to your consulate or embassy (see "Embassies & Consulates,"p 731).

Mail & Postage

Postcards, aerogrammes, and letters weighing up to 20 grams sent to the United States and Canada cost .85€; to the United Kingdom and Ireland, .65€; and to Australia and New Zealand, 1.05€. You can buy stamps (*francobolli*) at all post offices and at *tabacchi* (tobacco) stores.

Note that the Italian mail system is notoriously slow and that it can take a while for a letter to make it back home.

Money

Italy's currency is the euro (at press time, equal to $1.50). For details on the euro, the official currency of Italy, check out www.europa.eu.int/euro. Euro banknotes come in denominations of 5€, 10€, 20€, 100€, 200€, and 500€, and coins of .2€, .5€, .10€, .20€, .50€, 1€, and 2€. For the most up-to-date currency conversion information, go to www.xe.com.

The best way to get cash in Italy is at ATMs or Cashpoints (see "ATMs/Cashpoints," above). While credit cards are accepted at almost all shops, restaurants, and hotels, some places won't take them (and banks often levy a 2–3% conversion fee above the 1% the credit card company takes in order to convert purchases made in a foreign currency). Always have some cash on hand for incidentals and sightseeing admissions. Avoid exchanging money at commercial exchange bureaus and hotels, which often have the highest fees. Also be sure that you have a valid PIN number for your bank card or credit card (five- and six-digit numbers usually won't work in Europe—verify with your bank before you leave home that you can use your card in Italy).

Passports

Allow plenty of time before your trip to apply for a passport; processing normally takes 3 weeks but can take much longer during busy periods (especially spring). And keep in mind that if you need a passport in a hurry, you'll pay a higher processing fee.

FOR RESIDENTS OF AUSTRALIA

Contact the **Australian Passport Information Service** at ☎ 131-232, or visit the government website at www.passports.gov.au.

FOR RESIDENTS OF CANADA

Contact the central **Passport Office,** Department of Foreign Affairs and International Trade, Ottawa, ON K1A 0G3 (☎ 800/567-6868; www.ppt.gc.ca).

FOR RESIDENTS OF IRELAND

Contact the **Passport Office,** Setanta Centre, Molesworth Street, Dublin 2 (☎ 01/671-1633; www.irlgov.ie/iveagh).

FOR RESIDENTS OF NEW ZEALAND

Contact the **Passports Office** at ☎ 0800/225-050 in New Zealand or 04/474-8100, or log on to www.passports.govt.nz.

FOR RESIDENTS OF THE UNITED KINGDOM

Visit your nearest passport office, major post office, or travel agency or contact the **United Kingdom Passport Service** at ☎ 0870/521-0410 or search its website at www.ukpa.gov.uk.

FOR RESIDENTS OF THE UNITED STATES

To find your regional passport office, either check the U.S. State Department website or call the **National Passport Information Center** toll-free number (☎ 877/487-2778) for automated information. Note that to obtain a passport for a child in the U.S., the child must be present, with both parents at the place of issuance; *or* a notarized statement from the parents is required.

Pharmacies

Farmacie are recognizable by a neon green or red cross. Regular hours are Monday to Friday 9am to 12:30pm and 3:45 to 7:30pm; Saturday 9am to 12:45pm. At least one pharmacy in each town or neighborhood of larger cities is open all night on a rotating basis; the tourist office keeps a list and a sign posted outside all pharmacies indicates which pharmacy is currently remaining open.

Safety

The most common menace, especially in Rome and other large cities, is the plague of pickpockets and roving gangs of Gypsy children who surround you, distract you in all the confusion, and steal your purse or wallet. When touring and walking down city streets, take some basic precautions: Carry bags and cameras so they are on the side of you away from the street; never carry wallets or other valuables in your back pocket; when sitting in a public place, keep purses and valuables on your lap rather than on the floor or on the back of your chair; and do not wear valuable jewelry that can be snatched.

Never leave valuables in a car, and never travel with your car unlocked.

Single women should feel relatively safe in Italy, and attention paid from men may be persistent but will generally be courteous and nonthreatening. Women on their own should take the same precautions they would in any U.S. city, avoiding deserted areas in general and remaining on well-lighted and busy streets at night.

For more information and updates on travel safety in Italy, consult the U.S. State Department's website at www.travel.state.gov; in the U.K., consult the Foreign Office's website, www.fco.gov.uk; and in Australia, consult the government travel advisory service at www.smartraveller.gov.au.

Senior Travelers

Seniors over 62 are usually entitled to discounted admission to museums and other sights throughout Italy. Discounts may also extend to theater and other events, and seniors are sometimes entitled to discounts at hotels. For tours geared to seniors, see p 712.

Smoking

Smoking is banned in all public places, though restaurants and bars can provide ventilated smoking rooms. Smokers face fines from 29€ to 290€ if caught lighting up.

Spectator Sports

Most Italians focus their sports enthusiasm on soccer (calcio), and few events generate as much enthusiasm or conversation. You will find it hard to avoid games, which are broadcast in every bar and most other public places, and if possible, should find time to attend a match.

For more on this national pastime, see p 188.

The only event that comes close to generating as much excitement is the **Giro d'Italia,** a bicycle race that is second only to the Tour de France in worldwide prestige. The 100-year-old race, held in late May/early June, traverses 3,395km (2,110 miles), beginning in Venice and usually ending in Milan, after covering most the peninsula. Spectators crowd every centimeter of the route.

Taxes

As a member of the European Union, Italy imposes a value-added tax (called IVA in Italy) on most goods and services. The tax that most affects visitors is the one imposed on hotel rates, which ranges from 10% in first- and second-class hotels to 19% in deluxe hotels.

Non–E.U. (European Union) citizens are entitled to a refund of the IVA if they spend more than 155€ at any one store, before tax. To claim your refund, request an invoice from the cashier at the store and take it to the Customs office (dogana) at the airport to have it stamped before you leave. *Note:* If you're going to another E.U. country before flying home, have it stamped at the airport Customs office of the last E.U. country you'll be in (for example, if you're flying home via Britain, have your Italian invoices stamped in London). Once back home, mail the stamped invoice (keep a photocopy for your records) back to the original vendor within 90 days of the purchase. The vendor will, sooner or later, send you a refund of the tax that you paid at the time of your original purchase. Reputable stores view this as a matter of ordinary paperwork and are businesslike about it. Less-honorable stores might lose your dossier. It pays to deal with established vendors on large purchases. You can also request that the refund be credited to the credit card with which you made the purchase; this is usually a faster procedure.

Many shops are now part of the "Tax Free for Tourists" network (look for the sticker in the window). Stores participating in this network issue a check along with your invoice at the time of purchase. After you have the invoice stamped at Customs, you can redeem the check for cash directly at the Tax Free booth in the airport (in Rome, it's past Customs; in Milan's airport, the booth is inside the duty-free shop) or mail it back in the envelope provided within 60 days.

Telephones

To call Italy from abroad, dial the international prefix, 011; then Italy's country code, 39; and then the city code (for example, 06 for Rome and 055 for Florence), which is now built into every number. Then dial the actual phone number.

A local phone call in Italy costs around .10€. Public phones accept coins, precharged phone cards (*scheda* or *carta telefonica*), or both. You can buy a *carta telefonica* at any *tabacchi* (tobacconists; look for a white T on a brown background) in increments of 5€, 10€, and 20€. To make a call, pick up the receiver and insert .10€ or your card (break off the corner first). Most phones have a digital display to tell you how much money you inserted (or how much is left). Dial the number, and don't forget to take the card with you.

To call from one city code to another, dial the city code, complete with initial 0, and then dial the number. (Numbers in Italy range from four to eight digits. Even when you're calling within the same city, you must dial that city's area code—including the zero. A Roman calling another Rome number must dial 06 before the local number.)

To dial direct internationally, dial 00 and then the country code, the area code, and the number. Country codes are as follows: the United States and Canada, 1; the United Kingdom, 44; Ireland, 353; Australia, 61; New Zealand, 64.

Make international calls from a public phone, if possible, because hotels charge inflated rates for direct dial—but bring plenty of *schede* (change). A reduced rate is applied from 11pm to 8am on Monday through Saturday and all day Sunday. Direct-dial calls from the United States to Italy are much cheaper, so arrange for whomever to call you at your hotel.

International phone cards (*scheda telefonica internazionale*) for calling overseas come in increments of 50, 100, 200, and 400 *unita* (units), and they're available at *tabacchi* and bars. Each *unita* is worth .15€ of phone time; it costs 5 *unita* (.65€) per minute to call within Europe or to the United States or Canada, and 12 *unita* (1.55€) per minute to call Australia or New Zealand. You don't insert this card into the phone; merely dial ☎ 1740 and then *2 (star 2) for instructions in English, when prompted.

To call the free national telephone information (in Italian) in Italy, dial ☎ 12. International information is available at ☎ 176 but costs .60€ a shot.

To make collect or calling-card calls to the U.S., drop in .10€ or insert your card and dial one of the numbers here; an American operator will come on to assist you (because Italy has yet to discover the joys of the touch-tone phone). The following calling-card numbers work all over Italy: **AT&T** (☎ 172-1011), **MCI** (☎ 172-1022), and **Sprint** (☎ 172-1877). To make collect calls to a country besides the United States, dial ☎ 170 (.50€), and practice your Italian counting in order to relay the number to the Italian operator. Tell him or her that you want it *a carico del destinatario* (charged to the destination, or collect).

Time Zone

Italy is 6 hours ahead of Eastern Standard Time (EST) in the United States; it's 1 hour ahead of London and 9 hours behind Sydney. Daylight saving time goes into effect in Italy each year from the end of March through the end of October.

Tipping

In hotels, the service charge of 15% to 19% is already added to a bill. In addition, it's customary to tip the chambermaid .50€ per day, the doorman (for calling a cab) .50€, and the bellhop or porter 1.50€ to 1.95€ for carrying your bags to your room. A concierge expects about 15% of his or her bill.

In restaurants and cafes, 15% is usually added to your bill to cover most charges. If you're not sure whether this has been done, ask, *"È incluso il servizio?"* (ay een-*cloo*-soh eel sair-*vee*-tsoh?). An additional tip isn't expected, but it's nice to leave the equivalent of an extra couple of dollars if you've been pleased with the service. Checkroom attendants expect .75€, and washroom attendants should get .50€.

Taxi drivers expect at least 15% of the fare.

Toilets

Public toilets are found near many of the major sights. Usually they're designated as wc (water closet) or *DONNE* (women) and *UOMINI* (men). A more confusing designation is *SIGNORI* (gentlemen) and *SIGNORE* (ladies), so watch that final *i* and *e!* Many public toilets charge a fee (as much as 1€). While public toilets are in general clean and well maintained, it's a good idea to carry some tissues in your pocket or purse—they often come in handy.

Tourist Traps

Italy has been catering to tourists for centuries, and like elsewhere in the world, attendant touts and shills try to profit from sightseeing enthusiasm. A little common sense will protect you from being taking advantage of.

At Pompeii or other sites, never accept the services of a guide without asking to see credentials and agreeing on a price. If you are unconvinced, check with the ticket office to make sure the guide is officially sanctioned.

Never accept rides with a driver who is operating any vehicle other than a licensed taxi. Make sure the meter is running and pay no more than the official rate. In Venice, exercise the same caution with gondolas and accept rides only from licensed gondoliers charging official rates.

Do not offer to change large bills for strangers on the street—this a common scheme in which you will be slipped counterfeit notes.

Travelers with Disabilities

Laws in Italy require rail stations, airports, hotels, and most restaurants to follow a strict set of regulations about wheelchair accessibility to restrooms, ticket counters, and the like. Museums and other attractions have conformed to the regulations, and continue to be upgraded to meet codes. You still, however, will encounter many places in Italy that might pose a challenge. Crossing many bridges in Venice, for example, often involves mounting and descending steps, and the city has yet to implement plans to equip these crossings with ramps or lifts. Visitors to Venice should note that the Venice tourist office distributes a free map called *Veneziapertutti* ("Venice for All"), illustrating which parts of the city are accessible and listing accessible churches, monuments, gardens, public offices, hotels, and restrooms.

Always call ahead to check on the accessibility of hotels, restaurants, and sights. If you need assistance when traveling by rail, you can make special arrangements at many train stations as long as you notify them at least 24 hours in advance.

Accessible Italy (www.accessibleitaly.com) provides information on resources and options for those with disabilities. It also rents wheelchairs and other equipment, and organizes tours of Italy for those with disabilities.

Of special note for nature lovers is **Parco Nazionale del Gran Paradiso** (p 500, **4**), which has a 1km (¾ mile) trail especially laid out for travelers with disabilities (from mobility issues to the visually impaired).

Visitor Information

For information before you go, contact the **Italian Government Tourist Board** (www.enit.it and www.italiantourism.com). Another helpful website is www.initaly.com.

You can also write directly (in English or Italian) to the provincial or local tourist boards of the areas you plan to visit. Provincial tourist boards (Ente Provinciale per il Turismo) operate in the principal towns of the provinces. Local tourist boards (Azienda Autonoma di Soggiorno e Turismo) operate in all places of tourist interest; you can get a comprehensive list from the Italian Government Tourist Board or consult the "Visitor Information" listings in the "Fast Facts" of each destination chapter in this book.

Useful Phrases & Menu Terms

Phrases

ENGLISH	ITALIAN	PRONUNCIATION
thank you	grazie	*graht*-tzee-yey
please	per favore	*pehr* fah-*vohr*-eh
yes	sì	*see*
no	no	*noh*
good morning	buongiorno	bwohn-*djor*-noh
good evening	buona sera	*bwohn*-ah *say*-rah
How are you?	Come sta?	koh-may-*stah*
very well	molto bene	*mohl*-toh-*bhen*-eh
excuse me	scusi	*skoo*-zee
Where is___?	Dovè___?	doh-*vey*
a hotel	un albergo	oon ahl-*behr*-goh
a restaurant	un ristorante	oon reest-oh-*rahnt*-eh
the bathroom	il bagno	eel *bahn*-nyoh
to the right	a destra	ah *day*-stra
to the left	a sinistra	ah see-*nees*-tra
straight ahead	avanti	ahv-*vahn*-tee
good	buono	*bwoh*-noh
bad	cattivo	ka-*tee*-voh
open	aperto	ah-*pair*-toh
closed	chiuso	kee-*yoo*-soh
hot	caldo	*kahl*-doh
cold	freddo	*fray*-doh
big	grande	*grahn*-day
expensive	caro	*kahr*-roh
cheap	a buon prezza	ah bwon *pretz*-so
small	piccolo	*pee*-koh-loh
I'm sorry	mi dispiace	mee deez-pee-*ach*-ay
Do you speak English?	Parla inglese?	*pahr*-lah een-*gleh*-zeh
I would like___	Vorrei___	vor-*ray*
How much does it cost?	Quanto costa?	*kwan*-toh *coh*-sta

Emergencies

Help!	Aiuto!	eye-*yooh*-toh
Call the police!	Chiama la polizia!	kee-*ah*-mah lah poh-lee-*tsee*-ah
a doctor	un medico	oon *meh*-dee-koh
an ambulance	un ambulanza	oon am-boo-*lahn*-tsah

Numbers

ENGLISH	ITALIAN	PRONUNCIATION
1	uno	*oo*-noh
2	due	*doo*-ay
3	tre	tray
4	quattro	*kwah*-troh
5	cinque	*cheen*-kway
6	sei	say
7	sette	*set*-tay
8	otto	*oh*-toh
9	nove	*noh*-vay
10	dieci	dee-*ay*-chee
11	undici	*oon*-dee-chee
12	dodici	*doe*-dee-chee
13	tredici	*tray*-dee-chee
14	quattordici	kwah-*tohr*-dee-chee
15	quindici	*kween*-dee-chee
16	sedici	*say*-dee-chee
17	diciassette	dee-chah-*set*-tay
18	diciotto	dee-*choh*-toh
19	diciannove	dee-chah-*noh*-vay
20	venti	*vehn*-tee
30	trenta	*trehn*-tah
40	quaranta	kwah-*rahn*-tah
50	cinquanta	cheen-*kwan*-tah
60	sessanta	say-*sahn*-tah
70	settanta	seht-*tahn*-tah
80	ottanta	oht-*tahn*-tah
90	novanta	noh-*vahnt*-tah
100	cento	*chen*-toh
1,000	mille	*mee*-lay
2,000	duemila	*doo*-ay-*mee*-lah
5,000	cinquemila	*cheen*-kway *mee*-lah

Days of the Week

ENGLISH	ITALIAN	PRONUNCIATION
Monday	Lunedì	loo-nay-*dee*
Tuesday	Martedì	mart-ay-*dee*
Wednesday	Mercoledì	mehr-cohl-ay-*dee*
Thursday	Giovedì	joh-vay-*dee*
Friday	Venerdì	ven-nehr-*dee*
Saturday	Sabato	*sah*-bah-toh
Sunday	La Domenica	lah doh-*mehn*-nee-kah

Restaurant Phrases

ENGLISH	ITALIAN	PRONUNCIATION
Have you a table for___?	Avete una tavola per___?	ah-*veh*-te oon-ah *tah*-voe-lah?
I would like___	Vorrei___.	Vor-*ray*
a glass of___	un bicchiere di___	Oon beek-ee-*air*-ay dee
mineral water	acqua minerale	*ock*-wa meen-er-*ah*-lay
carbonated/uncarbonated water	acqua gassata/senza gas	*ock*-wa gazz-*ah*-ta/*sens*-za-gaz
white wine	vino bianco	*vee*-no bee-*ahn*-ko
red wine	vino rosso	*vee*-no *roh*-so
beer	birra	*behr*-ah
first course	il primo	eel-*pree*-mo
main course	il secondo	eel-say-*kon*-do
The bill, please.	Il conto, per favore.	eel-*kon*-toe, pear-fa-*vorr*-ray
Is the service included?	È incluso il servizio?	ay-een-*klu*-so eel ser-*veez*-zio

Menu Items

ENGLISH	ITALIAN	PRONUNCIATION
anchovies	acciughe	ah-*choo*-gay
butter	burro	*boor*-roh
cheeses	formaggi	for-*mahd*-jee
chicken	pollo	*poe*-lo
clams	vongole	*vahn*-goh-lee
desserts	dolci	*dol*-chee
eggplant	melanzana	meh-lan-*tsah*-nah
eggs	uova	*woh*-vah
fish	pesce	*pesh*-ay
lamb	agnello	ahn-*yell*-oh
liver	fegato	*fay*-gah-toh
meat sauce	ragù	rah-*goo*
mushrooms	funghi	*foon*-ghee
nuts	noci	*no*-chee
pork	maiale	my-*ah*-lay
rice	riso	*ree*-so
sauce	salsa	*sahl*-sa
sausages	salsiccie	sahl-*see*-chee-ay
shrimp	gamberoni	gam-ber-*oh*-nee
soup	zuppa	*tzoo*-pah
steak	bistecca	bee-*stehk*-kah
tomatoes	pomodori	pah-mo-*dor*-ee
veal	vitello	vi-*tell*-oh
vegetables	contorni	cohn-*tor*-nee
vinegar	aceto	ah-*chay*-toh

Index

Photo Credits

Note: l= left; r= right; t= top; b= bottom; c= center

Cover Photo Credits: Front cover (l to r): Portrait of Rodrigo Borgia (1431-1503) Pope Alexander VI, German School, (16th century)/ Musee des Beaux-Arts, Dijon France/The Bridgeman Art Library; © Vanessa Berberian; © Vanessa Berberian. Back cover: © Raffaele Capasso. Cover flap (t to b): © Corbis/SuperStock; National Geographic/Getty Images; © Louie Psihoyos/Sciene Faction/Corbis; Rama-Pathe/The Kobal Collection. Inside Front Cover (clockwise from tr:) © Cristina Fumi; © Sandro Di Fatta; © Anthony Woods; © Riccardo De Luca; © Jessica Hauf; © Riccardo De Luca; © Vanessa Berberian; © Vanessa Berberian; © Riccardo De Luca; © Riccardo De Luca.

Interior Photo Credits: AGE: © Giulio Andreini/age fotostock: p293; © ARCO/R Kiedrowski/age fotostock: p498; © Angelo Cavalli/age fotostock: p448(b), p449; © Atlantide S.N.C/age fotostock: pv(t), p240(r), p328; © B&Y Photography Inc./age fotostock: p181; © Richard Brine/VIEW/age fotostock: p702(l); © Wojtek Buss/age fotostock: p699(l); © Sunny Celeste/age fotostock: p14, p522(t); © Stefano Cellai/age fotostock: p507, p698(br); © Claudio Ciabochi/age fotostock: p232(b); © Alan Copson/age fotostock: p529; © DEA/G CIGO-LINI/age fotostock: p464; © Danilo Donadoni/age fotostock: p435, p454, p467; p550(r); © Damiano Fiorentini/age fotostock: p189 (2nd from tr); © Factoria Singular/age fotostock: p70; © Raga Jose Fuste/age fotostock: p158; © Ken Gillham/age fotostock: p646; © Tommaso di Girolamo/age fotostock: p442; © Robert Harding/age fotostock: 17; © INTERFOTO/age fotostock: p163(l); © Angelo Kruger/age fotostock: p308; © Frank Lukasseck/age fotostock: p434; © Brian Lawrence/age fotostock: 255(r); © Stefano Lunardi/age fotostock: p549; © Maurilio Mazzola/age fotostock: p440; © Giovanni Mereghetti/age fotostock: p496; © Raffaele Meucci/age fotostock: p469; © Mezzabarba/age fotostock: p691(b); © Bruno Morandi/age fotostock: p34-35, p608(t), p661, p696(r); © P. Narayan/age fotostock: p250; © The Print Collector/age fotostock: pxi, p693; © Alberto Ramella/age fotostock: p480-81, p506; © RENAULT Philippe/age fotostock: p664; © Ellen Rooney/age fotostock: p275, p645; © Marco Scataglini/age fotostock: p302; © Pietro Scozzari/age fotostock: p709(r); © Lorenzo Sechi/age fotostock: p106, p263; © Guy Thouvenin/age fotostock: p45(bl); © Nico Tondini/age fotostock: p276, p303; © Tramonto/age fotostock: p429(br); © Ken Welsh/age fotostock: piv(c), p288;© Walter Zerla/age fotostock: p45(tl), p490; Al Fonte Mocenigo: p407(l); **Alamy:** © Peter Adams Photography Ltd/Alamy: p422-23; © A Eastland/Alamy: p696(l); © David Angel/Alamy: piii(c) p153; © Arco Images GmbH/Alamy: p372;© Vito Arcomano/Alamy: p634-635; © Jon Arnold Images Ltd/Alamy: p39, p220, p598; © Claudio H. Artman/Alamy: p556; © Associated Sports Photography/Alamy: p189(cr); © Andrew Bargery/Alamy: p254; © Peter Barritt/Alamy: p180; © Michael Belardo/Alamy: p707(t); © blickwinkel/Alamy: p710-11; © Bon Appetit/Alamy: p241(t), p243(r); © Richard Broadwell/Alamy: p233, p280; © Cephas Picture Library/Alamy: p242; © Alan Copson City Pictures/Alamy: p508; © Marco Cristofori/Alamy: piii(t), p18; © Derek Croucher/Alamy: p694; © CuboImages srl/Alamy: p147, p212, p350(t), p444, p486, p495(l), p497(br), p554(b), p666(l and r), p679(l); © CW Images/Alamy: p98; © Ian Dagnall/Alamy: p246;© Danita Delimont/Alamy, p272; © dk/Alamy: 654(t); © EIGHTFISH/Alamy: p264;© John Elk III/Alamy: p382; © Mary Evans Picture Library/Alamy: p331(cr); © FAN travelstock/Alamy: p416, p713; © Foodcollection.com/Alamy: p708(l); © Domenico Farone/Alamy: p552; © Peter Forsberg/Alamy: p381; © Gaertner/Alamy: p265(b); © Paolo Gallo/Alamy: p306(l); © Misha Gordon/Alamy: p184; © Robert Harding Picture Library Ltd/Alamy: p142, pp150-51, p665, p696(c); © Hemis/Alamy: p30, p586(br), 655(t); © Tim Hill/Alamy: p689(r); © Angelo Hornak/Alamy: p544; © Peter Horree/Alamy: p145(tl), p266, p640; © imagebroker/Alamy: p364, p650; © INTERFOTO/Alamy: p515(bl); © International Photobank/Alamy: p437; © Isifa Image Service s.r.o./Alamy: p500; © Rainer Jahns/Alamy: p628; © Michael Jenner/Alamy: p309; © JLImages/Alamy: p232(t); © Boris Karpinski/Alamy: pvii(c), p615; © Justin Kase zelevenaz/Alamy: p618; © Art Kowalsky/Alamy: p056-57, p160; © Lautaro/Alamy: p112; © Lebrecht Music and Arts Photo Library/Alamy: p704; © The London Art Archive/Alamy: p331(bl); © Yannick Luthy/Alamy: p146; © David Lyons/Alamy: p673; © Tom Mackie/Alamy: pp218-19; © Vincent MacNamara/Alamy: 385; © MARKA/Alamy: p515(br); © Yvette McGreavy/Alamy: p367(t); © Chris McLennan/Alamy: pvi(t), p488; © DAVID NEWHAM/Alamy: pv(t), p365(t);© New Photo Service/Alamy: p45 (3rd from tl); © DAVID NOBLE PHOTOGRAPHY/Alamy: p178; © Martin Norris/Alamy: p229; © Anne-Marie Palmer/Alamy: p162; © PCL/Alamy: pviii(t), p179, p347, p588; © David Pearson/Alamy: p62; © Pictorial Press Ltd/Alamy: p429(bl), p691(c), p695(l); © Picture Contact/Alamy: p503; © PhotoBliss/Alamy: p692(r); © Photos 12/Alamy: p515(tl and bc); © Platinum GPics/Alamy: p533, p702(r); © Vova Pomortzeff/Alamy: p587(br); © Alex Ramsay/Alamy: p214; © Francesco Ridolfi/Alamy: p690(b); © Ray Roberts/Alamy: p548(t); © Phil Robinson/PjrFoto/Alamy: p282; © Rough Guides/Alamy: p141; © Witold Skrypczak/Alamy: p656, p658; © Stock Italia/Alamy: p315(r), p452; © David Sutherland/Alamy: pp586-87(tl); © Paul M Thompson/Alamy: p140; © Travelshots.com/Alamy: p624; © Christine Webb/Alamy: p196; © Wilmar Photography/Alamy: p93; © Peter M. Wilson/Alamy: p472; © WoodySka/Alamy: p418(r); **AP:** Associated Press: p33, p189(tl), p703; Arena di Verona, Photo by Gianfranco Fainello/from the Archives of Fondazione Arena di Verona/All rights reserved: pp686-87; Art Hotel Boston: Luca de Bellis of Magnetic Photo Studio: p513; **Art Resource:** Alinari/Art Resource, NY: pp22-23, p23 (2nd from bl and 3rd from bl); Erich Lessing/Art Resource, NY: p23(tr), p145(tr), p357, p691(t); © National Gallery, London/Art Resource, NY: p701(b); Scala/Art Resource, NY: p69(r), p331(tr), p550(l), p536, p547, p587(cr), p688(tr); Scala/Ministero per i Beni e le Attività culturali/Art Resource, NY: p22(bl and br), p23(bl and r), p425, p539(b), p606; Auditorium Parco della Musica, C. Moreno Maggi: p17; Banfi, Courtesy of Castello Banfi: p253; Bauer Palladio Hotel & Spa: p402; © Vanessa Berberian: piii(b), piv(t), p8-9, p19, p25, p26, p36, p38, p59(l and r), p63, p73(l and r), p77(l and r), p78, p80, p81, p82, p84, p88(tt), p89, p100, p103(t), p107, p108, p109(b), p113, p114, p115, p118, p120, p121, p124, p125, p126, p127, p128, p129(t and b), p136, p143, p156, p159(b), p166(l and r), p167, p168, p173(t), p182, p183, p186, p191, p194, p195(l and r), p197, p200, p201(t, c and r), p202, p203, p211, p221, p222, p223(t and b), p224(b), p228, p230, p234, p236, p237, p238, p239, p240(l), p241(b), p244, p247, p248(t), p252, p255(l), p257, p258, p259, p260, p261(t and b), p262, p265(t), p267, p268, p269, p271, p277, p279, p281, p283, p284(t), p285, p286, p287, p289, p290, p292, p295, p475, p688(l and tc), p689(bl), p700(l), p716-17; **Bridgeman:** Albert Moravia in Rome/Private Collection/The Bridgeman Art Library: p705(l); *Annunciation* by da Vinci/Galleria degli Uffizi/The Bridgeman Art Library: p177(t); *the Assumption of the Virgin* by Titian/Santa Maria Gloriosa dei Frari, Venice /The Bridgeman Art Library: p700(r); *Baker's Shop/*Pompeii, Italy/The Bridgeman Art Library: p587(tr); *Basket with Fruit* by Caravaggio/Ambrosiana, Milan/The Bridgeman Art Library: p448(t); *The Brera Altarpiece* by Francesca/Pinacoteca di Brera, Milan/The Bridgeman Art Library, 461; *Bust of Caligula*/Museo Archeologico, Venice/ the Bridgeman Art Library: p145 (2nd from tl); *Caldarium of the Forum Thermae*/Pompeii, Italy/The Bridgeman Art Library: p587(bl); *David* by Donatello/Museo Nazionale del Bargello, Florence/The Bridgeman Art Library: p172; *The Drunkeness of Bacchus* by Buonarroti/Bargello, Florence/The Bridgeman Art Library: p164; *Emperor Constantine I*/San Marcio, Venice/The Bridgeman Art Library: p690(c); *Emperor Lucius Aurrelius Commodus*/Museo Archeologico Nazionale, Naples/The Bridgeman Art Library: p145(3rd from tl); *The Expulsion of the Devils from Arezzo* by Bondone/San Francesco, Upper Church, Assisi/The Bridgeman Art Library: p270; *The Holy Family with St. Catherine of Alexandria* by Lotto/Galleria dell'Accademia Carrara, Bergamo/The Bridgeman Art Library: p451; *Holy Family with St. John* by Michelangelo/Galleria degli Uffizi, Florence/The Bridgeman Art Library,176(tr); Househould shrine from the Casa dei Vetti/Pompeii, Italy/The Bridgeman Art Library: p586(bl); Laurentian Library Staircase by Buonarroti/Biblioteca Medicea-Laurenziana, Florence/The Bridgeman Art Library: p163(r); *The Life of St. Benedict* by Signorelli & Sodoma/Monte Oliveto Maggiore, Tuscany/The Bridgeman Art Library: p249; *The Madonna of the Chair* by Raphael/Palazzo Pitti, Florence/The Bridgeman Art Library: p169; *The Marriage of the Virgin* by Raphael/Pinacoteca di Brera, Milan/The Bridgeman Art Library: p16; *Medusa* by Caravaggio/Galleria degli Uffizi, Florence/The Bridgeman Art Library: p176(tl); *The Nativity* by Lotto/Pinacoteca Nazionale, Siena/The Bridgeman Art Library: p248(b); *Niccolo Machiavelli* by Altissimo/Galleria Doria Pamphilj/The Bridgeman Art Library: p705(r); *Portrait of Dante* by Botticelli/Private Collection/The Bridgeman Art Library: p688(br); *Portrait of a Lady of the Court of Catherine of Bragnza* by Juysmans/© PhilipMould Ltd, London/The Bridgeman Art Library: p331(br); *Portrait of Rodrigo Borgia*/Musée des Beaux-Arts, Dijon, France/The Bridgeman Art Library: p331(tl); *The Presentation in the Temple* by Lorenzetti/Galleria degli Uffizi, Florence/The Bridgeman Art Library: p174; *The Salone del Cinquecento* by Polla/Palazzo Vecchio, Florence/The Bridgeman Art Library: p170; *The Sick Bacchus* by Caravaggio/Galleria Borghese, Rome/The Bridgeman Art Library: p85(b); Skyphos Cup with Incised Figure of a Warrior, Etruscan/Fitzwilliam Museum, University of Cambridge, UK/The Bridgeman Art Library: p690(t); *St. Francis* by Strozzi/Palazzo Bianco, Genoa/The Bridgeman Art Library, View of the Forum/Pompeii, Italy/The Bridgeman Art Library: p577; *The Story of Joseph* by Ghiberti/Museo dell'Opera del Duomo, Florence/The Bridgeman Art Library: p699(c); *Study of the Man* by da Vinci/Biblioteca Ambrosiana, Milan/The Bridgeman Art Library: p465; *Supper at Emmaus* by Caravaggio/Pinacoteca di Brera, Milan/The Bridgeman Art Library: p446; *The Triumph of Death*/Galerie Nationale, Palermo/The Bridgeman Art Library: p671; Warrior, Etruscan/© Museumslandschaft Hessen, Kassel/The Bridgeman Art Library International: p692(l); *The Wounded Chimera of Bellerophon*/Museo Archeologico, Florence/The Bridgeman Art Library: p173(b); Ca'della Corte: p405; Caesar Augustus hotel, Robert Miller pp566-67, p616; © Raffaele Capasso, pvii(c and b), p11, p12, p42, p570, p571(t and b), p572(b), p573, p574, p576(t and b), p578, p579, p580, p582(b), p583, p584, p585(t and b), p594, p595, p596, p597, p600, p602, p604, p605, p607(t and b), p608(b), p609, p611, p612, p614, p617, p619, p620, p621, p627, p708(r); Comune di Padova, Settore Musei e Biblioteche: p412, p413, p698(tr); Archives of the Ministry of Infrastructure and Transport–Venice Water Authority concessionary Consorzio Venezia Nuova: p367(b); Corbis: © Alinari Archives/CORBIS: p102; © Bernard Annebicque/CORBIS SYGMA: pp68-69; © Atlantide Phototravel/Corbis: p243(l); © Bettmann/CORBIS: p144, p330; © Araldo de Luca/CORBIS: p145(br); © Patrick Durand/Sygma/Corbis: p74; © Wilfried Krecichwost/Corbis p429(tr); © Louie Psihoyos/Science Faction/Corbis: p366; Danieli hotel: p401; Davanzati Hotel: p208; DD 724: p406; © Riccardo De Luca: pv(b), pvi(c), pxiii-1, p27, p50, p52, p53, p54, p58, p67, p72, p92, p96, p101, p103(b), p109(t), p110, p190, p210, p231, p298-99, p300, p301, p304, p305, p306(r), p307, p310, p312, p313, p314, p315(l), p316, p318, p320, p321(l and r), p322, p323, p325, p326, p327, p329, p334, p336, p338, p339, p340(t and b), p341, p344-45, p346, p350(b), p352, p353(l and r), p354, p356, p358, p360(l and r), p361, p362, p365(b), p368(r), p370(t and b), p371(t), p373(b), p374, p376(t and b), p377(l and r), p378, p380, p384(t and b), p386, p388, p390, p391, p392, p393, p394, p395, p398(l and r), p399(l and r), p400(l and r), p408, p409, p414, p415(t and b), p424, p426, p427, p450, p453, p456, p460, p462, p463, p466, p474, p476, p482, p484, p485, p489, p492, p493, p495(b), p497(bl, br, cr and tr), p502, p504, p509(t), p510(l and r), p511, p512, p516, p518, p519, p520, p521, p522(b), p526-27, p528, p530, p531, p532, p534, p535, p537, p539(t), p540, p542, p543, p546, p548(b), p551, p553, p558, p559, p560, p562, p563, p572(t), p581, p582(t), p590(t), p591, p592(t and b), p593, p698(tl), p706(l and r), p707(b), p709(l); © Sandro Di Fatta: p554(t); Everett: © Everett Collection: 515(tr); Jim Forest: p76, p697; Four Seasons: Mathias Hamel: p24; © Cristina Fumi: pv(b), p10, p28-29, p32, p43, p51, p332, p418(l), p419, p430, p432, p433, p438, p439, p441, p443; Getty: AFP/Getty Images: p428; After Antonio Niccolini: p587(bc); Dennis Flaherty: p226; Getty Images, p189 (tr, 2nd from br and br), pp470-71; National Geographic/Getty Images: p188; Popperfoto/Getty Images: p429 (2nd from bl); Time & Life Pictures/Getty Images: p695(r); Ingmar Wesemann: p256; Grand Hotel et de Milan: p468; Grand Hotel Rimini Archives: p311; Hevetia & Bristol: p204; Hilton Venice: p411; Hotel Antiche Mura, Michele Savarese: p626; Hotel Canal Grande: p21; Hotel Constantinopoli 104: p610; Hotel La Canna: p667; Hotel Milleluci: p501; Hotel Santa Caterina, Dr. Battistessa: p630; Hotel Villa Ducale: p21; Hotel Villa Schuler: p683; Inn at tRoman Forum: p134; JK Place, Massimo Listri: p205; Kobal: Rama-Pathe/The Kobal Collection: p514-515; The Kobal Collection: p 689(c); Mrs. Barbara Kraft: p209; Lebrecht: © Royal Academy of Music/Lebrecht Music & Arts: p689(tl); Locanda Borgonuovo: p335; Lonely Planet: Rachel Lewis/Lonely Planet Images: p274; Metropolitian Opera House, The Metropolitan Opera Archives p423 (3rd from bl); © Mr. Lorenzo Muner: p407(r); Palazzo Ravizza, Bruno Bruchi: p294; Palazzo Sasso: p623; © Giuseppe Piazza, WPN: pviii(b), p13, p15, p46, p49(t and b), p636, p637, p638, p639, p642, p643, p644, p648, p649, p651, p652, p654(b), p655(b), p657(t and b), p660, p662, p663, p668, p670(t and b), p672, p674, p676, p677, p678, p678(r), p680, p681, p682, p698(tc); Poggio Antico: p278; Portrait Suites: Lungarno Hotels: p130; Tim Reder: p189(bl); © Kelly Regan: p37; Santa Maria hotel p131; Lauren Sarah Photography: p689(tc); © 1978 Barrie M. Schwortz.: p509(b); StockFood: Schinharl, Michael - StockFood Munich: p706(c); Bill Strouse: p324; Superstock: © age fotostock/SuperStock: p45 (4th from tl); p85(t), p88(b), p91, p499, p699(r); © Bridgeman Art Library, London/SuperStock: p373(t); © Corbis/SuperStock: p44, p45 (2nd from tl), p371(b); © De Agostini/SuperStock: p45(br), p251, p368(l), p641; © Hemis.fr/SuperStock: p104; © Pixtal/SuperStock: p224(t); © Photononstop/SuperStock p41; © SuperStock/SuperStock: piv(b), p20, p45(tr), p69(l), p152, p159(t), p171, p176(bl), p177(b), p331(cl), p455, p688(bc) p701(t); Teatro Alla Scala: p457; Tuscan Summer Festival: p213; Università per Stranieri di Perugia: p284(b); Villa Bordoni, Francesco Bedini: 225; Villa Cimbrone, Roberto Vuilleumier: piii(c), p40, p568, p601, p622; Villa Laetitia, p135; Judy Witts Francini: p715